Mastering Machine Learning Algorithms

Second Edition

Expert techniques for implementing popular machine learning algorithms, fine-tuning your models, and understanding how they work

Giuseppe Bonaccorso

BIRMINGHAM - MUMBAI

Mastering Machine Learning Algorithms
Second Edition

Acquisition Editor: Tushar Gupta
Acquisition Editor – Peer Reviews: Divya Mudaliar
Content Development Editor: Alex Patterson
Technical Editor: Gaurav Gavas
Project Editor: Kishor Rit
Proofreader: Safis Editing
Indexer: Rekha Nair
Production Designer: Sandip Tadge

First published: May 2018

Second edition: January 2020

Production reference: 1300120

Published by Packt Publishing Ltd.
Livery Place
35 Livery Street
Birmingham B3 2PB, UK.

ISBN 978-1-83882-029-9

www.packt.com

`packt.com`

Subscribe to our online digital library for full access to over 7,000 books and videos, as well as industry leading tools to help you plan your personal development and advance your career. For more information, please visit our website.

Why subscribe?

- Spend less time learning and more time coding with practical eBooks and Videos from over 4,000 industry professionals
- Learn better with Skill Plans built especially for you
- Get a free eBook or video every month
- Fully searchable for easy access to vital information
- Copy and paste, print, and bookmark content

Did you know that Packt offers eBook versions of every book published, with PDF and ePub files available? You can upgrade to the eBook version at www.Packt.com and as a print book customer, you are entitled to a discount on the eBook copy. Get in touch with us at customercare@packtpub.com for more details.

At www.Packt.com, you can also read a collection of free technical articles, sign up for a range of free newsletters, and receive exclusive discounts and offers on Packt books and eBooks.

Contributors

About the author

Giuseppe Bonaccorso is an experienced data science manager with expertise in machine/deep learning. He got his M.Sc. Eng. in Electronics Engineering in 2005 from the University of Catania, Italy and continued his studies (MBA) at the University of Rome "Tor Vergata," Italy and the University of Essex, UK. His main interests include machine/deep learning, data science strategy, and digital innovation in the healthcare industry.

About the reviewer

Luca Massaron is a data scientist with more than a decade of experience in transforming data into smarter artifacts, in solving real-world problems and in generating value for businesses and stakeholders. He is also the author of best-selling books on AI, machine learning, and algorithms; a Kaggle master who reached no 7 in the worldwide user rankings for his performance in data science competitions; and a Google Developer Expert in machine learning.

My greatest thanks go to my family, Yukiko and Amelia, for their support and loving patience.

Table of Contents

Preface

In the last few years, machine learning has become an increasingly important field in the majority of industries. Several processes once considered impossible to automate are now completely managed by computers, allowing human beings to focus on more creative tasks. This revolution has been made possible by the dramatic improvement of standard algorithms, together with a continuous reduction in hardware prices. The complexity that was a huge obstacle only a decade ago is now a problem that even a personal computer can solve. The general availability of high-level open source frameworks has allowed everybody to design and train extremely powerful models.

The main goal of the second edition of *Mastering Machine Learning Algorithms* is to introduce the reader to complex techniques (such as semi-supervised and manifold learning, probabilistic models, and neural networks), balancing mathematical theory with practical examples written in Python (using the most advanced and common frameworks). I wanted to keep a pragmatic approach, focusing on the applications but never forgetting the theoretical foundations. A solid knowledge of this field, in fact, can be acquired only by understanding the underlying logic, which is always expressed using mathematical concepts. This extra effort is rewarded with a more solid awareness of every specific choice and helps the reader understand how to apply, modify, and improve all the algorithms in specific business contexts.

Machine learning is an extremely wide field and it's impossible to cover all the topics in a book. In this case, I've done my best to cover a selection of algorithms belonging to supervised, semi-supervised, unsupervised, and reinforcement learning, providing all the references necessary to further explore each of them. The examples have been designed to be easy to understand without any deep insight into the code; in fact, I believe it's more important to show general cases and let the reader improve and adapt them to cope with particular scenarios. I apologize for mistakes: even though many revisions have been made, it's possible that some details (both in the formulas and in the code) got away.

In particular, the second edition corrects some typos and mistakes present in the first one, improves the readability of some complex topics, and is based on the most recent version of production-ready frameworks (like TensorFlow 2.0). Given the overall complexity of the work, I apologize since despite the hard work of the author and all editors, it's always possible to find imprecisions or errors.

I've finished this book in a particular period of my life and I'd like to dedicate it to my father, an artist and art professor, who has been always a guide for me, teaching me how it's always possible to join scientific rigor with an artistic approach. At the end of the day, data science needs creativity and, conversely, creativity can find in data science an extremely fertile soil!

Who this book is for

This book is a relevant source of content (both theoretical and practical) for data science professionals and machine learning engineers who want to deep dive into the complex machine learning algorithms, the calibration of the models, and to improve the predictions of the trained model. A solid knowledge of basic machine learning is required to get the best out of this mastery guide. Moreover, given the complexity of some topics, a good mathematical background is necessary.

What this book covers

Chapter 1, Machine Learning Models Fundamentals, explains the most important theoretical concepts regarding machine learning models, including bias, variance, overfitting, underfitting, data normalization, and scaling.

Chapter 2, Loss Functions and Regularization, continues the exploration of fundamental concepts focusing on loss functions and discussing their properties and applications. The chapter also introduces the reader to the concept of regularization, which plays a fundamental role in the majority of supervised methods.

Chapter 3, Introduction to Semi-Supervised Learning, introduces the reader to the main elements of semi-supervised learning, discussing the main assumptions and focusing on generative algorithms, self-training, and cotraining.

Chapter 4, Advanced Semi-Supervised Classification, discusses the most important inductive and transductive semi-supervised classification methods, which overcome the limitations of simpler algorithms analyzed in *Chapter 3*.

Chapter 5, Graph-Based Semi-Supervised Learning, continues the exploration of semi-supervised learning algorithms belonging to the families of graph-based and manifold learning models. Label propagation and non-linear dimensionality reduction are analyzed in different contexts, providing some effective solutions that can be immediately exploited using scikit-learn functionalities.

Chapter 6, Clustering and Unsupervised Models, introduces some common and important unsupervised algorithms, such as k-Nearest Neighbors (based on K-d trees and Ball Trees), K-means (with K-means++ initialization). Moreover, the chapter discusses the most important metrics that can be employed to evaluate a clustering result.

Chapter 7, Advanced Clustering and Unsupervised Models, continues the discussion of more complex clustering algorithms, like spectral clustering, DBSCAN, and fuzzy clustering, which can solve problems that simpler methods fail to properly manage.

Chapter 8, Clustering and Unsupervised Models for Marketing, introduces the reader to the concept of biclustering, which can be employed in marketing contexts to create recommender systems. The chapter also presents the Apriori algorithm, which allows us to perform Market Basket Analysis on extremely large transaction databases.

Chapter 9, Generalized Linear Models and Regression, discusses the main concept of generalized linear models and how to perform different kinds of regression analysis (including regularized, isotonic, polynomial, and logistic regressions).

Chapter 10, Introduction to Time-Series Analysis, introduces the reader to the main concepts of time-series analysis, focusing on the properties of stochastic processes and on the fundamental models (AR, MA, ARMA, and ARIMA) that can be employed to perform effective forecasts.

Chapter 11, Bayesian Networks and Hidden Markov Models, introduces the concepts of probabilistic modeling using direct acyclic graphs, Markov chains, and sequential processes. The chapter focuses on tools like PyStan and algorithms like HMM, which can be employed to model temporal sequences.

Chapter 12, The EM Algorithm, explains the generic structure of the Expectation-Maximization (EM) algorithm. We discuss some common applications, such as generic parameter estimation, MAP and MLE approaches, and Gaussian mixture.

Chapter 13, Component Analysis and Dimensionality Reduction, introduces the reader to the main concepts of Principal Component Analysis, Factor Analysis, and Independent Component Analysis. These tools allow us to perform effective component analysis with different kinds of datasets and, if necessary, also a dimensionality reduction with controlled information loss.

Chapter 14, Hebbian Learning, introduces Hebb's rule, which is one of the oldest neuro-scientific concepts and whose applications are incredibly powerful. The chapter explains how a single neuron works and presents two complex models (Sanger networks and Rubner-Tavan networks) that can perform a Principal Component Analysis without the input covariance matrix.

Chapter 15, Fundamentals of Ensemble Learning, explains the main concepts of ensemble learning (bagging, boosting, and stacking), focusing on Random Forests and AdaBoost (with its variants both for classification and for regression).

Chapter 16, Advanced Boosting Algorithms, continues the discussion of the most important ensemble learning models focusing on Gradient Boosting (with an XGBoost example), and voting classifiers.

Chapter 17, Modeling Neural Networks, introduces the concepts of neural computation, starting with the behavior of a perceptron and continuing the analysis of the multi-layer perceptron, activation functions, back-propagation, stochastic gradient descent, dropout, and batch normalization.

Chapter 18, Optimizing Neural Networks, analyzes the most important optimization algorithms that can improve the performances of stochastic gradient descent (including Momentum, RMSProp, and Adam) and how to apply regularization techniques to the layers of a deep network.

Chapter 19, Deep Convolutional Networks, explains the concept of convolution and discusses how to build and train an effective deep convolutional network for image processing. All the examples are based on Keras/TensorFlow 2.

Chapter 20, Recurrent Neural Networks, introduces the concept of recurrent neural networks to manage time-series and discusses the structure of LSTM and GRU cells, showing some practical examples of time-series modeling and prediction.

Chapter 21, Auto-Encoders, explains the main concepts of an autoencoder, discussing its application in dimensionality reduction, denoising, and data generation (variational autoencoders).

Chapter 22, Introduction to Generative Adversarial Networks, explains the concept of adversarial training. We focus on Deep Convolutional GANs and Wasserstein GANs. Both techniques are extremely powerful generative models that can learn the structure of an input data distribution and generate brand new samples without any additional information.

Chapter 23, Deep Belief Networks, introduces the concepts of Markov random fields, Restricted Boltzmann Machines, and Deep Belief Networks. These models can be employed both in supervised and unsupervised scenarios with excellent performance.

Chapter 24, Introduction to Reinforcement Learning, explains the main concepts of Reinforcement Learning (agent, policy, environment, reward, and value) and applies them to introduce policy and value iteration algorithms and Temporal-Difference Learning (TD(0)). The examples are based on a custom checkerboard environment.

Chapter 25, Advanced Policy Estimation Algorithms, extends the concepts defined in the previous chapter, discussing the TD(λ) algorithm, TD(0) Actor-Critic, SARSA, and Q-Learning. A basic example of Deep Q-Learning is also presented to allow the reader to immediately apply these concepts to more complex environments. Moreover, the OpenAI Gym environment is introduced and a policy gradient example is shown and analyzed.

To get the most out of this book

- The reader must possess a basic knowledge of the most common machine learning algorithms, with a clear understanding of their mathematical structure and applications.

- As Python is the language chosen for the example, the reader must be familiar with this language and, in particular, frameworks like scikit-learn, TensorFlow 2, pandas, and PyStan.

- Considering the complexity of some topics, a good knowledge of calculus, probability theory, linear algebra, and statistics is strongly advised.

Download the example code files

You can download the example code files for this book from your account at http://www.packt.com. If you purchased this book elsewhere, you can visit http://www.packtpub.com/support and register to have the files emailed directly to you.

You can download the code files by following these steps:

1. Log in or register at http://www.packt.com.
2. Select the **Support** tab.
3. Click on **Code Download**.
4. Enter the name of the book in the **Search** box and follow the on-screen instructions.

Once the file is downloaded, please make sure that you unzip or extract the folder using the latest version of:

- WinRAR / 7-Zip for Windows
- Zipeg / iZip / UnRarX for Mac
- 7-Zip / PeaZip for Linux

The code bundle for the book is also hosted on GitHub at `https://github.com/PacktPublishing/Mastering-Machine-Learning-Algorithms-Second-Edition`. We also have other code bundles from our rich catalog of books and videos available at `https://github.com/PacktPublishing/`. Check them out!

Download the color images

We also provide a PDF file that has color images of the screenshots/diagrams used in this book. You can download it here: `https://static.packt-cdn.com/downloads/9781838820299_ColorImages.pdf`.

Conventions used

There are a number of text conventions used throughout this book.

`CodeInText`: Indicates code words in text, database table names, folder names, filenames, file extensions, pathnames, dummy URLs, user input, and Twitter handles. For example, "Mount the downloaded `WebStorm-10*.dmg` disk image file as another disk in your system."

A block of code is set as follows:

```
ax[0].set_title('L1 regularization', fontsize=18)
ax[0].set_xlabel('Parameter', fontsize=18)
ax[0].set_ylabel(r'$|\theta_i|$', fontsize=18)
```

When we wish to draw your attention to a particular part of a code block, the relevant lines or items are set in bold:

```
ax[0].set_title('L1 regularization', fontsize=18)
ax[0].set_xlabel('Parameter', fontsize=18)
ax[0].set_ylabel(r'$|\theta_i|$', fontsize=18)
```

Any command-line input or output is written as follows:

```
pip install -U scikit-fuzzy
```

Bold: Indicates a new term, an important word, or words that you see on the screen, for example, in menus or dialog boxes, also appear in the text like this. For example: "Select **System info** from the **Administration** panel."

 Warnings or important notes appear like this.

 Tips and tricks appear like this.

Get in touch

Feedback from our readers is always welcome.

General feedback: If you have questions about any aspect of this book, mention the book title in the subject of your message and email us at customercare@packtpub.com.

Errata: Although we have taken every care to ensure the accuracy of our content, mistakes do happen. If you have found a mistake in this book we would be grateful if you would report this to us. Please visit, www.packtpub.com/support/errata, selecting your book, clicking on the Errata Submission Form link, and entering the details.

Piracy: If you come across any illegal copies of our works in any form on the Internet, we would be grateful if you would provide us with the location address or website name. Please contact us at copyright@packt.com with a link to the material.

If you are interested in becoming an author: If there is a topic that you have expertise in and you are interested in either writing or contributing to a book, please visit authors.packtpub.com.

Reviews

Please leave a review. Once you have read and used this book, why not leave a review on the site that you purchased it from? Potential readers can then see and use your unbiased opinion to make purchase decisions, we at Packt can understand what you think about our products, and our authors can see your feedback on their book. Thank you!

For more information about Packt, please visit `packt.com`.

1
Machine Learning Model Fundamentals

Machine learning models are mathematical tools that allow us to uncover synthetic representations of external events, with the purpose of gaining better understanding and predicting future behavior. Sometimes these models have only been defined from a theoretical viewpoint, but advances in research now allow us to apply machine learning concepts to better understand the behavior of complex systems such as deep neural networks. In this chapter, we're going to introduce and discuss some fundamental elements. Skilled readers may already know these elements, but here we offer several possible interpretations and applications.

In particular, in this chapter, we're discussing the main elements of:

- Defining models and data
- Understanding the structure and properties of good datasets
- Scaling datasets, including scalar and robust scaling
- Normalization and whitening
- Selecting training, validation and test sets, including cross-validation
- The features of a machine learning model
- Learnability
- Capacity, including Vapnik-Chervonenkis capacity
- Bias, including underfitting
- Variance, including overfitting and the Cramér-Rao bound

Models and data

Machine learning models work with data. They create associations, find out relationships, discover patterns, generate new samples, and more, working with well-defined datasets, which are homogenous collections of data points (for example, observations, images, or measures) related to a specific scenario (for example, the temperature of a room sampled every 5 minutes, or the weights of a population of individuals)

Unfortunately, sometimes the assumptions or conditions imposed on machine learning models are not clear, and a lengthy training process can result in a complete validation failure. We can think of a model as a gray box (some transparency is guaranteed by the simplicity of many common algorithms), where a vectoral input X extracted from a dataset is transformed into a vectoral output Y:

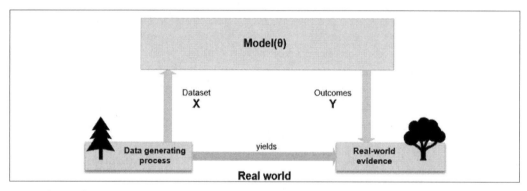

Schema of a generic model parameterized with the vector θ and its relationship with the real world

In the preceding diagram, the model has been represented by a function that depends on a set of parameters defined by the vector θ. The dataset is represented by data extracted from a real-world scenario, and the outcomes provided by the model must reflect the nature of the actual relationships. These conditions are very strong in logic and probabilistic contexts, where the inferred conditions must reflect *natural* ones.

For our purposes, it's necessary to define models that:

- Mimic animal cognitive functions
- Learn to produce outcomes that are *compatible* with the environment, given a proper training set
- Learn to overcome the boundaries of the training set, by outputting the correct (or the most likely) outcome when new samples are presented

The first point is a crucial element in the AI debate. As pointed out by Darwiche (in Darwiche A., *Human-Level Intelligence or Animal-Like Abilities?*, Communications of the ACM, Vol. 61, 10/2018), the success of modern machine learning is mainly due to the ability of deep neural networks to reproduce specific cognitive functions (for example, vision or speech recognition). It's obvious that the outcomes of such models must be based on real-world data and, moreover, that they must possess all the features of the outcomes generated by the animals whose cognitive functions we are trying to reproduce.

We're going to analyze these properties in detail. It's important to remember that they're not simple requirements, but rather the pillars that guarantee the success or the failure of an AI application in a production environment (that is, outside of the *golden world* of limited and well-defined datasets).

In this section, we're only considering **parametric** models, although there's a family of algorithms that are called **non-parametric** because they're only based on the structure of the data; we're going to discuss some of them in upcoming chapters.

The task of a **parametric learning process** is to find the best parameter set that maximizes a target function, the value of which is proportional to the accuracy of the model, given specific input X and output Y datasets (or proportional to the error, if we're trying to minimize the error). This definition isn't very rigorous, and we'll improve it in the following sections; however, it's useful as a way to introduce the structure and the properties of the data we're using, in the context of machine learning.

Structure and properties of the datasets

The first question to ask is: What are the natures of X and Y? A machine learning problem is focused on learning abstract relationships that allow a consistent generalization when new samples are provided. More specifically, we can define a stochastic data generating process with an associated joint probability distribution:

$$p_{data}(x, y) = p(y|x)p(x)$$

The process p_{data} represents the broadest and most abstract expression of the problem. For example, a classifier that must distinguish between male and female portraits will be based on a data generating process that theoretically defines the probabilities of all possible faces, with respect to the binary attribute male/female. It's clear that we can never work directly with p_{data}; it's only possible to find a well-defined formula describing p_{data} in a few limited cases (for example, the distribution of all images belonging to a dataset).

Even so, it's important for the reader to consider the existence of such a process, even when the complexity is too high to allow any direct mathematical modeling. A machine learning model must consider this kind of abstraction as a reference.

Limited Sample Populations

In many cases, we cannot derive a precise distribution and we're forced to work with a limited population of actual samples. For example, a pharmaceutical experiment is aimed to understand the effectiveness of a drug on human beings. Obviously, we cannot test the drug on every single individual, nor we can imagine including all dead and future people. Nevertheless, the limited sample population must be selected carefully, in order to represent the underlying data generating process. That is, all possible groups, subgroups, and reactions must be considered.

Since this is generally impossible, it's necessary to sample from a large population. Sampling, even in the optimal case, is associated with a loss of information (unless we remove only redundancies), and therefore when creating a dataset, we always generate a bias. This bias can range from a small, negligible effect to a widespread condition that mischaracterizes the relations present in the larger population and dramatically affects the performance of a model. For this reason, data scientists must pay close attention to how a model is tested, to be sure that new samples are generated by the same process as the training samples were. If there are strong discrepancies, data scientists should warn end users about the differences in the samples.

Since we can assume that similar individuals will behave in a similar way, if the numerosity of the sample set is large enough, we are statistically authorized to draw conclusions that we can extend to the larger, unsampled part of the population. Animals are extremely capable at identifying critical features from a family of samples, and generalizing them to interpret new experiences (for example, a baby learns to distinguish a teddy-bear from a person after only seeing their parents and a few other people). The challenging goal of machine learning is to find the optimal strategies to train models using a limited amount of information, to find all the necessary abstractions that justify their logical processes.

Of course, when we consider our sample populations, we always need to assume that they're drawn from the original data-generating distribution. This isn't a purely theoretical assumption – as we're going to see, if our sample data elements are drawn from a different distribution, the accuracy of our model can dramatically decrease.

For example, if we trained a portrait classifier using 10-megapixel images, and then we used it in an old smartphone with a 1-megapixel camera, we could easily start to find discrepancies in the accuracy of our predictions.

This isn't surprising; many details aren't captured by low-resolution images. You could get a similar outcome by feeding the model with very noisy data sources, whose information content could only be partially recovered.

N values are **independent and identically distributed (i.i.d.)** if they are sampled from the same distribution, and two different sampling steps yield statistically independent values (that is, $p(a, b) = p(a)p(b)$). If we sample N i.i.d. values from p_{data}, we can create a finite dataset X made up of k-dimensional real vectors:

$$X = \{x_0, x_1, \dots, x_{N-1}\} \text{ where } x_i \in R^k$$

In a supervised scenario, we also need the corresponding labels (with t output values):

$$Y = \{y_0, y_1, \dots, y_{N-1}\} \text{ where } y_i \in R^t$$

When the output has more than two classes, there are different possible strategies to manage the problem. In classical machine learning, one of the most common approaches is **One-vs-All**, which is based on training N different binary classifiers, where each label is evaluated against all the remaining ones. In this way, $N-1$ classifications are performed to determine the right class. With shallow and deep neural models, instead, it's preferable to use a **softmax function** to represent the output probability distribution for all classes:

$$\tilde{y}_i = \left(\frac{e^{z_0}}{\sum e^z}, \frac{e^{z_1}}{\sum e^z}, \dots, \frac{e^{z_{N-1}}}{\sum e^z} \right)$$

This kind of output, where z_i represents the intermediate values and the sum of the terms is normalized to 1, can be easily managed using the cross-entropy cost function, which we'll discuss in *Chapter 2, Loss functions and Regularization*. A sharp-eyed reader might notice that calculating the softmax output of a population allows one to obtain an approximation of the data generating process.

This is brilliant, because once the model has been successfully trained and validated with a positive result, it's reasonable to assume that the output corresponding to never-seen samples reflects the real-world joint probability distribution. That means the model has developed an internal representation of the relevant abstractions with a minimum error; which is the final goal of the whole machine learning process.

Before moving on to the discussion of some fundamental preprocessing techniques, it's worth mentioning the problem of **domain adaptation**, which is one of the most challenging and powerful techniques currently under development.

As discussed, animals can perform abstractions and extend the concepts learned in a particular context to similar, novel contexts. This ability is not only important but also necessary. In many cases, a new learning process could take too long, exposing the animal to all sorts of risks.

Unfortunately, many machine learning models lack this property. They can easily learn to generalize, but always under the condition of coping with samples originating from the same data generating process. Let's suppose that a model M has been optimized to correctly classify the elements drawn from $p_1(x, y)$ and the final accuracy is large enough to employ the model in a production environment. After a few tests, a data scientist discovers that $p_2(x, y) = f(p_1(x, y))$ is another data generating process that has strong analogies with $p_1(x, y)$. Its samples meet the requirements needed to be considered a member of the same global class. For example, $p_1(x, y)$ could represent family cars, while $p_2(x, y)$ could be a process modeling a set of trucks.

In this case, it's easy to understand that a transformation $f(z)$ is virtually responsible for increasing the size of the vehicles, their relative proportions, the number of wheels, and so on. At this point, can our model M also correctly classify the samples drawn from $p_2(x, y)$ by exploiting the analogies? In general, the answer is negative. The observed accuracy decays, reaching the limit of a purely random guess.

The reasons behind this problem are strictly related to the mathematical nature of the models and won't be discussed in this book (the reader who is interested can check the rigorous paper Crammer K., Kearns M., Wortman J., *Learning from Multiple Sources*, Journal of Machine Learning Research, 9/2008). However, it is helpful to consider such a scenario. The goal of domain adaptation is to find the optimal methods to let a model shift from M to M' and vice versa, in order to maximize its ability to work with a specific data generating process.

It's within the limits of reasonable change, for example, for a component of the model to recognize the similarities between a car and truck (for example, they both have a windshield and a radiator) and force some parameters to shift from their initial configuration, whose targets are cars, to a new configuration based on trucks. This family of methods is clearly more suitable to represent cognitive processes. Moreover, it has the enormous advantage of allowing reuse of the same models for different purposes without the need to re-train them from scratch, which is currently often a necessary condition to achieve acceptable performances.

This topic is still enormously complex; certainly, it's too detailed for a complete discussion in this book. Therefore, unless we explicitly declare otherwise, in this book you can always assume we are working with a single data generating process, from which all the samples will be drawn.

Now, let's introduce some important data preprocessing concepts that will be helpful in many practical contexts.

Scaling datasets

Many algorithms (such as logistic regression, **Support Vector Machines** (**SVMs**) and neural networks) show better performances when the dataset has a feature-wise null mean. Therefore, one of the most important preprocessing steps is so-called zero-centering, which consists of subtracting the feature-wise mean $E_x[X]$ from all samples:

$$\hat{x}_i = x_i - E_x[X] \quad \left(for \ a \ finite \ sample, \hat{x}_i = x_i - \frac{1}{N} \sum_{i=0}^{N-1} x_i = x_i - \mu \right)$$

This operation, if necessary, is normally reversible, and doesn't alter relationships either among samples or among components of the same sample. In deep learning scenarios, a zero-centered dataset allows us to exploit the symmetry of some activation functions, driving our model to a faster convergence (we're going to discuss these details in the next chapters).

Zero-centering is not always enough to guarantee that all algorithms will behave correctly. Different features can have very different standard deviations, and therefore, an optimization that works considering the norm of the parameter vector (see the section about regularization) will tend to treat all the features in the same way. This equal treatment can produce completely different final effects; features with a smaller variance will be affected more than features with a larger variance.

In a similar way, when single features contribute to finding the optimal parameters, features with a larger variance can take control over the other features, forcing them in the context of the problem to become similar to constant values. In this way, those less-varied features lose the ability to influence the end solution (for example, this problem is a common limiting factor when it comes to regressions and neural networks). For this reason, If $x_i \in R^n, \mu$, and $\sigma \in R^n$ and are computed considering every single feature for the whole dataset, it's often helpful to divide the zero-centered samples by the feature-wise standard deviation, obtaining the so-called z-score:

$$\hat{x}_i = \frac{x_i - \mu}{\sigma} \quad \left(for \ a \ finite \ sample, \sigma = \sqrt{\frac{1}{N-1} \sum_{i=0}^{N-1} (x_i - \mu)^2} \right)$$

The result is a transformed dataset where most of the internal relationships are kept, but all the features have a null mean and unit variance. The whole transformation is completely reversible when it's necessary to remap the vectors onto the original space.

We can now analyze other approaches to scaling that we might choose for specific tasks (for example, datasets with outliers).

Range scaling

Another approach to scaling is to set the range where all features should lie. For example, if $x_i \in [a, b]$ so that $(x_i) = a$ and $(x_i) = b$, the transformation will force all the values to lie in a new range $[a', b']$, as shown in the following figure:

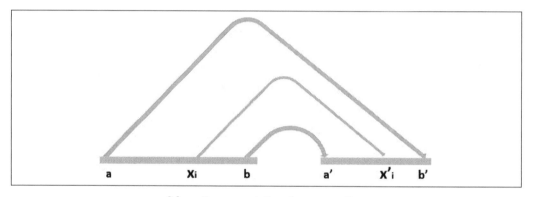

Schematic representation of a range scaling

Range scaling behaves in a similar way to standard scaling, but in this case, both the new mean and the new standard deviation are determined by the chosen interval. In particular, if the original features have symmetrical distributions, the new standard deviations will be very similar, even if not exactly equal. For this reason, this method can often be chosen as an alternative to a standard scaling (for example, when it's helpful to bound all the features in the range [0, 1]).

Robust scaling

The previous two methods have a common drawback: they are very sensitive to outliers. In fact, when the dataset contains outliers, their presence will affect the computation of both mean and standard deviation, shifting the values towards the outliers. An alternative, robust approach is based on the usage of quantiles. Given a distribution p over a range $[a, b]$, the most common quantile, called median, 50th percentile or second quartile (Q_2), is the value the splits the range $[a, b]$ into two subsets so that $P([a, m]) = P([m, b]) = 0.5$. That is to say, in a finite population, the median is the value in the central position.

For example, considering the set $A = \{1, 2, 3, 5, 7, 9\}$, we have:

$$Mean(A) \approx 4.67 \; and \; Median(A) = 4.5$$

If we add the value 10, the set A, we get $A' = A \cup \{10\}$:

$$Mean(A') \approx 5.43 \; and \; Median(A') = 6$$

In a similar way, we can define other percentiles or quantiles. A common choice for scaling the data is the **Interquartile Range** (**IQR**), sometimes called *H-spread*, defined as:

$$IQR = 75^{th} perc. - 25^{th} perc. = Q_3 - Q_1$$

In the previous formula, Q_1 is the cut-point the divides the range $[a, b]$ so that 25% of the values are in the subset $[a, Q_1]$, while Q_2 divides the range so that 75% of the values are in the subset $[a, Q_2]$. Considering the previous set A', we get:

$$Q_1 = 2.5 \; and \; Q_2 = 8 \Rightarrow IQR = 5.5 \; (std(A') \approx 3.24)$$

Given these definitions, it's easy to understand that IQR has a low sensitivity to outliers. In fact, let's suppose that a feature lies in the range [-1, 1] without outliers. In a larger dataset, we observe the interval [-2, 3]. If the effect is due to the presence of outliers (for example, the new value 10 added to A), their numerosity is much smaller than the one of normal points, otherwise they are part of the actual distribution. Therefore, we can cut them out from the computation by setting an appropriate quantile. For example, we might want to exclude from our calculations all those features whose probability is lower than 10%. In that case, we would need to consider the 5th and the 95th percentiles in a double-tailed distribution and use their difference $QR = 95^{th} - 5^{th}$.

Considering the set A', we get $IQR = 5.5$, while the standard deviation is 3.24. This implies that a standard scaling will compact the values less than a robust scaling. This effect becomes larger and larger as we increase the quantile range (for example, using the 95th and 5th percentiles, $QR \approx 8.4$). However, it's important to remember that this technique is not an outlier filtering method. All the existing values, including the outliers, will be scaled. The only difference is that the outliers are excluded from the calculation of the parameters, and so their influence is reduced, or completely removed.

The robust scaling procedure is very similar to the standard one, and the transformed values are obtained using the feature-wise formula:

$$\hat{z}_i = \frac{x_i - m}{QR}$$

Where m is the median and QR is the quantile range (for example, IQR).

Before we discuss other techniques, let's compare these methods using a dataset containing 200 points sampled from a multivariate Gaussian distribution with $\mu = (1,1)$ and $\Sigma = diag(2, 0.8)$:

```
import numpy as np

nb_samples = 200
mu = [1.0, 1.0]
covm = [[2.0, 0.0], [0.0, 0.8]]

X = np.random.multivariate_normal(mean=mu, cov=covm, size=nb_samples)
```

At this point, we employ the following scikit-learn classes:

- `StandardScaler`, whose main parameters are `with_mean` and `with_std`, both Booleans, indicating whether the algorithm should zero-center and whether it should divide by the standard deviations. The default values are both `True`.

- `MinMaxScaler`, whose main parameter is `feature_range`, which requires a tuple or list of two elements (a, b) so that $a < b$. The default value is $(0, 1)$.

- `RobustScaler`, which is mainly based on the parameter `quantile_range`. The default is $(25, 75)$ corresponding to the IQR. In a similar way to `StandardScaler`, the class accepts the parameters `with_centering` and `with_scaling`, that selectively activate/deactivate each of the two functions.

In our case, we're using the default configuration for `StandardScaler`, `feature_range=(-1, 1)` for `MinMaxScaler`, and `quantile_range=(10, 90)` for `RobustScaler`:

```
from sklearn.preprocessing import StandardScaler, RobustScaler,
MinMaxScaler

ss = StandardScaler()
X_ss = ss.fit_transform(X)

rs = RobustScaler(quantile_range=(10, 90))
```

```
X_rs = rs.fit_transform(X)

mms = MinMaxScaler(feature_range=(-1, 1))
X_mms = mms.fit_transform(X)
```

The results are shown in the following figure:

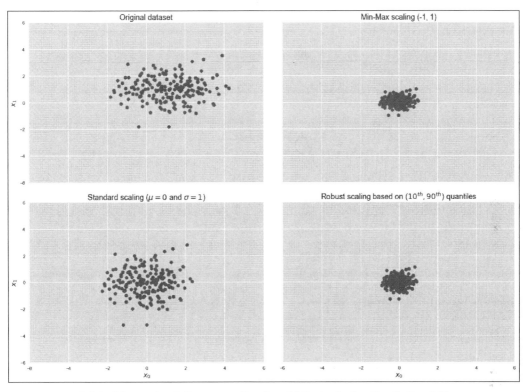

Original dataset (top left), range scaling (top right), standard scaling (bottom left),
and robust scaling (bottom right)

In order to analyze the differences, I've kept the same scale for all the diagrams.
As it's possible to see, the standard scaling performs a shift of the mean and adjusts
the points so that it's possible to consider them as drawn from $N(0, I)$. Range scaling
behaves in almost the same way and in both cases, it's easy to see how the variances
are negatively affected by the presence of a few outliers.

In particular, looking at the result of range scaling, the shape is similar to an ellipse
and the roundness — implied by a symmetrical distribution — is obtained by including
also the outliers. Conversely, robust scaling is able to produce an almost perfect
normal distribution $N(0, I)$ because the outliers are kept out of the calculations
and only the *central* points contribute to the scaling factor.

We can conclude this section with a general rule of thumb: standard scaling is normally the first choice. Range scaling can be chosen as a valid alternative when it's necessary to project the values onto a specific range, or when it's helpful to create sparsity. If the analysis of the dataset has highlighted the presence of outliers and the task is very sensitive to the effect of different variances, robust scaling is the best choice.

Normalization

One particular preprocessing method is called **normalization** (not to be confused with statistical normalization, which is a more complex and generic approach) and consists of transforming each vector into a corresponding one with a unit norm given a predefined norm (for example, L_2):

$$\hat{z}_i = f(x_i) \ \text{ and } \ \|\hat{z}_i\|_n = 1$$

Given a zero-centered dataset X, containing points $x_i \in R^n$, the normalization using the L_2 (or Euclidean) norm transforms each value into a point lying on the surface of a hypersphere with unit radius, and centered in $x_0 = (0, 0, \ldots, 0) \in R^n$ (by definition all the points on the surface have $d(x_i, x_0) = \|x_i - x_0\|_2 = 1$).

Contrary to the other methods, normalizing a dataset leads to a projection where the existing relationships are kept only in terms of angular distance. To understand this concept, let's perform a normalization of the dataset defined in the previous example, using the scikit-learn class `Normalizer` with the parameter `norm='l2'`:

```
from sklearn.preprocessing import Normalizer

nz = Normalizer(norm='l2')
X_nz = nz.fit_transform(X)
```

The result is shown in the following figure:

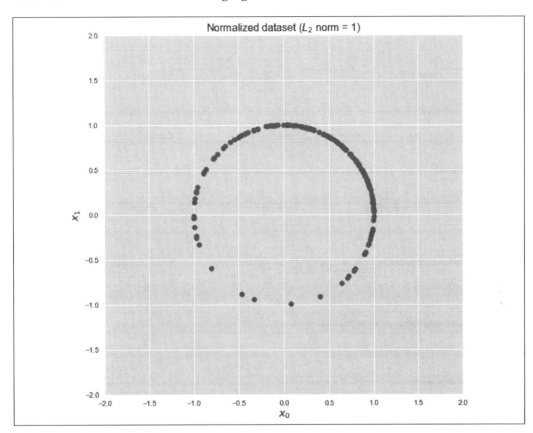

Normalized bidimensional dataset. All points lie on a unit circle

As we expected, all the points now lie on a unit circle. At this point, the reader might ask how such a preprocessing step could be helpful. In some contexts, such as **Natural Language Processing (NLP)**, two feature vectors are different in proportion to the angle they form, while they are almost insensitive to Euclidean distance.

For example, let's imagine that the previous diagram defines four semantically different concepts, which are located in the four quadrants. In particular, imagine that opposite concepts (for example, cold and warm) are located in opposite quadrants so that the maximum distance is determined by an angle of π radians (180°). Conversely, two points whose angle is very small can always be considered similar.

In this common case, we assume that the transition between concepts is *semantically smooth*, so two points belonging to different sets can always be compared according to their common features (for example, the boundary between warm and cold can be a point whose temperature is the average between the two groups). The only important thing to know is that if we move along the circle far from a point, increasing the angle, the dissimilarity increases. For our purposes, let's consider the points (-4, 0) and (-1, 3), which are almost orthogonal in the original distribution:

```
X_test = [
    [-4., 0.],
    [-1., 3.]
]

Y_test = nz.transform(X_test)

print(np.arccos(np.dot(Y_test[0], Y_test[1])))
```

The output of the previous snippet is:

`1.2490457723982544`

The dot product between two vectors x_1 and x_2 is equal to:

$$x_1 \cdot x_2 = \|x_1\|\|x_2\|\cos(\alpha_{12}) \quad \Rightarrow \quad \alpha_{12} = \cos^{-1}(x_1 \cdot x_2)$$

The last step derives from the fact that both vectors have unit norms. Therefore, the angle they form after the projection is almost $\frac{\pi}{2}$, indicating that they are indeed orthogonal. If we multiply the vectors by a constant, their Euclidean distance will obviously change, but the angular distance after normalization remains the same. I invite you to check it!

Therefore, we can completely get rid of the relative Euclidean distances and work only with the angles, which, of course, must be correlated to an appropriate similarity measure.

Whitening

Another very important preprocessing step is called **whitening**, which is the operation of imposing an identity covariance matrix to a zero-centered dataset:

$$E_x[X^T X] = I \quad \left(\overset{\textit{for a finite sample}}{\frac{1}{N-1} \left[\sum_{i=1}^{N} \left(x_i^{(p)} - \mu \right) \left(x_i^{(q)} - \mu \right)^T \right] = I} \right)$$

As the covariance matrix $E_x[X^T X]$ is real and symmetrical, it's possible to eigendecompose it without the need to invert the eigenvector matrix:

$$E_x[X^T X] = V \Omega V^T$$

The matrix V contains the eigenvectors as columns, and the diagonal matrix Ω contains the eigenvalues. To solve the problem, we need to find a matrix A, such that:

$$\hat{x}_i = A x_i \ \text{ and } \ E_x[\hat{X}^T \hat{X}] = I$$

Using the eigendecomposition previously computed, we get:

$$E_x[\hat{X}^T \hat{X}] = E_x[A X^T X A^T] = A E_x[X^T X] A^T = A V \Omega V^T A^T = I$$

Hence, the matrix A is:

$$A A^T = V \Omega^{-1} V^T \Rightarrow A = V \Omega^{-\frac{1}{2}}$$

One of the main advantages of whitening is the decorrelation of the dataset, which allows for an easier separation of the components. Furthermore, if X is whitened, any orthogonal transformation induced by the matrix P is also whitened:

$$Y = PX \Rightarrow E_x[Y^T Y] = P E_x[X^T X] P^T = P P^T = I$$

Moreover, many algorithms that need to estimate parameters that are strictly related to the input covariance matrix can benefit from whitening, because it reduces the actual number of independent variables. In general, these algorithms work with matrices that become symmetrical after applying the whitening.

Another important advantage in the field of deep learning is that the gradients are often higher around the origin and decrease in those areas where the activation functions (for example, the hyperbolic tangent or the sigmoid) saturate ($|x| \rightarrow \infty$). That's why the convergence is generally faster for whitened — and zero-centered — datasets.

In the following graph, it's possible to compare an **original dataset** and the result of **whitening**, which in this case is both zero-centered and with an identity covariance matrix:

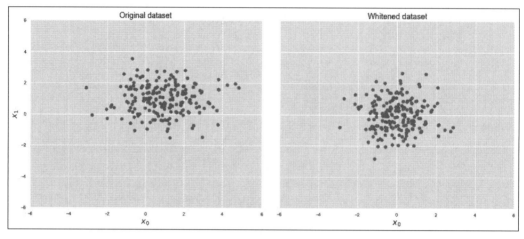

Original dataset (left) and whitened version (right)

When a whitening process is needed, it's important to consider some important details. The first one is that there's a scale difference between the real sample covariance and the estimation $X^T X$, often adopted with the **Singular Value Decomposition (SVD)**. The second one concerns some common classes implemented by many frameworks, such as scikit-learn's StandardScaler. In fact, while zero-centering is a feature-wise operation, a whitening filter needs to be computed considering the whole covariance matrix; StandardScaler implements only unit variance and feature-wise scaling.

Luckily, all scikit-learn algorithms that can benefit from a whitening preprocessing step provide a built-in feature, so no further actions are normally required. However, for all readers who want to implement some algorithms directly, I've written two Python functions that can be used for both zero-centering and whitening. They assume a matrix X with a shape ($N_{Samples} \times n$). In addition, the whiten() function accepts the parameter correct, which allows us to apply the scaling correction. The default value for correct is True:

```
import numpy as np
```

```
def zero_center(X):
    return X - np.mean(X, axis=0)

def whiten(X, correct=True):
    Xc = zero_center(X)
    _, L, V = np.linalg.svd(Xc)
    W = np.dot(V.T, np.diag(1.0 / L))
    return np.dot(Xc, W) * np.sqrt(X.shape[0]) if correct else 1.0
```

Training, validation, and test sets

As we have previously discussed, the numerosity of the sample available for a project is always limited. Therefore, it's usually necessary to split the initial set X, together with Y, each of them containing N i.i.d. elements sampled from p_{data}, into two or three subsets as follows:

- **Training set** used to train the model
- **Validation set** used to assess the score of the model without any bias, with samples never seen before
- **Test set** used to perform the final validation before moving to production

The hierarchical structure of the splitting process is shown in the following figure:

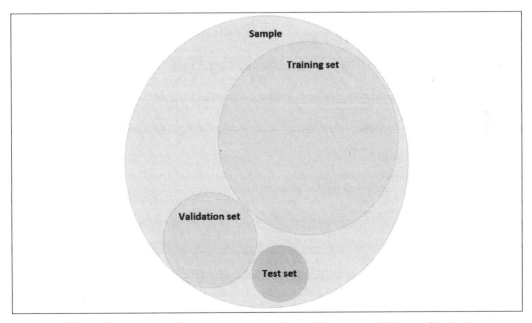

Hierarchical structure of the process employed to create training, validation, and test sets

Considering the previous diagram, generally, we have:

$$N > N_{training} > N_{Validation} > N_{test} \;\; and \; \begin{cases} Training \subset Sample \\ Validation \subset Sample \\ Test \subset Sample \\ Training \cap Test = \emptyset \\ Training \cap Validation = \emptyset \\ Test \cap Validation = \emptyset \end{cases}$$

The sample is a subset of the potential complete population, which is partially inaccessible. Because of that, we need to limit our analysis to a sample containing N elements. The training set and the validation/test set are disjoint (that is, the evaluation is carried out using samples never seen during the training phase).

The test set is normally obtained by removing N_{test} samples from the initial validation set and keeping them apart until the final evaluation. This process is quite straightforward:

1. The model M is trained using the training set
2. M is evaluated using the validation set and a designated Score($\bullet$) function
3. If Score(M) > Desired accuracy:

    perform the final test to confirm the results

4. Otherwise, the hyperparameters are modified and the process restarts

Since the model is always evaluated on samples that were not employed in the training process, the Score($\bullet$) function can determine the quality of the generalization ability developed by the model. Conversely, an evaluation performed using the training sample can help us understand whether the model is basically able to learn the structure of the dataset. We'll discuss these concepts further over the next few sections.

The choice of using two (training and validation) or three (training, validation, and test) sets is normally related to the specific context. In many cases, a single validation set, which is often called the test set, is used throughout the whole process. That's usually because the final goal is to have a reliable set of i.i.d. elements that will never be employed for training and, consequently, whose prediction results reflect the unbiased accuracy of the model. In this book, we'll always adopt this strategy, using the expression *test set* instead of *validation set*.

Depending on the nature of the problem, it's possible to choose a split percentage ratio of 70% – 30%, which is a good practice in machine learning, where the datasets are relatively small, or a higher training percentage of 80%, 90%, or up to 99% for deep learning tasks where the numerosity of the samples is very high. In both cases, we're assuming that the training set contains all the information we'll require for a consistent generalization.

In many simple cases, this is true and can be easily verified; but with more complex datasets, the problem becomes harder. Even if we draw all the samples from the same distribution, it can happen that a randomly selected test set contains features that are not present in other training samples. When this happens, it can have a very negative impact on global accuracy and, without other methods, it can also be very difficult to identify.

This is one of the reasons why, in deep learning, training sets are huge: considering the complexity of the features and structure of the data generating the distributions, choosing large test sets can limit the possibility of learning particular associations. This is a consequence of an effect called overfitting, which we'll discuss later in this chapter.

In scikit-learn, it's possible to split the original dataset using the `train_test_split()` function, which allows specifying the train/test size, and if we expect to have randomly shuffled sets (which is the default). For example, if we want to split X and Y, with 70% training and 30% test, we can use:

```
from sklearn.model_selection import train_test_split

X_train, X_test, Y_train, Y_test = train_test_split(X, Y, train_size=0.7, random_state=1000)
```

Shuffling the sets is always good practice, in order to reduce the correlation between samples (the method train_test_split has a parameter called shuffle that allows this to be done automatically). In fact, we have assumed that X is made up of i.i.d samples, but often two subsequent samples have a strong correlation, which reduces the training performance. In some cases, it's also useful to re-shuffle the training set after each training epoch; however, in the majority of our examples, we'll work with the same shuffled dataset throughout the whole process.

Shuffling has to be avoided when working with sequences and models with memory. In all those cases, we need to exploit the existing correlation to determine how the future samples are distributed. Whenever an additional test set is needed, it's always possible to reuse the same function: splitting the original test set into a larger component, which becomes the actual *validation set*, and a smaller one, the new *test set* that will be employed for the final performance check.

When working with NumPy and scikit-learn, it's always a good practice to set the random seed to a constant value, so as to allow other people to reproduce the experiment with the same initial conditions. This can be achieved by calling `np.random.seed(...)` and using the `random-state` parameter present in many scikit-learn methods.

Cross-validation

A valid method to detect the problem of wrongly selected test sets is provided by the **cross-validation (CV)** technique. In particular, we're going to use the **K-Fold** cross-validation approach. The idea is to split the whole dataset X into a moving test set and a training set made up of the remaining part. The size of the test set is determined by the number of folds, so that during k iterations, the test set covers the whole original dataset.

In the following diagram, we see a schematic representation of the process:

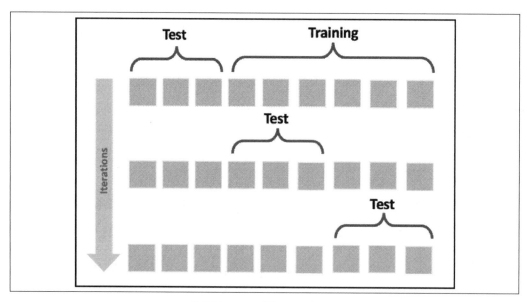

K-Fold cross-validation schema

In this way, we can assess the accuracy of the model using different sampling splits, and the training process can be performed on larger datasets; in particular, on $(k-1)N$ samples. In an ideal scenario, the accuracy should be very similar in all iterations; but in most real cases, the accuracy is quite below average.

This means that the training set has been built excluding samples that contain all the necessary examples to let the model fit the separating hypersurface considering the real p_{data}. We're going to discuss these problems later in this chapter. However, if the standard deviation of the accuracies is too large—a threshold must be set according to the nature of the problem/model—that probably means that X hasn't been drawn uniformly from p_{data}, and it's useful to evaluate the impact of the outliers in a preprocessing stage. In the following graph, we see the plot of 15-fold CV performed on a Logistic Regression:

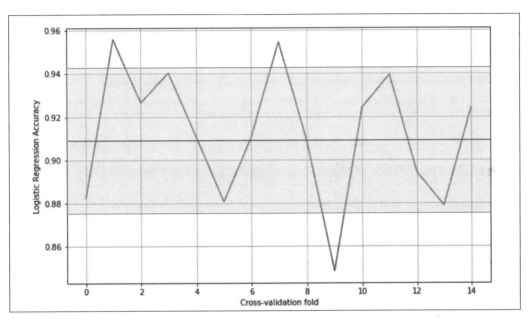

Cross-validation accuracies

The values oscillate from 0.84 to 0.95, with an average of 0.91, marked on the graph as a solid horizontal line. In this particular case, considering the initial purpose was to use a linear classifier, we can say that all folds yield high accuracies, confirming that the dataset is linearly separable; however, there are some samples, which were excluded in the ninth fold, that are necessary to achieve a minimum accuracy of about 0.88.

K-Fold cross-validation has different variants that can be employed to solve specific problems:

- **Stratified K-Fold**: A standard K-Fold approach splits the dataset without considering the probability distribution $p(y|x)$, therefore some folds may theoretically contain only a limited number of labels. Stratified K-Fold, instead, tries to split X so that all the labels are equally represented.

- **Leave-one-out (LOO):** This approach is the most drastic because it creates *N* folds, each of them containing *N-1* training samples and only one test sample. In this way, the maximum possible number of samples is used for training, and it's quite easy to detect whether the algorithm is able to learn with sufficient accuracy, or if it's better to adopt another strategy.

- The main drawback of this method is that *N* models must be trained, and when *N* is very large this can cause a performance issue. It's also an issue that with a large number of samples, the probability that two random values are similar increases, and therefore many of the folds will yield almost identical results. At the same time, LOO limits the possibilities for assessing the generalization ability of a model, because a single test sample is not enough for a reasonable estimation.

- **Leave-P-out (LPO):** In this case, the number of test samples is set to *p* non-disjoint sets, so the number of folds is equal to the binomial coefficient of *n* over *p*. This approach mitigates LOO's drawbacks, and it's a trade-off between K-Fold and LOO. The number of folds can be very high, but it's possible to control it by adjusting the number *p* of test samples; however, if *p* isn't small or big enough, the binomial coefficient can exponentially *explode*, as shown in the following figure in case of *n=20* and $p \in [1, 20]$:

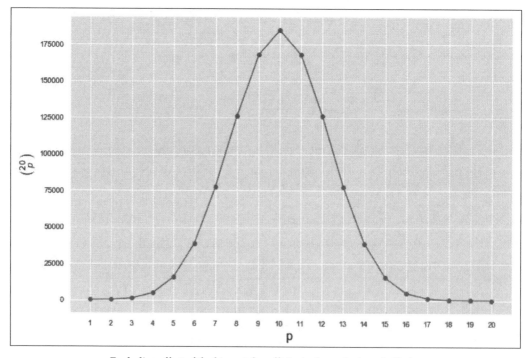

Exploding effect of the binomial coefficient when *p* is about half of *n*

Scikit-learn implements all those methods, with some other variations, but I suggest always using the `cross_val_score()` function, which is a helper that allows applying the different methods to a specific problem. It uses **Stratified K-Fold** for categorical classifications and **Standard K-Fold** for all other cases. Let's now try to determine the optimal number of folds, given a dataset containing 500 points $x_i \in R^{50}$ with redundancies, internal non-linearities, and belonging to 5 classes:

```
from sklearn.datasets import make_classification
from sklearn.preprocessing import StandardScaler

X, Y = make_classification(n_samples=500, n_classes=5,
                           n_features=50, n_informative=10,
                           n_redundant=5, n_clusters_per_class=3,
                           random_state=1000)

ss = StandardScaler()
X = ss.fit_transform(X)
```

As the first exploratory step, let's plot the learning curve using a Stratified K-Fold with 10 splits; this assures us that we'll have a uniform class distribution in every fold:

```
import numpy as np
from sklearn.linear_model import LogisticRegression


from sklearn.model_selection import learning_curve, StratifiedKFold

lr = LogisticRegression(solver='lbfgs', random_state=1000)

splits = StratifiedKFold(n_splits=10, shuffle=True, random_state=1000)
train_sizes = np.linspace(0.1, 1.0, 20)

lr_train_sizes, lr_train_scores, lr_test_scores = \
    learning_curve(lr, X, Y, cv=splits, train_sizes=train_sizes,
                   n_jobs=-1, scoring='accuracy',
                   shuffle=True, random_state=1000)
```

The result is shown in the following diagram:

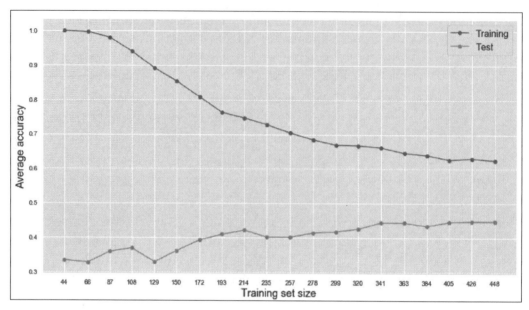

Learning curves for a Logistic Regression classification

The training curve decays when the training set size reaches its maximum, and converges to a value slightly larger than 0.6. This behavior indicates that the model is unable to fully capture the dynamics of x, and it has good performances only when the training set size is very small (that is, the actual data generating process is not fully covered). Conversely, the test performances improve when the training set is larger. This is an obvious consequence of the *wider experience* that the classifier gains when more and more points are employed.

Considering both the training and test accuracy trends, we can conclude that in this case a training set larger than about 270 points doesn't yield any strong benefit. On the other hand, since the test accuracy is extremely important, it's preferable to use the maximum number of points. As we're going to discuss later in this chapter, it indicates how well the model generalizes. In this case, the average training accuracy is worse, but there's a small benefit in the test accuracy. I've chosen this example because it's a particular case that requires a trade-off. In many cases, the curves grow proportionally, and determining the optimal number of folds is straightforward.

However, when the problem is harder, as it is in this case—considering the nature of the classifier—the choice is not obvious, and analyzing the learning curve becomes an indispensable step. Before we move on, we can try to summarize the rule. We need to find the optimal number of folds so that cross-validation guarantees an unbiased measure of the performances.

As a dataset X is drawn from an underlying data generating process, the amount of information that X carries is bounded by p_{data}. This means that an increase of the dataset's size over a certain threshold can only introduce redundancies, which cannot improve the performance of the model. The optimal number of folds, or the size of the folds, can be determined by considering the point at which both training and test average accuracies stabilize. The corresponding training set size allows us to use the largest possible test sample size for performance evaluations. Let's now compute the average CV accuracies for a different number of folds:

```
import numpy as np


from sklearn.linear_model import LogisticRegression
from sklearn.model_selection import cross_val_score

mean_scores = []
cvs = [x for x in range(5, 100, 10)]

for cv in cvs:
    score = cross_val_score(LogisticRegression(solver='lbfgs',
                            random_state=1000),
                            X, Y, scoring='accuracy', n_jobs=-1,
                            cv=cv)
    mean_scores.append(np.mean(score))
```

The result is shown in the following figure:

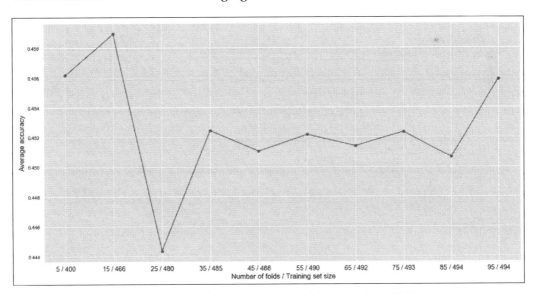

Average cross-validation accuracy for a different number of folds

The curve has a peak corresponding to 15-fold CV, which corresponds to a training set size of 466 points. In our previous analysis, we have discovered that such a value is close to the optimal one. On the other side, a larger number of folds implies smaller test sets.

We have seen that the average CV accuracy depends on a trade-off between training and test set sizes. Therefore, when the number of folds increases, we should expect an improvement in the performances. This result becomes clear with 85 folds. In this case, only 6 samples are used for testing purposes (1.2%), which means the validation is not particularly reliable, and the average value is associated with a very large variance (that is, in some *lucky* cases, the CV accuracy can be large, while in the remaining ones, it can be close to 0).

Considering all the factors, the best choice remains *k=15*, which implies the usage of 34 test samples (6.8%). I hope it's clear the right choice of *k* is a problem itself; however, in practice, a value in the range [5, 15] is often the most reasonable default choice. The goal of a good choice is also to maximize the stochasticity of CV and, consequently, to reduce the cross-correlations between estimations. Very small folds imply that many models are highly correlated, while over-large folds reduce the learning ability of the model. Therefore, a good trade-off should never prefer either very small values (acceptable only if the dataset is extremely small) nor over-large ones.

Of course, this value is strictly correlated to the nature of the task and to the structure of the dataset. In some cases, just 3 to 5% of test points can be enough to perform a correct assessment; in many other ones, a larger set is needed in order to capture the dynamics of all regions.

As a general rule, I always encourage the employment of CV for performance measurements. The main drawback of this method is its computational complexity. In the context of deep learning, for example, a training process can require hours or days, and repeating it without any modification of the hyperparameters can be unacceptable. In all these cases, a standard training-test set decomposition will be used, assuming that for both sets the numerosity is large enough to guarantee *full coverage* of the underlying data generating process.

Characteristics of a machine learning model

In this section, we're mainly going to consider supervised models, even though the concepts we'll discuss are valid in general. We'll try to determine how it's possible to measure the theoretical potential accuracy of a model, and a model's ability to generalize correctly over every possible sample drawn from p_{data}.

The majority of these concepts were developed long before the *deep learning age*, but continue to have an enormous influence on research projects.

The idea of *capacity*, for example, is an open-ended question that neuroscientists keep on asking themselves about the human brain. Modern deep learning models with dozens of layers and millions of parameters have reopened this theoretical question from a mathematical viewpoint. Together with this, other elements, such as the limits for the variance of an estimator, have again attracted the limelight because the algorithms are becoming more and more powerful, and performances that once were considered far from feasible are now a reality.

Being able to train a model, so as to exploit its full capacity, maximize its generalization ability, and increase its accuracy to overcome even human performances, is what a modern data scientist or deep learning engineer ought to expect from their work.

Learnability

Before starting the discussion of the features of a model, it's helpful to introduce some fundamental elements related to the concept of learnability, work not too dissimilar from the mathematical definition of generic computable functions. The first formal work on this was published by Valiant (in Valiant L., *A theory of the learnable*, Communications of the ACM, 27, 1984) and is mostly an introduction of the concept of **Probably Approximately Correct** (**PAC**) learning. We won't discuss the very technical mathematical details of PAC learning in this book, but it's useful to understand the possibility of finding a suitable way to describe a learning process, without referring to specific models.

For simplicity, let's assume we have a selector algorithm that can search a hypothesis h_i in a set H. This element can be interpreted in many ways according to the context. For example, the **set of hypotheses** might correspond to the set of reasonable parameters of a model, or, in another scenario, to a finite set of algorithms tuned to solve specific problems. As the definition is general, we don't have to worry about its structure.

On the other side of this landscape, there is the **set of concepts** C that we want to learn. A concept $c_i \in C$ is an instance of a problem belonging to a defined class. Again, the structure can vary, but for simplicity the reader can assume that a concept is associated with a classical training set containing a finite number of data points.

For our purposes, it's necessary to define the structure of an error measure (we're going to do that later, when talking about cost and loss functions). If you're not familiar with the concept, it's possible to consider the normalized average number of misclassified data points.

If the sample size is N, an error equal to 0 implies that there are no misclassifications, while an error equal to 1 means that all the samples have been misclassified. Just as for AUC diagrams, in a binary classifier we consider the threshold of 0.5 as lower bound, because it corresponds to a random choice of the label.

An informal definition states that a problem is PAC learnable if, given a desired maximum error ϵ and probability ψ, it's possible to set a minimum sample size N for every concept $c_i \in C$, so that a selector algorithm can find a hypothesis $h_i \in H$ such that the probability that the error is upper bounded by ϵ is greater than ψ.

As the problem is generally stochastic, the result must be expressed using probabilities. That means we can summarize the previous definition, saying that for a PAC learnable problem, $\forall \, \epsilon > 0 \; and \; \psi \in [0,1], \exists \, N : P(error_N < \epsilon) > \psi$. We also need to add that we expect the sample to have polynomial growth as a function of ϵ and ψ. This condition can be relaxed with respect to the original one, but it's enough to understand that a problem that requires an infinite sample size to achieve an error greater than 0 is not PAC learnable.

This characterization justifies the use of the word *approximately* in the definition, which could lead to misunderstandings if not fully mathematically defined. In our context, in fact, we cope with deterministic problems very rarely, and they generally don't require a machine learning algorithm. It's more helpful to know that the probability of obtaining a small error is always larger than a predefined threshold. Even if the theory is much more complex and rigorous, we can avoid all the theoretical details (which are available in Valiant's paper mentioned before) and limit our analysis to this concrete meaning of the concept.

Given a problem, we can generally find a model that can learn the associated concept and keep the accuracy above a minimum acceptable value. That's equivalent to saying that the concept is PAC learnable, a condition that we haven't proved, but that can reasonably be assumed to be true in most real-life contexts. Therefore, taking the PAC learnability for granted, we know that we can reach the desired accuracy for a specific scenario.

However, the price to pay for that isn't so easy to evaluate. For sure, when the requirements become stronger and stronger, we also need a larger training set and a more powerful model, but is this enough to achieve an optimal result? Moreover, is it possible to quantify how optimal the result is using a single measure? In the next sections, we'll introduce the elements that must be evaluated when defining, or evaluating, every machine learning model.

Capacity of a model

If we consider a supervised model as a set of parameterized functions, we can define the **representational capacity** as the intrinsic ability of a certain generic function to map a relatively large number of data distributions. To understand this concept, let's consider a function $f(x)$ that admits infinite derivatives, and rewrite it as a Taylor expansion around a starting point x_0:

$$f(x) = f(x_o) + \frac{f'(x_o)}{1!}(x - x_0) + \frac{f''(x_0)}{2!}(x - x_0)^2 + \cdots = \sum_{n=0}^{\infty} \frac{f^{(n)}(x_0)}{n!}(x - x_0)^n$$

We can decide to take only the first n terms, so to have an n-degree polynomial function around the starting point $x_0 = 0$:

$$f(x) \approx \theta_0 + \theta_1 x + \cdots + \theta_n x^n$$

Consider a simple bi-dimensional scenario with six functions, starting from a linear one. We can observe the different behaviors with a small set of data points:

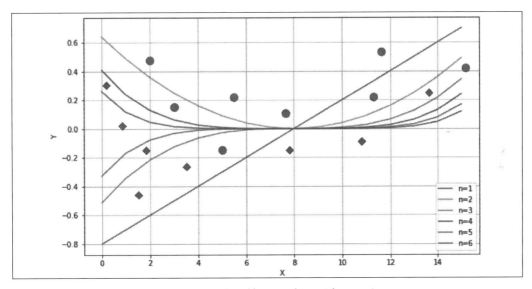

Different behavior produced by six polynomial separating curves

The ability to rapidly change the curvature is proportional to the degree. If we choose a linear classifier, we can only modify its slope—the example is always in a bi-dimensional space—and the intercept.

Instead, if we pick a higher-degree function, we have more possibilities to *bend* the curvature when it's necessary. If we consider **n=1** and **n=2** in the plot (on the top-right, they are the first and the second functions), with **n=2**, we can include the dot corresponding to *x=11*, but this choice has a negative impact on the dot at *x=5*.

Only a parameterized non-linear function can solve this problem efficiently. That's because this simple problem requires a representational capacity higher than the one provided by linear classifiers. Another classical example is the XOR function. For a long time, several researchers opposed **perceptrons** (linear neural networks) because they couldn't classify a dataset generated by the XOR function.

Fortunately, the introduction of **Multilayer Perceptrons (MLP)**, with non-linear functions, allowed us to overcome this problem, and many other problems whose complexity is beyond the possibilities of any classic machine learning model. For a better understanding of this concept, it's helpful to introduce a formalism that allows us to understand how different model families treat the same kind of problem, achieving better or worse accuracies.

Vapnik-Chervonenkis capacity

A common mathematical formalization of the capacity of a classifier is provided by the **Vapnik-Chervonenkis theory**. To introduce the definition, it's first necessary to define the concept of **shattering**. If we have a class of sets C and a set M, we say that C shatters M if:

$$\forall m_i \subseteq M \; \exists c_j \in C \Rightarrow m_j = c_i \cap M$$

In other words, given any subset of M, it can be obtained as the intersection of a particular instance of C (c_j) and M itself. Now, if we consider a model as a parameterized function:

$$C = f(\theta) \; where \; \theta \in R^p$$

Considering the variability of θ, C can be considered as a set of functions with the same structure, but different parameters:

$$C = \{f(\theta) \; with \; \theta \in \theta \subseteq R^p\}$$

We want to determine the capacity of this model family in relation to a finite dataset X:

$$X = \{x_0, x_1, ..., x_N\} \; where \; x_i \in R^k$$

According to the Vapnik-Chervonenkis theory, we can say that the model family C shatters X if there are no classification errors for every possible label assignment. Therefore, we can define the **Vapnik-Chervonenkis-capacity** or **VC-capacity** — sometimes called **VC-dimension** — as the maximum cardinality of a subset of X, so that any $f(\theta) \in C$ can shatter it (that is, the maximum number of points that $f(\theta)$ can shatter).

For example, if we consider a linear classifier in a bi-dimensional space, the VC-capacity is equal to 3, because it's always possible to label three samples so that $f(\theta)$ shatters them. However, it's impossible to do it in all situations where $N > 3$. The XOR problem is an example that needs a VC-capacity higher than three. Let's explore the following plot:

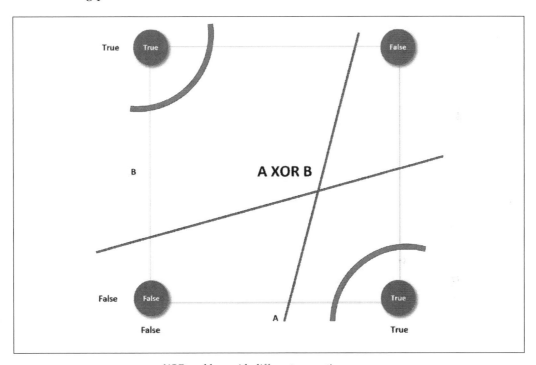

XOR problem with different separating curves

This particular label choice makes the set non-linearly separable. The only way to overcome this problem is to use higher-order functions, or non-linear ones. The curve lines — belonging to a classifier whose VC-capacity is greater than 3 — can separate both the upper-left and the lower-right regions from the remaining space, but no straight line can do the same, although it can always separate one point from the other three.

This definition of capacity is quite rigorous (the reader who's interested in the all theoretical aspects can read Mohri M., Rostamizadeh A., Talwalkar A., *Foundations of Machine Learning*, Second edition, The MIT Press, 2018), but it can help understand the relation between the complexity of a dataset and a suitable model family. According to the principle of **Occam's razor**, the simplest model that obtains an optimal accuracy (that is, the optimal set of measures that quantifies the performances of an algorithm) must be selected, and in this book, we are going to repeat this principle many times. However, the reason for this advice, which is strictly connected to the informal definition of PAC learning, will become obvious after having introduced the concepts of bias and variance of an estimator.

Bias of an estimator

Let's now consider a parameterized model with a single vectoral parameter. This isn't a limitation, just a didactic choice:

$$p(X; \bar{\theta}) \in C$$

The goal of a learning process is to estimate the parameter θ so as, for example, to maximize the accuracy of its classifications. We define the **bias of an estimator** in relation to a parameter $\tilde{\theta}$:

$$Bias[\tilde{\theta}] = E_{x|\bar{\theta}}[\tilde{\theta}] - \bar{\theta} \Rightarrow \left(\sum_{\bar{x}} \tilde{\theta} p(\bar{\theta}) \right) - \bar{\theta}$$

In other words, the bias of $p(X; \theta)$ is the difference between the expected value of the estimation and the real parameter value. Remember that the estimation is a function of X, and cannot be considered a constant in the sum.

An estimator is said to be **unbiased** if:

$$Bias[\tilde{\theta}] = 0 \Rightarrow E_{x|\bar{\theta}}[\tilde{\theta}] = \bar{\theta}$$

Moreover, the estimator is defined as **consistent** if the sequence of estimations $\{\theta_k\}$ of θ converges in probability to the real value when $k \to \infty$ (that is, it is **asymptotically unbiased**):

$$\theta_k = \theta \Rightarrow \forall \epsilon > 0 \ P(|\theta - \theta_k| > \epsilon) \to 0 \ when \ k \to \infty$$

It's obvious that this definition is weaker than the previous one, because in this case, we're only certain of achieving unbiasedness if the sample size becomes infinitely large. However, in practice, many asymptotically unbiased estimators can be considered unbiased when $k > N_k$. In other words, with samples containing at least N_k points, the results have a negligible error, and the estimation can be considered correct. From the theory, we know that some model families are unbiased (for example, linear regressions optimized using the ordinary least square), but confirming a model is unbiased is extremely different to test when the model is very complex.

For example, we can suppose that a deep neural network is prone to be unbiased, but as we are going to discuss throughout the book, the sample size is a fundamental parameter in achieving good results. Given a dataset X whose samples are drawn from p_{data}, the accuracy of an estimator is inversely proportional to its bias. Low-bias (or unbiased) estimators are able to map the dataset X with high-precision levels, while high-bias estimators are very likely to have too low a capacity for the problem to solve, and therefore their ability to detect the whole dynamic is poor.

This also implies that, in many cases, if $k << N_k$, the sample doesn't contain enough of the representative elements that are necessary to rebuild the data generating process, and the estimation of the parameters risks becoming clearly biased. Remember that the training set X is drawn from p_{data} and contains a limited number of points. Hence, given k different sets $X_1, X_2, ..., X_k$ obtained from the same data generating process, we are interested in understanding whether the initial estimation is still valid.

If X is truly representative of p_{data} and the estimator is unbiased, we should expect to always obtain the same mean, with a reasonable tolerance. This condition assures that, at least on average, the estimator yields results distributed around the true values. Let's now consider the extremes of this process: **underfitting** and **overfitting** a model.

Underfitting

A model with a large bias is likely to underfit the training set X (that is, it's not able to learn the whole structure of X). Let's consider the simple bidimensional scenario shown in the following figure:

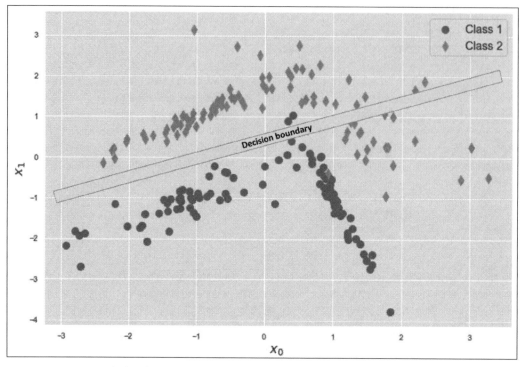

Underfitted classifier: The curve cannot separate correctly the two classes

Even if the problem is very hard, we could try to adopt a linear model and, at the end of the training process, the slope and the intercept of the separating line are about 1 and -1, as shown in the plot. However, if we measure the accuracy, we discover that it's not as large as expected—indeed, it's about 0.65—because there are too many class 2 samples in the region assigned to class 1.

Moreover, the sample size of 200 points is quite small and, therefore, X cannot be a true representative of the underlying data generating process. Considering the density for class 2 observed in the area $x_0 < 0$ and $1 < x_1 < 2$, it's reasonable to suppose that larger sample size could lead to a worse accuracy due to the increased number of misclassified class 2 points. Independent of the number of iterations, this model will never be able to learn a good association between X and Y.

This condition is called **underfitting**, and the major indicator of underfitting is very low training accuracy. Unfortunately, even if some data preprocessing steps can improve the accuracy, when a model is underfitted, the only valid solution is to adopt a higher-capacity model. In fact, when the estimation of the parameters is biased, its expected value is always different from the true value. That difference leads to a systematic prediction error that cannot be corrected.

Considering the previous example, a linear model (for example, a logistic regression) can only modify the slope and the intercept of the separating line. The reader can easily see that the number of degrees of freedom are too small to achieve, for example, an accuracy greater than 0.95. Instead, using a polynomial classifier (for example, a parabolic one), the problem can be easily solved. The introduction of another parameter. the coefficient of the square term, allows defining a curve separating line that surely leads to a better fit. Of course, the price to pay is double:

- A model with larger capacity needs a higher computational effort. This is often a secondary problem.

- The extra capacity could reduce the generalization ability, if X is not fully representative of p_{data} (we are going to discuss this problem in the next section).

In a machine learning task, our goal is to achieve the maximum accuracy, starting from the training set and then moving on to the validation set. More formally, we can say that we want to improve our models so to get as close as possible to **Bayes error**, which is the theoretical minimal generalization error achievable by an estimator. It can also be expressed as **Bayes accuracy**, which is the maximum achievable generalization accuracy.

In the following diagram, we can see a representation of this process:

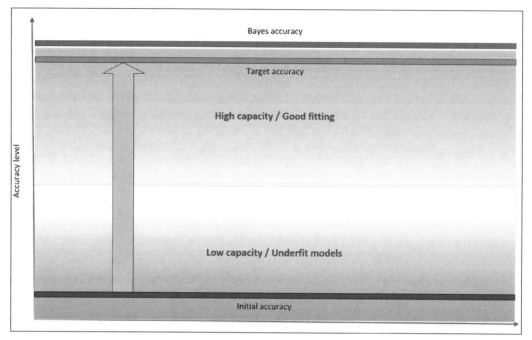

Accuracy level diagram

Bayes accuracy is often a purely theoretical limit and, for many tasks, it's almost impossible to achieve, even using biological systems. However, advancements in the field of deep learning allow creating models that have a target accuracy slightly below the Bayes one. In general, there's no closed form for determining the Bayes accuracy, therefore human abilities are considered as a benchmark.

In the previous classification example, a human being is immediately able to distinguish among different dot classes, but the problem can be very hard for a limited-capacity classifier. Some of the models we're going to discuss can solve this problem with a very high target accuracy, but at this point, we need to introduce the concept of variance of an estimator in order to understand the effects of excessive capacity.

Variance of an estimator

At the beginning of this chapter, we defined the data generating process p_{data}, and we've assumed that our dataset X has been drawn from this distribution. However, we don't want to learn existing relationships limited to X; we expect our model to be able to generalize correctly to any other subset drawn from p_{data}. A good measure of this ability is provided by the **variance of the estimator**:

$$Var[\theta] = Stderr[\tilde{\theta}]^2 = E\left[(\tilde{\theta} - E[\tilde{\theta}])^2\right]$$

The variance can be also defined as the square of the standard error, analogously to the standard deviation. A large variance implies dramatic changes in accuracy when new subsets are selected. In fact, even if the model is unbiased, and the estimated values of the parameters are spread around the true mean, they can show high variability.

For example, suppose that an estimated parameter $\theta \sim N(0, 2)$ and the true mean is actually 0. We know that the probability $P(-2 \leq \theta \leq 2) \approx 0.68$; hence, if a wrong estimation that $\theta = 0.5$ can lead to a significant error, there's a very high risk of misclassification with the majority of validation samples. This effect is related to the fact that the model has probably reached a very high training accuracy through over-learning a limited set of relationships, and it has almost completely lost its ability to generalize (that is, the average validation accuracy decays when never-seen samples are tested).

However, if it's possible to obtain unbiased estimators, it's almost impossible to reduce the variance under a well-defined threshold (see the later section related to the Cramér-Rao bound). Before discussing the implications of the variance, we need to introduce the opposite extreme situation to underfitting: overfitting a model.

Overfitting

If underfitting was the consequence of low capacity and large bias, **overfitting** is a phenomenon strictly related to large variance. In general, we can observe a very high training accuracy (even close to the Bayes level), but not a poor validation accuracy.

This means that the capacity of the model is high enough or even excessive for the task (the higher the capacity, the higher the probability of large variances), and that the training set isn't a good representation of p_{data}. To understand the problem, consider the following classification scenarios:

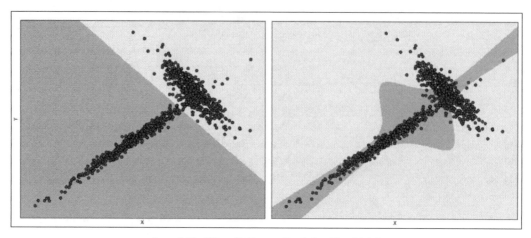

Acceptable fitting (left), overfitted classifier (right)

The left plot has been obtained using logistic regression, while the right plot was obtained with an SVM algorithm with a sixth-degree polynomial kernel. If we consider the second model, the decision boundaries seem much more precise, with some samples just over them. Considering the shapes of the two subsets, it would be possible to say that a non-linear SVM can better capture the dynamics; however, if we sample another dataset from p_{data} and the diagonal *tail* becomes wider, logistic regression continues to classify the points correctly, while the SVM accuracy decreases dramatically.

The second model is very likely to be overfitted, and some corrections are necessary. When the validation accuracy is much lower than the training one, a good strategy is to increase the number of training samples, to consider the real p_{data}. In fact, it can happen that a training set is built starting from a hypothetical distribution that doesn't reflect the real one, or the number of samples used for the validation is too high, reducing the amount of information carried by the remaining samples.

Cross-validation is a good way to assess the quality of datasets, but it can always happen that we misclassify completely new subsets (for example, generated when the application is deployed in a production environment), even if they were supposed to belong to p_{data}. If it's not possible to enlarge the training set, data augmentation could be a valid solution, because it allows creating artificial samples (for images, it's possible to mirror, rotate, or blur them) starting from the information stored in the known ones.

Other strategies to prevent overfitting are based on a technique called **regularization**, which we're going to discuss in the next chapter. For now, we can say that the effect of regularization is similar to a partial linearization, which implies a capacity reduction with a consequent variance decrease and a tolerable bias increase.

The Cramér-Rao bound

If it's theoretically possible to create an unbiased model, even asymptotically, this is not true for the variance. To understand this concept, it's necessary to introduce an important definition: the **Fisher information**. If we have a parameterized model and a data-generating process p_{data}, we can define a likelihood function by considering the following parameters:

$$L(X) = p(X|\theta)$$

This function allows us to measure how well the model describes the original data generating process. The shape of the likelihood can vary substantially, from well-defined, peaked curves, to almost flat surfaces. Let's consider the following graph, showing two examples based on a single parameter. The x-axis represents the value of a generic parameter, while the y-axis is the log-likelihood:

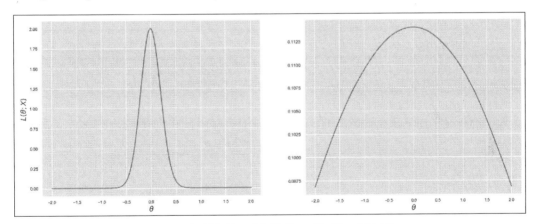

Very peaked likelihood (left), flatter likelihood (right)

We can immediately understand that, in the first case, the maximum likelihood (which represents the value for which the model has the highest probability to generate the training dataset – the concept will be discussed in a dedicated section) can be easily reached using classic optimization methods, because the surface is very peaked. In the second case, instead, the gradient magnitude is smaller, and it's rather easy to stop before reaching the actual maximum because of numerical imprecisions or tolerances. In worst cases, the surface can be almost flat in very large regions, with a corresponding gradient close to zero.

Of course, we'd like it if we could always work with very sharp and peaked likelihood functions, because they carry more information about their maximum. More formally, the Fisher information quantifies this value. For a single parameter, it is defined as follows:

$$I(\theta) = E_{\bar{x}|\theta}\left[\left(\frac{\partial}{\partial \theta} log\, p(\bar{x}\,|\theta)\right)^2\right]$$

The Fisher information is an unbounded, non-negative number, that is proportional to the amount of information carried by the log-likelihood; the use of logarithm has no impact on the gradient ascent, but it simplifies complex expressions by turning products into sums.

This value can be interpreted as the *speed* of the gradient when the function is reaching the maximum; therefore, higher values imply better approximations, while a hypothetical value of zero means that the probability to determine the right parameter estimation is also null.

When working with a set of K parameters, the Fisher information becomes a positive semidefinite matrix:

$$I(\widetilde{\theta}) = \begin{pmatrix} E_{\bar{x}|\bar{\theta}}\left[\left(\frac{\partial}{\partial \theta_0}log\, p(\bar{x}|\bar{\theta})\right)\left(\frac{\partial}{\partial \theta_0}log\, p(\bar{x}|\bar{\theta})\right)\right] & \cdots & E_{\bar{x}|\bar{\theta}}\left[\left(\frac{\partial}{\partial \theta_0}log\, p(\bar{x}|\bar{\theta})\right)\left(\frac{\partial}{\partial \theta_K}log\, p(\bar{x}|\bar{\theta})\right)\right] \\ \vdots & \ddots & \vdots \\ E_{\bar{x}|\bar{\theta}}\left[\left(\frac{\partial}{\partial \theta_K}log\, p(\bar{x}|\bar{\theta})\right)\left(\frac{\partial}{\partial \theta_0}log\, p(\bar{x}|\bar{\theta})\right)\right] & \cdots & E_{\bar{x}|\bar{\theta}}\left[\left(\frac{\partial}{\partial \theta_K}log\, p(\bar{x}|\bar{\theta})\right)\left(\frac{\partial}{\partial \theta_K}log\, p(\bar{x}|\bar{\theta})\right)\right] \end{pmatrix}$$

This matrix is symmetrical, and also has another important property: when a value is zero, it means that the corresponding parameters are orthogonal for the purpose of the maximum likelihood estimation, and they can be considered separately. In many real cases, if a value is close to zero, it determines a very low correlation between parameters. In that case, even if it's not mathematically rigorous, it's possible to decouple them anyway.

At this point, we can introduce the **Cramér-Rao bound**, which states that for every unbiased estimator that adopts $\bar{x}$ with probability distribution $p(\bar{x}; \bar{\theta})$ as a measure set, the variance of any estimator of a parameter θ is always lower-bounded according to the following inequality:

$$Var[\tilde{\theta}] \geq \frac{1}{I(\theta)}$$

In fact, if we initially consider a generic estimator, and exploit Cauchy-Schwarz inequality with the variance and the Fisher information, which are both expressed as expected values, we obtain:

$$E_{\bar{x}|\theta}\left[(\tilde{\theta}-E_{\bar{x}|\theta}[\tilde{\theta}])^2\right] E_{\bar{x}|\theta}\left[\left(\frac{\partial \log p(\bar{x}|\theta)}{\partial \theta}\right)^2\right] \geq E_{\bar{x}|\theta}\left[(\tilde{\theta}-E_{\bar{x}|\theta}[\tilde{\theta}])\frac{\partial \log p(\theta)}{\partial \theta}\right]^2$$

Now, if we need to compute the expression for derivatives of the bias with respect to θ:

$$\frac{\partial Bias[\tilde{\theta}]}{\partial \bar{\theta}} = \frac{\partial}{\partial \bar{\theta}}\left[\left(\sum_x \tilde{\theta} p(x|\bar{\theta})\right)-\bar{\theta}\right] = \left(\sum_x \tilde{\theta}\frac{\partial p(x|\bar{\theta})}{\partial \bar{\theta}}\right)-1 = \left(\sum_x \tilde{\theta} p(x|\bar{\theta})\frac{\partial p(x|\bar{\theta})}{\partial \bar{\theta}}\right)-1$$
$$= E_{x|\bar{\theta}}\left[\tilde{\theta}\frac{\partial \log p(x|\bar{\theta})}{\partial \bar{\theta}}\right]-1$$

Considering that the expected value of the estimation of θ doesn't depend on x, we can rewrite the right side of the inequality as:

$$E_{x|\theta}\left[(\tilde{\theta}-E_{x|\theta}[\tilde{\theta}])\frac{\partial \log p(\bar{x}|\theta)}{\partial \theta}\right]^2 = \left(\frac{\partial Bias[\tilde{\theta}]}{\partial \theta}+1\right)^2$$

If the estimator is unbiased, the derivative on the right side is equal to zero, and therefore, we get:

$$Var[\tilde{\theta}] \cdot I(\theta) \geq 1$$

In other words, we can try to reduce the variance, but it will be always lower-bounded by the inverse Fisher information. Therefore, given a dataset and a model, there's always a limit to the ability to generalize.

In some cases, this measure is easy to determine; however, its real value is theoretical, because it provides the likelihood function with another fundamental property: it carries all the information needed to estimate the worst case for the variance. This is not surprising: when we discussed the capacity of a model, we saw how different functions could lead to higher or lower accuracies. If the training accuracy is high enough, this means that the capacity is appropriate or even excessive for the problem; however, we haven't considered the role of the likelihood $p(X; \bar{\theta})$.

Large-capacity models, in particular, with small or low-informative datasets, can lead to flat likelihood surfaces with a higher probability than lower-capacity models. Therefore, the Fisher information tends to become smaller, because there are more and more parameter sets that yield similar probabilities; this, at the end of the day, leads to higher variances and an increased risk of overfitting.

At this point, it's possible to fully understand the meaning of the empirical rule derived from the **Occam's razor** principle: if a simpler model can explain a phenomenon with enough accuracy, it doesn't make sense to increase its capacity.

A simpler model is always preferable when the performance is good and it represents the specific problem accurately, because it's normally faster and more efficient in both the training and the inference phases. When we talk about deep neural networks, this principle can be applied in a more precise way, because it's easier to increase or decrease the number of layers and neurons until the desired accuracy has been achieved.

Summary

In this chapter, we discussed some fundamental concepts shared by almost any machine learning model.

In the first part, we introduced the data generating process, as a generalization of a finite dataset, and discussed the structure and properties of a good dataset. We discussed some common preprocessing strategies and their properties, such as scaling, normalizing, and whitening. We explained the most common strategies to split a finite dataset into a training block and a validation set, and we introduced cross-validation, with some of the most important variants, as one of the best approaches to avoid the limitations of a static split.

In the second part, we discussed the features of a machine learning model, and the concept of learnability. We discussed the main properties of an estimator: capacity, bias, and variance. We also introduced the Vapnik-Chervonenkis theory, which is a mathematical formalization of the concept of representational capacity, and we analyzed the effects of high biases and high variances. In particular, we discussed effects called underfitting and overfitting, defining the relationship with high bias and high variance.

In the next chapter, *Chapter 2, Loss functions and Regularization*, we're going to introduce loss and cost functions, which provide a simple and effective tool to fit machine learning models by minimizing an error measure or maximizing a specific objective.

Further reading

- Darwiche A., *Human-Level Intelligence or Animal-Like Abilities?*, Communications of the ACM, Vol. 61, 10/2018

- Crammer K., Kearns M., Wortman J., *Learning from Multiple Sources*, Journal of Machine Learning Research, 9/2008

- Mohri M., Rostamizadeh A., Talwalkar A., *Foundations of Machine Learning, Second edition*, The MIT Press, 2018

- Valiant L., *A theory of the learnable*, Communications of the ACM, 27, 1984

- Ng A. Y., *Feature selection, L1 vs. L2 regularization, and rotational invariance*, ICML, 2004

- Dube S., *High Dimensional Spaces, Deep Learning and Adversarial Examples*, arXiv:1801.00634 [cs.CV]

- Sra S., Nowozin S., Wright S. J. (edited by), *Optimization for Machine Learning*, The MIT Press, 2011

- Bonaccorso G., *Machine Learning Algorithms, Second Edition*, Packt, 2018

2
Loss Functions and Regularization

Loss functions are proxies that allow us to measure the error made by a machine learning model. They define the very structure of the problem to solve, and prepare the algorithm for an optimization step aimed at maximizing or minimizing the loss function. Through this process, we make sure that all our parameters are chosen in order to reduce the error as much as possible. In this chapter, we're going to discuss the fundamental loss functions and their properties. I've also included a dedicated section about the concept of regularization; regularized models are more resilient to overfitting, and can achieve results beyond the limits of a simple loss function.

In particular, we'll discuss:

- Defining loss and cost functions
- Examples of cost functions, including mean squared error and the Huber and hinge cost functions
- Regularization
- Examples of regularization, including Ridge, Lasso, ElasticNet, and early stopping techniques

We'll begin with some definitions related to loss and cost functions.

Defining loss and cost functions

Many machine learning problems can be expressed throughout a proxy function that measures the training error. The obvious implicit assumption is that, by reducing both training and validation errors, the accuracy increases, and the algorithm reaches its objective.

If we consider a supervised scenario (many considerations hold also for semi-supervised ones), with finite datasets X and Y:

$$X = \{\bar{x}_0, \bar{x}_1, \dots, \bar{x}_N\} \text{ where } \bar{x}_i \in \mathbb{R}^k$$

$$Y = \{\bar{y}_0, \bar{y}_1, \dots, \bar{y}_N\} \text{ where } \bar{y}_i \in \mathbb{R}^t$$

We can define the generic **loss function** for a single data point as:

$$J(\bar{x}_i, \bar{y}_i; \bar{\theta}) = J(f(\bar{x}_i; \bar{\theta}), \bar{y}_i) = J(\tilde{y}_i, \bar{y}_i)$$

J is a function of the whole parameter set and must be proportional to the error between the true label and the predicted label.

 A very important property of a loss function is convexity. In many real cases, this is an almost impossible condition; however, it's always useful to look for convex loss functions, because they can be easily optimized through the gradient descent method. We're going to discuss this topic in *Chapter 10, Introduction to Time-Series Analysis*.

However, for now, it's useful to consider a loss function as an intermediary between our training process and a pure mathematical optimization. The missing link is the complete data. As already discussed, X is drawn from p_{data}, so it should represent the true distribution. Therefore, when we minimize the loss function, we're considering a potential subset of points, and never the whole real dataset.

In many cases, this isn't a limitation. If the bias is null and the variance is small enough, the resulting model will show a good generalization ability, with high training and validation accuracy; however, considering the data generating process, it's useful to introduce another measure called **expected risk**:

$$E_{Risk}[f] = \int J(f(\bar{x}; \bar{\theta}), \bar{y}) p_{data}(\bar{x}, \bar{y}) d\bar{x} d\bar{y}$$

This value can be interpreted as an average of the loss function over all possible samples drawn from p_{data}. However, as p_{data} is generally continuous, it's necessary to consider an expected value and integrate over all possible $(\bar{x}, \bar{y})$ couples, which is often an intractable problem. The minimization of the expected risk implies the maximization of global accuracy, which, in turn, corresponds to the optimal outcome.

On the other hand, in real-world scenarios we work with a finite number of training samples. Since that's the case, it's preferable to define a **cost function**, which is often called a loss function as well, and is not to be confused with the log-likelihood:

$$L(X, Y; \bar{\theta}) = \sum_{i=0}^{N} J(\bar{x}_i, \bar{y}_i; \bar{\theta})$$

This is the actual function that we're going to minimize. Divided by the number of samples (a factor that doesn't have any impact) it's also called **empirical risk**. It's called that because it's an approximation, based on a finite sample X, of the expected risk. In other words, we want to find a set of parameters so that:

$$\bar{\theta}^* = \underset{\bar{\theta}}{\operatorname{argmin}} L(X, Y; \bar{\theta})$$

When the cost function has more than two parameters, it's very difficult and perhaps even impossible to understand its internal structure. However, we can analyze some potential conditions using a bidimensional diagram:

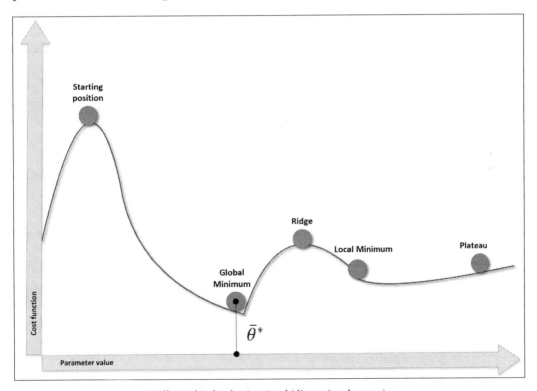

Different kinds of points in a bidimensional scenario

The different situations we can observe are:

- The **starting point**, where the cost function is usually very high due to the error.

- **Local minima**, where the gradient is null and the second derivative is positive. They're candidates for the optimal parameter set, but unfortunately, if the concavity isn't too deep, an inertial movement or noise can easily move the point away.

- **Ridges** (or **local maxima**), where the gradient is null, and the second derivative is negative. They are unstable points, because even minimal perturbation allows escape toward lower-cost areas.

- **Plateaus**, or regions where the surface is almost flat and the gradient is close to zero. The only way to escape a plateau is to keep some residual kinetic energy — we're going to discuss this concept when talking about neural optimization algorithms in *Chapter 18, Optimizing Neural Networks*.

- **Global minimum**, the point we want to reach to optimize the cost function.

Even if local minima are likely when the model has a small number of parameters, they become very unlikely when the model has a large number of parameters. In fact, an n-dimensional point $\bar{\theta}^*$ is a local minimum for a convex function (and here, we're assuming L to be convex) only if:

$$\begin{cases} \nabla_{\bar{\theta}} L(\bar{x}^*) = 0 \\ \mathcal{H}_{\bar{\theta}} L(\bar{x}^*) \; is \; positive \; definite \end{cases}$$

The second condition imposes a positive definite Hessian matrix — equivalently, all principal minors $\mathcal{H}_n$ made with the first n rows and n columns must be positive — therefore all its eigenvalues $\lambda_0, \lambda_1, \dots \lambda_n$ must be positive. This probability decreases with the number of parameters ($\mathcal{H}$ is an $n \times n$ square matrix and has n eigenvalues), and becomes close to zero in deep learning models where the number of weights can be in the order of millions, or even more. The reader interested in a complete mathematical proof can read Dube S., *High Dimensional Spaces, Deep Learning and Adversarial Examples*, arXiv:1801.00634 [cs.CV].

As a consequence, a more common condition to consider is instead the presence of **saddle points**, where the eigenvalues have different signs and the orthogonal directional derivatives are null, even if the points are neither local maxima nor local minima. Consider, for example, the following plot:

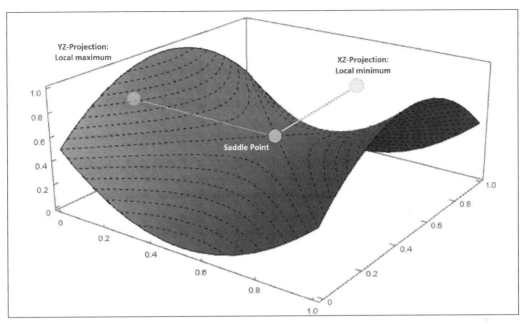

Saddle point in a three-dimensional scenario

The surface is very similar in shape to a horse saddle, and if we project the point on an orthogonal plane, XZ is a minimum, while on another plane (YZ) it is a maximum. It's straightforward that saddle points are quite *dangerous*, because many simpler optimization algorithms can slow down and even stop, losing the ability to find the right direction. In *Chapter 18, Optimizing Neural Networks*, we're going to discuss some methods that are able to mitigate this kind of problem, allowing deep models to converge.

Examples of cost functions

In this section, we'll discuss some common **cost functions** that are employed in both classification and regression tasks. Some of them will be repeatedly adopted in our examples over the next few chapters, particularly when we're discussing training processes in shallow and deep neural networks.

Mean squared error

Mean squared error is one of the most common regression cost functions. Its generic expression is:

$$L(X, Y; \bar{\theta}) = \frac{1}{N+1} \sum_{i=0}^{N} [f(\bar{x}_i; \bar{\theta}) - y_i]^2$$

This function is differentiable at every point of its domain and it's convex, so it can be optimized using the **stochastic gradient descent** (**SGD**) algorithm. This cost function is fundamental in regression analysis using the **Ordinary** or **Generalized Least Square** algorithms, where, for example, it's possible to prove that the estimators are always unbiased.

However, there's a drawback when employing it in regression tasks with outliers. Its value is always quadratic, and therefore, when the distance between the prediction and an actual outlier value is large, the relative error is large, and this can lead to an unacceptable correction.

Huber cost function

As explained, mean squared error isn't robust to outliers, because it's always quadratic, independent of the distance between actual value and prediction. To overcome this problem, it's possible to employ the **Huber cost function**, which is based on threshold t_H, so that for distances less than t_H its behavior is quadratic, while for a distance greater than t_H it becomes linear, reducing the entity of the error and thereby reducing the relative importance of the outliers.

The analytical expression is:

$$L(X, Y; \bar{\theta}, t_H) = \begin{cases} \dfrac{1}{2} \displaystyle\sum_{i=0}^{N-1} [f(\bar{x}_i; \bar{\theta}) - y_i]^2 & if \ \left| f(\bar{x}_i; \bar{\theta}) - y_i \right| \leq t_H \\ t_H \displaystyle\sum_{i=0}^{N-1} \left| f(\bar{x}_i; \bar{\theta}) - y_i \right| - \dfrac{t_H}{2} & if \ \left| f(\bar{x}_i; \bar{\theta}) - y_i \right| > t_H \end{cases}$$

Hinge cost function

This cost function is adopted by **Support Vector Machine** (**SVM**) algorithms, where the goal is to maximize the distance between the separation boundaries, where the support vectors lie. Its analytic expression is:

$$L(X, Y; \bar{\theta}) = \sum_{i=0}^{N-1} \max(0, 1 - f(\bar{x}_i; \bar{\theta})y_i)$$

Contrary to the other examples, this cost function is not optimized using classic SGD methods, because it's not differentiable when:

$$f(\bar{x}_i; \bar{\theta})y_i = 1 \implies \max(0,0)$$

For this reason, SVM algorithms are optimized using quadratic programming techniques.

Categorical cross-entropy

Categorical cross-entropy is the most diffused classification cost function, adopted by logistic regression and the majority of neural architectures. The generic analytical expression is:

$$L(X, Y; \bar{\theta}) = -\sum_{i=0}^{N-1} y_i \log f(\bar{x}_i; \bar{\theta})$$

This cost function is convex and can easily be optimized using SGD techniques. According to information theory, the entropy of a distribution p is a measure of the amount of uncertainty — expressed in **bit** if $\log_2 x$ is used and in **nat** is natural logarithm is employed — *carried* by a particular probability distribution. For example, if we toss a fair coin, then $P(Head) = P(Tail) = {}^1/_2$ according to a Bernoulli distribution. Therefore, the entropy of such a discrete distribution is:

$$H(p) = -\sum_i p_i \log_2 p_i = -\frac{1}{2}(-1) - \frac{1}{2}(-1) = 1 \; bit$$

The uncertainty is equal to 1 bit, which means that before any experiment there are 2 possible outcomes, which is obvious. What happens if we know that the coin is loaded, and *P(Head) = 0.1* and *P(Tail) = 0.9*? The entropy is now:

$$H(p) = -0.1 \log_2 0.1 - 0.9 \log_2 0.9 \approx 0.47 \; bit$$

As our uncertainty is now very low — we know that in 90% of the cases, the outcome will be tails — the entropy is less than half a bit. The concept must be interpreted as a continuous measure, which means that a single outcome is very likely to appear. The extreme case when $P(Head) \rightarrow 0$ and $P(Tail) \rightarrow 1$ asymptotically requires 0 bits, because there's no more uncertainty and the probability distribution is degenerate.

The concept of entropy, as well as cross-entropy and other information theory formulas, can be extended to continuous distributions using an integral instead of a sum. For example, the entropy of a normal distribution $N(0, \sigma^2)$ is $H(p) = \frac{1}{2} \log 2\pi e \sigma^2$. In general, the entropy is proportional to the variance or to the *spread* of the distribution.

This is an intuitive concept, in fact; the larger the variance, the larger the region in which the potential outcomes have a similar probability to be selected. As the uncertainty grows when the potential set of candidate outcomes does, the *price* in bits or nats we need to pay to remove the uncertainty increases. In the example of the coin, we needed to pay 1 bit for a fair outcome and only 0.47 bit when we already knew that $P(Tail) = 0.9$; our uncertainty was quite a lot lower.

Analogously, cross-entropy is defined between two distributions p and q:

$$H(p, q) = -\sum_i p_i \log q_i$$

Let's suppose that p is the data generating process we are working with. What's the meaning of $H(P, q)$? Considering the expression, what we're doing is computing the expected value $-E_p[\log q]$, while the entropy computed the expected value $-E_p[\log p]$. Therefore, if q is an approximation of p, the cross-entropy measures the additional uncertainty that we are introducing when using the model q instead of the original data generating process. It's not difficult to understand that we increase the uncertainty by only using an approximation of the true underlying process.

In fact, if we're training a classifier, our goal is to create a model whose distribution is as similar as possible to p_{data}. This condition can be achieved by minimizing the Kullback-Leibler divergence between the two distributions:

$$D_{KL}(p_{data} || \tilde{p}_M) = \sum_{i=0}^{N-1} p_{data}(\bar{x}_i, y_i) \log \frac{p_{data}(\bar{x}_i, y_i)}{\tilde{p}_M(\bar{x}_i, y_i; \bar{\theta})}$$

In the previous expression, p_M is the distribution generated by the model. Now, if we rewrite the divergence, we get:

$$D_{KL}(p_{data}||\tilde{p}_M) = \sum_{i=0}^{N-1} p_{data}(\bar{x}_i, y_i) \log p_{data}(\bar{x}_i, y_i)$$
$$- \sum_{i=0}^{N-1} p_{data}(\bar{x}_i, y_i) \log \tilde{p}_M(\bar{x}_i, y_i; \bar{\theta}) = H(p_{data}) + H(p_{data}||\tilde{p}_M)$$

The first term is the entropy of the data generating distribution, and it doesn't depend on the model parameters, while the second one is the cross-entropy. Therefore, if we minimize the cross-entropy, we also minimize the Kullback-Leibler divergence, forcing the model to reproduce a distribution that is very similar to p_{data}. That means that we are reducing the additional uncertainty that was induced by the approximation. This is a very elegant explanation as to why the cross-entropy cost function is an excellent choice for classification problems.

Regularization

When a model is ill-conditioned or prone to overfitting, **regularization** offers some valid tools to mitigate the problems. From a mathematical viewpoint, a regularizer is a penalty added to the cost function, to impose an extra condition on the evolution of the parameters:

$$L_R(X, Y; \bar{\theta}) = L(X, Y; \bar{\theta}) + \lambda g(\bar{\theta})$$

The parameter λ controls the strength of the regularization, which is expressed through the function $g(\bar{\theta})$. A fundamental condition on $g(\bar{\theta})$ is that it must be differentiable so that the new composite cost function can still be optimized using SGD algorithms. In general, any regular function can be employed; however, we normally need a function that can contrast the indefinite growth of the parameters.

To understand the principle, let's consider the following diagram:

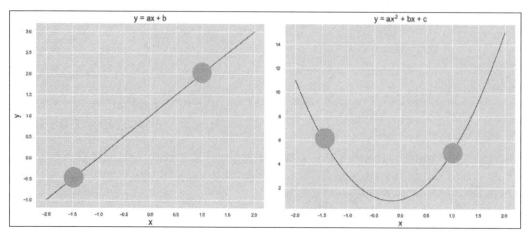

Interpolation with a linear curve (left) and a parabolic one (right)

In the first diagram, the model is linear and has two parameters, while in the second one, it is quadratic and has three parameters. We already know that the second option is more prone to overfitting, but if we apply a regularization term, it's possible to avoid the growth of the first quadratic parameter and transform the model into a linearized version.

Of course, there's a difference between choosing a lower-capacity model and applying a regularization constraint. In the first case, we are renouncing the possibility offered by the extra capacity with a consequent risk of large bias, while with regularization we keep the same model but optimize it to reduce the variance and only slightly increase the bias. I hope it's clear that regularization always leads to a suboptimal model M' and, in particular, if the original M is unbiased, M' will be biased proportionally to λ and to the kind of regularization used.

Generally speaking, if the absolute minimum of a cost function with respect to a training set is c_{opt}, any model with $c > c_{opt}$ is suboptimal. This means that the training error is larger, but the generalization error might be better controlled.

In fact, a perfectly trained model could have learned the structure of the training set and reached a minimum loss, but, when a new sample is checked, the performance is much worse.

Even if it's not very mathematically rigorous, we can say that regularization often acts as a brake that avoids perfect convergence. By doing this, it keeps the model in a region where the generalization error is lower, which is, generally, the main objective of machine learning. Hence, this *extra penalty* can be accepted in the context of the **bias-variance** trade-off.

A small bias can be acceptable when it's the consequence of a drastic variance reduction (that is, a smaller generalization error); however, I strongly suggest that you don't employ regularization as a black-box technique, but instead to check (for example, using cross-validation) which value yields the optimal result, intended as a trade-off.

Examples of Regularization Techniques

At this point, we can explore the most common regularization techniques and discuss their properties.

L$_2$ or Ridge regularization

L_2 or **Ridge** regularization, also known as **Tikhonov regularization**, is based on the squared L_2-norm of the parameter vector:

$$L_R(X, Y; \bar{\theta}) = L(X, Y; \bar{\theta}) + \lambda \left\| \bar{\theta} \right\|_2^2$$

This penalty avoids infinite growth of the parameters—for this reason, it's also known as **weight shrinkage**—and it's particularly useful when the model is ill-conditioned, or there is multicollinearity due to the fact that the samples are not completely independent, which is a relatively common condition.

In the following diagram, we see a schematic representation of the Ridge regularization in a bidimensional scenario:

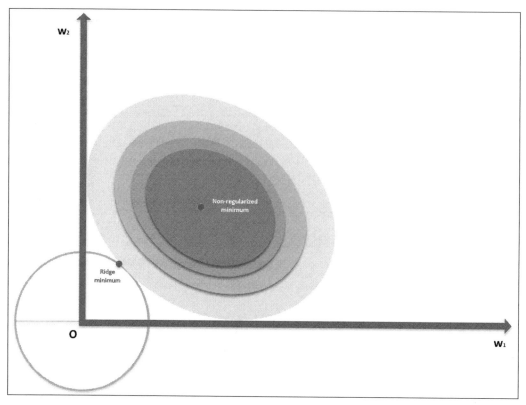

Ridge (L$_2$) regularization

The zero-centered circle represents the Ridge boundary, while the shaded surface is the original cost function. Without regularization, the minimum (w_1, w_2) has a magnitude (for example, the distance from the origin) which is about double the one obtained by applying a Ridge constraint, confirming the expected shrinkage.

When applied to regressions solved with the **Ordinary Least Squares (OLS)** algorithm, it's possible to prove that there always exists a Ridge coefficient, so that the weights are shrunk with respect to the OLS ones. The same result, with some restrictions, can be extended to other cost functions.

Moreover, Andrew Ng (in Ng A. Y., *Feature selection, L1 vs. L2 regularization, and rotational invariance*, ICML, 2004) proved that L_2 regularization, applied to the majority of classification algorithms, allows us to obtain rotational invariance. In other words, if the training set is rotated, a regularized model will yield the same prediction distribution as the original one. Another fundamental aspect to remember is that L_2-regularization shrinks the weights independent of the scale of the data. Therefore, if the features have different scales, the result may be worse than expected.

It's easy to understand this concept by considering a simple linear model with two variables, $y = ax_1 + bx_1 + c$. As the L_2 has a single control coefficient, the effect will be the same on both a and b (excluding the intercept c). If $x_1 \in (-1,1)$ and $x_2 \in (0,100)$, the shrinkage will affect x_1 much more than x_2.

For this reason, we recommend scaling the dataset before applying the regularization. Other important properties of this method will be discussed throughout the book, when specific algorithms are introduced.

L_1 or Lasso regularization

L_1 or **Lasso** regularization is based on the L_1-norm of the parameter vector:

$$L_R(X, Y; \bar{\theta}) = L(X, Y; \bar{\theta}) + \lambda \|\bar{\theta}\|_1$$

While Ridge shrinks all the weights inversely proportionally to their importance, Lasso can shift the smallest weight to zero, creating a sparse parameter vector.

The mathematical proof is beyond the scope of this book; however, it's possible to understand it intuitively by considering the following bidimensional diagram:

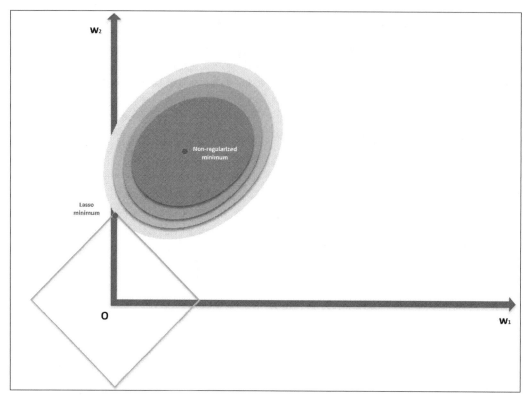

Lasso (L₁) regularization

The zero-centered square represents the Lasso boundaries in a bidimensional scenario (it will be a hyperdiamond in $\mathbb{R}^n$). If we consider a generic line, the probability of that line being tangential to the square is higher at the corners, where at least one parameter is null—exactly one parameter in a bidimensional scenario. In general, if we have a vectorial convex function $f(x)$ (we provide a definition of convexity in *Chapter 7, Advanced Clustering and Unsupervised Models*), we can define:

$$g(\bar{x}) = f(\bar{x}) + \|\bar{x}\|_p$$

As any L_p-norm is convex, as well as the sum of convex functions, $g(\bar{x})$ is also convex. The regularization term is always non-negative, and therefore the minimum corresponds to the norm of the null vector.

When minimizing $g(\bar{x})$, we also need to consider the contribution of the gradient of the norm in the ball centered in the origin, where the partial derivatives don't exist. Increasing the value of p, the norm becomes smoothed around the origin, and the partial derivatives approach zero for $|\bar{x}_i| \to 0$.

On the other hand, excluding the L_0-norm and all the norms with $p \in (0,1)$ allows an even stronger sparsity, but is non-convex (even if L_0 is currently employed in the quantum algorithm QBoost). With $p = 1$ the partial derivatives are always +1 or -1, according to the sign of x_i ($x_i \neq 0$). Therefore, it's *easier* for the L_1-norm to push the smallest components to zero, because the contribution to the minimization (for example, with gradient descent) is independent of x_i, while an L_2-norm decreases its *speed* when approaching the origin.

This is a non-rigorous explanation of the sparsity achieved using the L_1-norm. In practice, we also need to consider the term $f(\bar{x})$, which bounds the value of the global minimum; however, it may help the reader to develop an intuitive understanding of the concept. It's possible to find further, more mathematically rigorous details in Sra S., Nowozin S., Wright S. J. (edited by), *Optimization for Machine Learning*, The MIT Press, 2011.

Lasso regularization is particularly useful when a sparse representation of a dataset is needed. For example, we could be interested in finding the feature vectors corresponding to a group of images. As we expect to have many features, but only a subset of those features present in each image, applying the Lasso regularization allows us to force all the smallest coefficients to become null, which helps us by suppressing the presence of the secondary features.

Another potential application is latent semantic analysis, where our goal is to describe the documents belonging to a corpus in terms of a limited number of topics. All these methods can be summarized in a technique called **sparse coding**, where the objective is to reduce the dimensionality of a dataset by extracting the most representative atoms, using different approaches to achieve sparsity.

Another important property of L_1 regularization concerns its ability to perform an implicit **feature selection**, induced by the sparsity. In a generic scenario, a dataset can also include irrelevant features that don't contribute to increasing the accuracy of the classification. This can happen because real-world datasets are often redundant, and the data collectors are more interested in their *readability* than in their usage for analytical purposes. There are many techniques (some of them are described in Bonaccorso G., *Machine Learning Algorithms, Second Edition*, Packt, 2018) that can be employed to select only those features that really transport unique pieces of information and discard the remaining ones; however, L_1 is particularly helpful.

First of all, it's automatic and no preprocessing steps are required. This is extremely useful in deep learning. Moreover, as Ng pointed out in the aforementioned paper, if a dataset contains n features, the minimum number of samples required to increase the accuracy over a predefined threshold is affected by the logarithm of the number of redundant or irrelevant features.

This means, for example, that if dataset X contains 1000 points $\bar{x}_i \in \mathbb{R}^p$ and the optimal accuracy is achieved with this sample size when all the features are informative when $k < p$ features are irrelevant, we need approximately $1000 + O(\log k)$ samples. This is a simplification of the original result; for example, if $p = 5000$ and 500 features are irrelevant, assuming the simplest case, we need about $1000 + \log 500 \approx 1007$ data points.

Such a result is very important because it's often difficult and expensive to obtain a large number of new samples, in particular when they are obtained in experimental contexts (for example, social sciences, pharmacological research, and so on). Before moving on, let's consider a synthetic dataset containing 500 points $\bar{x}_i \in \mathbb{R}^{10}$ with only five informative features:

```
from sklearn.datasets import make_classification
from sklearn.preprocessing import StandardScaler

X, Y = make_classification(n_samples=500, n_classes=2, n_features=10,
                           n_informative=5,
                           n_redundant=3, n_clusters_per_class=2,
                           random_state=1000)

ss = StandardScaler()
X_s = ss.fit_transform(X)
```

We can now fit two logistic regression instances with the whole dataset: the first one using the L_2 regularization and the second one using L_1. In both cases, the strength is kept fixed:

```
from sklearn.linear_model import LogisticRegression

lr_l2 = LogisticRegression(solver='saga', penalty='l2', C=0.25,
random_state=1000)
lr_l1 = LogisticRegression(solver='saga', penalty='l1', C=0.25,
random_state=1000)

lr_l2.fit(X_s, Y)
lr_l1.fit(X_s, Y)
```

It's possible to see that, in both cases, the 10-fold cross-validation yields approximately the same average accuracy. However, in this case, we are more interested in checking the feature selection properties of L_1; therefore we are going to compare the 10 coefficients of the two models, available as an instance variable `coef_`. The results are shown in the following figure:

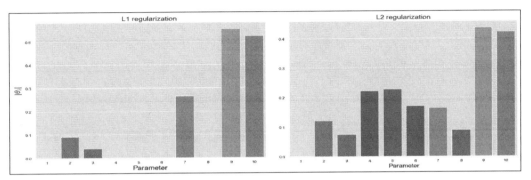

Logistic regression coefficients with L1 (left) and L2 (right) regularizations

As you can see, L_2 regularization tends to shrink all coefficients almost uniformly, excluding the dominance of 9 and 10, while L_1 performs a feature selection, by keeping only 5 non-null coefficients. This result is coherent with the structure of the dataset, in that it contains only 5 informative features and, therefore, a good classification algorithm can get rid of the remaining ones.

It's helpful to remember that we often need to create explainable models. That is to say, we often need to create models whose output can be immediately traced back to its causes. When there are many parameters, this task becomes more difficult. The usage of Lasso allows us to exclude all those features whose importance is secondary with respect to a primary group. In this way, the resulting model is smaller, and definitely more explainable.

As a general suggestion, in particular when working with linear models, I invite the reader to perform a feature selection to remove all non-determinant factors; and L_1 regularization is an excellent choice that avoids an additional preprocessing step.

Having discussed the main properties of both L_1 and L_2 regularizations, we can now explain how to combine them in order to exploit the respective benefits.

ElasticNet

In many real cases, it's useful to apply both Ridge and Lasso regularization in order to force weight shrinkage and a global sparsity. It is possible by employing the **ElasticNet** regularization, defined as:

$$L_R(X, Y; \bar{\theta}) = L(X, Y; \bar{\theta}) + \lambda_1 \left\| \bar{\theta} \right\|_2^2 + \lambda_2 \left\| \bar{\theta} \right\|_1$$

The strength of each regularization is controlled by the parameters λ_1 and λ_2. ElasticNet can yield excellent results whenever it's necessary to mitigate overfitting effects, while encouraging sparsity. We're going to apply all these regularization techniques when we discuss deep learning architectures.

Early stopping

Even though it's a pure regularization technique, **early stopping** is often considered a *last resort* when all other approaches to prevent overfitting, and maximize validation accuracy, fail. In many cases, above all in deep learning scenarios even though it can also happen with SVMs and other simpler classifiers, it's possible to observe a typical behavior of the training process, considering both training and the validation cost functions:

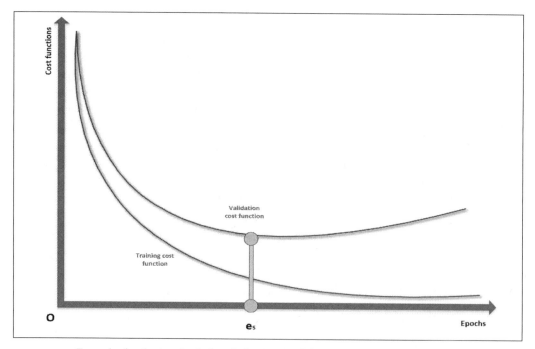

Example of early stopping before the beginning of the ascending phase of a U-curve

During the first epochs, both costs decrease, but it can happen that after a *threshold* epoch e_s, the validation cost starts increasing. If we continue with the training process, this results in overfitting the training set and increasing the variance.

For this reason, when there are no other options, it's possible to prematurely stop the training process. In order to do so, it's necessary to store the last parameter vector before the beginning of a new iteration and, in the case of no improvements or the accuracy worsening, to stop the process and recover the last set of parameters.

As explained, this procedure must never be considered as the best choice, because a better model or an improved dataset could yield higher performances. With early stopping, there's no way to verify alternatives, therefore it must be adopted only at the last stage of the process and never at the beginning.

Many deep learning frameworks such as Keras include helpers to implement early stopping callbacks. However, it's important to check whether the last parameter vector is the one stored before the last epoch or the one corresponding to e_s. In this case, it could be helpful to repeat the training process, stopping it at the epoch previous to e_s, where the minimum validation cost has been achieved.

Summary

In this chapter, we introduced the loss and cost functions, first as proxies of the expected risk, and then we detailed some common situations that can be experienced during an optimization problem. We also exposed some common cost functions, together with their main features and specific applications.

In the last part, we discussed regularization, explaining how it can mitigate the effects of overfitting and induce sparsity. In particular, the employment of Lasso can help the data scientist to perform automatic feature selection by forcing all secondary coefficients to become equal to 0.

In the next chapter, *Chapter 3, Introduction to Semi-Supervised Learning*, we're going to introduce semi-supervised learning, focusing our attention on the concepts of transductive and inductive learning.

Further reading

- Darwiche A., *Human-Level Intelligence or Animal-Like Abilities?*, Communications of the ACM, Vol. 61, 10/2018

- Crammer K., Kearns M., *Wortman J., Learning from Multiple Sources*, Journal of Machine Learning Research, 9/2008

- Mohri M., Rostamizadeh A., Talwalkar A., *Foundations of Machine Learning, Second edition*, The MIT Press, 2018

- Valiant L., *A theory of the learnable*, Communications of the ACM, 27, 1984

- Ng A. Y., *Feature selection, L1 vs. L2 regularization, and rotational invariance*, ICML, 2004

- Dube S., *High Dimensional Spaces, Deep Learning and Adversarial Examples*, arXiv:1801.00634 [cs.CV]

- Sra S., Nowozin S., Wright S. J. (edited by), *Optimization for Machine Learning*, The MIT Press, 2011

- Bonaccorso G., *Machine Learning Algorithms, Second Edition*, Packt, 2018

3
Introduction to Semi-Supervised Learning

Semi-supervised learning is a machine learning branch that tries to solve problems that include both labeled and unlabeled data, employing concepts that include characteristics of both clustering and classification methods.

The high availability of unlabeled samples, and the difficulty of labeling huge datasets correctly, drove many researchers to investigate the best approaches that allow extending the knowledge provided by the labeled samples to a larger unlabeled population, without loss of accuracy. In this chapter, we're going to introduce this branch of machine learning and we'll discuss:

- The semi-supervised scenario
- The different approaches to semi-supervised learning
- The assumptions needed to efficiently operate in such a scenario

We'll then move on to present several semi-supervised learning algorithms and show Python coded examples of them in practice. Example algorithms include:

- The Generative Gaussian Mixture algorithm
- Self-Training
- Co-Training

We'll start by describing how a semi-supervised scenario is defined, and how it differs from other data scenarios.

Semi-supervised scenario

A typical semi-supervised scenario is not very different from a supervised one. Let's suppose we have a data generating process, p_{data}:

$$p_{data}(\bar{x}, \bar{y}) = p(\bar{y}|\bar{x})p(\bar{x}) \ \text{ or } \ p(\bar{x}|\bar{y})p(\bar{y})$$

However, contrary to a supervised approach, where we can rely on a completely labeled dataset, we have only a limited number N of data points drawn from p_{data} and provided with a label, as follows:

$$\begin{cases} X_L = \{\bar{x}_0^L, \bar{x}_1^L, \dots, \bar{x}_N^L\} \ \text{ where } \ \bar{x}_i^L \in \mathbb{R}^p \\ Y_L = \{\bar{y}_0^L, \bar{y}_1^L, \dots, \bar{y}_N^L\} \ \text{ where } \ \bar{y}_i^L \in \mathbb{R}^q \end{cases}$$

As for other methods, the training sample is assumed to be drawn uniformly, so as not to exclude any region of p_{data}. When this condition is met, it's possible to consider a larger amount (M) of unlabeled samples drawn from the marginal distribution $p(\bar{x})$:

$$X_U = \{\bar{x}_0^U, \bar{x}_1^U, \dots, \bar{x}_M^U\} \ \text{ where } \ \bar{x}_i^U \in \mathbb{R}^p$$

The context of semi-supervised learning is then defined by the union of the two sets $\{X_L, Y_L\}$ and X_U. An important assumption about the unlabeled samples is that their labels are supposed to be **missing at random**, without any correlation with the actual label distribution. The unlabeled dataset is assumed to have a distribution that doesn't differ dramatically from the labeled one in terms of class balance (for example, we cannot expect 90% of unlabeled samples to belong to the same class and the remaining ones spread across all the remaining classes).

In a general framework, there are no restrictions on the values of N and M; however, a semi-supervised problem normally arises when the number of unlabeled points is (much) larger than the cardinality of the labeled set. If we can draw $N \gg M$ labeled points from p_{data}, it's probably useless to keep on working with semi-supervised approaches, and classical supervised methods are likely to be the best choice. The extra complexity we need is justified by $M \gg N$, which is a common condition in all those situations where the amount of available unlabeled data is large and the number of correctly labeled samples is quite a lot lower.

For example, we can easily access millions of free images, but detailed, labeled datasets are expensive, and include only a limited subset of possibilities.

However, is it always possible to apply semi-supervised learning to improve our models? The answer to this question is almost obvious: unfortunately, in some cases, it's impossible.

As a fundamental rule, we can say that if the knowledge of X_U increases our knowledge about the prior distribution $p(\bar{x})$, a semi-supervised algorithm is likely to perform better than a purely supervised — and thus limited to X_L — counterpart. On the other hand, if the unlabeled points are drawn from different distributions or from regions of p_{data} excluded from the training process, the final result can be quite a lot worse.

In real cases, there's no way to immediately understand whether or not a semi-supervised algorithm is the best choice; therefore, cross-validation and comparisons are the best practices to employ when evaluating a scenario. It should be also clear that, while in a supervised scenario, we are directly interested in the conditional probability distribution $p(\bar{y}|\bar{x})$ and we can get rid of $p(\bar{x})$, in a semi-supervised scenario, we are often forced to model $p(\bar{x})$ in order to exploit the unlabeled samples. Such a problem can also be analyzed in a different way, which unveils another limitation of semi-supervised learning.

Causal scenarios

As pointed out by Peters, Janzing, and Schölkopf (in Peters J., Janzing D., Schölkopf B., *Elements of Causal Inference*, The MIT Press, 2017), semi-supervised learning can be impossible in causal scenarios. In fact, let's consider a process that generates y as an effect of the cause x. Can we suppose that the knowledge of $p(\bar{x})$ increases the knowledge of $p(\bar{y}|\bar{x})$? The answer can be understood intuitively. If we have modeled a conditional distribution of effects given a set of causes, all the information needed to decide which cause is the most likely is already encoded in the model. The additional knowledge of $p(\bar{x})$ (that includes the density of regions excluded from $p(\bar{y}|\bar{x})$) cannot have any impact on the decision of selecting one effect instead of another, because such a process is governed only by the knowledge of the data $(\bar{x})$ that triggered all training effects $(\bar{y})$.

In other words, it doesn't matter if $p(\bar{x})$ is different from the distribution that we have already considered during the training phase (in general, this can be a problem, but to solve it it's necessary to sample more data from the actual generating process, without involving any semi-supervised approach). The reason for this behavior can be summarized by saying that the distribution of the effects, given some causes, is independent of the distribution of the causes.

In order to further simplify this concept, we can consider the causal scenario *button → light*. We know that it's necessary to press the button more times at specific frequencies in order to switch the light on and, to model this problem, we have collected a training set (X, Y) containing N observations. We are interested in the conditional probability *p(light | button = ON)*, which can be easily determined. What happens if someone tells us that he knows the exact probability *p(button = ON)*? Can we also take it into account in this causal scenario, like the one shown in the following figure?

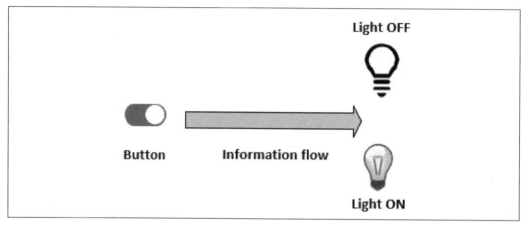

The status of the button determines the status of the light (causal scenario)

Remember that we are working in a semi-supervised scenario; therefore, we're not able to find the corresponding outcomes ($\bar{y}$). This means that, unfortunately, we can't employ *p(button = ON)* to improve our model because, for example, knowing that the probability of a frequency range is p_0 has no *right* to influence our knowledge *p(light | button = ON)*, which is based on observed evidence (that is, the effects have been conditioned on true outcomes and that's all we need to know to model the conditional probability). The same authors showed that, instead, an anti-causal scenario is fully compatible with semi-supervised learning. In this case, we are in fact modeling *p(cause | effect)* and, clearly, the knowledge of *p(effect)* can affect the conditional probability.

Considering our example, since the light is triggered by the button, if we have carried out N experiments, we can create an initial model *p(button = ON | light)*, but we're not sure that we are taking into account all possible outcomes *(light on/off)*. Therefore, in our first estimation, we are likely to introduce an error. The knowledge of *p(light)* can help us reduce such an error because we know that, whenever the probability to observe the light on is large, the probability of a correct button frequency is also large (and vice versa).

The majority of the examples discussed in this chapter are based on this assumption. We often consider the class as the cause and the attributes as the effects (that is, the fact that a flower belongs to a class in the Iris dataset determines a specific set of features, like petal length and sepal width). However, I invite the reader to evaluate this condition in every case and to test the algorithms anyway.

Different studies have, in fact, showed how semi-supervised learning can also have a non-negligible impact on performances related to causal scenarios, by improving the accuracy of the classification with respect to using only a smaller labeled dataset. Therefore, if a larger labeled dataset is not immediately available, these methods remain a good starting point. Of course, when the data scientist is sure to be working with a causal model, they must be also prepared to reevaluate it against standard supervised methods, in order to check whether there's an actual improvement or not. In the latter case, a set of unlabeled points is not helpful, and better accuracy can only be obtained by employing a larger labeled training set.

Transductive learning

When a semi-supervised model is aimed at finding the labels for the unlabeled samples, the approach is called transductive learning.

In this case, we're not interested in modeling the whole distribution $p(\bar{x}|\bar{y})$, which implies determining the density of both datasets, but rather in finding $p(\bar{y}|\bar{x})$ only for the unlabeled points. In many cases, this strategy can be time-saving and it's always preferable when our goal is more oriented at improving our knowledge about the unlabeled dataset. Of course, this scenario implies that the knowledge of $p(\bar{x})$ can improve our knowledge about $p(\bar{y}|\bar{x})$; therefore, as previously discussed, it's not suitable for purely causal processes.

Inductive learning

Contrary to transductive learning, inductive learning considers all the X data points, and tries to determine a complete $p(\bar{x}|\bar{y})$ or a function $y = f(\bar{x})$ that can map both labeled and unlabeled points to their corresponding labels.

In general, this method is more complex and requires more computational time. Therefore, according to **Vapnik's principle** – that we shouldn't solve a more general problem as an intermediate step in solving a specific problem – if it's not required or necessary, it's always better to pick the most pragmatic solution and, possibly, expand it if the problem requires further details.

Semi-supervised assumptions

As explained in the previous section, semi-supervised learning is not guaranteed to improve a supervised model. A wrong choice could lead to a dramatic worsening in performance. However, it's possible to state some fundamental assumptions that are required for semi-supervised learning to work properly. They're not always mathematically proven theorems, but rather empirical observations that justify the otherwise completely arbitrary choice of an approach.

Smoothness assumption

Let's consider a real-valued function $f(x)$ and the corresponding metric spaces X and Y. Such a function is said to be Lipschitz-continuous if:

$$\exists K : \forall x_1, x_2 \in X \Rightarrow d_Y\big(f(x_1), f(x_2)\big) \le K d_X(x_1, x_2)$$

In other words, if two points x_1 and x_2 are near, the corresponding output values y_1 and y_2 cannot be arbitrarily far from each other. This condition is fundamental in regression problems, where a generalization is often required for points that are between training samples.

For example, if we need to predict the output for a point $x_t : x_1 < x_t < x_2$ and the regressor is Lipschitz-continuous, we can be sure that y_t will be correctly bounded by y_1 and y_2. This kind of behavior is often called general smoothness, but in semi-supervised learning it's helpful to add an explicit restriction to it (correlated with the cluster assumption): if two points are in a high-density region (cluster) and they are close, then the corresponding outputs must be close too. In a more formal fashion, the smoothness assumption can be expressed as:

$$if\ f(\bar{x}_c; \bar{\theta}) = y_c, \exists\ \delta > 0 : \forall \bar{x} \in X : d(\bar{x}, \bar{x}_c) < \delta \Rightarrow f(\bar{x}; \bar{\theta}) = y_c$$

In this formula, $f(\bar{x}; \bar{\theta})$ is a generic parametric classifier. Hence, given a point $\bar{x}_c$ which is classified as y_c, there exists a ball where all points will be classified in the same way. This definition doesn't impose any restriction on δ, but, for our purposes, we need to assume that two margins greater than zero (δ_m and δ_M) exist, so to introduce both a lower and an upper bound to $\delta (\delta_m < \delta < \delta_M)$. In this way, we are restricting the family of suitable functions to the set of *relatively slowly-changing* ones.

In the context of semi-supervised learning, the smoothness assumption plays a fundamental role because, if two samples are in a low-density region they can belong to different clusters and their labels can be very different. This isn't always true, but it's useful to include this constraint to allow some further assumptions in many definitions of semi-supervised models.

Cluster assumption

This assumption is strictly linked to the previous one, and it's probably easier to accept. It can be expressed with a chain of interdependent conditions. Clusters are high-density regions; therefore, if two points are close, they're likely to belong to the same cluster, and their labels must be the same. Low-density regions are separation spaces; therefore, samples belonging to a low-density region are likely to be boundary points, and their classes can be different. To better understand this concept, it's useful to think about supervised SVM: only the support vectors should be in low-density regions. Let's consider the following bidimensional example:

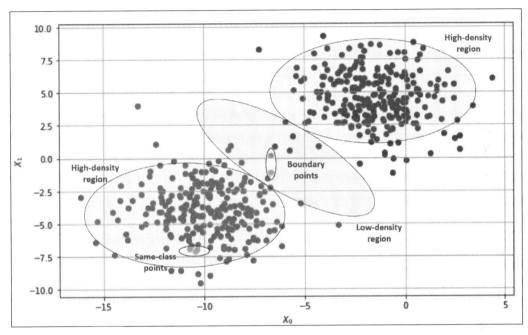

Representation of two separated bidimensional clusters

In a semi-supervised scenario, we couldn't know the label of a point belonging to a high-density region; however, if it's close enough to a labeled point that it's possible to build a ball where all the points have the same average density, then we're allowed to predict the label of our test sample. If instead we move to a low-density region, the process becomes harder, because two points can be very close but with different labels. We're going to discuss the semi-supervised, low-density separation problem in the next chapter, where different semi-supervised Support Vector Machines will be analyzed.

Manifold assumption

This is the least intuitive assumption, but it can be extremely useful to reduce the complexity of many problems. First of all, we need to provide a non-rigorous definition of a manifold. An *n*-manifold is a topological space that is globally curved, but locally homeomorphic to *n*-dimensional Euclidean space. In other words, it's possible to select a sufficiently small region and *deform* it into a standard Euclidean flat space. However, this is not true when considering the whole space.

For example, if we look at the Earth from space, we might think that its inhabitants are uniformly distributed over the whole volume. We know that this is false, and in fact, we can create maps and atlases which are represented on two-dimensional manifolds. It doesn't make sense to use three-dimensional vectors to map the position of a human being. It's easier to use a projection, and work with latitude and longitude.

In the following diagram, there's an example of a manifold: the surface of a sphere in $\mathbb{R}^3$:

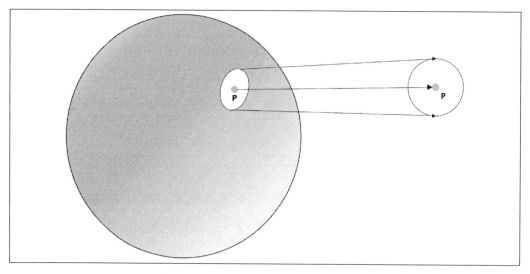

2D manifold obtained from a spherical surface

The small patch around P (for $\epsilon \to 0$) can be mapped to a flat circular surface. Therefore, the local properties of a manifold are based on Euclidean geometry, while globally, they need a proper mathematical extension, which is beyond the scope of this book (further information can be found in Belkin M., Niyogi P., *Semi-supervised learning on Riemannian manifolds*, Machine Learning 56, 2004).

The manifold assumption states that p-dimensional samples (where $p \gg 1$) approximately lie on a q-dimensional manifold with $p \ll q$. Without excessive mathematical rigor, we can say that, for example, if we have N 1000-dimensional bounded vectors, they are enclosed into a 1000-dimensional hypercube with edge-length equal to r. The corresponding n-volume is $r^p = r^{1000}$; therefore, the probability of filling the entire space is very small (and decreases with p). What we observe, instead, is a high density on a lower dimensional manifold.

This assumption authorizes us to apply dimensionality reduction methods in order to avoid the *Curse of Dimensionality* theorized by Bellman (the reader can find further information in Howard R. A., *Dynamic Programming and Markov Process*, The MIT Press, 1960). In the scope of machine learning, the main consequence of such an effect is that when the dimensionality of the samples increases, in order to achieve high accuracy, it's necessary to use more and more samples.

Moreover, Hughes observed (the phenomenon has been named after him and it's presented in the paper Hughes G. F., *On the mean accuracy of statistical pattern recognizers*, IEEE Transactions on Information Theory, 14/1, 1968) that the accuracy of statistical classifiers is inversely proportional to the dimensionality of the samples. This means that whenever it's possible to work on lower dimensional manifolds (in particular, in semi-supervised scenarios), two advantages are achieved:

- Less computational time and memory consumption
- Larger classification accuracy

Before we start to analyze some algorithms, I'd like to show the importance of the manifold assumption with a virtual example. Imagine I have a 2,000 × 1,000 RGB canvas. Each pixel is encoded with 24 bits, so it can have $2^{24} = 16,777,216$ possible values. If all the pixels in the canvas (2,000,000) are independent, the total number of images is $16,777,216^{2000000}$. It's not difficult to understand that this number is extremely huge (far beyond the computational power required to run a deep learning application). Now, let's think about a dataset of handwritten digits (like MNIST, which we are going to employ many times) and suppose the resolution is 100 × 100 with a greyscale 8-bit encoding. There are 10 classes of digit, so if the samples are uniformly collected, we can assume to have, for example, 250,000 examples of every digit. Since no repetitions are allowed, and small variations can be discarded by numerical approximations, each image must differ substantially. Even if we assume we have a high-resolution dataset, including the smallest variations, the percentage of digits with respect to the total possible number of images is definitely negligible (if you try to compute it with your smartphone or pocket calculator, you get 0 because the required precision is extremely high).

A more complex example is a face recognition application. It can succeed in generalizing effectively with a dataset of, for example, 1,000,000 images. So what about all the remaining combinations? Many of them are random noise, but since they are all possible combinations, if you take a picture of your desk, reduce the resolution to a 2,000 × 1,000 and start checking your monster dataset, you'll eventually find the image of your desk (together with the Mona Lisa, your portrait and whatever else you can imagine—assuming reasonable quality loss)! This might be surprising, but it's a normal consequence of basic combinatorics.

In all the following examples that involve random numbers, the seed is set to 1000 (np.random.seed(1000)). Other values, or subsequent experiments without resetting it, can yield slightly different results.

Therefore, we can conclude that the manifold assumption states that all instances of a universal family (for example, images) are implicitly clustered into separated subspaces. Some of them are semantically valid, while most of the other ones are noisy, and hence negligible. Our tasks are always focused on the former subsets, which, luckily, are rather structured and with reasonable numerosity and dimensionality. After having defined the main concepts regarding semi-supervised scenarios, we can start exploring some practical algorithms that rely on both labeled and unlabeled datasets to perform more accurate classifications.

Generative Gaussian Mixture

The first model we're going to discuss is called Generative Gaussian Mixture, and it aims to model the data generating process p_{data} using a sum of weighted Gaussian distributions. Since the model is generative, its structure allows us not only to cluster the existing dataset into well-defined regions (represented as Gaussians), but also to output the probability of any new data point to belong to each of the classes. This model is very flexible, and can be applied to solve all those problems where it's necessary to perform a clustering and a classification at the same time, obtaining the assignment probability vector that determines the likelihood of a data point to be generated by a specific Gaussian distribution.

Generative Gaussian Mixture theory

Generative Gaussian Mixture is an inductive algorithm for semi-supervised classification and clustering that's aimed at modeling the conditional probability $p(\bar{x}, \bar{y})$ given both a labeled and an unlabeled dataset (in this case, we are sure that the knowledge of $p(\bar{x})$ is helpful because we are going to derive $p(\bar{y}|\bar{x})$ using Bayes' theorem).

Generative Gaussian Mixtures are very helpful when it's necessary to find a model that explains the structure of the existing data points and, additionally, it has the ability to output the probability of new data points. For example, an anomaly detection system can be modeled starting from a dataset of normal and malicious activities. A Generative Gaussian Mixture will be able to distinguish between them, and to answer the question "Is a new data point representing an activity either normal or malicious?" by providing the probability of both cases.

Let's suppose we have a labeled dataset $\{X_i, Y_i\}$ containing N data points (drawn from the same p_{data}) and an unlabeled dataset X_u containing $M \gg N$ points (drawn from the marginal distribution $p(\bar{x})$). It's not necessary that $M \gg N$, but we want to create a real semi-supervised scenario, with only a few labeled samples. Moreover, we're assuming that all unlabeled samples are consistent with p_{data}. This can seem like a vicious cycle, but without this assumption, the procedure does not have a strong mathematical foundation.

Our goal is to determine a complete $p(\bar{x}, \bar{y})$ distribution using a generative model and then to obtain the conditional distribution $p(\bar{y}|\bar{x})$. In general, it's possible to use different priors, but we are now employing multivariate Gaussians to model our data:

$$f(\bar{x}; \bar{\mu}; \Sigma) = \frac{1}{\sqrt{\det 2\pi\Sigma}} e^{-\frac{(\bar{x}-\bar{\mu})^T \Sigma^{-1}(\bar{x}-\bar{\mu})}{2}}$$

Thus, our model parameters are means and covariance matrices for all Gaussians. In other contexts, it's possible to use binomial or multinomial distributions. However, the procedure doesn't change; therefore, let's assume that it's possible to approximate $p(\bar{x}|\bar{y})$ with a parametrized distribution $p(\bar{x}|\bar{y}; \theta)$. We can achieve this goal by minimizing the Kullback-Leibler divergence between the two distributions:

$$\operatorname*{argmin}_{\bar{\theta}} D_{KL}(p(\bar{x}|y)||p(\bar{x}|y; \bar{\theta})) = \sum_i p(\bar{x}_i|y_i) \log \frac{p(\bar{x}_i|y_i)}{p(\bar{x}_i|y_i; \bar{\theta})}$$

In *Chapter 12, The EM Algorithm*, we are going to show that this is equivalent to maximizing the likelihood of the dataset. To obtain the likelihood, it's necessary to define the number of expected Gaussians (which is known from the labeled samples) and a weight-vector that represents the marginal probability of a specific Gaussian:

$$\bar{w} = (p(y = 1), p(y = 2), \dots, p(y = M))$$

Using Bayes' theorem, we get:

$$p(y_i|\bar{x}_j;\ \bar{\theta},\bar{w}) \sim w_i p(\bar{x}_j|y_i;\ \bar{\theta})$$

Analogously, we can get an expression for the conditional distribution of the points X given the parameter vector $\bar{\theta}$ and the weight vector $\bar{w}$:

$$p(\bar{x}_j|y_i;\ \bar{\theta}) = \sum_i w_i p(\bar{x}_j|\bar{y}_i;\ \bar{\theta})$$

In this way, it's easy to understand the role of each Gaussian in determining the probability of a new point. The model can be also quickly visualized using the plate notation, as shown in the following figure, where the rectangle represents a repeating block (in this case, repeating M times) and the circles represent variables that are conditionally linked by arrows (for further details, please check Koller D., Friedman N., *Probabilistic Graphical Models*, The MIT Press, 2009):

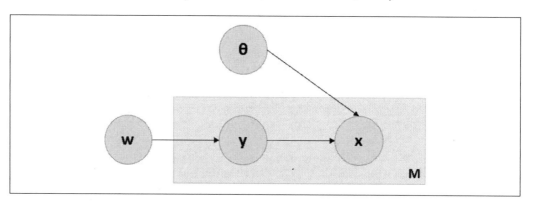

Plate diagram for the Generative Gaussian Mixture model

Let's now consider the complete expression of $p(y_i|\bar{x}_j;\ \bar{\theta},\bar{w})$:

$$p(y_i|\bar{x}_j;\ \bar{\theta},\bar{w}) = \frac{w_i p(\bar{x}_j|y_i;\ \bar{\theta})}{\sum_i w_i p(\bar{x}_j|y_i;\ \bar{\theta})}$$

Since we're working with both labeled and unlabeled samples, the previous formula has a double interpretation:

- For unlabeled samples, it's computed by multiplying the ith Gaussian weight times the probability $p(\bar{x}_i)$ relative to the ith Gaussian distribution.

- For labeled samples, it can be represented by a vector $\bar{p} = (0,0,\dots,1,\dots,0,0)$ where 1 is the ith element. In this way, we force our model to trust the labeled samples, in order to find the best parameter values that maximize the likelihood of the whole dataset.

With this distinction, we can consider a single log-likelihood function where the term $f_w(y_i|\bar{x}_j)$ has been substituted by a per sample weight:

$$L(\bar{\theta}; \bar{w}) = \sum_j \log \sum_i f_w(y_i|\bar{x}_j) \, p(\bar{x}_j|y_i; \bar{\theta}) = \sum_j \log \sum_i w_i \, p(\bar{x}_j|y_i; \bar{\theta})$$

It's possible to maximize the log-likelihood using the EM algorithm (see *Chapter 12, The EM Algorithm*). In this context, we provide the steps directly:

- $p(y_i|\bar{x}_j; \bar{\theta}, \bar{w})$ is computed according to the previously explained method.
- The parameters of the Gaussians are updated using these rules:

$$\begin{cases} w_i = \dfrac{\sum_j p(y_i|\bar{x}_j; \bar{\theta}, \bar{w})}{N} \\[2ex] \bar{\mu}_i = \dfrac{\sum_j \left[p(y_i|\bar{x}_j; \bar{\theta}, \bar{w}) \bar{x}_j \right]}{\sum_j p(y_i|\bar{x}_j; \bar{\theta}, \bar{w})} \\[2ex] \Sigma_i = \dfrac{\sum_j \left[p(y_i|\bar{x}_j; \bar{\theta}, \bar{w})(\bar{x}_j - \bar{\mu}_i)(\bar{x}_j - \bar{\mu}_i)^T \right]}{\sum_j p(y_i|\bar{x}_j; \bar{\theta}, \bar{w})} \end{cases}$$

N is the total number of samples. The procedure must be iterated until the parameters stop modifying or the modifications are lower than a fixed threshold. Now we can show a complete example of this model based on the theory just discussed.

Example of a Generative Gaussian Mixture

We can now implement this model in Python using a simple bidimensional dataset, created using the `make_blobs()` function provided by scikit-learn. This function allows creating synthetic datasets to test algorithms that require data points drawn from a set of normal distributions. The goal of the example is to show the dynamics of a Generative Gaussian Mixture, and therefore we have voluntarily avoided more complex datasets that cannot be easily visualized.

However, the reader will be able to apply the same code to any kind of scenario without any modification:

```
from sklearn.datasets import make_blobs
import numpy as np
nb_samples = 250
nb_unlabeled = 200

X, Y = make_blobs(n_samples=nb_samples, n_features=2, centers=2,
cluster_std=1.25, random_state=100)

unlabeled_idx = np.random.choice(np.arange(0, nb_samples, 1),
replace=False, size=nb_unlabeled)
Y[unlabeled_idx] = -1
```

We've created 200 samples belonging to 2 classes. 250 points have then been randomly selected to become our unlabeled dataset (the corresponding class has been set to -1). We can now initialize two Gaussian distributions by defining their mean, covariance, and weight. One possibility is to use random values; this choice is the simplest, and doesn't require any prior calculation. The algorithm has been proven to converge in any case, but the number of steps is a function of the difference between the initial and final states:

```
import numpy as np

m1 = np.random.uniform(-7.5, 10.0, size=2)
c1 = np.random.uniform(5.0, 15.0, size=(2, 2))
c1 = np.dot(c1, c1.T)
q1 = 0.5

m2 = np.random.uniform(-7.5, 10.0, size=2)
c2 = np.random.uniform(5.0, 15.0, size=(2, 2))
c2 = np.dot(c2, c2.T)
q2 = 0.5
```

However, the covariance matrices must be positive semi-definite. From a mathematical viewpoint, a matrix $A \in \mathbb{R}^{n \times n}$ is said to be positive semi-definite if $\bar{v}^T A \bar{v} \geq 0 \; \forall \; \bar{v} \in \mathbb{R}^n$ with $\bar{v} \neq \bar{0}$. Moreover, all eigenvalues are always non-negative. The variance is a squared quantity, therefore its's non-negative. A covariance-matrix is is an extension of the concept of variance that must inherit the same properties. In particular, when the Gaussian is aligned with the axis, all non-diagonal terms are null. On the diagonal there are the variances with respect to every component, which are also the eigenvalues. It's straightforward to understand that all these terms are non-negative.

If the same Gaussian is rotated, the non-diagonal elements can become different from zero but we expect the eigenvalues to remain non-negative because the two Gaussians differ only by rotation. Such a condition can be assured only by imposing that the matrix is positive semi-definite. Hence, after the definition, it's useful to alter the random values (by multiplying each matrix by the corresponding transpose) or to set hard-coded initial parameters. Since we don't know the structure of the dataset before training the model, we cannot easily define a criterion to initialize all the parameters in the optimal way without complex calculations.

A simple trade-off is based on setting the weights as $1/N_{classes}$ and setting the covariance matrices and means equal to the sample covariance and means. In this way, all the Gaussians will initially be overlapped, and the algorithm will move and deform them to match the input distribution.

In this case, we could pick the following example where $m_{1/2}$ are the mean vectors, $c_{1/2}$ are the covariance matrices, and $q_{1/2}$ are the weights:

```
m1 = np.array([-2.0, -2.5])
c1 = np.array([[1.0, 1.0],
               [1.0, 2.0]])
q1 = 0.5

m2 = np.array([1.0, 3.0])
c2 = np.array([[2.0, -1.0],
               [-1.0, 3.5]])
q2 = 0.5
```

If we project the Gaussians on the *xy* plane and we truncate them by limiting the range of independent variables, you'll be able to see that they appear as ellipses. In order to determine their structure and orientation, we need to observe that:

- The major axis $\bar{v}_{M1/2}$ is oriented as the eigenvector associated with the largest eigenvalue of the covariance matrix. In the same way, the minor axis $\bar{v}_{M1/2}$ is oriented as the eigenvector associated with the smallest eigenvalue (in a multi-dimensional case, it's necessary to take the eigenvalues in descending order).

- The eccentricity *e* is equal to the ratio between the two eigenvalues. When *e* = *1*, the ellipse is a circle because both axes have equal length. When *e* ≠ 1, the ellipse is a proper one, stretched along one of the two axes.

Let's start finding out the orientation angle $\alpha_{1/2}$ of the major axis $\bar{v}_{M1/2}$. If $\bar{e}_x$ is the x-versor, we get:

$$\bar{v}_{M1/2} \cdot \bar{e}_x = \left\|\bar{v}_{M1/2}\right\|\left\|\bar{e}_x\right\| \cos \alpha_{1/2} \Rightarrow \alpha_{1/2} = \arccos \frac{\bar{v}_{M1/2} \cdot \bar{e}_x}{\left\|\bar{v}_{M1/2}\right\|\left\|\bar{e}_x\right\|}$$

The Python code to perform this operation is shown in the following snippet:

```
w1, v1 = np.linalg.eigh(c1)
w2, v2 = np.linalg.eigh(c2)

nv1 = v1 / np.linalg.norm(v1)
nv2 = v2 / np.linalg.norm(v2)

a1 = np.arccos(np.dot(nv1[:, 1], [1.0, 0.0]) / np.linalg.norm(nv1[:,
1])) * 180.0 / np.pi
a2 = np.arccos(np.dot(nv2[:, 1], [1.0, 0.0]) / np.linalg.norm(nv2[:,
1])) * 180.0 / np.pi
```

The resulting plot is shown in the following graph, where the cross marks represent the unlabeled points, and the dots and diamonds the samples belonging to the known classes:

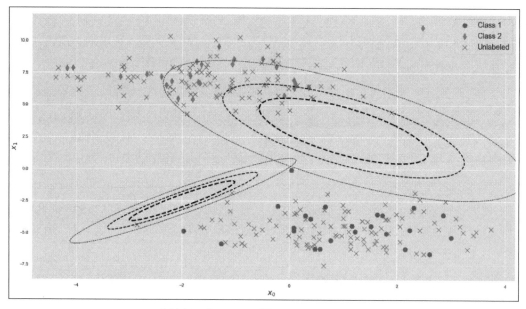

Initial configuration of the Gaussian mixture

The two Gaussians are represented by the concentric ellipses that don't capture the actual structure of the dataset. We can now execute the training procedure. Let's start by defining the temporary placeholders for the parameters computed at the previous iteration, and a function to compute the sum of the norms of all differences between current and previous values:

```
from scipy.stats import multivariate_normal

threshold = 1e-4

def total_norm():
    global m1, m1_old, m2, m2_old, c1, c1_old, c2, c2_old, q1, q1_old,
q2, q2_old
    return np.linalg.norm(m1 - m1_old) + \
            np.linalg.norm(m2 - m2_old) + \
            np.linalg.norm(c1 - c1_old) + \
            np.linalg.norm(c2 - c2_old) + \
            np.linalg.norm(q1 - q1_old) + \
            np.linalg.norm(q2 - q2_old)
```

We can now define the actual training procedure that will be iterated until the parameters become stable (that is, the sum of the norms `total_norm()` becomes smaller than the `threshold`):

```
m1_old = np.zeros((2,))
c1_old = np.zeros((2, 2))
q1_old = 0

m2_old = np.zeros((2,))
c2_old = np.zeros((2, 2))
q2_old = 0

while total_norm() > threshold:
    m1_old = m1.copy()
    c1_old = c1.copy()
    q1_old = q1

    m2_old = m2.copy()
    c2_old = c2.copy()
    q2_old = q2

    Pij = np.zeros((nb_samples, 2))

    # E Step
    for i in range(nb_samples):
```

```
        if Y[i] == -1:
            p1 = multivariate_normal.pdf(X[i], m1, c1, allow_
singular=True) * q1
            p2 = multivariate_normal.pdf(X[i], m2, c2, allow_
singular=True) * q2
            Pij[i] = [p1, p2] / (p1 + p2)

        else:
            Pij[i, :] = [1.0, 0.0] if Y[i] == 0 else [0.0, 1.0]

    # M Step
    n = np.sum(Pij, axis=0)
    m = np.sum(np.dot(Pij.T, X), axis=0)

    m1 = np.dot(Pij[:, 0], X) / n[0]
    m2 = np.dot(Pij[:, 1], X) / n[1]

    q1 = n[0] / float(nb_samples)
    q2 = n[1] / float(nb_samples)

    c1 = np.zeros((2, 2))
    c2 = np.zeros((2, 2))

    for t in range(nb_samples):
        c1 += Pij[t, 0] * np.outer(X[t] - m1, X[t] - m1)
        c2 += Pij[t, 1] * np.outer(X[t] - m2, X[t] - m2)

    c1 /= n[0]
    c2 /= n[1]
```

The first thing at the beginning of each cycle is to initialize the `Pij` matrix that will be used to store the $p(y_i|\bar{x}_j; \bar{\theta}; \bar{w})$ values. Then, for each sample, we can compute $p(y_i|\bar{x}_j; \bar{\theta}; \bar{w})$ considering whether it's labeled or not. The Gaussian probability is computed using the SciPy function `multivariate_normal.pdf()`. When the whole P_{ij} matrix has been populated, we can update the parameters (means and covariance matrix) of both Gaussians and the relative weights. The algorithm is very fast: after about five iterations, we get the stable state represented in the following plot:

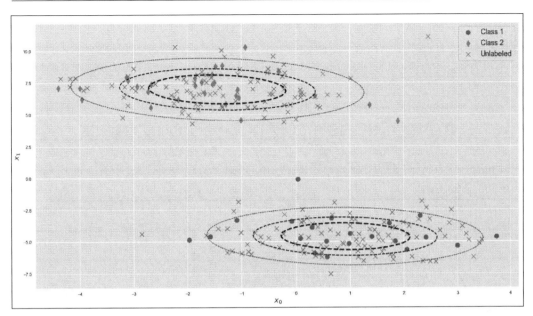

Final configuration of the Gaussian mixture

The two Gaussians have perfectly mapped the space by setting their parameters so as to cover the high-density regions. We can check for some unlabeled points, as follows:

```
print(np.round(X[Y==-1][0:5], 3))
```

The output of the previous snippet is:

```
[[-1.37   10.07 ]
 [ 0.398 -3.857]
 [-1.866   7.496]
 [-0.752 -4.314]
 [ 0.145 -5.932]]
```

It's easy to locate them in the previous plot. The corresponding classes can be obtained through the last P_{ij} matrix:

```
print(np.round(Pij[Y==-1][0:10], 3))
```

The output is:

```
[[0. 1.]
 [1. 0.]
 [0. 1.]
```

```
[1. 0.]
[1. 0.]]
```

This immediately verifies that they have been correctly labeled, and assigned to the right cluster.

Generative Gaussian Mixtures summary

Generative Gaussian Mixtures are models that can learn the structure of a dataset and output the probability of any data point. They are based on both labeled and unlabeled samples, which are assumed to be equally trustworthy. That is to say, the unlabeled points contribute to the final positioning of the Gaussians like the labeled ones. As we're discussing in the next section, this condition is not always met and it's necessary to introduce a slight modification in the algorithm.

This algorithm is very fast and produces excellent results in terms of density estimation. In *Chapter 12, The EM Algorithm*, we are going to discuss a general version of this algorithm, explaining the complete training procedure based on the EM algorithm.

Weighted log-likelihood

In the previous example, we have considered a single log-likelihood for both labeled and unlabeled samples:

$$L(\bar{\theta}; \bar{w}) = \sum_j \log \sum_i f_w(y_i|\bar{x}_j) \, p(\bar{x}_j|y_i; \bar{\theta}) = \sum_j \log \sum_i w_i \, p(\bar{x}_j|y_i; \bar{\theta})$$

This is equivalent to saying that we trust the unlabeled points just like the labeled ones. However, in some contexts, this assumption can lead to completely wrong estimations, as shown in the following graph:

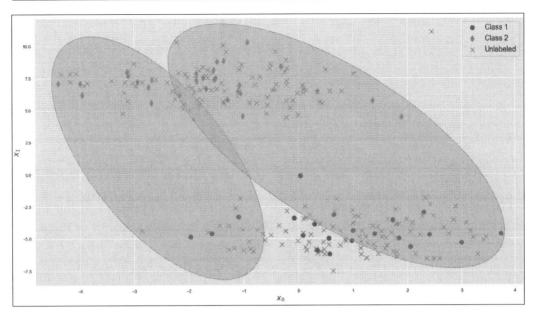

Biased final Gaussian mixture configuration

In this case, the means and covariance matrices of both Gaussian distributions have been biased by the unlabeled points and the resulting density estimation is clearly wrong. As the labeled points are supposed to be drawn from Gaussian distributions, it's always possible to train a model containing only this sample. If the unlabeled points have a *fair* contribution, the mean vectors and covariance matrices should be relatively similar in both cases (for example, the norms of the differences are expected to be smaller than a predefined threshold that might be set equal to 1/10 of the largest element). Moreover, it's possible to compare the non-diagonal elements of the covariance matrices to check whether the orientations are extremely different. In both cases, a large difference highlights a dominance of the unlabeled samples over the labeled ones, and the final log-likelihood is often less than the expected one (this is a natural consequence of the mispositioning of the Gaussians, whose probability density is smaller in the regions where the points lie).

When this phenomenon happens, the best thing to do is to consider a double weighted log-likelihood. If the first N samples are labeled and the following M are unlabeled, the log-likelihood can be expressed as follows:

$$L(\bar{\theta};\ \bar{w}) = \sum_{j=1}^{N} \log \sum_{i} p(y_i|\bar{\theta})\, p(\bar{x}_j|y_i;\ \bar{\theta}) + \lambda \sum_{j=N+1}^{N+M} \log \sum_{i} w_i\, p(\bar{x}_j|y_i;\ \bar{\theta})$$

In the previous formula, the term λ, if less than 1, can underweight the unlabeled terms, giving more importance to the labeled dataset. The modifications to the algorithm are trivial because each unlabeled weight has to be scaled according to λ, reducing its estimated probability. In Chapelle O., Schölkopf B., Zien A., (edited by), *Semi-Supervised Learning*, The MIT Press, 2010, the reader can find a very detailed discussion about the choice of the parameter λ.

As we explained before, there are many potential rules of thumb to determine the effect of the unlabeled sample over the labeled one. A possible strategy to find the optimal λ could be based on the cross-validation performed on the labeled dataset (for the reasons previously explained). Another more complex approach is to consider different increasing values of λ, and pick the first one where the log-likelihood is the maximum. In both cases, the goal is to find a value that avoids the dominance of the unlabeled samples, and at the same time, doesn't overestimate the role of the distribution $p(\bar{x}|\bar{y})$.

Given the nature of the problem, understanding which final configuration is optimal is not a trivial task, but in general, we expect better performance when taking into account unlabeled samples too (in particular, if the problem is anti-causal, hence the variables x_i represent the effects) and when the knowledge of $p(\bar{x})$ can increase the precision of the estimation of the likelihood.

If either an additional validation set is available, or the underlying clustering structure is at least partially known, the simplest approach is to test whether re-weighting the log-likelihood yields a better result. In such a case, the unlabeled dataset is forcing the model to *extend* the labeling knowledge in the wrong way, yielding a final biased full joint probability.

If the problem is a classification, it's therefore important to remember that we are trying to learn $p(\bar{y}|\bar{x})$, which could have only a weak dependence with $p(\bar{x})$. Hence, after checking the causal nature of the scenario (which is supposed to be anti-causal), a good practice is trying to understand how much prior information can be safely transferred to $p(\bar{y}|\bar{x})$ (that is, the amount of prior information that can be incorporated into the model without altering the existing $p(\bar{y}|\bar{x})$) and picking the smallest value λ that maximizes the log-likelihood.

Self-Training

Self-training is a very intuitive approach to semi-supervised classification, based on an extensive application of both the smoothness and cluster assumptions. Self-training is generally a valid choice when the labeled dataset contains enough information about the underlying data-generating process (that is, a CV shows a relatively high accuracy) and the unlabeled sample is assumed to be responsible only for a fine-tuning of the algorithm. Whenever this condition is not met, Self-training cannot be chosen, because it heavily relies on the completeness of the labeled sample.

Self-Training theory

Suppose we have a dataset of labeled samples $\{X_L, Y_L\}$, and assume that it has been drawn uniformly from a data generating process p_{data}. Moreover, there's another set of unlabeled data points X_U, which, of course, is assumed to have the same distribution of X_L. Let's suppose that a classifier is trained using the first labeled dataset (that is, the initial one containing only the pre-labeled points) and the final accuracy is large enough to consider its predictions as reliable. The generalization ability of the classifier guarantees that all predictions are consistent with the training data unless the samples are drawn from a different process. At this point, a **Self-Training** algorithm can try to include the unlabeled dataset with a simple iterative procedure:

1. All points $\bar{x}_u \in X_U$ are evaluated and each prediction is represented using a confidence vector $\bar{p}(\bar{x}_U) = (p_1, p_2, \dots, p_m)$ (assuming that there are m classes).
2. The first k values associated with the largest confidences are selected, removed from X_U, and added to the labeled dataset.
3. The classifier is retrained using the new training set.

The process must be repeated until all the unlabeled values have been labeled and there's no more need to retrain the classifier. The method is quite simple and intuitive, but how is it possible to trust it? The first fundamental assumption is that all X values are drawn from the same distribution. Therefore, when the training sample is not too small, the classifier can start learning the structure of the underlying process and develop a discrete generalization ability. The second element to consider is the effect of the smoothness and cluster assumptions. In particular, we need to assume that similar samples are very likely to be associated with similar outcomes, excluding *de facto* the possibility of abrupt jumps.

In the case of finite classes, if the distance (using an appropriate metrics, for example, Euclidean or Manhattan) between two values $d(\bar{x}_i, \bar{x}_j) < \epsilon$, their behaviors tend to *converge* to a single common class.

Hence, if the initial classifier is already well-trained with a sample uniformly drawn from the underlying process, there will be a few predictions whose confidence is large enough to justify their inclusion in the new training set. The number k of values can be either pre-determined or based on an adaptive approach. In the first case, we select always the k top samples, therefore, k must be small enough to guarantee the maximum accuracy, but, at the same time, large enough not to slow down excessively the training procedure. Instead, an adaptive approach can consider a minimum level of confidence and select only those samples that meet this requirement. Considering our experience, when such an alternative is employed, it's also important to consider a limit to the maximum number of values per iteration. In fact, it can happen that a classifier with small capacity will output very large confidence for a quite large subset, even if their predicted labels are different from the ground truth.

As for all the other methods discussed in this chapter, a self-learning algorithm must be carefully monitored during the whole training phase, in particular when the labeled set is particularly small. If $\{X_L, Y_L\}$, for example, is drawn considering only a limited region of p_{data}, only a few close unlabeled points will be correctly recognized. However, without any other further guidance, the algorithm will continue labeling the remaining values gaining more and more confidence despite the wrong outcomes. This problem is a consequence of the cluster assumption when the new extended training sets are created. Imagine that some new point has been added close to a boundary region of the initial training set. The classifier identified a subset of k values that were very similar to some $\bar{x}_i \in X_L$ and labeled them accordingly. As these points were indeed extremely close to the boundary, the predictions were correct and the new training set was consistent. However, while the process goes on, other points will be discovered as close to the new boundary, which was already *enlarged* by the previous sub-samples. The confidence could not have been affected, but the probability of error clearly grew step after step. In some particular cases, such a process might work, but in general, it's very likely to yield completely wrong outcomes, as shown in the following figure:

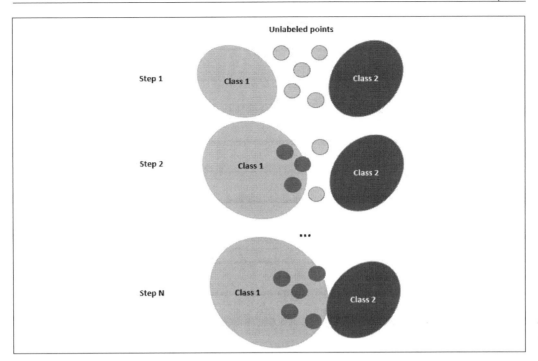

Wrong classification due to the enlargement of a boundary by a Self-Training algorithm

A possible way to mitigate the risk is to analyze the non-linear dimensionality reduction (if $n > 3$) of the whole dataset together with a plot of the initial decision surface. If the dataset is not extremely complex, it will be possible to highlight the correctness of the basic assumptions (that is, $\{X_L, Y_L\}$ uniformly covers the whole data generating process and that $X_U \sim p(X_L)$). If they are not respected, it's necessary to reanalyze the problem or to find more secure labeled samples. Let's now show the ability of self-learning of a Gaussian Naive Bayes algorithm applied to the Iris dataset.

Example of Self-Training with the Iris dataset

Let's start by loading and shuffling the dataset, to meet the requirement of missing unlabeled samples at random:

```
from sklearn.datasets import load_iris
from sklearn.utils import shuffle

iris = load_iris()
X, Y = shuffle(iris['data'], iris['target'], random_state=1000)
```

We can now suppose we have only 20 (out of 150) labeled samples. As the arrays X and Y are already shuffled, we can directly split them:

```
nb_samples = X.shape[0]
nb_labeled = 20
nb_unlabeled = nb_samples - nb_labeled
nb_unlabeled_samples = 2

X_train = X[:nb_labeled]
Y_train = Y[:nb_labeled]

X_unlabeled = X[nb_labeled:]
```

At this point, it's helpful to train a Gaussian Naive Bayes classifier (using the default parameters) with the whole original dataset and evaluate its performances:

```
from sklearn.naive_bayes import GaussianNB
from sklearn.metrics import classification_report

nb0 = GaussianNB()
nb0.fit(X, Y)

print(classification_report(Y, nb0.predict(X), target_
names=iris['target_names']))
```

The output of the previous snippet is:

	precision	recall	f1-score	support
setosa	1.00	1.00	1.00	50
versicolor	0.94	0.94	0.94	50
virginica	0.94	0.94	0.94	50
micro avg	0.96	0.96	0.96	150

macro avg	0.96	0.96	0.96	150
weighted avg	0.96	0.96	0.96	150

On average, the classifier has both precision and recall of about 0.96, indicating the presence of a very small number of false positives and false negatives. For our purposes, we can consider this value as a benchmark (this doesn't mean that another classifier can't achieve better performances). Let's now train a semi-supervised model based on Self-Training:

```python
import numpy as np

from sklearn.naive_bayes import GaussianNB

while X_train.shape[0] <= nb_samples:
    nb = GaussianNB()
    nb.fit(X_train, Y_train)

    if X_train.shape[0] == nb_samples:
        break

    probs = nb.predict_proba(X_unlabeled)
    top_confidence_idxs = np.argsort(np.max(probs, axis=1)).astype(np.int64)[::-1]
    selected_idxs = top_confidence_idxs[0:nb_unlabeled_samples]

    X_new_train = X_unlabeled[selected_idxs]
    Y_new_train = nb.predict(X_new_train)

    X_train = np.concatenate((X_train, X_new_train), axis=0)
    Y_train = np.concatenate((Y_train, Y_new_train), axis=0)

    X_unlabeled = np.delete(X_unlabeled, selected_idxs, axis=0)
```

The process is straightforward: a Gaussian Naive Bayes classifier is trained with a partial set, which is built incrementally as showed in the following figure where the blocks M_2 to M_n are created like M_1, by adding k points labeled by the model built in the previous block:

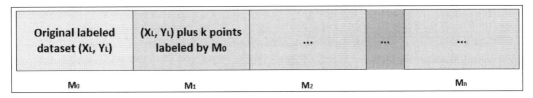

Incremental and sequential process involved in Self-Training

After each training step, the top-confidence `nb_unlabeled_samples` points (in our case, we preferred to be careful and limited this number to 2 elements) are selected using the `predict_proba()` method. They are then labeled using the previously trained classifier and added to the training set. On the next iteration, the new training set will also contain the *synthetic* points that will contribute to finding the updated separation hypersurface. The process is repeated until all unlabeled points have been labeled and added to the training set. Considering all semi-supervised learning assumptions, we can suppose that just 20 points might be enough to define the high-density regions to allow the first classifier to label correctly (that is, with high confidence) at least k unlabeled points. Once these new elements have been added to the training set, a new classifier can take advantage of the extra information in order to improve its performances. We can now evaluate the performances of the final classifier with the original complete dataset:

```
from sklearn.metrics import classification_report

print(classification_report(Y, nb.predict(X), target_
names=iris['target_names']))
```

The corresponding output is:

	precision	recall	f1-score	support
setosa	1.00	1.00	1.00	50
versicolor	0.95	0.70	0.80	50
virginica	0.76	0.96	0.85	50
micro avg	0.89	0.89	0.89	150
macro avg	0.90	0.89	0.88	150
weighted avg	0.90	0.89	0.88	150

As expected, the final performances are worse than the supervised approach, with an average precision and recall equal to about 0.9. However, they are quite reasonable considering that we used only 20 labeled samples (13% of the original dataset) and the benchmark was instead trained using the whole dataset.

This result confirms that both cluster and smoothness assumptions are valid and once the centroids of the clusters have been roughly determined, the remaining points can be labeled with high confidence. Of course, the price to pay is training the classifier a large number of times. In our case:

$$N_{training} = 1 + \frac{N_{total\ points} - N_{labeled\ points}}{N_{unlabled\ points}} = 1 + \frac{150 - 20}{2} = 66$$

It's possible to reduce this value by increasing the number of unlabeled points added at each iteration, but this can lead to worse final performances. In general, a higher accuracy can be achieved by reducing the number of unlabeled points and increasing consequently the number of iterations. Vice versa, the speed can be maximized by increasing the number of unlabeled points.

A reasonable strategy (when the training process must be repeated periodically) is to start with a baseline accuracy (obtained by a classifier trained using only the labeled sample) and a number of labeled samples equal, for example, to 1/5 of the total sample size. After a training session, the number can be reduced by 50% and the accuracy reevaluated. The optimal number of unlabeled points is the largest value corresponding to a null accuracy improvement. As an exercise, I invite the reader to find the optimal value for this problem. Surprisingly it is quite a bit larger than 2, confirming that the informational content of the dataset is concentrated in a small sample if it's drawn uniformly. In particular, the fundamental pieces of information are not relative to single points, but to a set of them.

Given a randomly drawn subset of X, if the number of points is large enough, the initial classifier already possesses all the elements needed to define the high-density regions. If we draw randomly, the probability that we've sampled from all the clusters is very large, and therefore we can conclude that the Iris dataset is intrinsically clustered and a few representatives of each cluster are sufficient to assign new samples to the right class.

Self-Training summary

Self-Training is a simple and effective algorithm that leverages the structure of the labeled dataset to find out a suitable separation hypersurface. Once this process is completed, the unlabeled sample is evaluated, and the points classified with sufficiently large confidence are included in the new training set. The procedure is repeated until all data points are successfully classified. This algorithm works quite well when the cluster assumption holds and only a few points lie in a boundary region. Moreover, it requires a classifier that outputs a probability (or any other confidence measure) in order to decide which points are optimal candidates to be included in the updated training set.

In the next section, we are going to analyze another simple classification algorithm that, contrary to Self-Training, relies on the simultaneous usage of two different models that operate on separate feature subsets.

Co-Training

Co-Training is another very simple but effective semi-supervised approach, proposed by Blum and Mitchell (in Blum A., Mitchell T., *Combining Labeled and Unlabeled Data with Co-Training*, 11th Annual Conference on Computational Learning Theory, 1998) as an alternative strategy when the dataset is a multidimensional one, and different groups of features encode different but still peculiar aspects of each class. Co-Training is effective only in scenarios where the data points can be theoretically classified using only a part of the features (even if with a light performance loss). As we're going to see, the redundancy becomes helpful in presence of an unlabeled sample, to compensate for the lack of knowledge that a single classifier might have. On the contrary, if every data point contains features that cannot be split into two separate and autonomous groups, this method is ineffective.

Co-Training theory

Let's suppose we have a labeled dataset $\{X_L, Y_L\}$ with $\bar{x}_i \in \mathbb{R}^n$, the main idea behind a **Co-Training** approach being that, in many cases, a subset $\bar{n}_0 = \{n_i, n_{i+1}, ..., n_k\}$ of features (n_i indicates the generic feature index) can be exploited by a specialized classifier, in order to model a particular behavior that drives the assignment of a class. Analogously, the remaining features (in a scenario based on two classifiers) are employed by another classifier, which should come to the same conclusions as the first one. This means that both classifiers must confidently assign a sample to the same class. Whenever they are discordant, it means that the training set didn't contain enough information to make a correct decision. The main assumption of Co-Training is that both classifiers must be able to assign the correct labels using only a specific *view* of the dataset (which is not always possible).

For example, a dataset might contain points representing the level of income and expenses of different individuals. We can fairly suppose that a classifier can work with only the income data, and arrive at the same conclusions as another classifier working with only the expense data. If such a requirement is not met (because all the features are needed to perform a valid classification), this method cannot be applied.

For our purposes, let's suppose that our data points can be easily split into two different views assigned respectively to the classifiers $c_0(\bar{x})$ and $c_1(\bar{x})$. We're interested in finding the optimal parameters so that $c(\bar{x}_{i0}) = c_1(\bar{x}_{i1})$ for all labeled points $\bar{x}_i \in X_L$ ($\bar{x}_{i0}$ and $\bar{x}_{i1}$ represent the views of $\bar{x}_i$). Moreover, we want to exploit the unlabeled dataset X_U in order to obtain a better knowledge of $p(\bar{x})$.

As pointed out by Chapelle, Schölkopf, and Zien (in Chapelle O., Schölkopf B., Zien A. (edited by), *Semi-Supervised Learning*, The MIT Press, 2010), this problem can be analyzed in a Bayesian framework. In other words, we start with prior knowledge about the classifiers and employ Bayes' theorem to find a posterior probability distribution that takes into account also the unlabeled samples.

Hence, the problem can be expressed using a *proxy* distribution $X_t \subseteq X$ over the complete data generating process $p_{data}(X)$ so that $c_0(\bar{x}_{i0}) = c_1(\bar{x}_{i1}) \; \forall \; \bar{x}_i \in X_t$ with not-null probability (that is, both classifiers are concordant about the assignments given the respective views). At this point, we can define $p(c_0, c_1|X_t)$ as the prior knowledge about the classifiers. The notation can be misleading, but, in this case, we are defining the probability of a joint parameter set $\{\bar{\theta}_0, \bar{\theta}_1\}$ given X_t and assuming implicitly the structure $c_i(\bar{x}; \theta_i)$ for both classifiers. Using Bayes' theorem we can derive the posterior distribution $p(c_0, c_1|X_L, Y_L X_U)$:

$$p(c_0, c_1|X_L, Y_L X_U) \propto p(c_0, c_1|X_t)p(X_t|X_L, X_U)$$

It's not difficult to understand that the posterior incorporates the knowledge derived from the unlabeled dataset given that both classifiers are able to posit the same label assignments for the labeled dataset and that X_t overlaps $X_L \cup X_U$. The process performs an implicit model selection by excluding all those classifiers that are discordant (that is, $p(c_0, c_1|X_t) = 0$) and restricting the parameter set to all those classifiers whose probability is the largest given $X_L \cup X_U$ (hence, the knowledge of the unlabeled samples directly influences the selection). Blum and Mitchell proposed a simple schema for implementing a Co-Training model, which is mainly based on the following steps:

1. X_L is split into two views X_{L0} and X_{L1} and X_U is kept as it is or subsampled.
2. The classifier $c_0(\bar{x})$ is trained using $\{X_{L0}, Y_L\}$.
3. The classifier $c_1(\bar{x})$ is trained using $\{X_{L1}, Y_L\}$.
4. Given a subset of unlabeled samples, both classifiers are asked to label n positive and m negative points (in our example, we are going to relax this rule by selecting k points corresponding to the highest confidence levels).
5. The new labeled samples are added to the training sets and the process is repeated starting from 2 until all unlabeled samples have been processed.

As already discussed, such an approach has a strong prerequisite ($c_0(\bar{x}_{i0}) = c_1(\bar{x}_{i1})$) that can't be met in many real-world applications. Moreover, it might be very difficult to identify the views of the same dataset when the features are not immediately splittable into two coherent groups (for example, when they represent the same kind of measurement from different sensors).

It's also important to remember that the unlabeled dataset can provide a valuable piece of information only under this assumption because, in all the other cases, the posterior distribution can be biased by the wrong assignments that are not corrected by one of the two classifiers (in other words, we are assuming that at the least one of the two classifiers is always quite confident of the correct label assignment, while, for example, the other one couldn't have already reached a stable configuration).

Therefore, Co-Training is helpful mainly in all those scenarios where the dataset is *naturally split* and can become unreliable in all the other ones because the views don't allow any of the two classifiers to find the correct assignments. To better understand the process, let's apply this method to the Wine dataset and draw some conclusions.

Example of Co-Training with the Wine dataset

Just as in the previous example, let's start by loading and shuffling the dataset:

```
from sklearn.datasets import load_wine
from sklearn.utils import shuffle

wine = load_wine()
X, Y = shuffle(wine['data'], wine['target'], random_state=1000)
```

The Wine dataset contains chemical data about different wines (178 data points). In particular, there are 13 attributes whose behavior is not assumed to be known (we don't know how they contribute, for example, to the flavor). Therefore, as this is an exercise with only a didactic purpose, we're assuming that it's possible to discriminate the class using the subsets containing only the first 7 features and the remaining 6 ones (it's not important whether this is chemically correct, but in a real-life scenario, the data scientist should never decide to split the features arbitrarily, because only a domain expert can have the specific awareness required to make a reasonable choice that is often counterintuitive). In this case, let's suppose we have 20 labeled points and 158 unlabeled ones:

```
nb_samples = X.shape[0]
nb_labeled = 20
nb_unlabeled = nb_samples - nb_labeled
nb_unlabeled_samples = 2
feature_cut = 7

X_unlabeled = X[-nb_unlabeled:]

X_labeled = X[:nb_labeled]
Y_labeled = Y[:nb_labeled]
```

```
X_labeled_1 = X_labeled[:, 0:feature_cut]
X_labeled_2 = X_labeled[:, feature_cut:]
```

The arrays `X_labeled_1/2` contain the training sets, which share the same `Y_labeled` array. As in the Self-Training example, we are going to employ two Gaussian Naive Bayes classifiers (the reader is invited to test other models, such as Logistic Regression or Kernel SVM). The first step is training a supervised model based only on the labeled so to obtain a baseline benchmark:

```
from sklearn.naive_bayes import GaussianNB
from sklearn.metrics import classification_report

nb0 = GaussianNB()
nb0.fit(X_labeled, Y_labeled)

print(classification_report(Y, nb0.predict(X), target_
names=wine['target_names']))
```

The output of the previous snippet is:

	precision	recall	f1-score	support
class_0	1.00	0.51	0.67	59
class_1	0.68	1.00	0.81	71
class_2	1.00	0.92	0.96	48
micro avg	0.81	0.81	0.81	178
macro avg	0.89	0.81	0.81	178
weighted avg	0.87	0.81	0.81	178

The result confirms that even a small sample can yield good performances, with a weighted precision average of about 0.87 and a slightly worse recall. We can now go on with the Co-Training approach, selecting `n_unlabeled_samples` points (the ones with the highest confidence) per classifier at each iteration:

```
import numpy as np

from sklearn.naive_bayes import GaussianNB

nb1 = None
    nb2 = None

    while X_labeled_1.shape[0] <= nb_samples:
        nb1 = GaussianNB()
        nb1.fit(X_labeled_1, Y_labeled)
```

```
        nb2 = GaussianNB()
        nb2.fit(X_labeled_2, Y_labeled)

        if X_labeled_1.shape[0] == nb_samples:
            break

        probs1 = nb1.predict_proba(X_unlabeled[:, 0:feature_cut])
        top_confidence_idxs1 = np.argsort(np.max(probs1, axis=1))[::-
1]

        selected_idxs1 = top_confidence_idxs1[0:nb_unlabeled_samples]

        probs2 = nb2.predict_proba(X_unlabeled[:, feature_cut:])
        top_confidence_idxs2 = np.argsort(np.max(probs2, axis=1))[::-
1]

        selected_idxs2 = top_confidence_idxs2[0:nb_unlabeled_samples]

        selected_idxs = list(selected_idxs1) + list(selected_idxs2)

        X_new_labeled = X_unlabeled[selected_idxs]
        X_new_labeled_1 = X_unlabeled[selected_idxs1, 0:feature_cut]
        X_new_labeled_2 = X_unlabeled[selected_idxs2, feature_cut:]

        Y_new_labeled_1 = nb1.predict(X_new_labeled_1)
        Y_new_labeled_2 = nb2.predict(X_new_labeled_2)

        X_labeled_1 = np.concatenate((X_labeled_1, X_new_labeled[:,
0:feature_cut]), axis=0)
        X_labeled_2 = np.concatenate((X_labeled_2, X_new_labeled[:,
feature_cut:]), axis=0)
        Y_labeled = np.concatenate((Y_labeled, Y_new_labeled_1, Y_new_
labeled_2), axis=0)

        X_unlabeled = np.delete(X_unlabeled, selected_idxs, axis=0)
```

The procedure is not very different from Self-Training, but in the end, we have two different classifiers. Let's start evaluating the first one:

```
print(classification_report(Y, nb1.predict(X[:, 0:feature_cut]),
target_names=wine['target_names']))
```

The output is:

	precision	recall	f1-score	support
class_0	1.00	0.75	0.85	59
class_1	0.77	0.97	0.86	71
class_2	0.95	0.88	0.91	48
micro avg	0.87	0.87	0.87	178

macro avg	0.91	0.86	0.87	178
weighted avg	0.89	0.87	0.87	178

As it's possible to see, the first classifier has achieved a better average precision with the worst performances for the second class. However, the result is better than the baseline benchmark and this partially confirms our initial hypothesis about the possibility to discriminate the classes using only a feature subset. It's not surprising to notice that, at least in a semi-supervised scenario, a smaller number of features allows us to obtain a more accurate prediction.

It's possible to explain such a behavior considering that, during each iteration, both classifiers *propose* the labelings with the largest confidence. If the smoothness assumption holds, the probability to find at least one point very close to a labeled cluster is quite large. As none of the two models is *forced* (at least until there are enough remaining values) to label points with low confidence (contrary to the supervised approach), Co-Training avoids risky decisions, letting the labeled dataset grow trying to maintain the optimal confidence level (which, of course, is subject to decay once the most difficult points have been added). This process is shown in the following figure, where the "risky" data point is kept unlabeled until the confidence level overcomes a minimum acceptable threshold:

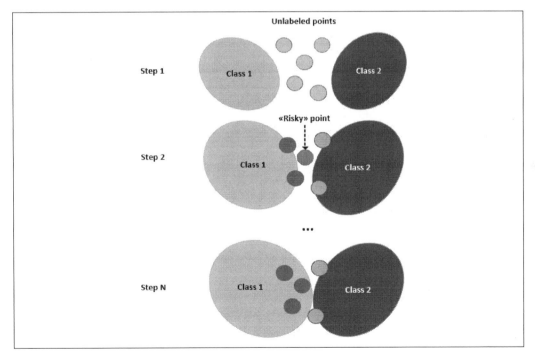

Example of the Co-Training labeling process

Let's now evaluate the second classifier:

```
print(classification_report(Y, nb2.predict(X[:, feature_cut:]),
target_names=wine['target_names']))
```

The output of the previous snippet is:

	precision	recall	f1-score	support
class_0	1.00	0.71	0.83	59
class_1	0.78	0.97	0.87	71
class_2	0.96	0.96	0.96	48
micro avg	0.88	0.88	0.88	178
macro avg	0.91	0.88	0.89	178
weighted avg	0.90	0.88	0.88	178

Again, the final performance is extremely positive and clearly superior to the benchmark. We can conclude that the second class is more problematic (with a small number of false negatives). This result can be directly connected with the larger support (71 points), which can drive the classifier to wrongly assign more points to this class. However, this is not the context to discuss the internal structure of the result, and it's not impossible that other algorithms can perform well for all classes.

Co-Training summary

If the final label of a point is decided by taking the assignment with the largest confidence, a Co-Training approach based on a limited number of unlabeled points performs better than a supervised alternative. As an exercise, I invite the reader to test other models and to find the minimum number of labeled points necessary to achieve an average precision equal to or greater than 0.85.

Summary

In this chapter, we introduced semi-supervised learning, starting from the scenario and the assumptions needed to justify the approaches. We discussed the importance of the smoothness assumption when working with both supervised and semi-supervised classifiers, in order to guarantee a reasonable generalization ability. Then we introduced the clustering assumption, which is strictly related to the geometry of the datasets, and allows coping with density estimation problems with a strong structural condition.

Finally, we discussed the manifold assumption and its importance in order to avoid the curse of dimensionality.

The chapter continued by introducing a generative and inductive model: Generative Gaussian mixtures, which allow clustering labeled and unlabeled samples starting from the assumption that the prior probabilities are modeled by multivariate Gaussian distributions. We also introduced the concepts of Self-Training and Co-learning. The former is an algorithm that leverages both the cluster and smoothness assumptions to adapt an initial separation hypersurface to the unlabeled dataset through an iterative procedure, and the latter is based on the simultaneous exploitation of two different "views" of the same dataset by two specialized classifiers.

In the next chapter, *Chapter 4, Advanced Semi-Supervised Classification*, we're continuing this exploration by discussing some more complex semi-supervised classification algorithms, like CPLE, S3VM, and Transductive SVM. These models can solve very complex problems where the basic algorithms discussed in this chapter can fail. The reader will learn their peculiarities and how to implement them using Python in real-life scenarios.

Further reading

- Chapelle O., Schölkopf B., Zien A. (edited by), *Semi-Supervised Learning*, The MIT Press, 2010

- Peters J., Janzing D., Schölkopf B., *Elements of Causal Inference*, The MIT Press, 2017

- Howard R. A., *Dynamic Programming and Markov Process*, The MIT Press, 1960

- Hughes G. F., *On the mean accuracy of statistical pattern recognizers*, IEEE Transactions on Information Theory, 14/1, 1968

- Belkin M., Niyogi P., *Semi-supervised learning on Riemannian manifolds*, Machine Learning 56, 2004

- Blum A., Mitchell T., *Combining Labeled and Unlabeled Data with Co-Training*, 11th Annual Conference on Computational Learning Theory, 1998

- Loog M., *Contrastive Pessimistic Likelihood Estimation for Semi-Supervised Classification*, arXiv:1503.00269, 2015

- Joachims T., *Transductive Inference for Text Classification using Support Vector Machines*, ICML Vol. 99/1999

- Koller D., Friedman N., *Probabilistic Graphical Models*, The MIT Press, 2009

- Bonaccorso G., *Machine Learning Algorithms, Second Edition*, Packt Publishing, 2018

4

Advanced Semi-Supervised Classification

In this chapter, we're going to introduce more advanced semi-supervised classification algorithms that are able to solve complex problems where simpler algorithms fail. In particular, we will discuss:

- **Contrastive Pessimistic Likelihood Estimation (CPLE)**
- **Semi-Supervised Support Vector Machines (S3VM)**
- **Transductive Support Vector Machines (TSVM)**

For each of these algorithms, we'll explain the theory behind them and then show a Python-coded example of them in practice. We'll start with the CPLE Algorithm.

Contrastive Pessimistic Likelihood Estimation

As we discussed in the previous chapter, in many real-life problems, it's cheaper to retrieve unlabeled samples, rather than correctly labeled ones. For this reason, many researchers have worked to find out the best strategies to carry out a semi-supervised classification that could outperform its supervised counterpart. The idea is to train a classifier with a few labeled samples and then improve its accuracy after adding weighted unlabeled samples. One of the best results is the CPLE algorithm, proposed by Loog (in Loog M., *Contrastive Pessimistic Likelihood Estimation for Semi-Supervised Classification*, arXiv:1503.00269, 2015).

Before we can explain this algorithm, it's necessary to define Platt scaling. If we have a labeled dataset (X, Y) containing N samples, it's possible to define the log-likelihood cost function of a generic estimator, as follows:

$$L(\bar{\theta}; \bar{x}, \bar{y}) = \sum_i \log p(\bar{x}_i, \bar{y}_i; \bar{\theta})$$

After training the model, it should be possible to determine $p(y_i|x_i, \theta)$, which is the probability of a label given a sample x_i. However, some classifiers are not based on this approach (such as SVM) and evaluate the right class, for example, by checking the sign of a parametrized function $f(x_i, \theta)$. As CPLE is a generic framework that can be used with any classification algorithm when the probabilities are not available, it's useful to implement a technique called **Platt scaling**, which allows us to transform the decision function into a probability, through a parametrized sigmoid. For a binary classifier, it can be expressed as follows:

$$p(y_i = +1|\bar{x}_i; \theta) = \frac{1}{1 + e^{\alpha f(\bar{x}_i; \bar{\theta}) + \beta}}$$

α and β are parameters that must be learned in order to maximize the likelihood. Luckily, scikit-learn provides the method `predict_proba()`, which returns the probabilities for all classes. Platt scaling is performed automatically or on demand; for example, the SCV classifier needs to have the parameter `probability=True` in order to compute the probability mapping. I always recommend checking the documentation before implementing a custom solution.

CPLE Theory

Consider a full dataset, made up of labeled and unlabeled samples. For simplicity, we can reorganize the original dataset, so that the first N samples are labeled, while the next M are unlabeled:

$$X_t = \{(\bar{x}_1, \bar{y}_1), (\bar{x}_2, \bar{y}_2), \dots, (\bar{x}_N, \bar{y}_N), \bar{x}^u_{N+1}, \dots, \bar{x}^u_{N+M}\}$$

As we don't know the labels for all x^u samples, we can decide to use M k-dimensional (k is the number of classes) soft-labels q_i that can be optimized during the training process:

$$Q = \{\bar{q}_1, \bar{q}_2, \dots, \bar{q}_M\} \ where \ \bar{q}_i \in \mathbb{R}^k \ and \ \sum_k \bar{q}_i^{(k)} = 1$$

The second condition in the previous formula is necessary to guarantee that each q_i represents a discrete probability (all the elements must sum up to 1.0). The complete log-likelihood cost function can, therefore, be expressed as follows:

$$L(\bar{\theta}; X_t, Q) = L(\bar{\theta}; \bar{x}, \bar{y}) + \sum_{i=N+1}^{N+M} \sum_k \bar{q}_i^{(k)} \log p(\bar{x}_i^u, \bar{y}_i^u = k; \bar{\theta})$$

The first term represents the log-likelihood for the supervised part, while the second one is responsible for the unlabeled points. If we train a classifier with only the labeled samples, excluding the second addend, we get a parameter set θ_{sup}. CPLE defines a contrastive condition (as a log-likelihood too), by defining the improvement in the total cost function given by the semi-supervised approach, compared to the supervised solution:

$$CL(\bar{\theta}, \bar{\theta}_{sup}, X_t, Q) = L(\bar{\theta}; X_t, Q) - L(\bar{\theta}_{sup}; X_t, Q)$$

This allows us to impose the condition that the semi-supervised solution must outperform the supervised one, in fact, maximizing it; we both increase the first term and reduce the second one, obtaining a proportional increase of CL (the term *contrastive* is very common in machine learning and it normally indicates a condition that is achieved as the difference between two opposite constraints). If CL doesn't increase, it probably means that the unlabeled samples have not been drawn from the marginal distribution $p(x)$ extracted from p_{data}.

In the previous expression, we implicitly used soft-labels, but since they're initially randomly chosen and there's no ground truth to support their values, it's a good idea not to trust them. We do that by imposing a pessimistic condition (as another log-likelihood):

$$CPL(\bar{\theta}, \bar{\theta}_{sup}, X_t, Q) = \min_{\bar{q}} CL(\bar{\theta}, \bar{\theta}_{sup}, X_t, Q)$$

By imposing this constraint, we try to find the soft-labels that minimize the contrastive log-likelihood; that's why this is defined as a pessimistic approach. It can seem a contradiction; however, trusting soft-labels can be dangerous, because the semi-supervised log-likelihood could be increased even with a large percentage of misclassification. Our goal is to find the best parameter set (the parameter set that guarantees the highest accuracy starting from the supervised baseline, which has been obtained using the labeled samples) and improve it, without forgetting the structural features provided by the labeled samples.

Therefore, our final goal can be expressed as follows:

$$\bar{\theta}_{semi} = \max_{\theta} CPL\left(\bar{\theta}, \bar{\theta}_{sup}, X_t, Q\right)$$

At this point, we can create a complete Python example to show the practical abilities of this algorithm.

Example of contrastive pessimistic likelihood estimation

We're going to implement the CPLE algorithm in Python, using a subset extracted from the MNIST dataset. For simplicity, we're going to use only the samples representing the digits 0 and 1:

```python
from sklearn.datasets import load_digits

import numpy as np

X_a, Y_a = load_digits(return_X_y=True)

X = np.vstack((X_a[Y_a == 0], X_a[Y_a == 1]))
Y = np.vstack((np.expand_dims(Y_a, axis=1)[Y_a==0], np.expand_
dims(Y_a, axis=1)[Y_a==1]))

nb_samples = X.shape[0]
nb_dimensions = X.shape[1]
nb_unlabeled = 150
Y_true = np.zeros((nb_unlabeled,))

unlabeled_idx = np.random.choice(np.arange(0, nb_samples, 1),
replace=False, size=nb_unlabeled)
Y_true = Y[unlabeled_idx].copy()
Y[unlabeled_idx] = -1
```

After creating the restricted dataset (*X*, *Y*) which contain 360 samples, we randomly select 150 samples (about 42%) to become unlabeled (the corresponding *y* is -1). At this point, we can measure the performance of logistic regression trained only on the labeled dataset:

```python
from sklearn.linear_model import LogisticRegression

lr_test = LogisticRegression(solver="lbfgs", max_iter=10000, multi_
class="auto", n_jobs=-1, (), random_state=1000)
```

```
lr_test.fit(X[Y.squeeze() != -1], Y[Y.squeeze() != -1].squeeze())
unlabeled_score = lr_test.score(X[Y.squeeze() == -1], Y_true)

print(unlabeled_score)
```

The output is:

```
0.573333333333
```

So, the logistic regression shows 57% accuracy for the classification of the unlabeled samples. We can also evaluate the cross-validation score on the whole dataset (before removing some random labels):

```
from sklearn.model_selection import cross_val_score

total_cv_scores = cross_val_score(LogisticRegression(solver="lbfgs",
max_iter=10000, multi_class="auto", random_state=1000),
  X, Y.squeeze(), cv=10, n_jobs=-1)

print(total_cv_scores)
```

The output of the previous snippet is:

```
[0.41666667 0.58333333 0.63888889 0.19444444 0.44444444 0.27777778

 0.44444444 0.38888889 0.5         0.41666667]
```

Thus, the classifier achieves an average 43% accuracy when using 10 folds (each test set contains 36 samples) if all the labels are known.

We can now implement a CPLE algorithm. The first thing is to initialize a LogisticRegression instance and the soft-labels:

```
lr = LogisticRegression(solver="lbfgs", max_iter=10000, multi_
class="auto", random_state=1000)

q0 = np.random.uniform(0, 1, size=nb_unlabeled)
```

q0 is a random array of values bounded in the half-open interval (0, 1), therefore, we also need a converter to transform q_i into an actual binary label:

$$y(q) = \begin{cases} 0 \ if \ q < 0.5 \\ 1 \ otherwise \end{cases}$$

We can achieve this using the NumPy function `np.vectorize()`, which allows us to apply a transformation to all the elements of a vector:

```
trh = np.vectorize(lambda x: 0.0 if x < 0.5 else 1.0)
```

In order to compute the log-likelihood, we also need a weighted log-loss (similar to the scikit-learn function `log_loss()`, which, however, computes the negative log-likelihood but doesn't support weights):

```
def weighted_log_loss(yt, p, w=None, eps=1e-15):
    if w is None:
        w_t = np.ones((yt.shape[0], 2))
    else:
        w_t = np.vstack((w, 1.0 - w)).T

    Y_t = np.vstack((1.0 - yt.squeeze(), yt.squeeze())).T
    L_t = np.sum(w_t * Y_t * np.log(np.clip(p, eps, 1.0 - eps)),
axis=1)

    return np.mean(L_t)
```

This function computes the following expression:

$$L(\bar{y}_i, \bar{p}, \bar{w}) = \frac{1}{N} \sum_i \left[y_{t_i} \log p_i + \left(1 - y_{t_i}\right) \log(1 - p_i) \right]$$

We also need a function to build the dataset with variable soft-labels q_i:

```
def build_dataset(q):
    Y_unlabeled = trh(q)

    X_n = np.zeros((nb_samples, nb_dimensions))
    X_n[0:nb_samples - nb_unlabeled] = X[Y.squeeze()!=-1]
    X_n[nb_samples - nb_unlabeled:] = X[Y.squeeze()==-1]

    Y_n = np.zeros((nb_samples, 1))
    Y_n[0:nb_samples - nb_unlabeled] = Y[Y.squeeze()!=-1]
    Y_n[nb_samples - nb_unlabeled:] = np.expand_dims(Y_unlabeled,
axis=1)

    return X_n, Y_n
```

At this point, we can define our contrastive log-likelihood:

```
def log_likelihood(q):
    X_n, Y_n = build_dataset(q)
```

```
Y_soft = trh(q)

lr.fit(X_n, Y_n.squeeze())

p_sup = lr.predict_proba(X[Y.squeeze() != -1])
p_semi = lr.predict_proba(X[Y.squeeze() == -1])

l_sup = weighted_log_loss(Y[Y.squeeze() != -1], p_sup)
l_semi = weighted_log_loss(Y_soft, p_semi, q)

return l_semi - l_sup
```

This method will be called by the optimizer, passing a different q vector each time. The first step is building the new dataset and computing Y_soft, which are the labels corresponding to q. Then, the logistic regression classifier is trained with the dataset (as Y_n is a $(k, 1)$ array, it's necessary to squeeze it to avoid a warning; the same thing is done when using Y as a Boolean indicator). At this point, it's possible to compute both p_{sup} and p_{sem} using the method predict_proba(), and finally, we can compute the semi-supervised and supervised log-loss, a function of q_i, which is the term that we want to minimize, while the maximization of θ is done implicitly when training the logistic regression.

The optimization is carried out using the **Broyden–Fletcher–Goldfarb–Shanno (BFGS)** algorithm implemented in SciPy:

```
from scipy.optimize import fmin_bfgs
q_end = fmin_bfgs(f=log_likelihood, x0=q0, maxiter=1000, disp=False)
```

This is a very fast algorithm, but the user is encouraged to experiment with methods or libraries. The two parameters we need in this case are f, which is the function to minimize, and x0, which is the initial condition for the independent variables. Maxiter is helpful for avoiding an excessive number of iterations when no improvements are achieved (considering the non-convex nature of the problem, this can be very frequent). Once the optimization is complete, q_end contains the optimal soft-labels. We can, therefore, rebuild our dataset:

```
X_n, Y_n = build_dataset(q_end)
```

With this final configuration, we can retrain the logistic regression and check the cross-validation accuracy:

```
final_semi_cv_scores = cross_val_score(
        LogisticRegression(solver="lbfgs", max_iter=10000, multi_
class="auto", random_state=1000),
        X_n, Y_n.squeeze(), cv=10, n_jobs=-1)

print(final_semi_cv_scores)
```

The output of the CPLE cross-validation is:

```
[0.97297297 0.86486486 0.94594595 0.86486486 0.89189189 0.88571429

 0.48571429 0.91428571 0.88571429 0.48571429]
```

The semi-supervised solution based on the CPLE algorithms achieves an average 81% accuracy, outperforming, as expected, the supervised approach.

CPLE Summary

CPLE is able to outperform standard classification methods with a limited computational cost, which can be relatively larger due to the re-evaluation of the log-likelihood by the optimization function. However, extra complexity is a normal condition in semi-supervised learning and, at this point, it should be clear when this cost is reasonable and when it's preferable to stick to a smaller, labeled, dataset. The reader can try other examples using different classifiers, such as SVM or Decision Trees, and verify when CPLE allows obtaining higher accuracy than other supervised algorithms.

Semi-supervised Support Vector Machines (S³VM)

When we discussed the cluster assumption in the previous chapter, we also defined the low-density regions as boundaries and the corresponding problem as low-density separation. A common supervised classifier based on this concept is a **Support Vector Machine (SVM)**, the objective of which is to maximize the distance between the dense regions where the samples must be.

S³VM Theory

For a complete description of linear and kernel-based SVMs, please refer to Bonaccorso G., *Machine Learning Algorithms, Second Edition*, Packt Publishing, 2018. However, it's useful to remind yourself of the basic model for a linear SVM with slack variables ξ_i:

$$\begin{cases} \min_{\bar{w},b,\xi} \dfrac{1}{2}\bar{w}^T\bar{w} + C\displaystyle\sum_i \xi_i \\ y_i(\bar{w}^T\bar{x}_i + b) \geq 1 - \xi_i \ and \ \xi_i \geq 0 \ \forall \ i \in (1,N) \end{cases}$$

This model is based on the assumption that y_i can be either -1 or 1. The slack variables ξ_i or soft-margins are variables, one for each sample, introduced to reduce the *strength* imposed by the original condition ($min \ ||w||$), which is based on a hard margin that misclassifies all the samples that are on the wrong side. They are defined by the Hinge loss, as follows:

$$\xi_i = \max\left(0, 1 - y_i(\bar{w}^T \bar{x}_i + b)\right)$$

With those variables, we allow some points to overcome the limit without being misclassified if they remain within a distance controlled by the corresponding slack variable (which is also minimized during the training phase, so as to avoid uncontrollable growth). In the following diagram, there's a schematic representation of this process:

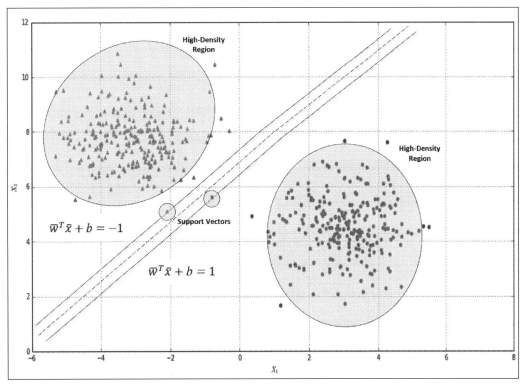

Linear SVM classification scenario

The last elements of each high-density region are the support vectors. Between them, there's a low-density region (it can also be zero-density in some cases) where our separating hyperplane lies.

In *Chapter 1*, *Machine Learning Model Fundamentals*, we defined the concept of *empirical risk* as a proxy for expected risk; therefore, we can turn the SVM problem into the minimization of empirical risk, under the Hinge cost function (with or without Ridge Regularization on w):

$$L(X, Y; \bar{w}, b) = \frac{1}{N} \sum_i \max\left(0, 1 - y_i(\bar{w}^T \bar{x}_i + b)\right)$$

Theoretically, every function that is always bounded by two hyperplanes containing the support vectors is a good classifier, but we need to minimize the empirical risk (and so, the expected risk); hence, we look for the maximum margin between high-density regions. This model can separate two dense regions with irregular boundaries; by adopting a kernel function, it can also work in non-linear scenarios. The natural question, at this point, is about the best strategy to integrate labeled and unlabeled samples when we need to solve this kind of problem in a semi-supervised scenario.

The first element to consider is the ratio: if we have a low percentage of unlabeled points, the problem is mainly supervised, and the generalization ability learned using the training set should be enough to correctly classify all the unlabeled points. On the other hand, if the number of unlabeled samples is much larger, we return to an almost pure clustering scenario (like the one discussed in the paragraph about the Generative Gaussian mixtures). That means that in order to exploit the strength of semi-supervised methods in low-density separation problems, we should consider situations where the ratio labeled/unlabeled is about 1.0.

However, even if we have the predominance of a class (for example, if we have a huge unlabeled dataset and only a few labeled samples), it's always possible to use the algorithms we're going to discuss, even if their performance can sometimes be equal to or lower than a pure supervised/clustering solution. Transductive SMVs, for example, show better accuracies when the labeled/unlabeled ratio is very small, while other methods can behave in a completely different way. When working with semi-supervised learning (and its assumptions), it's always important to bear in mind that each problem is supervised and unsupervised at the same time; the best solution must be evaluated in every different context.

A solution for this problem is offered by the *Semi-Supervised SVM* (also known as S^3VM) algorithm. If we have N labeled samples and M unlabeled samples, the objective function becomes as follows:

$$\min_{\bar{w}, b, \bar{\eta}, \bar{\xi}, \bar{z}} \left[\|\bar{w}\| + C \left(\sum_{i=1}^{N} \eta_i + \sum_{j=N+1}^{N+M} \min(\xi_j, z_j) \right) \right]$$

The first term imposes the standard SVM condition about the maximum separation distance, while the second block is divided into two parts:

- We need to add N slack variables η_i to guarantee a soft-margin for the labeled samples.

- At the same time, we have to consider the unlabeled points, which could be classified as +1 or -1. Therefore, we have two corresponding slack-variable sets ξ_i and z_i. However, we want to find the smallest variable for each possible pair, so as to be sure that the unlabeled sample is placed on the sub-space where the maximum accuracy is achieved.

The constraints necessary to solve the problems become as follows:

$$\begin{cases} y_i(\bar{w}^T\bar{x}_i + b) \geq 1 - \eta_i \; and \; \eta_i \geq 0 \; \forall \, i \in (1, N) \\ (\bar{w}^T\bar{x}_i - b) \geq 1 - \xi_j \; and \; \xi_j \geq 0 \; \forall \, j \in (N+1, N+M) \\ -(\bar{w}^T\bar{x}_i - b) \geq 1 - z_j \; and \; z_j \geq 0 \; \forall \, j \in (N+1, N+M) \end{cases}$$

The first constraint is limited to the labeled points and it's the same as a supervised SVM. The following two, instead, consider the possibility that an unlabeled sample could be classified as +1 or -1. Let's suppose, for example, that the label y_j for the sample x_j should be +1 and the first member of the second inequality is a positive number K (so the corresponding term of the third equation is -K). It's easy to verify that the first slack variable is $\xi_i \geq 1 - K$, while the second one is $z_j \geq 1 + K$. Therefore, in the objective, ξ_i is chosen to be minimized.

The choice of the hyperparameter C should be based on the same criteria employed for standard SVM. In particular, when $C \to 0$, the number of support vectors is reduced toward the minimum, while larger values (for example, $C=1$) imply an increased flexibility of the boundaries. Even if this model is structurally an SVM, the presence of unlabeled samples influences the optimization process, yielding very different results when, for example, C is increased from 0 to 1.

The reader must keep in mind that the algorithm will try to find the smallest slack values for the unlabeled samples, but since there are no guiding labels, the final choice could be incompatible with the problem. Considering both cluster and smoothness assumptions, the unlabeled samples should acquire the label of the closest coherent dense region. As it's possible to see by changing the value of C, this is not always true, because, in order to minimize the slack error, the algorithm could assign a label *geometrically* incompatible with the sample.

For example, the closest region to a point next to the boundary might be a cluster with fixed labels. In this case, we'd expect this point to have the same label.

However, if the objective is minimized by assigning a different label, the algorithm will make an inappropriate decision, because there are no penalties for not respecting the cluster assumption. Therefore, as a generic rule, we suggest starting with a larger value (for example, *C=1*) and reducing it only after having compared the results with an analogous supervised classifier. In most cases, the optimal value can be found with a few iterations, when a performance measure (for example, AUC, F1-score, or accuracy) of the S³VM overcomes the corresponding measure of the benchmark method.

This algorithm is inductive and generally yields good (if not excellent) performances. However, it has a very high computational cost, and should be solved using optimized (native) libraries. Unfortunately, it's a non-convex problem, and there are no methods to solve it in closed form; this also implies that the optimization might not reach the optimal configuration.

Let's now implement an S³VM in Python and evaluate the results.

Example of S³VM

We'll now implement an S³VM in Python using the SciPy optimization methods, which are mainly based on C and FORTRAN implementations. The reader can try it with other libraries, such as NLOpt and LIBSVM, and compare the results.

NLopt is a complete optimization library developed at MIT. It is available for different operating systems and programming languages. The website is https://nlopt.readthedocs.io.

LIBSVM is an optimized library for solving SVM problems and it is adopted by scikit-learn together with LIBLINEAR. It's also available for different environments. The home page is https://www.csie.ntu.edu.tw/~cjlin/libsvm/.

A possibility suggested by Bennet and Demiriz is to use the L1-norm for *w*, so as to linearize the objective function; however, this choice only seems to produce good results for small datasets. We're going to keep the original formulation based on the L2-norm, using a **Constrained optimization by linear approximation (COBYLA)** algorithm to optimize the objective.

Let's start by creating a bidimensional dataset, with both labeled and unlabeled samples (with 50% of each):

```
from sklearn.datasets import make_classification
```

```
nb_samples = 100
nb_unlabeled = 50

X, Y = make_classification(n_samples=nb_samples, n_features=2, n_
redundant=0, random_state=1000)
Y[Y==0] = -1
Y[nb_samples - nb_unlabeled:nb_samples] = 0
```

For simplicity (and without any impact, because the samples are shuffled), we set the last 50 samples as unlabeled ($y = 0$). The corresponding plot is shown in the following graph:

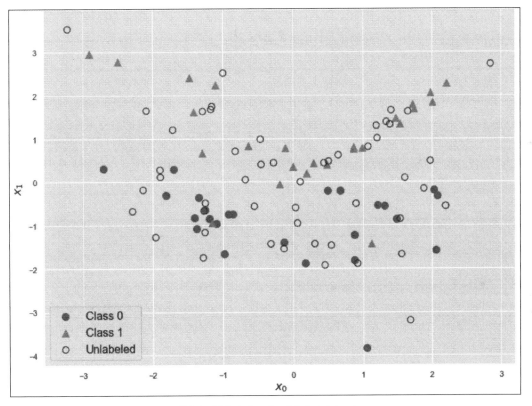

Original labeled and unlabeled dataset

The empty circles represent unlabeled points, which are spread throughout the entire dataset, while full circles and triangle markers are assigned respectively to class 0 ($y=-1$) and 1 ($y=1$). At this point, we need to initialize all variables required for the optimization problem:

```
import numpy as np
```

```
w = np.random.uniform(-0.1, 0.1, size=X.shape[1])
eta = np.random.uniform(0.0, 0.1, size=nb_samples - nb_unlabeled)
xi = np.random.uniform(0.0, 0.1, size=nb_unlabeled)
zi = np.random.uniform(0.0, 0.1, size=nb_unlabeled)
b = np.random.uniform(-0.1, 0.1, size=1)
C = 1.0


theta0 = np.hstack((w, eta, xi, zi, b))
```

Since the optimization algorithm requires a single array, we've stacked all vectors into a horizontal array `theta0` using the `np.hstack()` function. We also need to vectorize the `min()` function in order to apply it to arrays:

```
vmin = np.vectorize(lambda x1, x2: x1 if x1 <= x2 else x2)
```

Now, we can define the objective function:

```
def svm_target(theta, Xd, Yd):
    wt = theta[0:2].reshape((Xd.shape[1], 1))

    s_eta = np.sum(theta[2:2 + nb_samples - nb_unlabeled])
    s_min_xi_zi = np.sum(vmin(theta[2 + nb_samples - nb_unlabeled:2
                                    + nb_samples],
                              theta[2 + nb_samples:2
                                    + nb_samples + nb_unlabeled]))
    return C * (s_eta + s_min_xi_zi) + 0.5 * np.dot(wt.T, wt)
```

The arguments are the current `theta` vector, and the complete datasets `Xd` and `Yd`. The dot product of w has been multiplied by 0.5 to keep the conventional notation used for supervised SVMs. The constant can be omitted without any impact. At this point, we need to define all the constraints, since they are based on the slack variables; each function (which shares the same parameters of the objectives) is parametrized with an index, `idx`. The labeled constraint is as follows:

```
def labeled_constraint(theta, Xd, Yd, idx):
    wt = theta[0:2].reshape((Xd.shape[1], 1))

    c = Yd[idx] * (np.dot(Xd[idx], wt) + theta[-1]) + \
    theta[2:2 + nb_samples - nb_unlabeled][idx] - 1.0

    return (c >= 0)[0]
```

The unlabeled constraints, instead, are as follows:

```
def unlabeled_constraint_1(theta, Xd, idx):
    wt = theta[0:2].reshape((Xd.shape[1], 1))
```

```
    c = np.dot(Xd[idx], wt) - theta[-1] + \
        theta[2 + nb_samples - nb_unlabeled:2 + nb_samples][idx - nb_
samples + nb_unlabeled] - 1.0

    return (c >= 0)[0]

def unlabeled_constraint_2(theta, Xd, idx):
    wt = theta[0:2].reshape((Xd.shape[1], 1))

    c = -(np.dot(Xd[idx], wt) - theta[-1]) + \
        theta[2 + nb_samples:2 + nb_samples + nb_unlabeled ][idx - nb_
samples + nb_unlabeled] - 1.0

    return (c >= 0)[0]
```

They're parametrized with the current theta vector, the Xd dataset, and an idx index. We also need to include the constraints for each slack variable (≥ 0):

```
def eta_constraint(theta, idx):
    return theta[2:2 + nb_samples - nb_unlabeled][idx] >= 0

def xi_constraint(theta, idx):
    return theta[2 + nb_samples - nb_unlabeled:2 + nb_samples][idx -
nb_samples + nb_unlabeled] >= 0

def zi_constraint(theta, idx):
    return theta[2 + nb_samples:2 + nb_samples+nb_unlabeled ][idx -
nb_samples + nb_unlabeled] >= 0
```

We can now set up the problem using the SciPy convention:

```
svm_constraints = []

for i in range(nb_samples - nb_unlabeled):
    svm_constraints.append({
            'type': 'ineq',
            'fun': labeled_constraint,
            'args': (X, Y, i)
        })
    svm_constraints.append({
            'type': 'ineq',
            'fun': eta_constraint,
            'args': (i,)
        })

for i in range(nb_samples - nb_unlabeled, nb_samples):
```

```
svm_constraints.append({
        'type': 'ineq',
        'fun': unlabeled_constraint_1,
        'args': (X, i)
    })
svm_constraints.append({
        'type': 'ineq',
        'fun': unlabeled_constraint_2,
        'args': (X, i)
    })
svm_constraints.append({
        'type': 'ineq',
        'fun': xi_constraint,
        'args': (i,)
    })
svm_constraints.append({
        'type': 'ineq',
        'fun': zi_constraint,
        'args': (i,)
    })
```

Each constraint is represented by a dictionary, where `type` is set to `ineq` to indicate that it is an inequality, `fun` points to the callable object, and `args` contains all extra arguments (`theta` is the main `x` variable and it's automatically added). Using SciPy, it's possible to minimize the objective using either the **Sequential Least Squares Programming (SLSQP)** or **Constraint Optimization by Linear Approximation (COBYLA)** algorithms. We've chosen the latter, but the reader is free to employ any other method or library. In order to limit the number of iterations, we've also set the optional dictionary parameter `'maxiter': 5000`:

```
from scipy.optimize import minimize

result = minimize(fun=svm_target,
                  x0=theta0,
                  constraints=svm_constraints,
                  args=(X, Y),
                  method='COBYLA',
                  tol=0.0001,
                  options={'maxiter': 5000})
```

After the training process is complete, we can compute the labels for the unlabeled points:

```
theta_end = result['x']
w = theta_end[0:2]
```

```
b = theta_end[-1]

Xu= X[nb_samples - nb_unlabeled:nb_samples]
yu = -np.sign(np.dot(Xu, w) + b)
```

In the next graph, it's possible to compare the initial plot (left) with the final one where all points have been assigned a label (right):

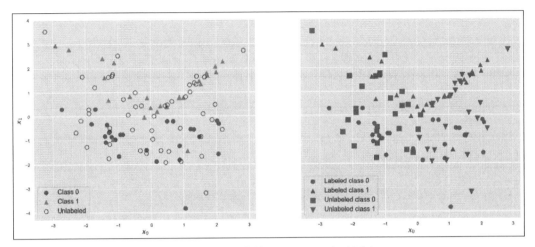

Original dataset (left). Training results (right)

As you can see, S³VM succeeded in finding the right label for most unlabeled points and it's also rather resistant to the noise induced by spurious points. Unfortunately, the problem is not linearly separable with the maximum accuracy and the final configuration tends to penalize the class 1 samples below a diagonal separation line (the dominant cluster is the stretched one in the upper-right quadrant). However, the result is promising and worth further investigations using different hyperparameters and optimization algorithms (COBYLA tends to remain stuck in local minima). I invite the reader to go on with such experiments to gain confidence in the method.

S³VM Summary

S³VM is a very powerful approach that offers high flexibility to adapt to different scenarios. It's particularly suitable when the structure of the unlabeled sample is partially (or even completely) unknown, and the main responsibility for labeling must be granted to the labeled samples.

Transductive Support Vector Machines (TSVM)

Another approach to the same problem is offered by **Transductive Support Vector Machines** (**TSVM**), proposed by T. Joachims (in Joachims T., *Transductive Inference for Text Classification using Support Vector Machines*, ICML Vol. 99/1999). TSVM are particularly suited when the unlabeled sample isn't very noisy, and the overall structure of the dataset is trustworthy. A common application of TSVM is classification on a dataset containing data points drawn from the same data-generating process (for example, medical photos collected using the same instrument) but only partially labeled due to, for example, economic reasons. Since all the images can be trusted, TSVM can exploit the structure of the dataset to achieve an accuracy larger than the one reachable by a supervised classifier.

TSVM Theory

The idea is to keep the original objective with two sets of slack variables – the first for the labeled samples and the other for the unlabeled ones:

$$\min_{\bar{w},b,\bar{\eta},\bar{\epsilon}} \left[\|\bar{w}\| + C_L \sum_{i=1}^{N} \eta_i + C_U \sum_{j=N+1}^{N+M} \xi_j \right]$$

Since this is a transductive approach, we need to consider the unlabeled samples as variable-labeled ones (subject to the learning process), imposing a constraint similar to the supervised points. From a certain viewpoint, this is equivalent to introducing a prior belief about the final classification, strongly based on both cluster and smoothness assumptions.

In other words, a TSVM can trust the structure of the dataset more than a S³VM, and the data scientist has more flexibility in the choice of behavior. Different combinations of C_L and C_U yield results that can shift from complete trust being granted to the labeled points to the opposite condition. As explained in the introduction, the goal of transductive learning is only to classify the unlabeled samples, leveraging both the labeled ones and the structure of the dataset to do so. However, contrary to inductive methods, the constraints imposed by the labeled samples can be weakened in favor of a more geometrically coherent solution.

As for the previous algorithm, we assume we have N labeled samples and M unlabeled ones; therefore, the conditions become as follows:

$$\begin{cases} y_i(\bar{w}^T \bar{x}_i + b) \geq 1 - \eta_i \ \ and \ \ \eta_i \geq 0 \ \ \forall i \in (1, N) \\ y_j^{(u)}(\bar{w}^T \bar{x}_j + b) \geq 1 - \xi_j \ \ and \ \ \xi_j \geq 0 \ \ \forall j \in (N+1, N+M) \\ y_j^{(u)} \in \{-1, 1\} \end{cases}$$

The first constraint is the classical SVM one and it works only on labeled samples. The second one uses the variable $y_j^{(u)}$ with the corresponding slack variables ξ_j to impose a similar condition on the unlabeled samples, while the third one is necessary to constrain the labels to be equal to -1 and 1.

Just like the semi-supervised SVMs, this algorithm is non-convex, and it's useful to try different methods to optimize it. Moreover, the author, in the aforementioned paper, showed how TSVM outperforms a standard supervised SVM when the test set (unlabeled) is large, and the training set (labeled) is relatively small. On the other hand, with large training sets and small test sets, a supervised SVM (or other algorithms) are always preferable, because they are faster and yield better accuracy.

We can now create a complete Python example of TSVM and evaluate the results.

Example of TSVM

In our Python implementation, we're going to use a bidimensional dataset similar to the one employed in the previous method. However, in this case, we'll impose 150 unlabeled samples out of a total of 200 points:

```
from sklearn.datasets import make_classification

nb_samples = 200
nb_unlabeled = 150

X, Y = make_classification(n_samples=nb_samples, n_features=2, n_
redundant=0, random_state=1000)
Y[Y==0] = -1
Y[nb_samples - nb_unlabeled:nb_samples] = 0
```

The corresponding plot is shown in the following figure:

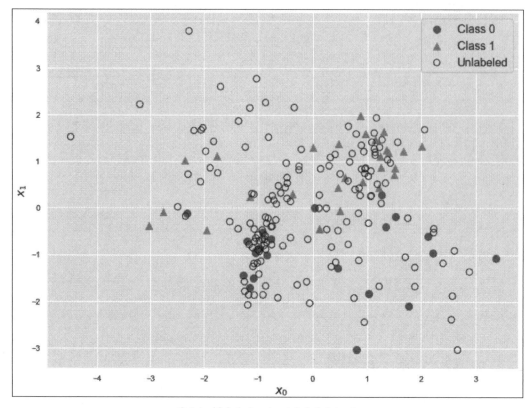

Original labeled and unlabeled dataset

The procedure's similar to the one we used before. First of all, we need to initialize our variables:

```
import numpy as np

w = np.random.uniform(-0.1, 0.1, size=X.shape[1])
eta_labeled = np.random.uniform(0.0, 0.1, size=nb_samples - nb_
unlabeled)
eta_unlabeled = np.random.uniform(0.0, 0.1, size=nb_unlabeled)
y_unlabeled = np.random.uniform(-1.0, 1.0, size=nb_unlabeled)
b = np.random.uniform(-0.1, 0.1, size=1)

C_labeled = 2.0
C_unlabeled = 0.1

theta0 = np.hstack((w, eta_labeled, eta_unlabeled, y_unlabeled, b))
```

In this case, we also need to define the y_unlabeled vector for variable labels. I also suggest using two C constants (C_labeled and C_unlabeled), in order to be able to weight the misclassification of labeled and unlabeled samples differently. We used a value of 2.0 for C_labeled and 0.1 for C_unlabled, because we want to accept the *guidance* of the labeled samples more than the structure of the unlabeled ones. In a further example, we'll compare the results with an opposite scenario.

The objective function to optimize is as follows:

```
def svm_target(theta, Xd, Yd):
    wt = theta[0:2].reshape((Xd.shape[1], 1))

    s_eta_labeled = np.sum(theta[2:2 + nb_samples - nb_unlabeled])
    s_eta_unlabeled = np.sum(theta[2 + nb_samples - nb_unlabeled:2 +
nb_samples])

    return (C_labeled * s_eta_labeled) + (C_unlabeled * s_eta_
unlabeled) + (0.5 * np.dot(wt.T, wt))
```

While the labeled and unlabeled constraints are as follows:

```
def labeled_constraint(theta, Xd, Yd, idx):
    wt = theta[0:2].reshape((Xd.shape[1], 1))

    c = Yd[idx] * (np.dot(Xd[idx], wt) + theta[-1]) + \
    theta[2:2 + nb_samples - nb_unlabeled][idx] - 1.0

    return int((c >= 0)[0])

def unlabeled_constraint(theta, Xd, idx):
    wt = theta[0:2].reshape((Xd.shape[1], 1))

    c = theta[2 + nb_samples:2 + nb_samples + nb_unlabeled][idx - nb_
samples + nb_unlabeled] * \
        (np.dot(Xd[idx], wt) + theta[-1]) + \
        theta[2 + nb_samples - nb_unlabeled:2 + nb_samples][idx - nb_
samples + nb_unlabeled] - 1.0

    return int((c >= 0)[0])
```

In this example, we want to employ the SLSQP algorithm to optimize the objective. This method computes the Jacobian (that is, the matrix containing the first partial derivatives) of all constraints (including the Boolean ones) and in NumPy 1.8+ the difference operator (-) between Boolean arrays has been deprecated and must be replaced with a logical XOR.

Unfortunately, this can cause incompatibilities with SciPy; since that's the case, we've transformed all Boolean outputs into integer values (0 and 1). This substitution doesn't affect either the performance or the final result. At this point, we can introduce the constraints for both labeled and unlabeled samples:

```
def eta_labeled_constraint(theta, idx):
    return int(theta[2:2 + nb_samples - nb_unlabeled][idx] >= 0)


def eta_unlabeled_constraint(theta, idx):
    return int(theta[2 + nb_samples - nb_unlabeled:2 + nb_samples][idx
- nb_samples + nb_unlabeled] >= 0)
```

As in the previous example, we can create the constraint dictionary needed by SciPy:

```
svm_constraints = []

for i in range(nb_samples - nb_unlabeled):
    svm_constraints.append({
            'type': 'ineq',
            'fun': labeled_constraint,
            'args': (X, Y, i)
        })
    svm_constraints.append({
            'type': 'ineq',
            'fun': eta_labeled_constraint,
            'args': (i,)
        })


for i in range(nb_samples - nb_unlabeled, nb_samples):
    svm_constraints.append({
            'type': 'ineq',
            'fun': unlabeled_constraint,
            'args': (X, i)
        })
    svm_constraints.append({
            'type': 'ineq',
            'fun': eta_unlabeled_constraint,
            'args': (i,)
        })
```

After having defined all the constraints, we can minimize the objective function using method='SLSQP' and the dictionary option 'maxiter': 2000. In general, convergence is achieved in a smaller number of iterations, but here we've made assumptions as though we're working in a more general scenario:

```
from scipy.optimize import minimize

result = minimize(fun=svm_target,
                  x0=theta0,
                  constraints=svm_constraints,
                  args=(X, Y),
                  method='SLSQP',
                  tol=0.0001,
                  options={'maxiter': 2000})
print(result['message'])
```

The output of the previous snippet is:

Optimization terminated successfully.

Such a message confirms that SLSQP successfully found a minimum. I always check the output of the optimization function, to make sure that nothing went wrong during the procedure, and I recommend that you do too. In particular, when using methods like COBYLA, it's important that all constraints are differentiable. When some of them are not, the algorithm can stop working properly, because the approximations of the Jacobian become unreliable.

When the process is complete, we can compute the labels for the unlabeled samples and compare the plots:

```
theta_end = result['x']
w = theta_end[0:2]
b = theta_end[-1]

Xu= X[nb_samples - nb_unlabeled:nb_samples]
yu = -np.sign(np.dot(Xu, w) + b)
```

The plot comparison is shown in the following figure:

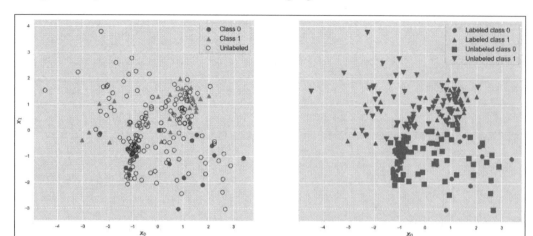

Original dataset (left). Final labeled dataset (right)

The misclassification (based on the density distribution) is slightly lower than S³VM, because we have decided to trust the labeled samples more. Of course, it's possible to change the C values and the optimization method until the expected result has been reached. A good benchmark is provided by a supervised SVM, which can have better performance when the training set is huge enough (and when it represents the whole p_{data} correctly). However, considering the clusters in the original dataset, we can conclude that TSVM achieved the expected result.

In particular, if we consider the separation region, we can observe that a slight modification of the slope will force the class 0 dense blob located at $x_0 \in [-1.5, -0.5]$ to be, at least partially, assigned to the label 1. The presence of separate slack variable sets, contrary to S³VM, has allowed the smoothness of the separation boundary to increase, with a final result similar to the ones achievable with non-linear methods.

Analysis of different TSVM configurations

It's interesting to evaluate different combinations of the C parameters, starting from a standard supervised linear SVM. The dataset is smaller, with a large number of unlabeled samples:

```
nb_samples = 100
nb_unlabeled = 90
```

```
X, Y = make_classification(n_samples=nb_samples, n_features=2, n_
redundant=0, random_state=100)
Y[Y==0] = -1
Y[nb_samples - nb_unlabeled:nb_samples] = 0
```

We use the standard SVM implementation provided by scikit-learn (the `SVC()` class) with a linear kernel and `C=1.0`:

```
from sklearn.svm import SVC

svc = SVC(kernel='linear', C=1.0)
svc.fit(X[Y != 0], Y[Y != 0])

Xu_svc= X[nb_samples - nb_unlabeled:nb_samples]
yu_svc = svc.predict(Xu_svc)
```

The SVM is trained with the labeled samples, and the vector `yu_svc` contains the prediction for the unlabeled samples. The resulting plot (in comparison with the original dataset) is shown in the following figure:

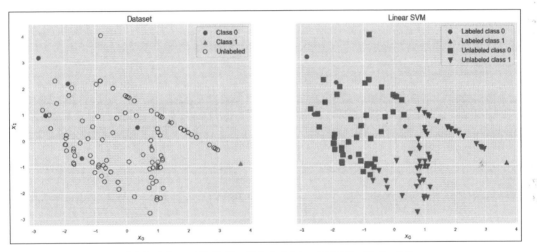

Original dataset (left). Final labeled dataset (right) with C = 1.0

All the labeled samples are represented with bigger squares and circles. The result meets our expectations, but there's an area *(X [-1, 0] - Y [-2, -1])*, where the SVM decided to impose the *circle* class (class 0) even if the unlabeled points are close to a square. This hypothesis might not be always acceptable considering the clustering assumption.

In fact, in a high-density region, there are samples belonging to two classes. A similar result is obtained using a TSVM with C_L=1 and C_U=10.0 (the reader can easily check it as an exercise):

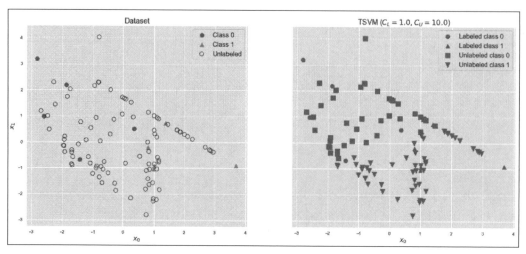

Original dataset (left). Final labeled dataset (right) with $C_L = 1$ and $C_U = 10$

In this case, we are trusting the labeled samples to determine the final result. As it's possible to see, the boundary position is slightly worse than SVM. For example, the class 1 points in the region $x_0 \in [1, 2]$ and $x_1 \in [0.75, 1]$ are aligned with a sequence of other points. We can consider the structure as a very long blob (with a strong directional cohesion). The standard SVM decided to split it into two regions with a separation line passing through the central empty area. This might be the most logical choice, considering the overall dataset.

On the other hand, using the TSVM, we have granted more responsibility to the labeled sample (that is, the unlabeled slack variables can have a larger variation so the configuration can more easily include the constraints imposed by the labeled sample) and such a choice led the algorithm to reduce the slope of the separation line. The result, although similar to the SVM one, has more *cluster-coherence* and the two classes are also more balanced. Remember that, in a semi-supervised scenario, we don't have any external guarantee about the class-balance, and it can only be obtained through the geometry of the dataset. In our case, we started with a balanced dataset; however, if it were potentially unbalanced, the only resources that a TSVM has in order to achieve this objective are the cluster and smoothness assumptions. By granting a larger weight to the unlabeled samples, we enforce this condition implicitly. In other words, we instruct the model to find the most appropriate labels according to the clustering structure of the dataset, and to minimize all abrupt transitions.

Let's try now to invert the responsibilities by setting C_L=**10** and C_U=**0.1**:

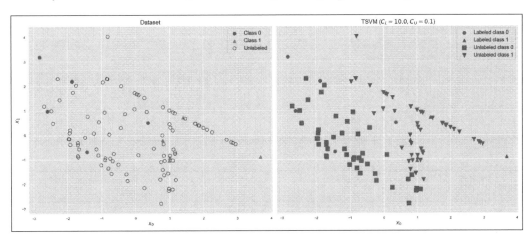

Original dataset (left). Final labeled dataset (right) with C_L = 10 and C_U = 0.1

In this case, the labeled samples are allowed to exploit more flexible margins, while the unlabeled ones are restricted to an almost hard margin. The separation line is now diagonal, and the misclassification error is lower or comparable to the previous configuration. However, in this case, we can fully appreciate the effectiveness of TSVMs. In fact, the result shows a more coherent geometrical separation. All the clusters are compact, and the slack variables for the unlabeled samples are kept smaller, while the labeled samples are allowed to be more flexible. This condition determines an increased ability to adapt the final configuration to the geometrical structure of the dataset.

Of course, the reader may wonder which of the two results is correct. As we are working in a semi-supervised scenario, to fully answer this question, it's necessary to have access to a larger labeled dataset, which is often impossible. My suggestion is to test several configurations (on sub-sampled datasets), before making the final decision. Whenever the labeled points must be trusted not only because they have been correctly pre-classified, but also because their position is *geometrically strategical* (for example, they are centroids of specific populations), the choice should be to pick a configuration similar to a standard SVM.

On the contrary, when the structure of the dataset is definitely more representative of the underlying data-generating process, a TSVM can grant more responsibility to the unlabeled sample and exploit the labeled one to find a reasonable classification that is also compatible with the position of the dense regions. Finally, it's also important to remember that the smoothness assumption is based on the idea that abrupt changes are very rare. Comparing the two previous examples, the reader will notice that, in the second configuration, the separation boundary is a little bit smoother than the first one.

In fact, while in the first configuration there are at least two abrupt class changes and all the central empty region is subject to the same behavior, the second one seems to transition from one class to another in a more flexible and smoother way, with only an abrupt (inevitable) separation. In this case, we can conclude that the second configuration is preferable.

In Chapelle O., Schölkopf B., Zien A. (edited by), *Semi-Supervised Learning*, The MIT Press, 2010, there are further details about possible optimization strategies, with strengths and weaknesses. I invite the reader to check the book if they're interested in studying other, more complex, problems and solution strategies.

TSVM Summary

TSVMs are powerful semi-supervised models that are particularly suited to scenarios where the geometrical structure of the dataset is trustworthy and all the points are drawn from the same data-generating process. If these conditions are met, the algorithm can leverage the structure of the dataset to find the most appropriate labeling for the unlabeled sample. On the other hand, if the unlabeled sample is noisy, or its structure can derive from multiple processes, TSVM is not an appropriate choice and might yield very inaccurate results.

Summary

The algorithms discussed in this chapter are generally more powerful than those analyzed in the previous one, but they have specific differences that must always be considered. CPLE and S³VM are inductive methods.

CPLE is an inductive, semi-supervised classification framework based on statistical learning concepts that can be adopted together with any supervised classifier. The main concept is to define a contrastive log-likelihood based on soft-labels that takes into account both labeled and unlabeled samples. The importance granted to the latter is conditioned to the maximization of the log-likelihood, and therefore the algorithm is less suited to tasks where fine control is needed.

Another inductive classification approach is provided by the S³VM algorithm, which is an extension of the classical SVM approach, based on two extra optimization constraints to address the unlabeled samples. This method is relatively powerful, but it's non-convex and, therefore, very sensitive to the algorithms employed to minimize the objective function. In both the S³VM and CPLE cases, the level of trust granted to the unlabeled sample is always relatively low, and the main responsibility for the classification lies with the labeled sample.

An alternative to S³VM is provided by TSVM, which tries to minimize the objective with a condition based on variable labels. The problem is, hence, divided into two parts: a supervised one, which is exactly the same as standard SVM, and a semi-supervised one, which has a similar structure but without fixed y labels. This problem is non-convex too and it's necessary to evaluate different optimization strategies to find the best trade-off between accuracy and computational complexity. TSVMs transductive approach relies heavily on the structure of the dataset; it's only a reasonably good choice when both labeled and unlabeled samples are known to be drawn from the same data-generating process.

In the *Further reading* section, there are some useful resources so you can examine all these problems in depth and find a suitable solution for each particular scenario.

In the next chapter, *Chapter 5, Graph-Based Semi-Supervised Learning*, we'll continue this exploration by discussing some important algorithms based on the structure underlying the dataset. In particular, we're going to employ graph theory to perform the propagation of labels to unlabeled samples, and to reduce the dimensionality of datasets in non-linear contexts.

Further reading

- Chapelle O., Schölkopf B., Zien A. (edited by), *Semi-Supervised Learning*, The MIT Press, 2010

- Peters J., Janzing D., Schölkopf B., *Elements of Causal Inference*, The MIT Press, 2017

- Howard R. A., *Dynamic Programming and Markov Process*, The MIT Press, 1960

- Hughes G. F., *On the mean accuracy of statistical pattern recognizers*, IEEE Transactions on Information Theory, 14/1, 1968

- Belkin M., Niyogi P., *Semi-supervised learning on Riemannian manifolds*, Machine Learning 56, 2004

- Blum A., Mitchell T., *Combining Labeled and Unlabeled Data with Co-Training*, 11th Annual Conference on Computational Learning Theory, 1998

- Loog M., *Contrastive Pessimistic Likelihood Estimation for Semi-Supervised Classification*, arXiv:1503.00269, 2015

- Joachims T., *Transductive Inference for Text Classification using Support Vector Machines*, ICML Vol. 99/1999

- Bonaccorso G., *Machine Learning Algorithms, Second Edition*, Packt Publishing, 2018

5

Graph-Based
Semi-Supervised Learning

In this chapter, we continue our discussion about semi-supervised learning, considering a family of algorithms that are based on the graph obtained from a dataset, and the existing relationships among samples. The problems that we are going to discuss belong to two main categories: the propagation of class labels to unlabeled samples, and the use of non-linear techniques based on the manifold assumption to reduce the dimensionality of the original dataset. In particular, this chapter covers the following propagation algorithms:

- Label propagation based on the weight matrix
- Label propagation in scikit-learn, based on transition probabilities
- Label spreading
- Laplacian regularization
- Propagation based on Markov random walks

For the manifold learning section, we're discussing the following:

- The Isomap algorithm and the multidimensional scaling approach
- Locally linear embedding
- Laplacian spectral embedding
- t-distributed Stochastic Neighbor Embedding (t-SNE)

Each algorithm is described mathematically and a coded example is provided. We'll start with label propagation, which covers a family of algorithms that rely on the dataset structure to find the missing labels.

Label propagation

Label propagation is a family of semi-supervised algorithms that rely on the graph representation of a dataset to exploit the existing relations among nodes in order to propagate the labels to unlabeled points. In particular, if we have N labeled points (with bipolar labels +1 and –1) and M unlabeled points (denoted by $y = 0$), it's possible to build an undirected graph based on a measure of geometric affinity among samples. In the following figure, there's an example of such a structure:

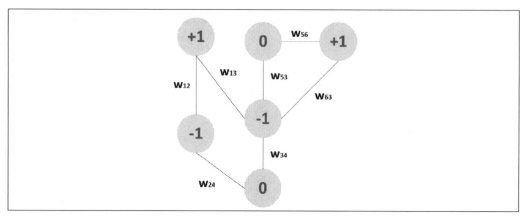

Example of binary graph

The graph is defined as a structure containing two sets $G = \{V, E\}$. E is the set of vertices (or nodes) and contains all sample labels $V = \{-1, +1, 0\}$, while the edge set E is based on an affinity measure that encodes the strength of the relation between two nodes. For practical reasons, it's helpful to introduce a matrix W whose elements w_{ij} are:

- The actual weight $w_{ij} \in \mathbb{R}$ of the edge (i, j). In this case, W is called the **affinity matrix**, and the elements w_{ij} are defined through an actual distance measure, so that when $w_{ij} > w_{iz}$ it means that the node i has a stronger connection with j rather than with z.

- A value from the set $K = \{0, 1\}$, where 1 indicates the presence of a connection, and 0 the opposite condition. In this case, W is often called the **adjacency matrix** and, contrary to the previous example, now W can also be singular when the graph is not fully connected (for example, if the outliers are too far away to be connected to any other nodes, their rows will be null and det $W = 0$). It's necessary to pay attention to these cases when the algorithms need to invert W, or its derived matrix, which will be singular too.

In the preceding example, there are four labeled points (two with $y = +1$ and two with $y = -1$), and two unlabeled points ($y = 0$). The affinity matrix W is normally symmetric and square with dimensions equal to $(N + M) \times (N + M)$. It can be obtained with different approaches. The most common ones, also adopted by scikit-learn, are:

- **k-Nearest Neighbors** (we are going to discuss this algorithm in further detail in *Chapter 6, Clustering and Unsupervised Models*), which yields an adjacency matrix:

$$W_{ij} = \begin{cases} 1 \; if \; \bar{x}_i \in neighbors_k(\bar{x}_j) \\ 0 \; otherwise \end{cases}$$

- **Radial basis function kernel**, which instead outputs an actual affinity matrix with not-null entries:

$$W_{ij} = e^{-\gamma \|\bar{x}_i - \bar{x}_j\|_2^2}$$

Sometimes, in the radial basis function kernel, the parameter γ is represented as the reciprocal of $2\sigma^2$; however, small γ values corresponding to a large variance increase the radius, including farther points and *smoothing* the class over a number of samples, while large γ values restrict the boundaries to a subset that tends to a single sample. Instead, in the KNN kernel, the parameter k controls the number of samples to consider as neighbors.

To describe the basic algorithm, we also need to introduce the **degree matrix** (D):

$$D = diag\left(\left|\sum_j W_{ij}\right| \; \forall \; i \in (1, N + M)\right) = \begin{pmatrix} \deg v_1 & \cdots & 0 \\ \vdots & \ddots & \vdots \\ 0 & \cdots & \deg v_{N+M} \end{pmatrix}$$

This is a diagonal matrix where each non-null element represents the *degree* of the corresponding vertex. This can be the number of incoming edges, or a measure proportional to it (as in the case of W based on the radial basis function). The degree matrix plays a fundamental role in the definition of a particular operator, called **graph Laplacian**, which is extremely helpful in many of the algorithms that we are going to discuss.

The general idea of label propagation is to let each node propagate its label to its neighbors and iterate the procedure until convergence.

Formally, if we have a dataset containing both labeled and unlabeled samples:

$$\begin{cases} X = \{\bar{x}_0, \bar{x}_1, \dots, \bar{x}_N, \bar{x}_{N+1}, \dots, \bar{x}_{N+M}\} \ where \ \bar{x}_i \in \mathbb{R}^k \\ Y = \{y_0, y_1, \dots, y_N, 0, 0, \dots, 0\} \ where \ y_i \in \{0, +1, -1\} \end{cases}$$

The steps of the main **label propagation** algorithm (as proposed by Zhu and Ghahramani in Zhu X., Ghahramani Z., *Learning from Labeled and Unlabeled Data with Label Propagation*, CMU-CALD-02-107, 2002), are:

1. Select an affinity matrix type (KNN or RBF) and compute W
2. Compute the degree matrix D
3. Define $\tilde{Y}^{(0)} = Y$
4. Define $Y_L = \{y_0, y_1, \dots, y_N\}$
5. Iterate until the convergence of the following steps:

$$\begin{cases} \tilde{Y}^{(t+1)} = D^{-1} W \tilde{Y}^{(t)} \\ \tilde{Y}_L^{(t+1)} = Y_L \end{cases}$$

The first update performs a propagation step with both labeled and unlabeled points. Each label is spread from a node through its outgoing edges, and the corresponding weight, normalized with the degree, increases or decreases the *effect* of each contribution. The second command instead resets all y values for the labeled samples. The final labels can be obtained with:

$$Y_{Final} = sign\left(\tilde{Y}^{(t_{end})}\right)$$

The proof of convergence is very easy. If we partition the matrix $D^{-1}W$ according to the relationship among labeled and unlabeled samples (identified respectively with the subscripts L and U), we get:

$$D^{-1}W = \begin{pmatrix} A_{LL} & A_{LU} \\ A_{UL} & A_{UU} \end{pmatrix}$$

If we consider that only the first N components of Y are non-null and they are clamped at the end of each iteration, the matrix can be rewritten as:

$$D^{-1}W = \begin{pmatrix} A_{LL} & A_{LU} \\ A_{UL} & A_{UU} \end{pmatrix} = \begin{pmatrix} I & 0 \\ A_{UL} & A_{UU} \end{pmatrix}$$

We are interested in proving the convergence for the part regarding the unlabeled samples (the labeled ones are fixed), so we can write the update rule as:

$$\tilde{Y}_U^{(t+1)} = A_{UL}Y_L + A_{UU}\tilde{Y}_U^{(t)}$$

Transforming the recursion into an iterative process, the previous formula becomes:

$$\tilde{Y}_U^{(t+1)} = \sum_{k=1}^{t+1}((A_{UU})^{k-1}A_{UL}Y_L) + (A_{UU})^{t+1}Y_U$$

In the previous expression, the second term is null, so we need to prove that the first term converges; however, it's easy to recognize a truncated matrix geometrical series (Neumann series), which has a limit if the matrix $(I - A)$ is invertible:

$$\sum_{i=0}^{\infty} A^i = (I - A)^{-1}$$

In our case, A_{UU} is constructed to have all eigenvalues $|\lambda_i| < 1$; therefore, $(I - A_{UU})$ is invertible and the series converges to:

$$\tilde{Y}_U^{(\infty)} = \lim_{t \to \infty} \sum_{k=1}^{t+1}(A_{UU})^{k-1}A_{UL}Y_L = (I - A_{UU})^{-1}A_{UL}Y_L$$

Therefore, the final labeling is unique (when $t \to \infty$) and depends on both the existing labels and on the unlabeled part of the Laplacian. From a mathematical viewpoint, the labeled part is responsible for *incorporating* the starting condition in the model, while the unlabeled part has the role of defining the dynamics of the propagation according to the structure of the graph.

Example of label propagation

We can implement the algorithm in Python, using a test bidimensional dataset:

```
from sklearn.datasets import make_classification

nb_samples = 100
nb_unlabeled = 75

X, Y = make_classification(n_samples=nb_samples, n_features=2, n_
```

```
informative=2, n_redundant=0, random_state=1000)
Y[Y==0] = -1
Y[nb_samples - nb_unlabeled:nb_samples] = 0
```

As in the other examples, we set $y = 0$ for all unlabeled samples (75 out of 100). The corresponding plot is shown in the following graph:

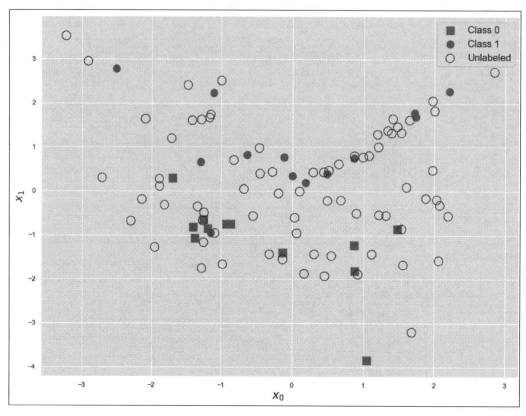

Partially labeled dataset

The dots marked with a cross are unlabeled. At this point, we can define the affinity matrix. In this case, we compute it using both methods:

```
from sklearn.neighbors import kneighbors_graph

nb_neighbors = 2

W_knn_sparse = kneighbors_graph(X, n_neighbors=nb_neighbors,
mode='connectivity', include_self=True)
W_knn = W_knn_sparse.toarray()
```

The KNN matrix is obtained using the scikit-learn function `kneighbors_graph()` with the parameters `n_neighbors=2` and `mode='connectivity'`; the alternative is `distance`, which returns the distances instead of 0 and 1 to indicate the absence/presence of an edge. The `include_self=True` parameter is useful, as we want to have $W_{ii} = 1$.

For the RBF matrix, we need to define it manually:

```python
import numpy as np

def rbf(x1, x2, gamma=10.0):
    n = np.linalg.norm(x1 - x2, ord=1)
    return np.exp(-gamma * np.power(n, 2))

W_rbf = np.zeros((nb_samples, nb_samples))

for i in range(nb_samples):
    for j in range(nb_samples):
        W_rbf[i, j] = rbf(X[i], X[j])
```

The default value for γ is 10, corresponding to a standard deviation σ equal to 0.22. When using this method, it's important to set a correct value for γ; otherwise, the propagation can degenerate in the predominance of a class (γ too small). As γ is analogous to the inverse of the double of the variance of a Gaussian distribution ($\gamma = 1/2\sigma^2$), its value should be computed by considering the sample standard deviation of the labeled dataset σ and by assuming that the influence of the function almost vanishes after about 3σ from the mean. Therefore, the value chosen for γ should always be computed considering this reference. A small γ is equivalent to a large variance; therefore, the affinity matrix will take into account also very far neighbors, while a large γ might result in an almost empty neighborhood.

Now, we can compute the degree matrix and its inverse. As the procedure is identical, from this point on, we continue using the RBF affinity matrix:

```python
D_rbf = np.diag(np.sum(W_rbf, axis=1))
D_rbf_inv = np.linalg.inv(D_rbf)
```

The algorithm is implemented using a variable threshold. The value adopted here is `0.01`. As the algorithm iterates until $\left\| Y^{(t)} - Y^{(t-1)} \right\|_1 > tolerance$, the value for the tolerance should be small enough to guarantee that the sign function applied to the final label vector doesn't make any mistake. A reasonable rule of thumb is to set the tolerance equal to $1/N$. Smaller values are always preferable, but they can lead to a larger number of iterations.

Ideally, it's possible to set a double stop criterion based on the threshold and a maximum number of iterations:

```
tolerance = 0.01

Yt = Y.copy()
Y_prev = np.zeros((nb_samples,))
iterations = 0

while np.linalg.norm(Yt - Y_prev, ord=1) > tolerance:
    P = np.dot(D_rbf_inv, W_rbf)
    Y_prev = Yt.copy()
    Yt = np.dot(P, Yt)
    Yt[0:nb_samples - nb_unlabeled] = Y[0:nb_samples - nb_unlabeled]

Y_final = np.sign(Yt)
```

The final result is shown in the following double plot:

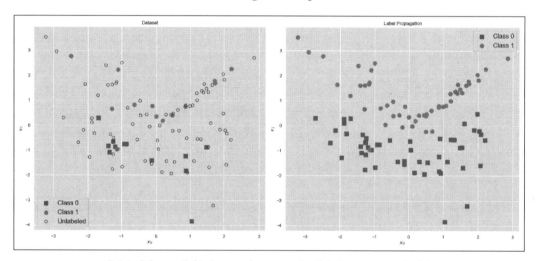

Original dataset (left); dataset after a complete label propagation (right)

As it's possible to see, in the original dataset, there's a round dot surrounded by square ones (-0.9, -1). As this algorithm keeps the original labels, we find the same situation after the propagation of labels. This condition could be acceptable, even if both the smoothness and clustering assumptions are contradicted. Assuming that it's reasonable (that is, the initial labeling can be considered as flexible and there are no explicit constraints), it's possible to force a *correction* by relaxing the algorithm:

```
tolerance = 0.01
```

```
Yt = Y.copy()
Y_prev = np.zeros((nb_samples,))
iterations = 0

while np.linalg.norm(Yt - Y_prev, ord=1) > tolerance:
    P = np.dot(D_rbf_inv, W_rbf)
    Yt = np.dot(P, Yt)
    Y_prev = Yt.copy()

Y_final = np.sign(Yt)
```

With this modification, the original labels are not clamped anymore, and the propagation algorithm is allowed to change all those values that disagree with the neighborhood. The result is shown in the following plot:

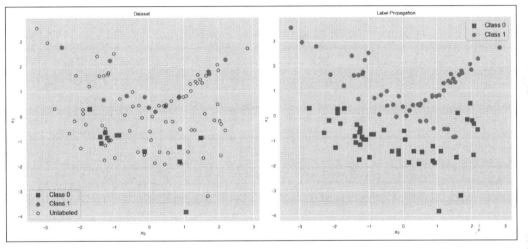

Original dataset (left); dataset after a complete label propagation with overwrite (right)

As you can see, the labeling process has been completed successfully and the point in the neighborhood centered at (-1, -1) has now been relabeled to match its neighbor's labels. We can now analyze an example using the scikit-learn API, which is slightly different from the algorithm previously discussed.

Label propagation in scikit-learn

Scikit-learn implements a slightly different algorithm proposed by Zhu and Ghahramani (in the aforementioned paper) that is equivalent in terms of results but has a slightly different internal dynamic based on a Markov random walk through the graph until a stationary configuration is found (that is, the labels don't change anymore).

The affinity matrix W can be computed using both methods (KNN and RBF), but it is normalized to become a probability transition matrix:

$$P_{ij}(i \to j) = \frac{w_{ij}}{\sum_k w_{kj}}$$

The algorithm operates like a Markov random walk, with the following sequence (assuming that there are Q different labels):

1. Define a matrix $Y_i^M = [P(label = y_0), P(label = y_1), \ldots, and\ P(label = y_Q)]$, where $P(label = y_i)$ is the probability of the label y_i, and each row is normalized so that all the elements sum up to 1

2. Define $\tilde{Y}^{(0)} = Y^M$

3. Iterate until convergence of the following steps:

$$\begin{cases} \tilde{Y}_M^{(t+1)} = P\tilde{Y}_M^{(t)} \\ \tilde{Y}_M^{(t+1)}(i,j) = \dfrac{\tilde{Y}_M^{(t+1)}(i,j)}{\sum_k \tilde{Y}_M^{(t+1)}(k,j)} \\ \tilde{Y}_{ML}^{(t+1)} = Y_L \end{cases}$$

The first update performs a label propagation step. As we're working with probabilities, it's necessary (second step) to renormalize the rows so that their element sums up to 1. The last update resets the original labels for all labeled samples. In this case, it means imposing a $P(label = y_i) = 1$ to the corresponding label and setting all the others to zero. The proof of convergence is very similar to the one for label propagation algorithms, and can be found in Zhu X., Ghahramani Z., *Learning from Labeled and Unlabeled Data with Label Propagation*, CMU-CALD-02-107. The most important result is that the solution can be obtained in closed form (without any iteration) through this formula:

$$Y_U = (I - P_{UU})^{-1} P_{UL} Y_L$$

The first term is the sum of a generalized geometric series, where P_{UU} is the unlabeled-unlabeled part of the transition matrix P. P_{UL}, instead, is the unlabeled-labeled part of the same matrix.

For our Python example, we need to build the dataset differently, because scikit-learn considers a sample unlabeled if $y = -1$:

```
from sklearn.datasets import make_classification

nb_samples = 1000
nb_unlabeled = 750

X, Y = make_classification(n_samples=nb_samples, n_features=2, n_
informative=2, n_redundant=0, random_state=100)
Y[nb_samples - nb_unlabeled:nb_samples] = -1
```

We can now train a `LabelPropagation` instance with an RBF kernel and `gamma=10.0`:

```
from sklearn.semi_supervised import LabelPropagation

lp = LabelPropagation(kernel='rbf', gamma=10.0)
lp.fit(X, Y)

Y_final = lp.predict(X)
```

The result is shown in the following double plot:

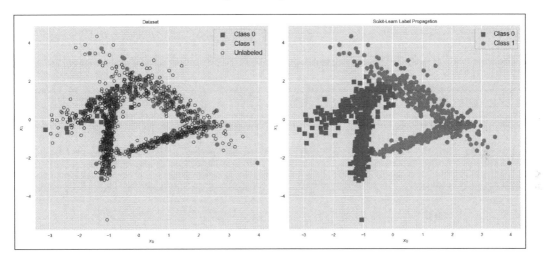

Original dataset (left). Dataset after a scikit-learn label propagation (right)

As expected, the propagation converged to a solution that respects both the smoothness and the clustering assumptions. In fact, as it's possible to see, the labels are assigned considering the clustering structure of the dataset (that is, the blobs are always coherent) and the transitions are relatively smooth (excluding the ones imposed by the labeled sample).

Label spreading

Another algorithm (proposed by Zhou et al.) that we need to analyze is called **label spreading**, which offers a slight better stability when the dataset is very noisy or dense. In these cases, standard label propagation might suffer a loss of precision due to the closeness of points with different labels. Conversely, label spreading is more robust because the Laplacian is normalized and abrupt transitions are more heavily penalized (all mathematical details are quite complex, but the reader can find all details in Biyikoglu T., Leydold J., Stadler P. F., *Laplacian Eigenvectors of Graphs*, Springer, 2007).

The algorithm is based on the normalized graph Laplacian, defined as:

$$\mathcal{L} = D^{-\frac{1}{2}} W D^{-\frac{1}{2}}$$

Considering it in matrix form, it has a diagonal element $\mathcal{L}_{ii}$ equal to 1, if the degree $\deg \mathcal{L}_{ii} > 0$ (0 otherwise), and all the other elements equal to:

$$\mathcal{L}_{ij} = -\frac{1}{\sqrt{\deg v_i} \sqrt{\deg v_j}} \; if \; v_i \in neighbors(v_j)$$

This operator is a particular case of a generic graph Laplacian:

$$\mathcal{L} = D - W$$

The behavior of such an operator is analogous to a discrete Laplacian operator, whose real-value version is the fundamental element of all diffusion equations. Let's suppose we have a small portion of a graph, as shown in the following figure:

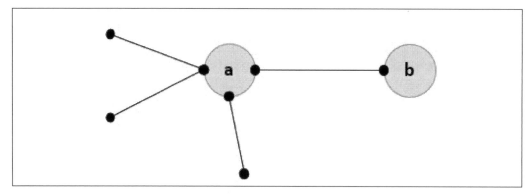

Portion of graph containing two nodes

If there are no other connections that involve either the node **a** or **b**, the degrees are: deg $a = 4$ and deg $b = 1$. Let's now consider the Laplacian value for the edge (a, b). As the nodes are connected, and D is diagonal, $\mathcal{L}_{ab} = -1$, while $\mathcal{L}_{aa} = 4$ and $\mathcal{L}_{bb} = 1$.

If we think about a path through the graph (that is, a Eulerian path, so to be sure to traverse each edge exactly once), the transition $a \to b$ can happen starting from three different previous states. Therefore, the *flow* is potentially greater than the case, for example, when the node a has a single connection. It's not difficult to understand that this concept is strictly related to the second derivative of a function (or, in case of multiple variables, to the Laplace-Beltrami operator $\mathcal{L} = \nabla \cdot \nabla$). As an analogy, let's consider the generic heat equation:

$$\frac{\partial Q}{\partial t} = \rho \nabla^2 Q$$

This equation describes the behavior of the temperature of a room when a point in the room is suddenly heated. From basic physics concepts, we know that heat will spread until the temperature reaches an equilibrium point and the speed of variation is proportional to the Laplacian of the distribution. If we consider a bidimensional grid at the equilibrium (the derivative with respect to when time becomes null) and we discretize the Laplacian operator $\nabla^2 = \nabla \cdot \nabla$ considering the incremental ratios, we obtain:

$$\rho\big(Q(x+1, y) + Q(x-1, y) + Q(x, y+1) + Q(x, y-1) - 4Q(x, y)\big) = 0 \Rightarrow$$

$$Q(x, y) = \frac{Q(x+1, y) + Q(x-1, y) + Q(x, y+1) + Q(x, y-1)}{4}$$

Therefore, at the equilibrium, each point has a value that is the mean of the direct neighbors (that is, in case of a graph, the number of neighbors is encoded in the degree of a node). It's possible to prove the finite-difference equation has a single fixed point that can be found iteratively, starting from every initial condition. Therefore, the graph Laplacian encodes both the structure of the graph and, consequently, its dynamic behavior when moving through it.

In addition to this fundamental idea, label spreading adopts a clamping factor α for the labeled samples. If $\alpha = 0$, the algorithm will always reset the labels to the original values (like for label propagation), while with a value in the interval $(0, 1]$, the percentage of clamped labels decreases progressively until $\alpha = 1$, when all the labels are overwritten.

The complete steps of the **label spreading** algorithm are:

1. Select an affinity matrix type (KNN or RBF) and compute W
2. Compute the degree matrix D
3. Compute the normalized graph Laplacian $\mathcal{L}$
4. Define $\tilde{Y}^{(0)} = Y$
5. Define α in the interval $(0, 1)$
6. Iterate until the convergence of the following step:

$$\tilde{Y}^{(t+1)} = \alpha \mathcal{L} \tilde{Y}^{(t)} + (1 - \alpha)\tilde{Y}^{(0)}$$

The structure of the equation (in particular, the first part) is straightforward and resembles a standard diffusion differential equation, with the main difference being that we're working with discrete time steps. However, also in this case, the variation $\Delta\tilde{Y}$ (analogous to time derivative) is proportional to the graph Laplacian applied to the labels (which are analogous, for example, to a scalar physical entity like the temperature). It's possible to show (as demonstrated in *Chapelle O., Schölkopf B., Zien A., (edited by), Semi-Supervised Learning, The MIT Press, 2010*) that this algorithm is equivalent to the minimization of a quadratic cost function with the following structure:

$$L(\tilde{Y}) = \left\| \tilde{Y}_L - Y_L \right\|^2 + \left\| \tilde{Y}_U \right\|^2 + \mu \left(D^{-\frac{1}{2}} \right)^T (D - W)(D^{-\frac{1}{2}}\tilde{Y})$$

The first term imposes consistency between original labels and estimated ones (for the labeled samples). The second term acts as a normalization factor, forcing the unlabeled terms to become zero, while the third term, which is probably the least intuitive, is needed to guarantee geometrical coherence in terms of smoothness. As we have seen in the previous paragraph, when hard clamping is adopted, the smoothness assumption can be violated. By minimizing this term (μ is proportional to α), it's possible to penalize the rapid changes inside the high-density regions. Also in this case, the proof of convergence is very similar to the one for label propagation algorithms, and will be omitted. The interested reader can find it in Chapelle O., Schölkopf B., Zien A., (edited by), *Semi-Supervised Learning*, The MIT Press, 2010.

Example of label spreading

We can test this algorithm using the scikit-learn implementation. Let's start by creating a very dense dataset:

```
from sklearn.datasets import make_classification

nb_samples = 5000
nb_unlabeled = 1000

X, Y = make_classification(n_samples=nb_samples, n_features=2, n_
informative=2, n_redundant=0, random_state=100)
Y[nb_samples - nb_unlabeled:nb_samples] = -1
```

We can train a `LabelSpreading` instance with a clamping factor `alpha=0.2`. We want to preserve 80% of the original labels but, at the same time, we need a smooth solution:

```
from sklearn.semi_supervised import LabelSpreading

ls = LabelSpreading(kernel='rbf', gamma=10.0, alpha=0.2)
ls.fit(X, Y)

Y_final = ls.predict(X)
```

The result is shown, as usual, together with the original dataset:

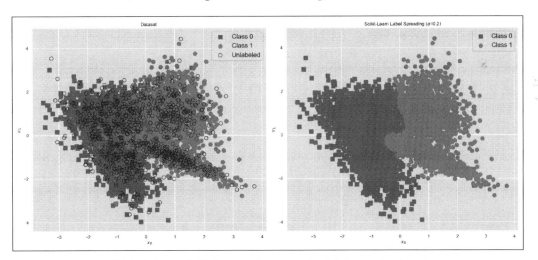

Original dataset (left). Dataset after a complete label spreading (right)

As it's possible to see in the first figure (left), in the central part of the cluster ($x \in [-1, 0]$), there's an area of circle dots. Using hard clamping, this *island* would remain unchanged, violating both the smoothness and clustering assumptions. Setting $\alpha > 0$, it's possible to avoid this problem. Of course, the correct choice of α is strictly limited to each single problem. If we know that the original labels are absolutely correct, allowing the algorithm to change them can be counterproductive.

In this case, for example, it would be better to preprocess the dataset, filtering out all those samples that violate the semi-supervised assumptions. If, instead, we are not sure that all samples are drawn from the same p_{data}, and it's possible to be in the presence of spurious elements, using a higher α value can smooth the dataset without any other operation.

Increasing the smoothness with Laplacian regularization

One of the problems of standard label propagation algorithms is that they tend to show abrupt label changes, which are incompatible with the smoothness assumption. There are many strategies to limit this behavior (most of them are analyzed in Belkin M., Niyogi P., Sindhwani V., *Manifold Regularization: A Geometric Framework for Learning from Labeled and Unlabeled Examples*, Journal of Machine Learning Research 7, 2006), and they are generally based on the introduction of a quadratic penalty term in the cost function. In a way similar to the one employed for label spreading, the authors proposed a cost function with the following form:

$$L(\tilde{Y}) = \left\| \tilde{Y}_L - Y_L \right\|^2 + \alpha \tilde{Y}^T L \tilde{Y} + \beta \left\| \tilde{Y} \right\|^2$$

The presence of the term $\alpha \tilde{Y}^T L \tilde{Y}$ forces the algorithm to penalize abrupt changes in the same neighborhood. As the Laplacian is directly connected to the affinity matrix, the quadratic penalty term $\tilde{Y}^T L \tilde{Y}$ behaves in a way similar to Ridge regularization. When two points have a large affinity and the algorithm tends to assign different labels, the penalty term forces the model to reduce the loss by selecting a smoother transition. Considering a generic classifier, this is equivalent to avoiding excessive oscillations of the separating hypersurface by inducing an implicit linearization.

The mathematical derivation of the algorithm, together with the theory, is a little bit complex. Therefore, we preferred to discuss another algorithm that is based on the behavior of manifolds (however, I invite the smartest readers to define the cost function and optimize it using a standard method such as BFGS).

The complete theory of Laplacian regularization methods is out of the scope of this book (many details can be found in Lee J. M., *Introduction to Smooth Manifolds*, Springer, 2012), but it's helpful for the reader to know that the graph Laplacian defines an operator on the underlying manifold. According to the theory, it's possible to eigendecompose the operator to find a basis of eigenfunctions. It can be proven that the smoothness of the basic functions is proportional to the associated eigenvalues. Therefore, the authors proposed to compute and select the first k smallest eigenvalues of $\mathcal{L}$ and to establish a labeling function (that is, a function that encodes the labeling for both labeled and unlabeled points) built using only the first k eigenfunctions (so as to maximize the smoothness). Therefore, given the matrix of the first k eigenvectors as columns $V_{\mathcal{L}} = \{\bar{v}_1, \bar{v}_2, \dots, \bar{v}_k\}$, and a variable vector $\bar{\theta}$ (subject to optimization), it's possible to build a cost function based on the labeled points:

$$L(Y_L; \bar{\theta}) = \sum_i (y_i - \bar{\theta} \cdot V_{\mathcal{L}}^T)^2$$

The minimum value corresponds to $\bar{\theta}_{opt} = \text{argmin } L(Y_L; \bar{\theta})$ and the labels can be determined by thresholding the dot product and taking the sign: $\tilde{y}_i = sign(\bar{\theta}_{opt} \cdot V_{\mathcal{L}}^T)$.

Let's try this method using a dataset containing 200 points with 150 unlabeled ones:

```
from sklearn.datasets import make_classification

nb_samples=200
nb_unlabeled=150
X, Y = make_classification(n_samples=nb_samples, n_features=2, n_
informative=2, n_redundant=0, random_state=1000)
Y[Y == 0] = -1
Y[nb_samples - nb_unlabeled:nb_samples] = 0
```

The original dataset is shown in the following figure:

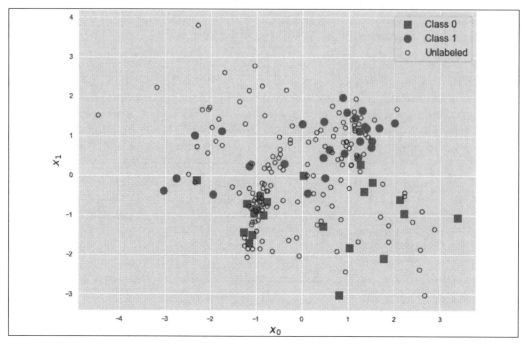

Original dataset employed in the example of Laplacian regularization

We can now build the graph Laplacian using an RBF affinity matrix. In this case, we have chosen $\gamma = 0.1$, but I invite the reader to test different values and compare the results:

```
import numpy as np
k = 50
def rbf(x1, x2, gamma=0.1):
    n = np.linalg.norm(x1 - x2, ord=1)
    return np.exp(-gamma * np.power(n, 2))
W_rbf = np.zeros((nb_samples, nb_samples))

for i in range(nb_samples):
    for j in range(nb_samples):
        if i == j:
            W_rbf[i, j] = 0.0
        else:
            W_rbf[i, j] = rbf(X[i], X[j])

D_rbf = np.diag(np.sum(W_rbf, axis=1))
L_rbf = D_rbf - W_rbf
```

Once the Laplacian is ready, we can eigendecompose it and select the first k eigenvectors (in our case, we have chosen $k = 50$, but, again, this is a hyperparameter that the data scientist should check in every specific scenario):

```
import numpy as np
w, v = np.linalg.eig(L_rbf)
sw = np.argsort(w)[0:k]
V = v[:, sw]
theta = np.random.normal(0.0, 0.1, size=(1, k))
Yu = np.zeros(shape=(nb_unlabeled,))
```

The last step is building the cost function and minimizing it (we have chosen to work with the BFGS algorithm):

```
from scipy.optimize import minimize

def objective(t):
    return np.sum(np.power(Y - np.dot(t, V.T), 2))

result = minimize(objective,
                  theta,
                  method="BFGS",
                  options={
                      "maxiter": 500000,
                  })
```

The final labeling is obtained by taking the result of the optimization and using the sign function:

```
Y_final = np.sign(np.dot(result["x"], V.T))
```

The result of the process is shown in the following figure:

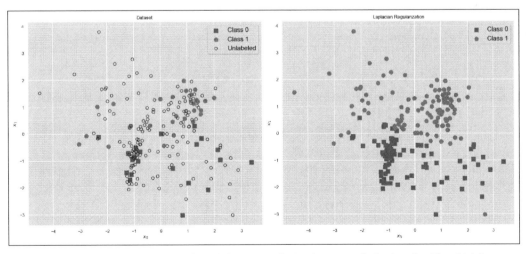

Original dataset (left). Dataset after labeling using the Laplacian regularization algorithm (right)

We can immediately observe that the labeling is very smooth, but the algorithm, analogous to a standard label propagation, has not clamped the labels and this has resulted in some changes (I invite the reader to modify the code as an exercise and to clamp the original labels). However, the main clusters kept their structure and, moreover, induced their labels to the neighbors. This behavior can be positive if the dataset is noisy and we can trust only the denser regions, but it might be undesirable when the labeled points have been controlled by an expert. The point at (2.7, -3) is an outlier that the algorithm failed to label correctly (indeed, it labeled it using the Class 1). Such kinds of problems are a consequence of the choice of the parameter γ. In fact, in this particular case, we have the presence of high-density and low-density regions. While the algorithm works fine with the high-density regions, it can have problems with outliers. A possible mitigation strategy is to increase γ while checking how many correctly labeled points change their labels. In some cases, an exploratory procedure is enough to find a slightly different γ value that avoids the mislabeling of outliers while keeping the correct labels unchanged.

The level of smoothness can be controlled by changing both the number of eigenfunctions and the value of the parameter γ. In this particular case, given the simplicity of the dataset, the RBF provides the larger contribution because it determines the structure of the neighborhoods and either limits or incentivizes the label propagation.

As an exercise, I invite the reader to test this approach using a more complex dataset (it can always be bidimensional, but possibly non-linear), comparing the results with a standard label propagation. In general, the main advantages are more tangible when the complexity of the dataset is very high (together with the dimensionality). In these cases, the reader can try to use one of the methods discussed in the remaining part of the chapter to project high-dimensional datasets into a bidimensional plane, so as to visualize the results and have a better understanding of the underlying dynamics.

Label propagation based on Markov random walks

The goal of this algorithm proposed by Zhu and Ghahramani is to find the probability distribution of target labels for unlabeled samples given a mixed dataset. This objective is achieved through the simulation of a stochastic process, where each unlabeled sample walks through the graph until it reaches a stationary absorbing state, a labeled sample, where it stops acquiring the corresponding label. The main difference with other similar approaches is that in this case, we consider the probability of reaching a labeled sample. In this way, the problem acquires a closed form and can be easily solved.

The first step is to always build a *k*-nearest neighbors graph with all N samples, and define a weight matrix W based on an RBF kernel:

$$W_{ij} = e^{-\gamma \|\bar{x}_i - \bar{x}_j\|_2^2}$$

$W_{ij} = 0$ means that $\bar{x}_i$, and $\bar{x}_j$ are not neighbors, and $W_{ii} = 0$. The transition probability matrix is built similarly to the scikit-learn label propagation algorithm, as:

$$P_{ij}(i \rightarrow j) = \frac{w_{ij}}{\sum_k w_{kj}}$$

In a more compact way, it can be rewritten as $P = D^{-1}W$. If we now consider a *test data point*, starting from the state $\bar{x}_i$ and randomly walking until an absorbing labeled state is found (we call this label y^∞), the probability (referred to as binary classification) can be expressed as:

$$p(y^\infty = 1|\bar{x}_i) = \begin{cases} I_{y_i=1} & \text{if } \bar{x}_i \text{ is labeled} \\ \sum_{k=1}^{N} p(y^\infty = 1|\bar{x}_k)p(\bar{x}_i|\bar{x}_k) & \text{if } \bar{x}_i \text{ is unlabeled} \end{cases}$$

When $\bar{x}_i$ is labeled, the state is final, and it is represented by the indicator function based on the condition $y_i = 1$. When the sample is unlabeled, we need to consider the sum of all possible transitions starting from $\bar{x}_i$ and ending in the closest absorbing state, with label $y = 1$ weighted by the relative transition probabilities.

We can rewrite this expression in matrix form. If we create a vector $P^\infty = [\,p_L(y^\infty = 1|X_L), p_U(y^\infty = 1|X_U)\,]$, where the first component is based on labeled points and the second on unlabeled ones, we can write:

$$P^\infty = D^{-1}WP^\infty$$

If we now expand the matrices, we get:

$$P^\infty = \begin{pmatrix} D_U^{-1} & 0 \\ 0 & D_{UU}^{-1} \end{pmatrix} \begin{pmatrix} W_U & W_{LU} \\ W_{UL} & W_{UU} \end{pmatrix} P^\infty = \begin{pmatrix} D_U^{-1}W_U & D_U^{-1}W \\ D_{UU}^{-1}W_{UL} & D_{UU}^{-1}W_{UU} \end{pmatrix} P^\infty$$

As we are interested only in the unlabeled points, we can consider just the second equation:

$$p_U(y^\infty = 1|X_U) = D_{UU}^{-1}W_{UL}p_L(y^\infty = 1|X_L) + D_{UU}^{-1}W_{UU}p_U(y^\infty = 1|X_U)$$

Simplifying the expression, we get the following linear system:

$$(D_{UU} - W_{UU})p_u(y^\infty = 1|X_U) = W_{UL}p_L(y^\infty = 1|X_L)$$

The term $(D_{uu} - W_{uu})$ is the unlabeled-unlabeled part of the unnormalized graph Laplacian $\mathcal{L} = D - W$. By solving this system, we can get the probabilities for the class $y = 1$ for all unlabeled points. By thresholding the probabilities (normally at 0.5), it's possible to transform the soft labeling into a hard one.

Example of label propagation based on Markov random walks

For this Python example of label propagation based on Markov random walks, we are going to use a bidimensional dataset containing 50 labeled points belonging to two different classes, and 1,950 unlabeled ones:

```python
from sklearn.datasets import make_blobs

nb_samples = 2000
nb_unlabeled = 1950
nb_classes = 2

X, Y = make_blobs(n_samples=nb_samples,
                  n_features=2,
                  centers=nb_classes,
                  cluster_std=2.5,
                  random_state=1000)

Y[Y == 0] = -1
Y[nb_samples - nb_unlabeled:nb_samples] = 0
```

The plot of the dataset is shown in the following diagram (the crosses represent the unlabeled samples):

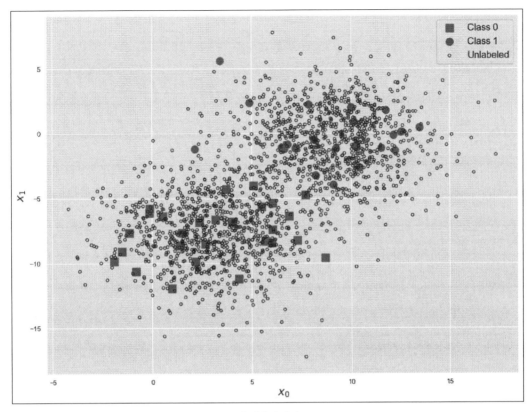

Partially labeled dataset

We can now create the graph (using n_neighbors=15) and the weight matrix:

```
from sklearn.neighbors import kneighbors_graph

W = kneighbors_graph(X, n_neighbors=15, mode='connectivity', include_
self=True).toarray()
```

Now, we need to compute the unlabeled part of the unnormalized graph Laplacian and the unlabeled-labeled part of the matrix W:

```
D = np.diag(np.sum(W, axis=1))
L = D - W
Luu = L[nb_samples - nb_unlabeled:, nb_samples - nb_unlabeled:]
Wul = W[nb_samples - nb_unlabeled:, 0:nb_samples - nb_unlabeled,]
Yl = Y[0:nb_samples - nb_unlabeled]
```

At this point, it's possible to solve the linear system using the NumPy function `np.linalg.solve()`, which accepts as parameters the matrix A and the vector $\bar{b}$ of a generic system in the form $A\bar{x} = \bar{b}$. When the matrix A is very large, the system could be ill-conditioned. I suggest checking the condition number ρ before solving the system. If it's large (for example, $\rho \gg 1$), it's preferable to use one of the other methods previously discussed.

Once we have the solution, we can merge the new labels with the original ones (where the unlabeled samples have been marked with -1). In this case, we don't need to convert the probabilities, because we are using 0 and 1 as labels. In general, it's necessary to use a threshold (0.5) to select the right label:

```
Yu = np.round(np.linalg.solve(Luu, np.dot(Wul, Yl)))
Y[nb_samples - nb_unlabeled:] = Yu.copy()
```

Replotting the dataset, we get:

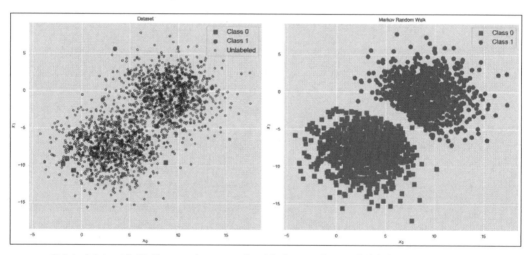

Original dataset (left). Dataset after a complete Markov random walk label propagation (right)

As expected, without any iteration, the labels have been successfully propagated to all data points, meeting the requirements of the clustering assumption. Both this algorithm and label propagation can work using a closed-form solution, so they are very fast even when the number of samples is high; however, there's a fundamental problem regarding the choice of σ/γ for the RBF kernel. As the same authors Zhu and Ghahramani remark, there is no standard solution, but it's possible to consider the cases where $\sigma \to 0$ and when $\sigma \to \infty$. In the first case, only the nearest point has an influence, while in the second case, the influence is extended to the whole sample space, and the unlabeled points all tend to acquire the same label.

The authors suggest considering the entropy of all samples, trying to find the best σ value that minimizes it. This solution can be very effective, but sometimes the minimum entropy corresponds to a label configuration that isn't impossible to achieve using these algorithms. The best approach is to try different values (at different scales) and select the one corresponding to a valid configuration with the lowest entropy. In our case, it's possible to compute the entropy of the unlabeled samples as:

$$H(X_U) = -\sum_{i=N+1}^{N+M} p(\bar{x}_i) \log p(\bar{x}_i)$$

The Python code to perform this computation is:

```
Pu = np.linalg.solve(Luu, np.dot(Wul, Yl))
H = -np.sum(Pu * np.log(Pu + 1e-6))
```

The term `1e-6` has been added to avoid numerical problems when the probability is null. Repeating this process for different values allows us to find a set of candidates that can be restricted to a single value with a direct evaluation of the labeling accuracy (for example, when there is no precise information about the real distribution, it's possible to consider the coherence of each cluster and the separation between them).

Another approach is called **class rebalancing,** and it's based on the idea of reweighting the probabilities of unlabeled samples to rebalance the number of points belonging to each class when the new unlabeled samples are added to the set. If we have N labeled points and M unlabeled ones, with K classes, the weight factor w_j for the class j can be obtained as:

$$w_j = \frac{\frac{1}{N}\sum_{t=1}^{N} y_t^{(j)}}{\frac{1}{M}\sum_{t=N+1}^{N+M} \tilde{y}_t^{(j)}}$$

The numerator is the average computed over the labeled samples belonging to class k, while the denominator is the average over the unlabeled ones whose estimated class is k. The final decision about a class is no longer based only on the highest probability, but on:

$$\tilde{y}_t^{(j)} = \underset{j}{\mathrm{argmax}}\big(w_j p(y_t = j)\big)$$

In this section, we have discussed some common strategies to perform an effective label propagation in different scenarios. In the next section, we are going to exploit the manifold assumption to perform non-linear dimensionality reduction of complex datasets.

Manifold learning

In *Chapter 3, Introduction to Semi-Supervised Classification*, we discussed the manifold assumption, saying that high-dimensional data normally lies on low-dimensional manifolds. Of course, this is not a theorem, but in many real cases, the assumption is proven to be correct, and it allows us to work with non-linear dimensionality reduction algorithms that would be otherwise unacceptable. In this section, we're going to analyze some of these algorithms. They are all implemented in scikit-learn, so it's easy to try them with complex datasets.

Isomap

Isomap is one of the simplest algorithms, and it's based on the idea of reducing dimensionality while trying to preserve the geodesic distances (which are the lengths of the shortest paths between a couple of points on the manifold) measured on the original manifold where the input data lies. The algorithm works in three steps. The first operation is a KNN clustering and the construction of the following graph. The vertices will be the samples, while the edges represent the connections among nearest neighbors, and their weight is proportional to the distance to the corresponding neighbor.

The second step adopts the **Dijkstra algorithm** (check Cormen T. H., Leiserson C. E., Rivest R. L., *Introduction to Algorithms*, The MIT Press, 2009, for further details) to compute the shortest pairwise distances on the graph of all couples of samples. In the following graph, there's a portion where some shorter distances are marked with a thicker line:

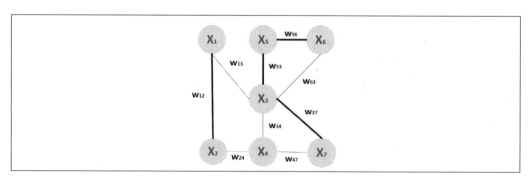

Example of a graph with marked shortest distances

For example, as $\mathbf{x}_3$ is a neighbor of $\mathbf{x}_5$ and $\mathbf{x}_7$, applying the Dijkstra algorithm, we could get the shortest paths $d(x_3, x_5) = w_{53}$ and $d(x_3, x_7) = w_{73}$. The computational complexity of this step is about $O(n^2 \log n + n^2 k)$, which is lower than $O(n^3)$ when $k << n$ (a condition normally met); however, for large graphs (with $n >> 1$), this is often the most expensive part of the whole algorithm.

The third step is called **metric multidimensional scaling**, which is a technique for finding a low-dimensional representation while trying to preserve the inner product among samples. If we have a P-dimensional dataset X, the algorithm must find a Q-dimensional set Φ, with $Q < P$ minimizing the function:

$$L_{MDS} = \sum_{(i,j)} \left(\bar{x}_i \cdot \bar{x}_j - \bar{\phi}_i \cdot \bar{\phi}_j \right)^2$$

As proven in Chapelle O., Schölkopf B., Zien A., *(edited by), Semi-Supervised Learning,* The MIT Press, 2010, the optimization is achieved by taking the top Q eigenvectors of the Gram matrix $G_{ij} = \bar{x}_i \cdot \bar{x}_j$ (or, in matrix form, $G = XX^T$ if $X \in \mathbb{R}^{n \times M}$); however, as the Isomap algorithm works with pairwise distances, we need to compute the matrix D of squared distances:

$$D_{ij} = \left\| \bar{x}_i - \bar{x}_j \right\|^2$$

If the X dataset is zero-centered, it's possible to derive a simplified Gram matrix from D, as described by M. A. A. Cox and T. F. Cox:

$$G_D = -\frac{1}{2}(I - \bar{v} \cdot \bar{v}^T)D(I - \bar{v} \cdot \bar{v}^T) \ \ with \ \bar{v} \in \mathbb{R}^p \ and \ \bar{v} = \left(\frac{1}{\sqrt{P}}, \frac{1}{\sqrt{P}}, ..., \frac{1}{\sqrt{P}} \right)$$

Isomap computes the top Q eigenvalues $\lambda_1, \lambda_2, \ldots, \lambda_Q$ of G_D and the corresponding eigenvectors $\bar{v}_1, \bar{v}_2, \ldots, \bar{v}_Q$ and determines the Q-dimensional vectors as:

$$\bar{\phi}_i = \left(\lambda_1^{\frac{1}{2}} \bar{v}_1, \lambda_2^{\frac{1}{2}} \bar{v}_2, ..., \lambda_Q^{\frac{1}{2}} \bar{v}_Q \right)$$

As we're going to discuss in *Chapter 13, Component Analysis and Dimensionality Reduction* (and also as pointed out by Saul, Weinberger, Sha, Ham, and Lee in Saul L. K., Weinberger K. Q., Sha F., Ham J., and Lee D. D., *Spectral Methods for Dimensionality Reduction,* UCSD, 2006), this kind of projection is also exploited by **Principal Component Analysis (PCA)**, which finds out the direction with the highest variance, corresponding to the top k eigenvectors of the covariance matrix.

In fact, when applying the SVD to the dataset X, we get:

$$X = U\Lambda V^T \ where \ U \in \mathbb{R}^{M \times M}, \Lambda = diag(n \times n) \ and \ V \in \mathbb{R}^{n \times n}$$

The diagonal matrix Λ contains the eigenvalues of both XX^T and X^TX; therefore, the eigenvalues λ_{G_i} of G are equal to $M\lambda_i^{\Sigma}$, where λ_i^{Σ} are the eigenvalues of the covariance matrix $\Sigma = M^{-1}X^TX$. Hence, Isomap achieves the dimensionality reduction, trying to preserve the pairwise distances, while projecting the dataset in the subspace determined by a group of eigenvectors, where the maximum explained variance is achieved. In terms of information theory, this condition guarantees the minimum loss with an effective reduction of dimensionality.

Scikit-learn also implements the Floyd-Warshall algorithm, which is slightly slower. For further information, please refer to Cormen T. H., Leiserson C. E., Rivest R. L., *Introduction to Algorithms*, The MIT Press, 2009.

Example of Isomap

We can now test the scikit-learn Isomap implementation using the Olivetti faces dataset (provided by AT&T Laboratories, Cambridge), which is made up of 400 64 × 64 grayscale portraits belonging to 40 different former employees. Examples of these images are shown here:

Subset of the Olivetti faces dataset

The original dimensionality is 4,096, but we want to visualize the dataset in two dimensions. It's important to understand that using the Euclidean distance for measuring the similarity of images might not the best choice, and it's surprising to see how well the samples are clustered by such a simple algorithm.

The first step is loading the dataset:

```
from sklearn.datasets import fetch_olivetti_faces

faces = fetch_olivetti_faces()
```

The `faces` dictionary contains three main elements:

- `images`: Image array with shape 400 × 64 × 64
- `data`: Flattened array with shape 400 × 4096
- `target`: Array with shape 400 × 1 containing the labels (0, 39)

At this point, we can instantiate the `Isomap` class provided by scikit-learn, setting `n_components=2` and `n_neighbors=5` (the reader can try different configurations), and then fitting the model:

```
from sklearn.manifold import Isomap

isomap = Isomap(n_neighbors=5, n_components=2)
X_isomap = isomap.fit_transform(faces['data'])
```

As the resulting plot with 400 elements is very dense, I preferred to show in the following plot only the first 100 samples:

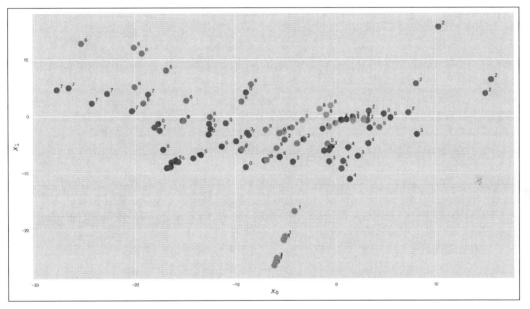

Isomap applied to 100 samples drawn from the Olivetti faces dataset

As it's possible to see, samples belonging to the same class (or sub-class, if, for example, the same person has different expressions or wears/doesn't wear glasses) are grouped in rather dense agglomerates.

The classes that seem better separated are 7 and 1. Checking the corresponding faces, for class 7, we get:

Samples belonging to class 7

The set contains portraits of a young woman with a fair complexion, quite different from the majority of the other people. Instead, for class 1, we get:

Samples belonging to class 1

In this case, it's a man with big glasses and a particular mouth expression. In the dataset, there are only a few people with glasses, and one of them has a dark beard. We can conclude that Isomap created a low-dimensional representation that is really coherent with the original geodesic distances. In some cases, there's a partial clustering overlap that can be mitigated by increasing the dimensionality or adopting a more complex strategy.

Locally linear embedding

Contrary to Isomap, which works with pairwise distances, this algorithm is based on the assumption that a high-dimensional dataset lying on a smooth manifold can have local linear structures that it tries to preserve during the dimensionality reduction process. **Locally Linear Embedding** (LLE), like Isomap, is based on three steps. The first one is applying the KNN algorithm to create a directed graph (in Isomap, it was undirected), where the vertices are the input samples and the edges represent a neighborhood relationship. As the graph is direct, a point $\bar{x}_i$ can be a neighbor of $\bar{x}_j$, but the opposite could be false. This means that the weight matrix can be asymmetric.

The second step is based on the main assumption of local linearity. For example, consider the following graph:

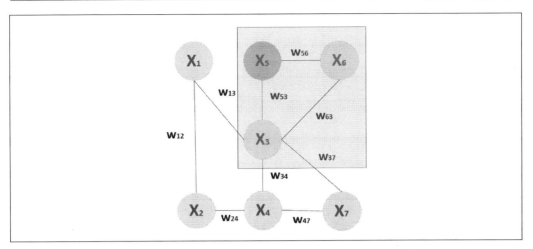

Graph where a neighborhood is marked with a shaded rectangle

The rectangle delimits a small neighborhood. If we consider the point x_5, the local linearity assumption allows us to think that $x_5 = w_{56}x_6 + w_{53}x_3$, without considering the cyclic relationship. This concept can be formalized for all N P-dimensional points through the minimization of the following function:

$$L_W = \sum_{i=1}^{N} \left\| \bar{x}_i - \sum_{k \in neighbors(\bar{x}_i)} W_{ik} \bar{x}_k \right\|^2 \quad subject\ to \quad \sum_{k \in neighbors(\bar{x}_i)} W_{ik} = 1$$

In order to address the problem of low-rank neighborhood matrices (think about the previous example, with a number of neighbors equal to 20), scikit-learn also implements a regularizer that is based on a small arbitrary additive constant that is added to the local weights (according to a variant called **Modified LLE** or **MLLE**). At the end of this step, the matrix W that better matches the linear relationships among neighbors will be selected for the next phase.

In the third step, LLE tries to determine the low-dimensional ($Q < P$) representation that best reproduces the original relationship among nearest neighbors. This is achieved by minimizing the following function:

$$L_\Phi = \sum_{i=1}^{N} \left\| \bar{\phi}_i - \sum_{k \in neighbors(\bar{\phi}_i)} W_{ik} \bar{\phi}_k \right\|^2 \quad subject\ to \quad \sum_{i} \bar{\phi}_i = 0 \ and \ Cov(\bar{\phi}_i, \bar{\phi}_j) = 1 \ \forall \ i,j$$

The solution for this problem is obtained through the adoption of the **Rayleigh-Ritz method**, an algorithm to extract a subset of eigenvectors and eigenvalues from a very large sparse matrix. For further details, read Schofield G. Chelikowsky J. R.; Saad Y., *A spectrum slicing method for the Kohn–Sham problem*, Computer Physics Communications. *183, 2012*. The initial part of the final procedure consists of determining the matrix D:

$$D = (I - W)^T (I - W)$$

It's possible to prove the last eigenvector (if the eigenvalues are sorted in descending order, it's the bottom one) has all components $\bar{v}_1^{(N)}, \bar{v}_2^{(N)}, \ldots, \bar{v}_N^N = \bar{v}$, and the corresponding eigenvalue is null. As Saul and Roweis (Saul L. K., Roweis S. T., *An introduction to locally linear embedding*, 2001) pointed out, all the other Q eigenvectors (from the bottom) are orthogonal, and this allows them to have zero-centered embedding. Hence, the last eigenvector is discarded, while the remaining Q eigenvectors determine the embedding vectors $\bar{\varphi}_i$.

 For further details about MLLE, please refer to Zhang Z., Wang J., *MLLE: Modified Locally Linear Embedding Using Multiple Weights*, NIPS, 2006.

Example of LLE

We can now apply this algorithm to the Olivetti faces dataset, instantiating the scikit-learn class `LocallyLinearEmbedding` with `n_components=2` and `n_neighbors=15`:

```
from sklearn.manifold import LocallyLinearEmbedding

lle = LocallyLinearEmbedding(n_neighbors=15, n_components=2)
X_lle = lle.fit_transform(faces['data'])
```

The result (limited to the first 100 data points) is shown in the following plot:

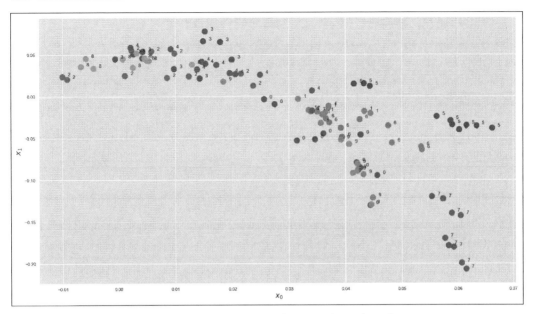

LLE applied to 100 samples drawn from the Olivetti faces dataset

Even if the strategy is different from Isomap, we can determine some coherent clusters. In this case, the similarity is obtained through the conjunction of small linear blocks; for the faces, they can represent particular micro-features, like the shape of the nose or the presence of glasses, that remain invariant in the different portraits of the same person. LLE is, in general, preferable when the original dataset is intrinsically locally linear, possibly lying on a smooth manifold.

In other words, LLE is a reasonable choice when small parts of a sample are structured in a way that allows the reconstruction of a point given the neighbors and the weights. This is often true for images, but it can be difficult to determine for a generic dataset. When the result doesn't reproduce the original clustering, it's possible to employ the next algorithm, Laplacian Spectral Embedding, or **t-SNE**, which is one of the most advanced and will be discussed later.

Laplacian Spectral Embedding

This algorithm, based on the spectral decomposition of a graph Laplacian, has been proposed in order to perform a non-linear dimensionality reduction to try to preserve the nearness of points in the P-dimensional manifold when remapping on a Q-dimensional (with $Q < P$) subspace.

The procedure is very similar to the other algorithms. The first step is a KNN clustering to generate a graph where the vertices (we can assume to have N elements) are the samples, and the edges are weighted using an RBF kernel:

$$W_{ij} = e^{-\gamma \|\bar{x}_i - \bar{x}_j\|_2^2}$$

The resulting graph is undirected and symmetric. We can now define a pseudo-degree matrix D:

$$D = diag\left(\sum_j W_{1j}, \sum_j W_{2j}, ..., \sum_j W_{Nj}\right)$$

The low-dimensional representation Φ is obtained by minimizing the function:

$$L_\Phi = \sum_{(i,j)} \frac{W_{ij}\|\bar{\phi}_i - \bar{\phi}_j\|^2}{\sqrt{D_{ii}D_{jj}}} \; subject \; to \; \sum_i \bar{\phi}_i = 0 \; and \; Cov(\bar{\phi}_i, \bar{\phi}_j) = 1 \, \forall \, i, j$$

If the two points $\bar{x}_i$ and $\bar{x}_j$ are near, the corresponding W_{ij} is close to 1, while it tends to 0 when the distance tends to ∞. D_{ii} is the sum of all weights originating from $\bar{x}_i$ (and the same for D_{jj}). Now, let's suppose that $\bar{x}_i$ is very close only to $\bar{x}_j$ so, to approximate $D_{ii} = D_{jj} \approx W_{ij}$. The resulting formula is a square loss based on the difference between the vectors $\bar{\phi}_i$ and $\bar{\phi}_j$. When instead there are multiple *closeness* relationships to consider, the factor W_{ij} divided by the square root of D_{ii} D_{jj} allows reweighting the new distances to find the best trade-off for the whole dataset. In practice, L_Φ is not minimized directly. In fact, it's possible to prove that the minimum can be obtained through the spectral decomposition of the symmetric normalized graph Laplacian (the name derives from this procedure):

$$\mathcal{L} = I - D^{-\frac{1}{2}} W D^{-\frac{1}{2}}$$

Just like for the LLE algorithm, Laplacian Spectral Embedding also works with the bottom $Q + 1$ eigenvectors. The mathematical theory behind the last step is always based on the application of the Rayleigh-Ritz method. The last one is discarded, and the remaining Q determines the low-dimensional representation $\bar{\phi}_i$.

Example of Laplacian Spectral Embedding

Let's apply this algorithm to the same dataset using the scikit-learn class `SpectralEmbedding`, with `n_components=2` and `n_neighbors=15`:

```
from sklearn.manifold import SpectralEmbedding

se = SpectralEmbedding(n_components=2, n_neighbors=15, random_
state=1000)
X_se = se.fit_transform(faces['data'])
```

The resulting plot (zoomed in due to the presence of a high-density region) is shown in the following graph:

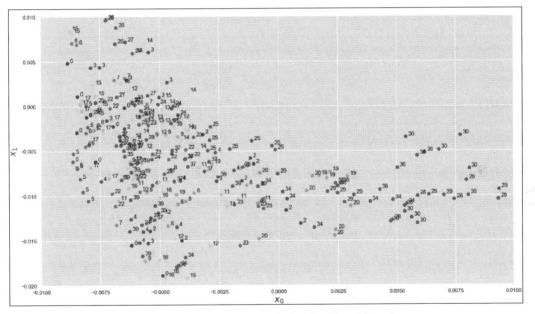

Laplacian Spectral Embedding applied to the Olivetti faces dataset

Even in this case, we can see that some classes are grouped into small clusters, but at the same time, we observe many agglomerates where there are mixed samples. Both this and the previous method work with local pieces of information, trying to find low-dimensional representations that could preserve the geometrical structure of micro-features.

This condition drives to a mapping where close points *share* local features (this is almost always true for images, but it's very difficult to prove for generic samples). Therefore, we can observe small clusters containing elements belonging to the same class, but also some *apparent* outliers, which, on the original manifold, can be globally different even if they share local *patches*. Instead, methods such as Isomap or t-SNE work with the whole distribution and try to determine a representation that is almost isometric with the original dataset considering its global properties.

t-SNE

This algorithm, proposed by Van der Mateen and Hinton, and formally known as t-Distributed Stochastic Neighbor Embedding, is one of the most powerful manifold dimensionality reduction techniques. Contrary to the other methods, this algorithm starts with a fundamental assumption: the similarity between two N-dimensional points $\bar{x}_i$ and $\bar{x}_j$ can be represented as the conditional probability $p(\bar{x}_j|\bar{x}_i)$ where each point is represented by a Gaussian distribution centered in $\bar{x}_i$ and with variance σ_i^2. The variances are selected starting from the desired perplexity, defined as:

$$Perplexity(p) = 2^{H(p)}$$

Low-perplexity values indicate low uncertainty and are normally preferable. In common t-SNE tasks, values in the range 5-50 are normally acceptable.

The assumption on the conditional probabilities can be interpreted thinking that if two samples are very similar, the probability associated with the first sample conditioned to the second one is high, while dissimilar points yield low conditional probabilities. For example, thinking about images, a point centered in the pupil can have as neighbors some points belonging to an eyelash. In terms of probabilities, we can think that $p(eyelash|pupil)$ is quite high, while $p(nose|pupil)$ is obviously lower. t-SNE models these conditional probabilities as:

$$p(\bar{x}_j|\bar{x}_i) = \frac{e^{-\frac{\|\bar{x}_i - \bar{x}_j\|^2}{2\sigma_i^2}}}{\sum_{k \neq i} e^{-\frac{\|\bar{x}_i - \bar{x}_k\|^2}{2\sigma_i^2}}}$$

The probabilities $p(\bar{x}_i|\bar{x}_i)$ are set to zero, so the previous formula can be extended to the whole graph. In order to solve the problem in an easier way, the conditional probabilities are also symmetrized:

$$p(\bar{x}_j|\bar{x}_i) = \frac{p(\bar{x}_i|\bar{x}_j) + p(\bar{x}_j|\bar{x}_i)}{2N}$$

The probability distribution so obtained represents the high-dimensional input relationship. As our goal is to reduce the dimensionality to a value $M < N$, we can think about a similar probabilistic representation for the target points $\bar{\phi}_i$, using a Student's-t distribution with one degree of freedom:

$$q(\bar{\phi}_i|\bar{\phi}_j) = \frac{\left(1 + \|\bar{\phi}_i - \bar{\phi}_j\|^2\right)^{-1}}{\sum_{k \neq j}\left(1 + \|\bar{\phi}_k - \bar{\phi}_j\|^2\right)^{-1}}$$

We want the low-dimensional distribution Q to be as close as possible to the high-dimensional distribution P; therefore, the aim of the **t-SNE** algorithm is to minimize the Kullback-Leibler divergence between P and Q:

$$D_{KL}(P\|Q) = \sum_{(i,j)} p(\bar{x}_j|\bar{x}_i) \log\frac{p(\bar{x}_j|\bar{x}_i)}{q(\bar{\phi}_j|\bar{\phi}_i)} = H(P) - \sum_{(i,j)} p(\bar{x}_j|\bar{x}_i) \log q(\bar{\phi}_j|\bar{\phi}_i)$$

The first term is the entropy of the original distribution P, while the second one is the cross-entropy $H(P, Q)$, which has to be minimized to solve the problem. The best approach is based on a gradient-descent algorithm (fully analyzed in *Chapter 17*, Modeling and Optimizing Neural Networks), but there are also some useful variations that can improve the performance discussed in Van der Maaten L.J.P., Hinton G.E., *Visualizing High-Dimensional Data Using t-SNE*, Journal of Machine Learning Research 9 (Nov), 2008.

Example of t-distributed stochastic neighbor embedding

We can apply this powerful algorithm to the same Olivetti faces dataset, using the scikit-learn class TSNE with n_components=2 and perplexity=20:

```
from sklearn.manifold import TSNE

tsne = TSNE(n_components=2, perplexity=20, random_state=1000)
X_tsne = tsne.fit_transform(faces['data'])
print("Final KL divergence: {}".format(tsne.kl_divergence_))
```

The output of the previous snippet is:

```
Final KL divergence: 0.5993183851242065
```

The final Kullback-Leibler divergence is about 0.6, which is a low value (the minimum achievable with a perplexity equal to 20), but probably not enough in some tasks. Let's start by looking at the graphical result for all 400 points:

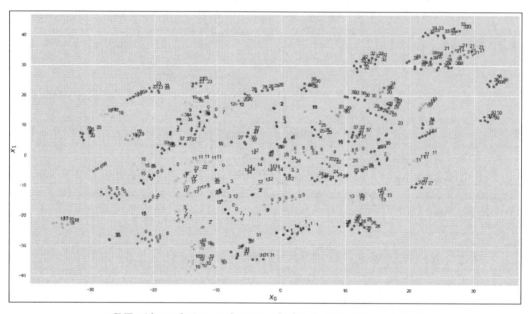

t-SNE with perplexity equal to 20 applied to the Olivetti faces dataset

A visual inspection of the label distribution can confirm that t-SNE recreated a very good clustering structure starting from the original high-dimensional distribution. We can reasonably suppose that the points belonging to the same blob are close, but also relatively separated. However, we want to try to push the algorithm toward its limit by reducing the perplexity to 2:

```
from sklearn.manifold import TSNE

tsne = TSNE(n_components=2, perplexity=2, random_state=1000)
X_tsne = tsne.fit_transform(faces['data'])
print("Final KL divergence: {}".format(tsne.kl_divergence_))
```

The output is now:

```
Final KL divergence: 0.37610241770744324
```

Clearly, the distributions are now more overlapped and it's very difficult to obtain better results. Let's check again the visual representation of the dataset:

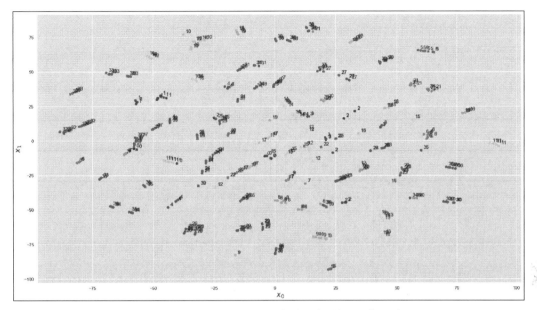

t-SNE with perplexity equal to 2 applied to the Olivetti faces dataset

The clusters are much more compact (unfortunately, the labels are often overlapped), confirming that the original dataset is naturally clustered and there are high-density regions split into groups of lower density (but still high) representing particular sets of pictures of the same person but with slightly different details. As t-SNE is strongly based on both cluster and smoothness assumptions, it seems that a larger perplexity yields smoother separations.

However, it's always helpful to consider the nature of the data-generating process. In this particular case, we have a set of portraits that can obviously be imagined as a coherent class of elements with respect, for example, to pictures of chairs. On the other side, we are interested in the sub-manifolds where the portraits of the same subject lie. Therefore, we need to get rid of some smoothness and rely more on the cluster assumption in order to achieve a better separation. This principle is general, and should be applied in all contexts where a homogeneous data-generating process must be analyzed at a local level.

The sub-manifolds are often less smooth than the overall manifold where the whole distribution lies (think about the surface of an orange).

Hence, we are not contradicting the initial assumptions when discovering that a higher detail yields a more abrupt class separation, as this is a consequence of a *zoom* process operating in an area that is already very smooth, but with some thin spots representing the sub-clusters with very similar features.

This algorithm can be employed in several non-linear dimensionality reduction tasks, such as images, word embeddings, or complex feature vectors. Its main strength is hidden in the assumption that we can consider similarities as probabilities, without the need to impose any constraint on the pairwise distances, either global or local. Under a certain viewpoint, it's possible to consider t-SNE as a reverse multiclass classification problem based on a cross-entropy cost function. Our goal is to find the labels (low-dimensional representation) given the original distribution and an assumption about the output distribution.

At this point, we could try to answer a natural question: which algorithm must be employed? The obvious answer is it depends on the single problem. When it's useful to reduce the dimensionality, preserving the global similarity among vectors (this is the case when the samples are long feature vectors without local properties, such as word embeddings or data encodings), t-SNE or Isomap are good choices. When, instead, it's necessary to keep the local distances (for example, the structure of a visual patch that can be shared by different samples also belonging to different classes) as close as possible to the original representation, LLE or spectral embedding algorithms are preferable.

Summary

In this chapter, we have introduced the most important label propagation techniques. In particular, we have seen how to build a dataset graph based on a weighting kernel, and how to use the geometric information provided by unlabeled samples to determine the most likely class. The basic approach works by iterating the multiplication of the label vector times the weight matrix until a stable point is reached and we have proven that, under simple assumptions, it is always possible.

Another approach, implemented by scikit-learn, is based on the transition probability from a state (represented by a sample) to another one, until the convergence to a labeled point. The probability matrix is obtained using a normalized weight matrix to encourage transitions associated with close points and discourage all the *long jumps*. The main drawback of these two methods is the hard clamping of labeled samples; this constraint can be useful if we *trust* our dataset, but it can be a limitation in the presence of outliers whose labels have been wrongly assigned.

Label spreading solves this problem by introducing a clamping factor that determines the percentage of clamped labels. The algorithm is very similar to label propagation, but it's based on graph Laplacian and can be employed in all those problems where the data-generating distribution is not well determined and the probability of noise is high.

The propagation based on Markov random walks is a very simple algorithm that can estimate the class distribution of unlabeled samples through a stochastic process. It's possible to imagine it as a *test sample* that walks through the graph until it reaches a final labeled state (acquiring the corresponding label). The algorithm is very fast and it has a closed-form solution that can be found by solving a linear system.

The next topic was the introduction of manifold learning with the Isomap algorithm, which is a simple but powerful solution based on a graph built using a KNN algorithm (this is a common step in most of these algorithms). The original pairwise distances are processed using the multidimensional scaling technique, which allows a low-dimensional representation to be obtained where the distances between samples are preserved.

Two different approaches, based on local pieces of information, are locally linear embedding and Laplacian Spectral Embedding. The former tries to preserve the local linearity present in the original manifold, while the latter, which is based on the spectral decomposition of the normalized graph Laplacian, tries to preserve the nearness of original samples. Both methods are suitable for all those tasks where it's important not to consider the whole original distribution, but the similarity induced by small data *patches*.

We closed this chapter by discussing t-SNE, which is a very powerful algorithm that tries to model a low-dimensional distribution that is as similar as possible to the original high-dimensional one. This task is achieved by minimizing the Kullback-Leibler divergence between the two distributions. t-SNE is a state-of-the-art algorithm, useful whenever it's important to consider the whole original distribution and the similarity between entire samples.

In the next chapter, we are going to introduce some common unsupervised algorithms to perform clustering and pattern discovery. Some of the concepts we are going to exploit have already been discussed in this chapter. Therefore, I suggest studying all the sections before continuing your reading.

Further reading

- Zhu X., Ghahramani Z., *Learning from Labeled and Unlabeled Data with Label Propagation*, CMU-CALD-02-107, 2002

- Chapelle O., Schölkopf B., Zien A. (edited by), *Semi-Supervised Learning*, The MIT Press, 2010

- Saul L. K., Weinberger K. Q., Sha F., Ham J., and Lee D. D., *Spectral Methods for Dimensionality Reduction*, UCSD, 2006

- Cormen T. H., Leiserson C. E., Rivest R. L., *Introduction to Algorithms*, The MIT Press, 2009

- Schofield G. Chelikowsky J. R.; Saad Y., *A spectrum slicing method for the Kohn–Sham problem*, Computer Physics Communications. 183, 2012

- Saul L. K., Roweis S. T., *An introduction to locally linear embedding*, 2001

- Zhang Z., Wang J., *MLLE: Modified Locally Linear Embedding Using Multiple Weights*, NIPS, 2006

- Belkin M., Niyogi P., Sindhwani V., *Manifold Regularization: A Geometric Framework for Learning from Labeled and Unlabeled Examples*, Journal of Machine Learning Research 7, 2006

- Van der Maaten L.J.P., Hinton G. E., *Visualizing High-Dimensional Data Using t-SNE*, Journal of Machine Learning Research 9 (Nov), 2008

- Biyikoglu T., Leydold J., Stadler P. F., *Laplacian Eigenvectors of Graphs*, Springer, 2007

- Lee J. M., *Introduction to Smooth Manifolds*, Springer, 2012

6
Clustering and Unsupervised Models

In this chapter, we are going to introduce some fundamental clustering algorithms and discuss their strengths and weaknesses. The field of unsupervised learning, as well as any other machine learning approach, must always be based on the concept of Occam's razor. Simplicity must always be preferred, so long as the performance of the model meets your requirements.

However, in this case, the ground truth can be unknown. When a clustering algorithm is adopted as an exploratory tool, we can only assume that the dataset represents a precise data-generating process. If this assumption is correct, the best strategy is to determine the number of clusters to maximize the internal cohesion (denseness) and the external separation. This means that we expect to find blobs (or isles) whose samples share some common and partially unique features.

In particular, the algorithms and the topics we are going to analyze are:

- **K-Nearest Neighbors (KNN)**, based on **k-dimensional (k-d)** trees and ball trees
- K-means and k-means++
- Evaluation of clustering models

We can now start analyzing one of the simplest approaches to clustering data, considering the pros and cons and how it's possible to improve your results.

K-nearest neighbors

This algorithm belongs to a particular family called *instance-based* algorithms (the methodology is called instance-based learning).

It differs from other approaches because it doesn't work with an actual mathematical model. On the contrary, the inference is performed by direct comparison of new samples with existing ones (which are defined as instances). KNN is an approach that can be easily employed to solve clustering, classification, and regression problems (even though, in this case, we are going to consider only the first technique). The main idea behind the clustering algorithm is very simple. Let's consider a data generating process p_{data} and finite a dataset drawn from this distribution:

$$X = \{\bar{x}_1, \bar{x}_2, ..., \bar{x}_n\} \ where \ \bar{x}_i \in \mathbb{R}^N$$

Each point has a dimensionality equal to N. We can now introduce a distance function $d(\bar{x}_1, \bar{x}_2)$, which in most cases can be generalized with the Minkowski distance:

$$d_p(\bar{x}_1, \bar{x}_2) = \left(\sum_{j=1}^{N} \left| \bar{x}_1^{(j)} - \bar{x}_2^{(j)} \right|^p \right)^{\frac{1}{p}}$$

When $p = 2$, $d_p(\bar{x}_1, \bar{x}_2)$ represents the classical Euclidean distance, that is normally the default choice in almost any scenario. In particular cases, it can be helpful to employ other variants, such as $p = 1$ (which is also known as Manhattan distance) or $p > 2$. Even if all the properties of a metric function remain unchanged, different values of p yield results that can be semantically diverse. As an example, we can consider the distance between points $\bar{x}_1 = (0, 0)$ and $\bar{x}_2 = (15, 10)$ as a function of p:

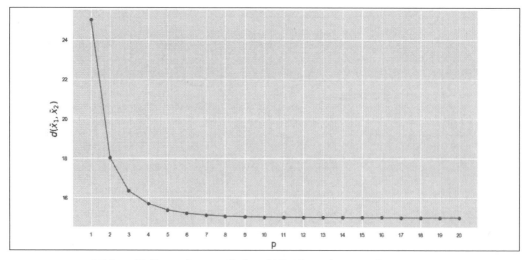

Minkowski distance between (0, 0) and (15, 10) as a function of parameter p

The distance decreases monotonically with p and converges to the largest component absolute difference $\left| \bar{x}_1^{(j)} - \bar{x}_2^{(j)} \right|$ when $p \rightarrow \infty$. Therefore, whenever it's important to weight all the components in the same way in order to have a consistent metric, small values of p are preferable (for example, $p = 1$ or 2). This result has also been studied and formalized by Aggarwal, Hinneburg, and Keim (in Aggarwal C. C., Hinneburg A., Keim D. A., *On the Surprising Behavior of Distance Metrics in High Dimensional Space*, ICDT, 2001), who proved a fundamental inequality.

If we consider a generic distribution G of M points $\bar{x}_i \in (0,1)^d$, a distance function based on the L_p norm, and the maximum D_{max}^p and minimum D_{min}^p distances (computed using the L_p norm) between two points, $\bar{x}_j$ and $\bar{x}_k$ drawn from G and the origin $O \in \mathbb{R}^d$, the following inequality holds:

$$C_p \leq \lim_{d \to \infty} E \left[\frac{D_{max}^p - D_{min}^p}{d^{\frac{1}{p} - \frac{1}{2}}} \right] \leq (M - 1)C_p \;\; where \;\; C_p \geq 0$$

It's clear that when the input dimensionality is very high and $p \gg 2$, the expected value $E\left[D_{max}^p - D_{min}^p \right]$ becomes bounded between two constants, $k_1 \left(C_p d^{1/p - 1/2} \right)$ and $(M - 1)k_2 \left(C_p d^{1/p - 1/2} \right) \rightarrow 0$, reducing the actual effect of almost any distance.

In fact, given two generic couples of points $(\bar{x}_1, \bar{x}_2)$ and $(\bar{x}_3, \bar{x}_4)$ drawn from G, the natural consequence of the following inequality is that $d_p(\bar{x}_1, \bar{x}_2) \approx d_p(\bar{x}_3, \bar{x}_4)$ when $p \rightarrow \infty$, independently of their relative positions. This important result confirms the importance of choosing the right metric according to the dimensionality of the dataset and that $p = 1$ is the best choice when $d \gg 1$, while $p \gg 1$ can produce inconsistent results due the ineffectiveness of the metric. To see direct confirmation of this phenomenon, it's possible to run the following snippet, which computes the average difference between the maximum and minimum distances considering 100 sets containing 100 data points drawn from a uniform distribution, $G \sim U(0, I)$. In the snippet, the case of $d = 5, 10, 15, 20$ is analyzed with Minkowski metrics with $P = 1, 2, 5, 10$ (the final values depend on the random seed and how many times the experiment is repeated):

```
import numpy as np
from scipy.spatial.distance import pdist

nb_samples = 100
nb_bins = 100

def max_min_mean(p=1.0, d=2):
```

```
Xs = np.random.uniform(0.0, 1.0,
    size=(nb_bins, nb_samples, d))

pd_max = np.zeros(shape=(nb_bins,))
pd_min = np.zeros(shape=(nb_bins,))

for i in range(nb_bins):
    pd = pdist(Xs[i], metric='minkowski', p=p)
    pd_max[i] = np.max(pd)
    pd_min[i] = np.min(pd)

return np.mean(pd_max - pd_min)
```

The result for different values grouped by metric value p is shown in the following figure:

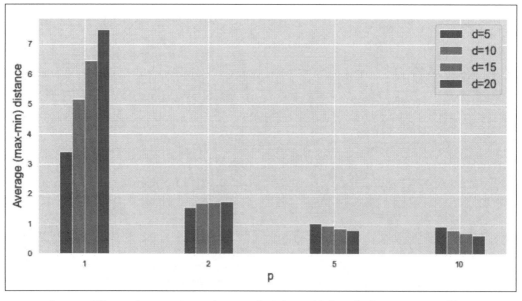

Average difference between the maximum and minimum Minkowski distances grouped by p

A particular case that is a direct consequence of the previous inequality is when the largest absolute difference between components determines the most important factor of a distance, large values of p can be employed. For example, if we consider three points: $\bar{x}_1 = (0,0), \bar{x}_2 = (15, 10)$, and $\bar{x}_3 = (15, 0)$, then $d_2(\bar{x}_1, \bar{x}_2) \approx 18$, and $d_2(\bar{x}_1, \bar{x}_3) = 15$. So, if we set a threshold at $d = 16$ centered at $\bar{x}_1$, the point $\bar{x}_2$ is outside the boundaries. If instead $p = 15$, both distances become close to 15 and the two points $\bar{x}_2$ and $\bar{x}_3$ are inside the boundaries. A particular use of large values of p is when it's important to take into account the inhomogeneity among components.

For example, some feature vectors can represent the age and height of a set of people. Considering a test person $\bar{x} = (30, 175)$, with large p values, the distances between x and two samples (35, 150) and (25, 151) are almost identical (about 25.0), and the only dominant factor becomes the height difference (independent of the age).

The KNN algorithm determines the k closest samples to each training point. When a new sample is presented, the procedure is repeated with two possible variants:

- With a predefined value of k, the KNN are computed.
- With a predefined radius/threshold r, all the neighbors whose distance is less than or equal to the radius are computed.

The philosophy of KNN is that similar samples can share their features. For example, a recommendation system can cluster users using this algorithm and, given a new user, find the most similar ones (based, for example, on the products they bought) to recommend the same category of items. In general, a similarity function is defined as the reciprocal of a distance (there are some exceptions, such as the cosine similarity, which is effective for any value of p):

$$s(\bar{x}_1, \bar{x}_2) = f\left(d_p(\bar{x}_1, \bar{x}_2)\right) = \frac{1}{d_p(\bar{x}_1, \bar{x}_2)} \quad for \; d_p(\bar{x}_1, \bar{x}_2) \neq 0$$

Two different users, A and B, who are classified as neighbors, will differ under some viewpoints, but at the same time, they will share some peculiar features. This statement authorizes us to increase the homogeneity by *suggesting the differences*. For example, if A liked book b_1 and B liked b_2, we can recommend b_1 to B and b_2 to A. If our hypothesis was correct, the similarity between A and B will be increased; otherwise, the two users will move toward other clusters that better represent their behavior.

Unfortunately, the vanilla algorithm (in scikit-learn, it is called the brute-force algorithm) can become extremely slow with a large number of samples because it's necessary to compute all the pairwise distances in order to answer any query. With M points, this number is equal to M^2, which is often unacceptable (if $M = 1,000$, each query needs to compute a million distances). More precisely, as the computation of a distance in an N-dimensional space requires N operations, the total complexity becomes $O(M^2 N)$, which can be reasonable only for small values of both M and N. That's why some important strategies, such as k-d trees and ball trees, have been implemented to reduce the computational complexity.

K-d trees

As all KNN queries can be considered search problems, one of the most efficient ways to reduce the overall complexity is to reorganize the dataset into a tree structure. In a binary tree (one-dimensional data), the average computational complexity of a query is $O(\log M)$ because we assume we have almost the same number of elements in each branch (if the tree is completely unbalanced, all the elements are inserted sequentially and the resulting structure has a single branch, so the complexity becomes $O(M)$). In general, the real complexity is slightly higher than $O(\log M)$ because of the unbalancing of the tree, but the operation is always much more efficient than a vanilla search, which is $O(M^2)$.

However, we normally work with N-dimensional data and the previous structure cannot be immediately employed. K-d trees extend the concept of binary trees for $N > 1$. In this case, a split cannot be immediately performed, and a different strategy must be chosen. The easiest way to solve this problem is to select a feature at each level (1, 2, …, N) and repeat the process until the desired depth is reached. In the following diagram, there's an example of k-d trees with three-dimensional points:

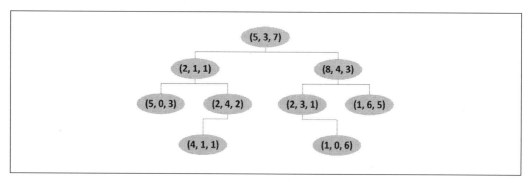

Example of a three-dimensional k-d tree

The root is point (5, 3, 7). The first split is performed considering the first feature, so two children are (2, 1, 1) and (8, 4, 3). The second one operates on the second feature, and so on. The average computational complexity is $O(N \log M)$, but if the distribution is very asymmetric, the probability that the tree will become unbalanced is very high. To mitigate this issue, it's possible to select the feature corresponding to the median of the (sub-)dataset and to continue splitting with this criterion. In this way, the tree is guaranteed to be balanced. However, the average complexity is always proportional to the dimensionality and this can dramatically affect the performance.

For example, if M = 10,000 and N = 10, using the $\log_{10} x$, O $(N \log M)$ = O (40), while with N = 1,000, the complexity becomes O (40,000). Generally, k-d trees suffer from the curse of dimensionality and when N becomes large, the average complexity is about O (MN), which is always better than the vanilla algorithm, but often too expensive for real-life applications. Therefore, k-d trees are only really effective when the dimensionality is not very high. In all other cases, the probability of having an unbalanced tree and the resulting computational complexity suggest employing a different method.

Ball trees

An alternative to k-d trees is provided by ball trees. The idea is to rearrange the dataset in a way that is almost insensitive to high-dimensional samples. A ball is defined as a set of points whose distance from a center sample is less than or equal to a fixed radius:

$$B_R(\bar{x}_c) = \left\{ \bar{x}_i : d_p(\bar{x}_i, \bar{x}_c) \leq R \right\}$$

Starting from the first main ball, it's possible to build smaller ones nested into the parent ball and stop the process when the desired depth has been reached. A fundamental condition is that a point can always belong to a single ball. In this way, considering the cost of the N-dimensional distance, the computational complexity is O $(N \log M)$ and doesn't suffer the curse of dimensionality that k-d trees suffers from. The structure is based on hyperspheres whose boundaries are defined by the equations (given a center point $\bar{x}$ and a radius R_i):

$$\bar{x}_{(1)}^2 + \bar{x}_{(2)}^2 \pm \cdots + \bar{x}_{(N)}^2 = R_i^2$$

Therefore, the only operation needed to find the right ball is measuring the distance between a sample and the centers starting from the smallest balls. If a point is outside the ball, it's necessary to move upward and check the parents, until the ball containing the sample is found.

In the following diagram, there's an example of ball trees with two levels:

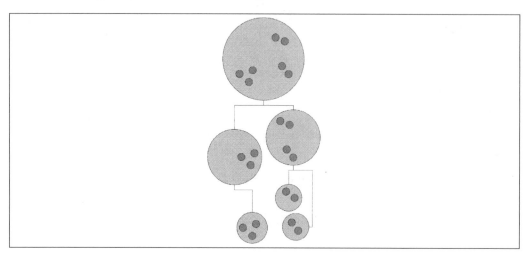

Example of ball trees with seven bidimensional points and two levels

In this example, the seven bidimensional points are split first into two balls containing three and four points. At the second level, the second ball is split again into two smaller balls containing two points each. This procedure can be repeated until a fixed depth is reached or by imposing the maximum number of elements that a leaf must contain (in this case, it can be equal to 3).

Fitting a KNN model

Both k-d trees and ball trees can be efficient structures to reduce the complexity of KNN queries. However, when fitting a model, it's important to consider both the k parameter (which normally represents the average or the standard number of neighbors computed in a query) and the maximum tree depth. These particular structures are not employed for common tasks (such as sorting) and their efficiency is maximized when all the requested neighbors can be found in the same sub-structure (with a size of $K << M$ to avoid an implicit fallback to the vanilla algorithm). In other words, the tree has the role of reducing the dimensionality of the search space by partitioning it into reasonably small regions.

At the same time, if the number of samples contained in a leaf is small, the number of tree nodes grows and the complexity is subsequently increased. The negative impact is doubled because on average it's necessary to explore more nodes, and if k is much greater than the number of elements contained in a node, it's necessary to merge the samples belonging to different nodes. On the other hand, a very large number of samples per node leads to a condition that is close to the vanilla algorithm.

For example, if M = 1,000 and each node contains 250 elements, once the right node is computed, the number of distances to compute is comparable with the initial dataset size and no real advantage is achieved by employing a tree structure. An acceptable practice is to set the size of a leaf equal to 5 to 10 times the average value of k to maximize the probability of finding all the neighbors inside the same leaf. However, every specific problem must be analyzed (while also benchmarking the performance) in order to find the most appropriate value. If different values of k are necessary, it's important to consider the relative frequencies of the queries. For example, if a program needs 10 5-NN queries and 1 50-NN query, it's probably better to set a leaf size equal to 25, even if the 50-NN query will be more expensive. In fact, setting a good value for a second query (for example, 200) will dramatically increase the complexity of the first 10 queries, leading to a loss of performance.

In this context, we are discussing KNN as an unsupervised algorithm. However, it can also be employed both in regression and classification scenarios. Most of the concepts discussed in the previous sections also apply when the problem needs a supervised approach. In particular, as the neighborhoods represent *uniform domains*, small numbers of neighbors lead to very low biases because, given a test sample, the values employed in computing the label (either categorical or continuous) are the ones of the most similar sample points. Obviously, such a low bias is the consequence of *intrinsic overfitting*, which leads to a naturally large variance. The problem can be mitigated by choosing larger neighborhoods.

This solution is a sort of regularization because the loss of precision is directly connected to an implicit and controlled linearization of the dataset. On the other hand, larger neighbors are more computationally expensive, therefore their size is often (and wrongly) reduced. In our context, we are always making our decisions without considering the bias-variance trade-off because the scenarios are unsupervised. However, it's helpful for the reader to keep in mind that instance-based methods are generally harder to manage than parametric ones, as the advantage of obtaining a synthetic model is absent and the predictions are strongly influenced by the structure (including noisy points and outliers) of the dataset.

We can now create a complete Python example using the scikit-learn API.

Example of KNN with scikit-learn

In order to test the KNN algorithm, we are going to use the MNIST handwritten digit dataset provided directly by scikit-learn. It is made up of 1,797 8 × 8 grayscale images representing the digits from 0 to 9.

The first step is loading it and normalizing all the values to be bounded between 0 and 1:

```
import numpy as np

from sklearn.datasets import load_digits

digits = load_digits()
X_train = digits['data'] / np.max(digits['data'])
```

The dictionary "digits" contains both the images, `digits['images']`, and the flattened 64-dimensional arrays, `digits['data']`. Scikit-learn implements different classes (for example, it's possible to work directly with k-d trees and ball trees using the `KDTree` and `BallTree` classes) that can be used in the context of KNN (as clustering, classification, and regression algorithms). However, we're going to employ the main class, `NearestNeighbors`, which allows us to perform clustering and queries based either on the number of neighbors or on the radius of a ball centered on a sample:

```
from sklearn.neighbors import NearestNeighbors

knn = NearestNeighbors(n_neighbors=50,
                       leaf_size=30,
                       algorithm='ball_tree')
knn.fit(X_train)
```

We have chosen to have a default number of neighbors equal to 50 and an algorithm based on a ball tree. The leaf size (`leaf_size`) parameter has been kept to its default value, equal to `30`. We have also employed the default metric (Euclidean), but it's possible to change it using the metric and p parameters (which is the order of the Minkowski metric). Scikit-learn supports all the metrics implemented by SciPy in the `scipy.spatial.distance` package (as not all metrics are compatible with k-d trees and ball trees, I invite the reader to check the official scikit-learn documentation). However, in the majority of cases, it's sufficient to use a Minkowski metric and adjust the value of p if the results are not acceptable with any number of neighbors. Other metrics, such as the cosine distance, can be employed when the similarity must not be affected by the Euclidean distance, but only by the angle between two vectors pointing at the samples. Applications that use this metric include, for example, deep learning models for natural language processing, where the words are embedded in feature vectors whose semantic similarity is proportional to their Cosine distance.

In general, when the dimensionality is high, Cosine distance is an effective choice, but I invite the reader to carefully evaluate every scenario to make the most appropriate decision.

We can now query the model in order to find 50 neighbors of a sample. For our purposes, we have selected the sample with index 100, which represents a 4 (the images have a very low resolution, but it's always possible to distinguish the digit):

Sample digit used to query the KNN model

The query can be performed using the instance method `kneighbors`, which allows specifying the number of neighbors (the `n_neighbors` parameter – the default is the value selected during the instantiation of the class) and whether we want to also get the distances of each neighbor (the `return_distance` parameter). In this example, we are also interested in evaluating how far the neighbors are from the center, so we set `return_distance=True`:

```
distances, neighbors = ( knn.kneighbors(X_train[100].reshape(1, -1),
                            return_distance=True))

print(distances[0])
```

The output of the previous snippet is:

```
[ 0. 0.91215747  1.16926793  1.22633855  ...
```

The first neighbor is always the center, so its distance is 0. The other ones range from 0.9 to 1.9. Considering that, in this case, the maximum possible distance is 8 (between a 64-dimensional vector $\bar{a} = (1, 1, \ldots, 1)$ and the null vector), the result could be acceptable. In order to get confirmation, we can plot the neighbors as bidimensional 8×8 arrays (the returned array, `neighbors`, contains the indexes of the samples).

The result is shown in the following figure:

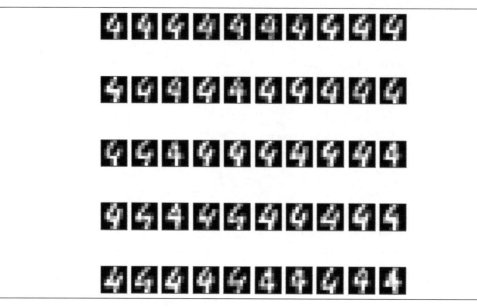

50 neighbors selected by the KNN model

As it's possible to see, there are no errors, but all the shapes are slightly different. In particular, the last one, which is also the farthest, has a lot of white pixels (corresponding to the value 1.0), explaining the reason for a distance equal to about 2.0. I invite the reader to test the `radius_neighbors` method until spurious values appear among the results. It's also interesting to try this algorithm with the Olivetti faces dataset, whose complexity is higher, and many more geometrical parameters can influence the similarity.

In this section, we have discussed the main concepts related to KNN, focusing our attention on pros and cons. We can now move on to another common clustering algorithm, K-means. We'll discuss its limitations and how to tune up the hyperparameters to obtain optimal performance.

K-means

When we discussed the Gaussian mixture algorithm, we defined it as soft K-means. The reason is that each cluster was represented by three elements: mean, variance, and weight. Each sample always belongs to all clusters with a probability provided by the Gaussian distributions. This approach can be very useful when it's possible to manage the probabilities as weights, but in many other situations, it's preferable to determine a single cluster per sample.

Such an approach is called hard clustering and K-means can be considered the hard version of a Gaussian mixture. In fact, when all variances $\Sigma_i \to 0$, the distributions degenerate to Dirac deltas $\delta(x - x_0)$, which represent perfect spikes centered at a specific point (even if they are not real functions but distributions). In this scenario, the only possibility to determine the most appropriate cluster is to find the shortest distance between a sample point and all the centers (from now on, we are going to call them centroids). This approach is also based on an important double principle that should be taken into account in every clustering algorithm. The clusters must be set up to maximize:

- The intra-cluster cohesion
- The inter-cluster separation

This means that we expect to label high-density regions that are well separated from each other. When this is not possible, the criterion must try to minimize the intra-cluster average distance between samples and centroid. This quantity is also called inertia and it's defined as:

$$S = \sum_{j=1}^{k} \sum_{\bar{x}_j \in C_j} \left\| \bar{x}_i - \bar{\mu}_j \right\|^2$$

Large levels of inertia imply low cohesion because there are probably too many points belongings to clusters whose centroids are too far away. The problem can be solved by minimizing the previous quantity. However, the computational complexity needed to find the global minimum is exponential (K-means belongs to the class of NP-hard problems). The alternative approach employed by the K-means algorithm, also known as Lloyd's algorithm, is iterative and starts from selecting k random centroids (in the next section, we're going to analyze a more efficient method) and adjusting them until their configuration becomes stable.

The dataset to cluster (with M data points) is represented as:

$$X = \{\bar{x}_1, \bar{x}_2, \dots, \bar{x}_M\} \text{ where } \bar{x}_i \in \mathbb{R}^N$$

An initial guess for the centroids could be:

$$M^{(0)} = \left\{ \bar{\mu}_0^{(0)}, \bar{\mu}_1^{(0)}, \dots, \bar{\mu}_k^{(0)} \right\} \text{ where } \bar{\mu}_i^{(0)} \in \mathbb{R}^N \left(e.g.\, \mu_i^{(0)} \sim N\big(0, Var(X)\big) \right)$$

There are no specific restrictions on the initial values. However, the choice can influence both the convergence speed and the minimum that is found.

The iterative procedure will loop over the dataset, computing the Euclidean distance between $\bar{x}_i$ and each $\bar{\mu}_j$ and assigning a cluster based on the criterion:

$$C^{(t)}(\bar{x}_i) = \underset{j}{\operatorname{argmin}}\, d\left(\bar{x}_i, \bar{\mu}_j^{(t)}\right)$$

Once all the points have been clustered, the new centroids are computed:

$$\bar{\mu}_j^{(t)} = \frac{1}{N_{C_j}} \sum_{\bar{x}_i \in C_j} \bar{x}_i \;\; \forall j \in (1, k)$$

The quantity N_{C_j} represents the number of points belonging to cluster j. At this point, the inertia is recomputed, and the new value is compared with the previous one. The procedure will stop either after a fixed number of iterations or when the variations in the inertia become smaller than a predefined threshold. Lloyd's algorithm is very similar to a particular case of the EM algorithm. In fact, the first step of each iteration is the computation of an expectation (the centroid configuration), while the second step maximizes the intra-cluster cohesion by minimizing the inertia.

Before moving forward, it's important to understand the structure of the inertia and the limitations that K-means inherits from it. Let's suppose we have a very dense blob and another less dense (and possibly with larger variance) one. The internal summation of S is limited to the points assigned to each cluster. In our case, the formula becomes:

$$S = \sum_{\bar{x}_j \in C_{dense}} \|\bar{x}_i - \bar{\mu}_{dense}\|^2 + \sum_{\bar{x}_j \in C_{sparse}} \|\bar{x}_i - \bar{\mu}_{sparse}\|^2.$$

As C_{dense} contains a (much) larger set of points than C_{sparse}, the first term dominates the sum. Therefore, when S is minimized there's a high chance of finding the optimal position of $\bar{\mu}_{dense}$, but a very low probability of obtaining a global optimum. In fact, the modifications to S due to the sparse blob are less and less negligible and the algorithm may stop before having explored all possibilities. When dealing with such scenarios, a possible solution is to up-sample the sparse blob by introducing n copies of the same points. This approach is equivalent to introducing a set of class weights $\bar{w} = \{w_1, w_2, \ldots, w_k\}$ in the computation of S to encode the prior knowledge about the geometrical structure:

$$S = \sum_{j=1}^{k} w_j \sum_{\bar{x}_j \in C_j} \|\bar{x}_i - \bar{\mu}_j\|^2$$

For example, in the previous scenario, $w_1 = 1$ and w_2 can be chosen as the ratio of points belonging to C_{dense} and C_{sparse} (of course, if this is not known before the first training, it can be included after an analysis of the results).

K-means can also be implemented with an incremental approach (formally known as mini-batch K-means). When the datasets are too large to fit into memory and no other solutions are feasible (such as a Dask or Spark cluster), it's possible to apply the same strategy to smaller batches with a slight modification of the algorithm. We are not covering all the details in this book (they are also available in Bonaccorso G., *Hands-On Unsupervised Learning with Python*, Packt Publishing, 2019), but it's not difficult to understand that the main problem is the incorrect allocation due to the fact that a part of the sample is not immediately available. For this reason, mini-batch K-means introduces a parametrized reallocation strategy to allow a point to be reassigned with a predefined sensitivity threshold (small values cause fluctuations, while larger ones yield sub-optimal final configurations). Even if the algorithm is less precise than standard K-means, it's possible to prove that the actual performance loss is generally extremely small, and it can therefore be employed in production scenarios without large risks.

The complete *vanilla* K-means algorithm (that is, the standard algorithm without any optimization or improvement) is:

- Set a maximum number of iterations N_{max}
- Set a tolerance *Thr*
- Set the value of k (the number of expected clusters)
- Initialize vector $C^{(0)}$ with random values. They can be points belonging to the dataset or sampled from a suitable distribution
- Compute the initial inertia $S^{(0)}$
- Set $N = 0$
- While $N < N_{max}$ or $\left\| S^{(t)} - S^{(t-1)} \right\| > Thr$:
    - $N = N + 1$
    - For $\bar{x}_i \in X$:

        Assign $\bar{x}_i$ to a cluster using the shortest distance between $\bar{x}_i$ and $\bar{\mu}_j$
    - Recompute the centroid vector $C^{(t)}$ considering the new assignments
    - Recompute the inertia $S^{(t)}$

The algorithm is quite simple and intuitive, and many real-life applications are based on it. However, there are two important elements to consider. The first one is the convergence speed.

It's easy to show that every initial guess drives to a convergence point, but the number of iterations is dramatically influenced by this choice and there's no guarantee of finding the global minimum. If the initial centroids are close to the final ones, the algorithm needs only a few steps to correct the values, but when the choice is totally random, it's not uncommon to need a very high number of iterations. If there are N data points and k centroids, N_k distances must be computed at each iteration, leading to an inefficient result. In the next paragraph, we'll show how it's possible to initialize the centroids to minimize the convergence time.

Another important aspect is that contrary to KNN, K-means needs to predefine the number of expected clusters. In some cases, this is a secondary problem because we already know the most appropriate value for k (for example, if the number of clusters is defined by external constraints, like in market segmentation). However, when the dataset is high-dimensional and our knowledge is limited, this choice could be hazardous. A good approach to solve the issue is to analyze the final inertia for a different number of clusters. As we expect to maximize the intra-cluster cohesion, a small number of clusters will lead to increased inertia. We try to pick the highest point below a maximum tolerable value. Theoretically, we can also pick $k = N$. In this case, the inertia becomes zero because each point represents the centroid of its cluster, but a large value of k transforms the clustering scenario into a fine-grained partitioning that might not be the best strategy to capture the feature of a consistent group. It's impossible to define a rule for the upper bound k_{max}, but we assume that this value is always much less than N. The best choice is to select k to minimize the inertia, selecting the values from a set bounded, for example, between 2 and k_{max}.

Even if the vanilla algorithm is quite effective, the optimal choice for the initial positions of the clusters can speed up the computation. This is the goal achieved by the variant called K-means++.

K-means++

We have said that a good choice for the initial centroids can improve the convergence speed and lead to a minimum that is closer to the global optimum of the inertia. Arthur and Vassilvitskii (in Arthur D., Vassilvitskii S., *The Advantages of Careful Seeding*, k-means++: Proceedings of the Eighteenth Annual ACM-SIAM Symposium on Discrete Algorithms, 2006) proposed a method called K-means++, which allows us to increase the accuracy of the initial centroid guess considering the most likely final configuration.

In order to explore the algorithm, it's useful to introduce a function, $D(\bar{x}, i)$, which is defined as:

$$D(\bar{x}, i) = \min_i d(\bar{x}, \bar{\mu}_i) \ \forall i \in (1, p \leq k)$$

$D(\bar{x}, i)$ defines the shortest distance between each sample and one of the centroids already selected. As the process is incremental, this function must be recomputed after all steps. For our purposes, let's also define an auxiliary probability distribution (we omit the index variable for simplicity):

$$G(\bar{x}) = \frac{D(\bar{x})^2}{\sum_{j=1}^{M} D(\bar{x}_j)^2}$$

The first centroid $\bar{\mu}_0$ is sampled from X using a uniform distribution. The next steps are:

- Compute $D(\bar{x}, i)$ for all $\bar{x} \in X$ considering the centroids already selected
- Compute $G(\bar{x})$
- Select the next centroid $\bar{\mu}_i$ from X with a probability $G(\bar{x})$

In the aforementioned paper, the authors showed a very important property. If we define S^* as the global optimum of S, a K-means++ initialization determines an upper bound for the expected value of the actual inertia:

$$E[S] \leq 8S^*(\log k + 2)$$

This condition is often expressed by saying that K-means++ is $O(\log k)$-competitive. When k is sufficiently small, the probability of finding a local minimum close to the global one increases. However, K-means++ is still a probabilistic approach and different initializations on the same dataset lead to different initial configurations. A good practice is to run a limited number of initializations (for example, 10) and pick the one associated with the smallest inertia. When training complexity is not a primary issue, this number can be increased, but different experiments showed that the improvement achievable with a very large number of trials is negligible when compared to the actual computational cost. The default value in scikit-learn is 10 and it's advisable to keep this value in most cases. If the result continues to be poor, it's preferable to pick another method.

Moreover, there are problems that cannot be solved using K-means (even with the best possible initialization) because one of the assumptions of the algorithm is that each cluster is a hypersphere and the distances are measured using a Euclidean function. In the next chapter, we're going to analyze other algorithms that are not constrained to working with such limitations and can easily solve clustering problems using asymmetric cluster geometries.

Example of K-means with scikit-learn

In this example, we continue using the MNIST dataset (the X_train array is the same as was defined in the earlier section dedicated to KNN), but we also want to analyze different clustering evaluation methods. The first step is visualizing the inertia corresponding to different numbers of clusters. We are going to use the KMeans class, which accepts the n_clusters parameter and employs the K-means++ initialization as the default method (as explained in the previous section, in order to find the best initial configuration, scikit-learn performs several attempts and selects the configuration with the lowest inertia; it's possible to change the number of attempts through the n_iter parameter):

```
import numpy as np

from sklearn.cluster import KMeans

min_nb_clusters = 2
max_nb_clusters = 20

inertias = np.zeros(shape=(max_nb_clusters - min_nb_clusters + 1,))

for i in range(min_nb_clusters, max_nb_clusters + 1):
    km = KMeans(n_clusters=i, random_state=1000)
    km.fit(X_train)
    inertias[i - min_nb_clusters] = km.inertia_
```

We are supposing to analyze the range [2, 20]. After each training session, the final inertia can be retrieved using the inertia_ instance variable. The following graph shows the plot of the gradient of the inertia as a function of the number of clusters. The plot is obtained using the NumPy function np.gradient():

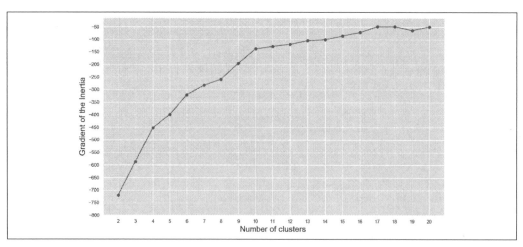

Gradient of the inertia as a function of the number of clusters

As expected, the function is decreasing (the gradient is negative) but the slope tends to reach 0 when $k \rightarrow \infty$. In this case, we know that the real number of clusters is 10, but it's also possible to discover this by observing the trend. The absolute value of the slope is quite high before 10, but it starts decreasing more and more slowly after this threshold. This is a signal that informs us that some clusters are not well separated, even if their internal cohesion is high. In order to confirm this hypothesis, we can set n_clusters=10 and, first of all, check the centroids at the end of the training process:

```
km = KMeans(n_clusters=10, random_state=1000)
Y = km.fit_predict(X_train)
```

The centroids are available through the cluster_centers_ instance variable. In the following screenshot, there's a plot of the corresponding bidimensional arrays:

K-means centroid at the end of the training process

All the digits are present and there are no duplicates. This confirms that the algorithm has successfully separated the sets, but the final inertia (which is about 4,500) informs us that there are probably incorrect assignments. To obtain confirmation, we can plot the dataset using a dimensionality reduction method, such as t-SNE (see *Chapter 5, Graph-Based Semi-Supervised Learning*, for further details):

```
from sklearn.manifold import TSNE

tsne = TSNE(n_components=2, perplexity=10.0,
            random_state=1000)
X_tsne = tsne.fit_transform(X_train)
```

At this point, we can plot the bidimensional dataset with the corresponding cluster labels:

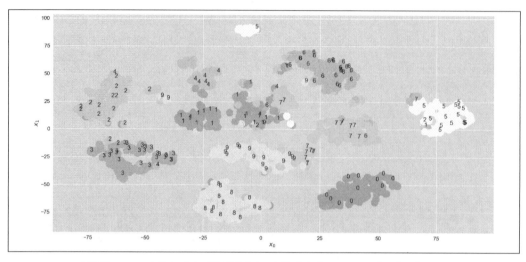

t-SNE representation of the MNIST dataset; the labels correspond to the clusters

The plot confirms that the dataset is made up of well separated blobs, but a few data points are assigned to the wrong cluster (this is not surprising considering the similarity between some pairs of digits). An important observation can further explain the trend of the inertia. In fact, the point where the slope changes almost abruptly corresponds to about 10 clusters. Observing the t-SNE plot, we can immediately discover the reason: the cluster corresponding to the digit 7 is indeed split into 3 blocks. The main one contains the majority of samples, but there are another 2 smaller blobs that are wrongly attached to clusters 1 and 9. This is not surprising, considering that the digit 7 can appear very similar to a distorted 1 or 9. However, these two spurious blobs are always at the boundaries of the wrong clusters (remember that the geometric structures are hyperspheres), confirming that the metric has successfully detected a low similarity. If a group of wrongly assigned samples were in the middle of a cluster, it would mean that the separation failed dramatically, and another method should be employed.

At this point, it's helpful to introduce some common evaluation metrics that can be employed both when the ground truth is known and when it's not.

Evaluation metrics

In many cases, it's impossible to evaluate the performance of a clustering algorithm using only a visual inspection. Moreover, it's important to use standard objective metrics that allow us to compare different approaches.

We are now going to introduce some methods based on the knowledge of the ground truth (the correct assignment for each data point) and one common strategy employed when the true labels are unknown.

Before discussing the scoring functions, we need to introduce a standard notation. If there are k clusters, we define the true labels as:

$$Y_{true} = \{y_1^{true}, y_2^{true}, \dots, y_M^{true}\} \ where \ y_i^{true} \in \{1, 2, \dots, k\}$$

In the same way, we can define the predicted labels:

$$Y_{pred} = \{y_1^{pred}, y_2^{pred}, \dots, y_M^{pred}\} \ where \ y_i^{pred} \in \{1, 2, \dots, k\}$$

Both sets can be considered as sampled from two discrete random variables (for simplicity, we denote them with the same names), whose probability mass functions are $P_{true}(y)$ and $P_{pred}(y)$ with a generic $y \in \{y_1, y_2, \dots, y_k\}$ (y_i represents the index of the ith cluster). These two probabilities can be approximated with a frequency count; so, for example, the probability $P_{true}(1)$ is computed as the number of data points whose true label is one $n_{true}(1)$ over the total number of data points M. In this way, we can define the entropies:

$$
\begin{cases}
H(Y_{true}) = -\displaystyle\sum_{i=1}^{k} p(y_i^{true}) \log p(y_i^{true}) \\
H(Y_{pred}) = -\displaystyle\sum_{i=1}^{k} p(y_i^{pred}) \log p(y_i^{pred})
\end{cases}
$$

These quantities describe the intrinsic uncertainty of the random variables. They are maximized when all the classes have the same probability, while, for example, they are null if all the samples belong to a single class (minimum uncertainty). We also need to know the uncertainty of a random variable Y given another one X. This can be achieved using the conditional entropy $H(Y|X)$. In this case, we need to compute the joint probability $p(\bar{x}, y)$ because the definition of $H(Y|X)$ is:

$$H(Y|X) = -\sum_{\bar{x}} \sum_{y} p(\bar{x}, y) \log \frac{p(\bar{x}, y)}{p(\bar{x})}$$

In order to approximate the previous expression, we can define the function $n(i_{true}, j_{pred})$, which counts the number of samples with the true label i assigned to cluster j.

In this way, if there are M samples, the approximated conditional entropies become:

$$\begin{cases} H(Y_{true}|Y_{pred}) = - \sum_{i_{true}=1}^{M} \sum_{j_{pred}=1}^{M} \frac{n(i_{true}, j_{pred})}{M} \log \frac{n(i_{true}, j_{pred})}{n_{pred}(j_{pred})} \\ H(Y_{true}|Y_{true}) = - \sum_{i_{pred}=1}^{M} \sum_{j_{true}=1}^{M} \frac{n(i_{true}, j_{pred})}{M} \log \frac{n(i_{true}, j_{pred})}{n_{true}(i_{true})} \end{cases}$$

Using these measures, we can now compute some scores that cover different aspects of the clustering result. They are often computed together because each of them has a peculiar feature.

Homogeneity score

This score is useful to check whether the clustering algorithm meets an important requirement: a cluster should contain only samples belonging to a single class. It's defined as:

$$h = 1 - \frac{H(Y_{true}|Y_{pred})}{H(Y_{true})}$$

It's bounded between 0 and 1, with low values indicating low homogeneity. In fact, when the knowledge of Y_{pred} reduces the uncertainty of Y_{true}, $H(Y_{true} | Y_{pred})$ becomes smaller ($h \rightarrow 1$) and vice versa. For our example, the homogeneity score can be computed as:

```
from sklearn.metrics import homogeneity_score

print(homogeneity_score(digits['target'], Y))
```

The output is:

```
0.739148799605
```

The `digits['target']` array contains the true labels, while `Y` contains the predictions (all the functions we are going to use accept the true labels as the first parameter and the predictions as the second one). The homogeneity score confirms that the clusters are rather homogeneous, but there's still a moderate level of uncertainty because some clusters contain incorrect assignments.

This method, together with the other ones, can be used to search for the right number of clusters and tune up all supplementary hyperparameters (such as the number of iterations or the metric function).

Completeness score

This score is complementary to the homogeneity score. Its purpose is to provide a piece of information about the assignment of samples belonging to the same class. More precisely, a good clustering algorithm should assign all samples with the same true label to the same cluster. From our previous analysis, we know that, for example, the digit 7 has been wrongly assigned to both clusters 9 and 1; therefore, we expect a non-perfect completeness score. The definition is symmetric to the homogeneity score:

$$c = 1 - \frac{H(Y_{pred}|Y_{true})}{H(Y_{pred})}$$

The rationale is very intuitive. When $H(Y_{pred} \mid Y_{true})$ is low ($c \rightarrow 1$), it means that the knowledge of the ground truth reduces the uncertainty about the predictions. Therefore, if we know that all the samples of subset A have the same label y_i, we are quite sure that all the corresponding predictions have been assigned to the same cluster. The completeness score for our example is:

```
from sklearn.metrics import completeness_score

print(completeness_score(digits['target'], Y))
```

The output is:

```
0.747718831945
```

Again, the value confirms our hypothesis. The residual uncertainty is due to a lack of completeness because a few samples with the same label have been split into blocks that are assigned to wrong clusters. It's obvious that a perfect scenario is characterized by having both homogeneity and completeness scores equal to 1.

Adjusted Rand index

This score is useful to compare the original label distribution with the clustering prediction. Ideally, we'd like to reproduce the exact ground truth distribution, but in general, this is very difficult in real-life scenarios. A way to measure the discrepancy is provided by the adjusted Rand index.

In order to compute this score, we need to define the auxiliary variables:

- a: Number of sample pairs (y_i, y_j) that have the same true label and that are assigned to the same cluster
- b: Number of sample pairs (y_i, y_j) that have a different true label and that are assigned to different clusters

The Rand index is defined as:

$$R = \frac{a + b}{\binom{M}{2}}$$

The adjusted Rand index is the Rand index corrected for chance and it's defined as:

$$R_A = \frac{R - E[R]}{\max R - E[R]}$$

The R_A measure is bounded between -1 and 1. A value close to -1 indicates a prevalence of wrong assignments, while a value close to 1 indicates that the clustering algorithm is correctly reproducing the ground truth distribution. The adjusted Rand score for our example is:

```
from sklearn.metrics import adjusted_rand_score

print(adjusted_rand_score(digits['target'], Y))
```

The output is:

```
0.666766395716
```

This value confirms that the algorithm is working well (because it's positive), but it can be further optimized by trying to reduce the number of incorrect assignments. The adjusted Rand score is a very powerful tool when the ground truth is known and can be employed as a single method to optimize all the hyperparameters.

Silhouette score

This measure doesn't need to know the ground truth and can be used to check, at the same time, the intra-cluster cohesion and the inter-cluster separation. In order to define the Silhouette score, we need to introduce two auxiliary functions. The first one is the average intra-cluster distance of a point $\bar{x}_i$ belonging to a cluster C_j:

$$a(\bar{x}_i) = \frac{1}{n(j)} \sum_p d(\bar{x}_i, \bar{x}_p) \ \forall \ \bar{x}_p \in C_j$$

In the previous expression, $n(k)$ is the number of samples assigned to the cluster C_j and $d(\bar{a},\bar{b})$ is a standard distance function (in the majority of cases, the Euclidean distance is the most reasonable choice). We also need to define the lowest inter-cluster distance, which can be interpreted as the average nearest-cluster distance. In the sample $\bar{x}_i \in C_j$, let's call C_t the nearest cluster; therefore, the function is defined as:

$$b(\bar{x}_i) = \frac{1}{n(t)} \sum_t d(\bar{x}_i, \bar{x}_t) \ \forall \ \bar{x}_t \in C_t$$

The Silhouette score for sample $\bar{x}_i$ is:

$$s(\bar{x}_i) = \frac{b(\bar{x}_i) - a(\bar{x}_i)}{\max[a(\bar{x}_i), b(\bar{x}_i)]}$$

The value of $s(\bar{x}_i)$, like for the adjusted Rand index, is bounded between -1 and 1. A value close to -1 indicates that $b(\bar{x}_i) \ll a(\bar{x}_i)$, so the average intra-cluster distance is greater than the average nearest-cluster index and sample $\bar{x}_i$ is wrongly assigned. Conversely, a value close to 1 indicates that the algorithm achieved a very good level of internal cohesion and inter-cluster separation (because $a(\bar{x}_i) \ll b(\bar{x}_i)$). Contrary to the other measure, the Silhouette score isn't a cumulative function and must be computed for each sample. A feasible strategy is to analyze the average value, but in this way, it's not possible to determine which clusters have the highest impact on the result. Another approach (the most common), is based on Silhouette plots, which display the score for each cluster in descending order. In the following snippet, we create plots for four different values of n_clusters (3, 5, 10, and 12):

```
import matplotlib.pyplot as plt
import matplotlib.cm as cm
import seaborn as sns

import numpy as np

from sklearn.cluster import KMeans
from sklearn.metrics import silhouette_samples

sns.set()

fig, ax = plt.subplots(2, 2, figsize=(15, 10))

nb_clusters = [3, 5, 10, 12]
mapping = [(0, 0), (0, 1), (1, 0), (1, 1)]

for i, n in enumerate(nb_clusters):
    km = KMeans(n_clusters=n, random_state=1000)
```

```
Y = km.fit_predict(X_train)

silhouette_values = silhouette_samples(X_train, Y)

ax[mapping[i]].set_xticks(
        [-0.15, 0.0, 0.25, 0.5, 0.75, 1.0])
ax[mapping[i]].set_yticks([])
ax[mapping[i]].set_title("{} clusters".format(n),
                        fontsize=16)
ax[mapping[i]].set_xlim([-0.15, 1])
ax[mapping[i]].grid(True)
y_lower = 20

for t in range(n):
    ct_values = silhouette_values[Y == t]
    ct_values.sort()

    y_upper = y_lower + ct_values.shape[0]

    color = cm.Accent(float(t) / n)
    ax[mapping[i]].fill_betweenx(
        np.arange(y_lower, y_upper), 0,
        ct_values,
        facecolor=color,
        edgecolor=color)

    y_lower = y_upper + 20
```

The result is shown in the following figure:

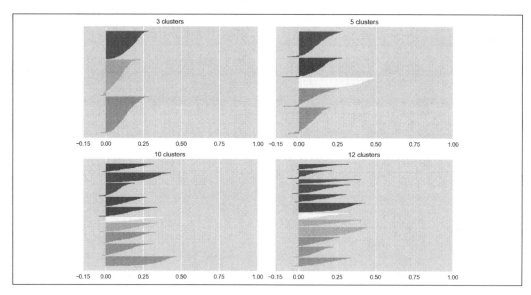

Silhouette plots for different numbers of clusters

The analysis of a Silhouette plot should follow some common guidelines:

- The width of each block must be proportional to the number of samples that are expected to belong to the corresponding cluster. If the label distribution is uniform, all the blocks must have a similar width. If the cluster distribution is originally balanced, any asymmetry indicates incorrect assignments. Of course, this is not true if the classes are intrinsically unbalanced. For example, in our case, we know that the right number of clusters is 10, but a couple of blocks are thinner than the other ones. This means that a cluster contains fewer samples than expected and the remaining ones have been assigned to incorrect partitions. On the contrary, if, for example, 50% of our dataset was zeros, a larger silhouette for this class would be perfectly fine. The correct interpretation of this plot requires background knowledge about the data-generating process. If such knowledge is missing (because, for example, the problem has never been studied), looking for symmetric silhouettes is generally good practice (particularly when the other scores confirm the result to be valid).

- The shape of a block shouldn't be sharp and peaked (like a knife) because it means that many samples have a low Silhouette score. The ideal (realistic) scenario is made up of shapes similar to cigars with a minimal difference between the highest and lowest values. Unfortunately, this is not always possible to achieve, but it's always preferable to tune up the algorithm if the shapes are like the ones plotted in the first diagram (three clusters).

- The maximum Silhouette score should be close to 1. Lower values (like in our example) indicate the presence of partial overlaps and wrong assignments. Negative values must be absolutely avoided (or limited to a very small number of samples) because they show a failure in the clustering process. Moreover, it's possible to prove that convex clusters (such as K-means hyperspheres) lead to higher values. This is due to the properties of the common distance functions (such as the Euclidean distance) that can suggest a low internal cohesion whenever the shape of a cluster is concave (think about a circle compared to a half-moon). In this case, the process of embedding the shape into a convex geometry leads to a lower density, and this negatively affects the Silhouette score.

In our particular case, we cannot accept having anything other than 10 clusters. However, the corresponding Silhouette plot is not perfect. We know the reasons for such imperfections (the structure of the samples and the high similarity of different digits) and it's quite difficult to avoid them using an algorithm such as K-means. The reader can try to improve the performance by increasing the number of iterations, but in these cases, if the result doesn't meet the requirements, it's preferable to adopt another method (such as the spectral clustering method described in the next chapter, which can manage asymmetric clusters and more complex geometries).

Summary

In this chapter, we presented some fundamental clustering algorithms. We started with KNN, which is an instance-based method that restructures the dataset to find the most similar samples to a given query point. We discussed three approaches: a naive one, which is also the most expensive in terms of computational complexity, and two strategies based respectively on the construction of a k-d tree and a ball tree. These two data structures can dramatically improve performance even when the number of samples is very large.

The next topic was a classic algorithm: K-means, which is a symmetric partitioning strategy comparable to a Gaussian mixture with variances close to zero that can solve many real-life problems. We discussed both a vanilla algorithm, which couldn't find a valid sub-optimal solution, and an optimized initialization method, called K-means++, which was able to speed up the convergence toward solutions quite close to the global minimum.

We also presented some evaluation methods that can be employed to assess the performance of a generic clustering algorithm. These metrics include homogeneity and completeness scores, which allow us to measure the between- and within-cluster separation. We also discussed a more complete measure, the Adjusted Rand index, and a very practical graphical tool, Silhouette plots, which show the structure of the clustering result and help the data scientist identify anomalies and overlapping clusters.

In the next chapter, *Chapter 7, Advanced Clustering and Unsupervised Models*, we're going to introduce more complex methodologies, like spectral and density-based clustering, that can easily solve problems where algorithms like K-means fail.

Further reading

- Aggarwal C. C., Hinneburg A., Keim D. A., *On the Surprising Behavior of Distance Metrics in High Dimensional Space*, ICDT, 2001

- Arthur D., Vassilvitskii S., *The Advantages of Careful Seeding*, k-means++: Proceedings of the Eighteenth Annual ACM-SIAM Symposium on Discrete Algorithms, 2006

- Pedrycz W., Gomide F., *An Introduction to Fuzzy Sets*, The MIT Press, 1998

- Shi J., Malik J., *Normalized Cuts and Image Segmentation*, IEEE Transactions on Pattern Analysis and Machine Intelligence, Vol. 22, 08, 2000

- Gelfand I. M., Glagoleva E. G., Shnol E. E., *Functions and Graphs Vol. 2*, The MIT Press, 1969

- Biyikoglu T., Leydold J., Stadler P. F., *Laplacian Eigenvectors of Graphs*, Springer, 2007

- Ester M., Kriegel H. P., Sander J., Xu X., *A Density-Based Algorithm for Discovering Clusters in Large Spatial Databases with Noise*, Proceedings of the 2nd International Conference on Knowledge Discovery and Data Mining, AAAI Press, pp. 226-231, 1996

- Kluger Y., Basri R., Chang J. T., Gerstein M., *Spectral Biclustering of Microarray Cancer Data: Co-clustering Genes and Conditions*, Genome Research, 13, 2003

- Huang, S., Wang, H., Li, D., Yang, Y., Li, T., *Spectral co-clustering ensemble.* Knowledge-Based Systems, 84, 46-55, 2015

- Bichot, C., *Co-clustering Documents and Words by Minimizing the Normalized Cut Objective Function.* Journal of Mathematical Modelling and Algorithms, 9(2), 131-147, 2010

- Agrawal R., Srikant R., *Fast Algorithms for Mining Association Rules*, Proceedings of the 20th VLDB Conference, 1994

- Li, Y., *The application of Apriori algorithm in the area of association rules.* Proceedings of SPIE, 8878, 88784H-88784H-5, 2013

- Bonaccorso G., *Hands-On Unsupervised Learning with Python*, Packt Publishing, 2019

7

Advanced Clustering and Unsupervised Models

In this chapter, we will continue to analyze clustering algorithms, focusing our attention on more complex models that can solve problems where K-means fails. These algorithms are extremely helpful in specific contexts (for example, geographical segmentation) where the structure of the data is highly non-linear and any approximation leads to a substantial drop in performance.

In particular, the algorithms and the topics we are going to analyze are:

- Fuzzy C-means
- Spectral clustering based on the Shi-Malik algorithm
- DBSCAN, including the Calinski-Harabasz and Davies-Bouldin scores

The first model is Fuzzy C-means, which is an extension of K-means to a soft-labeling scenario. Just like Generative Gaussian Mixtures, the algorithm helps the data scientist to understand the pseudo-probability (a measure similar to an actual probability) of a data point belonging to all defined clusters.

Fuzzy C-means

We have already talked about the difference between hard and soft clustering, comparing K-means with Gaussian mixtures. Another way to address this problem is based on the concept of fuzzy logic, which was proposed for the first time by Lotfi Zadeh in 1965 (for further details, a very good reference is Pedrycz W., Gomide F., *An Introduction to Fuzzy Sets*, The MIT Press, 1998). Classic logic sets are based on the law of excluded middle, which in a clustering scenario can be expressed by saying that a point $\bar{x}_i$ can belong only to a single cluster c_j.

Speaking more generally, if we split our universe into labeled partitions, a hard clustering approach would assign a label to each sample, while a fuzzy (or soft) approach would allow the management of a membership degree (in Gaussian mixtures, this is an actual probability) w_{ij}, which expresses how strong the relationship is between point $\bar{x}_i$ and cluster c_j.

Contrary to other methods, by employing fuzzy logic it's possible to define asymmetric sets that are not representable with continuous functions (such as trapezoids). This allows further flexibility and an increased ability to adapt to more complex geometries. The following graph shows examples of fuzzy sets:

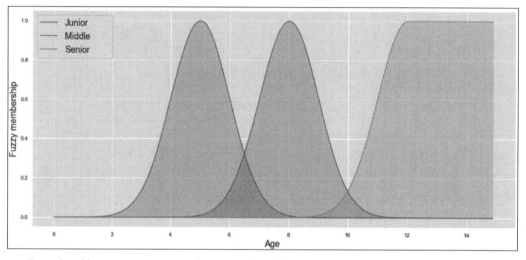

Examples of fuzzy sets representing the seniority level of an employee according to years of experience

The graph represents the seniority level of an employee given their years of experience. As we want to cluster the entire population into three groups (Junior, Middle, and Senior level employees), three fuzzy sets have been designed. We have assumed that a young employee is keen and can quickly reach the Junior level after an initial apprenticeship period. The opportunity to work on complex problems allows them to develop skills that are fundamental to the transition between the Junior and Middle levels. After about 10 years, the employee can begin to consider themselves as a Senior apprentice and, after about 25 years, their experience is enough to qualify them as a full Senior until the end of their career.

As this is an imaginary example, we haven't tuned all of the values, but it's easy to compare, for example, employee *A* who has 7 years of experience with employee *B* who has 18 years of experience. The former is about 25% Junior (decreasing even if with a minimum slope), 25% Middle (reaching its climax), and almost 0% Senior (increasing). The latter is 0% Junior (ending plateau), about 0% Middle (decreasing), and close to 100% Senior (ending plateau).

In both cases, the values are not normalized so always sum up to 1 because we are more interested in showing the process and the proportions. The fuzziness level is lower in extreme cases, while it is higher when two sets intersect. For example, at about 15%, the Middle and Senior are about 50%. As we're going to discuss, it's useful to avoid a very high fuzziness level when clustering a dataset because it can lead to a lack of precision as the boundaries fade out, becoming completely fuzzy.

Fuzzy C-means is a generalization of standard K-means, with a soft assignment and more flexible clusters. The dataset to cluster (containing M samples) is represented by:

$$X = \{\bar{x}_1, \bar{x}_2, \dots, \bar{x}_M\} \ where \ \bar{x}_i \in \mathbb{R}^N$$

If we assume we have k clusters, it's necessary to define a matrix $W \in \mathbb{R}^{M \times k}$ containing the membership degrees for each sample:

$$W = \begin{pmatrix} w_{11} & \cdots & w_{1k} \\ \vdots & \ddots & \vdots \\ w_{M1} & \cdots & w_{Mk} \end{pmatrix}$$

Each degree $w_{ij} \in (0,1)$ and all rows must be normalized so that they always sum up to 1. In this way, the membership degrees can be considered as probabilities (with the same semantics) and it's easier to make decisions with a prediction result. If a hard assignment is needed, it's possible to employ the same approach normally used with Gaussian mixtures: the winning cluster is selected by applying the argmax function. However, it's good practice to employ soft clustering only when it's possible to manage the vectorial output. For example, the probabilities/membership degrees can be fed into a classifier in order to yield more complex predictions.

As with K-means, the problem can be expressed as the minimization of generalized inertia:

$$S_f = \sum_{j=1}^{k} \sum_{\bar{x}_i \in C_j} w_{ij}^m \left\| \bar{x}_i - \bar{\mu}_j \right\|^2$$

The constant *m (m > 1)* is an exponent employed to re-weight the membership degrees. A value very close to 1 doesn't affect the actual values. Greater *m* values reduce their magnitude. The same parameter is also used when recomputing the centroids and the new membership degrees and can lead to a different clustering result. It's rather difficult to define a globally acceptable value; therefore, a good practice is to start with an average m (for example, 1.5) and perform a grid search (it's possible to sample from a Gaussian or uniform distribution) until the desired accuracy has been achieved.

Minimizing the previous expression is even more difficult than with standard inertia; therefore, a pseudo-Lloyd's algorithm is employed. After a random initialization, the algorithm proceeds, alternating two steps (like an EM procedure) in order to determine the centroids and recomputing the membership degrees to maximize the internal cohesion. The centroids are determined by a weighted average:

$$\bar{\mu}_j = \frac{\sum_{i=1}^{M} w_{ij}^m \, \bar{x}_i}{\sum_{i=1}^{M} w_{ij}^m}$$

Contrary to K-means, the sum is not limited to the points belonging to a specific cluster because the weight factor will force the farthest points ($w_{ij} \approx 0$) to produce a contribution close to 0. At the same time, as this is a soft-clustering algorithm, no exclusions are imposed, to allow a sample to belong to any number of clusters with different membership degrees. Once the centroids have been recomputed, the membership degrees must be updated using this formula:

$$w_{ij} = \frac{1}{\sum_{p=1}^{k} \left(\frac{\|\bar{x}_i - \bar{\mu}_j\|}{\|\bar{x}_i - \bar{\mu}_p\|} \right)^{\frac{2}{m-1}}}$$

This function behaves like a similarity. In fact, when sample x_i is very close to centroid $\bar{\mu}_j$ (and relatively far from $\bar{\mu}_p$ with $p \neq j$), the denominator becomes small and w_{ij} increases. The exponent m directly influences the fuzzy partitioning, because when $m \approx 1 (m > 1)$, the denominator is a sum of quasi-squared terms and the closest centroid can dominate the sum, yielding to a higher preference for a specific cluster. When $m \gg 1$, all the terms in the sum tend to 1, producing a flatter weight distribution with no well-defined preference.

It's important to understand that, even when working with soft clustering, a fuzziness excess leads to inaccurate decisions because there are no factors that push a sample to clearly belong to a specific cluster. This means that the problem is either ill-posed or, for example, the number of expected clusters is too high and doesn't represent the real underlying data structure. A good way to measure how much this algorithm is similar to a hard-clustering approach (such as K-means) is provided by the normalized Dunn's partitioning coefficient:

$$P_C = \frac{w_C - \frac{1}{k}}{1 - \frac{1}{k}} \quad where \quad w_C = \frac{1}{M} \sum_{i=1}^{M} \sum_{j=1}^{k} w_{ij}^2$$

When P_C is bounded between 0 and 1, when it's close to 0, it means that the membership degrees have a flat distribution and the level of fuzziness is the highest possible. On the other hand, if it's close to 1, each row of W has a single dominant value, while all the others are negligible. This scenario resembles a hard-clustering approach. Larger P_C values are normally preferable because, even without allowing a degree of fuzziness, they allow the making of more precise decisions.

Considering the previous example, P_C tends to 1 when the sets don't intersect, while it becomes 0 (complete fuzziness) if, for example, the three seniority levels are chosen to be identical and overlapping. Of course, we are interested in avoiding such extreme scenarios by limiting the number of borderline cases. A grid search can be performed by analyzing different numbers of clusters and m values (in the example, we're going to do this with the MNIST handwritten digit dataset). A reasonable rule of thumb is to accept P_C values higher than 0.8, but in some cases that can be impossible. If we are sure that the problem is well-posed, the best approach is to choose the configuration that maximizes P_C, considering, however, that a final value of less than 0.3 - 0.5 will lead to a very high level of uncertainty because the clusters will overlap extremely.

The complete Fuzzy C-means algorithm is:

1. Set a maximum number of iterations N_{max}
2. Set a tolerance *Thr*
3. Set the value of k (the number of expected clusters)
4. Initialize the matrix $W^{(0)}$ with random values and normalize each row, dividing it by its sum
5. Set $N = 0$
6. While $N < N_{max}$ or $\left\| W^{(t)} - W^{(t-1)} \right\| > Thr$:
    1. $N = N + 1$
    2. For $j = 1$ to k:
        a. Compute the centroid vectors $\bar{\mu}_j$
    3. Recompute the weight matrix $W^{(t)}$
    4. Normalize the rows of $W^{(t)}$

After the theoretical discussion, we can now analyze a concrete example of this algorithm using the scikit-fuzzy Python package, comparing the results with a classical hard-clustering approach.

Example of Fuzzy C-means with SciKit-Fuzzy

SciKit-Fuzzy (http://pythonhosted.org/scikit-fuzzy/) is a Python package based on SciPy (it can be installed using the `pip install -U scikit-fuzzy` command. For further instructions, please visit http://pythonhosted.org/scikit-fuzzy/install.html, which allows you to implement all the most important fuzzy logic algorithms (including fuzzy C-means).

In this example, we'll continue to use the MNIST dataset we used in the previous chapter, but with a major focus on fuzzy partitioning. To perform the clustering, SciKit-Fuzzy implements the `cmeans` method (in the `skfuzzy.cluster` package), which requires a few mandatory parameters: data, which must be an array $D \in \mathbb{R}^{N \times M}$ (N is the number of features; therefore, the array used with scikit-learn must be transposed); c, the number of clusters; the coefficient m, error, which is the maximum tolerance; and `maxiter`, which is the maximum number of iterations. Another useful parameter (not mandatory) is the seed parameter, which allows you to specify the random seed to be able to easily reproduce the experiments. I invite you to check the official documentation for further information.

The first step of this example is performing the clustering:

```
from skfuzzy.cluster import cmeans

fc, W, _, _, _, _, pc = \
    cmeans(X_train.T, c=10, m=1.25,
           error=1e-6, maxiter=10000, seed=1000)
```

The `cmeans` function returns many values, but for our purposes, the most important are: the first one, which is the array containing the cluster centroids; the second one, which is the final membership degree matrix; and the last one, the partition coefficient. In order to analyze the result, we can start with the partition coefficient:

```
print('Partition coeffiecient: {}'.format(pc))
```

The output is:

```
Partition coeffiecient: 0.6320708707346328
```

This value informs us that the clustering is not very far from a hard assignment, but there's still a residual fuzziness. In this particular case, such a situation may be reasonable because we know that many digit images are partially distorted, and may appear very similar to other digits (1, 7, and 9 are easily confused). However, I invite you to try different values for m and check how the partition coefficient changes. We can now display the centroids:

Centroids obtained by Fuzzy C-Means

All the different digit classes have been successfully found, but now, contrary to K-means, we can check the fuzziness of a problematic sample (representing a 7 with index 7), as shown in the following figure:

Sample (a 7) selected to test the fuzziness

The membership degrees associated with the previous sample are:

```
print('Membership degrees: {}'.format(W[:, 7]))
```

The output is:

```
Membership degrees: [0.00373221 0.01850326 0.00361638
                     0.01032591 0.86078292 0.02926149
                     0.03983662 0.00779066 0.01432076
                     0.0118298]
```

The corresponding plot is:

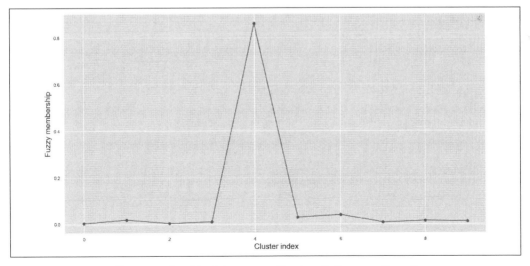

Fuzzy membership plot corresponding to a digit representing a 7

In this case, the choice of m has forced the algorithm to reduce the fuzziness. However, it's still possible to see three smaller peaks corresponding to the clusters centered respectively on the digits 1, 8, and 3 (remember that the cluster indexes – 1, 6, and 8, in this case – correspond to digits shown previously in the centroid plot). I invite you to analyze the fuzzy partitioning of different digits and replot it with different values of the m parameter. It will be possible to observe an increased level of fuzziness (also corresponding to smaller partitioning coefficients) with larger m values. This effect is due to a stronger overlap among clusters (also observable by plotting the centroids) and could be useful when it's necessary to detect the distortion of a sample. In fact, even if the main peak indicates the right cluster, the secondary ones, in descending order, inform us how much the sample is similar to other centroids and, therefore, if it contains features that are characteristics of other subsets.

Contrary to scikit-learn, in order to perform predictions, SciKit-Fuzzy implements the cmeans_predict method (in the same package), which requires the same parameters as cmeans, but instead of the number of clusters, c needs the final centroid array (the name of the parameter is cntr_trained). The function returns as a first value the corresponding membership degree matrix (the other ones are the same as cmeans). In the following snippet, we repeat the prediction for the same sample digit (representing a 7):

```
import numpy as np

from skfuzzy.cluster import cmeans_predict

new_sample = np.expand_dims(X_train[7], axis=1)
Wn, _, _, _, _, _ = \
    cmeans_predict(new_sample, cntr_trained=fc, m=1.25,
                   error=1e-6, maxiter=10000, seed=1000)

print('Membership degrees: {}'.format(Wn.T))
```

The output is:

```
Membership degrees: [[0.00373221 0.01850326 0.00361638
                      0.01032591 0.86078292 0.02926149
                      0.03983662 0.00779066 0.01432076
                      0.0118298]]
```

Spectral clustering

One of the most common problems with K-means and other similar algorithms is the assumption that we only have hyperspherical clusters. In fact, K-means is insensitive to the angle and assigns a label only according to the closest distance between a point and centroids. The resulting geometry is based on hyperspheres where all points share the same condition to be closer to the same centroid. This condition might be acceptable when the dataset is split into blobs that can be easily embedded into a regular geometric structure. However, it fails whenever the sets are not separable using regular shapes. Let's consider, for example, the following bidimensional dataset:

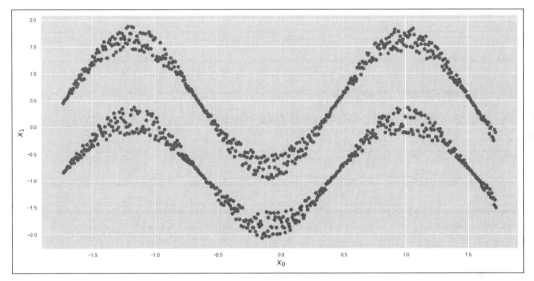

Sinusoidal dataset

As we are going to see in the example, any attempt to separate the upper sinusoid from the lower one using K-means will fail. The reason is obvious: a circle that contains the upper set will also contain part of the (or the whole) lower set. Considering the criterion adopted by K-means and imposing two clusters, the inertia will be minimized by a vertical separation corresponding to about $x_0 = 0$. Therefore, the resulting clusters are completely mixed and only a dimension is contributing to the final configuration. However, the two sinusoidal sets are well-separated and it's not difficult to check that, selecting a point x_i from the lower set, it's always possible to find a ball containing only samples belonging to the same set. We discussed this kind of problem when Label Propagation algorithms were discussed and the logic behind spectral clustering is essentially the same (for further details, I invite you to check out *Chapter 5, Graph-Based Semi-Supervised Learning*).

Let's suppose we have a dataset X sampled from a data generating process p_{data}:

$$X = \{\bar{x}_1, \bar{x}_2, \dots, \bar{x}_M\} \ where \ \bar{x}_i \in \mathbb{R}^N$$

We can build a graph $G = \{V, E\}$, where the vertices are the points and the edges are determined using an affinity matrix W. Each element w_{ij} must express the affinity between the points $\bar{x}_i$ and $\bar{x}_j$. W is normally built using two different approaches:

- **K-Nearest Neighbor (KNN)**: In this case, we can build the number of neighbors to take into account for each point $\bar{x}_i$. W can be built as a connectivity matrix (expressing only the existence of a connection between two samples) if we adopt the criterion:

$$w_{ij} = \begin{cases} 1 \ if \ \bar{x}_j \in neighborhood_k(\bar{x}_i) \\ 0 \ otherwise \end{cases}$$

  Alternatively, it's possible to build a *distance matrix*:

$$w_{ij} = \begin{cases} d(\bar{x}_i, \bar{x}_j) \ if \ \bar{x}_j \in neighborhood_k(\bar{x}_i) \\ 0 \ otherwise \end{cases}$$

- **Radial basis function (RBF)**: The previous methods can lead to graphs that are not fully connected because samples can exist that have no neighbors. In order to obtain a fully connected graph, it's possible to employ an RBF (this approach has also been used in the Kohonen map algorithm, discussed in *Chapter 15, Fundamentals of Ensemble Learning*):

$$w_{ij} = e^{-\gamma \|\bar{x}_i - \bar{x}_j\|^2}$$

  The parameter γ allows you to control the amplitude of the Gaussian function, reducing or increasing the number of samples with a large weight (actual neighbors). However, a weight is assigned to all points and the resulting graph will always be connected (even if many elements are close to zero).

In both cases, the elements of W will represent a measure of affinity (or closeness) between points and no restrictions are imposed on the global geometry (contrary to K-means). In particular, using a KNN connectivity matrix, we are implicitly segmenting the original dataset into smaller regions with a high level of internal cohesion. The problem that we need to solve now is to find out a way to merge all the regions belonging to the same cluster.

The approach we are going to present here has been proposed by Shi and Malik (in Shi J., Malik J., *Normalized Cuts and Image Segmentation*, IEEE Transactions on Pattern Analysis and Machine Intelligence, Vol. 22, 08, 2000), and it's based on the normalized graph Laplacian:

$$L_n = I - D^{-1}W$$

The matrix D, called the degree matrix, is the same as was discussed in *Chapter 5, Graph-Based Semi-Supervised Learning*, and it's defined as:

$$D = diag\left(\left[\sum_j w_{ij}\right] \forall i \in (1, M)\right)$$

It's possible to prove the following properties (the formal proofs are omitted but they can be found in texts such as Gelfand I. M., Glagoleva E. G., Shnol E. E., *Functions and Graphs Vol. 2*, The MIT Press, 1969 or Biyikoglu T., Leydold J., Stadler P. F., *Laplacian Eigenvectors of Graphs*, Springer, 2007):

- The eigenvalues λ_i and the eigenvectors $\bar{v}_i$ of L_n can be found by solving the problem $L\bar{v} = \lambda D\bar{v}$, where L is the unnormalized graph Laplacian $L = D - W$
- L_n always has an eigenvalue equal to 0 (with a multiplicity k) with a corresponding eigenvector $v_0 = (1, 1, \dots, 1)$
- As G is undirected and all $w_{ij} \geq 0$, the number of connected components k of G is equal to the multiplicity of the null eigenvalue

In other words, the normalized graph Laplacian encodes the information about the number of connected components and provides us with a new reference system where the clusters can be separated using regular geometric shapes (normally hyperspheres). To better understand how this approach works without a non-trivial mathematical approach, it's important to expose another property of L_n.

From linear algebra, we know that each eigenvalue λ of a matrix $M \in \mathbb{R}^{n \times n}$ spans a corresponding eigenspace, which is a subset of $\mathbb{R}^n$ containing all eigenvectors associated with λ plus the null vector. Moreover, given a set $S \subseteq \mathbb{R}^n$ and a countable subset C (it's possible to extend the definition to generic subsets but in our context, the datasets are always countable), we can define a vector $\bar{v} \in \mathbb{R}^n$ as an indicator vector, if $\bar{v}^{(i)} = 1$ if the vector $c_i \in S$ and $\bar{v}^{(i)} = 0$ otherwise. If we consider the null eigenvalues of L_n and we assume that their number is k (corresponding to the multiplicity of the eigenvalue 0), it's possible to prove that the corresponding eigenvectors are indicator vectors for eigenspaces spanned by each of them.

From the previous statements, we know that these eigenspaces correspond to the connected components of the graph G; therefore, performing standard clustering (like K-means or K-means++) with the points projected into these subspaces allows easy separation with symmetric shapes.

Since $L_n \in \mathbb{R}^{M \times M}$, its eigenvectors $\bar{v}_i \in \mathbb{R}^M$. Selecting the first k eigenvectors, it's possible to build a matrix $A \in \mathbb{R}^{M \times k}$:

$$A = \begin{pmatrix} v_1^{(1)} & \cdots & v_k^{(1)} \\ \vdots & \ddots & \vdots \\ v_1^{(M)} & \cdots & v_k^{(M)} \end{pmatrix}$$

Each row of A, $\bar{a}_j \in \mathbb{R}^k$, can be considered as the projection of an original point $\bar{x}_j$ in the low-dimensional subspace spanned by the eigenvectors associated with the null eigenvalues of L_n. At this point, the separability of the new dataset $A = \{\bar{a}_j\}$ depends only on the structure of the graph G and, in particular, on the number of neighbors or the γ parameter for RBFs. As in many other similar cases, it's impossible to define a standard value suitable for all problems, above all when the dimensionality doesn't allow a visual inspection. A reasonable approach should start with a small number of neighbors (for example, 5 or 10) or $\gamma = 1.0$ and increase the values until a performance metric (such as the Adjusted Rand Index) reaches its maximum.

Unfortunately, every problem has very specific requirements and it's quite difficult to provide the data scientist with rock-solid default values. All toolkits tend to use intermediate parameter levels, letting the user choose the most appropriate configuration. Considering a KNN scenario, for example, 5, 10, or 100 neighbors could be a reasonable choice if the underlying topology is compatible. It must be clear that a neighborhood should always be relatively small. More precisely, the user can imagine the neighborhood of a point as a building block (indeed, they are employed as bases in topology theory) to construct the overall hypersurface (or manifold) where the dataset lies. Given a metric function, the minimum number of neighbors can be determined considering the sample size S. Values corresponding to 0.1% - 0.5% of S could be good default choices when the density is large enough. On the other hand, excessive granularity might also yield incorrect results due to the large number of connected components.

Another important element to remember is that KNN often leads to non-connected affinity matrices. All the most common libraries can manage numeric instability problems (for example, if the degree matrix has $\det(D) = 0$, it's not invertible and more robust solutions must be employed), but in some particular cases, split graphs could hide relevant information about the structure.

Therefore, you should carefully evaluate the strategy to compute W and check the results when the software outputs warnings about the lack of connectivity (for example, scikit-learn outputs a precise warning, which must always be taken into account).

Considering the nature of the problems, it can also be helpful to measure homogeneity and completeness (discussed in the previous chapter) because these two measures are more sensitive to irregular geometric structures and can easily show when the clustering is not separating the sets correctly. If the ground truth is unknown, the Silhouette score can be employed to assess the intra-cluster cohesion and the inter-cluster separation as functions of all hyperparameters (the number of clusters, the number of neighbors, or γ).

The complete Shi-Malik spectral clustering algorithm is:

1. Select a graph construction method between KNN (1) and RBF (2):
   a. Select parameter k
   b. Select parameter γ

2. Select the expected number of clusters N_K
3. Compute the matrices W and D
4. Compute the normalized graph Laplacian L_n
5. Compute the first k eigenvectors of L_n
6. Build the matrix A

   a. Cluster the rows of A using K-means++ (or any other symmetric algorithm).

The output of this process is this set of clusters: $C_{km}^{(1)}, C_{km}^{(2)}, \dots, C_{km}^{(N_k)}$ At this point, we can create an example using scikit-learn with the goal being to compare the performances of K-means with spectral clustering.

Example of spectral clustering with scikit-learn

In this example, we are going to use the sinusoidal dataset previously shown. The first step is creating it (with 1,000 samples):

```
import numpy as np

from sklearn.preprocessing import StandardScaler
```

```
nb_samples = 1000

X = np.zeros(shape=(nb_samples, 2))

for i in range(nb_samples):
    X[i, 0] = float(i)

    if i % 2 == 0:
        X[i, 1] = 1.0 + (np.random.uniform(0.65, 1.0) *
                        np.sin(float(i) / 100.0))
    else:
        X[i, 1] = 0.1 + (np.random.uniform(0.5, 0.85) *
                        np.sin(float(i) / 100.0))

ss = StandardScaler()
Xs = ss.fit_transform(X)
```

At this point, we can try to cluster it using K-means (with `n_clusters=2`):

```
from sklearn.cluster import KMeans

km = KMeans(n_clusters=2, random_state=1000)
Y_km = km.fit_predict(Xs)
```

The result is shown in the following graph:

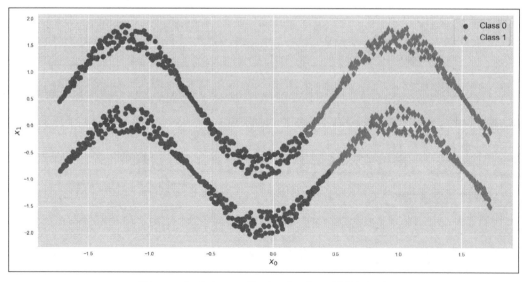

K-means clustering result using the sinusoidal dataset

As expected, K-means isn't able to separate the two sinusoids. You're free to try with different parameters, but the result will always be unacceptable because K-means bidimensional clusters are circles (when working in $\mathbb{R}^n$ they become hyperspheres, but the structural relations remain the same) and no valid configurations exist. It's easy to understand that both completeness and homogeneity are very low because each class contains about 50% of the samples of the other one.

We can now employ spectral clustering using an affinity matrix based on the KNN algorithm (in this case, scikit-learn can produce a warning because the graph is not fully connected, but this normally doesn't affect the results). Scikit-learn implements the `SpectralClustering` class, whose most important parameters are `n_clusters`, the number of expected clusters; affinity, which can be either `rbf` or `nearest_neighbors`; gamma (only for RBF); and `n_neighbors` (only for KNN). For our test, we have chosen to have `20` neighbors:

```
from sklearn.cluster import SpectralClustering

sc = SpectralClustering(n_clusters=2,
                        affinity='nearest_neighbors',
                        n_neighbors=20,
                        random_state=1000)
Y_sc = sc.fit_predict(Xs)
```

The result of the spectral clustering is shown in the following figure:

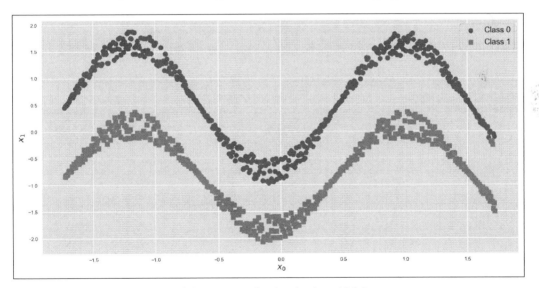

Spectral clustering result using the sinusoidal dataset

As expected, the algorithm was able to separate the two sinusoids perfectly. Even though the scenario is very simple, it perfectly illustrates the advantage of projecting a dataset onto a feature space whenever *standard* separation is not immediately achievable. The computational cost of computing the kernel is proportionate to the approach (RBF can be faster thanks to the parallelism achievable on modern architectures), but in general, there are no specific limitations except for what's already been discussed about KNN. The main *a posteriori* consideration with this algorithm concerns its internal structure. Feature spaces and kernels are very powerful tools, but they always require existing regularity in the geometry. In some cases, this is almost impossible to obtain (even using very complex projections) and, consequently, the results might not be extremely accurate.

As an exercise, I invite you to apply spectral clustering to the MNIST dataset, using both an RBF (with different gamma values) and KNN (with different numbers of neighbors). I also suggest replotting the t-SNE diagram and comparing all the assignment errors. As the clusters are strictly non-convex, we don't expect a high Silhouette score. Other useful exercises are drawing the Silhouette plot and checking the result, assigning ground truth labels, and measuring the homogeneity and completeness. Before moving forward, I'd like to remind you that bidimensional plots of high-dimensional datasets must always be carefully evaluated and, above all, obtained through non-linear dimensionality reduction algorithms (for example, t-SNE or LLE). Plotting two features excluding the remaining ones can yield misleading results where, for example, perfectly separated clusters appear as overlapped or vice versa.

In the next section, we are going to discuss an approach that is completely geometry-free and can segment irregular datasets more effectively than other methods.

DBSCAN

Most of the clustering methods discussed so far are based on assumptions about the geometrical structure of the dataset. For example, K-means can find the centroids of hyperspherical regions, while spectral clustering has less limitations (in particular, using a KNN affinity matrix), but it requires you to know the desired number of clusters and such a choice conditions the result. On the other hand, spectral clustering, as well as **DBSCAN** (which stands for **Density-Based Spatial Clustering of Applications with Noise**), can work with non-convex clusters, while K-means requires such a condition.

DBSCAN is an algorithm proposed by Ester et al. (in Ester M., Kriegel H. P., Sander J., Xu X., *A Density-Based Algorithm for Discovering Clusters in Large Spatial Databases with Noise*, Proceedings of the 2nd International Conference on Knowledge Discovery and Data Mining, AAAI Press, pp. 226-231, 1996) to overcome all these limitations.

The main assumption is that X represents a sample drawn from a multimodal distribution, with some dense areas sufficiently separated from one another by almost empty regions. We just said "sufficiently" because DBSCAN also assumes the presence of noisy points that normally lie on the boundaries and could be assigned to more than one cluster. In these cases, algorithms like K-means force the assignment in both possible scenarios:

- $\exists \bar{\mu}_j : d(\bar{x}_i, \bar{\mu}_j) < d(\bar{x}_i, \bar{\mu}_p) \, \forall p \in (1, 2, j-1, j+1, \dots, k)$. In this case, there is a cluster whose centroid is the closest one and the assignment is straightforward.

- $d(\bar{x}_i, \bar{\mu}_j) = d(\bar{x}_i, \bar{\mu}_p) \, \forall j, p \in (1, k)$. In this case (which is very unlikely), all distances are equal, therefore the algorithm will normally pick the first cluster (even if the choice could also be perfectly random).

Conversely, DBSCAN, which doesn't require you to specify the desired number of clusters, finds all the topological constraints necessary to separate highly dense and cohesive regions from separation regions. The process works by performing classification on each point, followed by a natural aggregation into labeled clusters and noisy points.

Given a point $\bar{x}_i \in X \subseteq \mathbb{R}^n$ and a predefined distance metric (for example, Euclidean), the algorithm determines the set of points belonging to the ball $B_\epsilon(\bar{x}_i) = \{\bar{x} \in \mathbb{R}^n : d(\bar{x}, \bar{x}_i) \leq \epsilon\}$. If $B_\epsilon(\bar{x}_i)$ contains more than n_{min} points (other than $\bar{x}_i$), $\bar{x}_i$ is marked as a core point. All other points $\bar{x} \in B_\epsilon(\bar{x}_i) \cap X$ are marked as *directly density-reachable* from the core point. A directly density-reachable point has the same importance as a core one, because, from a topological viewpoint, the relation is symmetric (that is, the core point becomes directly density-reachable when the ball is centered on the latter).

Let's now consider a sequence of points $\bar{x}_i, \bar{x}_{i+1}, \dots, \bar{x}_t, \dots, \bar{x}_j$. If $\bar{x}_{i+1}$ is directly density-reachable from $\bar{x}_i \, \forall i \in (i+1, j)$, the point $\bar{x}_j$ is marked as *density-reachable* from $\bar{x}_i$.

This concept is weaker than the previous one and it depends both on the radius ϵ and on the number n_{min}. This concept is shown in the following figure:

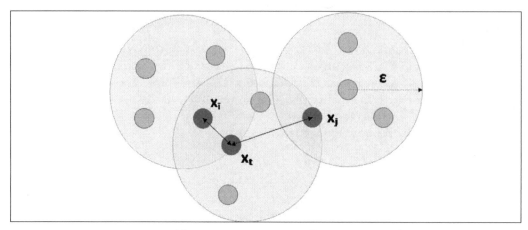

The point $\bar{x}_j$ is density-reachable from $\bar{x}_i$ when $n_{min} \geq 4$

It's easy to verify that $\bar{x}_j$ is density-reachable from $\bar{x}_i$ through the sequence $\bar{x}_i, \bar{x}_t, \bar{x}_j$ when $n_{min} \geq 4$. In fact, with a minimum number of four neighbors, all three points are core ones and each of them is also directly density-reachable from the neighbors, hence, the sequence leads to a density-reachable point.

Given three points $\bar{x}_i, \bar{x}_j, \bar{x}_t \in X$, if both $\bar{x}_i$ and $\bar{x}_j$ are density-reachable from $\bar{x}_k$, they are also marked as *density-connected* through $\bar{x}_k$. Density connection is an even weaker condition and it's not symmetric. In fact, it's possible to find density-connected triplets $\bar{x}_i, \bar{x}_j, \bar{x}_t$ where $\bar{x}_i$ is density-reachable from $\bar{x}_j$ but vice versa doesn't hold. As we move through a sequence in a predefined direction, the connecting point $\bar{x}_t$ can be directly density-reachable (and, therefore, implicitly a core point) only if its neighborhood contains enough points.

If we denote with $N(\cdot)$ the function that counts the number of points belonging to a ball, we can consider a scenario where $N(\bar{x}_i) > n_{min} + k$ and $N(\bar{x}_t) \ll N(\bar{x}_i)$, and it's possible to define $B_\epsilon(\bar{x}_i)$ such that $\bar{x}_t \in B_\epsilon(\bar{x}_i)$. This allows us to establish a density-reachability condition and we can move forward to the next step involving $\bar{x}_t$ and $\bar{x}_j$. Conversely, when $k >> 0$, $N(\bar{x}_t)$ can have less than n_{min} points, the reachability is broken and we cannot move in the direction $\bar{x}_t \to \bar{x}_i$. Density connection is a central concept in DBSCAN and most of the work necessary to tune up the hyperparameters concerns the right choice of both ϵ and n_{min} so as to minimize the number of noisy points and to allow the density-connection of all points that must belong to the same cluster. In fact, the algorithm will define a cluster C_p based on:

- All the couples $(\bar{x}_i, \bar{x}_j) \in X$ that are density-connected
- If $\bar{x}_t \in C_p$, all $\bar{x}_q \in X$ that are density-reachable from $\bar{x}_t$

After finishing this process, all density-reachable points have been assigned to a cluster. The remaining points, which are formally non-density-reachable by any $\bar{x}_i \in X$, are marked as *noisy* and grouped into an additional virtual cluster.

As anticipated, DBSCAN doesn't require any geometrical constraints but rather relies exclusively on the neighbors of each point. This property guarantees the separability of non-convex regions under the mild assumption that they are separated by low-density hypervolumes (as normally happens). For this reason, DBSCAN is particularly suited to spatial applications with many irregularities (for example, geographical or biomedical segmentation). However, it also works perfectly in many scenarios where simpler algorithms fail. The most important element to consider is its computational complexity, which ranges from $O(N \log N)$ to $O(N^2)$ according to the KNN strategy. As the neighbors are normally built using Ball and KD-trees, all considerations discussed in the previous sections are still valid and you should take care when choosing the most appropriate leaf size in order to reduce the number of comparisons and avoid the quadratic complexity (which can be too expensive for large datasets).

Before giving a practical example, it will also be helpful to remind you of the importance of the distance metric chosen for every specific task. When the dataset has high dimensionality, the discriminability of the points can become more difficult using the Minkowski distance with $p \geq 2$. As DBSCAN relies on the ability of the distance function to discover all density-connected chains, a high-dimensional dataset should be carefully evaluated before choosing the optimal clustering algorithm. Moreover, it's useful to consider the results obtained with the Manhattan distance (which is the most sensitive distance function) and compare them with the ones achieved using the default Euclidean distance. In some cases, the extra discriminability is enough to avoid too many noisy points and to detect most of the density-connected chains. Of course, there are no predefined recipes and the role of the data scientists is also to check the results (using appropriate evaluation metrics such as Calinski-Harabasz or Silhouette score) and validate them together with a business-domain expert.

Example of DBSCAN with scikit-learn

In this example, we are going to build a bidimensional dataset representing a territory where each point is a standardized group of buildings. The goal is to find all the agglomerates and categorize them.

Let's start creating the dataset using 11 partially overlapped bivariate Gaussian distributions:

```
import numpy as np
```

```
mus = [[-5, -3], [-5, 3], [-1, -4], [1, -4], [-2, 0],
       [0, 1], [4, 2], [6, 4], [5, 1], [6, -3], [-5, 3]]
Xts = []

for mu in mus:
    n = np.random.randint(100, 1000)
    covm = np.diag(np.random.uniform(0.2, 3.5, size=(2, )))
    Xt = np.random.multivariate_normal(mu, covm,
                                             size=(n, ))
    Xts.append(Xt)

X = np.concatenate(Xts)
```

A plot of the dataset is shown in the following figure:

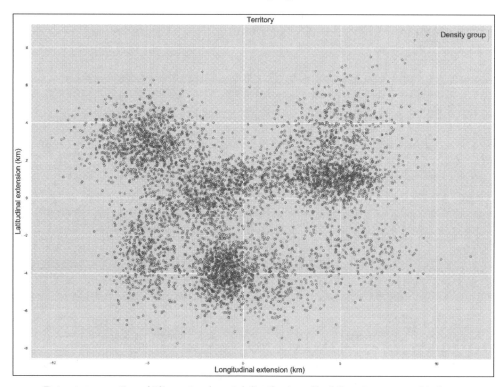

Dataset representing a bidimensional spatial distribution of buildings in a geographical area

As it's possible to see, the dataset represents an area where there are some main centers (large agglomerates), secondary ones (smaller agglomerates), and low-density regions (suburbs). Our goal is to employ DBSCAN to find out the optimal number of clusters representing homogeneous areas.

It should be clear that density-connected points make up intrinsically homogeneous regions because of the topological nature of this property (that is, as the balls have a common radius ϵ, all density-connected regions have the same average density of all sub-regions). However, as we don't know the ground truth, before starting the analysis, it's helpful to introduce two new evaluation measures: the Calinski-Harabasz and Davies-Boulding scores.

The Calinski-Harabasz score

This score doesn't need the ground truth and evaluates the result of a clustering procedure according to the double principle of maximum cohesion and maximum separation. A reasonable clustering result should show a low variance inside the clusters and a high variance between clusters and separation regions. To quantify this property, we need to introduce two supplementary measures.

Let's suppose that the dataset X has been clustered into k clusters identified by their centroids $\bar{\mu}_i \ \forall i \in (1, k)$. The **within-cluster-dispersion (WCD)** is defined as:

$$WCD_k = Tr\left(\sum_{i=1}^{k} \sum_{\bar{x}_j \in C_i} \left(\bar{x}_j - \bar{\mu}_j \right)\left(\bar{x}_j - \bar{\mu}_j \right)^T \right)$$

This measure provides a piece of information about the dispersion of the points assigned to each cluster around their respective centroids. In an ideal scenario, this value should be close to its theoretical minimum, indicating that the algorithm has achieved the maximum possible internal cohesion.

If we introduce the function $N(C_i)$ to count the number of points assigned to C_i and the average global centroid $\bar{\mu}$ (which corresponds to the geometrical center of mass of system containing all $\bar{\mu}_i$), we can also define the **between-cluster-dispersion (BCD)**:

$$BCD_k = Tr\left(\sum_{i=1}^{k} N(C_i)(\bar{\mu}_i - \bar{\mu})(\bar{\mu}_i - \bar{\mu})^T \right)$$

This measure encodes the separation of the clusters. A large BCD_k indicates that the dense regions are relatively far from each other, where the adjective *far* means that their centroids aren't near to the global one. Of course, this measure alone isn't helpful, because a cluster can have very large dispersion even when the centroid is far away, as measured by $\bar{\mu}$.

Therefore, the Calinski-Harabasz score for a dataset containing N points is computed as:

$$CH = \frac{N-k}{k-1} \cdot \frac{BCD_k}{WCD_k}$$

The first factor is a normalization term, while the second one measures the level of separation and cohesion at the same time. The values of CH have no upper bound (even if there's always a theoretical one, given the structure of X), hence, a larger CH indicates a better clustering result ($BCD_k \gg WCD_k \Rightarrow$ large separation and low internal dispersion).

The Davies-Bouldin score

Sometimes it's helpful to evaluate the separation of the clusters more than their internal cohesion. For example, in our case, we are more interested in finding out the agglomerates, even if they can be relatively low-cohesive because of urbanistic regulations.

If we have k clusters $C_i \; \forall i \in (1, k)$, we can start by finding out their diameters, which are proportional to the hypervolume where all possible points can be placed. If C_i is identified by its centroid $\bar{\mu}_i$ and $N(C_i)$ counts the number of points assigned to C_i, the diameter is defined as:

$$d_i = \frac{1}{N(C_i)} \sum_{\bar{x} \in C_i} d(\bar{x}, \bar{\mu}_i)$$

At this point, we can build a pseudo-distance matrix $D \in \mathbb{R}^{k \times k}$, whose elements D_{ij} are defined as $D_{ij} = (d_i + d_j)/d_{ij}$ where $d_{ij} = d(\bar{\mu}_i, \bar{\mu}_j)$. This choice allows us to have a proper distance matrix, where all elements $D_{ij} \geq 0$ and $D_{ij} = D_{ji}$. Every value D_{ij} measures the amount of separation existing between C_i and C_j. In fact, a large D_{ij} means that the sum of diameters is larger than the distance of the centroids, therefore the clusters are partially overlapped. On the contrary, a small D_{ij} implies, in the optimal case, that $d_{ij} > d_i + d_j$, hence the farthest points of both C_i and C_j (which make a greater contribution to the diameters) are separated by an empty region. To better clarify, let's suppose that both diameters are equal to d. We want to be sure that the sum of the two radiuses (each of them equal to $d/2$) is larger than the distance of the centroids. In fact, when $d_{ij} > d$ and assuming the work with convex clusters, there's always, on average, a separation space between C_i and C_j because the two hyperspheres don't intersect.

The Davies-Bouldin score is defined as:

$$DB = \frac{1}{k} \sum_{i=1}^{k} \max_{i \neq j} D_{ij}$$

It's easy to understand that DB quantifies the amount of average separation between clusters with the assumption of working with the maximum possible distance between couples (C_i, C_j). This allows us to have a *worst-case* measure that we need to minimize in order to obtain an optimal result.

At this point, we can evaluate DBSCAN on our geospatial dataset.

Analysis of DBSCAN results

The dataset X contains, on average, 5,000 points spread over a surface of $20 \times 15 = 300 \ km^2$. If we get rid of the units, there are about $5,000 \div 300 \approx 17$ points per square block. As the distribution is uneven, we can reasonably assume that each point must have a neighborhood of at least $\lfloor 17 \div 2 \rfloor = 8$ points. The choice of the radius ϵ is not immediate, therefore we want to employ both the Calinski-Harabasz and Davies-Bouldin scores together with the number of noisy points to find out the optimal configuration assuming $\epsilon \in (0.1, 0.5)$:

```
from sklearn.cluster import DBSCAN
from sklearn.metrics import calinski_harabasz_score
from sklearn.metrics import davies_bouldin_score
import numpy as np

ch = []
db = []
no = []

for e in np.arange(0.1, 0.5, 0.02):
    dbscan = DBSCAN(eps=e, min_samples=8, leaf_size=50)
    Y = dbscan.fit_predict(X)
    ch.append(calinski_harabasz_score(X, Y))
    db.append(davies_bouldin_score(X, Y))
    no.append(np.sum(Y == -1))
```

The resulting diagrams are shown in the following figure:

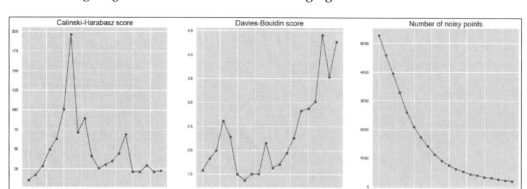

Calinski-Harabasz score (left), Davies-Bouldin score (center), the number of noisy points (right)

Let's start with the number of noisy points. As expected, the function monotonically decreases because larger ϵ values yield less cohesive clusters. However, there are two important considerations. The first one is that we need to assume a moderate number of noisy points because of the geographical structure of the map (that is, there are always suburbs or low-density areas around the centers). The second is that the function has a clear slope reduction in the range (0.2, 0.3). This indicates that, after a threshold, the number of noisy points almost stabilizes to a limit value corresponding to the total number of points that can be incorporated into clusters only when they become extremely overlapped. This is also confirmed by the Davies-Bouldin score, which increases abruptly in the same range. On the other hand, the Calinski-Harabasz score is at a maximum when $\epsilon = 0.2$ and the Davies-Bouldin score is at a minimum at the same value. Therefore, also thanks to the considerations about the noisy points, we can accept $\epsilon = 0.2$ as the optimal value and perform clustering with $n_{min} = 8$ and a leaf size equal to a reasonable value of $N(X) \div 100 = 50$ (however, you can test other values and compare the performance).

```
from sklearn.cluster import DBSCAN

dbscan = DBSCAN(eps=0.2, min_samples=8, leaf_size=50)
Y = dbscan.fit_predict(X)

print("No. clusters: {}".format(np.unique(dbscan.labels_).shape))
print("No. noisy points: {}".format(np.sum(Y == -1)))
print("CH = {}".format(calinski_harabasz_score(X, Y)))
print("DB = {}".format(davies_bouldin_score(X, Y)))
```

The output of the previous snippet is:

```
No. clusters: (54,)
No. noisy points: 2098
CH = 100.91669074221588
DB = 1.4949468861242001
```

DBSCAN has determined 53 clusters (1 label is reserved for noisy points) and 2,098 noisy points (it's important to remember that different random seeds might lead to slightly different results. In this book, we always set it equal to 1,000). This value might appear very large and, in some applications, it's actually unacceptable. However, in our case, noisy points are a valuable resource to identify all low-density regions surrounding the centers, therefore we are going to keep them.

The result of the clustering procedure is shown in the following figure, where the compact dots represent noisy points:

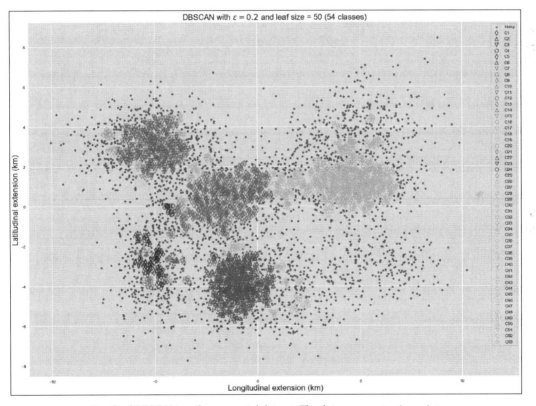

Result of DBSCAN on the geospatial dataset. The dots represent noisy points

It's interesting to notice that DBSCAN successfully identified four dense large areas and a series of smaller ones. Indeed, the blob in the lower-left corner is the least cohesive and, looking at the plot of X, it's possible to see that it corresponds to small areas (for example, towns) very close to each other but always separated by a number of isolated points. Moreover, there are also suburbs (for example, around the top-left cluster), which are dense enough to be considered as smaller clusters. This is also a peculiar property of geographical datasets and we are going to accept them because they are *semantically* valid. Of course, when submitting the results to a domain expert, it's possible to receive a request, for example, to reduce the number of noisy points. We already know that the cost to pay is to have less cohesive clusters. In fact, when $\epsilon \rightarrow 0.5$, it's possible to observe a drastic reduction in the number of clusters, because more and more areas become density-connected and, consequently, aggregated into single blocks.

In these cases, you can show a comparison of the results obtained using different parameter sets (including the metric – the default one is Euclidean) and explain the dynamics of DBSCAN. For instance, it's always possible to include a post-processing step to aggregate the smallest clusters, if they don't represent valid entities. Therefore, it's generally preferable to start with a lower ϵ (tuning up the value of n_{min}), trying to understand which blocks should be merged, instead of working with very large clusters with poor internal cohesion. As an exercise, find optimal configurations that yield less than 10, 20, and 30 clusters and compare the results that motivate the choice according to the structure of X.

Summary

In this chapter, we presented a soft-clustering method called Fuzzy C-means, which resembles the structure of standard K-means but allows managing membership degrees (analogous to probabilities) that encode the similarity of a sample with all cluster centroids. This kind of approach allows the processing of membership vectors in a more complex pipeline, where the output of a clustering process, for example, is fed into a classifier.

One of the most important limitations of K-means and similar algorithms is the symmetric structure of the clusters. This problem can be solved with methods such as spectral clustering, which is a very powerful approach based on the dataset graph and is quite similar to non-linear dimensionality reduction methods. We analyzed an algorithm proposed by Shi and Malik, showing how it can easily separate a non-convex dataset.

We also discussed a completely geometry-agnostic algorithm, DBSCAN, which is helpful when it's necessary to discover all dense regions in a complex dataset, and the Calinski-Harabasz and Davies-Boulding scores, two new evaluation measures.

In the next chapter, *Chapter 8, Clustering and Unsupervised Models for Marketing*, we're going to cover some unsupervised models that are very helpful for market segmentation and recommendations (in particular, biclustering) and to better understand the behavior of customers (Apriori) and suggest products according to their buyer profile.

Further reading

- Aggarwal C. C., Hinneburg A., Keim D. A., *On the Surprising Behavior of Distance Metrics in High Dimensional Space*, ICDT, 2001

- Arthur D., Vassilvitskii S., *The Advantages of Careful Seeding*, k-means++: Proceedings of the Eighteenth Annual ACM-SIAM Symposium on Discrete Algorithms, 2006

- Pedrycz W., Gomide F., *An Introduction to Fuzzy Sets*, The MIT Press, 1998

- Shi J., Malik J., *Normalized Cuts and Image Segmentation*, IEEE Transactions on Pattern Analysis and Machine Intelligence, Vol. 22, 08, 2000

- Gelfand I. M., Glagoleva E. G., Shnol E. E., *Functions and Graphs Vol. 2*, The MIT Press, 1969

- Biyikoglu T., Leydold J., Stadler P. F., *Laplacian Eigenvectors of Graphs*, Springer, 2007

- Ester M., Kriegel H. P., Sander J., Xu X., *A Density-Based Algorithm for Discovering Clusters in Large Spatial Databases with Noise*, Proceedings of the 2nd International Conference on Knowledge Discovery and Data Mining, AAAI Press, pp. 226-231, 1996

- Kluger Y., Basri R., Chang J. T., Gerstein M., *Spectral Biclustering of Microarray Cancer Data: Co-clustering Genes and Conditions*, Genome Research, 13, 2003

- Huang, S., Wang, H., Li, D., Yang, Y., Li, T., *Spectral co-clustering ensemble.* Knowledge-Based Systems, 84, 46-55, 2015

- Bichot, C., *Co-clustering Documents and Words by Minimizing the Normalized Cut Objective Function.* Journal of Mathematical Modelling and Algorithms, 9(2), 131-147, 2010

- Agrawal R., Srikant R., *Fast Algorithms for Mining Association Rules*, Proceedings of the 20th VLDB Conference, 1994

- Li, Y., *The application of Apriori algorithm in the area of association rules.* Proceedings of SPIE, 8878, 88784H-88784H-5, 2013

- Bonaccorso G., *Hands-On Unsupervised Learning with Python*, Packt Publishing, 2019

8
Clustering and Unsupervised Models for Marketing

This chapter is dedicated to two methods that can be extremely helpful in marketing applications. Unsupervised learning has many interesting applications in contexts where it's necessary to structure the knowledge a business has about customers, in order to optimize promotional campaigns, recommendations, or marketing strategies. This chapter shows how it's possible to exploit a particular kind of clustering to find similarities among sets of customers and products, and how to extract logic rules that describe and synthesize the behavior of customers selecting products from a catalog. Using these rules, marketeers can understand how to optimize their promotions, how to rearrange the position of their products, and what other items could be successfully suggested when a purchase is made.

In particular, the algorithms and topics we're going to analyze are:

- Biclustering based on a spectral biclustering algorithm
- An introduction to market basket analysis with the Apriori algorithm

The first algorithm we're going to analyze is a particular kind of clustering that operates on two levels at the same time. In general, these two levels are correlated by the presence of a medium (for example, customers and products can be correlated by a rating) and the goal of biclustering is to find the regions where such a medium is cohesive (for example, the rating is high or low) by rearranging the structure of both levels (or views).

Biclustering

Biclustering is a family of methods that operate on matrices $A \in \mathbb{R}^{n \times m}$ whose rows and columns represent different features connected with a precise rationale. For example, the rows can represent customers, and the columns products. Each element $a_{ij} \in A$ can indicate a rating or, if zero, the fact that a specific product, p_j, has not been bought/rated by the customer, c_i. As the behavior of the customers can generally be segmented into specific sets, we can assume that A has an underlying checkerboard structure, where the compact regions, called biclusters, represent sub-matrices with peculiar properties.

The nature of such properties depends on the specific context, but the structures share the common feature of being strongly separated from the remaining regions. In our example, the biclusters can be mixed segments containing sets of customers and products that agree on the rating (this concept will be clearer in the practical example), but more generally, the rearrangement of rows and columns of A can highlight highly inter-correlated regions that are not immediately detectable.

In this context, we are going to describe an algorithm developed by Kluger et al. (published in Kluger Y., Basri R., Chang J. T., and Gerstein M., *Spectral Biclustering of Microarray Cancer Data: Co-clustering Genes and Conditions*, Genome Research, 13, 2003) called spectral biclustering (the term *co-clustering* is often used as a synonym of biclustering, but it's important to avoid confusion when referring to different algorithms) and initially applied to bioinformatics tasks. The algorithm strongly relies on **Singular Value Decomposition (SVD)**, which will be extensively employed when discussing component analysis and reduction.

The first step, called *bistochatization*, is a preprocessing iterative phase that entails adjusting the values a_{ij} so that all column and row sums become equal to a constant common value (normally 1). The name derives from the definition of a stochastic matrix (in other words, all rows or columns total 1) and the result is therefore to have both A and A^T to be stochastic with respect to the columns. The advantage of this step is to reduce the noise caused, for example, by different scales and to unveil regions characterized by large/small variances.

The bistochastic matrix, A_b, is then decomposed using the SVD (further details will be discussed in *Chapter 13, Component Analysis and Dimensionality Reduction*):

$$\begin{cases} A_b = U \Sigma V^T \\ U \in \mathbb{R}^{m \times m}, V \in \mathbb{R}^{n \times n}, and \ \Sigma \in \text{diagonal}(\mathbb{R}^{n \times n}) \end{cases}$$

The eigenvectors of $A_b A_b^T$ and $A_b^T A_b$ are called, respectively, left and right singular vectors of A_b. The matrix U contains the left singular vectors as columns, while V contains the right singular vectors.

The values on the diagonal of Σ are the singular values, which are the square roots of the eigenvalues of $A_b A_b^T$ (and $A_b^T A_b$). SVD normally sorts the singular values in descending order and the singular vectors are rearranged according to this criterion.

The goal of biclustering is to highlight a checkerboard structure, which can be represented using a particular indicator vector, $\bar{v}_b$, built with a piecewise constant structure, for example:

$$\bar{v}_p = (0, 0, \dots, 0, 1, 1, \dots, 1, \dots, n, n, \dots, n)^T$$

It's not difficult to understand that such a vector is internally split into homogenous components that can represent (in one-dimensional projection) the biclusters we're looking for. The algorithm proceeds by ranking the singular vectors by analyzing their similarity with $\bar{v}_p$ (whose structure also depends on dimensions of the matrix A). If the desired number of biclusters is denoted with k, a projection matrix P_k is built using the top k singular vectors. The dataset (represented by A) is then projected onto the sub-space spanned by the columns of P_k. At this point, the checkerboard structure is easily discoverable because, in the new sub-space, the biclusters are made up of points close to one another (in other words, they make up dense regions separated by empty ones).

To better clarify this concept, let's consider the first column, c_1, of P_k. By definition, it contains the singular vector with the highest similarity to $\bar{v}_p$. After performing the projection, the original first component is rotated so as to overlap c_1. The process is repeated for all the remaining components. In this new reference system, the original points will therefore be associated by coordinates (features) indicating their similarity with respect to a particular bicluster.

The algorithm finishes by applying K-Means to find the labelling for the k clusters. This operation is performed in consideration of both rows and columns, yielding two label vectors, $\bar{r}$ and $\bar{c}$. It's easy to prove (but we are skipping this step) that the rearranged matrix with the checkerboard structure is obtained by applying the outer product to sorted vectors, $\bar{r}_s$ and $\bar{c}_s$ (which are simply the original vectors whose components have been sorted in ascending order):

$$A_c = \bar{r}_s \otimes \bar{c}_s = \begin{pmatrix} \bar{r}_s^{(1)} \\ \vdots \\ \bar{r}_s^{(m)} \end{pmatrix} \cdot \begin{pmatrix} \bar{c}_s^{(1)} & \cdots & \bar{c}_s^{(n)} \end{pmatrix} = \begin{pmatrix} \bar{r}_s^{(1)} \bar{c}_s^{(1)} & \cdots & \bar{r}_s^{(1)} \bar{c}_s^{(n)} \\ \vdots & \ddots & \vdots \\ \bar{r}_s^{(m)} \bar{c}_s^{(1)} & \cdots & \bar{r}_s^{(m)} \bar{c}_s^{(n)} \end{pmatrix}$$

We can now show a complete Python example based on a marketing dataset containing several purchase mixes.

Example of Spectral Biclustering with Scikit-Learn

In this and the following example, we are going to work with a synthetic transaction dataset containing 100 purchase mixes in the form$\{p_i, p_j, ...,p_k\}$ with 100 products and $k \sim U(2, 60)$. The dataset is enriched with a rating matrix $R \in \{0,10\}^{100 \times 100}$, where 0 indicates the absence of a rating and a value $R_{ij} > 0$ is considered an explicit rating. The goal of this example is to use biclustering to find the underlying checkerboard structure.

Let's start creating the dataset:

```python
import numpy as np

nb_users = 100
nb_products = 100

items = [i for i in range(nb_products)]

transactions = []
ratings = np.zeros(shape=(nb_users, nb_products),
                   dtype=np.int)

for i in range(nb_users):
    n_items = np.random.randint(2, 60)
    transaction = tuple(
        np.random.choice(items,
                         replace=False,
                         size=n_items))
    transactions.append(
        list(map(lambda x: "P{}".format(x + 1),
            transaction)))

    for t in transaction:
        rating = np.random.randint(1, 11)
        ratings[i, t] = rating
```

A heatmap of the initial rating matrix is shown in the following diagram:

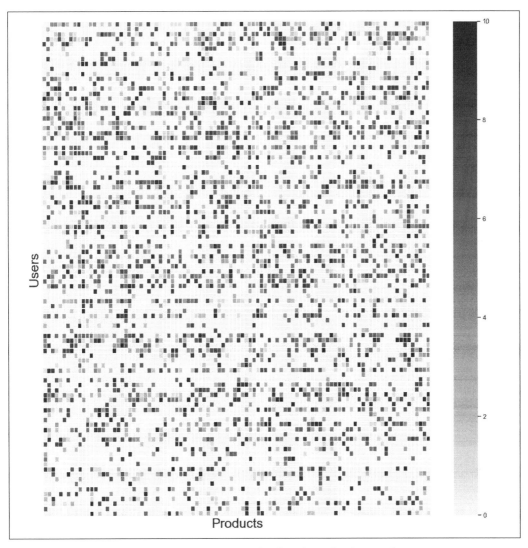

Heatmap of the rating matrix. Black cells indicate the absence of a rating

The matrix is sparse (when the dimensionality is larger, I suggest employing SciPy sparse matrices to save space), but every user has rated at least 2 products, with an approximate average of 30. In this example, we are interested in discovering the segments of user/product mixes characterized by the same rating. As each rating is in the range (1, 10), also considering the non-rating segment, there are 10 different possible biclusters with immediate semantics.

At this point, we can train the model using `n_best=5` to indicate that we want to project the dataset onto the top five singular vectors and `svd_solver="arpack"`, which is a very accurate SVD algorithm suitable for small/medium-sized matrices:

```
from sklearn.cluster.bicluster import SpectralBiclustering

sbc = SpectralBiclustering(n_clusters=10, n_best=5,
                           svd_method="arpack",
                           n_jobs=-1,
                           random_state=1000)
sbc.fit(ratings)

rc = np.outer(np.sort(sbc.row_labels_) + 1,
              np.sort(sbc.column_labels_) + 1)
```

As explained in the theoretical part, the final matrix is computed using the outer product of the sorted row and column indices.

Before showing the final result, we want to demonstrate how to find the mixes. Let's suppose that we are interested in determining the group of users $\{u_i, u_j, ..., u_t\}$ that rated a group of eight products $\{p_i, p_j, ..., p_t\}$ in order to send a periodical newsletter containing tailored recommendations. This operation can be easily achieved by selecting all the rows and columns associated with the biclusters with an index of 8 (remember that 0 corresponds to the absence of a rating):

```
import numpy as np

print("Users: {}".format(
      np.where(sbc.rows_[8, :] == True)))
print("Product: {}".format(
      np.where(sbc.columns_[8, :] == True)))
```

The raw output of the previous snippet (with a random seed set to 1,000) is as follows:

```
Users: (array([30, 35, 40, 54, 61, 86, 87, 91, 94], dtype=int64),)
Product: (array([49, 68, 93], dtype=int64),)
```

Therefore, we can check the family of the products {49, 68, 93}, select some similar items, and send them in the suggestion part of the newsletter to the users {30, 35, 40, 54, 61, 86, 87, 91, 94}. We can now show the final matrix with a checkerboard structure:

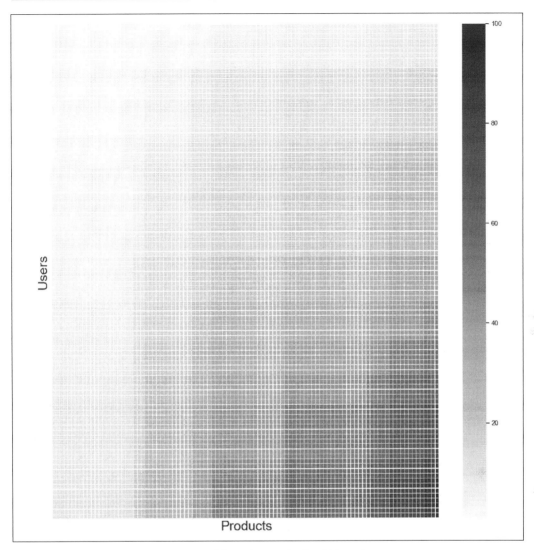

Heatmap of the rating matrix after biclustering

As it's possible to see, the matrix is split into homogeneous regions corresponding to the same rating. In practical applications, it can be helpful to select, for example, the mix corresponding to the ratings $r_{ij} \geq 8$ to recommend similar products, and the mix $\{u_i, r_{ij} < 6\}$ to ask for feedback regarding their negative ratings. I'll leave these two cases as exercises for the reader.

After this discussion about biclustering, let's now analyze a simple but effective way to perform market basket analysis and find association rules given a set of transactions.

Introduction to Market Basket Analysis with the Apriori Algorithm

In the previous example, we analyzed the ratings provided by different customers in order to perform mixed segmentation. However, sometimes, a company only has complete knowledge about the set of products bought by its customers. More formally, given a set $P = \{p_1, p_2, ..., p_n\}$ of products, a transaction, T_i, is a subset of P:

$$P \supseteq T_i = \{p_i, p_j, ..., p_k\}$$

A collection of transactions (often called a database) is a set of subsets, T_i:

$$C = \{T_1, T_2, ..., T_p\}$$

The main goal of market basket analysis is to mine all existing association rules that can be expressed in the generic form:

$$if \ (p_i, p_j, ..., p_k) \in T_g \Rightarrow P(p_t) > \pi$$

To avoid confusion, the previous expression means that, given a transaction containing a set of items, the probability of finding the item p_t is greater than a discriminant threshold, π (for example, 0.75). The value of this process is straightforward because a company can optimize its offers based on the evidence provided by the actual transactions. For example, a retailer can discover that customers buying a specific smartphone model also buy a case and, consequently, can create ad hoc offers and attract more customers.

Unfortunately, the number of all possible transactions, N_T, is equal to the cardinality of the power set of P. If we limit ourselves to the presence/absence of an item, $N_T = 2^n$, this can easily lead to intractable problems (for example, if there are just 1,000 products, N_T is a number with more than 300 digits). For this reason, Agrawal and Srikant (in Agrawal R., Srikant R., *Fast Algorithms for Mining Association Rules*, Proceedings of the 20th VLDB Conference, 1994) proposed an algorithm, called Apriori, whose goal is to allow the mining of relatively large datasets in a reasonable time (considering that the paper was published in 1994, the reader can easily imagine how simple this process is nowadays).

Given a discrete probability distribution over a set D the region $G \subseteq D$ where $P(x) > 0 \; \forall \; x \in G$ is called support of the distribution. Given a generic rule, $A \Rightarrow B$, its probabilistic confidence is the ratio between the support of $P(A, B)$ and the support of $P(A)$. We are going to employ and further analyze these concepts later, when defining the strategy adopted by this algorithm.

The main assumption of the Apriori algorithm is that only a small portion of the probability space with $P(\cdot) > 0$ (in other words, the support of $P \; S(P) \ll N_T$). In particular, when working with large datasets, the number of valid combinations is a very small fraction of the power set, therefore it doesn't make sense trying to model the full joint probability distribution.

As we are working with discrete variables, the support of an item p_i or of an item set $\{p_i, p_j, \dots, p_k\}$ can be computed with a frequency count. Given the maximum number of items in a transaction, Apriori starts computing the support of all products $S(p_i)$ and removing all the items with $S(p_i) < \tau$ (with $\tau > 0$). Indeed, we are not very interested in products that are seldom sold. Therefore, the first selection can be considered as a zoom into the region where all the most common transactions are located. Apriori proceeds by analyzing all couples, triplets, and so on and applying the same filter. The results of each pass are item sets that can be split into disjointed subsets to make up the association rules. For example:

$$\{p_i, p_j, \dots, p_k\} \Rightarrow if \; \{p_i, p_j\} \; then \; \{p_t, \dots, p_k\}$$

The rules have the standard format of logical implications, $A \Rightarrow B$, where A is the antecedent and A is the consequent. Of course, it must be clear that, while in propositional logic, the previous expression is deterministic, in market basket analysis, it's always probabilistic. Therefore, it's helpful to introduce a measure to evaluate the validity of each rule. Continuing with a logical approach, we can extend the concept of modus ponens, which states that:

$$if \; A \Rightarrow B \; and \; A \; is \; true, B \; is \; also \; true$$

In a probabilistic scenario, we are interested in quantifying how frequently the consequent is true when the whole rule is true. In other words, given the support of the original item set (before the split) $S(I)$ and, assuming that I has been split into $\{A, B\}$, a common measure is the confidence of a rule $C(I)$ (often represented as an item set):

$$C(I) = \frac{S(I)}{S(A)}$$

This value can always be computed as the threshold $\tau > 0$; therefore, neither the numerator nor the denominator can be null. If the rule always applies, $S(A) = S(I)$ and $C(I) = 1$, while all other values in the range $(0, 1)$ indicate increasingly infrequent rules. As the confidence is immediate to compute (all the data is already available during the steps), Apriori enables the setting of another threshold, excluding all those rules where $C(I) < \gamma$ (with $\gamma \in (0,1)$).

The algorithm is extremely simple and effective, but there are some evident drawbacks. The most problematic one is the necessity of setting large thresholds when the datasets are very large. In fact, most modern B2C companies have millions of users who are interested in small portions of items. The application of a vanilla Apriori algorithm might exclude a large number of custom rules that are valid for specific customers. Therefore, in all these cases, it's preferable to perform an initial segmentation of the customers and then apply Apriori to each subset of transactions. Another feasible strategy is based on a process of transaction generalization, which consists of transforming a transaction, T_i, in a particular feature vector containing dummy products that also represent large subsets of items:

$$T_i = \{p_i, p_j, ..., p_k\} \Rightarrow \{f_1, f_2, ..., f_m\}$$

The elements f_i are not real products, but rather classes that contain similar items. This method has the advantage of allowing fast recommendations based on the joint support of the rules or, in a more advanced scenario, on the joint subset of the last k rules activated by the transactions (in other words, the last product bought by the customer has higher priority than the ones present in non-recent transactions).

Example of Apriori in Python

We can now employ the `efficient-apriori` Python library (available on `https://pypi.org/project/efficient-apriori/` and installable by using the `pip install -U efficient-apriori` command) to mine the transaction dataset created in the previous example and detect all the rules with a maximum length equal to 3. As the dataset is quite small, we are going to set `min_support` = `0.15`, but we want to be sure to find reliable rules, hence the minimum confidence is set equal to `0.75`. We have also set the parameter `verbosity=1` to show the messages throughout the learning process:

```
from efficient_apriori import apriori

_, rules = apriori(transactions,
                   min_support=0.15,
                   min_confidence=0.75,
                   max_length=3,
                   verbosity=1)
```

The output of the previous snippet is:

```
Generating itemsets.
 Counting itemsets of length 1.
  Found 100 candidate itemsets of length 1.
  Found 100 large itemsets of length 1.
 Counting itemsets of length 2.
  Found 4950 candidate itemsets of length 2.
  Found 1156 large itemsets of length 2.
 Counting itemsets of length 3.
  Found 6774 candidate itemsets of length 3.
  Found 9 large itemsets of length 3.
Itemset generation terminated.


Generating rules from itemsets.
 Generating rules of size 2.
 Generating rules of size 3.
Rule generation terminated.
```

The reader can immediately identify the steps described in the theoretical part. In particular, the algorithm proceeds by defining the item sets (starting from a length of 1 and ending with the desired limit) and filtering out the elements with support below the minimum threshold (0.15). Let's now check the rules that have been found:

```
print("No. rules: {}".format(len(rules)))

for r in rules:
print(r)
```

The output is as follows:

```
No. rules: 22
{P31, P79} -> {P100} (conf: 0.789, supp: 0.150, lift: 2.024, conv: 2.897)
{P100, P79} -> {P31} (conf: 0.789, supp: 0.150, lift: 2.134, conv: 2.992)
{P66, P68} -> {P100} (conf: 0.789, supp: 0.150, lift: 2.024, conv: 2.897)
{P100, P68} -> {P66} (conf: 0.750, supp: 0.150, lift: 2.419, conv: 2.760)
{P11, P97} -> {P55} (conf: 0.750, supp: 0.150, lift: 2.143, conv: 2.600)
{P11, P55} -> {P97} (conf: 0.789, supp: 0.150, lift: 2.024, conv: 2.897)
{P21, P7} -> {P15} (conf: 0.789, supp: 0.150, lift: 2.134, conv: 2.992)
{P15, P7} -> {P21} (conf: 0.750, supp: 0.150, lift: 2.206, conv: 2.640)
```

```
{P15, P21} -> {P7}  (conf: 0.750, supp: 0.150, lift: 2.027, conv: 2.520)
{P46, P83} -> {P15} (conf: 0.789, supp: 0.150, lift: 2.134, conv: 2.992)
{P15, P83} -> {P46} (conf: 0.750, supp: 0.150, lift: 1.974, conv: 2.480)
{P15, P46} -> {P83} (conf: 0.789, supp: 0.150, lift: 2.322, conv: 3.135)
{P59, P65} -> {P15} (conf: 0.750, supp: 0.150, lift: 2.027, conv: 2.520)
{P15, P65} -> {P59} (conf: 0.789, supp: 0.150, lift: 2.078, conv: 2.945)
{P55, P68} -> {P36} (conf: 0.750, supp: 0.150, lift: 2.419, conv: 2.760)
{P36, P68} -> {P55} (conf: 0.789, supp: 0.150, lift: 2.256, conv: 3.087)
{P36, P55} -> {P68} (conf: 0.789, supp: 0.150, lift: 2.024, conv: 2.897)
{P4, P97} -> {P55}  (conf: 0.842, supp: 0.160, lift: 2.406, conv: 4.117)
{P4, P55} -> {P97}  (conf: 0.800, supp: 0.160, lift: 2.051, conv: 3.050)
{P56, P79} -> {P47} (conf: 0.762, supp: 0.160, lift: 2.116, conv: 2.688)
{P47, P79} -> {P56} (conf: 0.842, supp: 0.160, lift: 2.216, conv: 3.927)
{P47, P56} -> {P79} (conf: 0.842, supp: 0.160, lift: 2.477, conv: 4.180)
```

Hence, Apriori found 22 rules of length 2. The confidence ranges between (0.75, 0.84), while the support is always close to 0.15 (this is due to the cardinality of the dataset). The high confidence is helpful in excluding all the rules with a low probability. However, high confidence is not always enough to understand whether the rule is based on a large or small number of transactions.

As it's possible to see, after the support, the algorithm outputs a value called lift, which is defined as:

$$L(I) = \frac{C(I)}{S(B)} = \frac{S(I)}{S(A)S(B)}$$

This index is proportional to the ratio between the joint probability of the rule (in other words, $P(I) \sim S(I)$) and the product of the probabilities of the antecedent and consequent (in other words, $P(A)P(B) \sim S(A)S(B)$). The ratio $\frac{L(I)}{C(I)} = S(B)^{-1}$; therefore, taking into account that $S(B) \in (0,1)$ and $S(B)^{-1} \in (1, \infty)$, the lift will always be greater than or equal to the confidence. Moreover, as $C(I) = L(I)S(B)$, for a fixed confidence, the smaller $S(B)$ is, the larger $L(I)$ must be. Ideally, we'd like to have a lift equal to 1, indicating that all transactions contain the element(s) in B. In real cases, this is almost impossible; hence, the lift is generally greater than 1.

For example, for a rule with $C(I) = 0.75$ and $L(I) = 2$, the support of the consequent is $S(B) = \frac{0.75}{2} = 0.375$. In our example, all consequents contain a single value (which is the standard choice for market basket analysis).

Therefore, it's extremely easy to associate the lift with the probability of finding the product in a random transaction. In most real cases, a lift in the range (1.5, 2.5) is quite reasonable, while rules with, for example, a lift corresponding to $S(B) < 0.05$ cannot be considered solid enough to be trusted even if the confidence is large.

On the other hand, a support $S(B)$ close to 1 is associated with a trivial rule, because most of the transactions contain that product (for example, a convenience store could have accidently included the shopping bags in the transactions, and therefore their lift is often close to 1, but it doesn't make sense to recommend them). The optimal threshold for lift depends on the context and, contrary to confidence, it is better to define an interval because low and high values are both negative indicators for all affected rules.

For example, a B2C company could set up two sections of their newsletter. In the first one, they could include products with a large confidence ($C(I) > 0.8$) and a lift close to 2 (which normally corresponds to $S(B) \approx 0.5$). These recommendations are confirmed by a large number of customers. Therefore, there's a high conversion probability. Instead, in the second section, it's possible to include products with a smaller $S(B)$ (in other words, a larger lift) that have been selected by a niche group of customers.

Summary

In this chapter, we introduced two algorithms that are very helpful in marketing scenarios. Biclustering is a method for performing clustering on a matrix dataset with two different views correlated by a medium factor. The model facilitates the discovery of the checkerboard structure of such a dataset and can be employed whenever it's helpful to discover segments of elements (for example, customers or products) that share the same medium factor. A classic application is the creation of recommender systems that can immediately identify the similarities existing between a group of customers and products and help marketeers to provide suggestions with a high conversion likelihood.

Apriori is an efficient solution for performing market basket analysis on large transaction datasets. It enables discovery of the most important association rules existing in the dataset so as to plan optimal marketing strategies. Classical applications are product segmentation, promotion planning, and, in some cases, logistic planning, too. In fact, the algorithm can be applied to any kind of transactional dataset and, whenever it's helpful, it's also possible to rearrange the position of the items (generically speaking) so as to minimize the time necessary to complete the most important transactions.

In the next chapter, *Chapter 10, Introduction to Time-Series Analysis*, we're going to introduce the reader to the concepts of generalized linear models and time series, focusing attention on the main techniques and models that can be employed to implement complex scenarios.

Further reading

- Aggarwal C. C., Hinneburg A., Keim D. A., *On the Surprising Behavior of Distance Metrics in High Dimensional Space*, ICDT, 2001

- Arthur D., Vassilvitskii S., The Advantages of Careful Seeding, k-means++. *Proceedings of the Eighteenth Annual ACM-SIAM Symposium on Discrete Algorithms*, 2006

- Pedrycz W., Gomide F., *An Introduction to Fuzzy Sets*, The MIT Press, 1998

- Shi J., Malik J., *Normalized Cuts and Image Segmentation*, IEEE Transactions on Pattern Analysis and Machine Intelligence, Vol. 22, 08, 2000

- Gelfand I. M., Glagoleva E. G., Shnol E. E., *Functions and Graphs*, Vol. 2, The MIT Press, 1969

- Biyikoglu T., Leydold J., Stadler P. F., *Laplacian Eigenvectors of Graphs*, Springer, 2007

- Ester M., Kriegel H. P., Sander J., Xu X., *A Density-Based Algorithm for Discovering Clusters in Large Spatial Databases with Noise*. Proceedings of the 2nd International Conference on Knowledge Discovery and Data Mining, AAAI Press, pp. 226-231, 1996

- Kluger Y., Basri R., Chang J. T., Gerstein M., *Spectral Biclustering of Microarray Cancer Data: Co-clustering Genes and Conditions*, Genome Research, 13, 2003

- Huang, S., Wang, H., Li, D., Yang, Y., Li, T., *Spectral Co-clustering Ensemble*. Knowledge-Based Systems, 84, 46-55, 2015

- Bichot, C., *Co-clustering Documents and Words by Minimizing the Normalized Cut Objective Function*. Journal of Mathematical Modelling and Algorithms, 9(2), 131-147, 2010

- Agrawal R., Srikant R., *Fast Algorithms for Mining Association Rules*, Proceedings of the 20th VLDB Conference, 1994

- Li, Y., *The application of the apriori algorithm in the area of association rules*. Proceedings of the SPIE, 8878, 88784H-88784H-5, 2013

- Bonaccorso G., *Hands-On Unsupervised Learning with Python*, Packt Publishing, 2019

9

Generalized Linear Models and Regression

In this chapter, we're going to introduce the concept of **Generalized Linear Models (GLMs)** and regression, which remain essential pillars of topics such as econometrics and epidemiology. The goal is to explain the fundamental elements and expand them, showing both the advantages and limitations, while also focusing attention on practical applications that can be effectively solved using different kind of regression techniques.

In particular, we're going to discuss the following:

- GLMs
- Linear regression based on ordinary and weighted least squares
- Other regression techniques and when to use them, including:
    - Ridge regression and its implementation
    - Polynomial regression with coded examples
    - Isotonic regression
    - Risk modeling with lasso and logistic regression

The first concept we're going to discuss is at the center of all the other algorithms analyzed in this chapter, and which is based on the description of a dependent variable as a linear combination of different predictors. More formally, this concept is known as the GLM.

GLMs

Let's start our analysis of regression models by defining the context we're working with. A regression is a model that associates an input vector, $\bar{x} \in \mathbb{R}^m$, with one or more continuous dependent variables (for simplicity, we're going to refer to single outputs), $y \in \mathbb{R}$. In a general scenario, there's no explicit dependence on time, even if regression models are often employed to model time series. The main difference is that, in the latter, the order of the data points cannot be changed, because there are often inter-dependencies. On the other hand, a generic regression can be used to model time-independent phenomena, and, in the context of GLMs, we're initially assuming that we work with stateless associations where the output value depends only on the input vector. In such cases, it's also possible to shuffle the dataset without changing the final result (of course, this is not true if the output at time t depends, for example, on y_{t-1}, which is a function of $\bar{x}_{t-1}$, and so on).

Imagine having a dataset, $X \in \mathbb{R}^{N \times m}$, containing N m-dimensional observations drawn from the same data generating process, p_{data}. Each observation is associated with the corresponding continuous label contained in $Y \in \mathbb{R}^N$. A GLM models the relationship between y and $\bar{x}$ as:

$$y = \bar{\theta}^T \cdot \bar{x} + \bar{\epsilon} \quad where \quad \bar{\epsilon} \sim N(0, \Sigma)$$

The $\bar{x}$ values are called regressors, and we say that y has been regressed on the $\bar{x}$ set of variables. The noise term models the intrinsic uncertainty of a specific phenomenon and it's a fundamental element that cannot be discarded unless the relationship is purely linear (in other words, all the points $\bar{x}$ lie on the same hyperplane). However, there are two possible scenarios associated with the noise term, $\bar{\epsilon}$, which we always considered as conditioned to X for example, $E[\bar{\epsilon}|X] = 0$, while we generally don't know the value of $E[\bar{\epsilon}]$). This means that we can never estimate the moments of the noise directly, but always through the conditioning on an input sample.

Thanks to the Central Limit Theorem, we're generally allowed to model the noise using a normal distribution. The mean can be kept equal to 0 because other values only indicate a shift, but the covariance matrix, Σ, can assume two different forms:

$$\Sigma = E[\bar{\epsilon}_i \, \bar{\epsilon}_j | X] = \begin{cases} \sigma^2 I \\ Q \quad diagonal \, pos. def. with \, Q_{ii} \neq Q_{jj} \end{cases}$$

We have excluded the third case of a generic positive definite matrix because we assume that we have non-autocorrelated noise, $E[\bar{\epsilon}_i \, \bar{\epsilon}_j | X] = 0 \, \forall \, i \neq j$ (in other words, every regressor is affected by an *autonomous* noise component, which has no dependences on the other terms, which is a quite reasonable assumption in the majority of cases). If $\Sigma = \sigma^2 I$, the noise is called *homoscedastic*.

In this case, all the input variables are affected by noise with the same variance; therefore, we're often implicitly assuming that they all have the same scale. When this condition is not met, the effect of the noise will be different according to the scale of each regressor, $\bar{x}_i$. Therefore, it's important to pay attention to the structure of X before training a model and, if necessary, proceed by standardizing the variables.

Instead, if Σ is a generic, diagonal positive definite matrix (in other words, $\bar{v}^T \Sigma \bar{v} > 0 \; \forall \; \bar{v} \in \mathbb{R}^m$ and, moreover, all eigenvalues are positive), the noise is called *heteroscedastic* and every component can have its own variance. In the next sections, we're going to show the solutions in both cases, but, for simplicity, many results will refer to the homoscedastic case.

Least Squares Estimation

The simplest way to estimate the parameter vector $\bar{\theta}$ is based on the **Ordinary Least Squares (OLS)** procedure. The estimation, $\tilde{y}_i$, associated with the input vector, $\bar{x}_i$ also depends on the noise term, which is unknown. Therefore, we need to consider the expected value:

$$\tilde{y}_i = E[y_i | \bar{x}_i] = E[\bar{\theta} \cdot \bar{x}_i + \bar{\epsilon} | \bar{x}_i] = E[\bar{\theta} \cdot \bar{x}_i | \bar{x}_i] + E[\bar{\epsilon} | \bar{x}_i] = E[\bar{\theta} \cdot \bar{x}_i | \bar{x}_i]$$

The last term contains the estimation of the true parameter vector given the presence of noise. Just for simplicity, we're continuing to denote the estimation with $\bar{\theta}$, but it must be clear that the actual value is unknown. Therefore, we can write the following:

$$\tilde{y}_i = \bar{\theta} \cdot \bar{x}_i \;\; (\bar{\theta} \; etimated)$$

At this point, we can compute the square error for the entire training set:

$$L = \sum_{i=1}^{N} (y_i - \tilde{y}_i)^2 = \sum_{i=1}^{N} (y_i - \bar{\theta} \cdot \bar{x}_i)^2$$

It's obvious that the estimation of the noise is immediately transformed into the concept of *residual*, which is defined as:

$$e_i = y_i - \bar{\theta} \cdot \bar{x}_i$$

Again, I need to warn the reader about the meaning of e_i. This is not $\bar{\epsilon}_i$ because we're using an estimation of the true parameter vector; however, it's a good proxy of the true noise and, without loss of generality, we're going to consider it as the main disturbance component of our model.

Using a vectorial notation, we can rewrite the expression of L as:

$$L = (Y - X \cdot \bar{\theta})^T (Y - X \cdot \bar{\theta}) = Y^T Y + \bar{\theta}^T \cdot X^T X \cdot \bar{\theta} - 2Y^T X \cdot \bar{\theta}$$

The first derivative is equal to:

$$\frac{\partial L}{\partial \bar{\theta}} = 2X^T X \cdot \bar{\theta} - 2X^T Y$$

While the second derivative is as follows:

$$\frac{\partial^2 L}{\partial \bar{\theta} \partial \bar{\theta}^T} = 2X^T X$$

It's easy to see that the first derivative vanishes when $\bar{\theta} = (X^T X)^{-1} X^T Y$. Moreover, as we're looking for a minimum, $X^T X$ must be a positive definite matrix. The latter is one of the fundamental assumptions of GLMs. We're going to discuss it later, but for now, suffice to say that $X^T X$ must be invertible. Therefore, the determinant must be not null. This is always possible if the dataset X has full rank (with respect to the columns). If $rank(X) = m$, the regressors are linearly independent and $X^T X$ has no columns or rows that are proportional to other ones (a condition that leads to $\det(X^T X) = 0$). In fact, let's consider a simple model with two variables and two observations: $y = ax_1 + bx_2$. The matrix X is:

$$X = \begin{pmatrix} x_{11} & x_{12} \\ x_{21} & x_{22} \end{pmatrix}$$

Hence, $X^T X$ becomes:

$$X^T X = \begin{pmatrix} x_{11} & x_{21} \\ x_{12} & x_{22} \end{pmatrix} \begin{pmatrix} x_{11} & x_{12} \\ x_{21} & x_{22} \end{pmatrix} = \begin{pmatrix} x_{11}^2 + x_{21}^2 & x_{11}x_{12} + x_{21}x_{22} \\ x_{12}x_{11} + x_{22}x_{21} & x_{12}^2 + x_{22}^2 \end{pmatrix}$$

If $x_2 = kx_1$, $X^T X$ becomes:

$$X^T X = \begin{pmatrix} (1+k^2)x_{11}^2 & (1+k^2)x_{11}x_{12} \\ (1+k^2)x_{12}x_{11} & (1+k^2)x_{12}^2 \end{pmatrix} = (1+k^2) \begin{pmatrix} x_{11}^2 & x_{11}x_{12} \\ x_{12}x_{11} & x_{12}^2 \end{pmatrix}$$

Therefore, $\det(X^T X) = (1 + k^2)(x_{11}^2 x_{12}^2 - x_{11}^2 x_{12}^2) = 0$ and, consequently, $X^T X$ is not invertible. This principle is valid for any dimensionality and represents a problem that requires the maximum attention. We're going to discuss it when analyzing regularization techniques.

In the previous discussion, we assumed we were working with homoscedastic noise (in other words, $\Sigma = \sigma^2 I$). In case of heteroscedastic noise, expressed as $\Sigma = \sigma^2 Q$, the estimation of the parameter vector is very similar but it's necessary to employ a **Weighted Least Squares** (**WLS**) procedure. In this case, the cost function becomes:

$$L = (Y - X \cdot \bar{\theta})^T Q^{-1}(Y - X \cdot \bar{\theta})$$

Following the same method, we obtain the optimal estimation:

$$\bar{\theta} = (X^T Q^{-1} X)^{-1} X^T Q^{-1} Y$$

The matrix Q is assumed to be positive definite, and therefore always invertible.

A very instructive way to visualize a linear regression is based on an orthogonal decomposition, assuming that $\bar{y}_i$ is a vectorial output with m components. Let's start by expressing the regression as $\bar{y}_i = \tilde{y}_i + \bar{e}_i$. The residual can be computed using the parameter estimation: $\bar{e}_i = \bar{y}_i - X(X^T X)^{-1}X^T \bar{y}_i = (I - X(X^T X)^{-1}X^T)\bar{y}_i$.

Therefore, after substituting the different expressions, we obtain the following:

$$\bar{y}_i = \tilde{y}_i + \bar{e}_i = X(X^T X)^{-1}X^T \bar{y}_i + (I - X(X^T X)^{-1}X^T)\bar{y}_i$$

The previous expression can be written in a more compact form:

$$\bar{y}_i = P\bar{y}_i + E\bar{y}_i$$

To draw our conclusions, we need to analyze the nature of both matrices P and E. First, we can note that:

$$PE = X(X^T X)^{-1}X^T(I - X(X^T X)^{-1}X^T) = X(X^T X)^{-1}X^T - X(X^T X)^{-1}(X^T X)(X^T X)^{-1}X^T$$
$$= X(X^T X)^{-1}X^T - X(X^T X)^{-1}X^T = 0$$

The same result holds for the product EP. Therefore, the matrices are orthogonal. If we now look at the matrix, E, we can notice that $EX = 0$, in fact:

$$EX = (I - X(X^T X)^{-1}X^T)X = X - X(X^T X)^{-1}(X^T X) = X - X = 0$$

Hence, the residuals are orthogonal to the subspace where the input vectors, $\bar{x}$, lie. Moreover, considering the decomposition, $\bar{y}_i = P\bar{y}_i + E\bar{y}_i$, the vector $\bar{y}_i$ is decomposed into a component orthogonal to X (in other words, the residual) and one (the estimation) that must lie on X (since P and E are orthogonal). This result is shown for a bidimensional space X in the following diagram:

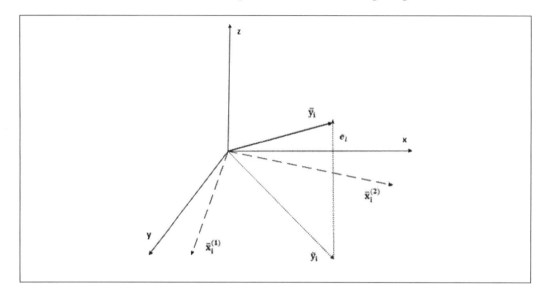

Decomposition of the regression into residual and estimated output vectors

Using this decomposition, it's possible to create a more comprehensible representation of the dynamics of a linear regression. The estimated output vector is a linear combination of $\bar{x}_i$, hence it lies on the same subspace of X. The original point, $\bar{y}_i$ requires an additional dimension, which is covered using the residual. Clearly, if $e_i = 0$, the target vectors, $\bar{y}_i$ are already linear combinations of the regressors (for example, with a single variable, all the points lie on a straight line) and there's no need for any regression. Therefore, in any realistic scenario, the extra dimension is a necessary and irreducible condition to describe the dispersion of the points around the mean.

Bias and Variance of Least Squares Estimators

Least squares estimators are extremely simple to obtain, and they don't even require an actual training procedure because there exists a closed-form formula. However, what can we say about their bias and variance?

Without proving the results (I leave all the steps to the reader as an exercise), the parameter vector estimation (to avoid confusion, we're denoting it with $\tilde{\theta}$) obtained using the least squares algorithm has the following properties:

$$\begin{cases} E[\tilde{\theta}] = \bar{\theta} \\ Var[\tilde{\theta}] = \sigma^2(X^TX)^{-1} \end{cases}$$

Hence, the estimation is unbiased and, thanks to the *Gauss-Markov Theorem*, it's also the **Best Unbiased Linear Estimation** (**BLUE**) achievable among all linear models. This implies that the variance, $\sigma^2(X^TX)^{-1}$, cannot be smaller than this value when the dependent variable is expressed as a linear combination of the regressors. To have a usable estimation of the variance, we need to know σ^2, which is generally unknown. The unbiased estimation for t degrees of freedom (number of parameters) is:

$$\tilde{\sigma}^2 = \frac{\left(Y - \tilde{\theta}^T \cdot X\right)^T \left(Y - \tilde{\theta}^T \cdot X\right)}{N - t}$$

Therefore, we can conclude by saying that the conditional distribution of the estimated parameter vector is normal:

$$\left(\tilde{\theta}|X\right) \sim N(\bar{\theta}, \tilde{\sigma}^2(X^TX)^{-1})$$

When discussing the assumptions, we have said that the matrix, X^TX, must have full rank. We can now add another important requirement because we want our estimator to be also *asymptotically consistent*. In other words, we want larger samples to improve the estimations. It's possible to prove that when the sequence of $(X_N^TX_N)^{-1}$ always has full rank, the sample covariance matrix, $\tilde{\sigma}^2$, converges in probability to σ^2, hence:

$$EVar[\tilde{\theta}] = \tilde{\sigma}^2(X^TX)^{-1}$$

In the previous formula, *EVar* indicates the estimation of the covariance. This result is extremely important because it provides us with the assurance that a more informative sample will always bring a positive contribution to the estimation, but, at the same, it states that there's a lower bound for the variance that cannot be overcome.

Example of Linear regression with Python

Let's begin by showing the results obtained previously with a simple example based on a one-dimensional dataset, X, containing 100 points:

```
import numpy as np

x_ = np.expand_dims(np.arange(0, 10, 0.1), axis=1)
y_ = 0.8*x_ + np.random.normal(0.0, 0.75, size=x_.shape)
x = np.concatenate([x_, np.ones_like(x_)], axis=1)
```

The reader can notice that we have added a column to X containing $(1, 1, …, 1)$ (in other words, each point is represented by $\bar{x}_t = (x_i, 1)$). The reason is that we also want to fit the intercept (the constant term). Packages such as scikit-learn do this by default and allow this option to be disabled, but, as we're initially going to perform manual calculations, it's helpful to include the constant column.

The estimation of the parameter set can be obtained as:

```
theta = (np.linalg.inv(x.T @ x) @ x.T) @ y_
```

Therefore, the fitted model is represented by the following equation:

```
print("y = {:.2f} + {:.2f}x".
        format(theta[1, 0], theta[0, 0]))
```

The output of the previous snippet is:

```
y = -0.04 + 0.82x
```

The true slope is 0.8 and the intercept is null. Therefore, the estimator is perfectly valid, the mean $E[\tilde{\theta}] = (0, 0.8)$, while the variance (excluding the intercept) can be computed as:

```
sigma2 = (1. / float(x_.shape[0] - 1)) * \
    np.sum(np.power(np.squeeze(y_) -   np.squeeze(x_) *
    theta[0, 0], 2))
variance = np.squeeze(
    np.linalg.inv(x_.T @ x_) * sigma2)
```

Hence, the asymptotic distribution of the parameter set (without the intercept) is:

```
print("theta ~ N(0.8, {:.5f})".
        format(variance))
```

The output is as follows:

```
theta ~ N(0.8, 0.00019)
```

The variance is very small. Hence, we expect an optimal fit considering the limits of a linear model. The result, together with the original dataset, is shown in the following diagram:

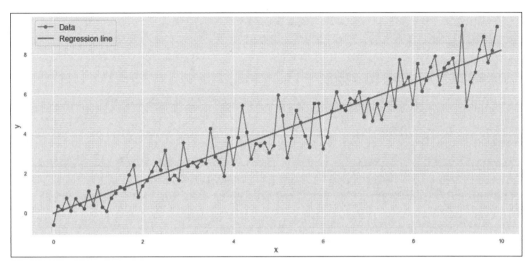

Dataset and regression line

We have voluntarily chosen a noisy dataset to show the effect of the residuals on the final estimation. In particular, we're interested in measuring the quality of the estimation to compare it with other linear regressions based, for example, on larger sample sizes. A common measure is the R^2 coefficient (also known as the *coefficient of determination*), which is defined as:

$$R^2 = 1 - \frac{SSR}{SST} = 1 - \frac{\sum_{i=1}^{N}(y_i - \tilde{y}_i)^2}{\sum_{i=1}^{N}(y_i - Mean[Y])^2}$$

The term SSR is the residual sum of squares and corresponds to the variation due to the prediction. Instead, the term SST is a property of Y and measures the total variation present in the original dataset. The difference, $SST - SSR$, corresponds to the variation that the model is able to explain. Therefore, when $R^2 \to 0$, $SSR \approx SST$. As the model is linear, the only way to achieve this condition is to have no variation from the mean in Y. When $R^2 \in (0,1)$, its value is proportional to a relative goodness of fit. In fact, if $R^2 \to 1$, $SSR \to 0$, and hence, the model is able to explain all the variations. However, $R^2 = 1$ is generally meaningless because it implies $y_i = \tilde{y}_i \; \forall \; i$ and, again, this is only possible when the points are aligned and the noise is null (a condition that clearly doesn't require any regression).

Another problem concerns a peculiar characteristic of R^2 (that we're in the process here of proving, but the interested reader can check Greene W. H., *Econometric Analysis (Fifth Edition)*, Prentice Hall, 2002): it can never decrease and it's possible to obtain larger values by adding new regressors. In fact, by adding new regressors, the fit improves and the bias decreases. Clearly, this is a bad practice that is helpful to penalize; hence, an *adjusted version* has been proposed:

$$AR^2 = 1 - \frac{N-1}{N-t}(1 - R^2)$$

This new measure (which is equivalent to R^2 when $t = 1$) is no longer bounded between 0 and 1 and takes into account the degrees of freedom, t, of the model. Moreover, when $N >> 1$ and $t << N$, $AR^2 \approx R^2$. Therefore, AR^2 becomes helpful when working with small datasets and large numbers of predictors. For example, if a model has achieved $R^2 = 0.9$ with 100 data points and 10 regressors, $AR^2 = 1 - \left(\frac{99}{90}\right)0.1 = 0.89$. This value is very close to R^2 and, generally, it's always less than it. Hence, the penalization becomes evident in rare cases, but it's always possible to employ it instead of R^2 in order to also consider the complexity of the model.

For our example, we can compute the R^2 coefficient as:

```
sst = np.sum(np.power(np.squeeze(y_) -
                      np.mean(y_), 2))
ssr = np.sum(np.power(np.squeeze(y_) -
                      np.squeeze(x_) * theta[0, 0], 2))

print("R^2 = {:.3f}".format(1 - ssr / sst))
```

The output (excluding the intercept) is:

```
R^2 = 0.899
```

In this case, we have excluded the intercept because it's equal to 0 and its contribution is null. However, in general, R^2 and AR^2 must always be computed while including the intercept, otherwise the values might become meaningless and unpredictable. We're omitting a full explanation, but it's a consequence of the algebraic derivation of the coefficients. However, it's not difficult to understand that the effect of the intercept is to shift the hyperplane along an axis (for example, in a bidimensional scenario, the line is shifted upward or backward), therefore *Mean[Y]* can be larger or smaller than the value corresponding to a null intercept, and *SSR* may represent a biased measure of the residual variation if the estimation term assumes a null intercept.

Returning to our example, the R^2 value we obtained is definitely acceptable and confirms the goodness of fit. However, the missing 10% is also a signal that the noise term is not negligible, and some residuals have a large relative magnitude. As this is a linear model and it's unbiased, there's nothing to do to improve the performances. However, the evaluation of R^2 must be considered as a decisional tool. If the value is too small (for example, $R^2 \leq 0.5$), the accuracy of the model (in terms of mean square or absolute error) is probably unacceptable and a non-linear solution must be employed. On the other hand, a large R^2, as explained, is not necessarily associated with a perfect model, but at least we have the guarantee that it explains a large percentage of the variations contained in the dataset.

Computing Linear regression Confidence Intervals with Statsmodels

When fitting a linear model using OLS, it's often helpful to estimate the confidence intervals for each parameter. Before showing you how to do it, I'd like to remind you that a confidence interval is defined as a range where the probability to find the true parameter value is greater or equal to a predefined threshold (for example, 95%), while the opposite statement is false (in other words, the probability that the estimation lies in the interval).

The procedure is very simple and depends mainly on the sample size. Given an estimated parameter, $\tilde{\theta}$, corresponding to the true value, θ (for simplicity, let's consider a scalar parameter), we know that $(\tilde{\theta}|X) \sim N(\theta, \tilde{\sigma}^2(X^TX)^{-1})$. Hence, we can define the associated z-score as:

$$z = \frac{\tilde{\theta} - \theta}{\sqrt{\sigma^2 D}} \text{ where } D \text{ is the diagonal element of } (X^TX)^{-1} \text{ corresponding to } \tilde{\theta}$$

The new variable, z, is normally distributed, and the 95% confidence interval for θ is:

$$P\left(\theta \in \left[\tilde{\theta} \pm 1.96\sqrt{\sigma^2 D}\right]\right) = 0.95$$

The previous well-known formula is valid only when the sample size is large enough to justify the normality assumption (the reader is advised not to take it for granted) and, in most cases, it provides accurate estimations. However, when N is small, the conditions for the Central Limit Theorem no longer hold and the z-score becomes distributed according to a t-student distribution with N - t degrees of freedom (t is equal to the number of free parameters, including the intercept).

Therefore, the β double-tailed confidence interval becomes:

$$P\left(\theta \in \left[\tilde{\theta} \pm t_{N-t}^{\beta/2}\sqrt{\sigma^2 D}\right]\right) = \beta$$

Computing such intervals manually is very easy. However, I prefer to show how to employ Statsmodels (which we're going to use also for other algorithms) to fit the model and to obtain a complete summary.

Let's start by creating a pandas DataFrame using the previously defined dataset, which simplifies the operations:

```
import pandas as pd

df = pd.DataFrame(data=np.concatenate((x_, y_), axis=1),
                  columns=("x", "y"))
```

We have excluded the intercept because Statsmodels includes it automatically. Hence, we want to fit the linear model:

$$y = a + bx + \epsilon$$

Using the standard R formula language supported by Statsmodels (through Patsy, which is a library that implements R-like formulas), the previous condition is expressed as:

$$y \sim x$$

In this case, the equals sign is transformed into $\sim$, which means that the left-hand side is the dependent part of a relation, while the right-hand side contains all the independent variables. A complete discussion about the formula language is beyond the scope of this book (it can be found in the official Patsy documentation). However, it's important to remember that the character + doesn't mean an arithmetic addition. It allows variables to be added to the dependent set and it also supports complex expressions based on NumPy (for example, $y \sim np.power(x, 2) + x$ for a quadratic regression).

We can now fit an OLS model and print a complete summary:

```
import statsmodels.formula.api as smf

slr = smf.ols("y ~ x", data=df)
r = slr.fit()

print(r.summary())
```

The output of the previous snippet is shown in the following diagram:

```
                            OLS Regression Results
==============================================================================
Dep. Variable:                      y   R-squared:                       0.900
Model:                            OLS   Adj. R-squared:                  0.899
Method:                 Least Squares   F-statistic:                     879.1
Date:                Sat, 14 Sep 2019   Prob (F-statistic):           9.78e-51
Time:                        09:42:00   Log-Likelihood:                -118.02
No. Observations:                 100   AIC:                             240.0
Df Residuals:                      98   BIC:                             245.3
Df Model:                           1
Covariance Type:            nonrobust
==============================================================================
                 coef    std err          t      P>|t|      [0.025      0.975]
------------------------------------------------------------------------------
Intercept      -0.0427      0.158     -0.270      0.787      -0.356       0.271
x               0.8173      0.028     29.650      0.000       0.763       0.872
==============================================================================
Omnibus:                        0.798   Durbin-Watson:                   2.145
Prob(Omnibus):                  0.671   Jarque-Bera (JB):                0.484
Skew:                           0.161   Prob(JB):                        0.785
Kurtosis:                       3.115   Cond. No.                         11.6
==============================================================================

Warnings:
[1] Standard Errors assume that the covariance matrix of the errors is correctly specified.
```

Statsmodels fit summary for an OLS

The summary is extremely detailed (some measures will be discussed in the following chapters), but it's helpful to focus attention on the central block containing the estimation of the parameters. As expected, the standard error is larger for the intercept than for the coefficient, x. The reason is that the strong noise impacts more on the vertical shift, but doesn't affect the slope too much (if the sample size is large enough). The confidence intervals are shown in the last two columns. Again, the true coefficient has 95% probability to be in the range (0.763, 0.872), which we know contains the actual true value (0.8) and has a mean equal to about 0.817, corresponding to the estimation.

On the contrary, the confidence interval for the intercept is much larger and, even if the estimation is correct (≈ 0), it informs us that a small noise variation could lead to a vertical shift. By way of an exercise, I invite the reader to change the noise distribution and check the corresponding variations in both standard errors and confidence intervals.

Increasing the robustness to outliers with Huber loss

Hitherto, we've implicitly assumed that our datasets don't contain any outliers. This is equivalent to saying that the estimated covariance matrix reflects the actual noise included in the model and no other external noise sources are allowed. However, in reality, many samples contain points that are affected by an unpredicted noise (for example, the instruments are temporarily out of order). Unfortunately, the least squares algorithm cannot distinguish between inliers and outliers and, moreover, the quadratic loss naturally gives a stronger weight to larger residuals, paradoxically increasing the importance of outliers.

A solution to this problem is provided by the Huber loss function, which is a valid replacement for the mean square error. It is defined as:

$$L = \begin{cases} \frac{1}{2}\left\|Y - \tilde{\theta}^T \cdot X\right\|_2^2 & \forall\, y: \; \left\|y - \tilde{\theta}^T \cdot X\right\|_1 \le \epsilon \\ \epsilon\left\|Y - \tilde{\theta}^T \cdot X\right\|_1 - \frac{1}{2}\epsilon^2 & otherwise \end{cases}$$

This loss function has a double behavior. When the absolute residual is less than a predefined threshold, $\epsilon > 1$, the loss is quadratic, just like in OLS. However, if the absolute residual is larger than ϵ, the point is considered as a potential outlier and the loss becomes linear, reducing the weight of the error. In this way, the outliers close to the inliers provide a stronger contribution than the ones that are very far from the remaining population and, consequently, are more likely to be spurious data points. The optimal value for the constant ϵ depends on the specific dataset. A simple strategy is to select the largest value that minimizes the **mean absolute error (MAE)** (for example, starting with a baseline of 1.5, the model is fitted, and the MAE is computed. The process is repeated by reducing ϵ until the MAE stabilizes to its minimum).

Now we can test the Huber loss function, with an altered version of the previously defined dataset:

```
x = np.expand_dims(np.arange(0, 10, 0.1), axis=1)
y = 0.8 * x + np.random.normal(0.0, 0.75, size=x.shape)
y[65:75] *= 5.0
```

This dataset has a systematic error that affects the points in the index range (65, 75). As we're not fully aware if they are either inliers or outliers, let's start by fitting a linear regression and evaluating the MAE (of course, we cannot employ R^2, as it is strongly influenced by the unexplained variation due to the outliers – in this case, such a variation does not have to be explained!):

```
from sklearn.linear_model import LinearRegression
from sklearn.metrics import mean_absolute_error
lr = LinearRegression()
lr.fit(x, y)


print("Linear: {:.2f}".
      format(mean_absolute_error(y, lr.predict(x))))
```

The output of the previous snippet is:

Linear: 3.66

If we analyze the distribution of the first 50 data points, assuming that a linear fit has a null intercept with a coefficient equal to 0.8, we obtain:

```
print("Mean Y[0:50] = {:.2f}".
      format(np.mean(y[0:50] - 0.8*x[0:50])))
print("Std Y[0:50] = {:.2f}".
      format(np.std(y[0:50] - 0.8*x[0:50])))
```

The output is as follows:

Mean Y[0:50] = 0.01

Std Y[0:50] = 0.63

Hence, assuming a null mean, all values outside the range ($\theta x \pm 1.2$) can be considered as outliers because, after two standard deviations, the probability drops below 5% (under a normal distribution). Hence, we can set $\epsilon = 1.2$ and train a Huber regressor:

```
from sklearn.linear_model import HuberRegressor


hr = HuberRegressor(epsilon=1.2)
hr.fit(x, y.ravel())


print("Huber: {:.2f}".
      format(mean_absolute_error(y, hr.predict(x))))
```

The output is now:

```
Huber: 2.65
```

Therefore, the Huber regressor has reduced the MAE by about 72%, increasing the robustness to outliers. A visual confirmation is shown in the following diagram:

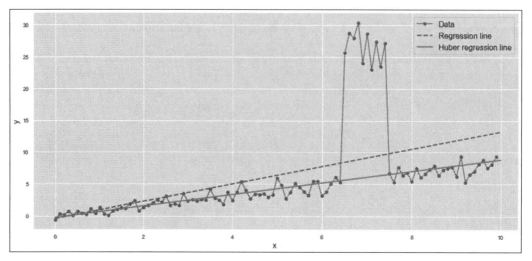

Comparison between standard linear regression and Huber regression

The diagram shows how negative the effect of the outliers might become when a simple linear regression is employed. Conversely, Huber loss keeps the regression line very close to the mean, with a minimum attraction by points that are about 10 times larger than the surrounding ones. Of course, the effect of ϵ is determinant; therefore, I invite the reader to repeat the exercise, changing this value and finding out the optimal trade-off when the set of outliers is larger.

Before moving on, it's helpful to remind ourselves how much R^2 can become dangerous when used without awareness. In this case, its value is larger for the linear regression because SSR is smaller when the slope gets closer to the outliers. The reason is simple: SSR is a quadratic measure, and 10 outliers whose magnitudes average 30 make a contribution that can easily overcome those of 70 inliers with an average equal to 5. In real-life cases, when the datasets are too complex to immediately identify the outliers, I suggest preprocessing the features using robust scaling. This will not affect the results, but avoids a situation where *hidden* outliers lead the model to a completely incorrect estimation.

Other regression techniques

A brief introduction to following regression techniques comes next, and why you may prefer to use them in comparison to least squares. In this section, we'll cover:

- Ridge regression, with a practical example in scikit-learn
- Lasso and logistic regression
- Polynomial regression with examples
- Isotonic regression

One of the most common problems with linear regression is the ill-conditioning that causes instabilities in the solution. Ridge regression has been introduced to overcome this problem.

Ridge Regression

A very common problem in regression models arises as a result of the structure of $X^T X$. We have previously shown that the presence of multi-collinearities forces $\det(X^T X) \to 0$, and this implies that the inversion becomes extremely problematic. A simple way to check the presence of multi-collinearities is based on the computation of the *condition number* of $X^T X$ (with normalized columns with a length equal to 1), defined as:

$$\kappa(X^T X) = \frac{\sigma_{max}(X^T X)}{\sigma_{min}(X^T X)}$$

In the previous formula, $\sigma_{max}(X^T X)$ and $\sigma_{min}(X^T X)$ are the largest and smallest singular values of $X^T X$, respectively. As $X^T X$ is positive definite, its eigenvalues, λ_i, are positive and the singular values, which are equal to $\sqrt{\lambda_i}$, are always defined. A small $\kappa(X^T X)$ is associated with a well-conditioned problem, hence the inversion is not problematic. On the contrary, when $\kappa(X^T X) > 15$, the problem is ill-posed, and the result can change dramatically following small variations in X.

A very simple and effective way to solve this problem is to employ a ridge (or Tikhonov) regularization, based on the L_2 norm of the parameter vector. Considering homoscedastic noise, the least-squares cost function becomes equal to:

$$L = (Y - X \cdot \bar{\theta})^T (Y - X \cdot \bar{\theta}) + \alpha \|\bar{\theta}\|_2 = (Y - X \cdot \bar{\theta})^T (Y - X \cdot \bar{\theta}) + \alpha \bar{\theta}^2 \bar{\theta}$$

The parameter α determines the strength of the regularization and its role is immediately clear when considering the solution:

$$\bar{\theta} = (X^T X + \alpha I)^{-1} X^T Y$$

In the context of a ridge regression, we need to invert $X^T X + \alpha I$, which can be made non-singular even when $X^T X$ is singular. Moreover, as α is added to all diagonal elements, the resulting coefficients will be shrunk (the first term is like the denominator in a division). The larger α is, the larger the amount of shrinkage obtained. As discussed in *Chapter 1*, *Machine Learning Models Fundamentals*, ridge regularization plays a fundamental role in preventing overfitting, but, in the context of linear regression, its main effect is to bias the model in order to lower the variance. We explained the concept of bias-variance trade-off earlier in this chapter, and this is a clear example of its necessity. Moreover, since $X^T X$ is proportional to the covariance matrix, $Cov[X]$, and α is constant, its effect will be stronger on low-variance components. Therefore, ridge performs a minimal feature selection by shrinking the coefficients more when they're associated with less explicative features.

Example of Ridge Regression with scikit-learn

Let's now employ scikit-learn to evaluate the effect of ridge regression with the Diabetes dataset included in scikit-learn. The dataset contains 442 observations of male and female diabetic patients with information about age, **body-mass index (BMI)**, and different blood pressure measures (average and 6 additional measures). The output is a numeric indicator regarding the progression of the disease. Without any further information, we can assume that the entries represent different patients and time is not included (for example, a different dataset might contain multiple entries for the same patients corresponding to different time periods). Hence, we want to check whether a linear regression can successfully fit the data.

The first step is to load the data and compute the condition number (the columns are already normalized):

```
import numpy as np

from sklearn.datasets import load_diabetes

data = load_diabetes()
```

```
X = data['data']
Y = data['target']

XTX = np.linalg.inv(X.T @ X)
print("k = {:.2f}".format(np.linalg.cond(XTX)))
```

The output of the previous snippet is:

```
k = 470.09
```

This value is extremely large, and indicates the presence of multi-collinearity. For our purposes, this result could be enough to proceed using a ridge regression, but as we want to perform a complete investigation, we want also to compute the Pearson correlation coefficients between the features. The elements of the resulting matrix, $R \in \mathbb{R}^{m \times m}$, are as follows:

$$R_{ij} = \frac{\sum_{k=1}^{N}(\bar{x}_k^{(i)} - Mean[\bar{x}^{(i)}])(\bar{x}_k^{(j)} - Mean[\bar{x}^{(j)}])}{\sqrt{\left(\sum_{k=1}^{N}\left(\bar{x}_k^{(i)} - Mean[\bar{x}^{(i)}]\right)^2\right)\left(\sum_{k=1}^{N}\left(\bar{x}_k^{(j)} - Mean[\bar{x}^{(j)}]\right)^2\right)}}$$

Every coefficient $R_{ij} \in (-1, 1)$ with a clear meaning:

- If the ith feature of X is positively correlated with the jth feature of X, $R_{ij} > 0$.
- Analogously, if the ith feature of X is negatively correlated with the jth feature of X, $R_{ij} > 0$.
- $R_{ij} = 0$ if the two features are completely uncorrelated.

Of course, when the absolute value $| R_{ij} |$ is close to 1, we can conclude that two features are correlated, and the problem is consequently ill-posed. A reasonable threshold depends on the specific context. However, a value $| R_{ij} | > 0.5$ should be considered carefully.

To have a better insight, let's compute the correlation matrix:

```
cm = np.corrcoef(X.T)
```

The output as a heatmap is shown in the following diagram:

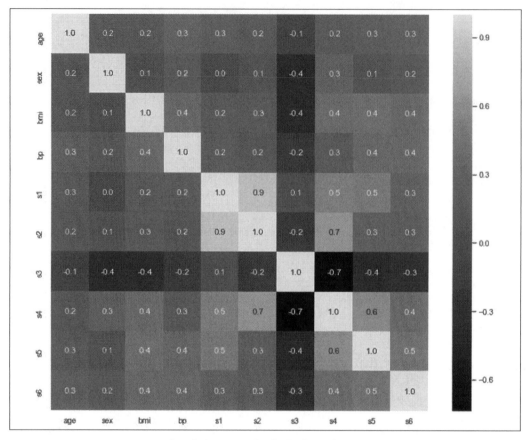

Correlation matrix for the Diabetes dataset

It should be noted immediately that there are different large correlations, in particular, between blood pressure values (this is not surprising, considering that these patients monitor their blood pressure regularly). At this point, we can decide to proceed in different ways:

- Evaluating a ridge regression
- Removing the correlated features (keeping only one of the members of each couple)
- Choosing another regression strategy

As we're going to see, a simple linear regression is not very effective. Therefore, it's necessary to adopt a more complex method. However, it's helpful to evaluate the benefits of employing an L_2 penalty.

As a first step, let's perform CV using the `RidgeCV` class and the default R^2 score to find the optimal α coefficient in the range $(0.1, 1.0)$:

```
from sklearn.linear_model import RidgeCV

rcv = RidgeCV(alphas=np.arange(0.1, 1.0, 0.01),
              normalize=True)
rcv.fit(X, Y)

print("Alpha: {:.2f}".format(rcv.alpha_))
```

The output of the previous snippet is:

```
Alpha: 0.10
```

The CV grid search established that the smallest α yields the best R^2 score. However, we know that ridge regression exacerbates the bias; therefore, we can check the condition number corresponding, for example, to $\alpha = \{0.1, 0.25, 0.5\}$:

```
print("k(0.1): {:.2f}".format(
        np.linalg.cond(X.T @ X +
                      0.1 * np.eye(X.shape[1]))))
print("k(0.25): {:.2f}".format(
        np.linalg.cond(X.T @ X +
                      0.25 * np.eye(X.shape[1]))))
print("k(0.5): {:.2f}".format(
        np.linalg.cond(X.T @ X +
                      0.5 * np.eye(X.shape[1]))))
```

The output is as follows:

```
k(0.1): 37.99
k(0.25): 16.53
k(0.5): 8.90
```

The condition numbers are definitely much better than before. As the value corresponding to $\alpha = 0.25$ is a good trade-off between penalization (in other words, bias) and variance, we can pick this choice instead of 0.1 and evaluate the ridge regression using both R^2 and the MAE:

```
from sklearn.linear_model import Ridge
from sklearn.metrics import r2_score, mean_absolute_error

lrr = Ridge(alpha=0.25, normalize=True,
            random_state=1000)
lrr.fit(X, Y)
```

```
print("R2 = {:.2f}".format(
        r2_score(Y, lrr.predict(X))))
print("MAE = {:.2f}".format(
        mean_absolute_error(Y, lrr.predict(X))))
```

The output is as follows:

```
R2 = 0.50
MAE = 44.26
```

Unfortunately, the performances are not excellent. In particular, the output Y has $Mean[Y] \approx 152$ and $Std[Y] \approx 77$. Therefore, an MAE equal to about 44 could be problematic. The R^2 score confirms that the regression is able to explain only a fraction of total variation and, moreover, different parameter choices yield minimum changes. Therefore, this is a good point when introducing a trick that brings the power of non-linear models to GLMs given a sufficiently large sample size.

Risk modeling with Lasso and Logistic Regression

Ridge regression produces a global parameter shrinkage, but, as shown in *Chapter 1, Machine Learning Models Fundamentals*, the constraint surface is a hypersphere centered at the origin. Independent from the dimensionality, it is smooth, and this prevents the parameters from becoming null.

On the other hand, an L_1 penalty has the advantage of performing an automatic feature selection, because the smallest weights are pushed toward an edge of the constraint hypercube. Lasso regression is formally equivalent to ridge, but it employs L_1 instead of L_2:

$$L = (Y - X \cdot \bar{\theta})^T (Y - X \cdot \bar{\theta}) + \alpha \|\bar{\theta}\|_1$$

The parameter α controls the strength of the regularization, which, in this case, corresponds to the percentage of parameters that are forced to become equal to zero. Lasso regression shares many of the properties of ridge, but its main application is feature selection. In particular, given that a linear model has a large number of parameters, we can consider the association:

$$effect \sim cause_1 + cause_2 + \cdots + cause_m$$

When $m \gg 1$ and all coefficients are different from zero, it's quite difficult to understand which causes are dominant and whether some contributions cancel out one another. Such a situation leads the model to be poorly explainable and, consequently, less helpful in contexts (for example, healthcare) where a study of the causes is necessary. Lasso regression helps to solve this problem without the need for any external intervention. In fact, one simple strategy might be manually removing some features that a domain expert considers secondary or not correlated to the effect. However, this operation can be long and prone to become biased by human beliefs. Automatic feature selection, on the other hand, acts on the single parameters without any prior piece of information and it's much easier to check whether the result is reasonable from a domain viewpoint because the parameter set is much smaller.

In this example, we want to employ a lasso logistic regression to model a risk, establishing also the dominant factors. Before discussing the application, let's recap the main ideas behind logistic regression. Suppose that we have a binary random variable describing the risk we want to model (the outcome *risk* = 1 indicates the presence of a risk and, analogously, *risk* = 0 indicates the absence of a risk). The algorithm is based on the linear description of the logit, which is the logarithm of the odd ratio:

$$log\left(\frac{P(risk=1)}{P(risk=0)}\right) = log\left(\frac{P(risk=1)}{1-P(risk=1)}\right) = logit(risk) = \bar{\theta}^T \cdot \bar{x}$$

The logit must be non-negative and monotonically increasing. A function that satisfies this requirement is the sigmoid, $\sigma(\bar{x})$. In fact, modeling $P(risk=1)$ with $\sigma(\bar{x})$, which is defined on $\mathbb{R}$ and whose values $\sigma(\bar{x}) \in (0,1)$, we obtain the following:

$$P(risk=1) = \sigma(\bar{x}) = \frac{1}{1+e^{-\bar{\theta}^T \cdot \bar{x}}}$$

Manipulating the logit expression, we get the required confirmation:

$$log\left(\frac{P(risk=1)}{1-P(risk=1)}\right) = log\left(\frac{\frac{1}{1+e^{-\bar{\theta}^T \cdot \bar{x}}}}{1-\frac{1}{1+e^{-\bar{\theta}^T \cdot \bar{x}}}}\right) = log\left(\frac{1}{e^{-\bar{\theta}^T \cdot \bar{x}}}\right) = \bar{\theta}^T \cdot \bar{x}$$

If we assume that all data points are i.i.d, we can model the log-likelihood as:

$$L = -\log \prod_{i=1}^{N} p(y_i|\bar{x}_i; \bar{\theta}) - \sum_{i=1}^{N} \log p(y_i|\bar{x}_i; \bar{\theta}) = -\sum_{i=1}^{N} [y_i \log \sigma(\bar{x}_i) + (1 - y_i) \log(1 - \sigma(x_i))]$$

The last term is a binary version of the cross-entropy between the distribution of the true labels, $p(y)$, and the predicted ones, $q(y)$:

$$L = -\sum_{i=1}^{N} p(y_i) \log q(y_i)$$

As $y_i \in \{0,1\}$, if $y_i = 0$, the first term $y_i \log \sigma(\bar{x}_i) = 0$, while the second one becomes equal to $\log(1 - \sigma(x_i))$. Conversely, when $y_i = 1$, the second term is null, and the first is equal to $\log \sigma(x_i)$. In both cases, the maximization of L forces the model to learn the actual distribution $p(y)$. If we explicit the dependence of the parameter vector and introduce a generic penalty term, L becomes:

$$L = -\sum_{y \in Y, \bar{x} \in X} p(y) \log q(\bar{x}; \bar{\theta}) + \alpha \|\bar{\theta}\|_p$$

When the p-norm is L_1, the model will perform a lasso feature selection while modeling the odd ratio.

We can now model the risk of breast cancer using Python and scikit-learn.

Example of Risk modeling with Lasso and Logistic Regression

Let's now consider a toy example based on the Breast Cancer dataset, which contains 569 data points with 30 biological features. Each point is associated with a binary label, $y_i \in \{0 = malignant, 1 = benign\}$. As this is only an exercise, we don't consider the real medical requirements for such kinds of studies (readers who are interested in the topic should read a book on epidemiology). However, as the true labels are guaranteed by medical experts, if a logistic regression succeeds in successfully classifying the sample (with a reasonable accuracy), the logit of the risk will also be correct.

Let's start by loading and normalizing the dataset using a robust scaler and the quantile range (15, 85) (the dataset is based on **real-world evidence** (**RWE**) and doesn't contain very noisy outliers):

```
from sklearn.datasets import load_breast_cancer
from sklearn.preprocessing import RobustScaler

data = load_breast_cancer()
X = data["data"]
Y = data["target"]

rs = RobustScaler(quantile_range=(15.0, 85.0))
X = rs.fit_transform(X)
```

At this point, we can evaluate the performances of a lasso logistic regression with $\alpha = 0.1$ (this choice has been made by testing the results corresponding to different values. I invite the reader to do the same as an exercise):

```
import joblib

from sklearn.linear_model import LogisticRegression
from sklearn.model_selection import cross_val_score
cvs = cross_val_score(
    LogisticRegression(C=0.1, penalty="l1", solver="saga",
                       max_iter=5000, random_state=1000),
        X, Y, cv=10, n_jobs=joblib.cpu_count())

print(cvs)
```

As it's possible to see, we have chosen to impose an L_1 penalty. Therefore, we expect to reduce the number of parameters from 31 (intercept and coefficients) to a much smaller value. The output of the previous snippet is as follows:

```
[0.98275862 0.94827586 0.94736842 0.98245614 0.96491228 0.98245614
 0.92982456 0.98214286 0.98214286 0.94642857]
```

The results are clearly positive. The worst accuracy is about 93%, with a maximum of 98%. Therefore, we can train the model with the entire dataset and use it for future predictions (assuming, of course, that they come from the same data-generating process – for example, the measures are taken using the same kind of instrument).

Let's now train the model and check the coefficients:

```
lr = LogisticRegression(C=0.05, penalty="l1",
                        solver="saga",
                        max_iter=5000,
```

```
                              random_state=1000)
lr.fit(X, Y)

for i, p in enumerate(np.squeeze(lr.coef_)):
    print("{} = {:.2f}".format(data['feature_names'][i], p))
```

The output of the previous snippet is as follows:

```
mean radius = 0.00
mean texture = 0.00
mean perimeter = 0.00
mean area = 0.00
mean smoothness = 0.00
mean compactness = 0.00
mean concavity = 0.00
mean concave points = -0.97
mean symmetry = 0.00
mean fractal dimension = 0.00
radius error = 0.00
texture error = 0.00
perimeter error = 0.00
area error = -0.90
smoothness error = 0.00
compactness error = 0.00
concavity error = 0.00
concave points error = 0.00
symmetry error = 0.00
fractal dimension error = 0.00
worst radius = -0.81
worst texture = -0.95
worst perimeter = -1.66
worst area = -0.16
worst smoothness = -0.08
worst compactness = 0.00
worst concavity = 0.00
worst concave points = -1.75
worst symmetry = -0.34
worst fractal dimension = 0.00
```

There are only nine non-null coefficients (out of 30) that can be rearranged so as to define the full relationship. As the risk is inverted (*malignant* = 0), in order to be coherent with the standard meaning, we're also inverting the sign of all coefficients (the sigmoid is symmetric; therefore, this is equivalent to swapping the labels):

```
model = "logit(risk) = {:.2f}".format(-lr.intercept_[0])
```

```
for i, p in enumerate(np.squeeze(lr.coef_)):
if p != 0:
    model += " + ({:.2f}*{}) ".\
    format(-p, data['feature_names'][i])

print("Model:\n")
print(model)
```

The output of the previous snippet is:

```
Model:

logit(risk) = -1.64 + (0.97*mean concave points)  + (0.90*area error)  +
(0.81*worst radius)  + (0.95*worst texture)  + (1.66*worst perimeter)
+ (0.16*worst area)  + (0.08*worst smoothness)  + (1.75*worst concave
points)  + (0.34*worst symmetry)
```

Such an expression is very simple and provides an immediate insight into the dominant factors. As it's possible to see, some redundant features have been discarded because their contribution is probably partially absorbed by other features (in other words, there are confounding factors). At this point, the model should also be evaluated by a domain expert to understand whether it can help to build a diagnostic algorithm. However, it should be clear to the reader how powerful a linear model can be when there's no need for the extra capacity provided by larger models.

As an exercise, I invite the reader to change the value of α (C for scikit-learn) until the number of non-null parameters stabilizes. Moreover, the reader can also incorporate an L_2 penalty through the ElasticNet loss (refer to *Chapter 1*, *Machine Learning Models Fundamentals*) to reduce the effect of multicollinearities.

Polynomial Regression

Linear regression is a simple and powerful algorithm because it can be fit very quickly and offers a high level of interpretability. For example, we can write the relation:

$$risk \sim \alpha Factor_a + \beta Factor_b + \epsilon$$

Even a non-technician can immediately understand the role played by the factors influencing the risk. To be more concrete, let's imagine that for the dependent variable $risk \in (-k, k)$, both factors are non-negative and:

$$risk \sim 5 \cdot Factor_a - 2 \cdot Factor_b$$

It's easy to observe that, while *Factor*$_a$ can increment the risk, the presence of *Factor*$_b$ can reduce it. Moreover, if *Factor*$_b$ > 2.5 *Factor*$_a$, the negative effect of *Factor*$_a$ is *neutralized* by *Factor*$_b$ (in other words, the risk becomes negative).

Even if this situation is almost ideal, the reality is quite often non-linear and the price to pay when working with linear models is a loss in terms of accuracy. When such a trade-off is acceptable, linear models are still the first choice (the Occam's razor principle), but when they don't meet the minimum requirements, it's necessary to look for other solutions. A simple but powerful alternative is offered by polynomial expansions of linear datasets.

Let's suppose that we have the following linear model (excluding the noise term):

$$\bar{y} = \bar{\theta}^T \cdot \bar{x} = \bar{\theta}_1 \bar{x}_1 + \bar{\theta}_2 \bar{x}_2 + \cdots + \bar{\theta}_m \bar{x}_m$$

Each of the $\bar{x}_i$ terms is a regressor and $\bar{y}$ is obtained as a linear combination of all regressors. Indeed, we're including any constraint regarding the real nature of $\bar{x}_i$. They can be simple factors, but they can also be, for example, square factors, or products of different factors. For the sake of rigor, we need to admit that the noise term cannot be easily discarded and what we're explaining is only correct when ϵ has the same *nature* of the regressors. For example, if we exchange $\bar{x}_i$ with $\bar{x}_i^2$, the noise contribution should also be squared, and the same happens for more complex transformations (such as log-linear models). However, in practice, we can often discard this control because we estimate the noise implicitly through the residuals and it's not always necessary to form confidence intervals (which rely on the distributional family of the noise). On the other hand, we know that the normality assumption can be relaxed when the sample size is large enough to justify application of the Central Limit Theorem; hence, we continue to employ the standard algorithms described in the previous section also when the distribution of each single noise term is no longer normal.

A polynomial regression is indeed a linear regression based on the transformation of the original feature set into its polynomial expansion. For example, a quadratic regression is obtained through the transformation:

$$\bar{x} = (x_1, x_2) \Rightarrow (x_1^2, x_1, x_1 x_2, x_2, x_2^2, 1) \Rightarrow (z_1, z_2, z_3, z_4, z_5, z_6) = \bar{z}$$

Unfortunately, this kind of transformation is prone to explode when the initial dimensionality is large. In fact, considering both polynomial and interaction features, the total number grows exponentially because of all combinations of every degree. For example, transforming the Diabetes dataset (13 original features) with a degree of 3, we obtain 560 features, which exceed the sample size (506). The drawbacks are obvious:

- The sample size can become too small due to the curse of dimensionality (for example, CV becomes extremely problematic because the folds are too small, and some regions can be easily cut out from the training set).

- The estimator can now overfit (hence, ridge is preferred over a standard linear regression).

- Both computational and memory complexities grow very rapidly.

In these cases, we can try to mitigate the problem by selecting only the interaction features, but this choice would not help us in capturing the oscillations due to the non-linearities. However, in many real cases, the main problem is due to the inability to manage the interactions (for example, in a lot of healthcare studies, comorbidities – which means the presence of different, linked pathologies at the same time – play a central role and it's not possible to model the interaction effects as a linear combination). Therefore, when the complexity of the datasets is very large, I suggest starting by generating interaction-only features and checking whether the result is acceptable. In case of poor performances, it's possible either to increase the degree or activate the full feature set.

Another important element to consider is the use of CV. If the sample size is very small, a low number (for example, less than 10) of folds results in training sets that might not cover the whole data-generating process. Consequently, the validation results are generally poor. The only way to address this problem is to use a **Leave-One-Out (LOO)** (if it's possible to evaluate a metric on a single data point) or **Leave-P-Out (LPO)**. Clearly, both strategies are extremely time consuming, but this is the only feasible way to manage CV effectively in these cases.

In any case, it's important to remember that K-fold CV is generally the most reliable choice because it avoids the cross-correlations that are almost inevitable with LOO and LPO. Alternatively, it's possible to perform a static train-test split after having shuffled the dataset properly. Obviously, the size of the test set must be small enough to allow the training set to capture the whole dynamic of p_{data}. If the regression is completely time-independent, a small training set might be large enough to train a model, but this problem can become very hard to manage when the data points are based on an evolution over time. In these cases, the exclusion of some points could lead to a biased model because of an under-estimation (or over-estimation) of the parameters.

Therefore, when working with time series, it's often preferable to employ specific models (which we're going to present in the next chapter) that are able to capture the internal dynamics and the interdependencies between time points. If a regression model is preferred, it's necessary to check whether the training set contains enough data points to describe the data-generating process.

Moreover, when working with polynomial regressions, the degrees of freedom, t, can be very large and, as generic rule of thumb, $N \gg t$. If, on the contrary, $N \approx t$ or, even worse, $N < t$, the model is partially undetermined, and the performances could become poorer than the linear counterpart.

Examples of Polynomial Regressions

As a first example, let's see how a ridge regression can be adapted to manage a non-linear 1-dimensional dataset defined as:

$$Y = 0.1(X + \epsilon_1)^3 + 3(X - 2 + \epsilon_2)^2 + 5(X + \epsilon_3)$$

We have also voluntarily included transformations of the noise terms to increase the complexity and we have also normalized the set, Y, to avoid a very large range:

```
import numpy as np

x = np.expand_dims(np.arange(-50, 50, 0.1), axis=1)
y = 0.1 * np.power(x +
    np.random.normal(0.0, 2.5, size=x.shape), 3) + \
    3.0 * np.power(x - 2 +                      np.random.normal(0.0,
1.5, size=x.shape), 2) - \
    5.0 * (x + np.random.normal(0.0, 0.5, size=x.shape))

y = (y - np.min(y)) / (np.abs(np.min(y)) + np.max(y))
```

At this point, we can train a standard ridge model (with $\alpha = 0.1$):

```
from sklearn.linear_model import Ridge

lr = Ridge(alpha=0.1, normalize=True, random_state=1000)
lr.fit(x, y)
```

Before moving on and comparing the results, it's helpful to evaluate both R^2 and the MAE:

```
from sklearn.metrics import r2_score, mean_absolute_error

print("R2 = {:.2f}".format(
        r2_score(y, lr.predict(x))))
print("MAE = {:.2f}".format(
        mean_absolute_error(y, lr.predict(x))))
```

The output of the previous snippet is:

```
R2 = 0.63
MAE = 0.10
```

This result might appear surprising because the dataset is highly non-linear. Indeed, the reader must pay attention to two important factors. The values of $Y \in (0, 1)$; therefore, we have about 10% of the MAE, which is generally too large for this kind of dataset. The reason will be clear when comparing the results, but generally speaking, the effect of the error is greater in the regions where the slope changes more abruptly. In this case, there are two such kinds of regions. The least squares algorithm successfully minimizes the error by selecting a slope that is more *compatible* with the first curved region and ineffective for the second one.

The second thing to remember is the informative value of R^2. As many authors have demonstrated, this score is very context-dependent and sometimes, it can also yield inconsistent results. In particular, R^2 must always be used in comparisons of compatible versions of a model (for example, the same dataset and different polynomial degrees), because it doesn't provide any information about the absolute goodness of fit. Moreover, it doesn't encode information about the turning points of polynomial curves. When working with linear regressions, this is not a problem. However, when using polynomial transformations, it's extremely important to understand whether the curve models the data correctly in its non-linear structure. A much more reliable alternative is provided by the U scores (also known as Theil scores), which are defined as:

$$U = \sqrt{\frac{\sum_{i=1}^{N}(y_i - \tilde{y}_i)^2}{\sum_{i=1}^{N} y_i^2}} \quad and \quad U\Delta = \sqrt{\frac{\sum_{i=1}^{N}(\Delta y_i - \Delta\tilde{y}_i)^2}{\sum_{i=1}^{N} \Delta y_i^2}} \quad where \quad \begin{cases} \Delta y_i = y_i - y_{i-1} \\ \Delta\tilde{y}_i = \tilde{y}_i - y_{i-1} \end{cases}$$

The standard U score is very similar to R^2 and encodes information about the total variation that the model is able to describe. Instead, $U\Delta$ is based on stepwise differences and enables the ability of the model to be measured in *turning on time*. Looking at the numerator, the first term is the difference between two consecutive outputs, while the second one is the difference between the predicted output and the true previous one. An ideal model should be characterized by $\Delta y_i = \Delta\tilde{y}_i$ and, consequently, $U\Delta = 0$.

In fact, in this case, the turning points are successfully predicted, and the model follows the non-linear structure of the data. In real cases, we look for the hyperparameter set that minimizes both scores (possibly including also the adjusted R^2 in order to take into account the degrees of freedom and penalize more complex models).

As a first step, let's define a function to compute both U scores:

```
import numpy as np

def u_scores(y_true, y_pred):
```

```
a = np.sum(np.power(y_true - y_pred, 2))
b = np.sum(np.power(y_true, 2))
u = np.sqrt(a / b)

d_true = y_true[:y_true.shape[0]-1] - y_true[1:]
d_pred = y_pred[:y_pred.shape[0]-1] - y_true[1:]
c = np.sum(np.power(d_true - d_pred ,2))
d = np.sum(np.power(d_true, 2))
ud = np.sqrt(c / d)

return u, ud
```

We can now check the values for a linear regression:

```
print("U = {:.2f}, UD = {:.2f}"

        .format(*u_scores(y, lr.predict(x))))
```

The output is as follows:

```
U = 0.37, UD = 3.38
```

Since U scores are also relative measures, we cannot draw any conclusion without comparing the results with a few polynomial regressions. Let's create three alternative datasets based on degrees 5, 3, and 2, including interactions using the `PolynomialFeatures` class:

```
from sklearn.preprocessing import PolynomialFeatures

pf5 = PolynomialFeatures(degree=5)
xp5 = pf5.fit_transform(x)

pf3 = PolynomialFeatures(degree=3)
xp3 = pf3.fit_transform(x)

pf2 = PolynomialFeatures(degree=2)
xp2 = pf2.fit_transform(x)
```

We can now fit the respective ridge regressions, keeping $\alpha = 0.1$:

```
lrp5 = Ridge(alpha=0.1, normalize=True, random_state=1000)
lrp5.fit(xp5, y)
yp5 = lrp5.predict(xp5)


lrp3 = Ridge(alpha=0.1, normalize=True, random_state=1000)
lrp3.fit(xp3, y)
yp3 = lrp3.predict(xp3)


lrp2 = Ridge(alpha=0.1, normalize=True, random_state=1000)
lrp2.fit(xp2, y)
yp2 = lrp2.predict(xp2)
```

At this point, we can evaluate the U scores:

```
print("2. U = {:.2f}, UD = {:.2f}".
        format(*u_scores(y, yp2)))
print("3. U = {:.2f}, UD = {:.2f}".
        format(*u_scores(y, yp3)))
print("5. U = {:.2f}, UD = {:.2f}".
        format(*u_scores(y, yp5)))
```

The output of the previous snippet is:

```
2. U = 0.21, UD = 1.92

3. U = 0.10, UD = 0.93

5. U = 0.09, UD = 0.83
```

The results confirm our hypotheses. If we look at $U\Delta$s, we already have a rapid decrease when the degree is 2, but the value seems to stabilize with $d = 3$. In fact, considering also the standard U score, there's a 50% drop between degree 2 and 3, while it remains almost constant for $d = 5$. This indicates that a degree 5 model is more prone to overfit, and the extra degrees of freedom are not to reduce the bias at the expense of the variance. In fact, the more complex model can explain the same variation, but it has more potential turning points that might be unnecessary.

The plot of all the models is shown in the following graph:

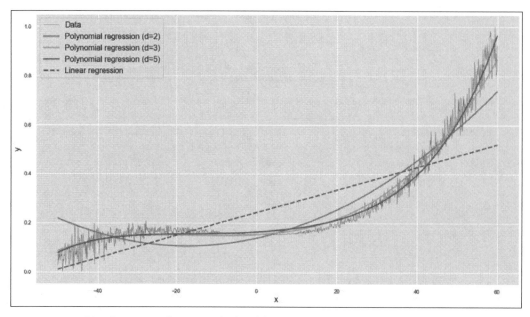

Non-linear noisy dataset overlaid with linear and three polynomial regressions

It's clear that a linear regression (dashed line) is totally inaccurate and should be excluded immediately. Assuming the structure of the dataset, the degree 2 polynomial is not a good choice either because it doesn't allow any saddle point. Looking at the dataset, there's a saddle point for $x \approx 0$ (the concavity changes direction) and the parabolic regression can only capture a side of the curve. Both degrees 3 and 5 are odd; therefore, they allow the concavity direction change and, indeed, the two curves almost overlap (with a slightly more precise prediction ability for $d = 5$).

However, the cost of the extra complexity is not justified by the results. Therefore, we prefer to employ a degree three model. Moreover, it's important to remember that the dataset should represent the entire data-generating process. In this particular case, it means that, when $x < -40$ and $x > 60$, the trend remains the same. This implies that $y \rightarrow \pm\infty$, which is clearly unrealistic in most actual cases. Hence, we're explicitly assuming that the independent variable, x, has a limited domain, which is fully captured by the training sample.

Returning to the Diabetes dataset, the U scores corresponding to a ridge regression with $\alpha = 0.25$ are as follows:

```
U = 0.32, UD = 0.51
```

These values don't seem too bad, but we know that $R^2 = 0.5$, and so we haven't achieved a high goodness of fit. We can test the effect of using polynomial features, but we also have to pay attention to the sample size. The original dataset contains 506 points with 13 features; therefore, the expansion must be limited, otherwise we risk having an undetermined system. Considering the nature of the dataset, it's reasonable to suppose that the lack of precision is mainly due to the inability to model the interactions between factors (this is a common scenario in healthcare studies). Therefore, we can limit the expansion to $d = 3$, including just the interactions:

```
pf = PolynomialFeatures(degree=3, interaction_only=True)
Xp = pf.fit_transform(X)
```

This transformation generates 176 features, fewer than the sample size, but it's still a very large number corresponding to a data-generating process that might not be fully captured by 506 points. However, we can retrain the ridge regression and compute the new measures:

```
lrr = Ridge(alpha=0.25, normalize=True, random_state=1000)
lrr.fit(Xp, Y)

print("R2 = {:.2f}".format(r2_score(Y, lrr.predict(Xp))))
print("MAE = {:.2f}".
        format(mean_absolute_error(Y, lrr.predict(Xp))))

print("U = {:.2f}, UD = {:.2f}".
format(*u_scores(Y, lrr.predict(Xp))))
```

The output is as follows:

```
R2 = 0.60
MAE = 39.24
U = 0.29, UD = 0.46
```

All the measures confirm an improvement, but it's obvious that a larger sample size could yield a much better fit. In particular, the reduction of $U\Delta$ indicates that the polynomial model is now capturing more turning points (a result that is also confirmed by the lower MAE). Unfortunately, all other combinations with higher degrees yield a total number of features larger than the training sample; therefore, they are not acceptable. Anyhow, it must be clear that polynomial regression is an extremely powerful tool for managing problems that are either naturally non-linear or with dependent features.

As an exercise, I invite the reader to test these models with other simple regression datasets, such as the Boston house pricing dataset, trying to establish the optimal trade-off between accuracy, degree, and the number of generated features.

Isotonic Regression

In some cases, the dataset is made up of a sample of a monotonic function $f(x): \forall x_1 > x_2 \Rightarrow f(x_1) \geq (\leq)f(x_2)$. A standard linear regression can easily capture the slope, but it fails when the curve is non-linear. On the other hand, polynomial regressions can also capture non-linear dynamics, but the models can easily become too complex because of the necessity of high degrees. Moreover, the boundary conditions cannot be easily managed, and the resulting regression will diverge to $\pm\infty$ when $x \to \pm\infty$. An isotonic regression assumes the monotonicity of the dependent variable and tries to find a set of N weights, w_i, so as to minimize the weighted least-square loss:

$$L = \sum_{i=1}^{N} w_i(y_i - \tilde{y}_i)^2 = \sum_{i=1}^{N} w_i \left(y_i - f(x_i; \bar{\theta}) \right)^2$$

The resulting function is an actual constrained interpolation of the points $\{(x_1, y_1), (x_2, y_2), ..., (x_N, y_N)\}$ and cannot generally be expressed as linear combination of the independent variables. The main advantage is that even complex non-linear dynamics with several slope changes can be easily captured. However, when the dataset is very noisy, the interpolation might become overfitted. To address this problem (and all related ones), it's possible to smooth the dataset before processing it, as discussed in the following section. For now, let's suppose that the noise is controlled, and we prefer a piecewise interpolation to a coarse approximation.

Example of Isotonic Regression

As an example, let's consider a dataset containing 600 points, where $y_{i+1} \geq y_i \ \forall \ i$ (this is the only condition required by an isotonic regression):

```
import numpy as np


x = np.arange(0, 60, 0.1)
y = 0.1 * np.power(x + np.random.normal(0.0, 1.0, size=x.shape), 3) + \
    3.0 * np.power(
    x - 2 + np.random.normal(0.0, 0.5, size=x.shape), 2) - \
    5.0 * (x + np.random.normal(0.0, 0.5, size=x.shape))

y = (y - np.min(y)) / (np.abs(np.min(y)) + np.max(y))
```

To have an immediate comparison, let's fit both a standard linear regression and an isotonic one:

```
from sklearn.linear_model import LinearRegression
from sklearn.isotonic import IsotonicRegression

lr = LinearRegression()
lr.fit(np.expand_dims(x, axis=1), y)

ir = IsotonicRegression()
ir.fit(x, y)
```

The result is shown in the following diagram:

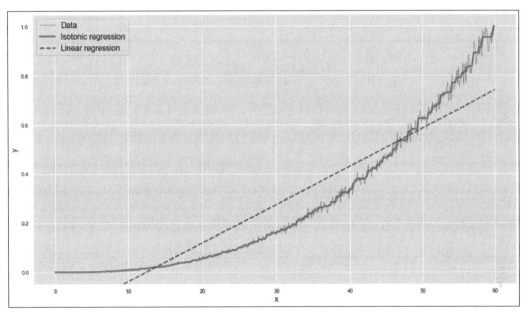

Linear regression compared to isotonic regression

The inner structure of the dataset is parabolic, and we could have been tempted to use a polynomial regression with degree 2. However, such a solution wouldn't capture the sub-dynamics due to noise, and this can be either positive or negative. As we have chosen to *trust* the noisy oscillations, the isotonic regression yielded an optimal result using a piecewise interpolation that minimizes the mean square error.

As an exercise, I invite the reader to compare the results (in terms of error) with a polynomial regression and select the model that best describes the underlying data-generating process (with and without noise).

Summary

In this chapter, we have introduced the reader to the most important concepts concerning linear models and regressions. In the first part, we discussed the features of a GLM, focusing attention on how to fit the models and how to avoid the most common problems.

We also analyzed how to include regularization penalties through ridge and lasso regressions and how it's possible to exploit the linear framework also when the dataset is non-linear through an appropriate polynomial transformation. We also compared the results with the one obtained using an isotonic regression and we analyzed the reasons for preferring either the former or the latter. Another important topic discussed in the chapter is risk modeling using logistic regression penalized with lasso to perform an automatic feature selection.

In the next chapter, we start discussing the basic concepts and of time-series analysis, focusing on the properties on the most important models (ARMA and ARIMA) that are commonly employed in econometrics and financial forecasting.

Further reading

- Greene W. H., *Econometric Analysis* (Fifth Edition), Prentice Hall, 2002

- Belsley D. A., Kuh E., Welsch R., *Regression Diagnostics: Identifying Influential Data and Sources of Collinearity*, Wiley, 1980

- Chakravarti N., *Isotonic Median Regression: A Linear Programming Approach*, Mathematics of Operations Research, 14/2, 1989

- Candanedo L. M., Feldheim V., Deramaix D., *Data-Driven Prediction Models of Energy Use of Appliances in a Low-Energy House*, Energy and Buildings, Volume 140, 04/2017

10
Introduction to Time-Series Analysis

The chapter comprises a brief introduction to time-series analysis, which is also a central topic in different contexts. A time-series is simply a sequence of values produced by a stochastic system over time. Contrary to regression, which often operates with stateless systems, time-series are based on an evolution that is based on the memory of the underlying process. For example, the level of water in a tank can be modeled by a time-series because the changes can be fully described only knowing the initial conditions (for example, if the tank is half full, it could have been empty and then half-filled, or full and then half-emptied). In this chapter, we are going to briefly describe some techniques that allow us to model time-series and make predictions about future states.

In particular, we are going to discuss:

- The main concepts of stochastic processes and time-series
- Autocorrelation and smoothing
- AR, MA, ARMA, and ARIMA models

We can now start our discussion by defining the main concepts associated with time-series and their underlying stochastic processes.

Time-series

In this chapter, we are going to briefly introduce the concepts of time-series and stochastic processes. As the topic is very wide, we are only discussing a few fundamental aspects and, at the same time, inviting the reader to refer to a complete book, such as Shumway R. H., Stoffer D. S., *Time Series Analysis and Its Applications*, Springer, 2017, for all the details.

The main concept of this chapter concerns the structure of a time-series. In this book, we are assuming that we are working with univariate series in the form:

$$y_1, y_2, \ldots, y_t, \ldots$$

Every value y_i depends implicitly on time (that is, $y_i = y(i)$); therefore, the series cannot be shuffled without losing information. If the values y_t are completely determined by a law (such as $y_t = t^2$), the underlying process is described as deterministic. This is the case with many physical laws, but it's almost useless for us because the future can not be predicted without uncertainty. On the other hand, if every y_i is a random variable, the process is stochastic, and we need to find good approximations to forecast values not contained in the training set.

The fundamental elements of stochastic processes that we are going to employ are:

- The process is generically denoted with y_t or $y(t)$.

- Setting a value t transforms the process into a random variable that, for simplicity, we are going to define as $y_t \sim D$. The distribution D is assumed to be the same for all realizations y_t.

- The temporal mean of the process is $\mu_t = E[y(t)]$. Analogously, the temporal variance is $\sigma_t^2 = E[(y(t) - E[y(t)])^2]$.

- The autocovariance function is defined as
$c_y(t_1, t_2) = E[(y(t_1) - E[y(t_1)])(y(t_2) - E[y(t_2)])]$.

- The process is *strongly stationary* if the full joint probability distribution is invariant to time shifts. This condition can be extremely difficult to meet and check; therefore, we often refer to *weakly stationary* processes, characterized by constant temporal mean and variance and $c_y(t_1, t_2) = c_y(t_2 - t_1) = c_y(\tau)$. Strong stationarity implies weak stationarity, but the opposite is true only for Gaussian processes, as they are fully defined by the first two moments.

- If the vertical mean (the mean obtained after having fixed a time instant) equals the temporal mean, the process is said to be ergodic.

- A white noise process is a Gaussian process (even if this is not a fundamental requirement), with null mean, fixed variance, and uncorrelated realizations (that is, $Cov[y_t, y_q] = 0 \ \forall \ t, q$).

In this section, we often refer to stationary processes because they offer evident advantages. However, it must be clear that a stationary process is not static. The latter is time-constant, while the former is ruled by static laws. In other words, a stationary process can be considered as a *simpler* stochastic process because once the first two moments are known (in the case of weak stationarity), the behavior can be predicted with controlled uncertainty.

On the other hand, a non-stationary process might become very difficult to model unless, for example, the non-stationarity only depends on trend components. In fact, given a process y_t, we can always decompose it as:

$$y_t = t_t + s_t + \epsilon_t$$

The first term is a trend component (for example, a linear trend, like in standard linear regression). The second term is called a seasonal component and models those effects that keep on repeating cyclically (for example, temperature measures during a long period), while ϵ_t is a purely random component that we cannot estimate. We consider the mean of the process $E[y_t] = E[t_t] + E[s_t] + E[\epsilon_t]$. Without a loss of generality, we can assume $E[s_t] = E[\epsilon_t] = 0$ because the seasonal effects tend to change very slowly and require many periods, and the noise is generally white.

However, if the trend is, for example, linear or quadratic, $E[t_t]$ cannot be constant. Therefore, the resulting process is non-stationary. However, this kind of non-stationarity is very easy to manage (for example, detrending a linear model simply requires fitting a linear regression and subtracting the estimation for each point). Unfortunately, some more complex models are not stationary for reasons that are not easy to detect, and modeling them could be complex and lead to poor performance. A simple example of non-stationarity is the presence of additive noise with a non-constant mean (for example, if an instrument records a signal and a component slowly loses its tuning, the resulting time-series will be non-stationary. On the other hand, if a component is broken, and the resulting signal is always affected by the same noise, the time-series will be stationary). The procedure described in the next section shows how to mitigate this problem and introduce the reader to the processing of time-series.

Smoothing

When we model a time-series, a common problem is non-stationarity caused by noise. A similar problem has been encountered when discussing isotonic regression. If a time-series is very noisy, many models can struggle to find an optimal configuration. Moreover, the interpretability of the behavior is consequently affected by sub-oscillations, which can hide more important elements. A solution to this problem is provided by a smoothing procedure. The idea is quite simple, and it's based on the assumption that the value y_t depends more on the immediately previous values $\{y_{t-1}, y_{t-2}, \ldots\}$ than the more distant ones. Therefore, we can re-express the original time-series y_t using a proxy series s_t defined as:

$$s_t = (1 - \lambda)y_t + \lambda s_{t-1}$$

We can manipulate the previous terms to obtain the following expression (which resembles a differential equation whose solution is exponential; that's why the method is also known as *exponential smoothing*):

$$\frac{s_t - \lambda s_{t-1}}{1 - \lambda} = y_t$$

Each term y_t is considered as the weighted difference of two consecutive terms of s_t, therefore, fast changes are absorbed by the difference as a function of the parameter λ. If $\lambda \to 0$, $s_t \to y_t$. On the contrary, when $\lambda \to 1$, s_t becomes more and more *conservative* and changes only when y_t is much larger in absolute value. This behavior allows us to transform a highly oscillating series into a much smoother one, avoiding all the problems caused by intense noise.

As an example, let's consider the energy consumption dataset available from UCI (`https://archive.ics.uci.edu/ml/datasets/Appliances+energy+prediction`). It contains several time-series about the environmental conditions of a house monitored every 10 mins for 4.5 months. In this example, we can consider the temperature recorded in the kitchen.

Let's start by loading the CSV dataset using Pandas (after setting the right path of the local CSV file):

```
import pandas as pd

data_file = "energydata_complete.csv"
df = pd.read_csv(data_file, header=0, index_col="date")
```

The time-series T1 (as well as all the other ones) contains 19,735 observations; therefore, if λ is too small, the smoothed series will tend to overlap the original one. A good strategy to find the optimal smoothing parameter λ is tricky and it's based on the idea of considering the parameterized sum of square errors, $y_t - s_t^\lambda$, and pick the λ value that minimizes the sum. Such a method is very effective but requires an additional computational step that might be not so immediate. Alternatively, it's possible to start with a standard value such as $\lambda = 0.5$, increasing or decreasing it if the time-series is either too fine or too coarse.

In our case, we are focusing on $\lambda = \{0.995, 0.999\}$, which may both seem very large but, as explained, considering the length of the time-series, yield very different results. We can now build the smoothed time-series:

```
Y = df["T1"].values
l1 = 0.995
l2 = 0.999
```

```
skt = np.zeros((Y.shape[0], 2))
skt[0, 0] = Y[0]
skt[0, 1] = Y[0]

for i in range(1, skt.shape[0]):
skt[i, 0] = ((1 - l1) * Y[i]) + (l1 * skt[i - 1, 0])
        skt[i, 1] = ((1 - l2) * Y[i]) + (l2 * skt[i - 1, 1])
```

The result is shown in the following figure:

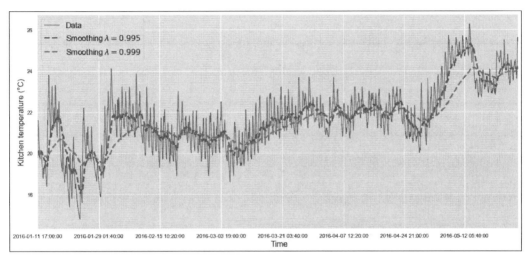

Original time-series with two exponential smoothing curves

As we can see, both smoothing curves are much less noisy than the original time-series, with a clear difference between $\lambda = 0.995$ and $\lambda = 0.999$. When the goal is modeling the overall trend (with its local variations), these choices can be very effective when trying to model the time-series using standard models. In these cases, the removal of the spurious oscillations can simplify the training process and yield better results with less complex models.

Introduction to linear models for time-series

In this section, we are going to employ an artificial time-series to show some common linear models for time-series. The goal is not to provide an exhaustive explanation (which would require an entire book), but to introduce the reader to this kind of modeling method. The reader who is interested in the topic (and would like to read a complete mathematical background) can check Shumway R. H., Stoffer D. S., *Time Series Analysis and Its Applications*, Springer, 2017.

A time-series containing 100 observations with a frequency of 0.5 (2 observations per time instant) is generated by the following snippet:

```
import numpy as np

x = np.expand_dims(np.arange(0, 50, 0.5), axis=1)
y = np.sin(5.*x) + np.random.normal(0.0, 0.5, size=x.shape)
y = np.squeeze(y)
```

A graphical representation is shown in the following figure:

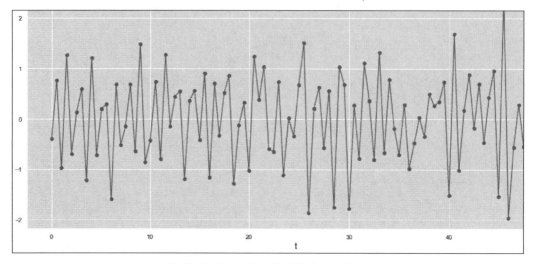

Synthetic time-series with 100 observations

This time-series has no particular characteristic except for a noisy periodicity. We explicitly wanted to avoid complex series in order to simplify this introduction. Of course, the reader is invited to apply the same models to more complex time-series (such as the ones contained in the energy consumption dataset).

Autocorrelation

A fundamental diagnostic tool for any time-series is the evaluation of its autocorrelation function. For a generic stochastic process $y(t)$, it is defined as:

$$r_y(t_1, t_2) = \frac{Cov[y_1, y_2]}{\sqrt{\sigma_1^2 \sigma_2^2}}$$

In the previous expression, we have assumed $y_i = y(t_i)$ and $\sigma_i^2 = \sigma^2(t_i)$. If the process is stationary, $Cov[y_1, y_2]$ depends only on the difference $\tau = t_2 - t_1$ and $\sigma_i^2 = \sigma^2 \; \forall \; i$, hence the autocorrelation can be simplified as:

$$r_y(\tau) = \frac{Cov[y_t, y_{t+\tau}]}{\sigma^2}$$

The covariance $Cov[y_t, y_{t+\tau}]$ integrates the variable t throughout; therefore, the result is only a function of the interval τ. As the name suggests, the autocorrelation function measures the correlation that the process has with itself when it is sampled at time t and $t + \tau$. The larger the randomness, the smaller the autocorrelation. Moreover, $r_y(\tau)$ very often naturally decays with τ because it's reasonable to assume a stronger correlation in a short time range and a weaker and weaker one when $\tau \to \infty$.

The autocorrelation plot for the synthetic time-series is shown in the following figure:

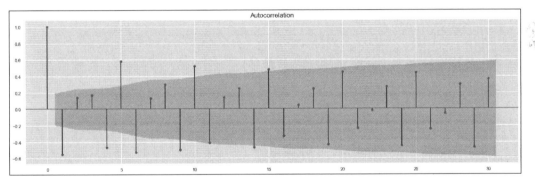

Autocorrelation plot

As it's possible to see, the first evaluation ($\tau = 0$) is always equal to 1 because, obviously, any y_i is fully correlated with itself. The remaining indicators are placed at fixed-distance lags. In our case, $r_y(1)$ is negative and it's followed by two smaller positive correlations. This means that the time-series y_t tends to invert the sign twice (at y_{t+1} and y_{t+2}), keep it for another lag with a slightly larger amplitude, and then invert it again. The main positive correlations ($\tau = 0, 5, 10, ...$) are dumped and decrease very slowly (this is mainly due to the periodicity).

The same happens for the two negative correlations before and after each main one ($\tau = 4$ and 6). It's easy to understand that this autocorrelation belongs to a process with a partially regular temporal dynamic because even after 30 lags, it's possible to observe the same periodic behavior.

On the contrary, the following plot shows the autocorrelation plot of a noise process:

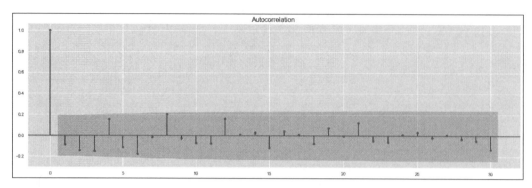

Autocorrelation plot of a noise process

In this case, after the first lag, the correlation drops under 0.2 and tends to vanish when $\tau \to \infty$. The larger correlations are mainly due to chance and to the internal random generation processes, which cannot easily produce pure white noise. However, the difference is evident, therefore $r_y(\tau)$ can be easily employed to evaluate the behavior of a time-series. As a last example, let's consider a linear process that is clearly non-stationary because it has a natural trend (that is, the mean obviously depends on instants t_1 and t_2):

$$y_t = t + \epsilon_t \ \ where \ \ \epsilon_t \sim N(0,0.5)$$

In this case, the autocorrelation plot is shown in the following image:

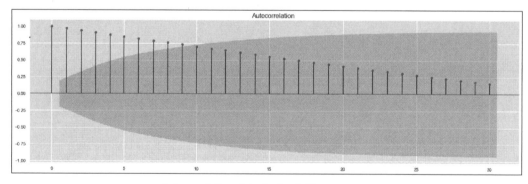

Autocorrelation plot of a simple linear process

Again, we can immediately identify the regularity. As two consequent instants $y_t - y_{t-1} = \epsilon$, the first difference is approximately 0, while it becomes smaller and smaller due to the magnitude of the main component. We can say that the initial lags are mainly dominated by the noise component, which produces a very slight decay, while when $\tau \gg 0$, the autocorrelation is dominated by the term proportional to the time instant.

In any case, given a lag, a large absolute autocorrelation means that the process tends to maintain an internal similarity, while a small value indicates that the evolution has *removed* most of the memory. In terms of prediction, a large autocorrelation implies a simple prediction given the preceding instants, while a small autocorrelation (as in the case of the noise process) informs us that the value y_t receives a very small influence from the previous values (that is, in a white noise process the outputs are uncorrelated; therefore, the prediction is theoretically impossible).

AR, MA, and ARMA processes

It's quite reasonable to suppose that a process at time t (y_t) is influenced by the value assumed in a number of previous instants. This concept can be expressed in the following way:

$$y_t = \alpha_1 y_{t-1} + \alpha_2 y_{t-2} + \cdots + \alpha_p y_{t-p} + \epsilon_t$$

This kind of process is called AR(p) or autoregressive of order p because y_t depends on past values of p (through a regression on itself). The term ϵ_t is white noise, therefore $Cov[\epsilon_t \epsilon_q] = 0 \ \forall \ t, q$. The stationarity of this process depends on the roots of the z-transform of the model, which is equivalent to computing the roots of the complex polynomial:

$$\alpha_p z^{-p} + \alpha_{p-1} z^{-p+1} + \cdots + 1 = 0$$

If the roots lie within the unit circle, the process is stationary. However, the theory required to understand these concepts is beyond the scope of this book, so we invite the interested reader to examine a specialized resource such as Shumway R. H., D. S., Stoffer, *Time Series Analysis and Its Applications*, Springer, 2017.

In a perfectly analogous way, it's possible to define a process that depends on the past q instants, expressed as a linear combination of white noise signals. That is, the model is expressed by:

$$y_t = \epsilon_t + \beta_1 \epsilon_{t-1} + \alpha_2 \epsilon_{t-2} + \cdots + \alpha_q \epsilon_{t-q}$$

This process is called MA(q) or the moving average of order q. Contrary to AR(p), MA(q) is always stationary if the noise terms ϵ_t are white. The reason is not simple, but it's very intuitive. A moving average process incorporates a sort of *behavioral stability* due to the fact that y_t always depends on the same combination assuming a limited variability. In other words, as the noise terms are limited, they assume large absolute values with a very low probability, and y_t tends to have a constant mean and variance (therefore, it is at least weakly stationary).

On the contrary, an AR(p) process has the potential ability to change its mean and variance if the effect of history is strong enough. This concept is equivalent to saying that model can be either stable (roots inside the unit circle) or unstable (roots outside the unit circle). In the latter case, the behavior becomes analogous to the linear process $y_t = \alpha t + \epsilon_t$, which diverges to $\pm\infty$. Therefore, even if they are simpler to understand, AR(p) processes must be tuned up more carefully, while MA(q) processes are always safe and, in the worst case, they simply produce bad predictions when the history is required to predict future states.

ARMA(p, q) processes are the natural combination of AR(p) and MA(q) and they have the following standard form (the signs of the coefficients are inverted):

$$y_t + \alpha_1 y_{t-1} + \alpha_2 y_{t-2} + \cdots + \alpha_p y_{t-p} = \epsilon_t + \beta_1 \epsilon_{t-1} + \alpha_2 \epsilon_{t-2} + \cdots + \alpha_q \epsilon_{t-q}$$

This process incorporates the positive and negative sides of both AR and MA processes, and it's possible to prove that it's stationary if the AR part taken alone is stationary. ARMA processes are extremely flexible and they are able to model many stationary processes (in particular, processes without a trend). Thanks to the presence of both an autoregressive and a moving average part, ARMA models can rely on the previous history, including also the variability brought by the MA part. Of course, an MA(q) process is an ARMA(0, q) and an AR(p) one is equivalent to an ARMA(p, 0).

The choice of the right model (in particular, the values p and q) depends on many factors that can be neither generalized nor immediately discovered. In order to find the optimal model, it's necessary to check different values, evaluating, for example, the **mean squared error** (**MSE**) of the predictions. The main principle is always the same: the simplest model that yields good performances must be selected; therefore, it's also helpful to evaluate specific metrics such as AIC or BIC (which we are going to discuss in later examples). They both penalize more complex models and provide an immediate insight into the most reasonable choice. As this part is introductory, we are not discussing more sophisticated techniques, but rather we are focusing on some examples based on the synthetic dataset.

Let's start by creating a training set containing the first 90 samples and a test set with the remaining ones:

```
y_train = y[0:90]
y_test = y[90:]
```

We can now use `statsmodels` to train an AR(15), MA(15), and ARMA(6, 4) model. Even if there are dedicated classes for all three families, it's preferable to employ the ARMA class, which provides a full set of features (including a specific plot function):

```
from statsmodels.tsa.arima_model import ARMA

ar = ARMA(y_train, order=(15, 0), missing="drop").\
        fit(transparams=True, trend="nc")

arma = ARMA(y_train, order=(6, 4), missing="drop").\
        fit(transparams=True, maxiter=500, trend="nc")

ma = ARMA(y_train, order=(0, 15), missing="drop").\
        fit(transparams=True, maxiter=500, trend="nc")
```

In all three models, we have chosen to drop the missing values (in this case, this choice is irrelevant), to standardize the parameters if the model is not stationary (`transparam=True`), and not to include any trend because the dataset doesn't contain it.

After the training phase, we can predict the results for the interval (90, 99) and compute the MSEs:

```
y_pred_ar = ar.predict(start=90, end=99)
y_pred_ma = ma.predict(start=90, end=99)
y_pred_arma = arma.predict(start=90, end=99)

print("MSE AR: {:.2f}".
        format(0.1*np.sum(np.power(y_test - y_pred_ar, 2))))
print("MSE MA: {:.2f}".
        format(0.1*np.sum(np.power(y_test - y_pred_ma, 2))))
print("MSE ARMA: {:.2f}".
        format(0.1*np.sum(np.power(y_test - y_pred_arma, 2))))
```

The output of the previous snippet is:

```
MSE AR: 0.83
MSE MA: 1.32
MSE ARMA: 0.71
```

As expected, the combination of AR and MA yielded the smallest error, while MA alone is the worst model (the reason is not complex to understand given the nature of the dataset, where the inversions follow a precise pattern).

Let's now visualize the predictions for AR and MA models:

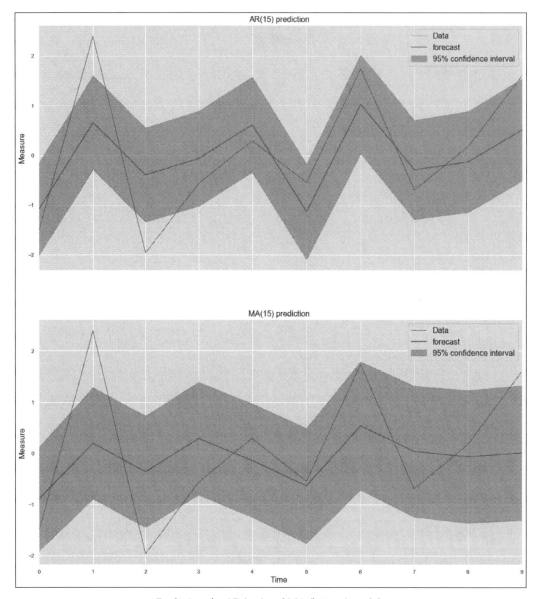

Predictions for AR (top) and MA (bottom) models

The plots confirm the error. While AR is able to follow the oscillations, MA is much slower and fails to capture some rapid variations. On the other hand, both AR and MA are evaluated with 15 lags.

More complex models might yield better performance, but the price could be too high in terms of computational complexity. Instead, the combination provided by the ARMA model achieves a smaller MSE with a total of 10 degrees of freedom. The result is shown in the following figure:

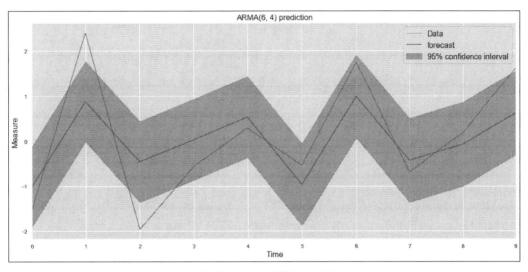

Predictions for ARMA model

As we can see, the ARMA model behaves almost like the AR model, but it uses fewer degrees of freedom. It fails to reach the data points only when the variations are extremely rapid, but it always follows the slope changes. This kind of behavior is strictly correlated with the frequency content of the system. The topic is out of scope; however, the reader must understand that fast-changing datasets contain higher frequencies. An ARMA model acts as a low-pass filter, which excludes the frequencies over a threshold that depends on the complexity of the model and on its parameter values. This problem is evident with the MA model, which tends to be almost flat, but it also appears in the ARMA model.

More accurate results require a larger training set and greater values for both p and q. However, as explained, we are not always interested in capturing all high-frequency oscillations because they can be caused by additive noise signals. Therefore, the low-pass filtering features provided by many linear systems performs both a smoothing and a signal modeling, reducing the risk of overfitting without compromising the information content.

Modeling non-stationary trend models with ARIMA

If the time-series contains a trend, ARMA will fail to model it correctly because of the non-stationarity.

However, as explained in the introduction, detrending a model is generally easy because it requires us to subtract a value proportional to the time instant. If we are not able to carry out this procedure or, alternatively, we don't know the actual kind of trend, a simpler approach is based on differencing the time-series. In other words, instead of using the values y_t, we employ an order d difference, defined as:

$$\nabla_1 y_t = y_t - y_{t-1}$$

$$\nabla_2 y_t = \nabla_1 y_t - \nabla_1 y_{t-1}$$

...

A first-order difference is able to detrend a model with a linear trend. For example, if $y_t = at + \epsilon_t$, $\nabla_1 y_t = at + \epsilon_t - a(t-1) + \epsilon_{t-1} = 1 + \epsilon_t - \epsilon_{t-1}$. If the noise has a null mean, $E[\nabla_1 y_t] = E[\epsilon_t] - E[\epsilon_{t-1}] = 0$. Analogously, it's possible to use second-order differencing to remove a quadratic trend, and so on. An ARIMA(p, d, q) model (where the letter I stands for integrated) is actually an ARMA model that performs d order differencing before training the ARMA(p, q) sub-model.

Let's test an ARIMA model with the same synthetic dataset as used in the previous example, where we have added a linear trend:

```
import numpy as np

x = np.arange(0, 50, 0.5)
y = np.sin(5.*x) + np.random.normal(0.0, 0.5, size=x.shape)
y += x/10.
```

A plot of the time-series is shown in the following figure:

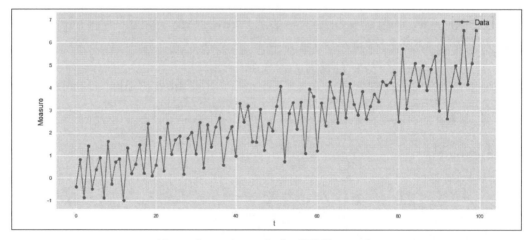

Non-stationary time-series for ARIMA example

At this point, we can proceed as done in the previous example. As we know that the trend is linear, we can employ an ARIMA(6, 1, 2) model:

```
from statsmodels.tsa.arima_model import ARIMA

y_train = y[0:90]
y_test = y[90:]

arima = ARIMA(y_train, order=(6, 1, 2), missing="drop").\
        fit(transparams=True, maxiter=500, trend="c")

y_pred_arima = arima.predict(start=90, end=99)
```

In this case, we have explicitly requested to include a constant for the trend. The prediction result is shown in the following figure:

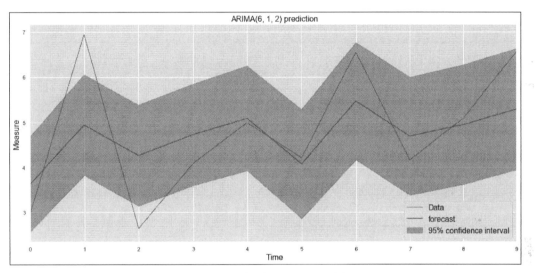

Predictions for the ARIMA model

As we can see, the prediction ranges in the interval (3, 7), which corresponds to the last part of the time-series and the accuracy is comparable to the one achieved by the ARMA model.

As an exercise, I invite the reader to repeat all these examples with the time-series contained in the energy consumption dataset. In that case, there are seasonal components and trends, so it's possible to test different models and evaluate the performances.

Summary

In this chapter, we have introduced the concept of time-series and discussed the properties of stationary processes and how to manipulate a dataset to remove irregularities through a process called smoothing. This method allows us to perform a data cleansing step when the time-series is heavily affected by white noise. It's also helpful when it's important to visualize the trends or seasonality without the secondary effects due to the noise. We have shown how AR, MA, and ARMA models can successfully forecast stationary time-series and how, using the technique of differencing, it's possible to train ARIMA models in order to also forecast non-stationary time-series. Another fundamental concept that we have discussed is auto-correlation, which allows us to have a clear insight into the behavior of the time-series with minimal effort. This kind of analysis helps the data scientist to choose the most appropriate model.

In the next chapter, we start discussing some fundamental elements of statistical learning, focusing the attention on Bayesian networks and hidden Markov models.

Further reading

- Greene W. H., *Econometric Analysis (Fifth edition)*, Prentice Hall, 2002

- Belsley D. A., Kuh E., Welsch R., *Regression diagnostics: Identifying Influential Data and Sources of Collinearity*, Wiley, 1980

- Chakravarti N., *Isotonic Median Regression: A Linear Programming Approach*, Mathematics of Operations Research, 14/2, 1989

- Shumway R. H., Stoffer D. S., *Time Series Analysis and Its Applications*, Springer, 2017

- Candanedo L. M., Feldheim V., Deramaix D., *Data driven prediction models of energy use of appliances in a low-energy house*, Energy and Buildings, Volume 140, 04/2017

11
Bayesian Networks and Hidden Markov Models

In this chapter, we're going to introduce the basic concepts of Bayesian models, which allow us to work with several scenarios where it's necessary to consider uncertainty as a structural part of the system. The discussion will focus on static (time-invariant) and dynamic methods that can be employed, where necessary, to model time sequences.

In particular, the chapter covers the following topics:

- Bayes' theorem and its applications
- Bayesian networks
- Sampling from a Bayesian network:
  - **Markov chain Monte Carlo (MCMC)**, Gibbs, and Metropolis-Hastings
- Modeling a Bayesian network with PyMC3 and PyStan
- **Hidden Markov Models (HMMs)**
- Examples with the library `hmmlearn`

Before discussing more advanced topics, we need to introduce the basic concept of Bayesian statistics with a focus on all those aspects that are exploited by the algorithms discussed in the chapter.

Conditional probabilities and Bayes' theorem

If we have a probability space Ω and two events A and B, the probability of A given B is called conditional probability, and it's defined as:

$$P(A|B) = \frac{P(A,B)}{P(B)}$$

As the joint probability is commutative, that is, $P(A, B) = P(B, A)$, it's possible to derive Bayes' theorem:

$$\begin{cases} P(A,B) = P(A|B)P(B) \\ P(B,A) = P(B|A)P(A) \end{cases} \Rightarrow P(A|B) = \frac{P(B|A)P(A)}{P(B)}$$

This theorem allows expressing a conditional probability as a function of the opposite one and the two marginal probabilities $P(A)$ and $P(B)$. This result is fundamental to many machine learning problems, because, as we're going to see in this and in the next chapters, normally it's easier to work with a conditional probability (for example, $p(A \mid B)$) in order to get the opposite (that is, $p(B \mid A)$), but it's hard to work directly with the probability $p(B \mid A)$. A common form of this theorem can be expressed as:

$$P(A|B) \propto P(B|A)P(A)$$

Let's suppose that we need to estimate the probability of an event A given some observations B, or using the standard notation, the posterior probability of A; the previous formula expresses this value as proportional to the term $P(A)$, which is the marginal probability of A, called prior probability, and the conditional probability of the observations B given the event A. $p(B \mid A)$ is called likelihood, and defines how event A is likely to determine B. Therefore, we can summarize the relation as:

posterior probability $\propto$ *likelihood $\cdot$ prior probability*

The proportion is not a limitation, because the term $P(B)$ is always a normalizing constant that can be omitted. Of course, the reader must remember to normalize $P(A, B)$ so that its terms always sum up to one. This is a key concept of Bayesian statistics, where we don't directly trust the prior probability, but we reweight it using the likelihood of our observations. To achieve this goal, we need to introduce the prior probability, which represents the initial knowledge (before observing the data).

This stage is very important and can lead to very different results as a function of the prior families. If the domain knowledge is consolidated, a precise prior distribution allows us to achieve a more accurate posterior distribution. Conversely, if the prior knowledge is limited, it's generally preferable to avoid specific distributions and, instead, default to so-called *low-* or *non-informative priors*.

In general, distributions that concentrate the probability in a restricted region are very informative and their entropy is low because the uncertainty is capped by the variance. For example, if we impose a prior Gaussian distribution $N(1.0, 0.01)$, we expect the posterior to be very peaked around the mean. In this case, the likelihood term has a limited ability to change the prior belief, unless the sample size is extremely large. Conversely, if we know that the posterior mean can be found in the range (0.5, 1.5) but we are not sure about the true value, it's preferable to employ a distribution with a larger entropy, like a uniform one. This choice is low-informative, because all the values (for a continuous distribution, we can consider arbitrary small intervals) have the same probability and the likelihood has more *room* to find the right posterior mean.

Conjugate priors

Another important family of prior distributions are the *conjugate priors* with respect to a specific likelihood. A distribution P is said to be conjugate prior to Q with respect to the likelihood L if, using the Bayes' formula, $Q \propto LP$, Q and P belong to same family. For example, if $L \sim N(\mu, \sigma^2)$ with known σ^2, the normal distribution is conjugate to itself, that is, the role of the likelihood is only to shift the Gaussian without altering the variance. Conjugate priors are helpful for many reasons. First, they simplify the calculations, because, given a likelihood, it's possible to find the posterior without any integration. Moreover, in some domains, the posterior is naturally expected to belong to same family of the prior distribution. For example, if we want to know whether a coin is either fair or loaded, the likelihood is obviously Bernoulli; there are only two discrete outcomes and the optimal prior distribution is the Beta, whose **probability density function (p.d.f.)** is defined as:

$$Beta(x; \alpha, \beta) \propto x^{\alpha-1}(1-x)^{\beta-1} \ with \ \alpha, \beta > 0$$

This probability distribution can easily model any binomial scenario. In fact, if $\alpha = \beta = 2$, the p.d.f. is perfectly symmetric, while it becomes peaked around the extremes when one parameter is larger than the other one. For a fair coin, we expect the likelihood to alter both constants in the same way. When $N \to \infty$, the likelihood becomes binomial (as the experiments are independent) and $\alpha \to \infty, \beta \to \infty$. Therefore, the distribution degenerates into a perfectly balanced Bernoulli with $p = 1/2$.

On the other side, if, for example, the number of heads (in a continuous model, this outcome can be equal exactly to 1) is much larger than the number of tails, $\alpha \gg \beta$ (or vice versa) and the Beta distribution starts to be very peaked in a region close to the extreme 1. If $N \to \infty \Rightarrow \alpha/\beta \to \infty$, and the distribution degenerates to a Bernoulli with $p = 1$ (corresponding to the heads). This scenario is shown in the following figure:

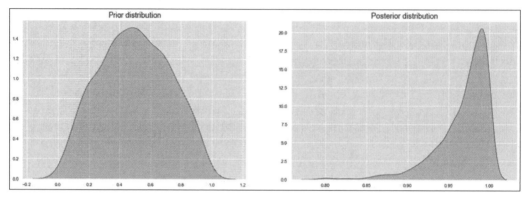

Beta prior (left) and posterior (right) distributions

It's not difficult to see that, when the likelihood is Bernoulli or binomial, the conjugate prior is Beta and, obviously, the effect of the likelihood is to shift α and β in order to reproduce the actual posterior distribution.

We can now think to toss the coin 10 times (event A). We know that $P(A) = 1/2$ if the coin is fair. If we'd like to know what the probability is to get 10 heads, we could employ the binomial distribution obtaining $P(k\ heads) = 1/2^k$. However, let's suppose that we don't know whether the coin is fair or not, but we suspect it's loaded with a prior probability $P(Coin = Loaded) = 0.7$ in favor of tails. We can define a complete prior probability $P(Coin)$ using the indicator functions:

$$P(Coin) = P(Coin = Loaded)I_{Coin=Loaded} + P(Coin = Fair)I_{Coin=Fair}$$

In the previous expression, we have assumed $P(Coin = Fair) = 0.5$ and $P(Coin = Loaded) = 0.7$, the indicator $I_{Coin=Fair} = 1$ only if the coin is fair, and 0 otherwise. The same happens with $I_{Coin=Loaded}$ when the coin is loaded. Our goal now is to determine the posterior probability $P(Coin \mid B_1, B_2, ..., B_n)$ to be able to confirm or to reject our hypothesis.

Let's imagine observing $n = 10$ events with $B_1 = Head$ and $B_2, ..., B_n = Tail$. We can express the probabilities of each outcome using the binomial distribution:

$$P(Coin|B_1, B_2, ..., B_n) \propto \left[\binom{10}{1} 0.5(1-0.5)^9 0.3 I_{Coin=Fair} + \binom{10}{1} 0.7(1-0.7)^9 0.7 I_{Coin=Loaded} \right]$$

After simplifying the expression, we get:

$$P(Coin|B_1, B_2, ..., B_n) \propto 0.003 I_{Coin=Fair} + 0.08 I_{Coin=Loaded}$$

We still need to normalize by dividing both terms by 0.083
(the sum of the two terms), so we get the final posterior probability
$P(Coin|B_1, B_2, ..., B_n) = 0.04 I_{Coin=Fair} + 0.96 I_{Coin=Loaded}$. This result confirms
and strengthens our hypothesis. The probability of a loaded coin is now about
96%, thanks to the sequence of nine tail observations after one head.

This example was presented to show how the data (observations) is plugged into the
Bayesian framework. If the reader is interested in studying these concepts in more
detail, in Pratt J., Raiffa H., Schlaifer R., *Introduction to Statistical Decision Theory*, The
MIT Press, 2008, it's possible to find many interesting examples and explanations;
however, before introducing Bayesian networks, it's useful to define two other
essential concepts.

The first concept is called conditional independence, and it can be formalized
considering two variables A and B, which are conditioned to a third one, C.
We say that A and B are conditionally independent given C if:

$$P(A, B|C) = P(A|C)P(B|C)$$

Now, let's suppose we have an event A that is conditioned to a series of causes C_1, C_2,
..., C_n. The conditional probability is, therefore, $P(A | C_1, C_2, ..., C_n)$. Applying Bayes'
theorem, we get:

$$P(A|C_1, C_2, ..., C_n) \propto P(C_1, C_2, ..., C_n|A)P(A)$$

If there is conditional independence, the previous expression can be simplified and
rewritten as:

$$P(A|C_1, C_2, ..., C_n) \propto P(C_1|A)P(C_2|A) ... P(C_n|A)P(A) = P(A) \prod_{i=1}^{n} P(C_i|A)$$

This property is fundamental in Naive Bayes classifiers, where we assume that the effect produced by a cause does not influence the other causes. For example, in a spam detector, we could say that the length of the mail and the presence of some particular keywords are independent events, and we only need to compute *P(Length | Spam)* and *P(Keywords | Spam)* without considering the joint probability *P(Length, Keywords | Spam)*.

The second important element, and the last we'll analyze in this chapter, is the chain rule of probabilities. Let's suppose we have the joint probability $P(X_1, X_2, \dots, X_n)$. It can be expressed as:

$$P(X_1, X_2, \dots, X_n) = P(X_1 | X_2, \dots, X_n) P(X_2, \dots, X_n)$$

Repeating the procedure with the joint probability on the right side, we get:

$$P(X_1, X_2, \dots, X_n) = P(X_1 | X_2, \dots, X_n) P(X_2 | X_3, \dots, X_n) \dots P(X_n) = \prod_{i=1}^{n} P(X_i | X_{i+1}, \dots, X_n)$$

In this way, it's possible to express a full joint probability as the product of hierarchical conditional probabilities, until the last term, which is a marginal distribution. We're going to use this concept extensively in the next section, where we'll explore Bayesian networks.

Bayesian networks

A Bayesian network is a probabilistic model represented by a direct acyclic graph $G = \{V, E\}$, where the vertices are random variables X_i, and the edges determine a conditional dependence among them. In the following diagram, there's an example of a simple Bayesian network with four variables:

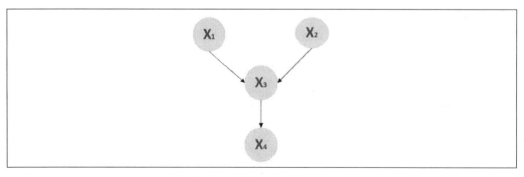

Example of Bayesian network

The variable X_4 is dependent on X_3, which is dependent on X_1 and X_2. To describe the network, we need the marginal probabilities $P(X_1)$ and $P(X_2)$ and the conditional probabilities $P(X_3 \mid X_1, X_2)$ and $P(X_4 \mid X_3)$. In fact, using the chain rule, we can derive the full joint probability as:

$$P(X_1, X_2, X_3, X_4) = P(X_4|X_3)P(X_3|X_1, X_2)P(X_2)P(X_1)$$

The previous expression shows an important concept: as the graph is direct and acyclic, each variable is conditionally independent of all other variables that are not successors given its predecessors. To formalize this concept, we can define the function $Predecessors(X_i)$, which returns the set of nodes that influence X_i directly, for example, $Predecessors(X_3) = \{X_1, X_2\}$. Using this function, it's possible to write a general expression for the full joint probability of a Bayesian network with N nodes:

$$P(X_1, X_2, ..., X_m) = \prod_{i=1}^{m} P(X_i|Predecessors(X_i))$$

The general procedure to build a Bayesian network should always start with the first causes, adding their effects one by one, until the last nodes are inserted into the graph. If this rule is not respected, the resulting graph can contain useless relations that can increase the complexity of the model. For example, if X_4 is caused indirectly by both X_1 and X_2, adding the edges $X_1 \rightarrow X_4$ and $X_2 \rightarrow X_4$ might seem like a good modeling choice; however, we know that the final influence on X_4 is determined by the value of X_3 only, whose probability is conditional on X_1 and X_2. As such, we can say with confidence that $X_1 \rightarrow X_4$ and $X_2 \rightarrow X_4$ are spurious edges, and they don't need to be added.

Sampling from a Bayesian network

Performing a direct inference on a Bayesian network can be quite a difficult operation when there's a high number of variables and edges, because the full joint probability can become extremely complex, as well as the integral needed to normalize the distribution. Since we need to compute the normalization constant to obtain the posterior probability, if this step is infeasible, we need to find other approaches to solve this problem. For this reason, several sampling methods have been proposed. In this paragraph, we're going to show how to determine the full joint probability sampling from a network using a direct approach, and two MCMC algorithms.

Let's start by considering a simple network with two connected nodes, X_1 and X_2, with the following distributions:

$$\begin{cases} X_1 \sim N(0.1, 2) \\ X_2 \sim N\left(X_1, 0.5 + \sqrt{|X_1|}\right) \end{cases}$$

We can now use a direct sampling to estimate the full joint probability $P(X_1, X_2)$ using the chain rule previously introduced.

Direct sampling

With direct sampling, our goal is to approximate the full joint probability through a sequence of samples drawn from each conditional distribution. If we assume that the graph is well structured (without unnecessary edges) and we have N variables, the algorithm is made up of the following steps:

1. Initialize the variable $N_{samples}$.
2. Initialize a vector S with shape $(N, N_{samples})$.
3. Initialize a frequency vector $F_{samples}$ with shape $(N, N_{samples})$. In Python, it's better to employ a dictionary where the key is a combination $(x_1, x_2, \ldots, x_n)$.
4. For $t = 1$ to $N_{samples}$:
    a. For $i = 1$ to N:
        i.   Sample from $P(X_i \mid Predecessor(X_i))$
        ii. Store the sample in $S[i, t]$
    b. If $F_{samples}$ contains the sampled tuple $S[: , t]$:
        $$F_{samples}\big[S[:,t]\big] \mathrel{+}= 1$$
    c. Else:
        $$F_{samples}\big[S[:,t]\big] = 1 \text{ (both these operations are immediate with}$$
        Python dictionaries)
5. Create a vector $P_{sampled}$ with shape $(N, 1)$.
6. Set $P_{samples}[i, 0] = {F_{sampled}[i]} \big/ {N}$.

From a mathematical viewpoint, we are first creating a frequency vector $F_{samples}(x_1, x_2, ..., x_N; N_{samples})$ and then approximating the full joint probability considering $N_{samples} \rightarrow \infty$:

$$P(x_1, x_2, ..., x_N) = \lim_{N_{samples} \rightarrow \infty} F_{samples}(x_1, x_2, ..., x_N; N_{samples})$$

Example of direct sampling

We can now implement this algorithm in Python. Let's start by defining the sample methods using the NumPy function `np.random.normal(u,s)` which draws a sample from a $N(u, s^2)$ distribution:

```
import numpy as np

def X1_sample():
    return np.random.normal(0.1, 2.0)

def X2_sample(x1):
    return np.random.normal(x1, 0.5 + np.sqrt(np.abs(x1)))
```

At this point, we can implement the main cycle. Since the variables are Boolean, the total number of probabilities is 16, so we set $N_{samples} = 10,000$ (smaller values are also acceptable):

```
Nsamples = 10000

X = np.zeros((Nsamples, ))
Y = np.zeros((Nsamples, ))

for i, t in enumerate(range(Nsamples)):
    x1 = X1_sample()
    x2 = X2_sample(x1)

    X[i] = x1
    Y[i] = x2
```

When the sampling is complete, it's possible to visualize the density estimation of the full joint probability:

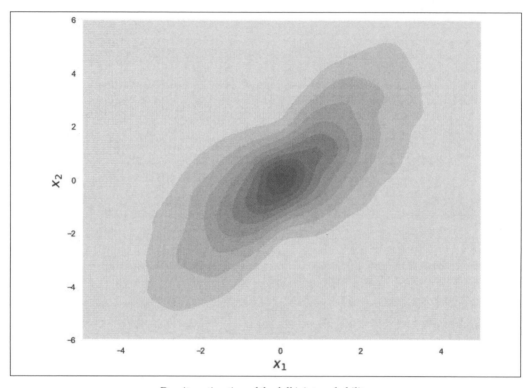

Density estimation of the full joint probability

A gentle introduction to Markov Chains

In order to discuss the MCMC algorithms, it's necessary to introduce the concept of Markov chains. In fact, while the direct sample method draws samples without any particular order, the MCMC strategies draw a sequence of samples according to a precise transition probability from a sample to the following one.

Let's consider a time-dependent random variable $X(t)$, and let's assume a discrete time sequence $X_1, X_2, \dots, X_t, X_{t+1}, \dots$ where X_t represents the value assumed at time t. In the following diagram, there's a schematic representation of this sequence:

Structure of a generic Markov chain

Suppose we have N different states $s_i \; \forall \; i = (1, N)$, in that case, it's possible to consider the probability $P(X_t = s_i | X_{t-1} = s_j, \dots, X_1 = s_p)$. $X(t)$ is defined as a first-order Markov process if:

$$P\big(X_t = s_i | X_{t-1} = s_j, \dots, X_1 = s_p\big) = P\big(X_t = s_i | X_{t-1} = s_j\big)$$

In other words, in a Markov process (from now on, we'll omit the specification *first-order* and assume that we're always working with this kind of chain, even if there are cases where it would be useful to consider a greater number of previous states), the probability that $X(t)$ is in a certain state depends only on the state assumed in the previous time instant. Therefore, we can define a transition probability for every couple (i, j):

$$P(j \to i) = P(X_t = s_i | X_{t-1} = s_j)$$

Considering all the couples (i, j), it's also possible to build a transition probability matrix $T(i, j) = P(i \to j)$. The marginal probability that $X_t = s_i$ using a standard notation is defined as:

$$\pi_i(t) = P(X_t = s_i)$$

At this point, it's easy to prove (using the Chapman-Kolmogorov equation) that:

$$\pi_i(t + 1) = \sum_k p(k \to i)\pi_k(t) \;\Rightarrow\; \bar{\pi}(t + 1) = T^T \bar{\pi}(t)$$

In the previous expression, in order to compute $\pi_i(t + 1)$, we need to sum over all possible previous states, considering the relative transition probability. This operation can be rewritten in matrix form, using a vector $\bar{\pi}(t)$ containing all states and the transition probability matrix T^T (the uppercase superscript T means that the matrix is transposed). The evolution of the chain can be computed recursively:

$$\bar{\pi}(t + 1) = T^T \bar{\pi}(t) = T^T (T^T \bar{\pi}(t - 1)) = \cdots = (T^T)^t \bar{\pi}(1)$$

For our purposes, it's important to consider Markov chains that are able to reach a *stationary distribution* $\bar{\pi}_s$:

$$\bar{\pi}_s = T^T \bar{\pi}_s$$

In other words, the state does not depend on the initial condition $\bar{\pi}(1)$, and it's no longer able to change. The stationary distribution is unique if the underlying Markov process is ergodic. This concept means that the process has the same properties if averaged over time (which is often impossible) or averaged vertically (freezing the time) over the states (which is simpler in the majority of cases).

The process of ergodicity for Markov chains is assured by two conditions. The first is aperiodicity for all states, which means that it is impossible to find a positive number p so that the chain returns in the same state sequence after a number of instants equal to a multiple of p. The second condition is that all states must be positive recurrent: this means that, given a random variable $N_{instants}(i)$, describing the number of time instants needed to return to the state s_i, $E[N_{instants}(i)] < \infty$; therefore, potentially, all the states can be revisited in a finite time.

The reason why we need the ergodicity condition, and hence the existence of a unique stationary distribution, is that we are considering the sampling processes modeled as Markov chains, where the next value is sampled according to the current state. The transition from one state to another is done in order to find better samples, as we're going to see in the Metropolis-Hastings sampler, where we can also decide to reject a sample and keep the chain in the same state. For this reason, we need to be sure that the algorithms converge to the unique stable distribution (that approximates the real full joint distribution of our Bayesian network). It's possible to prove that a chain always reaches a stationary distribution if:

$$\forall\, i, j \;\Rightarrow\; P(i \to j)\pi_{s_i} = P(j \to i)\pi_{s_j}$$

The previous equation is called *detailed balance* and implies the reversibility of the chain. Intuitively, it means that the probability of finding the chain in the state A times the probability of a transition to the state B is equal to the probability of finding the chain in the state B times the probability of a transition to A.

For both sampling algorithms that we're going to discuss, it's possible to prove that they satisfy the previous condition, and therefore their convergence is assured.

Gibbs sampling

Let's suppose that we want to obtain the full joint probability for a Bayesian network $P(X_1, X_2, ..., X_N)$; however, the number of variables is large and there's no way to solve this problem easily in a closed form. Moreover, imagine that we would like to get a marginal distribution, such as $P(X_2)$, but to do so we need to integrate the full joint probability, and this task is even harder. Gibbs sampling allows approximating of all marginal distributions with an iterative process. If we have N variables, the algorithm proceeds with the following steps:

- Initialize the variable $N_{iterations}$
- Initialize a vector S with shape $(N, N_{iterations})$
- Randomly initialize $x_1^{(0)}, x_2^{(0)}, \dots, x_N^{(0)}$ (the superscript index is referred to the iteration)
- For $t=1$ to $N_{iterations}$:

  ○ Sample $x_1^{(t)}$ from $p(x_1|x_2^{(t-1)}, x_3^{(t-1)}, \dots, x_N^{(t-1)})$ and store it in $S[0,t]$

  ○ Sample $x_2^{(t)}$ from $p(x_2|x_1^{(t-1)}, x_3^{(t-1)}, \dots, x_N^{(t-1)})$ and store it in $S[1,t]$

  ○ …

  ○ Sample $x_N^{(t)}$ from $p(x_N|x_2^{(t-1)}, x_3^{(t-1)}, \dots, x_{N-1}^{(t-1)})$ and store it in $S[N-1,t]$

At the end of the iterations, vector S will contain $N_{iterations}$ samples for each distribution. As we need to determine the probabilities, it's necessary to proceed like in the direct sampling algorithm, counting the number of single occurrences and normalizing dividing by $N_{iterations}$. If the variables are continuous, it's possible to consider intervals, counting how many samples are contained in each of them.

For small networks, this procedure is very similar to direct sampling, except that when working with very large networks, the sampling process could become slow; however, the algorithm can be simplified after introducing the concept of the Markov blanket of X_i, which is the set of random variables (excluding X_i) that are predecessors, successors, and successors' predecessors of X_i (in some books, they use the terms parents and children to denote these concepts). In a Bayesian network, a variable X_i is a conditional independent of all other variables given its Markov blanket. Therefore, if we define the function $MB(X_i)$, which returns the set of variables in the blanket, the generic sampling step can be rewritten as $P(X_i | MB(X_i))$, and there's no more need to consider all the other variables.

To understand this concept, let's consider the network shown in the following diagram:

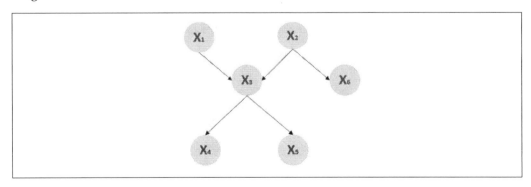

Bayesian network for the Gibbs sampling example

The Markov blankets of the variables are:

- $MB(X_1) = \{X_3\}$
- $MB(X_2) = \{X_1, X_3, X_6\}$
- $MB(X_3) = \{X_1, X_2, X_4, X_5\}$
- $MB(X_4) = \{X_3\}$
- $MB(X_5)=\{X_3\}$
- $MB(X_6)=\{X_2\}$

In general, if N is very large, the cardinality of $|MB(X_i)| \ll N$, thus simplifying the process (the vanilla Gibbs sampling needs $N - 1$ conditions for each variable). We can prove that the Gibbs sampling generates samples from a Markov chain that is in detailed balance:

$$P(i \rightarrow j)\pi_{s_i} = P(x_j|x_1, x_2, \dots, x_{j-1}, x_{j+1}, \dots, x_N)P(x_i) = P(x_j, x_i|x_1, x_2, \dots, x_{j-1}, x_{j+1}, \dots, x_{i-1}, x_{i+1}, \dots, x_N)$$
$$= P(x_i|x_1, x_2, \dots, x_{i-1}, x_{i+1}, \dots, x_N)P(x_j) = P(j \rightarrow i)\pi_{s_j}$$

Therefore, the procedure converges to the unique stationary distribution. This algorithm is quite simple; however, its performance is not excellent, because the random walks are not tuned up in order to explore the right regions of the state-space, where the probability to find good samples is high. Moreover, the trajectory can also return to bad states, slowing down the whole process. An alternative (also implemented by Stan for continuous random variables) is the No-U-Turn algorithm, which is not discussed in this book. The reader interested in this topic can find a full description in Hoffmann M. D., Gelman A., *The No-U-Turn Sampler: Adaptively Setting Path Lengths in Hamiltonian Monte Carlo*, arXiv:1111.4246, 2011.

The Metropolis-Hastings algorithm

We have seen that the full joint probability distribution of a Bayesian network $P(X_1, X_2 \dots, X_N)$ can become intractable when the number of variables is large. The problem can become even harder when it's needed to marginalize it in order to obtain, for example, $P(X_i)$, because it's necessary to integrate a very complex function. The same problem happens when applying the Bayes' theorem in simple cases.

Let's suppose we have the expression $P(A|B) = KP(B|A)P(A)$. I've expressly inserted the normalizing constant K because if we know it, we can immediately obtain the posterior probability; however, finding it normally requires integrating $P(B|A)P(A)$, and this operation can be impossible in closed form.

The Metropolis-Hastings algorithm can help us in solving this problem. Let's imagine that we need to sample from $P(X_1, X_2, ..., X_N)$, but we know this distribution up to a normalizing constant, so $P(x_1, x_2, ..., x_N) \propto g(x_1, x_2, ..., x_N)$. For simplicity, from now on we collapse all variables into a single vector, so $P(\bar{x}) \propto g(\bar{x})$.

Let's take another distribution $q(\bar{x}'|\bar{x}^{(t-1)})$, which is called *candidate-generating distribution*. There are no particular restrictions on this choice, only that $q(\bar{x})$, is easy to sample. In some situations, q can be chosen as a function very similar to the distribution $P(\bar{x})$, which is our target, while in other cases, it's possible to use a normal distribution with mean equal to $x^{(i-1)}$. As we're going to see, this function acts as a proposal-generator, but we're not obliged to accept all the samples drawn from it; therefore, potentially any distribution with the same domain of $P(X)$ can be employed.

When a sample is accepted, the Markov chain transitions to the next state. Otherwise, it remains in the current one. This decision process is based on the idea that the sampler must explore the most important state-space regions and discard the ones where the probability of finding good samples is low.

The algorithm proceeds with the following steps:

- Initialize the variable $N_{iterations}$
- Initialize $x^{(0)}$ randomly
- For $t=1$ to $N_{iterations}$:

    ○ Draw a candidate sample x' from $q(\bar{x}'|\bar{x}^{(i-1)})$

    ○ Compute the following value: $\alpha = \dfrac{g(\bar{x}')q(\bar{x}^{(t-1)}|\bar{x}')}{g(\bar{x}^{(t-1)})q(\bar{x}'|\bar{x}^{(t-1)})}$

    ○ If $\alpha \geq 1$:

    Accept the sample $\bar{x}^{(t-1)} = \bar{x}'$

    ○ Else if $\alpha \in (0,1)$:

    Accept the sample $\bar{x}^{(t-1)} = \bar{x}'$ with probability α

    Or:

    Reject the sample $\bar{x}'$ setting $\bar{x}^{(t)} = \bar{x}^{(t-1)}$ with probability $1 - \alpha$

It's possible to prove (the proof will be omitted, but it's available in Walsh B., *Markov Chain Monte Carlo and Gibbs Sampling*, Lecture Notes for EEB 596z, 2002) that the transition probability of the Metropolis-Hastings algorithm satisfies the detailed balance equation ($\forall i, j \Rightarrow P(i \rightarrow j)\pi_{s_i} = P(j \rightarrow i)\pi_{s_j}$), and therefore the algorithm converges to the true posterior distribution.

Example of Metropolis-Hastings sampling

We can implement this algorithm to find the posterior distribution $P(A\,|\,B)$ given the product of $P(B\,|\,A)$ and $P(A)$, without considering the normalizing constant that requires a complex integration.

Suppose that:

$$\begin{cases} P(A) \sim Exponential\ (\lambda = 0.1) \\ \quad P(B|A) \sim Laplace(\mu = 0, \alpha = 0.2) \end{cases}$$

Therefore, the resulting $g(x)$ (which is voluntarily relatively simple) is:

$$g(x) = \begin{cases} 0.1e^{-0.1x} \cdot \dfrac{1}{2}e^{-|x|} \ \ if\ x \geq 0 \\ 0 \quad otherwise \end{cases}$$

To solve this problem, we adopt the random walk Metropolis-Hastings, which consists of choosing $q \sim N(x^{(t-1)}, 1)$. This choice allows simplifying the value α, because the two terms $q(\bar{x}^{(t-1)}|\bar{x}')$ and $q(\bar{x}'|\bar{x}^{(t-1)})$ are equal (thanks to the symmetry around the vertical axis passing through x_{mean}) and can be canceled out, so α becomes the ratio between $g(\bar{x}')$ and $g(\bar{x}^{(t-1)})$.

The first thing is defining the functions:

```
import numpy as np

def prior(x):
    return 0.1 * np.exp(-0.1 * x)

def likelihood(x):
    if x >= 0:
        return 0.5 * np.exp(-np.abs(x))
    return 0
def g(x):
    return likelihood(x) * prior(x)

def q(xp):
    return np.random.normal(xp)
```

Now, we can start our sampling process with 100,000 iterations and $x^{(0)} = 1$:

```
nb_iterations = 100000
x = 1.0
samples = []
```

```
for i in range(nb_iterations):
    xc = q(x)

    alpha = g(xc) / g(x)
    if np.isnan(alpha):
        continue

    if alpha >= 1:
        samples.append(xc)
        x = xc
    else:
        if np.random.uniform(0.0, 1.0) < alpha:
            samples.append(xc)
            x = xc
```

We can visualize the kernel density estimation and the cumulative distribution:

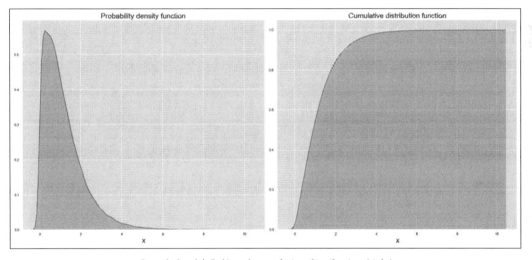

Sampled p.d.f. (left) and cumulative distribution (right)

Sampling using PyMC3

PyMC3 is a powerful Python Bayesian framework that relies on Theano to perform high-speed computations (it can also work using NumPy alone). It implements all the most important continuous and discrete distributions, and performs the sampling process mainly using the No-U-Turn and Metropolis-Hastings algorithms.

For all the details about the PyMC3 API (distributions, functions, and plotting utilities), I suggest visiting the documentation home page `http://docs.pymc.io/index.html`, where it's also possible to find some very intuitive tutorials.

The example we want to model and simulate is based on this scenario: a daily flight from London to Rome has a scheduled departure time of 12:00 am, and a standard flight time of two hours. We need to organize the operations at the destination airport, but we don't want to allocate resources too long before the plane has landed. Therefore, we want to model the process using a Bayesian network, and consider some common factors that can influence the arrival time.

In particular, we know that the onboarding process can be longer than expected, as well as the refueling one, even if they're carried out in parallel. London air traffic control can impose a delay, and the same can happen when the plane is approaching Rome. We also know that the presence of rough weather can cause another delay due to rough weather forcing a change of route. We can summarize this analysis with the following plot:

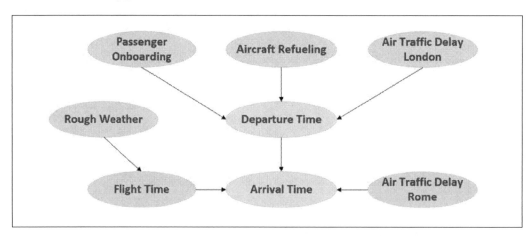

Bayesian network representing the air traffic control problem

Considering our real-world experience, we decide to model the random variables using the following distributions:

- Passenger Onboarding $\sim$ Wald($\mu = 0.5, \lambda = 0.2$)
- Refueling $\sim$ Wald($\mu = 0.25, \lambda = 0.5$)
- Departure Traffic Delay $\sim$ Wald($\mu = 0.1, \lambda = 0.2$)
- Arrival Traffic Delay $\sim$ Wald($\mu = 0.1, \lambda = 0.2$)

- Departure Time = 12 + Departure Traffic Delay + max(Passenger Onboarding, Refueling)
- Rough Weather ~ Bernoulli(p=0.35)
- Flight Time ~ Exponential(λ=0.5 - (0.1 Rough Weather)) (The output of a Bernoulli distribution is `0` or `1`, corresponding to `False` and `True`.)
- Arrival Time = Departure Time + Flight Time + Arrival Traffic Delay

The variables Departure Time and Arrival Time are functions of random variables, and the parameter λ of Flight Time is also a function of Rough Weather.

Even if the model's not very complex, the direct inference is rather inefficient, and therefore we want to simulate the process using PyMC3 (the package can be installed using the standard `pip`/`conda` commands as shown in `http://docs.pymc.io/index.html`).

The first step is to create a model instance:

```
import pymc3 as pm


model = pm.Model()
```

From now on, all operations must be performed using the context manager provided by the model variable. We can now set up all the random variables of our Bayesian network:

```
import pymc3.distributions.continuous as pmc
import pymc3.distributions.discrete as pmd
import pymc3.math as pmm

with model:
passenger_onboarding = \
        pmc.Wald("Passenger Onboarding",
                mu=0.5, lam=0.2)
    refueling = \
        pmc.Wald("Refueling",
                mu=0.25, lam=0.5)
    departure_traffic_delay = \
        pmc.Wald("Departure Traffic Delay",
                mu=0.1, lam=0.2)

    departure_time = \
        pm.Deterministic(
            "Departure Time",
            12.0 +
```

```
            departure_traffic_delay +
            pmm.switch(
                passenger_onboarding >= refueling,
                passenger_onboarding,
                refueling))

    rough_weather = \
        pmd.Bernoulli("Rough Weather",
                    p=0.35)

    flight_time = \
        pmc.Exponential("Flight Time",
                    lam=0.5 - (0.1 * rough_weather))
    arrival_traffic_delay = \
        pmc.Wald("Arrival Traffic Delay",
                mu=0.1, lam=0.2)

    arrival_time = \
        pm.Deterministic("Arrival time",
                        departure_time +
                        flight_time +
                        arrival_traffic_delay)
```

We've imported two namespaces, pymc3.distributions.continuous and pymc3.distributions.discrete, because we are using both kinds of variable. Wald and exponential are continuous distributions, while Bernoulli is discrete. In the first three rows, we declare the variables passenger_onboarding, refueling, and departure_traffic_delay. The structure is always the same: we need to specify the class corresponding to the desired distribution, passing the name of the variable and all the required parameters.

The `departure_time` variable is declared as `pm.Deterministic`. In PyMC3, this means that, once all the random elements have been set, its value becomes completely determined. Indeed, if we sample from `departure_traffic_delay`, `passenger_onboarding`, and `refueling`, we get a determined value for `departure_time`. In this declaration, we've also used the utility function `pmm.switch`, which operates a binary choice based on its first parameter (for example, *if A>B return A else return B*).

The other variables are very similar, except for `flight_time`, which is an exponential variable with a parameter λ, which is a function of another variable (`rough_weather`). Since a Bernoulli variable outputs 1 with probability p and 0 with probability $1 - p$ $\lambda = 0.4$ if there's rough weather, and 0.5 otherwise.

Running the Sampling Process

Once the model has been set up, it's possible to simulate it through a sampling process. PyMC3 picks the best sampler automatically, according to the type of variables.

As the model is not very complex, we can limit the process to 500 samples using a default value of 4 chains (for more complex scenario this parameter can be increased). Moreover, as default setting, PyMC3 will skip the first 500 samples (set through the parameter draws) as the chains could have not reached the stationary distribution yet. This warm-up period is extremely important because the first samples are unreliable, and their inclusion reduces the accuracy of the posterior probability prediction. Conversely, the usage of more than one chain can help reduce the variance.

Therefore, we are going to sample a total of (500 + 500) x 4 = 4,000 data points:

```
nb_samples = 500

with model:
samples = pm.sample(draws=nb_samples,
                            random_seed=1000)
```

The output can be analyzed using the built-in `pm.traceplot()` function, which generates the plots for each of the sample's variables (and each chain), as shown in the following diagram:

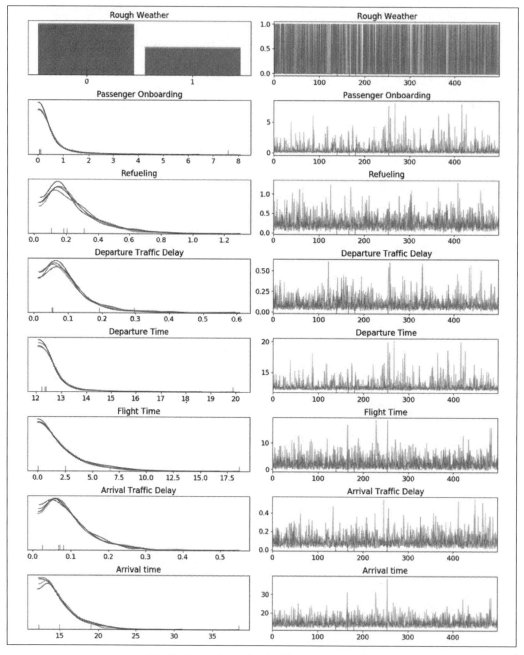

Distribution and samples for all random variables

The right column shown the samples generated for the random variable, while the left column shows the relative frequencies. This plot can be useful to get visual confirmation of our initial ideas; in fact, the arrival time has the majority of its mass concentrated in the interval 14:00 to 16:00 (the numbers are always decimal, so it's necessary to convert the times); however, we should integrate to get the probabilities. Instead, through the `pm.summary()` function, PyMC3 provides a statistical summary that can help us in making the right decisions. In the following snippet, the output containing the whole summary (which is a Pandas DataFrame) is shown:

```
import pandas as pd

with pd.option_context('display.max_rows', None,
                       'display.max_columns', None):
    print(pm.summary(samples))
```

The output is:

	mean	sd
Rough Weather	0.349500	0.476812
Passenger Onboarding	0.508697	0.792440
Refueling	0.248637	0.171351
Departure Traffic Delay	0.100411	0.073563
Departure Time	12.689327	0.775027
Flight Time	2.231149	2.264649
Arrival Traffic Delay	0.097987	0.066614
Arrival time	15.018463	2.410993

	mc_error	hpd_2.5	hpd_97.5
Rough Weather	0.008015	0.000000	1.000000
Passenger Onboarding	0.021105	0.014012	1.933437
Refueling	0.003331	0.038644	0.596968
Departure Traffic Delay	0.001905	0.016522	0.239186
Departure Time	0.020998	12.102561	14.099915
Flight Time	0.053354	0.004454	6.763558
Arrival Traffic Delay	0.001526	0.015110	0.228818
Arrival time	0.057962	12.267486	19.823165

	n_eff	Rhat
Rough Weather	3518.788680	0.999277
Passenger Onboarding	1607.397261	0.999506
Refueling	2032.614196	0.999326
Departure Traffic Delay	1588.997795	0.999700
Departure Time	1396.024578	0.999855
Flight Time	1800.353758	0.999524
Arrival Traffic Delay	1715.607331	0.999116
Arrival time	1787.109205	0.999169

For each variable, it contains mean, standard deviation, Monte Carlo error, 95% highest posterior density interval, and the posterior quantiles. The last two parameters (n_eff and Rhat) are extremely important to understand whether the model has reached or not a good convergence level; further details about the interpretation of these concepts will be revealed as we continue to discuss the results.

If there are more k chains, we expect that all of them become stationary, but, moreover, we need for them to all reproduce the same underlying distribution (that is, they are mixed). This goal, as proposed by Stan creators (in A. Gelman, J. B. Carlin, H. S. Stern, *Bayesian Data Analysis*, CRC Press, 2013), can be achieved by splitting the sequences into two parts and checking if each part is mixed with the corresponding half and with all other half parts.

The coefficient $\hat{R}$ (which is called Rhat in most computer packages) has been designed to measure this result by employing a weighted average between the in-sequence $V_{in}(\pi|p)$ and between-sequence $V_b(\pi|p)$ variances of each estimated parameter π (assuming N draws and the observation p):

$$\widetilde{var}(\pi|p) = \frac{V_b(\pi|p) + (N-1)V_{in}(\pi|p)}{N}$$

If the distributions become stationary and the chains are properly mixed, we expect $\widetilde{var}(\pi|p)$ to become closer and closer to $V_{in}(\pi|p)$. Intuitively, it's possible to understand, that the effect of $V_b(\pi|p)$ yields an overestimation of the variance, but, on the other side, when $N \to \infty$, if the model has been properly set up, the variance between sequence should approach the in-variance. Therefore, the coefficient $\hat{R}$ is defined as:

$$\hat{R}(\pi|p) = \sqrt{\frac{var(\pi|p)}{V_{in}(\pi|p)}}$$

In particular, when $N \to \infty$, if $\left|\hat{R}(\pi|p) - 1\right| > 0.1$, it means that the sequences are not properly mixed (the threshold 0.1 can be considered as a best practice), and the estimations could be inaccurate (even if theoretically $\left|\hat{R}(\pi|p)\right| \to 1$ *when* $N \to \infty$, the convergence speed might be too low to assure accurate results). As it's possible to see, in our example, all $\hat{R}(\pi|p) \approx 1$, therefore we can trust the mixing result.

As the mixing is not immediate, the effective sample size (often denoted as n_eff) corresponds to the number of *reliable* draws (that is, obtained after the mixing). This value is less informative than $\hat{R}$, but it helps to understand whether the number of iterations is enough or it's preferable to increase it. For example, if we expect at least 1,000 draws, the result obtained in the example is satisfactory.

Conversely, if the complexity of the posterior distribution is high and we prefer at least 2,000 drawn, the simulation must be extended because the mixing time doesn't allow us to achieve this value for all parameters.

Sampling using PyStan

Let's now consider a slightly simpler example using another popular framework (Stan). Imagine that you want to model the arrival time of an airplane as a linear combination of three factors:

- Departure delay
- Travel time
- Arrival delay

Given a set of existing observations, we can assume:

$$arrival\ time \sim N(departure\ delay + travel\ time + arrival\ delay, \sigma_a^2)$$

However, we cannot treat the independent variables as deterministic because they are influenced by many factors which are out of our control. For example, the departure delay depends on the origin airport. The travel time is influenced by the traffic and weather conditions (moreover, there can be speed limitations imposed by the company to reduce fuel consumption). Finally, the arrival delay depends on incoming traffic. For simplicity, we're avoiding interdependencies (but I invite the reader to include them as an exercise). Given the nature of each random variable, we've decided to model them as:

$$\begin{cases} departure\ delay \sim Exponential(0.5) \\ travel\ time \sim N(2, 0.2) \\ arrival\ delay \sim Exponential(0.1) \end{cases}$$

As the goal of the airline is to minimize the departure delay, we've chosen an exponential distribution, whose p.d.f. is:

$$f(x) = \beta e^{-\beta x}$$

This distribution has a peak for $x = 0$ and then decreases exponentially. As longer departure delays become less and less likely, this distribution is quite reasonable. The travel time is generally the same, with limited variations around the mean; therefore, a normal distribution is the best choice.

For the arrival delay, we've made the same assumptions as we did with the departure, therefore employing another exponential with a lower β (since the airplane has only a limited possibility of flying around for a long time).

Stan is based on a meta-language that is transformed into highly optimized C++ code; therefore, the first step is defining the whole model:

```
code = """
data {
    int<lower=0> num;
    vector[num] departure_delay;
    vector[num] travel_time;
    vector[num] arrival_delay;
    vector[num] arrival_time;
}
parameters {
    real beta_a;
    real beta_b;
    real mu_t;
    real sigma_t;
    real sigma_a;
}
model {
    departure_delay ~ exponential(beta_a);
    travel_time ~ normal(mu_t, sigma_t);
    arrival_delay ~ exponential(beta_b);
    arrival_time ~ normal(departure_delay +
                          travel_time +
                          arrival_delay,
                          sigma_a);
}
"""
```

The code is split into four main blocks:

- `data`, which describes the parameters that are passed as input observations. The details of the meta-language can be found in the official documentation; however, they are very intuitive. In this case, we are declaring an integer variable num to define the number of observations and four vectors to store their values (as real – double/float – variables).

- `parameters`, that contains the list of estimated parameters. Each value in this block will be considered as a variable that must be estimated using a Monte Carlo algorithm.

- `transformed parameters`, which is missing in this case, but that normally contains all those parameters that are obtained through specific transformations (for example, functions).

- `model`, which contains the main structure of the code, describing the nature of every random variable and how they combine to yield to desired result. In our case, we have declared all p.d.f.s and the structure of the arrival time, which has a well-defined mean, but a variable standard deviation that is subject to estimation.

At this point, since this is an example, we can create some observations:

```
import numpy as np

nb_samples = 10

departure_delay = np.random.exponential(0.5, size=nb_samples)
travel_time = np.random.normal(2.0, 0.2, size=nb_samples)
arrival_delay = np.random.exponential(0.1, size=nb_samples)
arrival_time = np.random.normal(departure_delay +
                                travel_time +
                                arrival_delay,
                                0.5, size=nb_samples)
```

In a real case, we should have collected these data through actual observations. Once the model is ready, we can compile it using PyStan (the package can be generally installed using the command `pip install pystan`, but the reader can find detailed instructions in the page `https://pystan.readthedocs.io/en/latest/installation_beginner.html`):

```
import pystan

model = pystan.StanModel(model_code=code)
```

In this way, PyStan will transform the code into a C++ module in order to achieve the best performance. Once the model has been compiled (the process can take some time depending on the available hardware), it's necessary to fit it using our data. To do that, we first need to create a dictionary where each key matches the variable name declared in the data section of the code:

```
data = {
    "num": nb_samples,
    "departure_delay": departure_delay,
    "arrival_time": arrival_time,
    "travel_time": travel_time,
    "arrival_delay": arrival_delay
}
```

Once the dictionary is ready, we can fit the model. In this case, we want to perform 10,000 iterations, with a warm-up of 1,000 draws using 2 chains:

```
fit = model.sampling(data=data, iter=10000,
                     refresh=10000, warmup=1000,
                     chains=2, seed=1000)
```

The result of the training procedure can be visualized directly:

```
print(fit)
```

The output of the previous code is (as a pretty print):

```
Inference for Stan model: anon_model_ba33d205f088c2a56ee1c983cd549ac9.
2 chains, each with iter=10000; warmup=1000; thin=1;
post-warmup draws per chain=9000, total post-warmup draws=18000.

          mean se_mean    sd   2.5%    25%    50%    75%  97.5%  n_eff   Rhat
beta_a    2.24  6.0e-3  0.66   1.12   1.76   2.18   2.65    3.7  12139    1.0
beta_b   10.63    0.03  3.22   5.35   8.32  10.31  12.63  17.74  11654    1.0
mu_t      1.98  5.4e-4  0.06   1.86   1.94   1.98   2.02    2.1  12721    1.0
sigma_t   0.19  6.5e-4  0.05   0.11   0.15   0.18   0.21   0.32   6551    1.0
sigma_a    0.5  2.0e-3  0.14   0.32   0.41   0.48   0.57   0.85   5069    1.0
lp__     24.14    0.03   1.8  19.76   23.2   24.5  25.48  26.53   5149    1.0

Samples were drawn using NUTS at Wed Oct  2 19:47:03 2019.
For each parameter, n_eff is a crude measure of effective sample size,
and Rhat is the potential scale reduction factor on split chains (at
convergence, Rhat=1).
```

The summary provides information about each estimated parameter. The minimum effective sample size is greater than 5,000 and $\hat{R} = 1$ for all parameters (this is not surprising since we created the dataset, but I invite the reader to employ different distributions and check the results). In order to have a confirmation of the estimations, we can ask the model to sample from the posterior distribution:

```
ext = fit.extract()
beta_a = ext["beta_a"]
beta_b = ext["beta_b"]
mu_t = ext["mu_t"]
sigma_t = ext["sigma_t"]
```

The density estimations of the parameters are shown in the following figure:

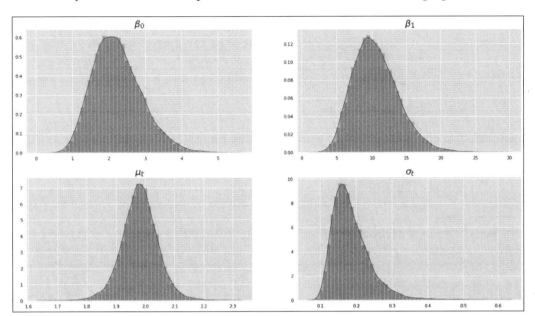

Distribution of sampled estimations

The reader must pay attention to the difference between Stan and NumPy when working with exponential distributions. In fact, NumPy considers the parameter β as β^{-1}, therefore, the diagrams are correct, with a peak corresponding to the true value. Considering the travel time, μ_t is normally distributed around the actual mean, while σ_t is asymmetric, indicating that larger variances are less likely than analogous smaller ones. However, the distribution has a long positive tail as $\sigma_t > 0$. Using these values, it's possible to determine the averages and, consequently the average arrival time. In this model, we've included all the uncertainty in the prior distributions (plus the standard deviation of the arrival time), however, it's possible to work in the same way as a linear regression, structuring the model as:

$$arrival\ time \sim N(\alpha_0 + \alpha_1 departure\ delay + \alpha_2 travel\ time + \alpha_3 arrival\ delay, \sigma_a^2)$$

In this case, the parameters α_i can be assumed to be normally distributed, while the observed values are deterministic. It's not difficult to understand that the result is analogous to a classical regression with normally distributed residuals.

The advantage of this approach is that it's more explainable, because the magnitude of the coefficients α_i (for example, their average and standard deviation) is directly correlated to the impact of each factor to the arrival time. The choice of a specific strategy depends on the context; however, given the flexibility of the frameworks and the computational power, I strongly suggest avoiding using deterministic variables whenever there are unmanaged uncertainty sources.

If the prior information is limited, it's always possible to default on non-informative priors (for example, uniform distributions), letting the model find the optimal parameters itself. On the other side, if the observation dataset is limited, it could be helpful to rely on domain experts to define the most reliable prior distributions (for example, in our case, we might have observed just a few flights, while an Air Traffic Controller can confirm that normally the arrival delay is close to 0 because the airport hasn't got a lot of incoming traffic).

The advantage of a Bayesian approach is evident when it's necessary to trade-off between prior knowledge and data evidence. In some cases, the former might be biased or limited, hence it's much better to rely exclusively on the data (assuming to collect enough data points). Conversely, when an expert can provide accurate details and the data points are limited, it's preferable to model the priors as expected and let the model adjust the parameters accordingly.

Hidden Markov Models

Hidden Markov Models are probabilistic algorithms that can be employed in all those contexts where it's impossible to measure the state of a system (we can only model it as a stochastic variable with a known transition probability), but it's possible to access some data connected to it. An example can be a complex engine that is made up of a large number of parts. We can define some internal states and learn a transition probability matrix (we're going to learn how to do that), but we can only receive measures provided by specific sensors.

Let's consider a stochastic process $X(t)$ that can assume N different states: $s_1, s_2, ..., s_N$ with first-order Markov chain dynamics. Let's also suppose that we cannot observe the state of $X(t)$, but we have access to another process $O(t)$, connected to $X(t)$, which produces observable outputs (often known as emissions). The resulting process is called a **Hidden Markov Model (HMM)**, and a generic schema is shown in the following diagram:

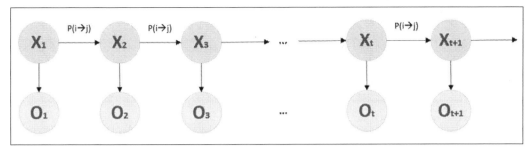

Structure of a generic Hidden Markov Model

For each hidden state s_i, we need to define a transition probability $P(i \rightarrow j)$, normally represented as a matrix if the variable is discrete. For the Markov assumption, we have:

$$P(j \rightarrow i) = P(X_t = s_i | X_{t-1} = s_j)$$

Moreover, given a sequence of observations $o_1, o_2, \dots, o_M$ we also assume the following assumption about the independence of the emission probability:

$$P(o_i | o_1, o_2, \dots, o_k, x_1, x_2, \dots, x_k) = P(o_i | x_i)$$

In other words, the probability of the observation o_i (in this case, we mean the value at time i) is conditioned only by the state of the hidden variable at time i (x_i). Conventionally, the first state x_0 and the last one x_{ending} are never emitted, and therefore all the sequences start with the index *1* and end with an extra timestep corresponding to the final state.

Sometimes, even if it's not extremely realistic, it's useful to include the Markov assumption and the emission probability independence in our models. The latter can be justified considering that we can sample all the peak emissions corresponding to precise states and, as the random process $O(t)$ is implicitly dependent on $X(t)$, it's not unreasonable to think of it like a pursuer of $X(t)$.

The Markov assumption holds for many real-life processes if either they are naturally first-order Markov ones, or if the states contain all the history needed to justify a transition. In other words, in many cases, if the state is A, then there's a transit to B and finally to C. We assume that when in C, the system moved from a state (B) that carries a part of the information provided by A.

For example, if we are filling a tank, we can measure the level (the state of our system) at time t, $t + 1$, ... If the water flow is modeled by a random variable because we don't have a stabilizer, we can find the probability that the water has reached a certain level at time t, $P(L_t = x \mid L_{t-1})$. Of course, it doesn't make sense to check the conditions over all the previous states, because if the level is, for example, 80m at time $t - 1$ then all the information needed to determine the probability of a new level (state) at time t is already contained in this state (80m).

At this point, we can start analyzing how to train an HMM, and how to determine the most likely hidden states given a sequence of observations. For simplicity, we call A the transition probability matrix, and B the matrix containing all $P(o_i \mid x_t)$. The resulting model can be determined by the knowledge of those elements: $HMM = \{A, B\}$.

The Forward-Backward algorithm

The forward-backward algorithm is a simple but effective method to find the transition probability matrix T given a sequence of observations o_1, o_2, ..., o_t. The first step is called the forward phase and consists of determining the probability of a sequence of observations $P(o_1, o_2, ..., o_{sequence\ length} \mid A, B)$. This piece of information can be directly useful if we need to know the likelihood of a sequence and it's necessary, together with the backward phase, to estimate the structure (A and B) of the underlying HMM.

Both algorithms are based on the concept of dynamic programming, which consists of splitting a complex problem into sub-problems that can be easily solved and reusing the solutions to solve more complex steps in a recursive/iterative fashion. For further information on this, please refer to R. A. Howard, *Dynamic Programming and Markov Process*, The MIT Press, 1960.

Forward phase

If we call p_{ij} the transition probability $P(i \rightarrow j)$, we define a recursive procedure considering the following probability:

$$f_t^i = P(o_1, o_2, ..., o_t, x_t = i \mid A, B)$$

The variable f_t^i represents the probability that the HMM is in the state i (at time t) after t observations (from 1 to). Considering the HMM assumptions, we can state that f_t^i depends on all possible f_{t-1}^i. More precisely, we have:

$$f_t^i = \sum_j f_{t-1}^j p_{ji} \, P(o_t|x_j)$$

With this process, we consider that the HMM can reach any of the states at time $t - 1$ (with the first $t - 1$ observations), and transition to the state i at time t with probability p_{ij}. We need also to consider the emission probability for the final state o_t conditioned to each of the possible previous states.

By definition, the initial and ending states are not emitting. It means that we can write any sequence of observations as $0, o_1, o_2, \ldots, o_{sequence\ length}, 0$ where the first and the final values are null. The procedure starts with computing the forward message at time 1:

$$f_1^i = p_{0i} P(o_1|x_0)$$

The non-emitting ending state must be also considered:

$$f_{Sequence\ length}^{ending} = \sum_i f_{Sequence\ lenght-1}^i \, p_{iending}$$

The expression for the last state x_{ending} is interpreted here as the index of the ending state in both A and B matrices. For example, we indicate p_{ij} as $A[i, j]$, meaning the transition probability at a generic time instant from the state $x_t = i$ to the state $x_{t+1} = j$. In the same way $p_{iending}$, is represented as $A[i, ending]$ meaning the transition probability from the penultimate state $x_{sequence\ length-1} = i$ to the ending one $x_{sequence\ length-1} = ending$.

The Forward algorithm can, therefore, be summarized in the following steps (we assume to have N states, hence we need to allocate $N + 2$ positions, considering the initial and the ending states):

1. Initialization of a *Forward* vector with shape ($N + 2$, *Sequence length*)

2. Initialization of A (transition probability matrix) with shape (N, N). Each element is $P(x_i \mid x_j)$

3. Initialization of B with shape (*Sequence length, N*). Each element is $P(o_i \mid x_j)$

4. For $i = 1$ to N:

   Set *Forward*$[i, 1] = A[0, i]B[1, i]$

5. For $t = 2$ to *Sequence length* – 1:

   a. For $i = 1$ to N:

$$\text{Set } S = 0$$

    b.   For $j = 1$ to N:

$$\text{Set } S = S + Forward[j, t - 1]A[j, i]B[t, i]$$

    c.   Set *Forward* $[i, t] = S$

6.   Set $S = 0$

7.   For $i = 1$ to N:

$$\text{Set } S = S + Forward[i, Sequence\ length]A[i, x_{ending}]$$

8.   Set *Forward* $[x_{ending}, Sequence\ length] = S$

Now it should be clear that the name "forward" derives from the procedure of propagating the information from the previous step to the next one, until the ending state, which is not emitted.

Backward phase

During the backward phase, we need to compute the probability of a sequence starting at time $t + 1$: $o_{t+1}, o_{t+2}, \ldots, o_{sequence\ length}$, given that the state at time t is i. Just like we did before, we define the following probability:

$$b_t^i = P(o_{t+1}, o_{t+2}, \ldots, o_{Sequence\ length} | x_t = i, A, B)$$

The backward algorithm is very similar to the forward one, but in this case, we need to move in the opposite direction, assuming we know that the state at time t is i. The first state to consider is the last one x_{ending}, which like the initial state is not emitting; therefore, we have:

$$b_{Sequence\ length}^i = p_{iending}$$

We terminate the recursion with the initial state:

$$b_1^0 = \sum_i b_1^i\, p_{0i} P(o_1 | x_i)$$

The steps are as follows:

1.   Initialization of a vector *Backward* with shape $(N + 2, Sequence\ length)$.
2.   Initialization of A (transition probability matrix) with shape (N, N). Each element is $P(x_i | x_j)$.

3. Initialization of B with shape (*Sequence length*, N). Each element is $P(o_i \mid x_j)$.

4. For $i = 1$ to N:

   Set $Backward[x_{ending}, Sequence\ length] = A[i, x_{ending}]$

5. For $t = Sequence\ length - 1$ to 1:

   For $i = 1$ to N:

       i. Set $S = 0$

       ii. For $j = 1$ to N:

           Set $S = S + Backward[j, t + 1]A[j, i]B[t + 1, i]$

       iii. Set $Backward[i, t] = S$

6. Set $S = 0$

7. For $i = 1$ to N:

   Set $S = S + Backward[i, 1]A[0,i]B[1,i]$

8. Set $Backward[0, 1] = S$

Now that we have defined both the forward and the backward algorithms, we can use them to estimate the structure of the underlying HMM.

HMM parameter estimation

The procedure we follow to estimate the parameters of the HMM is an application of the Expectation-Maximization algorithm, which will be discussed in the next chapter, *Chapter 12, The EM Algorithm*. Its goal can be summarized as defining how we want to estimate the values of A and B. If we define $N(i, j)$ as the number of transitions from the state i to the state j, and $N(i)$ the total number of transitions from the state i, we can approximate the transition probability $P(i \rightarrow j)$ with:

$$\tilde{a}_{ij} = \tilde{P}(i \rightarrow j) = \frac{Mean[N(i,j)]}{Mean[N(i)]}$$

In the same way, if we define $M(i, p)$ the number of times we have observed the emission o_p in the state i, we can approximate the emission probability $P(o_p \mid x_i)$ with:

$$\tilde{b}_{ip} = \tilde{P}(o_p | x_i) = \frac{Mean[M(i,p)]}{Mean[N(i)]}$$

Let's start with the estimation of the transition probability matrix A. If we consider the probability that the HMM is in the state i at time t, and in the state j at time $t + 1$ given the observations, we have:

$$\tilde{\alpha}_{ij}^t = P(x_t = i, x_{t+1} = j | o_1, o_2, \ldots, o_{Sequence\ length}, A, B)$$

We can compute this probability using the forward and backward algorithms, given a sequence of observations $o_1, o_2, \ldots o_{sequence\ length}$. In fact, we can use both the forward message f_t^i, which is the probability that the HMM is in the state i after t observations, and the backward message b_{t+1}^j, which is the probability of a sequence $o_{t+1}, o_{t+2}, \ldots, o_{sequence\ length}$, starting at time $t + 1$, given that the HMM is in state j at time $t + 1$. Of course, we need also to include the emission probability and the transition probability p_{ij}, which is what we are estimating. The algorithm, in fact, starts with a random hypothesis and iterates until the values of A become stable. The estimation $\tilde{\alpha}_{ij}$ at time t is equal to:

$$\tilde{\alpha}_{ij}^t = \frac{f_t^i p_{ij} b_{t+1}^j P(o_{t+1}|x_j)}{f_{Sequence\ length}^{ending}}$$

In this context, we are omitting the full proof due to its complexity; however, the reader can find it in Rabiner L. R., *A tutorial on hidden Markov models and selected applications in speech recognition*, Proceedings of the IEEE 77.2, 1989.

To compute the emission probabilities, it's easier to start with the probability of being in the state i at time t given the sequence of observations:

$$\tilde{\beta}_i^t = P(x_t = i | o_1, o_2, \ldots, o_{Sequence\ length}, A, B)$$

In this case, the computation is immediate, because we can multiply the forward and backward messages computed at the same time t and state i (remember that considering the observations, the backward message is conditioned to $x_t = i$, while the forward message computes the probability of the observations joined with $x_t = i$. Hence, the multiplication is the unnormalized probability of being in the state i at time t). Therefore, we have:

$$\tilde{\beta}_i^t = \frac{f_t^i b_t^i}{f_{Sequence\ length}^{ending}}$$

The proof of how the normalizing constant is obtained can be found in the aforementioned paper. We can now plug these expressions to the estimation of a_{ij} and b_{ip}:

$$\begin{cases} \tilde{a}_{ij} = \dfrac{\sum_{t=1}^{Sequence\ length-1} \tilde{\alpha}_{ij}^t}{\sum_{t=1}^{Sequence\ length-1} \sum_{j=1}^{N} \tilde{\alpha}_{ij}^t} \\[3ex] \tilde{b}_{ip} = \dfrac{\sum_{t=1}^{Sequence\ length} \tilde{\beta}_i^t I_{o_t=p}}{\sum_{t=1}^{Sequence\ length} \tilde{\beta}_i^t} \end{cases}$$

In the numerator of the second formula, we adopted the indicator function (it's 1 only if the condition is true, 0 otherwise) to limit the sum only where those elements are $o_t = p$. During an iteration k, p_{ij} is obtained through the estimated value $\tilde{a}_{ij}$ found in the previous iteration $k - 1$.

The algorithm is based on the following steps:

1. Randomly initialize the matrices A and B.

2. Initialize a tolerance variable Tol (for example, $Tol = 0.001$)

3. While $||A_k - A_{k-1}|| > Tol$ and $||B_k - B_{k-1}|| > Tol$ (k is the iteration index):

    a. For $t = 1$ to *Sequence length* – 1:

        i. For $i = 1$ to N:

            1. For $j = 1$ to N:

                a. Compute $\tilde{\alpha}_{ij}^t$

        ii. Compute $\tilde{\beta}_i^t$

    b. Compute the estimations of $\tilde{a}_{ij}$ and $\tilde{b}_{ip}$ and store them in A_k.

Alternatively, it's possible to fix the number of iterations, even if the best solution is using both a tolerance and a maximum number of iterations, to terminate the process when the first condition is met.

Example of HMM training with hmmlearn

For this example, we are going to use `hmmlearn` (installable through the command `pip install hmmlearn`), which is a package for HMM computations (see the information box at the end of this section for further details).

For simplicity, let's consider the airport example we discussed in the section about the Bayesian networks, and let's suppose we have a single hidden variable that represents the weather (of course, this is not a real hidden variable!), modeled as a multinomial distribution with two components (good and rough).

We observe the arrival time of our flight London-Rome (which partially depends on the weather conditions), and we want to train an HMM to infer future states and compute the posterior probability of hidden states corresponding to a given sequence.

The schema for our example is shown in the following diagram:

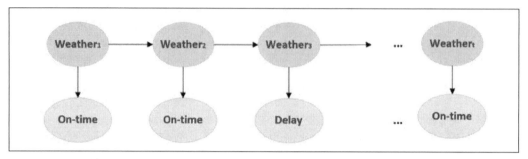

HMM for the weather-arrival delay problem

Let's start by defining our observation vector. As we have two states, its values will be 0 and 1. Let's assume that 0 means **On-time** and 1 means **Delay**:

```
import numpy as np

observations = np.array([[0], [1], [1],
                         [0], [1], [1],
                         [1], [0], [1],
                         [0], [0], [0],
                         [1], [0], [1],
                         [1], [0], [1],
                         [0], [0], [1],
                         [0], [1], [0],
                         [0], [0], [1],
                         [0], [1], [0],
                         [1], [0], [0],
                         [0], [0], [0]],
                        dtype=np.int32)
```

We have 35 consecutive observations whose values are either 0 or 1.

To build the HMM, we are going to use the `MultinomialHMM` class, with `n_components=2`, `n_iter=100`, and `random_state=1000` (it's important to always use the same seed to avoid differences in the results). The number of iterations is sometimes hard to determine; for this reason, `hmmlearn` provides a utility `ConvergenceMonitor` class that can be checked to be sure that the algorithm has successfully converged.

Now we can train our model using the `fit()` method, passing as argument the list of observations (the array must be always bidimensional with shape *Sequence length* x $N_{components}$):

```
from hmmlearn import hmm

hmm_model = hmm.MultinomialHMM(n_components=2,
                               n_iter=100,
                               random_state=1000)
hmm_model.fit(observations)

print(hmm_model.monitor_.converged)
```

The output of the previous snippet is:

True

The process is very fast, and the monitor (available as instance variable monitor) has confirmed the convergence. If the model is very big and needs to be retrained, it's also possible to check smaller values of `n_iter`). Once the model is trained, we can immediately visualize the transition probability matrix, which is available as an instance variable `transmat_`:

```
print('\nTransition probability matrix:')
print(hmm_model.transmat_)
```

The output is:

Transition probability matrix:
[[0.0025384 0.9974616]
 [0.69191905 0.30808095]]

We can interpret these values as saying that the probability to transition from 0 (good weather) to 1 (rough weather) is higher (p_{01} is close to 1) than the opposite, and it's more likely to remain in state 1 than in state 0 (p_{00} is almost null). We could deduce that the observations have been collected during the winter! After explaining the Viterbi algorithm in the next section, we can also check, given some observations, what the most likely hidden state sequence is.

The Viterbi algorithm

The Viterbi algorithm is one of most common decoding algorithms for HMM. Its goal is to find the most likely hidden state sequence corresponding to a series of observations. The structure is very similar to the forward algorithm, but instead of computing the probability of a sequence of observations joined with the state at the last time instant, this algorithm looks for:

$$v_t^i = \max_{x_j} P(o_1, o_2, \dots, o_t, x_1, x_2, \dots, x_{t-1}, x_t = i | A, B)$$

The variable v_t^i represents that maximum probability of the given observation sequence joint with $x_t = i$, considering all possible hidden state paths (from time instant 1 to $t - 1$). We can compute v_t^i recursively by evaluating all the v_{t-1}^j multiplied by the corresponding transition probabilities p_{ji} and emission probability $P(o_t \mid x_i)$. and always picking the maximum overall possible values of j:

$$v_t^i = \max_j v_{t-1}^j p_{ji} P(o_t | x_i)$$

The algorithm is based on a backtracking approach, using a back pointer bp_t^i whose recursive expression is the same as v_t^i but with the argmax function instead of max:

$$bp_t^i = \underset{j}{\operatorname{argmax}}\, v_{t-1}^j p_{ji} P(o_t | x_i)$$

Therefore, bp_t^i represents the partial sequence of hidden states $x_1, x_2, \dots, x_{t-1}$ that maximizes v_t^i. During the recursion, we add the timesteps one by one, so the previous path could be invalidated by the last observation. That's why we need to backtrack the partial result and replace the sequence built at time t that doesn't maximize v_{t+1}^i anymore.

The algorithm is based on the following steps (like in the other cases, the initial and ending states are not emitting):

1. Initialization of a vector V with shape ($N + 2$, *Sequence length*).
2. Initialization of a vector BP with shape ($N + 2$, *Sequence length*).
3. Initialization of A (transition probability matrix) with shape (N, N). Each element is $P(x_i \mid x_j)$.
4. Initialization of B with shape (*Sequence length*, N). Each element is $P(o_i \mid x_j)$.
5. For $i = 1$ to N:
   a. Set $V[i, 1] = A[i, 0]B[1, i]$

b. *BP[i, 1] = Null* (or any other value that cannot be interpreted as a state)

6. For *t* = 1 to *Sequence length*:

    a. For *i* = 1 to *N*:

        i. Set $V[i, t] = \max_j V[j, t-1]A[j, i]B[t, i]$.

        ii. Set $BP[i, t] = \operatorname{argmax}_j V[j, t-1]A[j, i]B[t, i]$.

7. Set
$$V\left[x_{ending}, Sequence\ length\right] = \max_j V[j, Sequence\ length]A\left[j, x_{ending}\right].$$

8. Set
$$BP\left[x_{ending}, Sequence\ length\right] = \operatorname{argmax}_j V[j, Sequence\ length]A\left[j, x_{ending}\right].$$

9. Reverse *BP*.

The output of the Viterbi algorithm is a tuple with the most likely sequence *BP* and the corresponding probabilities *V*.

Finding the most likely hidden state sequence using the Viterbi algorithm and hmmlearn

At this point, we can continue with the previous example, using our model to find the most likely hidden state sequence given a set of possible observations. We can use either the decode() method or the predict() method. The first one returns the log probability of the whole sequence and the sequence itself; however, they all use the Viterbi algorithm as a default decoder:

```
sequence = np.array([[1], [1], [1],
                     [0], [1], [1],
                     [1], [0], [1],
                     [0], [1], [0],
                     [1], [0], [1],
                     [1], [0], [1],
                     [1], [0], [1],
                     [0], [1], [0],
                     [1], [0], [1],
                     [1], [1], [0],
                     [0], [1], [1],
                     [0], [1], [1]],
                     dtype=np.int32)

lp, hs = hmm_model.decode(sequence)
```

```
print('\nMost likely hidden state sequence:')
print(hs)

print('\nLog-propability:')
print(lp)
```

The output of the previous snippet is:

Most likely hidden state sequence:

`[0 1 1 0 1 1 1 0 1 0 1 0 1 0 1 1 0 1 1 0 1 0 1 0 1 0 1 1 1 1 0 1 1 0 1 1]`

Log-propability:

`-30.4899924688786`

The sequence is coherent with the transition probability matrix; in fact, it's more likely the persistence of rough weather (1) than the opposite. Consequently, the transition from 1 to 0 is less likely than the one from 0 to 1. The choice of state is made by selecting the highest probability; however, in some cases, the differences are minimal (in our example, it can happen to have $p = (0.49, 0.51)$, meaning that there's a high error chance), so it's useful to check the posterior probabilities for all the states in the sequence, as shown in the following figure:

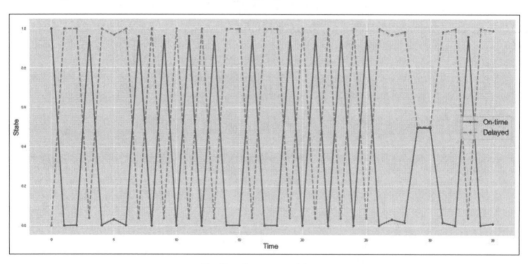

Predicted state transitions

In our case, there are a couple of states that have $p \approx (0.495, 0.505)$, so even if the output state is 1 (rough weather), it's also useful to consider a moderate probability of observing good weather. In general, if a sequence is coherent with the transition probability previously learned (or manually input), those cases are not very common. Suppose that we want to evaluate a sequence where the weather is always good (0):

```
sequence0 = np.array([[0], [0], [0],
                      [0], [0], [0],
                      [0], [0], [0],
                      [0], [0], [0],
                      [0], [0], [0],
                      [0], [0], [0],
                      [0], [0], [0],
                      [0], [0], [0],
                      [0], [0], [0],
                      [0], [0], [0],
                      [0], [0], [0]],
                     dtype=np.int32)
pp0 = hmm_model.predict_proba(sequence0)
```

This case is very particular because we know that the transition from good to rough weather is very likely (close to 1); therefore, we can't expect a stable output. The probabilities of state transitions are shown in the following figure:

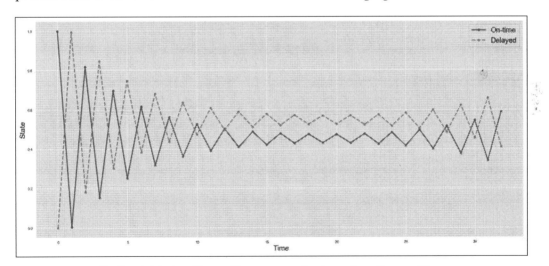

Predicted state transitions with a sequence of only good weather conditions

At the beginning, the model predicts alternate states with high probabilities. This is due to the knowledge previously acquired and encoded in the transition matrix. However, after a few steps, the probabilities tend to become close to $1/2$, increasing the uncertainty. The reason of such behavior is straightforward. We have trained a model using observations that describe a scenario where a day with good weather is almost always followed by a rough weather one. Therefore, a sequence of 0s (good weather) is an anomaly that the model is unable to manage properly, defaulting to a maximum entropy sequence where both states are equally likely. This example is helpful to understand how HMMs work and where it's needed to retrain them using additional special sequences.

If, for example, during summer, a period of 15-20 sunny days is observed, this block should be included in the training set, considering a frequency of $\frac{15/20}{365}$ observations (to avoid biasing the model). If this approach is not sufficient because of the prevalence of good-rough weather transitions, more HMMs can be trained for each period of the year. In general, I always suggest trying different configurations and observations sequences, and to also assess the probabilities for the strangest situations (like a sequence of zero second). At that point, it's possible to retrain the model and recheck that the new evidence has been correctly processed.

The data scientist has a responsibility to understand whether the models are accurate enough, or if they require more data or alternative approaches. As an exercise, I invite the reader to alter the training sequence using also a block of consecutive good-weather observations and check if the predictions become less uncertain (closer to 0 or 1).

Summary

In this chapter, we introduced Bayesian networks, describing their structure and relations. We have seen how it's possible to build a network to model a probabilistic scenario where some elements can influence the probability of others. We have also described how to obtain the full joint probability using the most common sampling methods, which allow reducing the computational complexity through an approximation.

The most common sampling methods belong to the family of MCMC algorithms, which model the transition probability from a sample to another one as a first-order Markov chain. In particular, the Gibbs sampler is based on the assumption that it's easier to sample from a conditional distribution than work directly with the full joint probability. The method is very easy to implement, but it has some performance drawbacks that can be avoided by adopting more complex strategies.

The Metropolis-Hastings sampler, instead, works with a candidate-generating distribution and a criterion to accept or reject the samples. Both methods satisfy the detailed balance equation, which guarantees their convergence (the underlying Markov chain will reach the unique stationary distribution).

In the last part of the chapter, we introduced HMMs, which allow modeling time sequences based on observations corresponding to a series of hidden states. The main concept of such models, in fact, is the presence of unobservable states that condition the emission of a particular observation (which is observable). We discussed the main assumptions and how to build, train, and infer from a model. In particular, the Forward-Backward algorithm can be employed when it's necessary to learn the transition probability matrix and the emission probabilities, while the Viterbi algorithm is adopted to find the most likely hidden state sequence given a set of consecutive observations.

In *Chapter 12*, *The EM Algorithm*, we're going to briefly discuss the Expectation-Maximization algorithm, focusing on some important applications based on the **Maximum Likelihood Estimation** (MLE) approach.

Further reading

- Pratt J., Raiffa H., Schlaifer R., *Introduction to Statistical Decision Theory*, The MIT Press, 2008

- Hoffmann M. D., Gelman A., *The No-U-Turn Sampler: Adaptively Setting Path Lengths in Hamiltonian Monte Carlo*, arXiv:1111.4246, 2011

- A. Gelman, J. B. Carlin, H. S. Stern, *Bayesian Data Analysis, CRC Press*, 2013

- Walsh B., *Markov Chain Monte Carlo and Gibbs Sampling*, Lecture Notes for EEB 596z, 2002

- R. A. Howard, *Dynamic Programming and Markov Process*, The MIT Press, 1960

- Rabiner L. R., *A tutorial on hidden Markov models and selected applications in speech recognition*, Proceedings of the IEEE 77.2, 1989

- W. K. Hastings, *Monte Carlo sampling methods using Markov chains and their applications*, Biometrik, 57/1, 04/1970

- Kevin B. Korb, Ann E. Nicholson, *Bayesian Artificial Intelligence*, CRC Press, 2010

- Pearl J., *Causality*, Cambridge University Press, 2009

- L. E. Baum, T. Petrie, *Statistical Inference for Probabilistic Functions of Finite State Markov Chains*, The Annals of Mathematical Statistics, 37, 1966

12

The EM Algorithm

In this chapter, we're going to introduce a very important algorithmic framework for many statistical learning tasks: the **Expectation Maximization** (**EM**) algorithm. Contrary to what its name might suggest, this is not an algorithm used to solve a single problem, but a methodology that can be applied in several contexts where the objective of the algorithm is learning the structure of the data-generating process through an iterative and flexible approach. Generative models, for example, are extremely powerful tools that help the data scientist in describing the existing data and generating new data. Unfortunately, direct optimization of these models is often impossible.

The EM algorithm, on the other hand, can often be applied with a minimum of effort. The goal of this chapter is to explain the rationale of this method and show the mathematical derivation, together with some practical examples. In particular, we are going to discuss the following topics:

- **Maximum Likelihood Estimation** (**MLE**) and **Maximum A Posteriori** (**MAP**) learning approaches
- The EM algorithm with a simple application for the estimation of unknown parameters
- The Gaussian Mixture algorithm, evaluation methods, and component selection

We can now start discussing the problems of MLE and MAP, which are the fundamental building blocks of most statistical learning algorithms.

MLE and MAP Learning

In many statistical learning tasks, our goal is to find the optimal parameter set $\bar{\theta}$ according to a maximization criterion. The most common approach is based on the likelihood $L(\bar{\theta}; X)$ and is called MLE.

In fact, given a statistical model $p(X; \bar{\theta})$ parametrized with the vector $\bar{\theta}$, the likelihood can be interpreted as the probability of such a model generating the training data. Therefore, given a suitable structure of $p(X; \bar{\theta})$, the MLE provides a simple but extremely effective tool to define a generative model that is never biased by prior belief. For our purposes, let's suppose we have a data-generating process p_{data}, used to draw a dataset X:

$$X = \{\bar{x}_1, \bar{x}_2, \ldots, \bar{x}_N\} \text{ where } \bar{x}_i \in \mathbb{R}^k$$

In this case, the optimal set $\bar{\theta}_{opt}$ that maximizes the likelihood of a generic statistical model $p(X; \bar{\theta})$ parametrized with $\bar{\theta}$ is found as follows:

$$\bar{\theta}_{opt} = \underset{\bar{\theta}}{\mathrm{argmax}}\, L(\bar{\theta}; X) = \underset{\bar{\theta}}{\mathrm{argmax}}\, p(X; \bar{\theta})$$

This approach has the advantage of being unbiased by incorrect preconditions, because the optimal value $\bar{\theta}_{opt}$ depends exclusively on the observed data. However, at the same time, this approach excludes any possibility of incorporating prior knowledge (that very often can be trusted) into the model. It simply looks for the best $\bar{\theta}$ in a wider subspace, so that $p(X; \bar{\theta})$ is maximized. Even if this approach is almost unbiased, there's a higher probability of finding a sub-optimal solution that can also be quite different from a reasonable prior. After all, several models are too complex to allow us to define a suitable prior probability (think, for example, of reinforcement learning strategies where there's a huge number of complex states). Therefore, MLE offers the most reliable solution. Moreover, it's possible to prove that the MLE of a parameter $\bar{\theta}$ converges in probability to the real value:

$$\forall \epsilon > 0 \;\; P\left(\left|\tilde{\theta}_k - \bar{\theta}\right| < \epsilon\right) \to 1 \;\; when \; k \to \infty$$

On the other hand, if we consider Bayes' theorem, we can derive the following relation:

$$p(\bar{\theta}|X) = \alpha p(X|\bar{\theta}) p(\bar{\theta})$$

The posterior probability, $p(\bar{\theta}|X)$, is obtained using both the likelihood and a prior probability, $p(\bar{\theta})$, and hence takes into account existing knowledge encoded in $p(\bar{\theta})$. The choice to maximize $p(\bar{\theta}|X)$ is called the MAP approach and it's often a good alternative to MLE when it's possible to formulate trustworthy priors or, as in the case of **Latent Dirichlet Allocation (LDA)**, where the model is purposely based on some specific prior assumptions.

Unfortunately, an incorrect or incomplete prior distribution can bias the model, leading to unacceptable results. For this reason, MLE is often the default choice even when it's possible to formulate reasonable assumptions on the structure of $p(\bar{\theta})$. To understand the impact of a prior on an estimation, let's consider having observed n = 1,000 binomial distributed (θ corresponds to the parameter p) experiments and k = 800 had a successful outcome. The likelihood is as follows:

$$p(X|\theta) = \binom{n}{k} \theta^k (1 - \theta)^{n-k}$$

For simplicity, let's compute the log-likelihood, which eliminates the products by turning them into sums:

$$\log p(X|\theta) = \log \binom{n}{k} + k \log \theta + (n - k) \log(1 - \theta)$$

If we compute the derivative with respect to θ and set it equal to zero, we get the following:

$$\frac{\partial}{\partial \theta} \log p(X|\theta) = \frac{k}{\theta} - \frac{n-k}{1-\theta} = 0 \Rightarrow \frac{\frac{1}{n-k}}{\frac{1}{k} + \frac{1}{n-k}} = \frac{k}{n}$$

So, the MLE for θ is 0.8, which is consistent with the observations (we can say that after observing 1,000 experiments with 800 successful outcomes, $p(X \mid Success) = 0.8$). If we have only the data X, we could say that success is more likely than a failure because 800 out of 1,000 experiments are positive.

However, after this simple exercise, an expert might tell us that considering the largest possible population, the marginal probability $p(Success) = 0.001$ (Bernoulli distributed with $p(Failure) = 1 - p(Success)$) and our sample is not representative. If we trust the expert, we need to compute the posterior probability using Bayes' theorem:

$$p(Success|X) = \frac{P(X|Success)P(Success)}{p(X|Success)p(Success) + p(X|Failure)(1 - p(Success))}$$
$$= \frac{0.8 \cdot 0.001}{(0.8 \cdot 0.001) + (0.2 \cdot 0.999)} = \frac{0.0008}{0.0008 + 0.1998} \approx 0.004$$

Surprisingly, the posterior probability is very close to zero and we should reject our initial hypothesis! At this point, there are two options: if we want to build a model based only on our data, the MLE is the only reasonable choice, because, considering the posterior, we need to accept that we have a very poor dataset (this is probably a bias when drawing the samples from the data-generating process p_{data}).

On the other hand, if we really trust the expert, we have a few options for managing the problem:

- Checking the sampling process in order to assess its quality (we can discover that better sampling leads to a much lower k value)
- Increasing the number of samples
- Computing the MAP estimation of $\bar{\theta}$

I suggest that the reader tries both approaches with simple models, to be able to compare the relative accuracies. In this book, we're always going to adopt the MLE when it's necessary to estimate the parameters of a model with a statistical approach. This choice is based on the assumption that our datasets are correctly sampled from p_{data}. If this is not possible (think about an image classifier that must distinguish between horses, dogs, and cats, built with a dataset where there are pictures of 500 horses, 500 dogs, and 5 cats), we should expand our dataset or use data augmentation techniques to create artificial samples in order to rebalance the classes.

At this point, we assume to have a dataset drawn from a well-defined data-generating process and that our goal is to optimize a parametrized statistical model through the maximization of its likelihood. The EM algorithm, which we're going to describe, makes no assumption about the structure of the model $P(X; \bar{\theta})$. Immediately after the theoretical part, a couple of concrete examples will be shown and discussed.

EM Algorithm

The EM algorithm is a generic framework that can be employed in the optimization of many generative models. It was originally proposed in Dempster A. P., Laird N. M., Rubin D. B., *Maximum likelihood from incomplete data via the EM algorithm,* Journal of the Royal Statistical Society, B, 39(1):1–38, 11/1977, where the authors also proved its convergence at different levels of genericity. Many machine learning problems have the objective of finding a flexible way to express the data-generating process behind datasets. For example, given a set of pictures representing faces $X = \{\bar{x}_1, \bar{x}_2, \dots \bar{x}_n\}$, we are generally interested in discovering at least an approximation of the distribution p_{data} from where the training sample has been drawn.

The reason is obvious: we can never work with all possible data points and, moreover, a synthetic expression (for example, a neural network or a mixture of distributions) allows us to draw new samples or to evaluate the likelihood of other datasets.

The EM algorithm allows us to find the optimal parameter set $\bar{\theta}_{opt}$ so that $P(X; \bar{\theta}_{opt})$ is maximized. This means that, assuming no prior knowledge, we have found a proxy for the real underlying distribution. At this point, any $\bar{x}_i \sim P(X; \bar{\theta}_{opt})$ is a data point compatible with the data-generating process (for example, if $P(\bar{x}_i; \bar{\theta}_{opt}) \to 1$, this means that $\bar{x}_i$ is a valid representation of a face, even if it was never employed in the training phase).

For our purposes, we are going to consider a dataset X and a set of latent variables Z that we cannot observe. They can be part of the original model or introduced artificially as a trick to simplify the problem. In general, the set Z helps to model the *hidden* dynamics of the model, that is, those mathematical relationships that we need to postulate but are too complex to be directly included in the model. For example, in **Hidden Markov Models (HMMs)**, the latent variables are a structural part of the algorithm that takes part in the description and in the synthesis of new sequences. Let's now analyze the theoretical part of the EM algorithm, focusing the attention on the key steps that make this approach so flexible and helpful.

A generic generative model parameterized with the vector $\bar{\theta}$ has a log-likelihood equal to the following:

$$L(\bar{\theta}|X, Z) = \log P(X, Z|\bar{\theta})$$

Of course, a large log-likelihood implies that the model is able to generate the original distribution with a small error. Therefore, our goal is to find the optimal set of parameters $\bar{\theta}$ that maximizes the marginalized log-likelihood (we need to sum — or integrate out for continuous variables — the latent variables out because we cannot observe them):

$$\bar{\theta}_{opt} = \underset{\bar{\theta}}{\operatorname{argmax}} \log \sum_z L(\bar{\theta}|X, z) = \underset{\bar{\theta}}{\operatorname{argmax}} \log \sum_z P(X, z|\bar{\theta})$$

Theoretically, this operation is correct, but, unfortunately, it's almost always impracticable because of its complexity (in particular, the logarithm of a sum is often very problematic to manage). However, the presence of the latent variables can help us in finding a good proxy that is easy to compute and whose maximization corresponds to the maximization of the original log-likelihood.

Let's start by rewriting the expression of the likelihood using the chain rule:

$$\log \sum_z P(X, z|\bar{\theta}) = \log \sum_z P(X|z, \bar{\theta})P(z|\bar{\theta})$$

If we consider an iterative process, our goal is to find a procedure that satisfies the following condition:

$$L(\bar{\theta}_{opt}|X, Z) > L(\bar{\theta}_t|X, Z) > L(\bar{\theta}_{t-1}|X, Z) > \cdots > L(\bar{\theta}_0|X, Z)$$

We can start by considering a generic step:

$$L(\bar{\theta}|X) - L(\bar{\theta}_t|X) = \log \sum_z P(X|z, \bar{\theta})P(z|\bar{\theta}) - \log P(X|\bar{\theta}_t)$$

The first problem to solve is the logarithm of the sum. Fortunately, we can employ the Jensen's inequality, which allows us to move the logarithm inside the summation.

Convex functions and the Jensen's inequality

Let's first define the concept of a convex function: a function, $f(x)$, defined on a convex set D is said to be convex if the following applies:

$$f(\lambda x_1 + (1 - \lambda)x_2) \leq \lambda f(x_1) + (1 - \lambda)f(x_2) \ \forall \ x_1, x_2 \in D \ and \ \lambda \in [0,1]$$

If the inequality is strict, the function is said to be *strictly convex*. Intuitively, and considering a function of a single variable $f(x)$, the previous definition states that the function is never above the segment that connects two points $(x_1, f(x_1))$ and $(x_2, f(x_2))$. In the case of strict convexity, $f(x)$ is always below the segment. Inverting these definitions, we obtain the conditions for a function to be *concave* or *strictly concave*. In the following figure, there are examples of convex and non-convex functions:

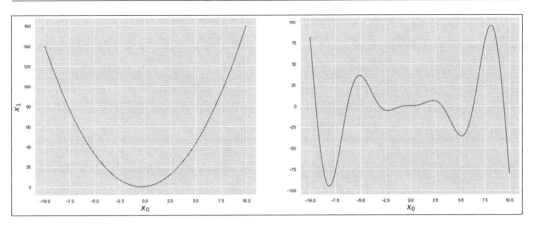

Examples of convex (left) and non-convex (right) functions

Convex functions aren't just helpful in this one context. They are, in fact, an extremely important concept in different machine learning branches (for example, deep learning). The reason is very simple: convex functions can be easily optimized (that is, minimized or maximized) using simple algorithms, while non-convex functions have multiple local maxima and minima. If, for example, we consider $f(x)$ = $-x^2 + x$, the first derivative $f'(x) = -2x + 1$ and there's only one point where $f'(x) =$ 0, which is $x = \frac{1}{2}$. As the second derivative is negative, we are sure that this point is the only global maximum of the function. On the other hand, if $f'(x)$ has many solutions, an automatic procedure cannot easily understand whether a minimum/ maximum is local or global and, very often, the algorithm remains stuck in a sub-optimal solution. After this important digression, we can continue analyzing the problem related to the EM algorithm, introducing some important considerations.

If (and only if) a function $f(x)$ is convex in D, the function $-f(x)$ is concave in D. However, if $f(x)$ is non-convex, there are no guarantees that $-f(x)$ is convex and vice versa.

As the function $\log x$ is monotonically increasing and concave in $[0, \infty)$, $-\log x$ is monotonically decreasing and convex in $[0, \infty)$, as shown in the following figure:

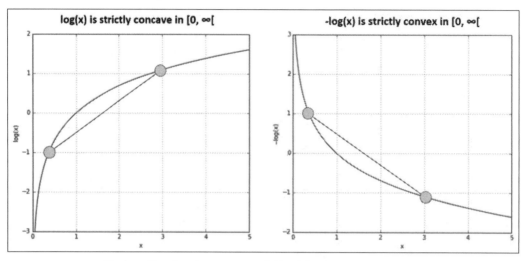

The logarithm function is concave (left), while $-\log x$ is convex (right)

The *Jensen's inequality* (the proof is omitted but further details can be found in Hansen F., Pedersen G. K. *Jensen's Operator Inequality*, arXiv:math/0204049 [math. OA]) states that if $f(x)$ is a convex function defined on a convex set D, if we select n points $x_1, x_2, \dots, x_N \in D$ and n constants $\lambda_1, \lambda_2, \dots, \lambda_N \geq 0$ satisfying the condition $\lambda_1 + \lambda_2 + \dots + \lambda_N = 1$, then the following applies:

$$f\left(\sum_i \lambda_i x_i\right) \leq \sum_i \lambda_i f(x_i)$$

Therefore, considering that $-\log x$ is convex, the *Jensen's inequality* for $\log x$ becomes as follows:

$$\log\left(\sum_i \lambda_i x_i\right) \geq \sum_i \lambda_i \log x_i$$

Hence, the generic iterative step can be rewritten as follows:

$$\Delta L = L(\bar{\theta}|X) - L(\bar{\theta}_t|X) = \log \sum_z P(z|X, \bar{\theta}_t) \frac{P(X|z, \bar{\theta})P(z|\bar{\theta})}{P(z|X, \bar{\theta}_t)} - \log P(X|\bar{\theta}_t)$$

Application of the Jensen's inequality to the EM algorithm

Applying the Jensen's inequality, we obtain the following:

$$\Delta L \geq \sum_z P(z|X, \bar{\theta}_t) \log \frac{P(X|z, \bar{\theta})P(z|\bar{\theta})}{P(z|X, \bar{\theta}_t)P(X|\bar{\theta}_t)}$$

All conditions are met, because the terms $P(z_i|X, \bar{\theta}_t)$ are, by definition, bounded between [0, 1] and the sum over all z must always be equal to 1 (laws of probability). The previous expression implies that the following is true:

$$L(\bar{\theta}|X) \geq L(\bar{\theta}_t|X) + \sum_z P(z|X, \bar{\theta}_t) \log \frac{P(X|z, \bar{\theta})P(z|\bar{\theta})}{P(z|X, \bar{\theta}_t)P(X|\bar{\theta}_t)}$$

Therefore, if we maximize the right side of the inequality, we also maximize the log-likelihood. However, the problem can be further simplified, considering that we are optimizing only the parameter vector θ and we can remove all the terms that don't depend on it. Hence, we can define a Q function (there is no relation to Q-learning, which we're going to discuss in *Chapter 24, Introduction to Reinforcement Learning*) whose expression is as follows:

$$Q(\bar{\theta}|\bar{\theta}_t) = \sum_z P(z|X, \bar{\theta}_t) \log P(X, z|\bar{\theta}) = E_{Z|X, \bar{\theta}_t}[\log P(X, z|\bar{\theta})]$$

$Q(\bar{\theta}|\bar{\theta}_t)$ is the expected value of the log-likelihood considering the complete data $Y = (X, Z)$ and the current iteration parameter set $\bar{\theta}_t$. At each iteration, $Q(\bar{\theta}|\bar{\theta}_t)$ is computed considering the current estimation $\bar{\theta}_t$, and it's maximized considering the variable $\bar{\theta}$. It's now clearer why the latent variables can often be artificially introduced: they allow us to apply the Jensen's inequality and transform the original expression into an expected value that is easy to evaluate and optimize. This doesn't mean that the set Z is always *artificial* and necessary only for practical purposes. In many contexts, the hidden variables are necessary to achieve a better description of the problem. For example, in the Gaussian Mixture context that we are going to discuss later in this chapter, the latent variables are required to model the contribution of each Gaussian to the generation of a generic point. As we don't know how the components will mix together, we can only postulate the existence of these variables (that is, factors), incorporating them in the model, but avoiding any speculation about their behavior.

The EM algorithm, through its genericity, will optimize the whole parameter set (including the hidden variables) so as to maximize the likelihood. When this process is complete, we can reasonably assume that the set Z has been chosen in an optimal way and each $\bar{z}_i \in Z$ describes a precise behavior that was initially unknown.

At this point, we can formalize the EM algorithm:

- Set a threshold *Thr* (for example, *Thr* = 0.001)
- Set a random parameter vector $\bar{\theta}_0$

While $\left| L(\bar{\theta}_t | X, Z) - L(\bar{\theta}_{t-1} | X, Z) \right| > Thr$:

- ○ **E-Step**: Compute $Q(\bar{\theta} | \bar{\theta}_t)$. In general, this step consists of computing the conditional probability $P(z | X, \bar{\theta}_t)$ or some of its moments (sometimes, the sufficient statistics are limited to mean and covariance) using the current parameter estimation $\bar{\theta}_t$.
- ○ **M-Step**: Find $\bar{\theta}_{t+1} = \underset{\bar{\theta}}{\text{argmax}} \, Q(\bar{\theta} | \bar{\theta}_t)$. The new parameter estimation is computed to maximize the Q function.

The procedure ends when the log-likelihood stops increasing or after a fixed number of iterations. At this point, the EM algorithm has found the optimal parameter set $\bar{\theta}_{opt}$ that maximizes the likelihood of the model $P(X; \bar{\theta}_{opt})$ and it's possible to use it to perform classifications, clustering, or new data synthesis tasks. Next, we'll analyze a simple example where the EM algorithm is employed to estimate the parameters of a partially unknown distribution.

An example of parameter estimation

In this example, we see how it's possible to apply the EM algorithm for the maximum likelihood estimation of unknown parameters given a set of observations (inspired by an example discussed in the original paper Dempster A. P., Laird N. M., Rubin D. B., *Maximum likelihood from incomplete data via the EM algorithm*, Journal of the Royal Statistical Society, B, 39(1):1–38, 11/1977). The problem is rather simple, but it helps us understand how the proxy function $Q(\bar{\theta} | \bar{\theta}_t)$ can be used with an iterative approach to find $\bar{\theta}_{opt}$.

Let's consider a sequence of n independent experiments modeled with a multinomial distribution with three possible outcomes x_1, x_2, x_3 and corresponding probabilities p_1, p_2, p_3. The probability mass function is as follows:

$$f(x_1, x_2, x_3; p_1, p_2, p_3) = \frac{n!}{\prod_{i=1}^{3} x_i!} \prod_{i=1}^{3} p_i^{x_i}$$

Let's suppose that we can observe $z_1 = x_1 + x_2$ and x_3, but we don't have any direct access to the single values x_1 and x_2. Therefore, x_1 and x_2 are latent variables, while z_2 and x_3 are observed ones. In other words, the set $Z = \{x_1, x_2\}$ takes part in the process, but we have no elements that help us in determining their precise behavior. Therefore, in this case, the knowledge of the set Z is not only functional but also a requirement that we need to meet in order to solve the problem.

The probability vector $\bar{p}$ is parameterized in the following way:

$$\bar{p} = (p_1 \quad p_2 \quad p_3)^T = \left(\frac{\theta}{6} \quad 1 - \frac{\theta}{4} \quad \frac{\theta}{12}\right)^T$$

Our goal is to find the MLE for θ given n, z_1, x_3. Let's start computing the log-likelihood:

$$
\begin{aligned}
L(\theta|x_1, x_2, x_3, z_1) \quad &= \log \frac{n!}{\prod_{i=1}^{3} x_i!} \prod_{i=1}^{3} p_i^{x_i} \\
&= c + \sum_{i=1}^{3} x_i \log p_i = c + x_1 \log \frac{\theta}{6} + x_2 \log\left(1 - \frac{\theta}{4}\right) + x_3 \log \frac{\theta}{12}
\end{aligned}
$$

We can derive the expression for the corresponding Q function, exploiting the linearity of the expected value operator $E[\bullet]$:

$$Q(\bar{\theta}|\bar{\theta}_t) = E[x_1|z_1, \bar{p}^{(t)}] \log \frac{\theta}{6} + E[x_2|z_1, \bar{p}^{(t)}] \log\left(1 - \frac{\theta}{4}\right) + x_3 \log \frac{\theta}{12}$$

The variables x_1 and x_2 given z_1 are binomially distributed and can be expressed as a function of $\bar{\theta}_t$ (we need to recompute them at each iteration). Hence, the expected value of $x_1^{(t+1)}$ becomes as follows:

$$E[x_1|z_1, \bar{p}^{(t)}] = z_1 \frac{p_1^{(t)}}{p_1^{(t)} + p_2^{(t)}} = z_1 \frac{\frac{\theta_t}{6}}{\frac{\theta_t}{6} + 1 - \frac{\theta_t}{4}} = z_1 \frac{2\theta_t}{12 - \theta_t}$$

While the expected value of $x_2^{(t+1)}$ is as follows:

$$E\left[x_2|z_1,\bar{p}^{(t)}\right] = z_1 \frac{p_2^{(t)}}{p_1^{(t)} + p_2^{(t)}} = z_1 \frac{1 - \frac{\theta_t}{4}}{\frac{\theta_t}{6} + 1 - \frac{\theta_t}{4}} = z_1 \frac{3(4 - \theta_t)}{12 - \theta_t}$$

If we apply these expressions in $Q(\bar{\theta}|\bar{\theta}_t)$ and compute the derivative with respect to θ, we get the following:

$$\frac{\partial Q}{\partial \theta} = 0 \Rightarrow \frac{E\left[x_1|z_1,\bar{p}^{(t)}\right] + x_3}{\theta} + \frac{E\left[x_2|z_1,\bar{p}^{(t)}\right]}{\theta - 4} = 0$$

Therefore, solving for θ, we get the following:

$$\theta = \frac{4\left(E\left[x_1|z_1,\bar{p}^{(t)}\right] + x_3\right)}{z_1 + x_3}$$

At this point, we can derive the iterative expression for θ:

$$\theta = \frac{4\left(z_1 \frac{2\theta_t}{12 - \theta_t} + x_3\right)}{z_1 + x_3} = \frac{8z_1\theta_t + 4x_3(12 - \theta_t)}{(z_1 + x_3)(12 + \theta_t)}$$

Let's compute the value of θ for $z_1 = 50$ and $x_3 = 10$:

```
def theta(theta_prev, z1=50.0, x3=10.0):
    num = (8.0 * z1 * theta_prev) + \
          (4.0 * x3 * (12.0 - theta_prev))
    den = (z1 + x3) * (12.0 - theta_prev)
    return num / den

theta_v = 0.01

for i in range(1000):
    theta_v = theta(theta_v)

print(theta_v)
```

The output is:

```
1.999999999999999
```

Let's now compute the probability vector:

```
p = [theta_v / 6.0,
     (1 - (theta_v / 4.0)),
     theta_v / 12.0]

print("P=[{:.2f}, {:.2f}, {:.2f}]".
      format(p[0], p[1], p[2]))
```

The resulting output is:

```
P=[0.33, 0.50, 0.17]
```

In this example, we have parameterized all probabilities and, considering that $z_1 = x_1 + x_2$, we have one degree of freedom for the choice of θ. The reader can repeat the example by setting the value of one of p_1 or p_2 and leaving the other probabilities as functions of $\bar{\theta}$. The computation is almost identical but, in this case, there are no degrees of freedom.

Once we have completed this example, we can return to a purely machine learning application, Gaussian Mixture, to fully understand how to derive the iterative procedure that is employed to optimize the parameters.

Gaussian Mixture

In *Chapter 3, Introduction to Semi-Supervised Learning*, we discussed the Generative Gaussian Mixture model in the context of semi-supervised learning. In this section, we're going to apply the EM algorithm to derive the formulas for the parameter updates.

Let's start considering a dataset X, drawn from a data-generating process p_{data}:

$$X = \{\bar{x}_1, \bar{x}_2, \dots, \bar{x}_N\} \ where \ \bar{x}_i \in \mathbb{R}^m$$

We assume that the whole distribution is generated by the sum of k Gaussian distributions so that the probability of each sample can be expressed as follows:

$$p(\bar{x}_i) = \sum_{j=1}^{k} P(N = j) N(\bar{x}_i | \bar{\mu}_j, \Sigma_j) = \sum_{j=1}^{k} w_j N(\bar{x}_i | \bar{\mu}_j, \Sigma_j)$$

In the previous expression, the term $w_j = P(N = j)$ is the relative weight of the jth Gaussian, while $\bar{\mu}_j$ and Σ_j are the mean and the covariance matrix. For consistency with the laws of probability, we also need to impose the following:

$$\sum_j w_j = 1$$

Unfortunately, if we try to solve the problem directly, we need to manage the logarithm of a sum and the procedure becomes very complex. However, we have learned that it's possible to use latent variables as helpers whenever this trick can simplify the solution.

Let's consider a single parameter set $\bar{\theta} = (w_j, \bar{\mu}_j, \Sigma_j)$ and a latent indicator matrix Z, where each element z_{ij} is equal to 1 if the point $\bar{x}_j$ has been generated by the jth Gaussian and 0 otherwise. Therefore, each z_{ij} is Bernoulli distributed with parameters equal to $p(j|\bar{x}_i, \bar{\theta}_t)$. At this point, the role of the latent variables Z should be clearer. We know that each Gaussian contributes to the overall probability of a point $\bar{x}_i \in X$, but we have no further pieces of information. Therefore, the latent variables describe a known behavior that is, however, initially too complex to be mathematically described (even if it must be included in the model).

The joint log-likelihood can hence be expressed using the exponential-indicator notation, as follows:

$$L(\bar{\theta}; X, Z) = \log \prod_i \prod_j p(\bar{x}_i, j|\bar{\theta})^{z_{ij}} = \sum_i \sum_j z_{ij} \log p(\bar{x}_i, j|\bar{\theta})$$

The index i refers to the samples, while j refers to the Gaussian distributions. If we apply the chain rule and the properties of a logarithm, the expression becomes as follows:

$$L(\bar{\theta}; X, Z) = \sum_i \sum_j z_{ij} \log p(\bar{x}_i, j|\bar{\theta}) + z_{ij} \log p(j|\bar{\theta})$$

The first term represents the probability of $\bar{x}_i$ under the jth Gaussian, while the second one is the relative weight of the jth Gaussian. We can now compute the $Q(\bar{\theta}|\bar{\theta}_t)$ function using the joint log-likelihood:

$$Q(\bar{\theta}|\bar{\theta}_t) = E_{Z|X,\bar{\theta}_t}\left[\sum_i\sum_j z_{ij}\log p(\bar{x}_i,j|\bar{\theta}) + z_{ij}\log p(j|\bar{\theta})\right]$$

Exploiting the linearity of $E[\bullet]$, the previous expression becomes as follows:

$$Q(\bar{\theta}|\bar{\theta}_t) = \sum_i\sum_j p(j|\bar{x}_i,\bar{\theta}_t)\log p(\bar{x}_i,j|\bar{\theta}) + p(j|\bar{x}_i,\bar{\theta}_t)\log p(j|\bar{\theta})$$

The term $p(j|\bar{x}_i,\bar{\theta}_t)$ corresponds to the expected value of z_{ij} considering the complete data and expresses the probability of the jth Gaussian given the sample $\bar{x}_i$. It can be simplified considering Bayes' theorem:

$$p(j|\bar{x}_i,\bar{\theta}_t) = \alpha p(\bar{x}_i|j,\bar{\theta}_t)p(j,\bar{\theta}_t)$$

The first term is the probability of $\bar{x}_i$ under the jth Gaussian with parameters $\bar{\theta}_t$, while the second one is the weight of the jth Gaussian considering the same parameter set $\bar{\theta}_t$. In order to derive the iterative expressions for the parameters, it's useful to write the complete formula for the logarithm of a multivariate Gaussian distribution:

$$\log p(\bar{x}_i|j,\bar{\theta}_t) = \log\frac{1}{\sqrt{2\pi\det\Sigma_j}}e^{-\frac{(\bar{x}_i-\bar{\mu}_j)^T\Sigma_j^{-1}(\bar{x}_i-\bar{\mu}_j)}{2}} = -\frac{m}{2}\log 2\pi - \frac{1}{2}\log\det\Sigma_j - \frac{1}{2}(\bar{x}_i-\bar{\mu}_j)^T\Sigma_j^{-1}(\bar{x}_i-\bar{\mu}_j)$$

To simplify this expression, we use the trace trick. In fact, as $(\bar{x}_i-\bar{\mu}_j)^T\Sigma_j^{-1}(\bar{x}_i-\bar{\mu}_j)$ is a scalar, we can exploit the properties $tr(AB) = tr(BA)$ and $tr(C) = C$, where A and B are matrices and $c \in \mathbb{R}$:

$$\log p(\bar{x}_i|j,\bar{\theta}_t) = -\frac{m}{2}\log 2\pi - \frac{1}{2}\log\det\Sigma_j - \frac{1}{2}tr\left(\Sigma_j^{-1}(\bar{x}_i-\bar{\mu}_j)(\bar{x}_i-\bar{\mu}_j)^T\right)$$

Let's start considering the estimation of the mean (only the first term of $Q(\bar{\theta}|\bar{\theta}_t)$ depends on the mean and covariance):

$$\frac{\partial Q}{\partial\bar{\mu}_j} = -\frac{1}{2}\sum_i p(j|\bar{x}_i,\bar{\theta}_t)tr\left(\Sigma_j^{-1}(\bar{x}_i-\bar{\mu}_j)\right)$$

Setting the derivative equal to zero, we get the following:

$$\bar{\mu}_j = \frac{\sum_i p(j|\bar{x}_i, \bar{\theta}_t)\, \bar{x}_i}{\sum_i p(j|\bar{x}_i, \bar{\theta}_t)}$$

In the same way, we obtain the expression of the covariance matrix:

$$\Sigma_j = \frac{\sum_i p(j|\bar{x}_i, \bar{\theta}_t)\left[(\bar{x}_i - \bar{\mu}_j)(\bar{x}_i - \bar{\mu}_j)^T\right]}{\sum_i p(j|\bar{x}_i, \bar{\theta}_t)}$$

To obtain the iterative expressions for the weights, the procedure is a little bit more complex, because we need to use the Lagrange multipliers. Considering that the sum of the weights must always be equal to 1, it's possible to write the following equation:

$$P = Q - \lambda\left(\sum_j w_j - 1\right) \Rightarrow \frac{\partial P}{\partial w_j} = \frac{\partial Q}{\partial w_j} - \lambda \;\; and \;\; \frac{\partial P}{\partial \lambda} = \sum_j w_j - 1$$

Setting both derivatives equal to zero, from the first one, considering that $w_j = p(j|\bar{\theta})$, we get the following:

$$w_j = \frac{\sum_i p(j|\bar{x}_i, \bar{\theta}_t)}{\lambda}$$

While from the second derivative, we obtain the following:

$$\frac{\partial P}{\partial \lambda} = \frac{\sum_i \sum_j p(j|\bar{x}_i, \bar{\theta}_t)}{\lambda} - 1 \Rightarrow \lambda = N$$

The last step derives from the fundamental condition:

$$\sum_j p(j|\bar{x}_i, \bar{\theta}_t) = 1$$

Therefore, the final expression of the weights is as follows:

$$w_j = \frac{\sum_i p(j|\bar{x}_i, \bar{\theta}_t)}{N}$$

At this point, we can formalize the Gaussian Mixture algorithm:

- Set random initial values for $w_j^{(0)}, \bar{\mu}_j^{(0)}, \Sigma_j^{(0)}$
- E-Step – Compute $p(j|\bar{x}_i, \bar{\theta}_t)$ using Bayes' theorem:
  $$p(j|\bar{x}_i, \bar{\theta}_t) = \alpha w^{(t)} p(\bar{x}_i|j, \bar{\theta}_t)$$

- M-Step – Compute $w_j^{(t+1)}, \bar{\mu}_j^{(t+1)}, \Sigma_j^{(t+1)}$ using the formulas provided previously

The process must be iterated until the parameters become stable. In general, the best practice is using both a threshold and a maximum number of iterations.

Example of Gaussian Mixture with scikit-learn

We can now implement the Gaussian Mixture algorithm using the scikit-learn implementation. The direct approach has already been shown in *Chapter 3, Introduction to Semi-Supervised Learning*. The dataset is generated to have three cluster centers and a moderate overlap due to a standard deviation equal to 1.5:

```
from sklearn.datasets import make_blobs

nb_samples = 1000
X, Y = make_blobs(n_samples=nb_samples,
                  n_features=2,
                  centers=3, cluster_std=1.5,
                  random_state=1000)
```

The corresponding plot is shown in the following figure:

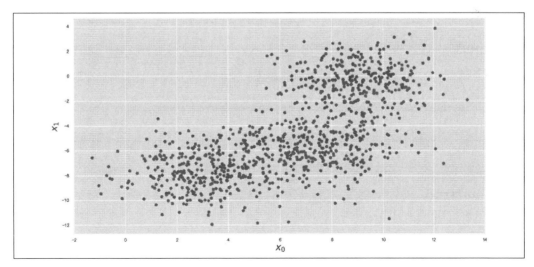

Dataset for Gaussian Mixture

The scikit-learn implementation is based on the `GaussianMixture` class, which accepts as parameters the number of Gaussians (`n_components`) and the type of covariance (`covariance_type`), which can be `full` (the default value) if all components have their own matrix, `tied` if the matrix is shared, `diag` if all components have their own diagonal matrix (this condition imposes an uncorrelation among the features), and `spherical` when each Gaussian is symmetric in every direction. The other parameters allow the setting of regularization and initialization factors (for further information, the reader can directly check the documentation). Our implementation is based on full covariance:

```
from sklearn.mixture import GaussianMixture

gm = GaussianMixture(n_components=3)
gm.fit(X)
```

After fitting the model, it's possible to access the learned parameters through the instance variables `weights_`, `means_`, and `covariances_`:

```
print(gm.weights_)
```

The output is:

```
[0.33021183 0.32825195 0.34153622]
```

We can do the same for the means:

```
print(gm.means_)
```

The resulting vectors are:

```
[[ 9.04405804 -0.37402889]
 [ 3.03380714 -7.69379648]
 [ 7.36636358 -5.77704133]]
```

Finally, we can compute the covariance matrices:

```
print(gm.covariances_)
```

The output is:

```
[[[ 2.11018067  0.02628044]
  [ 0.02628044  2.21420326]]

 [[ 2.34039729  0.08198461]
  [ 0.08198461  2.36352386]]
```

```
[[ 2.72613075 -0.00423492]
 [-0.00423492  2.40306437]]]
```

Considering the covariance matrices, we can already see that the features are very uncorrelated, and the Gaussians are almost spherical. The final plot can be obtained by assigning each point to the corresponding cluster (Gaussian distribution) through the `Yp = gm.transform(X)` command:

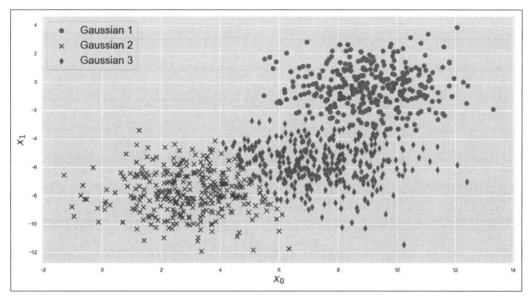

Labeled dataset obtained through the application of a Gaussian mixture with three components

The reader should have noticed a strong similarity between Gaussian Mixture and k-means (which we're going to discuss in *Chapter 6, Clustering and Unsupervised Models*). In particular, we can state that k-means is a particular case of spherical Gaussian Mixture with a covariance matrix $\Sigma \rightarrow 0$. This condition transforms the approach from a soft clustering, where each sample belongs to all clusters with a precise probability distribution, into a hard clustering, where the assignment is done by considering the shortest distance between the sample and centroid (or mean). For this reason, in some books, the Gaussian Mixture algorithm is also called soft k-means. A conceptually similar approach that we are going to present in that chapter is fuzzy k-means, which is based on assignments characterized by membership functions, which are analogous to probability distributions.

Determining the optimal number of components using AIC and BIC

In general, the optimal number of Gaussians is not known and depends on the structure of the underlying data-generating process. In this section, we show two relatively simple methods (without mathematical proofs) to find this value as a trade-off between maximum log-likelihood and model complexity. The first approach is called AIC, or Akaike Information Criterion, and is defined as follows:

$$AIC(L_{opt}, n) = 2n - 2L_{opt}$$

In the previous expression, L_{opt} is the maximum achieved log-likelihood, while n is the number of parameters (in general, n is based on the total number of parameters involved in the model, but, very often, the number of components is proportional to n; therefore we are using n as a proxy for the number of components). The goal of AIC is to measure the impact of having more components on the log-likelihood and, as it's easy to understand, the lower the AIC, the more optimal the solution is. In fact, L_{opt} is considered as the negative log-likelihood. Therefore, large AIC values imply an excessive model complexity that is not balanced by a corresponding improvement in the MLE. The penalty term $2n$ might not always be appropriate because the linearity as a function of n is not able to penalize models that yield a slightly better MLE with the cost of an unjustified extra complexity. An alternative to AIC is provided by **Bayesian Information Criterion (BIC)**, which employs a stronger penalty term:

$$BIC(L_{opt}, n) = n \log n - 2L_{opt}$$

In this case, the proportionality is no longer linear, and the number of components must produce a larger MLE to be selected. In practical applications, AIC is often preferred but, as it tends to overfit, it's necessary to use an appropriately large sample size. On the other hand, when this condition is met (from a theoretical viewpoint, it's necessary to consider the problem asymptotically, so when $n \rightarrow \infty$), the minimum value of BIC corresponds to a model p_m that minimizes the Kullback-Leibler divergence with p_{data} (that is, $D_{KL}(p_m||p_{data}) \rightarrow 0$). However, as this condition often requires an extremely large sample size, AIC and BIC often tend to select the same models.

Considering our example, we know that the ground truth is $n = 3$, but we want to check both AIC and BIC for different values to be sure that the choice is correct:

```
nb_components = [2, 3, 4, 5, 6, 7, 8]
```

```
aics = []
bics = []

for n in nb_components:
gm = GaussianMixture(n_components=n,
                                max_iter=1000,
                                random_state=1000)
        gm.fit(X)
aics.append(gm.aic(X))
bics.append(gm.bic(X))
```

The results are shown in the following figure:

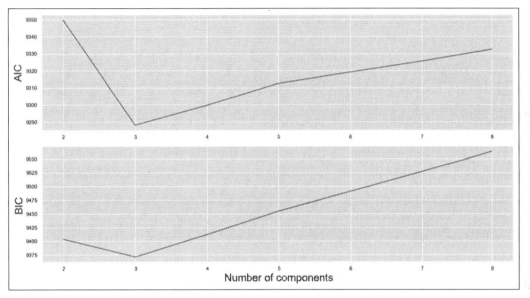

AIC and BIC for different numbers of components

Both AIC and BIC confirm that $n = 3$ is the optimal choice, but it's interesting to notice the penalty effect of AIC and BIC when $n = 2$. While the former has a peak, the latter is slightly larger than the optimal value. This is a consequence of the penalty $n \log n$ (equal to about 1.38), which is smaller than 4 ($2n$). Conversely, both indexes are very similar when n increases with a stronger penalty effect from BIC (the trend is almost linear, while AIC reduces the slope when $n > 5$). As a generic rule, we suggest analyzing both values and selecting BIC (in case the two minima are different) only when the score reduction is sensibly large with respect to AIC (for example, it's possible to compare the relative reduction considering the two neighboring values and pick BIC only if this value is greater than a predefined threshold, for example, 0.3).

Automatic component selection using Bayesian Gaussian Mixture

Sometimes, the determination of the most appropriate number of components is a problem that can be solved by exploiting a full Bayesian framework and by imposing a prior distribution on the weights (full details of the method can be found in Nasios N., Bors A. G., *Variational Learning for Gaussian Mixture Models*, IEEE Transactions on Systems, Man, and Cybernetics, 36/4, 2006). In particular, we can derive the posterior distribution of the weights with:

$$p(\bar{w}|X) \propto p(X|\bar{w})p(\bar{w})$$

In a standard EM approach, we maximize $p(X|\bar{\theta})$, which is the likelihood (to avoid confusion, we have generalized the parameter vector using the notation $\bar{\theta}$). However, if we have prior information about the parameters, we can try to find the optimal posterior. Unfortunately, while the EM algorithm employs the MLE, which can be solved in closed form, a MAP estimation is often extremely complex because it's necessary to find the normalizing constant and this step requires an integration. A simplification can be obtained by employing conjugate priors. A distribution $p(y)$ is a conjugate prior with respect to a posterior $q(y \mid X)$ and a likelihood $L(X \mid y)$, if $p(y)$ and $q(y \mid X)$ belong to the same family and:

$$q(y|X) = \alpha L(X|y)p(y)$$

The employment of conjugate priors allows us to work directly with the posterior by understanding the effect of the likelihood (which generally acts on the parameters of the prior distribution). In this particular context, we are not interested in discussing all conjugate priors (with respect to means, covariance, and weights), but we are focusing only on the weights (the reader who's interested in the details can check the aforementioned paper). As discussed in the main section, we want to impose the condition:

$$\sum_j w_j = 1$$

The likelihood considering only the weights is multinomial because we need to find the weights that maximize the probability that the points are assigned to the closest Gaussian (or, considering the problem from the opposite viewpoint, we need to adjust the weights so as to maximize the probability that the Gaussian generates the sample).

The conjugate prior for a multinomial distribution is the Dirichlet distribution parametrized with a vector $\bar{\alpha}$ with the same dimensionality of $\bar{w}$. A Dirichlet distribution is intrinsically sparse, that is, it tends to generate samples with many null components. Therefore, this choice perfectly meets our requirement to find the optimal number of Gaussian (a Gaussian associated with $w_i \approx 0$ is to be considered as non-existing). Solving the problem using a Dirichlet distribution directly is feasible, but there are still too many parameters (the components of the vector $\bar{\alpha}$) to manage. Alternatively, it's possible to employ a Dirichlet process parametrized with a single weight concentration coefficient w_c. Such a process outputs a probability distribution when sampled and the level of sparsity is proportional to w_c.

Let's now consider the previously defined dataset and apply a Bayesian Gaussian Mixture with $n = 8$ and $w_c = 1$:

```
from sklearn.mixture import BayesianGaussianMixture

gm = BayesianGaussianMixture(n_components=8,
                             max_iter=10000,
                             weight_concentration_prior=1,
                             random_state=1000)
gm.fit(X)

print("Weights (wc = 1):")
for w in gm.weights_:
    print("{:.2f}".format(w))
```

The output is:

```
Weights (wc = 1):
0.00
0.35
0.00
0.32
0.00
0.00
0.00
0.32
```

As it's possible to see, only three components have been selected, while all the other weights have been pushed toward zero. According to the dataset, very different results can be obtained by changing the weight concentration prior parameter, and this represents probably the most tedious weakness of this algorithm.

Therefore, the exploration should start by selecting very different values (for example, $w_c = \{0.1, 10, 1000\}$), observing the differences, and then analyzing the range where the number of active components remains constant. For example, in our case, as the dataset is intrinsically a Gaussian Mixture (because it has been generated by sampling 3 Gaussians), the weight concentration coefficient has a limited effect and $n = 4$ is naturally selected.

Conversely, if p_{data} has a more complex structure, low w_c values tend to reduce the number of active components (according to the strength of the L_1 norm), while large values make the Dirichlet distribution denser and denser. However, an ideal scenario should include both a grid search of the optimal concentration parameter and a continuous analysis of AIC and BIC. When the uncertainty is high, it's also possible to start by selecting a potential range for n using AIC and then *zooming* into it by adjusting the weight concentration parameter. For further details about this method, refer to Bonaccorso G., *Hands-On Unsupervised Learning with Python*, Packt Publishing, 2018.

Summary

In this chapter, we presented the EM algorithm, explaining the reasons that justify its application in many statistical learning contexts. We also discussed the fundamental role of hidden (latent) variables in order to derive an expression that is easier to maximize (the Q function).

We applied the EM algorithm to solve a simple parameter estimation problem and afterward to prove the Gaussian Mixture estimation formulas. We showed how it's possible to employ the scikit-learn implementation instead of writing the whole procedure from scratch (like in *Chapter 3, Introduction to Semi-Supervised Learning*).

In the next chapter, we are going to introduce and analyze three different approaches to component extraction: Factor Analysis, PCA, and FastICA.

Further reading

- Dempster A. P., Laird N. M., Rubin D. B., *Maximum likelihood from incomplete data via the EM algorithm*, Journal of the Royal Statistical Society, B, 39(1):1–38, 11/1977

- *Hansen F., Pedersen G. K. Jensen's Operator Inequality*, arXiv:math/0204049 [math.OA]

- Rubin D., Thayer D., *EM algorithms for ML factor analysis*, Psychometrika, 47/1982, Issue 1

- Ghahramani Z., Hinton G. E., *The EM algorithm for Mixtures of Factor Analyzers*, CRC-TG-96-1, 05/1996

- Hyvarinen A., Oja E., *Independent Component Analysis: Algorithms and Applications*, Neural Networks 13/2000

- Luenberger D. G., *Optimization by Vector Space Methods, Wiley, 1997*

- Ledoit O., Wolf M., *A Well-Conditioned Estimator for Large-Dimensional Covariance Matrices*, Journal of Multivariate Analysis, 88, 2/2004

- Minka T.P., *Automatic Choice of Dimensionality for PCA*, NIPS 2000

- Nasios N., Bors A. G., *Variational Learning for Gaussian Mixture Models*, IEEE Transactions on Systems, Man, and Cybernetics, 36/4, 2006

- Bonaccorso G., *Hands-On Unsupervised Learning with Python*, Packt Publishing, 2018

13
Component Analysis and Dimensionality Reduction

In this chapter, we're going to introduce the most common and important techniques to perform component analysis and dimensionality reduction. When working with large datasets, it's often necessary to optimize the performance of the algorithms, and one of the most reasonable ways of achieving this goal is to remove those features whose information content is negligible. The models discussed in this chapter allow us to perform a complete analysis of the components of a dataset and to select only those components that make a valuable contribution to the results. In particular, we're going to discuss the following topics:

- Factor analysis
- **Principal Component Analysis (PCA)**, Kernel PCA, and Sparse PCA
- **Independent Component Analysis (ICA)**
- A brief explanation of the **Hidden Markov Models (HMMs)** Forward-Backward algorithm considering the EM steps

We can now start our exploration of these models by discussing a very flexible algorithm to analyze the components of a dataset where there are noise terms present.

Factor Analysis

Let's suppose we have a Gaussian data-generating process $p_{data} \sim N(0, \Sigma)$, and M n-dimensional zero-centered samples drawn from it:

$$X = \{\bar{x}_1, \bar{x}_2, \dots, \bar{x}_M\} \ where \ \bar{x}_i \in \mathbb{R}^n$$

If p_{data} has a mean $\bar{\mu} \neq 0$, it's also possible to use this model, but it's necessary to account for this non-null value with slight changes to some of the formulas. As the zero-centering normally has no drawbacks, it's easier to remove the mean to simplify the model.

One of the most common problems in unsupervised learning is finding a lower dimensional distribution p_{lower} such that the Kullback-Leibler divergence with p_{data} is minimized. When performing a **factor analysis** (**FA**), following the original proposal published in Rubin D., Thayer D., *EM algorithms for ML factor analysis*, Psychometrika, 47/1982, Issue 1, and Ghahramani Z., Hinton G. E., *The EM algorithm for Mixtures of Factor Analyzers*, CRC-TG-96-1, 05/1996, we start from the assumption that we can model the generic data point $\bar{x}$ as a linear combination of Gaussian latent variables $\bar{z}$,
(whose dimension p is normally $p < n$) plus an additive and decorrelated Gaussian noise term $\bar{v}$:

$$\bar{x} = A\bar{z} + \bar{v} \ where \ \bar{z} \sim N(0, I) \ and \ \bar{v} \sim N(0, \Omega) \ with \ \Omega = diag(\omega_0^2, \omega_1^2, \ldots, \omega_n^2)$$

The matrix, A, is called a *factor loading matrix* because it determines the contribution of each latent variable (factor) to the reconstruction of $\bar{x}$. Factors and input data are assumed to be statistically independent. Instead, considering the last term, if $\omega_0^2 \neq \omega_1^2 \neq \cdots \neq \omega_n^2$, the noise is called heteroscedastic, while it's defined as homoscedastic if the variances are equal $\omega_0^2 = \omega_1^2 = \cdots = \omega_n^2$. To understand the difference between these two kinds of noise, think about a signal $\bar{x}$ that is the sum of two identical voices, recorded in different places (for example, an airport and a wood). In this case, we can easily imagine how these recordings have different noise variances; that is to say, heteroscedastic noise (the recording from the airport should have higher variance than the forest recording, considering the number of different noise sources). If, instead, both voices are recorded in a soundproofed room — or even in the same airport — homoscedastic noise is surely more likely (we're not considering the amplitude of the noise, just the difference between the variances).

One of the most important strengths of FA with respect to other methods (such as PCA) is its intrinsic robustness to heteroscedastic noise. In fact, including the noise term in the model (with only the constraint to be decorrelated) allows partial denoising filtering based on the single components, while one of the preconditions for the PCA is to impose only homoscedastic noise (which, in many cases, is very similar to the total absence of noise). Considering the previous example, we could assume the first variance would be $\omega_0^2 = k\omega_1^2$ with $k > 1$. In this way, the model will be able to understand that a high variance in the first component should be considered (with a higher probability) as the product of the noise, and not an intrinsic property of the component.

Linear relation analysis

Let's now analyze the linear relation:

$$\bar{x} = A\bar{z} + \bar{v}$$

Considering the properties of Gaussian distributions, we know that $\bar{x} \sim N(\bar{\mu}, \Sigma)$ and it's easy to determine either the mean or the covariance matrix:

$$\begin{cases} \bar{\mu} = E[X] = AE[Z] + E[\bar{v}] = 0 \\ \Sigma = E[X^T X] = AE[Z^T Z]A^T + E[\bar{v}^T \bar{v}] = AA^T + \Omega \end{cases}$$

Therefore, in order to solve the problem, we need to find the best $\theta = (A, \Omega)$ so that $AA^T + \Omega \approx \Sigma$ (with a zero-centered dataset, the estimation is limited to the input covariance matrix Σ). The ability to cope with noisy variables should be clearer now. If $AA^T + \Omega$ is exactly equal to Σ and the estimation of Ω is correct, the algorithm will optimize the factor loading matrix A, excluding the interference produced by the noise term; therefore, the components will be approximately denoised.

In order to adopt the EM algorithm, we need to determine the joint probability $p(X, \bar{z}; \bar{\theta}) = p(X|\bar{z}; \bar{\theta})p(\bar{z}|\bar{\theta})$. The first term on the right-hand side can be easily determined, considering that $\bar{x} - A\bar{z} \sim N(0, \Sigma)$. Therefore, we get the following:

$$p(X, \bar{z}; \bar{\theta}) = \prod_{i=1}^{M} \left(\frac{1}{\sqrt{(2\pi)^n \det \Omega}} e^{-\frac{(\bar{x}_i - A\bar{z})^T \Omega^{-1}(\bar{x}_i - A\bar{z})}{2}} \right) \left(\frac{1}{\sqrt{(2\pi)^p}} e^{-\frac{\bar{z}^T \bar{z}}{2}} \right)$$

We can now determine the $Q(\bar{\theta}|\bar{\theta}_t)$ function, discarding the constant terms and the term $\bar{z}^T \bar{z}$, because they don't depend on $\bar{\theta}$ (in this particular case, as we're going to see, we don't need to compute the probability $p(\bar{z}|X; \bar{\theta})$ because it's enough to obtain sufficient statistics for the expected value and second moment). Moreover, it's useful to expand the multiplication in the exponential:

$$Q(\bar{\theta}|\bar{\theta}_t) = E_{Z|X;\bar{\theta}}[\log p(X|\bar{z}; \bar{\theta})] = E_{Z|X;\bar{\theta}} \left[-\frac{M}{2}\log \det \Omega - \frac{1}{2}\sum_{i=1}^{M}\left(\bar{x}_i^T \Omega^{-1} \bar{x}_i - 2\bar{x}_i^T \Omega^{-1} A\bar{z} + \bar{z}^T A^T \Omega^{-1} A\bar{z} \right) \right]$$

Using the trace trick with the last term (which is a scalar), we can rewrite it as follows:

$$\bar{z}^T A^T \Omega^{-1} A\bar{z} = tr(\bar{z}^T A^T \Omega^{-1} A\bar{z}) = tr(A^T \Omega^{-1} A\bar{z}\bar{z}^T)$$

Exploiting the linearity of the operator $E[\cdot]$, we obtain the following:

$$Q(\bar{\theta}|\bar{\theta}_t) = -\frac{M}{2}\log\det\Omega - \frac{1}{2}\sum_{i=1}^{M}(\bar{x}_i^T\Omega^{-1}\bar{x}_i - 2\bar{x}_i^T\Omega^{-1}AE[\bar{z}|\bar{x}_i] + A^T\Omega^{-1}E[\bar{z}\bar{z}^T|\bar{x}_i])$$

This expression is similar to what we have seen in the Gaussian mixture model, but in this case, we need to compute the conditional expectation and the conditional second moment of $\bar{z}$. Unfortunately, we cannot do this directly, but it's possible to compute them exploiting the joint normality of $\bar{x}$ and $\bar{z}$. In particular, using a classic theorem, we can partition the full joint probability $p(\bar{z}, \bar{x})$, considering the following equations:

$$\bar{v} = \begin{pmatrix} \bar{z} \\ \bar{x} \end{pmatrix} \quad \bar{\mu}^* = \begin{pmatrix} E[\bar{z}] \\ E[\bar{x}] \end{pmatrix} = 0 \quad \Sigma^* = \begin{pmatrix} I & A^T \\ A & AA^T + \Omega \end{pmatrix}$$

The conditional distribution $p(\bar{z}|\bar{x} = \bar{x}_i)$ has a mean equal to the following:

$$E[\bar{z}|\bar{x} = \bar{x}_i] = E[\bar{z}] + E[\bar{z}\bar{x}^T]E[\bar{x}\bar{x}^T]^{-1}(\bar{x}_i - E[\bar{x}]) = A^T(AA^T + \Omega)^{-1}\bar{x}_i$$

The conditional variance is as follows:

$$E[(\bar{z} - E[\bar{z}|\bar{x} = \bar{x}_i])^2] = E[\bar{z}\bar{z}^T|\bar{x} = \bar{x}_i] - E[\bar{z}|\bar{x} = \bar{x}_i]E[\bar{z}|\bar{x} = \bar{x}_i]^T$$

Therefore, the conditional second moment is equal to the following:

$$E[\bar{z}\bar{z}^T|\bar{x} = \bar{x}_i] = I - A^T(AA^T + \Omega)^{-1}A + E[\bar{z}|\bar{x} = \bar{x}_i]E[\bar{z}|\bar{x} = \bar{x}_i]^T$$

If we define the auxiliary matrix $K = (AA^T + \Omega)^{-1}$, the previous expressions become as follows:

$$\begin{cases} E[\bar{z}|\bar{x} = \bar{x}_i] = A^T K \bar{x}_i \\ E[\bar{z}\bar{z}^T|\bar{x} = \bar{x}_i] = I - A^T KA + A^T K \bar{x}_i \bar{x}_i^T K^T A \end{cases}$$

Using the previous expression, it's possible to build the inverse model (sometimes called a *recognition model* because it starts with the effects and rebuilds the causes), which is still Gaussian distributed:

$$\bar{z} = B\bar{x} + \bar{\lambda} \text{ where } p(\bar{z}|\bar{x}; \bar{\theta}) \sim N(A^T K\bar{x}, I - A^T KA)$$

We are now able to maximize $Q(\bar{\theta}|\theta_t)$ with respect to A and Ω, considering $\bar{\theta}_t = (A_t, \Omega_t)$ and both the conditional expectation and the second moment computed according to the previous estimation $\bar{\theta}_{t-1} = (A_{t-1}, \Omega_{t-1})$. For this reason, they are not involved in the derivation process. We are adopting the convention that the term subject to maximization is computed at time t, while all the others are obtained through the previous estimations $(t-1)$:

$$\frac{\partial Q}{\partial A} = -\sum_{i=1}^{M} \Omega_{t-1}^{-1} \bar{x}_i E[\bar{z}|\bar{x} = \bar{x}_i]^T + \sum_{j=1}^{M} \Omega_{t-1}^{-1} A_t\, E[\bar{z}\bar{z}^T|\bar{x} = \bar{x}_i] = 0$$

The expression for A_t is therefore as follows (Q is the biased input covariance matrix $E[X^T X]$ for a zero-centered dataset):

$$A_t = (Q K_{t-1}^T A_{t-1})(I - A_{t-1}^T K_{t-1} A_{t-1} + A_{t-1}^T K_{t-1} Q K_{t-1}^T A_{t-1})^{-1}$$

In the same way, we can obtain an expression for Ω_t by computing the derivative with respect to Ω^{-1} (this choice simplifies the calculation and doesn't affect the result, because we must set the derivative equal to zero):

$$\frac{\partial Q}{\partial \Omega^{-1}} = \frac{M}{2} \Omega_t - \frac{1}{2} \sum_{i=1}^{M} (\bar{x}_i\, \bar{x}_i^T - A_{t-1} E[\bar{z}|\bar{x} = \bar{x}_i] \bar{x}_i^T) = 0$$

The derivative of the first term, which is the determinant of a real diagonal matrix, is obtained using the adjugated matrix $Adj(\Omega)$ and exploiting the properties of the inverse matrix $T^{-1} = \det(T)^{-1} Adj(T)$ and the properties $(\det T)^{-1} = \det T^{-1}$ and $\det T^T = \det T$:

$$\frac{\partial}{\partial \Omega^{-1}} \log \det \Omega = (\det \Omega)(Adj(\Omega)^T)^{-1} = \Omega^T = \Omega$$

The expression for Ω_t (imposing the diagonality constraint) is as follows:

$$\Omega_t = diag(Q - A_{t-1} A_{t-1}^T K_{t-1} Q)$$

Summarizing the steps, we can define the complete FA algorithm:

- Set random initial values for $A^{(0)}$ and $\Omega^{(0)}$
- Compute the biased input covariance matrix $Q = E[X^T X]$
- E-Step: Compute $A^{(t)}, \Omega^{(t)}, K^{(t)}$

- M-Step: Compute $A^{(t+1)}, \Omega^{(t+1)}, K^{(t+1)}$ using the previous estimations and the formulas provided previously

- Compute the matrices B and Ψ for the inverse model

The process must be repeated until $A^{(t)}, \Omega^{(t)}, K^{(t)}$ stop modifying their values (using a threshold) together with a constraint on the maximum number of iterations. The factors can be easily obtained using the inverse model.

Example of Factor Analysis with scikit-learn

We can now code an example of FA with scikit-learn using the MNIST handwritten digits dataset (70,000 28 × 28 grayscale images) in the original version and with added heteroscedastic normal noise (ω_i randomly selected in the range (0, 0.25)).

The first step is to load and zero-center the original dataset (I'm using the functions defined in *Chapter 1, Machine Learning Model Fundamentals*):

```python
import numpy as np

from sklearn.datasets import fetch_openml

def zero_center(X):
    return X - np.mean(X, axis=0)

digits = fetch_openml("mnist_784")
X = zero_center(digits['data'].
                astype(np.float64) / 255.0)
np.random.shuffle(X)

Omega = np.random.uniform(0.0, 0.25,
                          size=X.shape[1])
Xh = X + np.random.normal(0.0, Omega,
                          size=X.shape)
```

After this step, the X variable will contain the zero-center original dataset, while Xh is the noisy version. The following screenshot shows a random selection of samples from both versions:

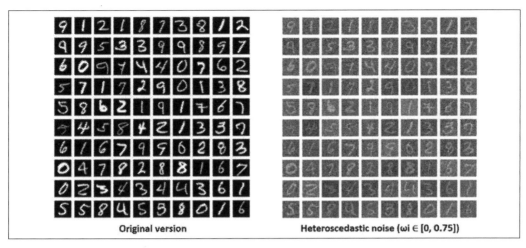

MNIST sample (left). Noisy version (right)

We can perform FA on both datasets using the scikit-learn `FactorAnalysis` class with the `n_components=64` parameter, and check the score (the average log-likelihood over all samples). If the noise variance is known (or there's a good estimation), it's possible to include the starting point through the `noise_variance_init` parameter; otherwise, it will be initialized with the identity matrix:

```
from sklearn.decomposition import FactorAnalysis

fa = FactorAnalysis(n_components=64,
                    random_state=1000)
fah = FactorAnalysis(n_components=64,
                     random_state=1000)

Xfa = fa.fit_transform(X)
Xfah = fah.fit_transform(Xh)

print('Factor analysis score X: {:.3f}'.
      format(fa.score(X)))
print('Factor analysis score Xh: {:.3f}'.
      format(fah.score(Xh)))
```

The output showing the average log-likelihood is:

```
Factor analysis score X: 1821.404
Factor analysis score Xh: 311.249
```

As expected, the presence of noise has reduced the final accuracy (MLE). Following an example provided by A. Gramfort and D. A. Engemann in the original scikit-learn documentation, we can create a benchmark for the MLE using the Ledoit-Wolf algorithm (a shrinking method for improving the condition of the covariance that is beyond the scope of this book). For further information, read Ledoit O., Wolf M., *A Well-Conditioned Estimator for Large-Dimensional Covariance Matrices*, Journal of Multivariate Analysis, 88, 2/2004:

```
from sklearn.covariance import LedoitWolf

ldw = LedoitWolf()
ldwh = LedoitWolf()

ldw.fit(X)
ldwh.fit(Xh)
```

The average log-likelihood is:

```
print('Ledoit-Wolf score X: {:.3f}'.
        format(ldw.score(X)))
print('Ledoit-Wolf score Xh: {:.3f}'.
        format(ldwh.score(Xh)))
```

The output is:

```
Ledoit-Wolf score X: 1367.221

Ledoit-Wolf score Xh: 346.825
```

With the original dataset, FA performs much better than the benchmark, while it's slightly worse in the presence of heteroscedastic noise. The reader can try other combinations using the grid search with different numbers of components and noise variances, and experiment with the effect of removing the zero-centering step. It's possible to plot the extracted components using the `components_` instance variable:

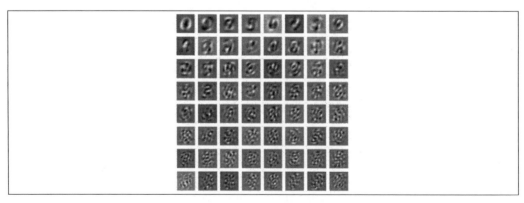

A plot of the 64 components extracted with the factor analysis on the original dataset

A careful analysis shows that the components are a superimposition of many low-level visual features. This is a consequence of the assumption that we have a Gaussian prior distribution over the components ($\bar{z} \sim N(0, I)$). In fact, one of the disadvantages of this distribution is its intrinsic denseness (the probability of sampling values far from the mean is often too high, while in some cases, it would be desirable to have a peaked distribution that discourages values not close to its mean, to be able to observe components more selectively).

Moreover, considering the distribution $p(Z|X; \bar{\theta})$, the covariance matrix Ψ might not be diagonal (trying to impose this constraint can lead to an unsolvable problem), leading to a resulting multivariate Gaussian distribution, which isn't normally made up of independent components. In general, the single variables $\bar{z}_i$, (conditioned to an input point $\bar{x}_i$) are statistically dependent and the reconstruction $\bar{x}_i$, is obtained with the participation of almost all extracted features. In all these cases, we say that the coding is dense and the dictionary of features in under-complete (the dimensionality of the components is lower than dim $\bar{x}_i$). The lack of independence can also be an issue considering that any orthogonal transformation Q applied to A (the factor loading matrix) doesn't affect the distribution $p(X|Z; \bar{\theta})$. In fact, as $QQ^T = I$, the following applies:

$$AA^T + \Omega = AQQ^T A^T + \Omega$$

In other words, any feature rotation ($\bar{x} = AQ\bar{z} + \bar{v}$) is always a solution to the original problem and it's impossible to decide which is the real loading matrix. All these conditions lead to the further conclusion that the mutual information among components is not equal to zero and neither close to a minimum (in this case, each of them carries a specific portion of information). On the other hand, our main goal was to reduce the dimensionality. Since that's the case, it's not surprising that we have dependent components because we aim to preserve the maximum amount of original information contained in $p(X)$ (remember that the amount of information is related to the entropy and the latter is proportional to the variance).

The same phenomenon can be observed in the PCA (which is still based on the Gaussian assumption), but in the last paragraph, we're going to discuss a technique called ICA, whose goal is to create a representation of each sample (without the constraint of the dimensionality reduction) after starting from a set of statistically independent features. This approach, even if it has its peculiarities, belongs to a large family of algorithms called sparse coding. In this scenario, if the corresponding dictionary has dim $\bar{z}_i >$ dim $\bar{x}_i$ it is called over-complete (of course, the main goal is no longer dimensionality reduction). However, we're going to consider only the case when the dictionary is at most complete dim $\bar{z}_i =$ dim $\bar{x}_i$, because ICA with over-complete dictionaries requires a more complex approach. The level of sparsity, of course, is proportional to dim $\bar{z}_i$, and with ICA, it's always achieved as a secondary goal (the primary one is always the independence between components).

Principal Component Analysis

Another common approach to the problem of reducing the dimensionality of a high-dimensional dataset is based on the assumption that, normally, the total variance is not explained equally by all components. If p_{data} is a multivariate Gaussian distribution with covariance matrix Σ, then the entropy (which is a measure of the amount of information contained in the distribution) is as follows:

$$H(p) = \frac{1}{2}\log \det 2\pi e\Sigma$$

Therefore, if some components have a very low variance, they also have a limited contribution to the entropy, and provide little additional information. Hence, they can be removed without a high loss of accuracy.

Just as we've done with FA, let's consider a dataset drawn from $p_{data} \sim N(0, \Sigma)$ (for simplicity, we assume that it's zero-centered, even if it's not necessary):

$$X = \{\bar{x}_1, \bar{x}_2, \ldots, \bar{x}_M\} \; where \; \bar{x}_i \in \mathbb{R}^n$$

Our goal is to define a linear transformation, $\bar{z} = A^T\bar{x}$ (a vector is normally considered a column, therefore, $\bar{x}$ has a shape $(n \times 1)$), such as the following:

$$\begin{cases} \dim \bar{z}_i \ll n \\ H(p(\bar{z})) \approx H(p(\bar{x})) \end{cases}$$

As we want to find out the directions where the variance is higher, we can build our transformation matrix A, starting from the eigendecomposition of the input covariance matrix Σ (which is real, symmetric, and positive definite):

$$\Sigma = V\Omega V^T$$

V is an $(n \times n)$ matrix containing the eigenvectors (as columns), while Ω is a diagonal matrix containing the eigenvalues. Moreover, V is also orthogonal, hence the eigenvectors constitute a basis. An alternative approach is based on the **Singular Value Decomposition (SVD)**, which has an incremental variant. There are also algorithms that can perform a decomposition truncated at an arbitrary number of components, speeding up the convergence process (such as the scikit-learn implementation TruncatedSVD). In this case, it's immediately noticeable that the sample covariance is as follows (if $M \gg 1$, $M \approx M - 1$ and the estimation is almost unbiased):

$$\Sigma_s = \frac{1}{M} X^T X \ where \ X \in \mathbb{R}^{M \times n} \ and \ \Sigma_s \in \mathbb{R}^{n \times n}$$

If we apply the SVD to the matrix X (each row represents a single data point with a shape $(1 \times n)$), we obtain the following:

$$X = U \Lambda V^T \ where \ U \in \mathbb{R}^{M \times M}, \Lambda \in diag(n \times n) \ and \ V \in \mathbb{R}^{n \times n}$$

U is a unitary matrix containing (as rows) the left singular vectors (the eigenvectors of XX^T), V (also unitary) contains (as rows) the right singular vectors (corresponding to the eigenvectors of $X^T X$), while Λ is a diagonal matrix containing the singular values of Σ_s (which are the square roots of the eigenvalues of both XX^T and $X^T X$). Conventionally, the eigenvalues are sorted by descending order and the eigenvectors are rearranged to match the corresponding position.

Hence, we can directly use the matrix Λ to select the most relevant eigenvalues (the square root is an increasing function and doesn't change the order) and the matrix V to retrieve the corresponding eigenvectors (the factor $^1/_M$ is a proportionality constant). In this way, we don't need to compute and eigendecompose the covariance matrix Σ (contains $n \times n$ elements) and we can exploit some very fast approximate algorithms that work only with the dataset (without computing $X^T X$). Using the SVD, the transformation of X can be done directly, considering that U and V are unitary matrices (this means that $UU^T = U^T U = I$; therefore, the conjugate transpose is also the inverse):

$$Z = XA = U \Lambda V^T V = U \Lambda$$

Right now, X has only been projected in the eigenvector space (it has been simply rotated) and its dimensionality hasn't changed. However, from the definition of the eigenvector, we know that the following is true:

$$\Sigma \bar{v} = \lambda \bar{v}$$

If λ is large, the projection of $\bar{v}$ will be amplified proportionally to the variance explained by the direction of the corresponding eigenvector. Therefore, if it has not already been done, we can sort (and rename) the eigenvalues and the corresponding eigenvectors to have the following:

$$\lambda_1 > \lambda_2 > \cdots > \lambda_n$$

If we select the first top k eigenvalues, we can build a transformation matrix based on the corresponding eigenvectors (principal components) that projects X onto a subspace of the original eigenvector space:

$$A_k = \{\bar{v}_1, \bar{v}_2, \dots, \bar{v}_k\} \text{ where } A_k \in \mathbb{R}^{n \times k}$$

Using the SVD, instead of A_k, we can directly truncate U and Λ, creating the matrices U_k (which contains only the top k eigenvectors) and Λ_k, a diagonal matrix with the top k eigenvalues.

Component importance evaluation

When choosing the value for k, we are assuming that the following is true:

$$Explained\ Variance[A_k] \approx Explained\ Variance[V]$$

To achieve this goal, it is normally necessary to compare the performances with a different number of components. In the following graph, there's a plot where the variance ratio (*variance explained by component n/total variance*) and the cumulative variance are plotted as functions of the components:

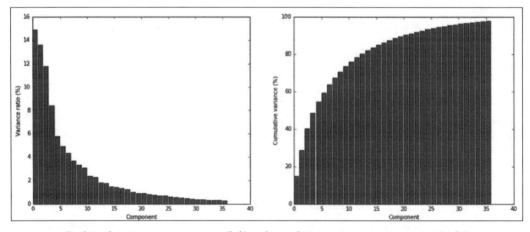

Explained variance per component (left) and cumulative variance per component (right)

In this case, the first 10 components are able to explain 80% of the total variance. The remaining 25 components have an increasingly minimal impact and could be removed. However, the choice must always be based on the specific context, considering the loss of value induced by the loss of information.

A trick for determining the correct number of components is based on the analysis of the eigenvalues of X. After sorting them, it's possible to consider the differences between subsequent values $d = \{\lambda_1 - \lambda_2, \dots, \lambda_{k-1} - \lambda_k\}$. The highest difference $\lambda_{k-1} - \lambda_k$ determines the index k of a potential optimal reduction (obviously, it's necessary to consider a constraint on the minimum value, because normally $\lambda_1 - \lambda_2$ is the highest difference). For example, if $d = \{4, 4, 3, 0.2, 0.18, 0.05\}$, the original dimensionality is $n = 6$; however, $\lambda_4 - \lambda_5$ is the smallest difference, so, it's reasonable to reduce the dimensionality to $(n + 1) - k = 3$. The reason is straightforward; the eigenvalues determine the magnitude of each component, but we need a relative measure because the scale changes. In the example, the last three eigenvectors point to directions where the explained variance is negligible when compared to the first three components.

Once we've defined the transformation matrix A_k, it's possible to perform the actual projection of the original vectors in the new subspace, through the relation:

$$\bar{z} = A_k^T \bar{x} \ \ where \ \ \bar{z} \in \mathbb{R}^{k \times 1}, A_k^T \in \mathbb{R}^{n \times k} \ \ and \ \ \bar{x} \in \mathbb{R}^{n \times 1}$$

The complete transformation of the whole dataset is simply obtained as follows:

$$Z = X A_k = U_k \Lambda_k$$

Now, let's analyze the new covariance matrix $E[Z^T Z]$. If the original distribution is $p_{data} \sim N(0, \Sigma)$, $p(\bar{z})$ will also be Gaussian with mean and covariance:

$$\begin{cases} \bar{\mu}_z = E[Z] = A^T E[X] = 0 \\ \Sigma_z = E[Z^T Z] = A^T E[X^T X] A = A^T \Sigma A = A^T V \Omega V^T A \end{cases}$$

Considering that Ω is diagonal, the resulting matrix Σ_z will be diagonal as well. This means that the PCA decorrelates the transformed covariance matrix. At the same time, we can state that every algorithm that decorrelates the input covariance matrix performs a PCA (with or without dimensionality reduction). For example, the whitening process is a particular PCA without dimensionality reduction, while Isomap (see *Chapter 5, Graph-Based Semi-Supervised Learning*) performs the same operation working with the Gram matrix with a more geometric approach. This result will be used in *Chapter 14, Hebbian Learning*, to show how some particular neural networks can perform a PCA without eigendecomposing Σ.

Let's now consider an FA with homoscedastic noise. We have seen that the covariance matrix of the conditional distribution $(X|Z; \bar{\theta})$ is equal to $AA^T + \Omega$. In the case of homoscedastic noise, it becomes $AA^T + \omega I$. For a generic covariance matrix, Σ, it's possible to prove that adding a constant diagonal matrix $\Sigma + aI$ doesn't modify the original eigenvectors and shifts the eigenvalues by the same quantity:

$$\Sigma + aI = V\Psi V^T + aI = V\Psi V^T + aVIV^T = V(\Psi + aI)V^T$$

Therefore, we can consider the generic case of absence of noise without loss of generality. We know that the goal of FA (with $\Omega = (0)$) is finding the matrix A, so that $AA^T \approx Q$ (the input covariance). Hence, thanks to the symmetry and imposing the asymptotic equality, we can write the following:

$$A_\infty A_\infty^T = Q \Rightarrow A_\infty A_\infty^T = V\Omega V^T = \left[V\left(\Omega^{1/2}\right)\left(\Omega^{1/2}\right)^T V^T \right] \Rightarrow A_\infty = V\Omega^{1/2}$$

This result implies that the FA is a more generic and robust way to manage the dimensionality reduction in the presence of heteroscedastic noise, and the PCA is a restriction to homoscedastic noise. When a PCA is performed on datasets affected by heteroscedastic noise, the MLE worsens because the different noise components altering the magnitude of the eigenvalues at different levels can drive the selection of eigenvectors that only explain a low percentage of the variance in the original dataset (and in a noiseless scenario, these eigenvectors would normally be discarded in favor of more important directions).

If you think back to the example we discussed at the beginning of the previous paragraph, we know that the noise is strongly heteroscedastic, but we don't have any tools to tell the PCA how to cope with it. That means that the variance of the first component will be much higher than expected, considering that the two sources are identical. Unfortunately, in a real-life scenario, the noise is correlated and neither a factor nor a PCA can efficiently solve the problem when the noise power is very high. In all those cases, more sophisticated denoising techniques must be employed. Whenever, instead, it's possible to define an approximate diagonal noise covariance matrix, FA is certainly more robust and efficient than PCA. The latter should be considered only in noiseless or *quasi*-noiseless scenarios. In both cases, the results can never lead to well-separated features. For this reason, the ICA has been studied and many different strategies have been engineered.

Example of PCA with scikit-learn

We can repeat the same experiment made with the FA and heteroscedastic noise to assess the MLE score of the PCA. We are going to use the PCA class with the same number of components (n_components=64). To achieve the maximum accuracy, we also set the svd_solver='full' parameter, to force scikit-learn to apply a full SVD instead of the truncated version. In this way, the top eigenvalues are only selected after the decomposition, avoiding the risk of imprecise estimations:

```
from sklearn.decomposition import PCA

pca = PCA(n_components=64,
            svd_solver='full',
            random_state=1000)
Xpca = pca.fit_transform(Xh)

print('PCA score: {:.3f}'.
        format(pca.score(Xh)))
```

The output is:

```
PCA score: 162.927
```

The result is not surprising: the MLE is much lower than it was with FA because of the incorrect estimations made due to the heteroscedastic noise. I invite the reader to compare the results with different datasets and noise levels, considering that the training performance of PCA is normally higher than FA. Therefore, when working with large datasets, a good trade-off is surely desirable. As with FA, it's possible to retrieve the components through the components_ instance variable.

It's interesting to check the total explained variance (as a fraction of the total input variance) through the component-wise instance array explained_variance_ratio_:

```
print('Explained variance ratio: {:.3f}'.
        format(np.sum(pca.explained_variance_ratio_)))
```

The output is:

```
Explained variance ratio: 0.677
```

With 64 components, we are explaining about 68% of the total input variance. Of course, it's also useful to compare the explained variance using a plot:

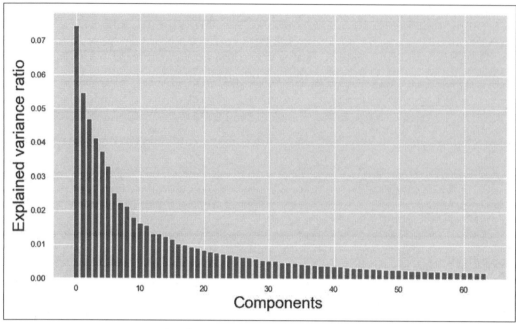

Bar plot of the explained variances per components

As usual, the first components explain the largest part of the variance; however, after about the twentieth component, each contribution becomes lower than 1% (decreasing till about 0%). This analysis suggests two observations: it's possible to further reduce the number of components with an acceptable loss (using the previous snippet, it's easy to extend the sum of just the first n components and compare the results) and, at the same time, the PCA will be able to overcome a higher threshold (such as 95%) only by adding a large number of new components. In this particular case, we know that the dataset is made up of handwritten digits; therefore, we can suppose that the tail is due to secondary differences (a line slightly longer than average, a marked stroke, and so on); hence, we can drop all the components with $n > 64$ (or less) without problems (it's also easy to verify visually a rebuilt image using the `inverse_transform()` method). However, it is always best practice to perform a complete analysis before moving on to further processing steps, particularly when the dimensionality of X is high.

Another interesting approach to determine the optimal number of components has been proposed by Minka (in Minka T. P., *Automatic Choice of Dimensionality for PCA*, NIPS 2000) and is based on the Bayesian model selection.

The idea is to use the MLE to optimize the likelihood $p(X \mid k)$ where k is a parameter indicating the number of components. In other words, it doesn't start analyzing the explained variance, but determines a value of $k < n$ so that the likelihood keeps being the highest possible (implicitly, k will explain the maximum possible variance under the constraint of max $k = k_{max}$). The theoretical foundation (with tedious mathematical derivations) of the method is presented in the previously mentioned paper. However, it's possible to use this method with scikit-learn by setting the `n_components='mle'` and `svd_solver='full'` parameters.

Kernel PCA

When the dataset is non-linearly separable, the true principle components might not be correctly detected. Consider, for example, the following radial dataset:

```
from sklearn.datasets import make_circles

X, _ = make_circles(n_samples=1000,
                    factor=0.25,
                    noise=0.1)
```

A graphical representation is shown in the following figure:

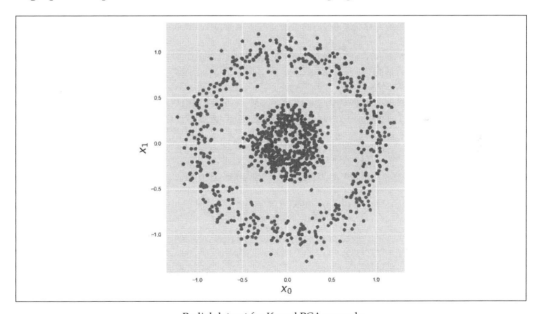

Radial dataset for Kernel PCA example

The dataset is almost symmetrical; therefore, a standard PCA can easily detect the principal components that are orthogonal and with about the same magnitude. However, this couldn't be enough to perform a dimensionality reduction that takes into account the actual semantics of the dataset. In fact, in this case, the inner blob is clearly a dense component separated by the surrounding circle, and it can be necessary to highlight this property in order to understand which components have a larger impact on the explained variance.

To solve this problem, it's necessary that we perform a preprocessing transformation. Imagine having a function $\Psi(\bar{x}) : D \subseteq \mathbb{R}^n \to G \subseteq \mathbb{R}^m$ with m generally (but not necessarily) larger than n. The new points $\bar{z}_i = \Psi(\bar{x}_i)$ are projections of the original ones onto a feature space G where the non-linearities are removed and the components can be linearly separated. Such spaces are extremely common and, in general, the price to pay is only increased complexity (because of the transformation). However, many algorithms (for example, SVMs) are based on the dot product among data points $\Psi(\bar{x}_i)^T \Psi(\bar{x}_j)$ and don't require the explicit transformation. Luckily, these problems can often be solved by employing the so-called kernel trick. We are not going to delve into all the mathematical theory (which requires more space and is beyond the scope of this book), but it suffices to say that, given a feature map $\Psi(\bar{x}_i)$, under mild conditions, it's possible to find a kernel that is equal to:

$$K\left(\bar{x}_i, \bar{x}_j\right) = \Psi(\bar{x}_i)^T \Psi\left(\bar{x}_j\right)$$

In other words, the dot product in the feature space is simply the kernel evaluated for the two points. The PCA is based on the eigendecomposition of the covariance matrix. It's straightforward to understand that working with the Gram matrix induced by the kernel is analogous to working with a covariance matrix in the feature space. In fact, the Gram matrix entries are $G(i,j) = \bar{z}_i^T \cdot \bar{z}_j = \Psi(\bar{x}_i)^T \Psi(\bar{x}_j) = K\left(\bar{x}_i, \bar{x}_j\right)$. At this point, considering the standard PCA transformation $\bar{y}_i = \bar{x}_i^T W$, and applying the feature projection, we get $\Psi(\bar{y}_i) = \Psi(\bar{x}_i)^T W_G$.

The matrix W_G is the kernel PCA projection matrix and is simply obtained by computing the eigenvectors $\{\bar{v}_G\}$ of the Gram matrix and performing the multiplication $W_G = \Psi(\bar{x})\bar{v}_G$. Therefore, the final transformation in the feature space becomes $\Psi(\bar{y}_i) = \Psi(\bar{x}_i)^T \Psi(\bar{x})\bar{v}_G = K(\bar{x}_i, \bar{x})\bar{v}_G$. The last step is the kernel trick itself, that allows us to perform the PCA projection directly in the feature space without the need of transforming all points. We have already analyzed some kernels when discussing Spectral Clustering; therefore, we're not showing them again. However, it should now be easy to understand that our example can be easily solved by employing a **radial basis function** (RBF) kernel:

$$K\left(\bar{x}_i, \bar{x}_j\right) = e^{-\gamma \|\bar{x}_i - \bar{x}_2\|^2}$$

Obviously, the corresponding feature space is radial (so invariant to the angle) and, through the parameter λ, it is possible to control the amplitude of the Gaussian curve (so as to capture or exclude specific regions).

Let's now perform the kernel PCA using an RBF kernel:

```
from sklearn.decomposition import KernelPCA

kpca = KernelPCA(n_components=2,
                 kernel='rbf',
                 fit_inverse_transform=True,
                 gamma=5,
                 random_state=1000)
X_kpca = kpca.fit_transform(X)
```

In this case, we have chosen $\gamma = 5$ because the average separation between the center and border is about 0.5, and so the standard deviation of the Gaussian is $\sigma = \frac{1}{\gamma} = 0.2$. After about three standard deviations, the value is approximately null, and therefore we should be able to perfectly separate the regions. The result is shown in the following figure:

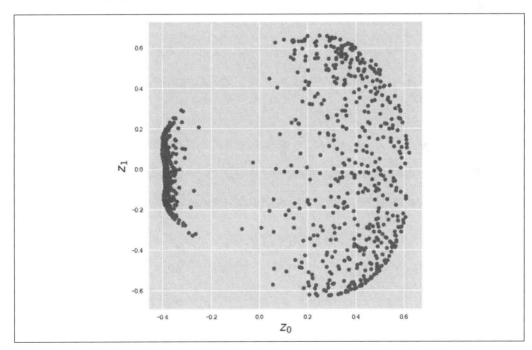

Kernel PCA projection

As it's possible to see, it's possible to use a single component ($\bar{z}_0$) to separate the dataset, while the second one (corresponding to the angle) is negligible because the dispersion is only due to the noise.

Sparse PCA

Sparse PCA is a particular dimensionality reduction technique also known as dictionary learning. The goal is to determine a dictionary of atoms (in other words, unique elements that can be *assembled* to make up any other existing data point) so as to express each training and new point $\bar{x}_i$ as a combination of them. Just as in natural language, where a limited number of words allows the composition of an infinite number of texts, the goal of sparse PCA is to determine those elements whose reusability make them perfect candidates to make up a dictionary. To achieve this goal, we need to formulate the problem in a more rigorous way.

Given a dataset $X = \{\bar{x}_1, \bar{x}_2, \ldots, \bar{x}_n\}$ where $\bar{x}_i \in \mathbb{R}^m$, we need to determine a dictionary $D \in \mathbb{R}^{m \times k}$ containing k atoms (note that every atom has the same dimensionality of the data points) with $k << n$ and a set of weights $A = \{\bar{a}_1, \bar{a}_2, \ldots, \bar{a}_m\}$. Using these elements, we can compute the transformation:

$$\bar{x}_i = D\bar{a}_i \ \forall \, i \in (1, n)$$

The problem can be solved by employing a specific cost function that minimizes the mean square error of the reconstructions and the L_1 norm of the weights (to induce sparsity):

$$L(D, A) = \frac{1}{n} \sum_{i=1}^{n} \|\bar{x}_i - D\bar{a}_i\|_2^2 + \gamma \|\bar{a}_i\|_1$$

The parameter γ controls the level of sparsity. It's obvious that a stronger sparsity will force the algorithm to run for a longer time, and the optimum might not be acceptable to obtain high-quality reconstructions. However, this technique is generally employed when the dataset is intrinsically split into elements subject to reuse (like words – that's why the method is also known as dictionary learning). Indeed, the components that are found by the algorithm are somehow *principal* because their reuse implies an underlying distribution where these components have a quite large variance, but formally, sparse PCA is not a true PCA but rather a dimensionality reduction algorithm. Moreover, the cost function doesn't guarantee to find decorrelated components, even if the sparsity constraint tends to avoid (or to limit) the redundancies.

Let's now apply the algorithm to the MNIST dataset (given the complexity, we will work only on 10 pictures):

```
from sklearn.datasets import fetch_openml

digits = fetch_openml("mnist_784")
X = zero_center(digits['data'].
                astype(np.float64) / 255.0)
np.random.shuffle(X)
```

Let's now apply the sparse PCA to obtain 10 components (hence $D \in \mathbb{R}^{784 \times 10}$ because each image has 28 x 28 = 784 features):

```
from sklearn.decomposition import SparsePCA


spca = SparsePCA(n_components=10,
                 alpha=0.1,
                 normalize_components=True,
                 n_jobs=-1,
                 random_state=1000)
X_spca = spca.fit_transform(X[0:10, :])

print('SPCA components shape:')
print(spca.components_.shape)
```

The parameter alpha corresponds to the L_1 penalty constraint γ. We have also used the library joblib to have a parallel computation as this algorithm can be extremely slow. The output of the previous snippet is:

```
SPCA components shape:
(10, 784)
```

The dictionary is transposed but the dimensions are correct. The 10 components are also shown in the following figure:

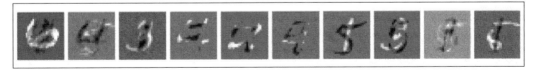

Components found by sparse PCA

The training set is very small but it's interesting to notice how the components can be assembled to generated different digits. However, as the dataset was subsampled, the resulting dictionary is almost over-complete. Therefore, the components are strongly cross-correlated.

As an exercise, I invite the reader to train the model using more data points (possibly the whole dataset) and check the final result. Given the geometrical structure of digits, it's not surprising that we've found a dictionary in which the pen strokes are almost oriented orthogonally.

Independent Component Analysis

We've seen that the factors extracted by a PCA are decorrelated, but not independent. A classic example is a cocktail party: we have a recording of many overlapped voices and we would like to separate them. Every single voice can be modeled as a random process and it's possible to assume that they are statistically independent (this means that the joint probability can be factorized using the marginal probabilities of each source). Using FA or PCA, we can find uncorrelated factors, but there's no way to assess whether they're also independent (normally, they aren't). In this section, we're going to study a model that's able to produce sparse representations (when the dictionary isn't under-complete) with a set of statistically independent components.

Let's assume we have a zero-centered and whitened dataset X sampled from $N(0, I)$ and noiseless linear transformation:

$$\bar{x} = A\bar{z} \ \ where \ \ \bar{x} \sim N(0, I) \ and \ p(\bar{z}; \ \bar{\theta}) = \alpha \prod_k e^{f_k(\bar{z})}$$

In this case, the prior over $\bar{z}$ is modeled as a product of independent variables (α is the normalization factor), each of them represented as a generic exponential where the function $f_k(\bar{z})$ must be non-quadratic, that is, $p(\bar{z}; \theta)$ cannot be Gaussian. Furthermore, we assume that the variance of $\bar{z}_i$ is equal to 1, therefore $p(\bar{x}|\bar{z}; \ \bar{\theta}) \sim N(A\bar{z}, AA^T)$. The joint probability $p(X, \bar{z}; \ \bar{\theta}) = p(X|\bar{z}; \ \bar{\theta})p(\bar{z}|\bar{\theta})$ is equal to the following:

$$p(X, \bar{z}; \ \bar{\theta}) = \left(\prod_{i=1}^{M} \frac{1}{\sqrt{(2\pi)^n \det AA^T}} e^{-\frac{(\bar{x}_i - A\bar{z})^T (AA^T)^{-1} (\bar{x}_i - A\bar{z})}{2}} \right) \left(\alpha \prod_k e^{f_k(\bar{z})} \right)$$

If X has been whitened, A is orthogonal (the proof is straightforward); hence, the previous expression can be simplified. However, applying the EM algorithm requires determining $p(\bar{z}|X; \ \bar{\theta})$ and that is quite difficult. The process could be easier after choosing a suitable prior distribution for $\bar{z}$, that is, $f_k(\bar{z})$, but, as we discussed at the beginning of the chapter, this assumption can have dramatic consequences if the real factors are distributed differently. For these reasons, other strategies have been studied.

The main concept that we need to enforce is having a non-Gaussian distribution of the factors. In particular, we'd like to have a peaked distribution (inducing sparseness) with heavy tails. From the theory, we know that the standardized fourth moment (also called **Kurtosis**) is a perfect measure:

$$Kurt[X] = E_x\left[\left(\frac{x - \mu_x}{\sigma_x}\right)^4\right]$$

For a Gaussian distribution, $Kurt[X]$ is equal to three (which is often considered as the reference point, determining the so called *Excess Kurtosis*$[X] = Kurt[X] - 3$), while it's larger for a family of distributions, called *Leptokurtotic or super-Gaussian*, which are peaked and heavy-tailed (also, the distributions with $Kurt[X] < 3$, called *Platykurtotic* or *sub-Gaussian*, can be good candidates, but they are less peaked and normally only the super-Gaussian distributions are taken into account). However, even if accurate, this measure is very sensitive to outliers because of the fourth power. For example, if $x \sim N(0,1)$ and $z = x + v$, where v is a noise term that alters a few samples, increasing their value to two, the result can be a super-Gaussian ($Kurt[X] > 3$) even if, after filtering the outliers out, the distribution has $Kurt[X] > 3$ (Gaussian).

To overcome this problem, Hyvärinen and Oja (in Hyvärinen A., Oja E., *Independent Component Analysis: Algorithms and Applications*, Neural Networks 13/2000) proposed a solution based on another measure, the negentropy. We know that the entropy is proportional to the variance and, given the variance, the Gaussian distribution has the maximum entropy. Therefore, we can define the measure:

$$H_N(X) = H\left(X_{\bar{x} \sim N(0,\Sigma)}\right) - H(X)$$

Formally, the negentropy of X is the difference between the entropy of a Gaussian distribution with the same covariance and the entropy of X (we are assuming both zero-centered). It's immediately possible to understand that $H_N(X) \geq 0$, hence, the only way to maximize it is by reducing $H(X)$. In this way, X becomes less random, concentrating the probability around the mean (in other words, it becomes super-Gaussian). However, the previous expression cannot be easily adapted to closed-form solutions because $H(X)$ needs to be computed over the entire distribution of X, which must be estimated. For this reason, the same authors proposed an approximation based on non-quadratic functions (remember that in the context of ICA, a quadratic function can never be employed because it would lead to a Gaussian distribution) that is useful for deriving a fixed-point iterative algorithm called *FastICA* (indeed, it's really faster than EM).

Using k functions $f_k(\bar{z})$, the approximation becomes as follows:

$$H_N(X) \approx \sum_{i=1}^{k} \alpha_i (E[f_i(\bar{x})] - E[f_i(\bar{n})])^2 \ where \ \bar{n} \sim N(0.I) \ and \ \alpha_i > 0$$

In many real-life scenarios, a single function is enough to achieve a reasonable accuracy and one of the most common choices for $f(x)$ is as follows:

$$f(x) = \frac{1}{a} \log \cosh ax = \frac{1}{a} \log \frac{e^{ax} + e^{-ax}}{2}$$

In the aforementioned paper, the reader can find some alternatives that can be employed when this function fails in forcing statistical independence between components.

If we invert the model, we get $\bar{z} = W\bar{x}$ with $W = A^{-1}$; therefore, considering a single sample, the approximation becomes as follows:

$$H_N(X) \approx (E[f(\bar{w}^T \bar{x}] - E[f(\bar{n})])^2 \ where \ \bar{n} \sim N(0,I)$$

Clearly, the second term doesn't depend on w (in fact, it's only a reference) and can be excluded from the optimization. Moreover, considering the initial assumptions, $E[Z^TZ] = WE[X^TX]W^T = I$, therefore $WW^T = I$, that is, $\|\bar{w}\| = 1$. Hence, our goal is to find the following:

$$\bar{w}_{opt} = \underset{\bar{w}}{\operatorname{argmax}} E[f(\bar{w}^T \bar{x})]^2 \ subject \ to \ \|\bar{w}\|^2 = 1$$

In this way, we're forcing the matrix W to transform the input vector $\bar{x}$, so that $\bar{z}$ has the lowest possible entropy; therefore, it's super-Gaussian. The maximization process is based on convex optimization techniques that are beyond the scope of this book (the reader can find all the details of Lagrange theorems in Luenberger D. G., *Optimization by Vector Space Methods*, Wiley, 1997). Therefore, I'll directly provide the iterative step that must be performed:

$$\bar{w}_{t+1} = E\left[\bar{x} f'(\bar{w}_t^T \bar{x})\right] - E\left[f''(\bar{w}_t^T \bar{x})\right] \bar{w}_t$$

Of course, to ensure $\|\bar{w}\|_2 = 1$, after each step, the weight vector must be normalized ($\bar{w}_{t+1} = \bar{w}_{t+1}/\|\bar{w}_{t+1}\|_2$).

In a more general context, the matrix W contains more than one weight vector and, if we apply the previous rule to find out the independent factors, it can happen that some elements, $\bar{w}_i^T \bar{x}$, are correlated. A strategy to avoid this problem is based on the Gram-Schmidt orthonormalization process, which decorrelates the components one by one, subtracting the projections of the current component ($\bar{w}_n$) onto all the previous ones ($\bar{w}_1, \bar{w}_2, \ldots, \bar{w}_{n-1}$) to $\bar{w}_n$. In this way, $\bar{w}_n$ is forced to be orthogonal to all the other components.

Example of FastICA with scikit-learn

Using the same dataset, we can now test the performance of the ICA. However, in this case, as explained, we need to zero-center and whiten the dataset, but fortunately, these preprocessing steps are done by the scikit-learn implementation (if the parameter `whiten=True` is omitted).

To perform the ICA on the MNIST dataset, we're going to instantiate the `FastICA` class, passing the arguments `n_components=64` and the maximum number of iterations `max_iter=5000`. It's also possible to specify which function will be used to approximate the negentropy; however, the default is $\log \cosh x$, which is normally a reasonable choice:

```
from sklearn.decomposition import FastICA

fastica = FastICA(n_components=64,
                  max_iter=5000,
                  random_state=1000)
fastica.fit(X)
```

At this point, we can visualize the components (which are always available through the `components_` instance variable):

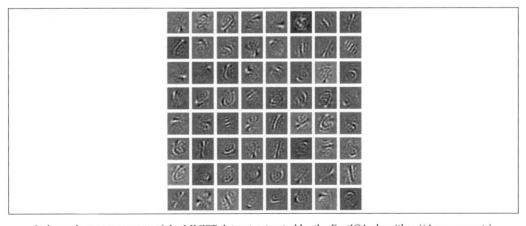

Independent components of the MNIST dataset extracted by the FastICA algorithm (64 components)

There are still some redundancies (the reader can try to increase the number of components) and background noise; however, it's now possible to distinguish some low-level features (such as oriented stripes) that are common to many digits. This representation isn't very sparse yet. In fact, we're always using 64 components (like for FA and PCA); therefore, the dictionary is under-complete (the input dimensionality is 28 × 28 = 784). To see the difference, we can repeat the experiment with a dictionary ten times larger, setting n_components=640:

```
fastica = FastICA(n_components=640,
                  max_iter=5000,
                  random_state=1000)
fastica.fit(X)
```

A subset of the new components (100) is shown in the following plot:

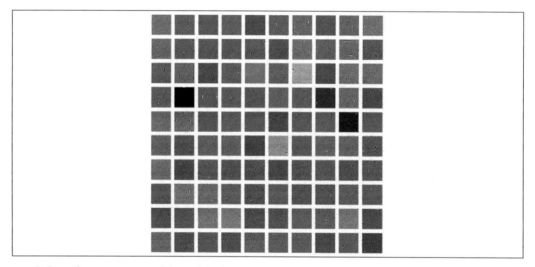

Independent components of the MNIST dataset extracted by the FastICA algorithm (640 components)

The structure of these components is almost elementary. They represent oriented stripes and positional dots. To check how an input is rebuilt, we can consider the mixing matrix A (which is available as the mixing_ instance variable). Considering the first input sample, we can check how many factors have a weight less than half of the average:

```
import numpy as np

M = fastica.mixing_
M0 = M[0] / np.max(M[0])

print(len(M0[np.abs(M0) < (np.mean(np.abs(M0)) / 2.0)]))
```

The output is:

233

The sample is rebuilt using approximately 410 components. The level of sparsity is higher, but considering the granularity of the factors, it's easy to understand that many of them are needed to rebuild even a single structure (like the image of a 1) where long lines are present. However, this is not a drawback because, as already mentioned, the main goal of the ICA is to extract independent components. Considering an analogy with the cocktail party example, we could deduce that each component represents a phoneme, not the complete sound of a word or a sentence.

The reader can test a different number of components and compare the results with the ones achieved by other sparse coding algorithms (such as dictionary learning or sparse PCA).

Addendum to Hidden Markov Models

In the previous chapter, we discussed how it's possible to train an HMM using the forward-backward algorithm and we have seen that it is a particular application of the EM algorithm. The reader can now understand the internal dynamic in terms of E and M steps. In fact, the procedure starts with randomly initialized A and B matrices and proceeds in an alternating manner:

- E-Step:
    - The estimation of the probability α_{ij}^t that the HMM is in the state i at time t and in the state j at time $t + 1$, given the observations and the current parameter estimations (A and B)
    - The estimation of the probability β_i^t that the HMM is in the state i at time t given the observations and the current parameter estimations (A and B)

- M-Step:
    - Computing the new estimation for the transition probabilities a_{ij} (A) and for the emission probabilities b_{ip} (B)

The procedure is repeated until convergence is reached. Even if there's no explicit definition of a Q function, the E-step determines a split expression for the expected complete data likelihood of the model given the observations (using both the Forward and Backward algorithms), while the M-Step corrects parameters A and B to maximize this likelihood.

Summary

In this chapter, we analyzed three different approaches to component extraction. FA assumes that we have a small number of Gaussian latent variables and a Gaussian decorrelated noise term. The only restriction on the noise is to have a diagonal covariance matrix, so two different scenarios are possible. When we are in the presence of heteroscedastic noise, the process is an actual FA. When, instead, the noise is homoscedastic, the algorithm becomes the equivalent of a PCA. In this case, the process is equivalent to check the sample space in order to find the directions where the variance is higher. Selecting only the most important directions, we can project the original dataset onto a low-dimensional subspace, where the covariance matrix becomes decorrelated.

One of the problems of both FA and PCA is their assumption to model the latent variables with Gaussian distributions. This choice simplifies the model but, at the same time, yields dense representations where the single components are statistically dependent. For this reason, we have investigated how it's possible to force the factor distribution to become sparse. The resulting algorithm, which is generally faster and more accurate than the MLE, is called FastICA and its goal is to extract a set of statistically independent components with the maximization of an approximation of the negentropy.

In the end, we provided a brief explanation of the HMM forward-backward algorithm (discussed in the previous chapter) considering the subdivision into E and M steps. Other EM-specific applications will be discussed in the next chapters.

In the next chapter, we are going to introduce the fundamental concepts of Hebbian learning and self-organizing maps, which are still very useful for solving many specific problems, such as principal component extraction, and have a strong neurophysiological foundation.

Further reading

- Dempster A. P., Laird N. M., Rubin D. B., *Maximum likelihood from incomplete data via the EM algorithm*, Journal of the Royal Statistical Society, B, 39(1):1–38, 11/1977

- Hansen F., Pedersen G. K., *Jensen's Operator Inequality*, arXiv:math/0204049 [math.OA]

- Rubin D., Thayer D., *EM algorithms for ML factor analysis, Psychometrika*, 47/1982, Issue 1

- Ghahramani Z., Hinton G. E., *The EM algorithm for Mixtures of Factor Analyzers*, CRC-TG-96-1, 05/1996

- Hyvärinen A., Oja E., *Independent Component Analysis: Algorithms and Applications*, Neural Networks 13/2000

- Luenberger D. G., *Optimization by Vector Space Methods*, Wiley, 1997

- Ledoit O., Wolf M., *A Well-Conditioned Estimator for Large-Dimensional Covariance Matrices*, Journal of Multivariate Analysis, 88, 2/2004

- Minka T. P., *Automatic Choice of Dimensionality for PCA*, NIPS 2000

- Nasios N., Bors A. G., *Variational Learning for Gaussian Mixture Models*, IEEE Transactions on Systems, Man, and Cybernetics, 36/4, 2006

- Bonaccorso G., *Hands-On Unsupervised Learning with Python*, Packt Publishing, 2018

14
Hebbian Learning

In this chapter, we're going to introduce the concept of Hebbian learning, based on the methods defined by the psychologist Donald Hebb. These theories immediately showed how a very simple biological law is able to describe the behavior of multiple neurons in achieving complex goals and was a pioneering strategy that linked the research activities in the fields of artificial intelligence and computational neuroscience.

In particular, we are going to discuss the following topics:

- The Hebb rule for a single neuron, which is a simple but biologically plausible behavioral law.
- Some variants on the Hebb rule, like Oja's and Covariance rules, that have been introduced to overcome a few stability problems.
- The final result achieved by a Hebbian neuron, which consists of computing the first principal component of the input dataset.
- Two neural network models (Sanger's network and Rubner-Tavan's network) that can extract a generic number of principal components.
- The concept of **Self-organizing maps (SOMs)** with a focus on the Kohonen Networks.

We can now start discussing the basic concepts of Hebb's rule and its implications in all models that are based on its dynamics.

Hebb's rule

Hebb's rule has been proposed as a conjecture in 1949 by the Canadian psychologist Donald Hebb to describe the synaptic plasticity of natural neurons.

A few years after its publication, this rule was confirmed by neurophysiological studies, and many research studies have also shown its validity in many applications of artificial intelligence. Before introducing the rule, it's useful to describe the generic Hebbian neuron, as shown in the following diagram:

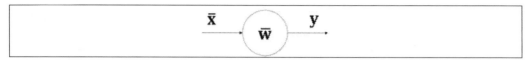

Generic Hebbian neuron with a vectorial input

The neuron is a simple computational unit that receives an input vector $\bar{x}$, from the pre-synaptic units (other neurons or perceptive systems) and outputs a single scalar value, y. The internal structure of the neuron is represented by a weight vector, $\bar{w}$, that models the strength of each synapse. For a single multi-dimensional input, the output is obtained as follows:

$$y = \bar{w}^T \cdot \bar{x}$$

In this model, we are assuming that each input signal is encoded in the corresponding component of the vector $\bar{x}$; therefore, $\bar{x}_i$ is processed by the synaptic weight $\bar{w}_i$, and so on.

Hebb's rule states that when two neurons in the same chain (a presynaptic and a postsynaptic one) have the same behavior, their connection strengthens more and more. If, on the other hand, they have different behaviors, so that when one neuron is excited, the other is depressed, their connection weakens.

The scientist S. Löwel expressed this concept in plain language with the famous sentence: "Neurons that fire together wire together".

In the original version of Hebb's theory, the input vectors represent neural firing rates, which are always non-negative. This means that the synaptic weights can only be strengthened (the neuroscientific term for this phenomenon is "long-term potentiation" - LTP). However, for our purposes, we assume that $\bar{x}$ is a real-valued vector, as is $\bar{w}$. This condition allows modeling more artificial scenarios without a loss of generality.

The same operation performed on a single vector holds when it's necessary to process many input samples organized in a matrix. If we have N m-dimensional input vectors, the formula becomes as follows:

$$\bar{y} = X\bar{w}^T \ \ where \ X \in \mathbb{R}^{N \times m}, \bar{w} \in \mathbb{R}^m \ and \ \bar{y} \in \mathbb{R}^N$$

The basic form of Hebb's rule in a discrete form can be expressed (for a single input) as follows:

$$\Delta \bar{w} = \eta y \bar{x} = \eta (\bar{w}^T \cdot \bar{x}) \bar{x}$$

The weight correction is hence a vector that has the same orientation of $\bar{x}$ and magnitude equal to $|\bar{x}|$ multiplied by a positive parameter η which is called the learning rate, and the corresponding output y which can have either a positive or a negative sign. The sense of $\Delta \bar{w}$ is determined by the sign of y; therefore, under the assumption that $\bar{x}$ and y are real values, two different scenarios arise from this rule:

- if $\bar{x}_i > 0$ (< 0) and $y > 0$ (< 0), $\bar{w}_i$ is strengthened
- If $\bar{x}_i > 0$ (< 0) and $y < 0$ (> 0), $\bar{w}_i$ is weakened

It's easy to understand this behavior considering two-dimensional vectors:

$$sign(y) = sign(\bar{w}^T \cdot \bar{x}) = sign(|\bar{w}||\bar{x}| \cos \alpha)$$

Therefore, if the initial angle α between $\bar{w}$ and $\bar{x}$ is less than 90° ($\pi/2$), $\bar{w}$ will have the same orientation of $\bar{x}$; if the initial angle α is greater than 90°, $\bar{w}$ will have the opposite orientation to $\bar{x}$. In case of $\alpha = 0$, the cosine is equal to 1 and the sign of y is always positive (assuming that $sign(0) = 1$). In the following diagram, there's a schematic representation of this process:

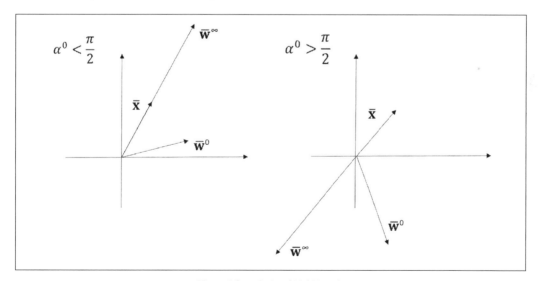

Vectorial analysis of Hebb's rule

It's possible to simulate this behavior using a very simple Python snippet. Let's start with a scenario where α is less than 90° and 50 iterations:

```python
import numpy as np

w = np.array([1.0, 0.2])
x = np.array([0.1, 0.5])
alpha = 0.0

for i in range(50):
    y = np.dot(w.T, x)
    w += x*y
    alpha = np.arccos(np.dot(w, x.T) /
                      (np.linalg.norm(w) *
                       np.linalg.norm(x)))
```

We can now measure the final values:

```python
print(w)
print("{:.3f}".format(alpha * 180.0 / np.pi))
```

The output is:

```
[8028.48942243 40137.64711215]
```

```
0.001
```

As expected, the final angle α is close to zero and $\bar{w}$ has the same orientation and sense of $\bar{x}$. We can now repeat the experiment with α greater than 90° (we change only the value of $\bar{w}$ because the procedure is the same):

```python
w = np.array([1.0, -1.0])
```

The final values are now:

```
[-16053.97884486 -80275.89422431]
```

```
179.999
```

In this case, the final angle α is about 180° and, of course, $\bar{w}$ has the opposite sense with respect to $\bar{x}$. As S. Löwel said: "Neurons that fire together wire together".

We can re-express this concept (adapting it to a machine learning scenario) by saying that the main assumption of this approach is based on the idea that when pre- and post-synaptic units are coherent (their signals have the same sign), the connection between neurons becomes stronger and stronger. On the other side, if they are discordant, the corresponding synaptic weight is decreased. For the sake of precision, if $\bar{x}$ is a spiking rate, it should be represented as a real function $\bar{x}(t)$ as well as $y(t)$.

According to the original Hebbian theory, the discrete equation must be replaced by a differential equation:

$$\frac{d\bar{w}}{dt} = \eta y \bar{x}$$

If $\bar{x}(t)$ and $y(t)$ have the same fire rate, the synaptic weight is strengthened proportionally to the product of both rates. If instead there's a relatively long delay between the pre-synaptic activity $\bar{x}(t)$ and the post-synaptic one $y(t)$, the corresponding weight is weakened. This is a more biologically plausible explanation of the relation fire together $\rightarrow$ wire together.

However, even if the theory has a strong neurophysiological basis, some modifications are necessary. In fact, it's easy to understand that the resulting system is always unstable. If two inputs are repeatedly applied (both real values and firing rates), the norm of the vector, $\bar{w}$ grows indefinitely and this isn't a plausible assumption for a biological system. In fact, if we consider a discrete iteration step, we have the following equation:

$$\bar{w}_{k+1} = \bar{w}_k + \eta(\bar{w}_k^T \cdot \bar{x})\bar{x}$$

Multiplying all terms times $\bar{x}$, we obtain:

$$\bar{w}_{k+1} \cdot \bar{x} = \bar{w}_k \cdot \bar{x} + \eta(\bar{w}_k^T \cdot \bar{x})\bar{x} \cdot \bar{x} \Rightarrow y_{k+1} = y_k(1 + \eta|\bar{x}|^2)$$

The previous output y_k is always multiplied by a factor greater than 1 (except in the case of null input), therefore it grows without a bound. As $y = \bar{w}^T \cdot \bar{x}$, this condition implies that the magnitude of $\bar{w}$ increases (or remains constant if the magnitude of $\bar{x}$ is null) at each iteration (a more rigorous proof can be easily obtained considering the original differential equation).

Such a situation is not only biologically unacceptable, but it's also necessary to properly manage it in machine learning problems in order to avoid a numerical overflow after a few iterations. In the next paragraph, we're going to discuss some common methods to overcome this issue. For now, we can continue our analysis without introducing a correction factor.

Let's now consider a dataset X:

$$X = \{\bar{x}_1, \bar{x}_2, \dots, \bar{x}_N\} \; where \; \bar{x}_i \in \mathbb{R}^m$$

We can apply the rule iteratively to all elements, but it's easier (and more useful) to average the weight modifications over the input samples (the index now refers to the whole specific vector, not to the single components):

$$\Delta \bar{w} = \frac{\eta}{N} \sum_{i=1}^{N} y_i \bar{x}_i = \frac{\eta}{N} \sum_{i=1}^{N} (\bar{w}^T \cdot \bar{x}_i) \bar{x}_i = \frac{\eta}{N} \sum_{i=1}^{N} (\bar{x}_i^T \cdot \bar{x}_i) \bar{w} = \eta C \bar{w}$$

In the previous formula, C is the input correlation matrix:

$$C = \begin{pmatrix} \frac{1}{N} \sum_i x_1^i x_1^i & \cdots & \frac{1}{N} \sum_i x_1^i x_m^i \\ \vdots & \ddots & \vdots \\ \frac{1}{N} \sum_i x_m^i x_1^i & \cdots & \frac{1}{N} \sum_i x_m^i x_m^i \end{pmatrix} = \frac{1}{N} X^T X$$

For our purposes, however, it's useful to consider a slightly different Hebbian rule based on a threshold θ for the input vector (there's also a biological reason that justifies this choice, but it's beyond the scope of this book; the reader who is interested can find it in Dayan P., Abbott F. L., *Theoretical Neuroscience*, The MIT Press, 2003).

It's easy to understand that in the original theory where $\bar{x}(t)$ and $y(t)$ are firing rates, this modification allows a phenomenon opposite to LTP called **long-term depression (LTD)**. In fact, when $\bar{x}(t) < \theta$ and $y(t)$ is positive, the product $(\bar{x}(t) - \theta)y(t)$ is negative and the synaptic weight is weakened.

If we set $\theta = \langle \bar{x} \rangle \approx E[X]$, we can derive an expression very similar to the previous one, but based on the input covariance matrix (unbiased through Bessel's correction):

The sample (co-)variance is biased if the formula is divided by N. To avoid the bias, it's necessary to divide by $N - 1$. Of course, the difference tends to vanish when $N \to \infty$, but it's generally helpful to take always in consideration this correction. The reader who wants to see further details about Bessel's correction can read Warner R., *Applied Statistics*, SAGE Publications, 2013.

$$\Delta \bar{w} = \frac{\eta}{N-1} \sum_{i=1}^{N} y_i (\bar{x}_i - \langle \bar{x}_i \rangle) = \frac{\eta}{N-1} \sum_{i=1}^{N} \left[\bar{w} \cdot (\bar{x}_i - \langle \bar{x}_i \rangle) \right] (\bar{x}_i - \langle \bar{x}_i \rangle)$$

$$= \frac{\eta}{N-1} \sum_{i=1}^{N} (\bar{x}_i - \langle \bar{x}_i \rangle)^T (\bar{x}_i - \langle \bar{x}_i \rangle) \bar{w} = \eta \Sigma \bar{w}$$

For obvious reasons, this variant of the original Hebb's rule is called the covariance rule. It's also possible to use the **Maximum Likelihood Estimation** (MLE) (or biased) covariance matrix (dividing by N), but it's important to check which version is adopted by the mathematical package that is employed. When using NumPy, it's possible to decide the version using the `np.cov()` function and setting the `bias=True/False` parameter (the default value is `False`, hence Bessel's correction is applied). However, when $N >> 1$, the difference between versions decreases and can often be discarded. In this book, we'll use the unbiased version.

Analysis of the Covariance Rule

The covariance matrix Σ is real and symmetric. If we apply the eigendecomposition, we get (for our purposes it's more useful to keep V^{-1} instead of the simplified version V^T):

$$\Sigma = V \Omega V^{-1}$$

V is an orthogonal matrix (thanks to the fact that Σ is symmetric) containing the eigenvectors of Σ (as columns), while Ω is a diagonal matrix containing the eigenvalues. Let's suppose we sort both eigenvalues $(\lambda_1, \lambda_2, \dots, \lambda_m)$ and the corresponding eigenvectors $(\bar{v}_1, \bar{v}_2, \dots, \bar{v}_m)$ so that:

$$\lambda_1 > \lambda_2 > \cdots > \lambda_m$$

Moreover, let's suppose that λ_1 is dominant over all the other eigenvalues (it's enough that $\lambda_1 > \lambda_i \; \forall \, i \neq 1$). As the eigenvectors are orthogonal, they constitute a basis and it's possible to express the vector w, with a linear combination of the eigenvectors:

$$\bar{w} = u_1 \bar{v}_1 + u_2 \bar{v}_2 + \cdots + u_m \bar{v}_m = V \bar{u}$$

The vector $\bar{u}$ contains the coordinates in the new basis. Let's now consider the modification to the covariance rule:

$$\Delta \bar{w} = \eta \Sigma \bar{w} = \eta V \Omega V^{-1} \bar{u} = \eta \Sigma \bar{w} = \eta V \Omega \bar{u}$$

If we apply the rule iteratively, we get a matrix polynomial:

$$\bar{w}^{(0)}$$

$$\bar{w}^{(1)} = \bar{w}^{(0)} + \eta \Sigma \bar{w}^{(0)}$$

$$\bar{w}^{(2)} = \bar{w}^{(1)} + \eta \Sigma \bar{w}^{(1)} = \bar{w}^{(0)} + 2\eta \Sigma \bar{w}^{(0)} + \eta^2 \Sigma^2 \bar{w}^{(0)}$$

$$\bar{w}^{(3)} = \bar{w}^{(2)} + \eta \Sigma \bar{w}^{(2)} = \bar{w}^{(0)} + 3\eta \Sigma \bar{w}^{(0)} + 3\eta^2 \Sigma^2 \bar{w}^{(0)} + \eta^3 \Sigma^3 \bar{w}^{(0)}$$

$$...$$

Exploiting the binomial theorem and considering that $\Sigma^0 = I$, we can get a general expression for $\bar{w}^{(k)}$ as a function of $\bar{w}^{(0)}$:

$$\bar{w}^{(k)} = \sum_{i=0}^{k} \binom{k}{i} \eta^i \Sigma^i \bar{w}^{(0)}$$

Let's now rewrite the previous formula using the change of basis:

$$\bar{w}^{(k)} = \sum_{i=0}^{k} \binom{k}{i} \eta^i \Sigma^i \bar{w}^{(0)} = \sum_{i=0}^{k} \binom{k}{i} \eta^i V \Omega^i V^{-1} \bar{w}^{(0)} = \sum_{i=0}^{k} \binom{k}{i} \eta^i V \Omega^i \bar{u}^{(0)}$$

The vector $\bar{u}^{(0)}$ contains the coordinates of $\bar{w}^{(0)}$ in the new basis; hence, $\bar{w}^{(k)}$ is expressed as a polynomial where the generic term is proportional to $V \Omega^i \bar{u}^{(0)}$.

Let's now consider the diagonal matrix Ω^k:

$$\Omega^k = \begin{pmatrix} \lambda_1^k & \cdots & 0 \\ \vdots & \ddots & \vdots \\ 0 & \cdots & \lambda_m^k \end{pmatrix} \approx \begin{pmatrix} \lambda_1^k & \cdots & 0 \\ \vdots & \ddots & \vdots \\ 0 & \cdots & 0 \end{pmatrix}$$

The last step derives from the hypothesis that λ_1 is greater than any other eigenvalue and when $k \to \infty$ all $\lambda_{j \neq i}^k \ll \lambda_i^k$. Of course, if $\lambda_{j \neq i} > 1$, $\lambda_{j \neq i}^k$ will grow as well as λ_i^k.

However, the contribution of the *secondary* eigenvalues to $\bar{w}^{(k)}$ becomes significantly weaker when $k \to \infty$. Just to understand the validity of this approximation, let's consider the following situation where λ_1 is slightly larger than λ_2:

$$\Omega = \begin{pmatrix} 1.1 & 0 \\ 0 & 1.05 \end{pmatrix} \Rightarrow \Omega^{1000} \approx \begin{pmatrix} 2.5 \cdot 10^{41} & 0 \\ 0 & 1.5 \cdot 10^{21} \end{pmatrix}$$

The result shows a very important property: not only is the approximation correct, but as we're going to show, if an eigenvalue λ_i is larger than all the other ones, the covariance rule will always converge to the corresponding eigenvector v_i. No other stable fixed points exist!

This hypothesis is no more valid if $\lambda_1 = \lambda_2 = \cdots = \lambda_m$. In this case, the total variance is explained equally by the direction of each eigenvector (a condition that implies a symmetry that isn't very common in real-life scenarios). This situation can also happen when working with finite-precision arithmetic, but in general, if the difference between the largest eigenvalue and the second one is less than the maximum achievable precision (for example, 32-bit floating point), it's plausible to accept the equality.

Of course, we assume that the dataset is not whitened, because our goal (also in the next paragraphs) is to reduce the original dimensionality considering only a subset of components with the highest total variability (the decorrelation, like in **Principal Component Analysis (PCA)**, must be an outcome of the algorithm, not a precondition). On the other side, zero-centering the dataset could be useful to exploit the symmetry of post-processing functions like sigmoid or hyperbolic tangent. However, it's not necessary to guarantee the correctness of this kind of algorithm.

If we rewrite the expression for $\bar{w}^{(k)}$ considering this approximation, we obtain the following:

$$\bar{w}^{(k)} = \sum_{i=0}^{k} \binom{k}{i} \eta^i V \Omega^i \bar{u}^{(0)} \approx \sum_{i=0}^{k} \binom{k}{i} \eta^i \left[(\bar{v}_1 \quad \cdots \quad \bar{v}_m) \begin{pmatrix} \lambda_1^k & \cdots & 0 \\ \vdots & \ddots & \vdots \\ 0 & \cdots & 0 \end{pmatrix} \begin{pmatrix} u_1^{(0)} \\ \vdots \\ u_m^{(0)} \end{pmatrix} \right] = \left[\sum_{i=0}^{k} \binom{k}{i} \eta^i \lambda_1^i u_1^{(0)} \right] \bar{v}_1$$

As $a_1 \bar{v} + a_2 \bar{v} + \cdots + a_k \bar{v} \propto \bar{v}$, this result shows that, when $k \to \infty$, $\bar{w}^{(k)}$ will become proportional to the first eigenvector of the covariance matrix Σ (if $u_1^{(0)}$ is not null) and its magnitude, without normalization, will grow indefinitely. The spurious effect due to the other eigenvalues becomes negligible (above all, if w is divided by its norm, so that the length is always $\|\bar{w}\| = 1$) after a limited number of iterations.

However, before drawing our conclusions, an important condition must be added:

$$\bar{w}^{(0)} \cdot \bar{v}_1 \neq 0$$

In fact, if $\bar{w}^{(0)}$ were orthogonal to $\bar{v}_1$, we would get (the eigenvectors are orthogonal to each other):

$$\bar{w}^{(0)} \cdot \bar{v}_1 = u_1^{(0)} \bar{v}_1 \cdot \bar{v}_1 + u_2^{(0)} \bar{v}_2 \cdot \bar{v}_1 + \cdots + u_m^{(0)} \bar{v}_m \cdot \bar{v}_1 = u_1^{(0)} \bar{v}_1 \cdot \bar{v}_1 = u_1^{(0)} |\bar{v}_1|^2 = 0 \Rightarrow u_1^{(0)} = 0$$

This important result shows how a Hebbian neuron working with the covariance rule is able to perform a PCA limited to the first component without the need for eigendecomposing Σ. In fact, the vector $\bar{w}$ (we're not considering the problem of the increasing magnitude, which can be easily managed) will rapidly converge to the orientation where the input dataset X as the highest variance. In *Chapter 13, Component Analysis and Dimensionality Reduction,* we discussed the details of PCA; in the next paragraph, we're going to discuss a couple of methods to find the first N principal components using a variant of the Hebb's rule. As we are going to see, one of the main advantages is that those methods have limited memory requirements and can easily perform the PCA of extremely complex datasets in an iterative fashion. Moreover, the networks can also exploit the computational libraries based on GPUs, providing an additional speed gain.

Example of application of the covariance rule

Before moving on, let's simulate this behavior with a simple Python example. We first generate 1,000 values sampled from a bivariate Gaussian distribution (the variance is voluntarily asymmetric) and then we apply the covariance rule to find the first principal component ($\bar{w}^{(0)}$ has been chosen so not to be orthogonal to $\bar{v}_1$):

```python
import numpy as np

rs = np.random.RandomState(1000)
X = rs.normal(loc=1.0, scale=(20.0, 1.0),
              size=(1000, 2))

w = np.array([30.0, 3.0])

S = np.cov(X.T)

for i in range(10):
    w += np.dot(S, w)
    w /= np.linalg.norm(w)
```

```
w *= 50.0
```

At the end of the training phase, we can check $\bar{w}^{(\infty)}$:

```
print(np.round(w, 1))
```

The output is:

Final w: [50.   0.]

The algorithm is straightforward, but there are a couple of elements that we need to comment on. The first one is the normalization of vector $\bar{w}$ at the end of each iteration. This is one of the techniques needed to avoid the uncontrolled growth of w. The second tricky element is the final multiplication, $\bar{w} \cdot 50$. As we are multiplying by a positive scalar, the direction of $\bar{w}$ is not impacted, but it's easier to show the vector in the complete plot.

The result is shown in the following diagram:

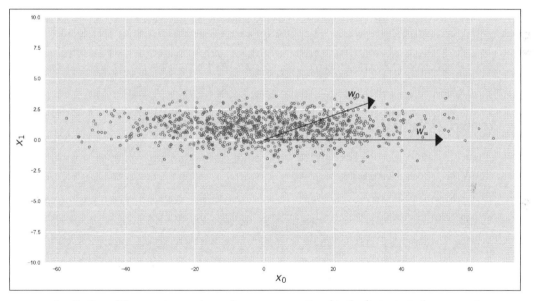

Application of the covariance rule. w∞ becomes proportional to the first principal component

After a limited number of iterations, $\bar{w}^{(\infty)}$ has the same orientation of the principal eigenvector which is, in this case, parallel to the x axes. The sense depends on the initial value $\bar{w}^{(0)}$; however, in a PCA, this isn't an important element.

Weight vector stabilization and Oja's rule

The easiest way to stabilize the weight vector is normalizing it after each update. In this way, its length will be always kept equal to one. In fact, in this kind of neural networks we are not interested in the magnitude, but only in the direction (that remains unchanged after the normalization). However, there are two main reasons that discourage this approach.

The first is that it's non-local. To normalize vector w, we need to know all its values, and this isn't biologically plausible. A real synaptic weight model should be self-limiting, without the need to have access to external pieces of information that cannot be available.

The second is that the normalization must be performed after having applied the correction, and hence needs a double iterative step.

In many machine learning contexts, these conditions are not limiting, and they can be freely adopted, but when it's necessary to work with neuroscientific models, it's better to look for other solutions. In a discrete form, we need to determine a correction term for the standard Hebb's rule:

$$\Delta \bar{w} = \bar{w}_{k+1} - \bar{w}_k = \eta y \bar{x} - f(\bar{w}_k, y_k, \bar{x})$$

The $f(\cdot)$ function can work both as a local and non-local normalizer. An example of the first type is Oja's rule:

$$\Delta \bar{w} = \eta y_k \bar{x}_k - \alpha y_k^2 \bar{w}_k$$

The α parameter is a positive number that controls the strength of the normalization. A non-rigorous proof of the stability of this rule can be obtained considering the condition:

$$\bar{w}^{\mathrm{T}} \cdot \Delta \bar{w} \to 0 \;\Rightarrow\; y_k(\bar{w}^T \cdot \bar{x}) - \alpha y_k^2(\bar{w}^T \cdot \bar{w}) \to 0$$

The second expression implies that:

$$y_k^2(1 - \alpha|\bar{w}|^2) \to 0 \;\Rightarrow\; |\bar{w}|^2 \to \frac{1}{\alpha}$$

Therefore, when $t \to \infty$, the magnitude of the weight correction becomes close to zero and the length of the weight vector $\bar{w}$ will approach a finite limit value:

$$\lim_{k \to \infty} |\bar{w}_k| = \frac{1}{\sqrt{\alpha}}$$

Sanger's network

A Sanger's network is a neural network model for online principal component extraction, proposed by T. D. Sanger in Optimal Unsupervised Learning in Sanger T. D., *Single-Layer Linear Feedforward Neural Network*, Neural Networks, 1989/2. The author started with the standard version of Hebb's rule and modified it to be able to extract a variable number of principal components $\{\bar{v}_1, \bar{v}_2, ..., \bar{v}_m\}$ in descending order ($\lambda_1 \geq \lambda_2 \geq \cdots \geq \lambda_m$). The resulting approach, which is a natural extension of Oja's rule, has been called the **Generalized Hebbian Rule (GHA)** — you might also sometimes see it called **Generalized Hebbian Learning (GHL)**. The structure of the network is represented in the following diagram:

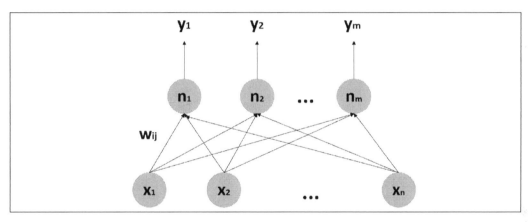

Structure of a Sanger's Network

The network is fed with samples extracted from an n-dimensional dataset:

$$X = \{\bar{x}_1, \bar{x}_2, ..., \bar{x}_N\} \ where \ \bar{x}_i \in \mathbb{R}^n$$

The *m* output neurons are connected to the input through a weight matrix, $W = \{w_{ij}\}$, where the first index refers to the input components (pre-synaptic units) and the second one to the neuron. The output of the network can be easily computed with a scalar product; however, in this case, we are not interested in it, because just like for the covariance (and Oja's) rules, the principal components are extracted through the weight updates.

The problem that arose after the formulation of Oja's rule was about the extraction of multiple components. In fact, if we applied the original rule to the previous network, all weight vectors (the rows of w) would converge to the first principal component. The main idea (based on the Gram-Schmidt orthonormalization method) to overcome this limitation is based on the observation that once we have extracted the first component $\bar{w}_1$, the second one $\bar{w}_2$ can be forced to be orthogonal to $\bar{w}_1$, the third one $\bar{w}_3$ can be forced to be orthogonal to $\bar{w}_1$ and $\bar{w}_2$, and so on. Consider the following representation:

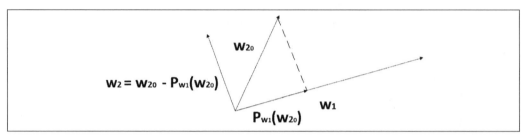

Orthogonalization of two weight vectors

In this case, we are assuming that $\bar{w}_1$ is stable and $\bar{w}_{2_0}$ is another weight vector that is converging to $\bar{w}_1$. The projection of $\bar{w}_{2_0}$ onto $\bar{w}_1$ is as follows:

$$P_{\bar{w}_1}\left(\bar{w}_{2_0}\right) = (\bar{w}_1^T \cdot \bar{w}_{2_0}) \frac{\bar{w}_1}{\|\bar{w}_1\|}$$

In the previous formula, we can omit the norm if we don't need to normalize (in the network, this process is done after a complete weight update). The orthogonal component of $\bar{w}_{2_0}$ is simply obtained with a difference:

$$\bar{w}_2 = \bar{w}_{2_0} - P_{\bar{w}_1}\left(\bar{w}_{2_0}\right)$$

Applying this method to the original Oja's rule, we obtain a new expression for the weight update (called Sanger's rule):

$$\Delta w_{ij} = \eta \left(y_i x_j - y_i \sum_{k=1}^{i} w_{kj} y_k \right)$$

The rule is referred to a single input vector $\bar{x}$, hence x_j is the jth component of $\bar{x}$. The first term is the classic Hebb's rule, which forces weight $\bar{w}$ to become parallel to the first principal component, while the second one acts in a way similar to the Gram-Schmidt orthogonalization, by subtracting a term proportional to the projection of w onto all the weights connected to the previous post-synaptic units and considering, at the same time, the normalization constraint provided by Oja's rule (which is proportional to the square of the output).

In fact, expanding the last term, we get the following:

$$y_i \sum_{k=1}^{l} w_{kj} y_k = y_i \sum_{k=1}^{l} w_{kj} (\bar{w}_k^T \cdot \bar{x}) = (\bar{w}_i^T \cdot \bar{x})[w_{1j}(\bar{w}_1^T \cdot \bar{x}) + w_{2j}(\bar{w}_2^T \cdot \bar{x}) + \cdots + w_{ij}(\bar{w}_i^T \cdot \bar{x})]$$

The term subtracted to each component w_{ij} is proportional to all the components where the index j is fixed and the first index is equal to $1, 2, \ldots, i$. This procedure doesn't produce an immediate orthogonalization but requires several iterations to converge. The proof is non-trivial, involving convex optimization and dynamic systems methods, but it can be found in the aforementioned paper. Sanger showed that the algorithm converges always to the sorted first n principal components (from the largest eigenvalue to the smallest one) if the learning rate $\eta(t)$ decreases monotonically and converges to zero when $t \to \infty$. Even if necessary for the formal proof, this condition can be relaxed (a stable value $\eta < 1$ is normally sufficient). In our implementation, matrix W normalized after each iteration, so that, at the end of the process, W^T (the weights are in the rows) is orthonormal and constitutes a basis for the eigenvector subspace.

In matrix form, the rule becomes as follows:

$$\Delta W = \eta[\bar{y} \cdot \bar{x}^T - Tril(\bar{y} \cdot \bar{y}^T)W]$$

$Tril(\cdot)$ is a matrix function that transforms its argument into a lower-triangular matrix and the term $\bar{y} \cdot \bar{y}^T$ is equal to $W\bar{y} \cdot \bar{y}^T W^T$.

The algorithm for a Sanger's network is as follows:

1. Initialize $W^{(0)}$ with random values. If the input dimensionality is n and m principal components must be extracted, the shape will be $(m \times n)$.
2. Set a learning rate η (for example, $\eta = 0.01$).
3. Set a threshold Thr (for example, $Thr = 0.001$).

4. Set a counter $T = 0$.

5. While $\left\| W^{(t)} - W^{(t-1)} \right\|_F > Thr$:

   a. Set $\Delta W = 0$ (same shape of W).

   b. For each $\bar{x} \in X$::

      i. Set $T = T + 1$.

      ii. Compute $\bar{y} = W(t)\bar{x}$

      iii. Compute and accumulate $\Delta W += \eta[\bar{y} \cdot \bar{x}^T - Tril(\bar{y} \cdot \bar{y}^T)W(t)]$

   c. Update $W(t+1) = W(t) + \left(\eta/T\right)\Delta W$.

   d. Set $W(t+1) = W(t+1) \Big/ \left\| W(t+1) \right\|_{rows}$ (the norm must be computed row-wise)

The algorithm can also be iterated a fixed number of times (like in our example), or the two stopping approaches can be used together. We can now implement a Sanger's network to evaluate its performances and to compare the results with a standard eigendecomposition.

Example of Sanger's network

For this Python example, we consider a bidimensional zero-centered dataset X with 500 data points (we are using the function defined in the first chapter). After the initialization of X, we also compute the eigendecomposition, to be able to double-check the result:

```python
import numpy as np

from sklearn.datasets import make_blobs

def zero_center(X):
    return X - np.mean(X, axis=0)

X, _ = make_blobs(n_samples=500, centers=2,
                  cluster_std=5.0, random_state=1000)
Xs = zero_center(X)

Q = np.cov(Xs.T)
eigu, eigv = np.linalg.eig(Q)
```

Let's start by evaluating the initial covariance matrix and its eigendecomposition:

```python
print('Covariance matrix:\n {}'.format(Q))
```

```
print('Eigenvalues:\n {}'.format(eigu))
print('Eigenvectors:\n {}'.format(eigv))
```

The output is:

Covariance matrix:

```
[[34.94435892 12.10674377]
 [12.10674377 38.55858945]]
```

Eigenvalues:

```
[24.5106037  48.99234467]
```

Eigenvectors:

```
[[-0.75750566 -0.6528286 ]
 [ 0.6528286  -0.75750566]]
```

As the dataset has been zero-centered, the result is coherent. We can now implement the training procedure:

```
n_components = 2
learning_rate = 0.01
nb_iterations = 5000
t = 0.0

W_sanger = np.random.normal(scale=0.5,
                    size=(n_components, Xs.shape[1]))
W_sanger /= np.linalg.norm(W_sanger, axis=1).\
        reshape((n_components, 1))

for i in range(nb_iterations):
dw = np.zeros((n_components, Xs.shape[1]))
        t += 1.0

        for j in range(Xs.shape[0]):
            Ysj = np.dot(W_sanger, Xs[j]).\
                    reshape((n_components, 1))
            QYd = np.tril(np.dot(Ysj, Ysj.T))
            dw += np.dot(Ysj, Xs[j].
                        reshape((1, X.shape[1]))) - \
                    np.dot(QYd, W_sanger)

W_sanger += (learning_rate / t) * dw
W_sanger /= np.linalg.norm(W_sanger, axis=1).\
            reshape((n_components, 1))

print('Final weights:\n {}'.format(W_sanger.T))
```

At the end of the procedure the output is:

```
Final weights:
  [[-0.6528286   0.75750566]
  [-0.75750566 -0.6528286 ]]
```

As expected, w has converged to the eigenvectors of the input correlation matrix (the sign – which is associated with the sense of w – is not important because we care only about the orientation). The second eigenvalue is the highest, so the columns are swapped. The graphical result is shown in the following plot:

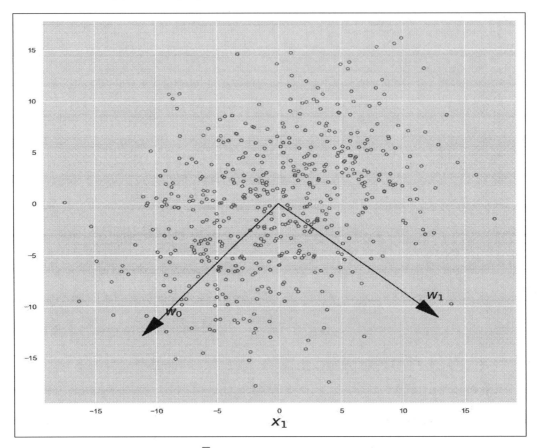

Final configuration, $\overline{W}$ has converged to the two principal components

The two components are perfectly orthogonal (the final orientations can change according to the initial conditions or the random state) and $\overline{w}_0$ points in the direction of the first principal component, while $\overline{w}_1$ points in the direction of the second component.

Considering this nice property, it's not necessary to check the magnitude of the eigenvalues; therefore, this algorithm can operate without eigendecomposing the input covariance matrix. Even if a formal proof is needed to explain this behavior, it's possible to understand it intuitively. Every single neuron converges to the first principal component given a full eigenvector subspace. This property is always maintained, but after the orthogonalization, the subspace is implicitly reduced by a dimension. The second neuron will always converge to the first component, which now corresponds to the global second component, and so on.

One of the advantages of this algorithm (and also of the next one) is that a standard PCA is normally a bulk process (even if there are batch algorithms), while a Sanger's network is an online algorithm that is trained incrementally. In general, the time performance of a Sanger's network is worse than the direct approach because of the iterations. Some optimizations can be achieved using more vectorization or GPU support or using optimized libraries like Numba (http://numba.pydata.org/) to speed up the loops and implement an internal parallelization. On the other side, a Sanger's network is memory-saving when the number of components is less than the input dimensionality (for example, the covariance matrix for $n = 1000$ has 10^6 elements, if $m = 100$ the weight matrix has 10^4 elements).

Rubner-Tavan's network

In *Chapter 13, Component Analysis and Dimensionality Reduction*, we mentioned that any algorithm that decorrelates the input covariance matrix is performing a PCA without dimensionality reduction. Starting from this approach, Rubner and Tavan (in the paper Rubner J., Tavan P., *A Self-Organizing Network for Principal-Components Analysis*, Europhysics, Letters, 10(7), 1989) proposed a neural model whose goal is decorrelating the output components to force the consequent decorrelation of the output covariance matrix (in lower-dimensional subspace). Assuming a zero-centered dataset and $E[y] = 0$, the output covariance matrix for m principal components is as follows:

$$
Q = \begin{pmatrix} \dfrac{1}{N}\sum_i y_1^i y_1^i & \cdots & \dfrac{1}{N}\sum_i y_1^i y_m^i \\ \vdots & \ddots & \vdots \\ \dfrac{1}{N}\sum_i y_m^i y_1^i & \cdots & \dfrac{1}{N}\sum_i y_m^i y_m^i \end{pmatrix}
$$

Hence, it's possible to achieve an approximate decorrelation, forcing the terms $y_i y_j \ \forall \ i \neq j$ to become close to zero.

The main difference with a standard approach (such as whitening or vanilla PCA) is that this procedure is local, while all the standard methods operate globally, directly with the covariance matrix. The neural model proposed by the authors is shown in the following diagram (the original model was proposed for binary units, but it works quite well also for linear ones):

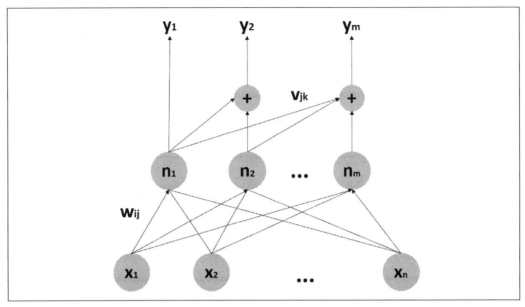

Rubner-Tavan network. The connections V_{jk} are based on the anti-Hebbian rule

The network has m output units and the last $m - 1$ neurons have a summing node that receives the weighted output of the previous units (hierarchical lateral connections). The dynamic is simple: the first output isn't modified. The second one is forced to become decorrelated with the first one. The third one is forced to become decorrelated with both the first and the second one and so on. This procedure must be iterated a number of times because the inputs are presented one by one and the cumulative term that appears in the correlation/covariance matrix (it's always easier to zero-center the dataset and work with the correlation matrix) must be implicitly split into its addends. It's not difficult to understand that the convergence to the only stable fixed point (which has been proven to exist by the authors) needs some iterations to correct the wrong output estimations.

The output of the network is made up of two contributions:

$$\bar{y}^{(i)} = \sum_{j=1}^{m} w_{ij}\bar{x}^{(j)} + \sum_{k=1}^{i-1} v_{jk}\bar{y}^{(k)}$$

The notation $y/x^{(i)}$ indicates the ith element of y/x. The first term produces a partial output based only on the input, while the second one uses hierarchical lateral connections to correct the values and enforce the decorrelation. The internal weights w_{ij} are updated using the standard version of Oja's rule (this is mainly responsible for the convergence of each weight vector to the first principal component):

$$\Delta w_{ij} = \eta y_i (x_j - w_{ij} y_i)$$

Instead, the external weights v_{jk} are updated using an anti-Hebbian rule:

$$\Delta v_{jk} = -\eta y_j (y_k + v_{jk} y_j) \ \forall \ i \neq k$$

The previous formula can be split into two parts: the first term $-\eta y_j y_k$ acts in the opposite direction of a standard version of Hebb's rule (that's why it's called anti-Hebbian) and forces the decorrelation. The second one $-\eta y_j v_{jk} y_j$ acts as a regularizer and it's analogous to Oja's rule. The term $-\eta y_j y_k$ works as a feedback signal for the Oja's rule that readapts the updates according to the new magnitude of the actual output. In fact, after modifying the lateral connections, the outputs are also forced to change and this modification impacts on the update of w_{ij}. When all the outputs are decorrelated, the vectors $\bar{w}_i$ are implicitly obliged to be orthogonal.

It's possible to imagine an analogy with the Gram-Schmidt orthogonalization, even if in this case the relation between the extraction of different components and the decorrelation is more complex. Like for Sanger's network, this model extracts the first m principal components in descending order (the reason is the same that has been intuitively explained), but for a complete (non-trivial) mathematical proof, please refer to the aforementioned paper.

If input dimensionality is n and the number of components is equal to m, it's possible to use a lower-triangular matrix V ($m \times m$) with all diagonal elements set to 0 and a standard matrix for W ($n \times m$).

The structure of W is as follows:

$$W = (\bar{w}_1 \quad \cdots \quad \bar{w}_m)$$

Therefore, $\bar{w}_i$ is a column-vector that must converge to the corresponding eigenvector. The structure of V is instead:

$$V = Tril_{(if \ i=j \ V(i,j)=0)} \begin{pmatrix} \bar{v}_1 \\ \vdots \\ \bar{v}_m \end{pmatrix} = \begin{pmatrix} 0 & \cdots & 0 \\ \vdots & \ddots & \vdots \\ v_{41} & \cdots & 0 \end{pmatrix}$$

Using this notation, the output becomes as follows:

$$y^{(t+1)} = W^T \bar{x} + V \bar{y}^{(t)}$$

As the output is based on recurrent lateral connections, its value must be stabilized by iterating the previous formula for a fixed number of times or until the norm between two consecutive values becomes smaller than a predefined threshold. In our example, we use a fixed number of iterations equal to five. The update rules cannot be written directly in matrix notation, but it's possible to use the vectors $\bar{w}_i$ (columns) and $\bar{v}_j$ (rows):

$$\begin{cases} \Delta \bar{w}_i = \eta \bar{y}^{(i)} \left(\bar{x} - \bar{y}^{(i)} \bar{w}_i \right) \\ \Delta \bar{v}_i = -\eta \bar{y}^{(i)} \left(\bar{y} - \bar{y}^{(i)} \bar{v}_i \right) \end{cases}$$

In this case, $\bar{y}^{(i)}$ means the ith component of $\bar{y}$. The two matrices must be populated with a loop.

The complete Rubner-Tavan's network algorithm is (the dimensionality of $\bar{x}$ is n, the number of components is denoted with m):

1. Initialize $W^{(0)}$ randomly. The shape is (n x m).
2. Initialize $V^{(0)}$ randomly. The shape is (m x m).
3. Set $V^{(0)} = Tril(V^{(0)})$. The function $Tril(\cdot)$ transforms the input argument in a lower-triangular matrix.
4. Set all diagonal components of $V^{(0)}$ equal to 0.
5. Set the learning rate ($\eta = 0.001$).
6. Set a threshold Thr (for example, $Thr = 0.0001$).
7. Set a cycle counter $T = 0$.
8. Set a maximum number of iterations N_{max} (for example, $N_{max} = 1000$).
9. Set a number of stabilization cycles N_{stab} (for example, $N_{stab} = 5$):
     a. While $\left\| W^{(t)} - W^{(t-1)} \right\|_F > Thr$ and $T < N_{max}$:
          i. Set $T = T + 1$.
          ii. For each $\bar{x}$ in X:
               1. Set $\bar{y}_{prev}$ to zero. The shape is (m x 1).
               2. For $i = 1$ to N_{stab}:
                    a. $\bar{y} = W^T \bar{x} + V \bar{y}_{prev}$

  b. $\bar{y}_{prev} = \bar{y}$

3. Compute the updates for W and V:

  a. Create two empty matrices ΔW $(n \times m)$ and ΔV $(m \times m)$

  b. For $t = 1$ to m:

   i. $\Delta \bar{w}^{(t)} = \eta \bar{y}^{(t)} \left(\bar{x} - \bar{y}^{(t)} \bar{w}_t \right)$

   ii. $\Delta \bar{v}^{(t)} = -\eta \bar{y}^{(t)} \left(\bar{y} - \bar{y}^{(t)} \bar{v}_t \right)$

  c. Update W and V:

   i. $W^{(t+1)} = W^{(t)} + \Delta W$

   ii. $V^{(t+1)} = V^{(t)} + \Delta V$

  d. Set $V = Tril(V)$ and set all the diagonal elements to 0.

  e. Set $W(t+1) = W(t+1) / \|W(t+1)\|_{columns}$
(The norm must be computed column-wise)

In this case, we have adopted both a threshold and a maximum number of iterations, because this algorithm normally converges very quickly. Moreover, I suggest the reader always checks the shapes of vectors and matrices when performing dot products.

Example of Rubner-Tavan's Network

For our Python example, we are going to use the same dataset already created for the Sanger's network (which is expected to be available in the variable Xs). In this example, as well as in all the other ones, the NumPy random seed is set equal to 1000 (np.random.seed(1000)). Using different values (or repeating the experiments more times without resetting the seed) can lead to slightly different results (which are always coherent).

We can start setting up all the constants and variables:

```
import numpy as np

n_components = 2
learning_rate = 0.0001
max_iterations = 1000
stabilization_cycles = 5
```

```
threshold = 0.00001

W = np.random.normal(0.0, 0.5,
                     size=(Xs.shape[1], n_components))
V = np.tril(np.random.normal(0.0, 0.01,
                    size=(n_components, n_components)))
np.fill_diagonal(V, 0.0)

prev_W = np.zeros((Xs.shape[1], n_components))
t = 0
```

At this point, it's possible to implement the training loop:

```
while (np.linalg.norm(W - prev_W, ord='fro') >
        threshold and t < max_iterations):
prev_W = W.copy()
    t += 1

    for i in range(Xs.shape[0]):
        y_p = np.zeros((n_components, 1))
        xi = np.expand_dims(Xs[i], 1)
        y = None

        for _ in range(stabilization_cycles):
            y = np.dot(W.T, xi) + np.dot(V, y_p)
            y_p = y.copy()

        dW = np.zeros((Xs.shape[1], n_components))
        dV = np.zeros((n_components, n_components))

        for t in range(n_components):
            y2 = np.power(y[t], 2)
            dW[:, t] = np.squeeze((y[t] * xi) +
                (y2 * np.expand_dims(W[:, t], 1)))
            dV[t, :] = -np.squeeze((y[t] * y) +
                (y2 * np.expand_dims(V[t, :], 1)))
            W += (learning_rate * dW)
            V += (learning_rate * dV)

            V = np.tril(V)
            np.fill_diagonal(V, 0.0)

            W /= np.linalg.norm(W, axis=0).\
                reshape((1, n_components))
```

We can now compute the final w:

```
print(W)
```

The output is:

```
[[-0.65992841  0.75897537]
 [-0.75132849 -0.65111933]]
```

The output covariance matrix can be computed using the following snippet:

```
Y_comp = np.zeros((Xs.shape[0], n_components))

for i in range(Xs.shape[0]):
y_p = np.zeros((n_components, 1))
        xi = np.expand_dims(Xs[i], 1)

    for _ in range(stabilization_cycles):
        Y_comp[i] = np.squeeze(np.dot(W.T, xi) +
                                np.dot(V.T, y_p))
        y_p = y.copy()

print(np.cov(Y_comp.T))
```

The output is:

```
[[ 48.9901765   -0.34109965]
 [ -0.34109965  24.51072811]]
```

As expected, the algorithm has successfully converged to the eigenvectors (in descending order) and the output covariance matrix is almost completely decorrelated (the sign of the non-diagonal elements can be either positive or negative). Rubner-Tavan's networks are generally faster than Sanger's network, thanks to the feedback signal created by the anti-Hebbian rule; however, it's important to choose the right value for the learning rate. A possible strategy is to implement a temporal decay (as done in Sanger's network) starting with a value not greater than 0.0001. However, it's important to reduce η when n increases (for example, $\eta = {0.0001}/{n}$), because the normalization strength of Oja's rule on the lateral connections v_{jk} is often not enough to avoid over-and underflows when n >>1. I don't suggest any extra normalization on v (which must be carefully analyzed considering that v is singular) because it can slow down the process and reduce the final accuracy.

Self-organizing maps

Self-organizing maps (SOMs) have been proposed by Willshaw and Von Der Malsburg (in Willshaw D. J., Von Der Malsburg C., *How patterned neural connections can be set up by self-organization*, Proceedings of the Royal Society of London, B/194, N. 1117, 1976) to model different neurobiological phenomena observed in animals. In particular, they discovered that some areas of the brain develop structures with different areas, each of them with a high sensitivity for a specific input pattern. The process behind such a behavior is quite different from what we have discussed up until now, because it's based on competition among neural units based on a principle called winner-takes-all. During the training period, all the units are excited with the same signal, but only one will produce the highest response. This unit is automatically candidate to become the receptive basin for that specific pattern. The particular model we are going to present has been introduced by Kohonen (in the paper Kohonen T., *Self-organized formation of topologically correct feature maps*, Biological Cybernetics, 43/1, 1982) and it's named after him.

The main idea is to implement a gradual winner-takes-all paradigm, to avoid the premature convergence of a neuron (as a definitive winner) and increment the level of plasticity of the network. This concept is expressed graphically in the following figure (where we are considering a linear sequence of neurons):

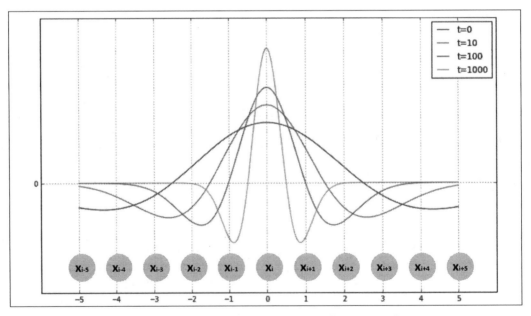

Mexican-hat dynamic implemented by a Kohonen network

In this case, the same pattern is presented to all the neurons. At the beginning of the training process ($t = 0$), a positive response is observed in $\bar{x}_{i-2}$ to $\bar{x}_{i+2}$ with a peak in $\bar{x}_i$. The potential winner is obviously $\bar{x}_i$, but all these units are potentiated according to their distance from $\bar{x}_i$. In other words, the network (which is trained sequentially) is still receptive to change if other patterns produce a stronger activation. If instead $\bar{x}_i$ keeps on being the winner, the radius is slightly reduced, until the only potentiated unit will be $\bar{x}_i$. Considering the shape of this function, which develops a peak around the winning unit, this dynamic is often called *Mexican Hat*. With this approach, the network remains plastic until all the patterns have been repeatedly presented. If, for example, another pattern elicits a stronger response in $\bar{x}_i$, it's important that its activation is still not too high, to allow a fast reconfiguration of the network. At the same time, the new winner will probably be a neighbor of $\bar{x}_i$, which has received a partial potentiation and can easily take the place of $\bar{x}_i$.

Self-organizing maps exhibit a very interesting behavior also in the context of non-linear dimensionality reduction. In fact, when the dataset $X \in \mathbb{R}^n$ is projected onto a m-dimensional space with $m << n$ (for example, images are projected onto a bidimensional matrix), the winning units act like pseudo-centroids of clusters developed around a specific recurring pattern. Assuming that X lies on a lower-dimensional manifold, the projection tends to remove the redundancies and, at the same time, preserve the topological similarities. However, contrary to other manifold learning algorithms, SOMs obtain this result in a different way. As explained, the winning units become stable only after a (long) series of iterations. During each iteration, the radius is incrementally reduced. Therefore, initially, the same topological structure is shared by a neighborhood. As the process continues in a smooth fashion, the manifold distances are preserved until the end of the training process. At that point, adjacent units are topologically similar and, in particular on 2D maps, it's almost impossible to observe abrupt changes. Moreover, as every data point $\bar{x}_i \in X$ elicits only a single maximal response, a SOM is also an implicit clustering space. However, if algorithms like K-Means arrange the centroids by minimizing the distance measured in the original space, SOMs perform also an implicit projection of the dataset.

This peculiar behavior allows us to work with these models considering them as *proxies* of the clustered dataset. In fact, when the projection is stable and adjacent units are elicited by similar patterns, it's possible to consider the position on the map as a real indicator with metric properties (that is, the closer two units are, the more similar they are and vice-versa). The applications of this ability are several and they include eye-tracking systems, denoising filters, and voice decoders (like the pioneering voice-controlled type-writing machine designed by T. Kohonen to validate his ideas).

Considering the very effectiveness of the latter kind of models, we can now dedicate the last part of this chapter to analyze how a Kohonen Map works and how to implement it using an image dataset.

Kohonen Maps

A Kohonen SOM (also known as Kohonen network or simply Kohonen Map) is normally represented as a bidimensional map (for example, a square matrix m x m, or any other rectangular shape), but 3D surfaces, such as spheres or toruses are also possible (the only necessary condition is the existence of a suitable metric). In our case, we always refer to a square matrix where each cell is a receptive neuron characterized by a synaptic weight w with the dimensionality of the input patterns:

$$X = \{\bar{x}_1, \bar{x}_2, \dots, \bar{x}_N\} \ where \ \bar{x}_i \in \mathbb{R}^n$$

During both training and working phases, the winning unit is determined according to a similarity measure between a sample and each weight vector. The most common metric is the Euclidean; hence, if we consider a bidimensional map W with a shape $(k \ x \ p)$ so that $W \in \mathbb{R}^{k \times p \times n}$, the winning unit (in terms of its coordinates) is computed as follows:

$$u^* = \underset{k,p}{\operatorname{argmin}} \ \|W(k,p) - \bar{x}\|_2$$

As explained before, it's important to avoid the premature convergence because the complete final configuration could be quite different from the initial one. Therefore, the training process is normally subdivided into two different stages. During the first one, whose duration is normally about 10-20% of the total number of iterations (let's call this value t_{max}), the correction is applied to the winning unit and its neighbors (computed by adopting a decaying radius). Instead, during the second one, the radius is set to 1.0 and the correction is applied only to the winning unit. In this way, it's possible to analyze a larger number of possible configurations, automatically selecting the one associated with the least error. The neighborhood can have different shapes; it can be square (in closed 3D maps, the boundaries don't exist anymore), or, more easily, it's possible to employ a radial basis function based on an exponentially decaying distance-weight:

$$n(i,j) = e^{-\frac{\|u^* - (i,j)\|^2}{2\sigma(t)^2}} \ where \ \sigma(t) = \sigma_0 e^{-\frac{t}{\tau}}$$

The relative weight of each neuron is determined by the $\sigma(t)$ function. σ_0 is the initial radius and τ is a time-constant that must be considered as a hyperparameter that determines the slope of the decaying weight. Suitable values are 5-10% of the total number of iterations. Adopting a radial basis function, it's not necessary to compute an actual neighborhood because the multiplication factor $n(i,j)$ becomes close to zero outside of the boundaries. A drawback is related to the computational cost, which is higher than a square neighborhood (as the function must be computed for the whole map); however, it's possible to speed up the process by precomputing all the squared distances (the numerator) and exploiting the vectorization features offered by packages such as NumPy (a single exponential is computed every time).

The update rule is very simple, and it's based on the idea to move the winning unit synaptic weights closer to the pattern $\bar{x}_i$, (repeated for the whole dataset X):

$$\Delta \bar{w}_{ij} = \eta(t) n(i,j)(\bar{x}_i - \bar{w}_{ij})$$

The $\eta(t)$ function is the learning rate, which can be fixed, but it's preferable to start with a higher value, η_0 and let it decay to a target final value, η_∞:

$$\eta(t) = \begin{cases} \eta_0 e^{-\frac{t}{\tau}} & \text{if } t < t_{max} \\ \eta_\infty & \text{if } t \geq t_{max} \end{cases}$$

In this way, the initial changes force the weights to align with the input patterns, while all the subsequent updates allow slight modifications to improve the overall accuracy. Therefore, each update is proportional to the learning rate, the neighborhood weighted distance, and the difference between each pattern and the synaptic vector. Theoretically, if $\Delta \bar{w}_{ij}$ is equal to 0 for the winning unit, it means that a neuron has become the attractor of a specific input pattern, and its neighbors will be receptive to noisy/altered versions. The most interesting aspect is that the complete final map will contain the attractors for all patterns that are organized to maximize the similarity between adjacent units. In this way, when a new pattern is presented, the area of neurons that maps the most similar shapes will show a higher response. For example, if the patterns are made up of handwritten digits, attractors for the digit 1 and for digit 7 will be closer than the attractor, for example, for digit 8. A malformed 1 (which could be interpreted as 7) will elicit a response that is between the first two attractors, allowing us to assign a relative probability based on the distance. As we're going to see in the example, this feature yields to a smooth transition between different variants of the same pattern class avoiding rigid boundaries that oblige a binary decision (like in a K-Means clustering or in a hard classifier).

The complete Kohonen SOM algorithm is as follows:

1. Randomly initialize $W^{(0)}$ (for example, $W_{ij}^{(0)} \sim N(0,1)$). The shape is $(k \times n \times p)$.

2. Initialize the total number of iterations N_{max} and t_{max} (for example, $N_{max} = 1000$ and $t_{max} = 150$).

3. Initialize τ (for example, $\tau = 100$).

4. Initialize η_0 and η_∞ (for example, $\eta_0 = 1.0$ and $\eta_\infty = 0.05$).

5. For $t = 0$ to N_{max}:

    a. If $t < t_{max}$:

        i. Compute $\eta(t)$

        ii. Compute $\sigma(t)$

    b. Otherwise:

        i. Set $\eta(t) = \eta_\infty$

        ii. Set $\sigma(t) = \sigma_\infty$

    c. For each $\bar{x}_i \in X$:

        i. Compute the winning unit u^* (let's assume that the coordinates are (i,j)

        ii. Compute $n(i,j)$

        iii. Apply the weight correction $\Delta \bar{w}_{ij}^{(t)}$ to all synaptic weights $W^{(t)}$

    d. Renormalize $W(t+1) = \left. W(t+1) \middle/ \|W(t+1)\|_{columns} \right.$ (the norm must be computed column-wise)

After discussing the theoretical part, we are ready to see a practical implementation of a Kohonen map using dataset containing different pictures of a group of people. The example is also helpful to understand how to tune up the hyperparameters in order to speed up the convergence and to increase the accuracy.

Example of SOM

We can now implement a SOM using the Olivetti faces dataset. As the process can be very long, in this example we limit the number of input patterns to 100 (with a 4 x 4 matrix). The reader can try with the whole dataset and a larger map.

The first step is loading the data, normalizing it so that all values are bounded between 0.0 and 1.0, and setting the constants:

```
import numpy as np

from sklearn.datasets import fetch_olivetti_faces

faces = fetch_olivetti_faces(shuffle=True)

Xcomplete = faces['data'].astype(np.float64) / np.max(faces['data'])
np.random.shuffle(Xcomplete)
X = Xcomplete[0:100]
```

We can now define the main constants and the initial matrices:

```
nb_iterations = 5000
nb_startup_iterations = 1000
pattern_length = 64 * 64
pattern_width = pattern_height = 64
eta0 = 1.0
sigma0 = 2.0
tau = 80.0
matrix_side = 4

W = np.random.normal(0, 0.1,
                     size=(matrix_side,
                           matrix_side,
                           pattern_length))
```

Now, we need to define the functions to determine the winning unit based on the least distance:

```
def winning_unit(xt):
    global W
    distances = np.linalg.norm(W - xt, ord=2, axis=2)
    max_activation_unit = np.argmax(distances)
    return int(np.floor(max_activation_unit /
                   matrix_side)), \
           max_activation_unit % matrix_side
```

It's also useful to define the functions $\eta(t)$ and $\sigma(t)$:

```
def eta(t):
    return eta0 * np.exp(-float(t) / tau)

def sigma(t):
    return float(sigma0) * np.exp(-float(t) / tau)
```

As explained before, instead of computing the radial basis function for each unit, it's preferable to use a precomputed distance matrix (in this case, 4 x 4 x 4 x 4) containing all the possible distances between couples of units. In this way, NumPy allows a faster calculation thanks to its vectorization features:

```
precomputed_distances = np.zeros((matrix_side,
                                  matrix_side,
                                  matrix_side,
                                  matrix_side))


for i in range(matrix_side):
    for j in range(matrix_side):
        for k in range(matrix_side):
            for t in range(matrix_side):
                precomputed_distances[i, j, k, t] = \
                    np.power(float(i) - float(k), 2) + \
                        np.power(float(j) - float(t), 2)

def distance_matrix(xt, yt, sigmat):
    global precomputed_distances
    dm = precomputed_distances[xt, yt, :, :]
    de = 2.0 * np.power(sigmat, 2)
    return np.exp(-dm / de)
```

The `distance_matrix` function returns the value of the radial basis function for the whole map given the center point (the winning unit) xt, yt and the current value of σ sigmat. Now, it's possible to start the training process (in order to avoid correlations, it's preferable to shuffle the input sequence at the beginning of each iteration):

```
sequence = np.arange(0, X.shape[0])
t = 0

for e in range(nb_iterations):
    np.random.shuffle(sequence)
    t += 1

    if e < nb_startup_iterations:
        etat = eta(t)
        sigmat = sigma(t)
    else:
        etat = 0.2
        sigmat = 1.0

    for n in sequence:
```

```
        x_sample = X[n]

        xw, yw = winning_unit(x_sample)
        dm = distance_matrix(xw, yw, sigmat)

        dW = etat * np.expand_dims(dm, axis=2) \
            * (x_sample - W)
        W += dW

    W /= np.linalg.norm(W, axis=2).\
        reshape((matrix_side, matrix_side, 1))
```

In this case, we have set $\eta_\infty = 0.2$ but I invite the reader to try different values and evaluate the final result. After training for 5000 epochs, we got the following weight matrix (each weight is plotted as a bidimensional array):

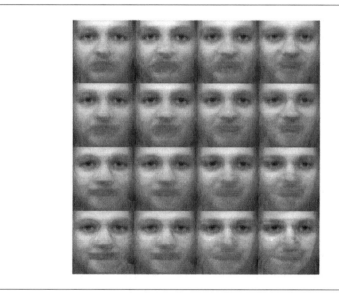

Final SOM weight matrix

As it's possible to see, the weights have converged to faces with slightly different features. In particular, looking at the shapes of the faces and the expressions, it's easy to notice the transition between different attractors (some faces are smiling, while others are more serious; some have glasses, mustaches, and beards, and so on). It's also important to consider that the matrix is larger than the minimum capacity (there are ten different individuals in the dataset). This allows mapping more patterns that cannot be easily attracted by the right neuron.

For example, an individual can have pictures with and without a beard and this can lead to confusion. If the matrix is too small, it's possible to observe an instability in the convergence process, while if it's too large, it's easy to see redundancies. The right choice depends on each different dataset and on the internal variance and there's no way to define a standard criterion. A good starting point is picking a matrix whose capacity is between 2.0 and 3.0 times larger than the number of desired attractors and then increasing or reducing its size until the accuracy reaches a maximum.

The last element to consider is the labeling phase. At the end of the training process, we have no knowledge about the weight distribution in terms of winning neurons, so it's necessary to process the dataset and annotate the winning unit for each pattern. In this way, it's possible to submit new patterns to get the most likely label. This process has not been shown, but it's straightforward and the reader can easily implement it for every different scenario.

Summary

In this chapter, we have discussed Hebb's rule, showing how it can drive the computation of the first principal component of the input dataset. We have also seen that this rule is unstable because it leads to the infinite growth of the synaptic weights and how it's possible to solve this problem using normalization or Oja's rule.

We have introduced two different neural networks based on Hebbian learning (Sanger's and Rubner-Tavan's networks), whose internal dynamics are slightly different, and which are able to extract the first n principal components in the right order (starting from the largest eigenvalue) without eigendecomposing the input covariance matrix.

Finally, we have introduced the concept of SOM and presented a model called a Kohonen network, which is able to map the input patterns onto a surface where some attractors (one per class) are placed through a competitive learning process. Such a model is able to recognize new patterns (belonging to the same distribution) by eliciting a strong response in the attractor that is most similar to the pattern. In this way, after a labeling process, the model can be employed as a soft classifier that can easily manage noisy or altered patterns.

In the next chapter, we are going to discuss the main concepts of ensemble learning and the most important and diffused bagging and boosting algorithms.

Further reading

- Dayan P., Abbott F. L., *Theoretical Neuroscience*, The MIT Press, 2003

- Warner R., *Applied Statistics*, SAGE Publications, 2013

- Sanger T. D., *Single-Layer Linear Feedforward Neural Network*, Neural Networks, 1989/2

- Rubner J., Tavan P., *A Self-Organizing Network for Principal-Components Analysis, Europhysics, Letters*, 10(7), 1989

- Principe J. C., Euliano N. R., Lefebvre W. C., *Neural and Adaptive Systems: Fundamentals Through Simulation*, Wiley 1997/1999

- Willshaw D. J., Von Der Malsburg C., *How patterned neural connections can be set up by self-organization*, Proceedings of the Royal Society of London, B/194, N. 1117, 1976

- Kohonen T., *Self-organized formation of topologically correct feature maps*, Biological Cybernetics, 43/1, 1982

- Kohonen T., *Learning Vector Quantization, Self-Organizing Maps*. Springer Series in Information Sciences, vol 30. Springer, 1995

15
Fundamentals of Ensemble Learning

In this chapter, we are going to discuss some important algorithms that exploit different estimators to improve the overall performance of an ensemble or committee. These techniques work either by introducing a medium level of randomness in every estimator belonging to a predefined set or by creating a sequence of estimators where each new model is forced to improve the performance of the previous ones. These techniques allow us to reduce both the bias and the variance (thereby increasing validation accuracy) when employing models with a limited capacity or more prone to overfit the training set.

In particular, the topics covered in the chapter are as follows:

- Introduction to ensemble learning
- A brief and propaedeutic introduction to decision trees
- Random forest and extra randomized forests
- AdaBoost (algorithms M1, SAMME, SAMME.R, and R2)

We can now start our exploration of ensemble learning algorithms by discussing the fundamental concepts of weak and strong learners and how to combine simple estimators to create much better performing committees.

Ensemble learning fundamentals

The main concept behind ensemble learning is the distinction between strong and weak learners. In particular, a strong learner is a classifier or a regressor which has enough capacity to reach the highest potential accuracy, minimizing both bias and variance (thus also achieving a satisfactory level of generalization).

On the other hand, a weak learner is a model that is generically able to achieve an accuracy slightly higher than a random guess, but whose complexity is very low (they can be trained very quickly but can never be used alone to solve complex problems).

To define a strong learner more formally, if we consider a parametrized binary classifier $f(\bar{x}; \bar{\theta})$, we define it as a strong learner if the following is true:

$$\forall\, \epsilon > 0 \ and \ \delta \leq \frac{1}{2} \ \exists\, \bar{\theta}_c \ : \ with\, p \geq 1 - \delta \ \Rightarrow p[f(\bar{x}_i; \bar{\theta}_c) \neq y_i] \leq \epsilon$$

This expression can initially appear cryptic; however, it's very easy to understand. It simply expresses the concept that a strong learner is theoretically able to achieve any non-null probability of misclassification with a probability greater than or equal to 0.5 (that is, the threshold for a binary random guess).

All the models normally employed in Machine Learning tasks are normally strong learners, even though their domain can be limited (for example, a logistic regression cannot solve non-linear problems).

There is a formal definition for weak learners, too, but it's simpler to consider that the real main property of a weak learner is a limited ability to achieve a reasonable accuracy. In some very particular and small regions of the training space, a weak learner could reach a low probability of misclassification, but in the whole space its performance is only a little bit superior to a random guess. The previous one is more a theoretical definition than a practice one, because all the models currently available are normally quite a lot better than a random oracle. However, an ensemble is defined as a set of weak learners that are trained together (or in a sequence) to make up a committee. Both in classification and regression problems, the final result is obtained by averaging the predictions or employing a majority vote.

At this point, a reasonable question is – Why do we need to train many weak learners instead of a single strong one? The answer is two-pronged – in ensemble learning, we normally work with medium-strong learners (such as decision trees or linear support vector machines – SVMs) and we use them as a committee to increase the overall accuracy and reduce the variance thanks to a wider exploration of the sample space.

In fact, while a single strong learner is often able to overfit the training set, it's more difficult to keep a high accuracy over the whole sample subspace without saturating the capacity. In order to avoid overfitting, a trade-off must be found, and the result is a less accurate classifier/regressor with a simpler separation hyperplane.

The adoption of many weak learners (that are actually quite strong, because even the simplest models are more accurate than a random guess), allows us to force them to focus only on a limited subspace, so as to be able to reach a very high local accuracy with a low variance. The committee, employing an averaging technique, can easily find out which prediction is the most suitable. Alternatively, it can ask each learner to vote, assuming that a successful training process must always lead the majority to propose the most accurate classification or prediction.

The most common approaches to ensemble learning are as follows:

- **Bagging** (**bootstrap aggregating**): This approach trains n weak learners $f_{w_1}, f_{w_2}, \dots, f_{w_n}$ (very often they are decision trees) using n training sets (D_1, D_2, ..., D_n) created by randomly sampling the original dataset D. The sampling process (called *bootstrap sampling*) is normally performed with replacement (which is known as proper bagging), so as to determine different data distributions. Moreover, in many real algorithms, the weak learners are also initialized and trained using a medium degree of randomness. In this way, the probability of having clones becomes very small and, at the same time, it's possible to increase the accuracy by keeping the variance under a tolerable threshold (thus avoiding overfitting). Breiman (in Breiman L., *Pasting small votes for classification in large databases and on-line*, Machine Learning, 36, 1999) proposed an alternative approach, called *Pasting*, where random selections of D are sampled without replacement. In this case, the specialization of the weak learners is more selective and focused on specific regions of the sample space without overlaps. Moreover, Ho (in Ho T., *The random subspace method for constructing decision forests, Pattern Analysis and Machine Intelligence*, 20, 1998), before Breiman, analyzed the possibility to create subsets by working exclusively on the features. Contrary to Pasting, this method forces the weak learners to specialize on subspaces (with sample overlaps). Such an approach resembles Cotraining, where different classifiers are employed to carry out a semi-supervised task by focusing on two different views of the dataset. However, in both cases, the requested capacity is limited, and weak learners can easily find a suitable separation hypersurface. The combination of such models, analogously to bagging, allows us to solve very complex problems through wise usage of randomness.

- **Boosting**: This is an alternative approach that builds an incremental ensemble starting with a single weak learner f_{w_1} and adding a new one f_{w_i} at each iteration. The goal is to reweight the dataset, so as to force the new learner to focus on the data points that were previously misclassified. This strategy yields a very high accuracy because the new learners are trained with a positively biased dataset that allows them to adapt to the most difficult internal conditions.

However, in this way, the control over the variance is weakened and the ensemble can more easily overfit the training set. It's possible to mitigate this problem by reducing the complexity of the weak learners or imposing a regularization constraint.

- **Stacking**: This method can be implemented in different ways, but the philosophy is always the same — use different algorithms (normally a few strong learners) trained on the same dataset and filter the final result using another classifier, averaging the predictions or using a majority vote. This strategy can be very powerful if the dataset has a structure that can be partially managed with different approaches. Each classifier or regressor should discover some data aspects that are peculiar; that's why the algorithms must be structurally different. For example, it can be useful to mix a decision tree with an SVM or linear and kernel models. The evaluation performed on the test set should clearly show the prevalence of a classifier only in some cases. If an algorithm is finally the only one that produces the best prediction, the ensemble becomes useless and it's better to focus on a single strong learner.

Random forests

A random forest is the bagging ensemble model based on decision trees. If the reader is not familiar with this kind of model, I suggest reading Alpaydin E., *Introduction to Machine Learning*, The MIT Press, 2010, where a complete explanation can be found. However, for our purposes, it's useful to provide a brief explanation of the most important concepts.

Random forest fundamentals

A decision tree is a model that resembles a standard hierarchical decision process. In the majority of cases, a special family is employed, called *binary decision trees*, as each decision yields only two outcomes. This kind of tree is often the simplest and most reasonable choice and the training process (which consists of building the tree itself) is very intuitive. The root contains the whole dataset:

$$X = \{\bar{x}_1, \bar{x}_2, \dots, \bar{x}_M\} \ \text{where} \ \bar{x}_i \in \mathbb{R}^n$$

Each level is obtained by applying a selection tuple, defined as follows:

$$\sigma_i = \langle i, t_i \rangle \ \text{where} \ i \in (1, n) \ \text{and} \ t_i \in \left(\min x^{(i)}, \max x^{(i)} \right)$$

The first index of the tuple corresponds to an input feature, while the threshold t_i is a value chosen in the specific range of each feature. The application of a selection tuple leads to a split and two nodes that each contain a non-overlapping subset of the input dataset. In the following diagram, there's an example of a slip performed at the level of the root (initial split):

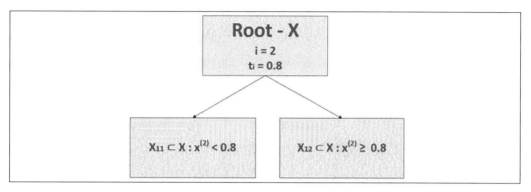

Example of initial split in a decision tree

The set X is split into two subsets defined as X_{11} and X_{12} whose data points have respectively the feature with $i = 2$ less or greater than the threshold $t_i = 0.8$. The intuition behind classification decision trees is to continue splitting until the leaves contain points belonging to a single category y_i (these nodes are defined as pure). In this way, a new point $\bar{x}_j$ can traverse the tree with a computation complexity $O(\log M)$ and reach a final node that determines its category. In a very similar way, it's possible to build regression trees whose output is continuous (even if, for our purposes, we are going to consider only classification scenarios).

At this point, the main problem is how to perform each split. We cannot pick any feature and any threshold, because the final tree will be completely unbalanced and very deep. Our goal is to find the optimal selection tuple at each node considering the final goal, which is classification into discrete categories (the process is almost identical for regressions). The technique is very similar to a problem based on a cost function that must be minimized, but, in this case, we operate locally, applying an impurity measure proportional to the heterogeneity of a node. A high impurity indicates that samples belonging to many different categories are present, while an impurity equal to 0 indicates that a single category is present. As we need to continue splitting until a pure leaf appears, the optimal choice is based on a function that scores each selection tuple, allowing us to select the one that yields the lowest impurity (theoretically, the process should continue until all the leaves are pure, but normally a maximum depth is provided, so as to avoid excessive complexity).

If there are p classes, the category set can be defined as follows:

$$Y = \{y_1, y_2, \ldots, y_M\} \ where \ y_i \in (1, p)$$

A very common impurity measure is called *Gini impurity* and it's based on the probability of a misclassification if a data point is categorized using a label randomly chosen from the node subset distribution. Intuitively, if all the points belong to the same category, any random choice leads to a correct classification (and the impurity becomes 0). On the other side, if the node contains points from many categories, the probability of a misclassification increases. Formally, the measure is defined as follows:

$$I_{Gini}(X_k) = \sum_{j=1}^{q} p(j|k)(1 - p(j|k))$$

The subset is indicated by X_k and $p(j \mid k)$ is obtained as the ratio of the data points belonging to the class j over the sample size. The selection tuple must be chosen so as to minimize the Gini impurity of the children. Another common approach is the cross-entropy impurity, defined as follows:

$$I_{CE}(X_k) = -\sum_{j=1}^{q} p(j|k) \log p(j|k)$$

The main difference between this measure and the previous one is provided by some fundamental information theory concepts. In particular, the goal we want to reach is the minimization of the uncertainty, which is measured using the *(cross-)entropy*. If we have a discrete distribution and all the data points belong to the same category, a random choice can fully describe the distribution; therefore, the uncertainty is null. On the contrary, if, for example, we have a fair die, the probability of each outcome is 1/6 and the corresponding entropy is about 2.58 bits (if the base of the logarithm is 2). When the nodes become purer and purer, the cross-entropy impurity decreases and reaches 0 in an optimal scenario. Moreover, adopting the concept of mutual information, we can define the information gain obtained after a split has been performed:

$$IG(\sigma) = H(X_{parent}) - H(X_{parent}|X_{children})$$

Given a node, we want to create two children to maximize the information gain. In other words, by choosing the cross-entropy impurity we implicitly grow the tree until the information gain becomes null. Considering again the example of a fair die, we need 2.58 bits of information to decide which is the right outcome. If, instead, the die is loaded and the probability of an outcome is 1 (100%), we need no information to make a decision. In a decision tree, we'd like to resemble this situation, so that, when a new data point has completely traversed the tree, we don't need any further information to classify it. If a maximum depth is imposed, the final information gain cannot be null. This means that we need to pay an extra cost to finalize the classification. This cost is proportional to the residual uncertainty and should be minimized to increase the accuracy.

Other methods can also be employed (even if Gini and cross-entropy are the most common) and I invite the reader to check the references for further information. However, at this point, a consideration naturally arises. Decision trees are simple models (they are not weak learners!), but the procedure for building them is more complex than, for example, training a logistic regression or a linear SVM. Why are they so popular?

Why use Decision Trees?

One reason for the popularity of decision trees is already clear—they represent a structural process that can be shown using a diagram; however, this is not enough to justify their usage. Two important properties allow the employment of decision trees without any data preprocessing.

In fact, it's easy to understand that, contrary to other methods, there's no need for any scaling or whitening and it's possible to use continuous and categorical features at the same time. For example, if in a bidimensional dataset a feature has a variance equal to 1 and the other equal to 100, the majority of classifiers will achieve a low accuracy; therefore, a preprocessing step becomes necessary. In a decision tree, a selection tuple has the same effect also when the ranges are very different. It goes without saying that a split can be easily performed considering also categorical features and there's no need, for example, to use techniques such as one-hot encoding (which is necessary in most cases to avoid generalization errors). However, unfortunately, the separation hypersurface obtained with a decision tree is normally much more complex than the one obtained using other algorithms and this drives to a higher variance with a consequential loss of generalization ability.

To understand the reason, it's possible to imagine a very simple bidimensional dataset made up of two blobs located in the second and fourth quarters. The first set is characterized by $(x < 0, y > 0)$, but the second one by $(x < 0, y < 0)$. Let's also suppose that we have a few outliers, but our knowledge about the data generating process is not enough to qualify them as noisy points or outliers (the original distribution can have tails that are extended over the axes; for example, it may be a mixture of two Gaussians). In this scenario, the simplest separation line is a diagonal splitting the plane into two sub-planes containing regions belonging also to the first and third quarters. However, this decision can be made only considering both coordinates at the same time. Using a decision tree, we need to split initially, for example, using the first feature and again with the second one. The result is a piece-wise separation line (for example, splitting the plane into the region corresponding to the second quarter and its complement), leading to a very high classification variance. Paradoxically, a better solution can be obtained with an incomplete tree (limiting the process, for example, to a single split) and with the selection of the y-axis as the separation line (this is why it's important to impose a maximum depth), but the price you pay is an increased bias (and a consequently worse accuracy).

Another important element to consider when working with decision trees (and related models) is the maximum depth. It's possible to grow the tree until all the leaves are pure, but sometimes it's preferable to impose a maximum depth (and, consequently, a maximum number of terminal nodes). A maximum depth equal to 1 drives to binary models called *decision stumps*, which don't allow any interaction among the features (they can simply be represented as *If ... Then* conditions). Higher values yield more terminal nodes and allow an increasing interaction among features (it's possible to think about a combination of many *If ... Then* statements together with *AND* logical operators). The right value must be tuned considering every single problem and it's important to remember that very deep trees are more prone to overfitting than pruned ones.

In some contexts, it's preferable to achieve a slightly worse accuracy with a higher generalization ability and, in those cases, a maximum depth should be imposed. The most commonly used tool to determine the best value is always a grid search together with a cross-validation technique.

Random forests and the bias-variance trade-off

Random forests provide us with a powerful tool to solve the bias-variance trade-off problem. They were proposed by Breiman (in Breiman L., *Random Forests, Machine Learning*, 45, 2001) and their logic is very simple.

As already explained in the previous section, the bagging method starts with the choice of the number of weak learners, N_c. The second step is the generation of N_c datasets (called *bootstrap samples*) $D_1, D_2, \dots, D_{N_c}$:

$$D_p = \{\bar{x}_1^S, \bar{x}_2^S, \dots, \bar{x}_M^S\} \; where \; \bar{x}_i^S \sim X \; and \; p \in (1, N_c)$$

Each decision tree is trained using the corresponding dataset using a common impurity criterion; however, in a random forest, in order to reduce the variance, the selection splits are not computed considering all the features, but only via a random subset containing a reduced number of features (common choices are the rounded square root, $\log_2 x$ or natural logarithm). This approach indeed weakens each learner, as the optimality is partially lost, but allows us to obtain a drastic variance reduction by limiting the over-specialization. At the same time, a bias reduction and an increased accuracy are a result of the ensemble (in particular for a large number of estimators). In fact, as the learners are trained with slightly different data distributions, the average of a prediction converges to the right value when $N_c \to \infty$ (in practice, it's not always necessary to employ a very large number of decision trees, however, the correct minimum value must be found using a grid search with cross-validation). Once all the models, represented with a function $d_i(\bar{x})$, have been trained, the final prediction can be obtained as an average:

$$\hat{y} = \frac{1}{N_c} \sum_{i=1}^{N_c} d_i(\bar{x})$$

Alternatively, it's possible to employ a majority vote (but only for classifications):

$$\hat{y} = \underset{d_i(\bar{x})}{\operatorname{argmax}} \, d_i(\bar{x})$$

These two methods are very similar, and, in most cases, they yield the same result. However, averaging is more robust and allows an improved flexibility when the points are almost on the boundaries. Moreover, it can be used for both classification and regression tasks.

Random forests limit their randomness by picking the best selection tuple from a smaller sample subset. In some cases, for example, when the number of features is not very large, this strategy drives to a minimum variance reduction and the computational cost is no longer justified by the result. It's possible to achieve better performances with a variant called *extra-randomized trees* (or simply extra-trees).

The procedure is almost the same; however, in this case, before performing a split, n random thresholds are computed (for each feature) and the one which leads to the least impurity is chosen. This approach further weakens the learners but, at the same time, reduces residual variance and prevents overfitting. The dynamic is not very different from many techniques, such as regularization or dropout (we're going to discuss this approach in the next chapter); in fact, the extra-randomness reduces the capacity of the model, forcing it to a more linearized solution (which is clearly sub-optimal).

The price to pay for this limitation is a consequent bias worsening, which, however, is compensated by the presence of many different learners. Even with random splits, when N_c is large enough, the probability of a wrong classification (or regression prediction) becomes smaller and smaller because both the average and the majority vote tend to compensate the outcome of trees whose structure is strongly sub-optimal in particular regions. This result is easier to obtain, in particular, when the number of training data points is large. In this case, in fact, sampling with replacement leads to slightly different distributions that could be considered (even if this is not formally correct) as partially and randomly boosted. Therefore, every weak learner will implicitly focus on the whole dataset with extra attention to a smaller subset that, however, is randomly selected (differently from actual boosting). Another important point to remember is that decision trees are extremely prone to overfitting (indeed, they tend to reach the final leaves with a single element per leaf). Such a condition is clearly undesirable and must be properly controlled by setting the maximum depth for each tree. In this way, the bias is kept a little bit above its potential minimum, but the ensemble has a smaller variance and can generalize better.

The complete random forest algorithm is as follows:

1. Set the number of decision trees N_c

2. For $i = 1$ to N_c:

    Create a dataset D_i sampling with replacements from the original dataset X

3. Set the number of features to consider during each split N_f (for example, $sqrt(n)$)

4. Set an impurity measure (for example, Gini impurity)

5. Define an optional maximum depth for each tree

6. For $i = 1$ to N_c:

    a. **Random forest**:

        Train the decision tree $d_i(\bar{x})$ using the dataset D_i and selecting the best split among N_f features randomly sampled

b. **Extra-trees**:

Train the decision tree $d_i(\bar{x})$ using the dataset D_i, computing before each split n random thresholds and selecting the one that yields the least impurity

7. Define an output function averaging the single outputs or employing a majority vote

Example of random forest with scikit-learn

In this example, we are going to use the famous Wine dataset (178 13-dimensional samples split into three classes) that is directly available in scikit-learn. Unfortunately, it's not so easy to find good and simple datasets for ensemble learning algorithms, as they are normally employed with large and complex sets that require too long a computational time. Anyway, the goal of the example is to show the properties of random forests with examples that can be run multiple times with different parameters. With this knowledge, the reader will be able to apply these models to real-life scenarios and to get the maximum advantage.

As the Wine dataset is not particularly complex, the first step is to assess the performances of different classifiers (simple Logistic Regression, Decision Tree with max depth set to 5 and cross-entropy impurity measure, and an RBF SVM of automatic tuning of γ) using a 10-fold cross-validation. Even if Decision Trees and random forest are not sensitive to different scales, Logistic Regression and SVM are, therefore, after loading the dataset, we are going to scale it:

```python
import numpy as np


from sklearn.datasets import load_wine
from sklearn.model_selection import cross_val_score
from sklearn.preprocessing import StandardScaler
from sklearn.linear_model import LogisticRegression
from sklearn.tree import DecisionTreeClassifier
from sklearn.svm import SVC

wine = load_wine()
X, Y = wine["data"], wine["target"]
ss = StandardScaler()
Xs = ss.fit_transform(X)

lr = LogisticRegression(max_iter=5000,
                        solver='lbfgs',
```

```
                        multi_class='auto',
                        random_state=1000)
  scores_lr = cross_val_score(lr, Xs, Y, cv=10,
                        n_jobs=-1)

  dt = DecisionTreeClassifier(criterion='entropy',
                        max_depth=5,
                        random_state=1000)
  scores_dt = cross_val_score(dt, Xs, Y, cv=10,
                        n_jobs=-1)

  svm = SVC(kernel='rbf',
            gamma='scale',
            random_state=1000)
  scores_svm = cross_val_score(svm, Xs, Y, cv=10,
                        n_jobs=-1)

  print("Avg. Logistic Regression CV Score: {:.3f}".
            format(np.mean(scores_lr)))
  print("Avg. Decision Tree CV Score: {:.3f}".
            format(np.mean(scores_dt)))
  print("Avg. SVM CV Score: {:.3f}".
            format(np.mean(scores_svm)))
```

The output is:

```
Avg. Logistic Regression CV Score: 0.978

Avg. Decision Tree CV Score: 0.933

Avg. SVM CV Score: 0.978
```

As expected, the performances are quite good, with a top value of average cross-validation accuracy equal to about 97.8% achieved by the Logistic Regression and RBF SVM. A very interesting element is the performance of the decision tree, which is slightly worse than the other classifiers. Other impurity measures (for example, Gini) or deeper trees don't improve this result, therefore, in this task, a decision tree is on average weaker than a Logistic Regression and, even if it's not fully correct, we can define this model as a candidate for our bagging test. The three curves with CV scores are shown in the following figure:

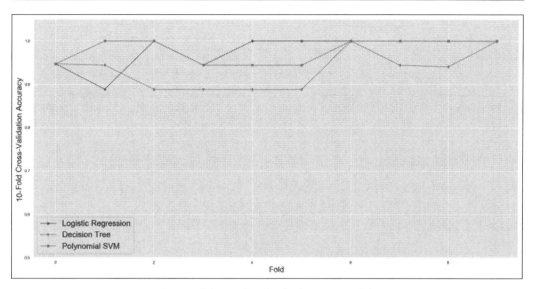

Cross-validation plots for the three test models

As it's possible to see, all classifiers tend easily to reach CV scores larger than 0.9 with 8 folds where the score is about 1.0 (no misclassifications). This means that the random forest has limited room for improvement and the ensemble must focus on the subsamples with *unique* features. For example, the second fold corresponds to the lowest CV scores for both classifiers, hence the data points contained in this set are the only representatives of a subregion of p_{data} that would be otherwise discarded. We expect the bagging ensemble to fill this gap by training some weak learners on that specific region so as to increase the final prediction confidence.

To test our hypothesis, we can now fit a random forest by instantiating the class RandomForestClassifier and selecting n_estimators=150 (I invite the reader to try different values). Considering the performances of the Decision Tree, also in this case, we are employing a cross-entropy impurity:

```
from sklearn.ensemble import RandomForestClassifier

rf = RandomForestClassifier(n_estimators=150,
                            n_jobs=-1,
                            criterion='entropy',
                            random_state=1000)
scores = cross_val_score(rf, Xs, Y, cv=10,
                         n_jobs=-1)
print("Avg. Random Forest CV score: {:.3f}".
        format(np.mean(scores)))
```

The output of the previous snippet is:

```
Avg. Random Forest CV score: 0.984
```

As expected, the average cross-validation accuracy is the highest, about 98.4%. Therefore, the random forest has successfully found a global configuration of decision trees, so as to specialize them in almost any region of the sample space. The parameter n_jobs=-1 or n_jobs=joblib.cpu_count() (including the joblib library) tells scikit-learn to parallelize the training process using all available CPU cores.

Even if we know that the random forest achieved a better average CV score, it should be helpful to also compare the standard deviation to gain a better insight about the distribution. However, in this case, it's easier to plot the scores directly:

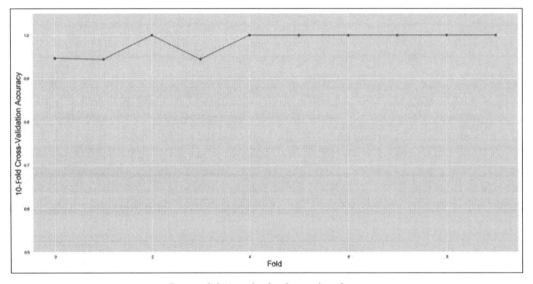

Cross-validation plot for the random forest

Even without any other confirmation, we can be sure that the random forest has achieved a better result because all the CV scores are larger than 0.9 and 7 are close to 1.0. Of course, considering the Occam's razor principle, we should select the smallest number of trees that guarantees the largest average CV score. In the following diagram, we have plotted the average CV score as a function of the number of trees:

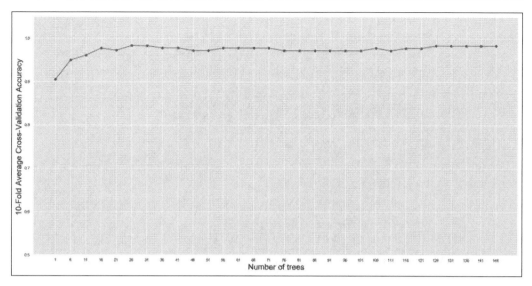

Average cross-validation score as a function of the number of trees

It's not surprising to observe some oscillations and a plateau when the number of trees becomes greater at about 60. The effect of the randomness can cause a performance loss, even increasing the number of learners. In fact, even if the training accuracy grows, the validation accuracy on different folds can be affected by an over-specialization. Another slight improvement appears when the number of trees becomes greater than 125 and remains almost constant for larger values. As the other classifiers have already achieved high accuracies, we have chosen N_c = 150, which should guarantee the best performances on this dataset. However, even when the computational cost is not a problem, I always suggest performing at least a grid search, in order not only to achieve the best accuracy but also to minimize the complexity of the model.

Feature importance

Another important element to consider when working with decision trees and random forests is feature importance (also called *Gini importance* when this impurity criterion is chosen), which is a measure proportional to the impurity reduction that a particular feature allows us to achieve. For a decision tree, it is defined as follows:

$$Importance\left(\bar{x}^{(i)}\right) = \sum_{j} \frac{n(j)}{M} \Delta I_j^i$$

In the previous formula, $n(j)$ denotes the number of samples reaching the node j (the sum must be extended to all nodes where the feature is chosen) and ΔI_j^i is the impurity reduction achieved at node j after splitting using the feature i. In a random forest, the importance must be computed by averaging over all trees:

$$Importance\left(\bar{x}^{(i)}\right) = \frac{1}{N_c} \sum_{k=1}^{N_c} \sum_j \frac{n(j)}{M} \Delta I_j^i$$

After fitting a model (decision tree or random forest), scikit-learn outputs the feature importance vector in the `feature_importances_` instance variable. In the following graph, there's a plot showing the importance of each feature in descending order:

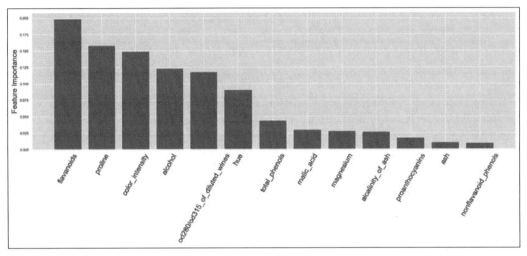

Feature importances for the Wine dataset

We don't want to analyze the chemical meaning of each element, but it's clear that, for example, the presence of flavonoids, proline, and color intensity are much more important than the presence of non-flavonoid phenols. As discussed in the context of regressions, when a dataset is normalized, the magnitude of the coefficients is proportional to the importance of the feature in terms of predictive power. For example, a simple logistic model can have the following structure:

$$logit(r) = ax_0 + bx_1 + c$$

If $x_0, x_1 \sim N(0, 1)$ and $a \gg b$, the value of x_0 can be strong enough to push the predicted value above or below the threshold independently from x_1. Analogously, the feature importance in a decision tree (or in an ensemble of trees) provides us with a measure of the ability of a feature to reduce the impurity and, consequently, to lead to a final prediction.

This concept is becoming more and more important and it's now called **Explainable AI (XAI)**. The reason for such an interest derives from the requests of domain experts that want to know:

- The reasons (factors) that drove a prediction
- Which factors are negligible?
- What happens to the prediction if a factor changes (for example a patient quits smoking or takes a different medication)?
- What the prediction would be with another factor setting (for example, a domain expert can suppose a hypothesis and validate it using the model)

All these kinds of questions (and many others) cannot be easily answered using black-box models and this situation can increase the scepticism with regard to AI. On the other side, decision trees are not black-box models. The whole decision process can be plotted and it's easy to justify a prediction given the input features (even if there are more sophisticated techniques that can be employed with more complex models). Therefore, I strongly encourage the reader to analyze the feature importances and to show them to the domain experts. Moreover, as the model is working with features that are semantically independent (it's not the same for the pixels of an image), it's possible to reduce the dimensionality of a dataset by removing all those features whose importance doesn't have a high impact on the final accuracy. This process, called *feature selection*, should be performed using more complex statistical techniques, such as Chi-square, but when a classifier is able to produce an importance index, it's also possible to use a scikit-learn class called `SelectFromModel`. Passing an estimator (that can be fitted or not) and a threshold, it's possible to transform the dataset by filtering out all the features whose value is below the threshold. Applying it to our model and setting a minimum importance equal to 0.02, we get the following:

```
from sklearn.feature_selection import SelectFromModel

rf.fit(X, Y)
sfm = SelectFromModel(estimator=rf,
                      prefit=True,
                      threshold=0.02)
X_sfm = sfm.transform(X)

print('Feature selection shape: {}'.
        format(X_sfm.shape))
```

The new dataset now contains 10 features instead of the 13 of the original Wine dataset (for example, it's easy to verify that ash and non-flavonoid phenols have been removed).

Of course, as for any other dimensionality reduction method, it's always suggested you verify the final accuracy with a cross-validation and make decisions only if the trade-off between loss of accuracy and complexity reduction is reasonable. Moreover, given a dataset, it's important to remember that the predictive power of the features changes with the predicted value(s).

In other words, the feature importance is not an intrinsic property of the dataset (like the principal components), but rather is a function of the specific task. It can happen that a large dataset containing thousands of features can be reduced to a fraction of them for particular predictions, while it could completely discard them if the goal is changed. If there are more targets to predict and each of them is associated with specific predictor sets, it can be a good idea to create a pipeline that outputs the training/validation sets for each task. This approach has a clear advantage with respect to using the whole dataset, in fact, in terms of XAI, it's much easier to show the responsibilities of the important features while discarding all those factors that don't play a primary role. Moreover, the computational cost is still higher than the space cost, therefore it's not an issue to have multiple specialized copies of the same dataset if this improves the model performances and helps the domain experts in understanding the outcomes.

AdaBoost

In the previous section, we saw that sampling with a replacement leads to datasets where the data points are randomly reweighted. However, if the sample size M is very large, most of the points will appear only once and, moreover, all the choices will be totally random. AdaBoost is an algorithm proposed by Schapire and Freund that tries to maximize the efficiency of each weak learner by employing adaptive boosting (the name derives from this). In particular, the ensemble is grown sequentially, and the data distribution is recomputed at each step so as to increase the weight of those points that were misclassified and reduce the weight of the ones that were correctly classified. In this way, every new learner is forced to focus on those regions that were more problematic for the previous estimators. The reader can immediately understand that, contrary to random forests and other bagging methods, boosting doesn't rely on randomness to reduce the variance and improve the accuracy; the improvement is mainly based on weighting, rather than randomness. In fact, this method works in a deterministic way and each new data distribution is chosen with a precise goal. In this paragraph, we are going to consider a variant called *Discrete AdaBoost* (formally AdaBoost.M1), which needs a classifier whose output is thresholded (for example, -1 and 1). However, real-valued versions (whose output behaves like a probability) have been developed (a classical example is shown in Friedman J., Hastie T., Tibshirani R., *Additive Logistic Regression: A Statistical View of Boosting*, Annals of Statistics, 28/1998).

As the main concepts are always the same, the reader interested in the theoretical details of other variants can immediately find them in the referenced papers.

For simplicity, the training dataset of **AdaBoost.M1** is defined as follows:

$$\begin{cases} X = \{\bar{x}_1, \bar{x}_2, \dots, \bar{x}_M\} \ where \ \bar{x}_i \in \mathbb{R}^n \\ Y = \{y_1, y_2, \dots, y_M\} \ where \ y_i \in \{-1, 1\} \end{cases}$$

This choice is not a limitation because, in multi-class problems, a one-versus-the-rest strategy can be easily employed, even if algorithms like AdaBoost.SAMME guarantee a much better performance. In order to manipulate the data distribution, we need to define a weight set:

$$\begin{cases} W^{(t)} = \left\{ w_1^{(t)}, w_2^{(t)}, \dots, w_M^{(t)} \right\} \ where \ w_i^{(t)} \in \mathbb{R}^+ \cup \{0\} \\ W^{(1)} = \left\{ \dfrac{1}{M}, \dfrac{1}{M}, \dots, \dfrac{1}{M} \right\} \end{cases}$$

The weight set allows defining an implicit data distribution $D^{(t)}(\bar{x})$, which initially is equivalent to the original one but that can be easily reshaped by changing the values w_i. Once the family and the number of estimators, N_c, have been chosen, it's possible to start the global training process. The algorithm can be applied to any kind of learner that is able to produce thresholded estimations (while the real-valued variants can work with probabilities, for example, obtained through the Platt scaling method).

The first instance $d_1(\bar{x})$ is trained with the original dataset, which means with the data distribution $D^{(1)}(\bar{x})$. The next instances, instead, are trained with the reweighted distributions $D^{(2)}(\bar{x})$, $D^{(3)}(\bar{x})$, ... $D^{(N_c)}(\bar{x})$. In order to compute them, after each training process, the normalized weighted error sum $\epsilon^{(t)}$ is computed:

$$\epsilon^{(t)} = \frac{\sum_{d_t(\bar{x}_i) \neq y_i} w_i}{\sum_{i=1}^{M} w_i}$$

This value is bounded between 0 (no misclassifications) and 1 (all data points have been misclassified) and it's employed to compute the estimator weight $\alpha^{(t)}$:

$$\alpha^{(t)} = \log \frac{1 - \epsilon^{(t)}}{\epsilon^{(t)}}$$

To understand how this function works, it's useful to consider its plot (shown in the following diagram):

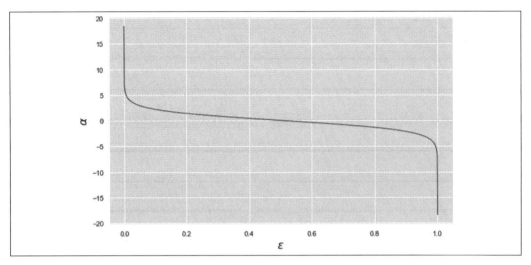

Estimator weight plot as a function of the normalized weighted error sum

This diagram unveils an implicit assumption: the worst classifier is not the one that misclassifies all points ($\epsilon^{(t)} = 1$), but a totally random binary guess (corresponding to $\epsilon^{(t)} = 0.5$). In this case, $\alpha^{(t)}$ is null and, therefore, the outcome if the estimator is completely discarded. When $\epsilon^{(t)} < 0.5$, a boosting is applied (between about 0.05 and 0.5, the trend is almost linear), but it becomes greater than 1 only when $\epsilon^{(t)} \leq 0.25$ (larger values drive to a penalty because the weight is smaller than 1). This value is a threshold to qualify an estimator as trusted or very strong and $\alpha^{(t)} \to +\infty$ in the particular case of a perfect estimator (no errors).

In practice, an upper bound should be imposed in order to avoid overflows or divisions by zero. Instead, when $\epsilon^{(t)} > 0.5$, the estimator is unacceptably weak, because it's worse than a random guess and the resulting boosting would be negative. To avoid this problem, real implementations must invert the output of such estimators, transforming them de facto into learners with $\epsilon^{(t)} < 0.5$ (this is not an issue, as the transformation is applied to all output values in the same way). It's important to consider that this algorithm shouldn't be directly applied to multi-class scenarios because, as pointed out in Zhu J., Rosset S., Zou H., Hastie T., *Multi-class AdaBoost*, Statistics and Its Inference, 02/2009, the threshold 0.5 corresponds to a random guess accuracy only for binary choices. When the number of classes is larger than two, a random estimator outputs a class with a probability $1/N_y$ (where N_y is the number of classes) and, therefore, AdaBoost.M1 will boost the classifiers in the wrong way, yielding poor final accuracies (the real threshold should be $1 - 1/N_y$, which is larger than 0.5 when $N_y > 2$).

The AdaBoost.SAMME algorithm (implemented by scikit-learn) has been proposed to solve this problem and exploit the power of boosting also in multi-class scenarios.

The global decision function is defined as follows:

$$d(\bar{x}) = sign\left(\sum_{i=1}^{N_c} \alpha^{(i)} d_i(\bar{x})\right)$$

In this way, as the estimators are added sequentially, the importance of each of them will decrease while the accuracy of $d_i(\bar{x})$ increases. However, it's also possible to observe a plateau if the complexity of X is very high. In this case, many learners will have a high weight, because the final prediction must take into account a sub-combination of learners in order to achieve an acceptable accuracy.

As this algorithm specializes the learners at each step, a good practice is to start with a small number of estimators (for example, 10 or 20) and increase the number until no improvement is achieved. Sometimes, a minimum number of good learners (like SVM or decision trees) is sufficient to reach the highest possible accuracy (limited to this kind of algorithm), but in some other cases, the number of estimators can be some thousands. Grid search and cross-validation are again the only good strategies to make the right choice.

After each training step it is necessary to update the weights in order to produce a boosted distribution. This is achieved using an exponential function (based on bipolar outputs {–1, 1}):

$$w_i^{(t+1)} = w_i^{(t)} e^{\alpha^{(t)} o_i} \ where \ o_i = \begin{cases} 1 \ if \ d_i(\bar{x}_i) \neq y_i \\ -1 \ if \ d_i(\bar{x}_i) = y_i \end{cases}$$

Given a data point $\bar{x}_i$, if it has been misclassified, its weight will be increased considering the overall estimator weight. This approach allows a further adaptive behavior because a classifier with a high $\alpha^{(t)}$ is already very accurate and a higher attention level is necessary to focus only on the (few) misclassified points.

On the contrary, if $\alpha^{(t)}$ is small, the estimator must improve its overall performance and the over-weighting process must be applied to a large subset (therefore, the distribution won't peak around a few points, but will penalize only the small subset that has been correctly classified, leaving the estimator free to explore the remaining space with the same probability).

Even if not present in the original proposal, it's also possible to include a learning rate η that multiplies the exponent:

$$w_i^{(t+1)} = w_i^{(t)} e^{\eta \alpha^{(t)} o_i}$$

A value $\eta = 1$ has no effect, while smaller values have been proven to increase the accuracy by avoiding a premature specialization. Of course, when $\eta \ll 1$, the number of estimators must be increased in order to compensate the minor reweighting and this can drive to a training performance loss. As for the other hyperparameters, the right value for η must be discovered using a cross-validation technique (alternatively, if it's the only value that must be fine-tuned, it's possible to start with one and proceed by decreasing its value until the maximum accuracy has been reached).

The complete AdaBoost.M1 algorithm is as follows:

1. Set the family and the number of estimators N_c
2. Set the initial weights $W^{(1)}$ equal to $1/M$
3. Set the learning rate η (for example, $\eta = 1$)
4. Set the initial distribution $D^{(1)}$ equal to the dataset X
5. For $i = 1$ to N_c:
    a. Train the ith estimator $d_i(\bar{x})$ with the data distribution $D^{(i)}$
    b. Compute the normalized weighted error sum $\epsilon^{(i)}$:
        If $\epsilon^{(i)} > 0.5$, invert all estimator outputs
    c. Compute the estimator weight $\alpha^{(i)}$
    d. Update the weights using the exponential formula (with or without the learning rate)
    e. Normalize the weights
6. Create the global estimator applying the sign($\bullet$) function to the weighted sum $\alpha^{(i)} d_i(\bar{x}) \ \forall \ i \in (1, N_c)$

AdaBoost.SAMME

This variant, called **Stagewise Additive Modeling using a Multi-class Exponential (SAMME)** loss, was proposed by Zhu, Rosset, Zou, and Hastie in Zhu J., Rosset S., Zou H., Hastie T., *Multi-class AdaBoost, Statistics and Its Inference*, 02/2009. The goal is to adapt AdaBoost.M1 in order to work properly in multi-class scenarios.

As this is a discrete version, its structure is almost the same, with a difference in the estimator weight computation. Let's consider a label dataset Y:

$$Y = \{y_1, y_2, \dots, y_M\} \text{ where } y_i \in (1, p)$$

Now, there are p different classes and it's necessary to consider that a random guess estimator cannot reach an accuracy equal to 0.5; therefore, the new estimator weights are computed as follows:

$$\alpha^{(t)} = \log \frac{1 - \epsilon^{(t)}}{\epsilon^{(t)}} + \log(p - 1) = \log \frac{(1 - \epsilon^{(t)})(p - 1)}{\epsilon^{(t)}}$$

In this way, the threshold is pushed forward and $\alpha^{(t)}$ will be zero when the following condition is true:

$$\epsilon^{(t)} = 1 - \frac{1}{p}$$

The following graph shows the plot of $\alpha^{(t)}$ with $p = 10$:

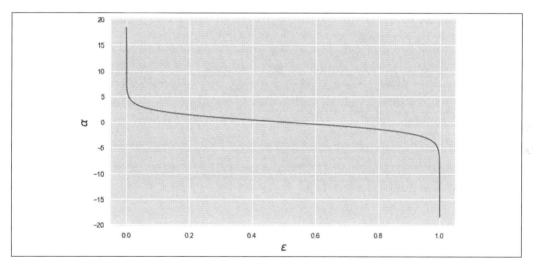

Estimator weight plot as a function of the normalized weighted error sum when $p = 10$

Employing this correction, the boosting process can successfully cope with multi-class problems without the bias normally introduced by AdaBoost.M1 when $p > 2$ ($\alpha^{(t)} > 0$ when the error is less than an actual random guess, which is a function of the number of classes).

As the performance of this algorithm is clearly superior, the majority of AdaBoost implementations aren't based on the original algorithm anymore (as already mentioned, for example, scikit-learn implements AdaBoost.SAMME and the real-valued version AdaBoost.SAMME.R). Of course, when $p = 2$, AdaBoost.SAMME is exactly equivalent to AdaBoost.M1.

AdaBoost.SAMME.R

AdaBoost.SAMME.R is a variant that works with classifiers that can output prediction probabilities. This is normally possible employing techniques such as Platt scaling, but it's important to check whether a specific classifier implementation is able to output the probabilities without any further action. For example, SVM implementations provided by scikit-learn don't compute the probabilities unless the parameter `probability=True` (because they require an extra step that could be useless in some cases).

In this case, we assume that the output of each classifier is a probability vector:

$$\hat{y}^{(t)} = d_t(\bar{x}_t) \ where \ \hat{y}^{(t)} = \left(p^{(t)}(y_t = 1|\bar{x}_t), p^{(t)}(y_t = 2|\bar{x}_t), \dots, p^{(t)}(y_t = p|\bar{x}_t) \right)^T$$

Each component is the conditional probability that the jth class is output given the input $\bar{x}_i$. When working with a single estimator, the winning class is obtained through the argmax x function; however, in this case, we want to re-weight each learner so as to obtain a sequentially grown ensemble. The basic idea is the same as AdaBoost.M1, but, as we now manage probability vectors, we also need an estimator weighting function that depends on the single point $\bar{x}_i$ (this function indeed wraps every single estimator that is now expressed as a probability vectorial function $p^{(t)}(y_t = i|\bar{x}_t)$):

$$\alpha_i^{(t)}(\bar{x}) = (p-1)\log\left(p_i^{(t)}(y = i|\bar{x}) \right) - \frac{p-1}{p}\sum_{j=1}^{p}\log\left(p_j^{(t)}(y = i|\bar{x}) \right)$$

Considering the properties of logarithms, the previous expression is equivalent to a discrete $\alpha_i^{(t)}(\bar{x})$; however, in this case, we don't rely on a weighted error sum. (The theoretical explanation is rather complex and is beyond the scope of this book. The reader can find it in the aforementioned paper, even though the method presented in *Chapter 16, Advanced Boosting Algorithms*, discloses a fundamental part of the logic.) To better understand the behavior of this function, let's consider a simple scenario with $p = 2$. The first case is a data point that the learner isn't able to classify ($p = (0.5, 0.5)$):

$$\alpha_i^{(t)}(\bar{x}) = \log\frac{1}{2} - \frac{1}{2}\left(\log\frac{1}{2} + \log\frac{1}{2}\right) = 0$$

In this case, the uncertainty is maximal, and the classifier cannot be trusted for this point, so the weight becomes null for all output probabilities. Now, let's apply the boosting, obtaining the probability vector $p = (0.7, 0.3)$:

$$\begin{cases} \alpha_1^{(t)}(\bar{x}) = \log 0.7 - \frac{1}{2}(\log 0.7 + \log 0.3) \approx 0.42 \\ \alpha_2^{(t)}(\bar{x}) = \log 0.3 - \frac{1}{2}(\log 0.7 + \log 0.3) \approx -0.42 \end{cases}$$

The first class will become positive and its magnitude will increase when $p \to 1$, while the other one is the opposite value. Therefore, the functions are symmetric and allow working with a sum:

$$d(\bar{x}) = \underset{j}{\operatorname{argmax}} \sum_{i=1}^{N_c} \alpha_j^{(i)}(\bar{x})$$

This approach is very similar to a weighted majority vote because the winning class y_i is computed taking into account not only the number of estimators whose output is y_i but also their relative weight and the negative weight of the remaining classifiers. A class can be selected only if the strongest classifiers predicted it and the impact of the other learners is not sufficient to overturn this result.

In order to update the weights, we need to consider the impact of all probabilities. In particular, we want to reduce the uncertainty (which can degenerate to a purely random guess) and force a superior attention focused on all those points that have been misclassified. To achieve this goal, we need to define the $\bar{y}_i$ and $p^{(t)}(\bar{x}_i)$ vectors, which contain, respectively, the one-hot encoding of the true class (for example, $(0, 0, 1, ..., 0)$) and the output probabilities yielded by the estimator (as a column vector). Hence, the update rule becomes as follows:

$$w_i^{(t+1)} = w_i^{(t)} e^{-\frac{\eta(p-1)}{p}(\bar{y}_i \cdot \log p^{(t)}(\bar{x}_i))}$$

If, for example, the true vector is $(1, 0)$ and the output probabilities are $(0.1, 0.9)$, with $\eta = 1$, the weight of the point will be multiplied by about 3.16. If instead, the output probabilities are $(0.9, 0.1)$, meaning the data point has been successfully classified, the multiplication factor will become closer to 1.

In this way, the new data distribution $D^{(t+1)}$, analogously to AdaBoost.M1, will be more peaked on the points that need more attention. All implementations include the learning rate as a hyperparameter because, as already explained, the default value equal to 1.0 cannot be the best choice for specific problems. In general, a lower learning rate allows reducing the instability when there are many outliers and improves the generalization ability thanks to a slower convergence towards the optimum. When $\eta < 1$, every new distribution is slightly more focused on the misclassified points, allowing the estimators to search for a better parameter set without big jumps (that can lead the estimator to skip an optimal point). However, contrary to neural networks that normally work with small batches, AdaBoost can also often perform quite well with $\eta = 1$ because the correction is applied only after a full training step. As usual, I recommend performing a grid search to select the right values for each specific problem.

The complete AdaBoost.SAMME.R algorithm is as follows:

1. Set the family and the number of estimators N_c

2. Set the initial weights $W^{(1)}$ equal to $1/M$

3. Set the learning rate η (for example, $\eta = 1$)

4. Set the initial distribution $D^{(1)}$ equal to the dataset X

5. For $i = 1$ to N_c:

    1. Train the ith estimator $d_i(\bar{x})$ with the data distribution $D^{(i)}$

    2. Compute the output probabilities for each class and each training sample

    3. Compute the estimator weights $\alpha_j^{(i)}(\bar{x})$

    4. Update the weights using the exponential formula (with or without the learning rate)

    5. Normalize the weights

6. Create the global estimator applying the argmax x function to the sum $\alpha_j^{(i)}(\bar{x})$ (for $i = 1$ to N_c)

After discussing algorithms that work with classifiers, we can now analyze a variant that has been designed and optimized to address regression problems.

AdaBoost.R2

A slightly more complex variant has been proposed by Drucker (in Drucker H., *Improving Regressors using Boosting Techniques*, ICML 1997) to manage regression problems. The weak learners are commonly decision trees and the main concepts are very similar to the other variants (in particular, the re-weighting process applied to the training dataset). The real difference is the strategy adopted in order to choose the final prediction y_i given the input data point $\bar{x}_i$. Assuming that there are N_c estimators and each of them is represented as function $d_t(\bar{x})$, we can compute the absolute residual $r_i^{(t)}$ for every input data point:

$$r_i^{(t)} = |d_t(\bar{x}_i) - y_i|$$

Once the set R_i containing all the absolute residuals has been populated, we can compute the quantity $Sr = \sup R_i$ and compute the values of a cost function that must be proportional to the error. The common choice that is normally implemented (and suggested by the author himself) is a linear loss:

$$L_i^{(t)} = \frac{r_i^{(t)}}{S_r}$$

This loss is very flat and it's directly proportional to the error. In most cases, it's a good choice because it avoids premature over-specialization and allows the estimators to readapt their structure in a gentler way. The most obvious alternative is the square loss, which starts giving more importance to those points whose prediction error is larger. It is defined as follows:

$$L_i^{(t)} = \frac{r_i^{(t)2}}{S_r^2}$$

The last cost function is strictly related to AdaBoost.M1 and it's exponential:

$$L_i^{(t)} = e^{-\frac{r_i^{(t)}}{S_r}}$$

This is normally a less robust choice because, as we are also going to discuss in the next section, it penalizes small errors in favor of larger ones. Considering that these functions are also employed in the re-weighting process, an exponential loss can force the distribution to assign very high probabilities to points whose misclassification error is high, driving the estimators to become over-specialized with effect from the first iterations. In many cases (such as in neural networks), the loss functions are normally chosen according to their specific properties but, above all, according to the ease with which they can be minimized. In this particular scenario, loss functions are a fundamental part of the boosting process and they must be chosen considering the impact on the data distribution. Testing and cross-validation provide the best tool to make a reasonable decision.

Once the loss function has been evaluated for the training sample, it's possible to build the global cost function as the weighted average of all losses. Contrary to many algorithms that simply sum or average the losses, in this case, it's necessary to consider the structure of the distribution. As the boosting process reweights the points, also the corresponding loss values must be filtered to avoid a bias. At iteration t, the cost function is computed as follows:

$$C^{(t)} = \frac{1}{\sum_j w_j^{(t)}} \sum_{i=1}^{M} \frac{L_i^{(t)}}{w_i^{(t)}}$$

This function is proportional to the weighted errors, which can be either linearly filtered or emphasized using a quadratic or exponential function. However, in all cases, a point whose weight is lower will yield a smaller contribution, letting the algorithm focus on the subsamples more difficult to predict. Consider that, in this case, we are working with classifications; therefore, the only measure we can exploit is the loss. Good points yield lower losses, hard ones yield proportionally higher losses. Even if it's possible to use $C^{(t)}$ directly, it's preferable to define a confidence measure:

$$\gamma^{(t)} = \frac{C^{(t)}}{1 - C^{(t)}}$$

This index is inversely proportional to the average confidence at iteration t. In fact, when $C^{(t)} \to 0$, $\gamma^{(t)} \to 0$ and when $C^{(t)} \to \infty$, $\gamma^{(t)} \to 1$. The weight update is performed considering the overall confidence and the specific loss value:

$$w_i^{(t+1)} = w_i \gamma^{(t)^{1-L_i^{(t)}}}$$

A weight will be decreased proportionally to the loss associated with the corresponding absolute residual. However, instead of using a fixed base, the global confidence index is chosen. This strategy allows a further degree of adaptability, because an estimator with a low confidence doesn't need to focus only on a small subset and, considering that $\gamma^{(t)}$ is bounded between 0 and 1 (worst condition), the exponential becomes ineffective when the cost function is very high, so that the weights remain unchanged. This procedure is not very dissimilar to the one adopted in other variants, but it tries to find a trade-off between global accuracy and local misclassification problems, providing an extra degree of robustness.

The most complex part of this algorithm is the approach employed to output a global prediction. Contrary to classification algorithms, we cannot easily compute an average, because it's necessary to consider the global confidence at each iteration. Drucker proposed a method based on the weighted median of all outputs. In particular, given a point $\bar{x}_i$, we define the set of predictions:

$$Y_i = \left\{ y_i^{(1)}, y_i^{(2)}, \dots, y_i^{(N_c)} \right\}$$

As weights, we consider the $\log 1/_{\gamma^{(t)}}$, so we can define a weight set:

$$\Gamma = \left\{ \log \frac{1}{\gamma^{(1)}}, \log \frac{1}{\gamma^{(2)}}, \dots, \log \frac{1}{\gamma^{(N_c)}} \right\}$$

The final output is the median of Y weighted according to Γ (normalized so that the sum is 1.0). As $\gamma^{(t)} \to 1$ when the confidence is low, the corresponding weight will tend to 0. In the same way, when the confidence is high (close to 1.0), the weight will increase proportionally and the chance to pick the output associated with it will be higher. For example, if the outputs are Y = {1, 1.2, 1.3, 2.0, 2.0, 2.5, 2.6} and the weights are Γ = { 0.35, 0.15, 0.12, 0.11, 0.1, 0.09, 0.08 }, the weighted median corresponds to the second index, therefore the global estimator will output 1.2 (which is, also intuitively, the most reasonable choice).

The procedure to find the median is quite simple:

1. The $y_i^{(t)}$ must be sorted in ascending order, so that $y_i^{(1)} \le y_i^{(2)} \le \cdots \le y_i^{(N_c)}$
2. The set Γ is sorted accordingly to the index of $y_i^{(t)}$ (each output $y_i^{(t)}$ must carry its own weight)
3. The set Γ is normalized, dividing it by its sum
4. The index corresponding to the smallest element that splits Γ into two blocks (whose sums are less than or equal to 0.5) is selected
5. The output corresponding to this index is chosen

The complete AdaBoost.R2 algorithm is as follows:

1. Set the family and the number of estimators N_c
2. Set the initial weights $W^{(1)}$ equal to $1/M$
3. Set the initial distribution $D^{(1)}$ equal to the dataset X
4. Select a loss function L
5. For $i=1$ to N_c:
   a. Train the ith estimator $d_i(\bar{x})$ with the data distribution $D^{(i)}$
   b. Compute the absolute residuals, the loss values, and the confidence measures
   c. Compute the global cost function
   d. Update the weights using the exponential formula
6. Create the global estimator using the weighted median

After a theoretical discussion about the most common AdaBoost variants, we can now focus on a practical example based on scikit-learn that can help the reader to understand how to tune up the hyperparameters and evaluate the performances.

Example of AdaBoost with scikit-learn

Let's continue using the Wine dataset in order to analyze the performance of AdaBoost with different parameters. scikit-learn, like almost all algorithms, implements both a classifier `AdaBoostClassfier` (based on the algorithm SAMME and SAMME.R) and a regressor `AdaBoostRegressor` (based on the algorithm R2). In this case, we are going to use the classifier, but I invite the reader to test the regressor using a custom dataset or one of the built-in toy datasets. In both classes, the most important parameters are `n_estimators` and `learning_rate` (default value set to 1.0).

The default underlying weak learner is always a decision tree, but it's possible to employ other models creating a base instance and passing it through the parameter `base_estimator` (of course, don't forget to normalize the dataset if the base classifier is sensitive to different scales). As explained in the chapter, real-valued AdaBoost algorithms require an output based on a probability vector. In scikit-learn, some classifiers/regressors (such as SVM) don't compute the probabilities unless it is explicitly required (setting the parameter `probability=True`); therefore, if an exception is raised, I invite you to check the documentation in order to learn how to force the algorithm to compute them.

The examples we are going to discuss have only a didactic purpose because they focus on a single parameter. In a real-world scenario, it's always better to perform a grid search (which is more expensive), so as to analyze a set of combinations. Let's start analyzing the cross-validation score as a function of the number of estimators (the vectors X and Y are the ones defined in the previous example):

```python
import numpy as np

from sklearn.ensemble import AdaBoostClassifier
from sklearn.model_selection import cross_val_score

scores_ne = []

for ne in range(10, 201, 10):
adc = AdaBoostClassifier(n_estimators=ne,
                                learning_rate=0.8,
                                random_state=1000)
    scores_ne.append(np.mean(
        cross_val_score(adc, X, Y,
                    cv=10,
                    n_jobs=-1)))
```

We have considered a range starting from 10 trees and ending with 200 trees with steps of 10 trees. The learning rate is kept constant and equal to 0.8. The resulting plot is shown in the following graph:

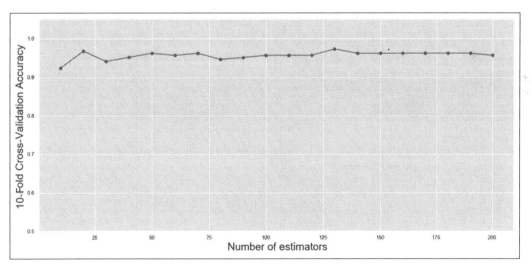

10-fold cross-validation accuracy as a function of the number of estimators

The maximum is reached with about 125 estimators. Larger values cause slight performance worsening due to the over-specialization and a consequent variance increase, while lower values suffer a marginal lack of specialization. As explained in other chapters, the capacity of a model must be tuned according to the Occam's Razor principle, not only because the resulting model can be faster to train, but also because a capacity excess is normally saturated, overfitting the training set and reducing the scope for generalization. Cross-validation can immediately show this effect, which, instead, can remain hidden when a standard training/test set split is done (above all when the samples are not shuffled).

Let's now check the performance with different learning rates (keeping the number of trees fixed to 125):

```
import numpy as np

scores_eta_adc = []

for eta in np.linspace(0.01, 1.0, 100):
adc = AdaBoostClassifier(n_estimators=125,
                         learning_rate=eta,
                         random_state=1000)
        scores_eta_adc.append(
            np.mean(cross_val_score(adc, X, Y,
                    cv=10, n_jobs=-1)))
```

The final plot is shown in the following graph:

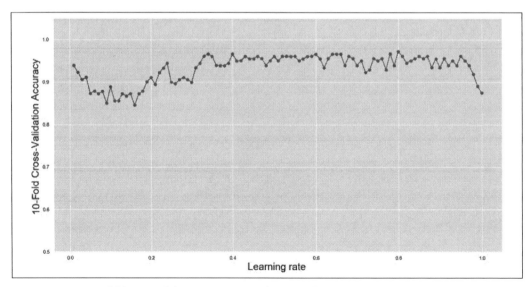

10-fold cross-validation accuracy as a function of the learning rate ($N_c = 125$)

Again, different learning rates yield different accuracies. The choice of $\eta = 0.8$ seems to be reasonable, as higher and lower values lead to performance worsening (even if they are quite similar in a small range around 0.8). This kind of analysis should be done together with the analysis of the optimal number of trees (for example, in a grid search), however a large number of combinations might result in an extremely long search time. To avoid this problem, it's possible to perform a manual check:

1. The number of estimators is set to a default initial value (for example, $N_c = 50$)

2. After setting an average learning rate η, the accuracy $a(X, Y, \bar{\theta})$ is assessed and compared with an expected baseline β

3. If $a(X, Y, \bar{\theta}) \ll \beta$:

    a. A lower/higher learning rate is selected, and the process is repeated

4. If $a(X, Y, \bar{\theta}) \geq \beta$:

    a. The optimal number of trees is searched after fixing η

This method is not effective as a grid search, but it can leverage the data scientist's experience to simplify the process, while guaranteeing a good compromise. Of course, all the other hyperparameters might be assessed in the same way. This can make the complexity explode, but it's possible to avoid such an overhead by starting with a single base classifier alone (for example, a Decision Tree) and tuning the specific hyperparameters. As some of them (for example, the impurity measure) have a direct impact on the ensemble, the choice can be extended to the whole model without a sensible precision loss.

As explained, the learning rate η has a direct impact on the re-weighting process. Very small values require a larger number of estimators because subsequent distributions are very similar. On the other side, large values can lead to a premature over-specialization. Even if the default value is 1.0, I always suggest checking the accuracy also with smaller values. There's no golden rule for picking the right learning rate in every case, but it's important to remember that lower values allow the algorithm to smoothly adapt to fit the training set in a gentler way, while higher values reduce the robustness to outliers, because the samples that have been misclassified are immediately boosted and the probability of sampling them increases very rapidly. The result of this behavior is a constant focus on those samples that may be affected by noise, almost forgetting the structure of the remaining sample space.

The last experiment we want to perform is analyzing the performance after a dimensionality reduction performed with **Principal Component Analysis (PCA)** and **Factor Analysis (FA)** (with 125 estimators and $\eta = 0.8$):

```
import numpy as np
```

```
from sklearn.decomposition import PCA, FactorAnalysis

scores_pca = []

for i in range(13, 1, -1):
if i < 12:
        pca = PCA(n_components=i,
                    random_state=1000)
        X_pca = pca.fit_transform(X)
    else:
        X_pca = X

    adc = AdaBoostClassifier(n_estimators=125,
                            learning_rate=0.8,
                            random_state=1000)
    scores_pca.append(np.mean(
cross_val_score(adc, X_pca, Y,
        n_jobs=-1, cv=10)))

scores_fa = []

for i in range(13, 1, -1):
if i < 12:
        fa = FactorAnalysis(n_components=i,
                            random_state=1000)
        X_fa = fa.fit_transform(X)
    else:
        X_fa = X

    adc = AdaBoostClassifier(n_estimators=125,
                            learning_rate=0.8,
                            random_state=1000)
    scores_fa.append(np.mean(
        cross_val_score(adc, X_fa, Y,
                    n_jobs=-1,
                    cv=10)))
```

The resulting plot is shown in the following graph:

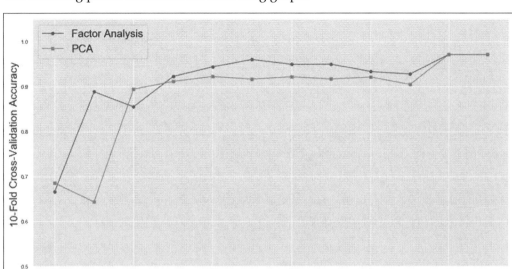

10-fold cross-validation accuracy as a function of the number of components (PCA and factor analysis)

This exercise confirms some important features analyzed in *Chapter 13, Component Analysis and Dimensionality Reduction.* First of all, performances are not dramatically affected even by a 50% dimensionality reduction. This consideration is further confirmed by the feature importance analysis performed in the previous example. Decision trees can perform quite a good classification considering only 6/7 features because the remaining ones offer a marginal contribution to the characterization of a sample. Moreover, FA is almost always superior to PCA. With 7 components, the accuracy achieved using the FA algorithm is higher than 0.95 (very close to the value achieved with no reduction), while PCA reaches this value with 12 components. The reader should remember that PCA is a particular case of FA, with the assumption of homoscedastic noise. The diagram confirms that this condition is not acceptable with the Wine dataset. Assuming different noise variances allows remodelling the reduced dataset in a more accurate way, minimizing the cross-effect of the missing features. Even if PCA is normally the first choice, with large datasets, I suggest you always compare the performance with a Factor Analysis (FA) and choose the technique that guarantees the best result (given also that FA is more expensive in terms of computational complexity).

Summary

In this chapter, we introduced the main concepts of ensemble learning, focusing on both bagging and boosting techniques. In the first section, we explained the difference between strong and weak learners, and we presented the big picture of how it's possible to combine the estimators to achieve specific goals.

The next topic focused on the properties of decision trees and their main strengths and weaknesses. In particular, we explained that the structure of a tree causes a natural increase in the variance. The bagging technique called random forests allow mitigating this problem, improving at the same time the overall accuracy. A further variance reduction can be achieved by increasing the randomness and employing a variant called extra randomized trees. In the example, we have also seen how it's possible to evaluate the importance of each input feature and perform dimensionality reduction without involving complex statistical techniques.

In the third section, we presented the most famous boosting technique, AdaBoost, which is based on the concept of creating a sequential additive model, when each new estimator is trained using a reweighted (boosted) data distribution. In this way, every learner is added to focus on the misclassified data points without interfering with the previously added models. We analyzed the original M1 discrete variant and the most effective alternatives called SAMME and SAMME.R (real-valued), and R2 (for regressions), which are implemented in many Machine Learning packages.

In the next chapter, we are going to discuss Gradient Boosting (together with some specific highly-optimized variants) and other generalized ensemble techniques.

Further reading

- Alpaydin E., *Introduction to Machine Learning*, The MIT Press, 2010
- Breiman L., *Bagging predictors*, Machine Learning, 24, 1996
- Breiman L., *Random Forests*, Machine Learning, 45, 2001
- Breiman L., *Pasting small votes for classification in large databases and on-line*, Machine Learning, 36, 1999
- Ho T., *The random subspace method for constructing decision forests*, Pattern Analysis and Machine Intelligence, 20, 1998
- Friedman J., Hastie T., Tibshirani R., *Additive Logistic Regression: A Statistical View of Boosting*, Annals of Statistics, 28/1998
- Zhu J., Rosset S., Zou H., Hastie T., *Multi-class AdaBoost*, Statistics and Its Inference, 02/2009

- Drucker H., *Improving Regressors using Boosting Techniques*, ICML 1997
- Lundberg S. M., Lee S., *A Unified Approach to Interpreting Model Predictions*, Advances in Neural Information Processing Systems 30, NIPS, 2017
- Bonaccorso G., *Machine Learning Algorithms Second Edition*, Packt Publishing, 2018

16
Advanced Boosting Algorithms

In this chapter, we are going to discuss some important algorithms that exploit different estimators to improve the overall performance of an ensemble or committee. These techniques work either by introducing a medium level of randomness in every estimator belonging to a predefined set, or by creating a sequence of estimators where each new model is forced to improve the performance of the previous ones. These techniques allow us to reduce both the bias and the variance (thereby increasing validation accuracy) when employing models with a limited capacity or that are more prone to overfit the training set.

In particular, the topics covered in the chapter are as follows:

- Gradient boosting
- Ensembles of voting classifiers, stacking, and bucketing

We can now start the exploration of the main concepts related to gradient boosting, which is an extremely flexible model that exploits both the simplicity of simpler algorithms (like decision trees) and the power of well-tuned ensembles.

Gradient boosting

At this point, we can introduce a more general method of creating boosted ensembles. Let's choose a generic algorithm family, represented as follows:

$$d_i(\bar{x}) = f(\bar{x}; \bar{\theta}_i)$$

Each model is parametrized using the vector $\bar{\theta}_i$ and there are no restrictions on the kind of method that is employed. In this case, we are going to consider decision trees (which is one of the most diffused algorithms when this boosting strategy is employed — in this case, the algorithm is known as gradient tree boosting), but the theory is generic and can be easily applied to more complex models, such as neural networks. In a decision tree, the parameter vector $\bar{\theta}_i$ is made up of selection tuples, so the reader can think of this method as a pseudo-random forest where, instead of randomness, we look for extra optimality exploiting the previous experience. In fact, as with AdaBoost, a gradient boosting ensemble is built sequentially, using a technique that is formally defined as *Forward Stage-wise Additive Modeling*. The resulting estimator is represented as a weighted sum:

$$d(\bar{x}) = \sum_{i=1}^{N_c} \alpha_i d_i(\bar{x}) + \beta\Omega(d_i) = \sum_{i=1}^{N_c} \alpha_i f(\bar{x}; \bar{\theta}_i) + \beta\Omega(f(\bar{x}; \bar{\theta}_i))$$

Therefore, the variables to manage are the single estimator weights α_i and the parameter vectors $\bar{\theta}_i$. The term $\Omega(d_i)$ is a regularization/penalty factor that is not always implemented. In the original formulation, this element was absent, but it has been introduced, for example, in the XGBoost framework. Generally, the possible penalty functions are L_1 (to achieve more sparsity) and L_2 (to prevent overfitting). In particular, the latter can be very helpful when the number of estimators grows because, even if, for example, the single decision trees have a limited maximum depth, the ensemble is potentially led to overfit given the extreme capacity. I invite the reader to always check whether the machine learning framework supports the regularization and to evaluate the performances with different values of β. However, from now on, we are excluding this term from the explanation because its role is straightforward and doesn't alter the structure of the problem (excluding the extra complexity).

In the training process, we don't have to work with the whole set, but with a single tuple $(\bar{\alpha}_i, \bar{\theta}_i)$, without modifying the values already chosen during the previous iterations. The general procedure can be summarized with a loop:

1. The estimator sum is initialized to a null value.

2. For $i = 1$ to N_c:
    ○ The best tuple $(\bar{\alpha}_i, \bar{\theta}_i)$ is chosen and the estimator $f(\bar{x}; \bar{\theta}_i)$ is trained.
    ○ $d_i(\bar{x}) = d_{i-1}(\bar{x}) + \alpha_i f(\bar{x}; \bar{\theta}_i)$.

3. The final estimator $d(\bar{x})$ is output.

How is it possible to find out the best tuple? We have already presented a strategy for improving the performance of every learner through boosting the dataset. In this case, instead, the algorithm is based on a cost function that we need to minimize:

$$C(X;Y;\bar{\alpha};\bar{\theta}) = \sum_{i=1}^{M} L(y_i, \alpha_i f(\bar{x};\bar{\theta}_i))$$

In particular, the generic optimal tuple is obtained as follows:

$$(\bar{\alpha}^*, \bar{\theta}^*) = \underset{\bar{\alpha},\bar{\theta}}{\operatorname{argmin}}\, C(X;Y;\bar{\alpha};\bar{\theta})$$

As the process is sequential, each estimator is optimized to improve the previous one's accuracy. However, contrary to AdaBoost, we are not constrained to impose a specific loss function (it's possible to prove that AdaBoost.M1 is equivalent to this algorithm with an exponential loss but the proof is beyond the scope of this book). As we are going to discuss, other cost functions can yield better performances in several different scenarios because they avoid the premature convergence toward sub-optimal minima.

The problem could be considered as solved by employing the previous formula to optimize each new learner; however, the argmin x function needs a complete exploration of the cost function space and, as $C(\cdot)$ depends on each specific model instance and, therefore, on $\bar{\theta}_i$, it's necessary to perform several retraining processes in order to find the optimal solution. Moreover, the problem is generally non-convex, and the number of variables can be very high. Numerical algorithms such as L-BFGS or other quasi-Newton methods need too many iterations and a prohibitive computational time. It's clear that such an approach is not affordable in the vast majority of cases and the gradient boosting algorithm has been proposed as an intermediate solution. The idea is to find a sub-optimal solution with a gradient descent strategy limited to a single step for each iteration.

In order to present the algorithm, it's useful to rewrite the additive model with an explicit reference to the optimal goal:

$$d_i(\bar{x}) = d_{i-1}(\bar{x}) + \underset{f}{\operatorname{argmin}} \sum_{j=1}^{M} L(y_j, d_{i-1}(\bar{x}_j) + f(\bar{x}_j;\bar{\theta}_i))$$

Note that the cost function is computed carrying on all the previously trained models; therefore, the correction is always incremental. If the cost function $L(\cdot)$ is differentiable (a fundamental condition that is not difficult to meet), it's possible to compute the gradient with respect to the current additive model (at the ith iteration, we need to consider the additive model obtained summing all the previous $i - 1$ models):

$$\nabla_d \left[\sum_{j=1}^{M} L\left(y_j, d_{i-1}(\bar{x}_j) + f(\bar{x}_j; \bar{\theta}_i)\right) \right] = \sum_{j=1}^{M} \nabla_d L\left(y_j, d_{i-1}(\bar{x}_j)\right)$$

At this point, a new classifier can be added by moving the current additive model into the negative direction of the gradient:

$$d_i(\bar{x}) = d_{i-1}(\bar{x}) - \eta \alpha_i \sum_{j=1}^{M} \nabla_d L\left(y_j, d_{i-1}(\bar{x}_j)\right)$$

We haven't considered the parameter α_i yet (nor the learning rate η, which is a constant). However, the reader familiar with some basic calculus can immediately understand that the effect of an update is to reduce the value of the global loss function by forcing the next model to improve its accuracy with respect to its predecessors. However, a single gradient step isn't enough to guarantee an appropriate boosting strategy. In fact, as discussed previously, we also need to weight each classifier according to its ability to reduce the loss. Once the gradient has been computed, it's possible to determine the best value for the weight α_i with a direct minimization of the loss function (using a line search algorithm) computed considering the current additive model with α as an extra variable:

$$\alpha_i = \underset{\alpha}{\operatorname{argmin}} \sum_{j=1}^{M} L\left(y_j, d_i(\bar{x}_j, \alpha)\right) = \underset{\alpha}{\operatorname{argmin}} \sum_{j=1}^{M} L\left(y_j, d_{i-1}(\bar{x}_j) - \eta \alpha \sum_{j=1}^{M} \nabla_d L\left(y_j, d_{i-1}(\bar{x}_j)\right)\right)$$

When using the gradient tree boosting variant, an improvement can be achieved by splitting the weight α_i into m sub-weights $\alpha_i^{(j)}$ associated with each terminal node of the tree. The computational complexity is slightly increased, but the final accuracy can be higher than the one obtained with a single weight. The reason derives from the functional structure of a tree. As the boosting forces a specialization in specific regions, a single weight could drive to an over-estimation of a learner also when a specific data point cannot be correctly classified.

Instead, using different weights, it's possible to operate a fine-grained filtering of the result, accepting or discarding an outcome according to its value and to the properties of the specific tree.

This solution cannot provide the same accuracy of a complete optimization, but it's rather fast and it's possible to compensate for this loss using more estimators and a lower learning rate. Like many other algorithms, gradient boosting must be tuned up in order to yield the maximum accuracy with a low variance. The learning rate is normally quite smaller than 1.0 and its value should be found by validating the results and considering the total number of estimators (it's better to reduce it when more learners are employed). Moreover, a regularization technique could be added in order to prevent overfitting. When working with specific classifier families (such as logistic regression or neural networks), it's very easy to include an L_1 or L_2 penalty, but it's not so easy with other estimators. For this reason, a common regularization technique (implemented also by scikit-learn) is the downsampling of the training dataset. Selecting $P < N$ random data points allows the estimators to reduce the variance and prevent overfitting.

Alternatively, it's possible to employ a random feature selection (for gradient tree boosting only) as in a random forest; picking a fraction of the total number of features increases the uncertainty and avoids over-specialization. Of course, the main drawback to these techniques is a loss of accuracy (proportional to the downsampling/feature selection ratio) that must be analyzed in order to find the most appropriate trade-off.

Loss functions for gradient boosting

Before moving to the next section, it's useful to briefly discuss the main loss/ cost functions that are normally employed with this kind of algorithm. In the first chapter, we have presented some common cost functions, like mean squared error, Huber Loss (very robust in regression contexts), and cross-entropy. They are all valid examples, but there are other functions that are peculiar to classification problems. The first one is exponential loss, defined as follows:

$$L\left(y_i, f(\bar{x}_i;\, \bar{\theta})\right) = e^{-y_i\, f(\bar{x}_i;\, \bar{\theta})}$$

As pointed out by Hastie, Tibshirani, and Friedman, this function transforms the gradient boosting into an AdaBoost.M1 algorithm. The corresponding cost function has a very precise behavior that sometimes is not the most adequate to solve particular problems. In fact, the result of an exponential loss has a very high impact when the error is large, yielding distributions that are strongly peaked around a few points.

The subsequent classifiers can be consequently driven to over-specialize their structure to cope only with a small data region, with a concrete risk of losing the ability to correctly classify other points. In many situations, this behavior is not dangerous and the final bias-variance trade-off is absolutely reasonable; however, there are problems where a softer loss function can allow a better final accuracy and generalization ability. The most common choice for real-valued binary classification problems is **binomial negative log-likelihood loss** (deviance), defined as follows (in this case, we are assuming that the classifier $f(\cdot)$ is not thresholded, but outputs a positive-class probability):

$$L\left(y_i, f(\bar{x}_i; \bar{\theta})\right) = y_i \log f(\bar{x}_i; \bar{\theta}) + (1 - y_i)\log(1 - f(\bar{x}_i; \bar{\theta}))$$

This loss function is the same employed in logistic regressions and, unlike exponential loss, doesn't yield peaked distributions. Two misclassified points with different probabilities are boosted proportionally to the error (not the exponential value), so as to force the classifiers to focus on all the misclassified population with almost the same probability (of course, a higher probability assigned to points whose error is very large is desirable, assuming that all the other misclassified points have always a good chance to be selected). The natural extension of the Binomial Negative Log-Likelihood Loss to multi-class problems is the **multinomial negative log-likelihood loss**, defined as follows (the classifier $f(\cdot)$ is represented as a probability vector with p components):

$$L\left(y_i, \bar{f}(\bar{x}_i; \bar{\theta})\right) = -\sum_{j=1}^{p} I_{y_i=j} \log f_j(\bar{x}_i; \bar{\theta})$$

In the previous formula, the notation $I_{y=j}$ must be interpreted as an indicator function, which is equal to 1 when $y = j$ and 0 otherwise. The behavior of this loss function is perfectly analogous to the binomial variant and, in general, it is the default choice for classification problems. The reader is invited to test the examples with both exponential loss and deviance and compare the results. Before showing the complete algorithm, it's helpful to consider also a more complete version of the cost functions, including the regularization terms:

$$L_R\left(y_i, f(\bar{x}_i; \bar{\theta})\right) = L\left(y_i, f(\bar{x}_i; \bar{\theta})\right) + \beta g(\bar{\theta})$$

The function $g(\bar{\theta})$ has no particular restrictions. In general, however, it's either the square L_2 norm $\left(g(\bar{\theta}) = \|\bar{\theta}\|_2^2\right)$, or the L_1 norm $\left(g(\bar{\theta}) = \|\bar{\theta}\|_1\right)$. The constant β controls the strength of the regularization.

Considering the nature of these models, which have a very large capacity and might easily overfit, it's always a good idea to evaluate a trade-off between, for example, the maximum depth of a decision tree and L_2 regularization. In fact, while the former incentivizes the reduction of the bias (with, sometimes, a dramatic increase of the variance), the latter has the opposite effect, guaranteeing always a reasonable generalization ability. The L_1 norm, which is mainly employed to induce sparsity, is less helpful in the context of gradient boosting because, even if many parameters become null, the ensemble will always use them all to operate.

The complete gradient boosting algorithm is as follows:

1. Set the family and the number of estimators N_c.
2. Select a loss function L (for example, deviance).
3. Select a regularization strategy and the value of the parameter β.
4. Initialize the base estimator $d_0(\bar{x})$ as a constant (such as 0) or using another model.
5. Set the learning rate η (for example, $\eta = 1$).
6. For $i = 1$ to N_c:

    a. Compute the gradient $\nabla_d L$ using the additive model at the step $i - 1$.
    b. Train the ith estimator $d_i(\bar{x})$ with the data distribution $\{(\bar{x}_i, \quad \nabla_d L(y_i, d_{i-1}(\bar{x}_i)))\}$.
    c. Perform a line search to compute α_i.
    d. Add the estimator to the ensemble.

Example of gradient tree boosting with scikit-learn

In this example, we want to employ a gradient tree boosting classifier (class `GradientBoostingClassifier`) and check the impact of the maximum tree depth (parameter `max_depth`) on performance. Considering the previous example, we start by setting `n_estimators=50` and `learning_rate=0.8`:

```
import numpy as np
import joblib

from sklearn.ensemble import GradientBoostingClassifier
from sklearn.model_selection import cross_val_score

scores_md = []
eta = 0.8
```

```
for md in range(2, 13):
gbc = GradientBoostingClassifier(n_estimators=50,
                                 learning_rate=eta,
                                 max_depth=md,
                                 random_state=1000)
    scores_md.append(np.mean(
        cross_val_score(gbc, X, Y,
                        n_jobs=joblib.cpu_count(), cv=10)))
```

The result is shown in the following diagram:

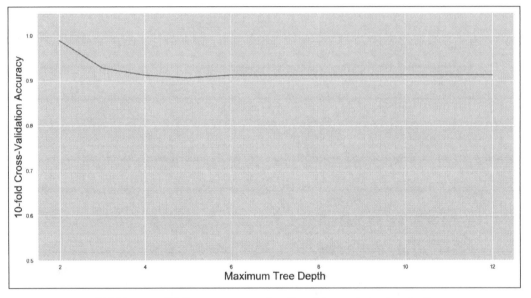

10-fold cross-validation accuracy as a function of the maximum tree depth

As explained in the first section, the maximum depth of a decision tree is strictly related to the possibility of interaction among features. This can be a positive or negative aspect when the trees are employed in an ensemble. A very high interaction level can create over-complex separation hyperplanes and reduce the overall variance. In other cases, a limited interaction results in a higher bias.

With this particular (and simple) dataset, the gradient boosting algorithm can achieve better performances when the max depth is two (consider that the root has a depth equal to zero) and this is partially confirmed by both the feature importance analysis and dimensionality reductions.

In many real-world situations, the result of such research could be completely different, with increased performance. Therefore, I suggest you cross-validate the results (it's better to employ a grid search) starting from a minimum depth and increasing the value until the maximum accuracy has been achieved. With `max_depth=2`, we now want to tune up the learning rate η, which is a fundamental parameter in this algorithm:

```python
import numpy as np

scores_eta = []

for eta in np.linspace(0.01, 1.0, 100):
gbr = GradientBoostingClassifier(n_estimators=50,
                                 learning_rate=eta,
                                 max_depth=2,
                                 random_state=1000)
        scores_eta.append(
            np.mean(cross_val_score(gbr, X, Y,
                        n_jobs=-1, cv=10)))
```

The corresponding plot is shown in the following diagram:

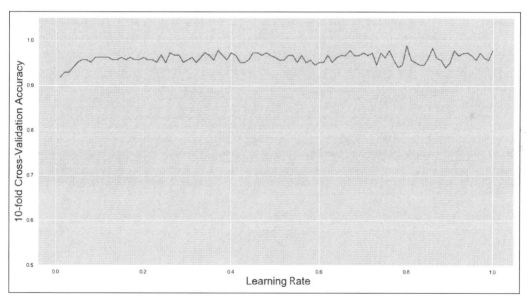

10-fold cross-validation accuracy as a function of the learning rate (max depth equal to 2)

Unsurprisingly, gradient tree boosting outperforms AdaBoost with $\eta \approx 0.8$, achieving a cross-validation accuracy slightly lower than 0.99. The example is very simple, but it clearly shows the power of this kind of techniques. The main drawback is the complexity.

Contrary to single models, ensembles are more sensitive to changes to the hyperparameters and more detailed research must be conducted in order to optimize the models. When the datasets are not excessively large, cross-validation remains the best choice. If, instead, we are pretty sure that the dataset represents almost perfectly the underlying data-generating process, it's possible to shuffle it and split it into two (training/test) or three blocks (training/test/validation) and proceed by optimizing the hyperparameters and trying to overfit the test set; this expression can seem strange, but overfitting the test set means maximizing the generalization ability while learning perfectly the training set structure.

Example of gradient boosting with XGBoost

XGBoost (`https://xgboost.readthedocs.io/en/latest`) is a popular distributed framework for modeling and training gradient boosting algorithms. It has been designed to be extremely fast (the backend is written in C++) and parallelizable using the majority of distributed infrastructures (for example, Yarn or Dask). Moreover, it offers interfaces for different languages and can help solve problems with extremely huge datasets through the implementations of not only gradient boosting, but also parallel random forests and AdaBoost models. The framework is quite complex and requires a dedicated resource to analyze all its features (two good starting points are the official documentation and the video course *Starttech Educational Services LLP, Decision Trees, Random Forests, AdaBoost, and XGBoost in Python*, Packt Publishing, 2019). In this context, we are more interested in showing how to train a gradient boosting model using XGBoost and how to evaluate the feature importance to increase the interpretability of the model. As we are already familiar with it, we are continuing using the Wine dataset, but, in this case, our analysis will be a little bit deeper.

As a first step, we need to load the dataset and, for our convenience, split it into training and test sets (15% of the sample size):

```
from sklearn.datasets import load_wine
from sklearn.model_selection import train_test_split

wine = load_wine()
X, Y = wine["data"], wine["target"]

X_train, X_test, Y_train, Y_test = \
        train_test_split(X, Y,
```

```
                        test_size=0.15,
                        random_state=1000)
```

At this point, we need to prepare the data in a format called DMatrix, which is compatible with XGBoost. Luckily, the framework allows us to load almost any kind of data structure. Therefore, we just need to instantiate the classes:

```
import xgboost as xgb

dall = xgb.DMatrix(X, label=Y,
                        feature_names=wine['feature_names'])
dtrain = xgb.DMatrix(X_train, label=Y_train,
                        feature_names=wine['feature_names'])
dtest = xgb.DMatrix(X_test, label=Y_test,
                        feature_names=wine['feature_names'])
```

Some of the main advantages of DMatrices is that they are ready to be parallelized and encode all necessary information about the data (in a way similar to a pandas DataFrame).

The Wine dataset is multiclass (there are 3 classes); therefore we cannot use a binary representation for the output. XGBoost offers two valid alternatives for multiclass problems: Softmax and Softprob. We are employing the latter, which is often known as Softmax. In fact, the output will be a probability vector $y^i = (p(c = 1), p(c = 2), \dots p(c = m))$ where each term $p(c = i)$ represents the relative probability that the right class is i. This method is extremely helpful in deep learning and also enables an analysis of borderline cases (for example, given three classes, $p(c = i) \approx 0.33 \ \forall i \in (1,3)$). Considering that we are working with probabilities, a loss function can employ the log-loss, which, for a sample size equal to N and N_y classes, is defined as:

$$L_{log} = -\frac{1}{N} \sum_{i=1}^{N} \sum_{j=1}^{N_c} I_{y_i=j} \log p(y_i = j)$$

In the previous formula, $I_{y_i=j} = 1$ if the point $\bar{x}_i$ is associated with the jth label and 0 otherwise. Of course, L_{log} must be minimized because $L_{log} \to 0$ if all samples have probability 1 associated with their actual class. In order to start performing an initial CV, we need to prepare a parameter dictionary:

```
import joblib
params = {
    'n_estimators': 50,
    'max_depth': 2,
    'eta': 1.0,
    'objective': 'multi:softprob',
```

```
'eval_metric': 'mlogloss',
'num_class': 3,
'lambda': 1.0,
'seed': 1000,
'nthread': joblib.cpu_count(),
}
```

The max depth of the trees (N_c = 50) has been set to 2 to avoid overfitting. The learning rate η has been set to 1.0 and the parameter λ, which controls the L_2 regularization, has been kept to its default value (1.0). This choice has been made after a simple grid search, but I invite the reader to re-implement the exercise using the XGClassifier class, which is compatible with scikit-learn and can be analyzed using GridSearchCV. It's always important to repeat that such large-capacity models, when working with small datasets, can easily overfit. This behavior would be paradoxical, because the validation accuracy could be lower than a simpler linear model. The use of L_2 regularization prevents the model (or, at least, mitigates the tendency) from overlearning the training set, hence its usage is always a factor to consider.

At this point, we can perform a CV with 10 folds:

```
nb_rounds = 20
cv_model = xgb.cv(params, dall,
                  nb_rounds,
                  nfold=10,
                  seed=1000)
print(cv_model.describe())
```

The output variable `cv_model` is a pandas DataFrame containing the train/test means and standard deviations computed using all the folds. A pretty print is shown in the following figure:

	train-mlogloss-mean	train-mlogloss-std	test-mlogloss-mean	test-mlogloss-std
count	20.000000	20.000000	20.000000	20.000000
mean	0.033196	0.001857	0.148413	0.092082
std	0.064994	0.003283	0.066968	0.005618
min	0.008251	0.000152	0.116997	0.079161
25%	0.008623	0.000274	0.119181	0.090248
50%	0.009486	0.000468	0.122765	0.091888
75%	0.016936	0.001275	0.136085	0.092663
max	0.284897	0.012273	0.399082	0.110782

Summary of CV statistics

As we have performed 20 rounds (iterations), the statistics are collected after each of them. The minimum average test log-loss is about 0.117 ± 0.08, which can be reasonable for this task. If better performances are required, it's possible to try to increase the number of estimators, the number of rounds, the max depth, and the regularization term.

Let's try now to train the classifier and to test it using the test set previously prepared:

```
evals = [(dtest, 'test'), (dtrain, 'train')]
model = xgb.train(params, dtrain,
                  nb_rounds, evals)
```

The output of the previous snippet is:

```
[0]     test-mlogloss:0.458516     train-mlogloss:0.278145
[1]     test-mlogloss:0.287964     train-mlogloss:0.113728

...

[18]    test-mlogloss:0.137905     train-mlogloss:0.00886
[19]    test-mlogloss:0.137903     train-mlogloss:0.00886
```

The classifier is almost overfitting, but, as there's a small decrease in the test log-loss and the train log-loss is constant, we can accept the results. Moreover, the final test log-loss is compatible with the CV scores (even if it's in the higher part of the tail). In a real-life case, a larger training set is probably the best choice (if feasible), but in our case, we do not have this possibility. On the other side, the CV scores are based on 18 test samples ($^1/_{10}$), while 15% of 178 is about 27. Therefore, we are training with fewer data points and the test is proportionally worse. The reader can change this value (for example, 10%), taking care not to reduce the test size too much because the sample size is already quite small (178) and it's easy to overfit the classifier.

Let's now test the model:

```
from sklearn.metrics import confusion_matrix

Y_pred = model.predict(dtest)
print(confusion_matrix(Y_test,
                       np.argmax(Y_pred, axis=1)))
```

The output of the previous snippet containing the confusion matrix is:

```
[[ 6  0  0]
 [ 0 13  1]
 [ 0  0  7]]
```

Hence, there is only one misclassification, which corresponds to about 96% accuracy. This value is compatible with our previous results, but it suffers from a common phenomenon due to the exclusion of data regions from the training sample. Considering the CV scores, this test set corresponds to one of the worst situations, also if the number of misclassifications will always be very small due the sample size. In the next example, we are going to see how a simple trick can solve this problem (given the nature of this dataset). For now, we can consider this result as acceptable, but the reader is warned not to give up immediately, nor to accept a validation result as an immutable value. The grid search of the optimal hyperparameter configuration remains the best choice in most cases (possibly including some prior knowledge about the most appropriate search regions – for example, it often doesn't make sense to evaluate too small or too large learning rates).

Evaluating the predictive power of the features

As the base estimators are decision trees, we can ask XGBoost to output the feature importances, but in this case, we want to employ a more interesting solution called SHAP (`https://github.com/slundberg/shap`), which is a very promising XAI approach. The idea is discussed in Lundberg S. M., Lee S., *A Unified Approach to Interpreting Model Predictions, Advances in Neural Information Processing Systems 30*, NIPS, 2017, and it's based on a common strategy to create interpretable models. As previously discussed, when a model has the form $y = ax_1 + bx_2 + \ldots + k$ and the variables are standardized, the coefficients are directly proportional to the predictive power of each specific feature. Unfortunately, only a few models are so simple, but it's possible to find an approximation of a model $f(\bar{x}; \bar{\theta})$ using an additive approach:

$$g(\bar{x}_i; \bar{\psi}) = \psi_0 + \sum_j \psi_k \bar{x}^{(j)}$$

The model $g(\bar{x}_i; \bar{\psi})$ plays the role of an explanatory one and it is generally built employing some techniques that limit the sample space to avoid a complexity explosion. As we are going to employ this method many other times, we can limit our discussion now, saying that the ψ_i coefficients are chosen to exploit a game theory result (they are called Shapley values after their creator) that allow us to understand how much a prediction is affected when conditioning on a particular feature. In a very simplified way, we can suppose that a function with N features has values in the range (a, b). If we have no knowledge about the parameters, we can only average the function (maximum uncertainty) $E[f(\bar{x}; \bar{\theta})]$. When some features are added, the expected value can be conditioned on the knowledge of these variables $E[f(\bar{x}; \bar{\theta})|x_1, x_2, \ldots, x_k]$.

This process (in an additive fashion) increases the accuracy of the prediction until we reach a point value $f(\bar{x}_i; \bar{\theta})$ that doesn't require any averaging (because the features saturate all degrees of freedom). In this way, when a feature is added to the model, its contribution can be evaluated from two viewpoints:

- The sign, which determines the direction of the influence (toward the real value or in the opposite direction)

- The magnitude, which provides the essential content in terms of importance (the larger it is, the more important the feature is)

To better understand (even without all the details) this process, let's compute the feature importance summary associated with our XGBoost model using SHAP (installable using the standard command `pip install shap`):

```
import shap

xg_explainer = shap.TreeExplainer(model)
shap_values = xg_explainer.shap_values(X)
```

The first command instantiates an explainer (which creates the structure of the explanation model), while the second fits the explanation model by finding the coefficients (the SHAP values). The output of the summary is shown in the following plot:

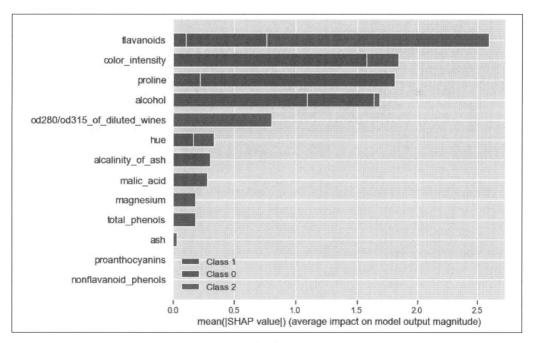

SHAP summary for the XGBoost model

The features are sorted in descending order and it's not surprising to find almost the same order yielded by other algorithms. The main difference is that now we have a measure of the predictive power of the features also with respect to the three classes. For example, flavonoids give a very strong contribution to choose/reject **Class 2**, while color intensity is dominant for **Class 1**. Taking the first three attributes, we have almost a complete explanation of every prediction. In fact, when, for example, the output is **Class 0**, the strongest contribution comes from proline (with a secondary contribution provided by the alkalinity of ash and total phenols).

In this case, it's easy to establish that the average value of proline for **Class 0** is about double the value for the other two classes (with similar standard deviations) and the class with the smallest proline content is 1 (this justifies the marginal contribution to the prediction). A domain expert might immediately recognize this pattern, but when the models (and the datasets) are much more complex, the interpretability becomes essential to understand the processes that led to a prediction. In this example, we haven't explicitly discussed the dependence between features, assuming that it is encoded in the tree structures. However, there are SHAP explainer instances and specific hyperparameters that allow independent features to be assumed or to model more complex scenarios (like deep neural networks). Over the next few chapters, we are going to show other interesting features.

Ensembles of voting classifiers

A simpler but no less effective way to create an ensemble is based on the idea of exploiting a limited number of strong learners whose peculiarities allow them to yield better performances in particular regions of the sample space. Let's start considering a set of N_c discrete-valued classifiers, $f_1(\bar{x}), f_2(\bar{x}), \dots, f_{N_c}(\bar{x})$. The algorithms are different, but they are all trained with the same dataset and output the same label set. The simplest strategy is based on a hard-voting approach:

$$\hat{y}_i = \text{argmax}\big(n(y_1), n(y_2), \dots, n(y_{N_c})\big)$$

In this case, the function $n(\cdot)$ counts the number of estimators that output the label y_i. This method is rather powerful in many cases but has some limitations. If we rely only on a majority vote, we are implicitly assuming that a correct classification is obtained by a large number of estimators. Even if, $^{N_c}/_2 + 1$ votes are necessary to output a result, in many cases, their number is much higher. Moreover, when k is not very large, also $^{N_c}/_2 + 1$ votes imply a symmetry that involves a large part of the population. This condition often drives to the training of useless models that could be simply replaced by a single well-fitted strong learner.

In fact, let's suppose that the ensemble is made up of three classifiers and one of them is more specialized in regions where the other two can easily be driven to misclassifications. A hard-voting strategy applied to this ensemble could continuously penalize the more complex estimator in favor of the other classifiers. A more accurate solution can be obtained by considering real-valued outcomes. If each estimator outputs a probability vector, the confidence of a decision is implicitly encoded in the values. For example, a binary classifier whose output is (0.52, 0.48) is much more uncertain than another classifier outputting (0.95, 0.05). Applying a threshold is equivalent to flattening the probability vectors and discarding the uncertainty.

Let's consider an ensemble with three classifiers and a data point that is hard to classify because it's very close to the separation hyperplane. A hard-voting strategy decides for the first class because the thresholded output is (1, 1, 2). Then, we check the output probabilities, obtaining (0.51, 0.49), (0.52, 0.48), (0.1, 0.9). After averaging the probabilities, the ensemble output becomes about (0.38, 0.62) and by applying argmax x, we get the second class as the final decision. In general, it's also a good practice to consider a weighted average, so that the final class is obtained as follows (assuming the output of the classifier is a probability vector):

$$\hat{y}_i = \operatorname{argmax} \frac{1}{N_c} \sum_{j=1}^{N_c} w_i \bar{f}_j(\bar{x}_i) \ where \ \bar{f}_j(\bar{x}_i) = \left(p_j(\hat{y}_j = 1), p_j(\hat{y}_j = 2), \dots, p_j(\hat{y}_j = p) \right)$$

The weights can be simply equal to 1.0 if no weighting is required or they can reflect the level of trust we have for each classifier. An important rule is to avoid the dominance of a classifier in the majority of cases because it would be an implicit fallback to a single estimator scenario. A good voting example should always allow a minority to overturn a result when their confidence is quite higher than the majority. In these strategies, the weights can be considered as hyperparameters and tuned up using a grid search with cross-validation. However, contrary to other ensemble methods, they are not fine-grained. Therefore, the optimal value is often a compromise among some different possibilities.

A slightly more complex technique is called stacking and consists of using an extra classifier as a post-filtering step. The classical approach consists of training the classifiers separately, then the whole dataset is transformed into a prediction set (based on class labels or probabilities), and the combining classifier is trained to associate the predictions with the final classes. Using even very simple models such as logistic regressions or perceptrons, it's possible to mix up the predictions so as to implement a dynamic reweighting that is a function of the input values.

A more complex approach is feasible only when a single training strategy can be used to train the whole ensemble (including the combiner). For example, it could be employed with neural networks that, however, already have an implicit flexibility and can often perform quite better than complex ensembles.

Example of voting classifiers with scikit-learn

In this example, we are going to employ again the Wine dataset. As the concept is very simple, our goal is to show how to combine two completely different estimators to improve the overall cross-validation accuracy. For this reason, we have selected a logistic regression and a non-linear classifier (an RBF SVM), which are structurally different. In particular, while the former is a linear model, the latter is a kernel-based classifier that can solve complex non-linear problems.

The reason why we are employing these algorithms is that we'd like to classify correctly the majority of data points using the linear model and exploit the non-linear abilities of the SVM to reduce the uncertainty associated with borderline points. As already pointed out, this dataset is quite simple and it's surprising how accurate a soft voting classifier can be compared to the complexity of other methods.

This observation has to be considered from two opposite viewpoints. The first one is about the complexity of the datasets employed in the examples (which often require an ensemble). We have already explained that our goal is to show the effectiveness of the methodologies and not to apply them in real-life cases that require long training phases. Therefore, the results previously obtained are absolutely valid and show how such models can overcome the limits of simpler algorithms.

On the other side, it's helpful to consider this example as an actual application of the Occam's razor principle. Sometimes, more complex models seem to perform better, but slight modifications of simpler ones can make them much more accurate and cost-effective. Considering that this is a didactic book, the reader should pay attention to this kind of compromise and learn when it makes sense to dedicate some time to optimize simpler models instead of switching to more complex (and often unmanageable) solutions.

As usual, the first step of the exercise consists in loading and normalizing the dataset:

```
import numpy as np

from sklearn.datasets import load_wine
from sklearn.preprocessing import StandardScaler

wine = load_wine()
```

```
X, Y = wine["data"], wine["target"]
ss = StandardScaler()
X = ss.fit_transform(X)
```

At this point, we need to evaluate the performances of both estimators individually:

```
from sklearn.linear_model import LogisticRegression
from sklearn.svm import SVC


svm = SVC(kernel='rbf',
            gamma=0.01,
            random_state=1000)
print('SCM score: {:.3f}'.format(
        np.mean(cross_val_score(svm, X, Y,
                n_jobs=-1, cv=10))))

lr = LogisticRegression(C=2.0,
                        max_iter=5000,
                        solver='lbfgs',
                        multi_class='auto',
                        random_state=1000)

print('Logistic Regression score: {:.3f}'.format(
        np.mean(cross_val_score(lr, X, Y,
                n_jobs=joblib.cpu_count(), cv=10))))
```

The output of the previous snippet is:

SVM score: 0.984

Logistic Regression score: 0.984

As expected, the logistic regression achieved a similar average CV accuracy as the SVM (about 98.4%). Therefore, considering the different nature of the classifiers, a hard-voting strategy is not the best choice. As we trust both classifiers and we'd like to exploit the individual features, we have chosen a soft voting with a weight vector set to (0.5, 0.5). In this way, no classifier is dominant and each of them will contribute equally to the prediction. Of course, we expect the SVM to be determinant in all those borderline cases where the linearity of the logistic regression loses the ability to capture small deviances.

The class VotingClassifier accepts a list of tuples (name of the estimator, instance) that must be supplied through the estimators parameter.

The strategy can be specified using parameter voting (it can be either "soft" or "hard") and the optional weights, using the parameter with the same name:

```
from sklearn.ensemble import VotingClassifier

vc = VotingClassifier(estimators=[
        ('LR', LogisticRegression(C=2.0,
                                  max_iter=5000,
                                  solver='lbfgs',
                                  multi_class='auto',
                                  random_state=1000)),
        ('SVM', SVC(kernel='rbf',
                gamma=0.01,
                probability=True,
                random_state=1000))],
        voting='soft',
        weights=(0.5, 0.5))

print('Voting classifier score: {:.3f}'.format(
        np.mean(cross_val_score(vc, X, Y,
                n_jobs=-1, cv=10))))
```

The output is:

```
Voting classifier score: 0.994
```

Using a soft-voting strategy, the resulting estimator is able to outperform both the logistic regression and the SVM by reducing the global uncertainty and reaching an average CV score of about 99.4%. Indeed, the Wine dataset is almost linearly separable, but there are a few data points that lie in the region that must always be misclassified with a linear model. The presence of the RBF SVM enables this limit to be overcome and *helps* the logistic regression when the sigmoid value is close to 0.5. In those cases, the contribution of the SVM is enough to push the output above or below the threshold so as to obtain a precise final classification.

As a further exercise, I invite the reader to test this algorithm with other datasets, using more estimators, and try to find out the optimal combination using both the hard-and soft-voting strategies.

Ensemble learning as model selection

This is not a proper ensemble learning technique, but it is sometimes known as bucketing. In the previous section, we have discussed how a few strong learners with different peculiarities can be employed to make up a committee.

However, in many cases, a single learner is enough to achieve a good bias-variance trade-off, but it's not so easy to choose among the whole machine learning algorithm population. For this reason, when a family of similar problems must be solved (they can differ but it's better to consider scenarios that can be easily compared), it's possible to create an ensemble containing several models and use cross-validation to find the one whose performances are the best. At the end of the process, a single learner will be used, but its choice can be considered like a grid search with a voting system.

Sometimes, this technique can unveil important differences even using similar datasets. For example, during the development of a system, a first dataset (X_1, Y_1) is provided. Everybody expects that it is correctly sampled from an underlying data-generating process p_{data} and, so, a generic model is fitted and evaluated. Let's imagine that an SVM achieves a very high validation accuracy (evaluated using a k-fold cross-validation) and, therefore, it is chosen as the final model. Unfortunately, a second, larger dataset (X_2, Y_2) is provided and the final mean accuracy worsens. We might simply think that the residual variance of the model cannot let it generalize correctly or, as sometimes happens, we can say that the second dataset contains many outliers that are not correctly classified.

The real situation is a little more complex: given a dataset, we can only suppose that it represents a complete data distribution. Even when the number of data points is very high or we use data augmentation techniques, the population might not represent some particular points that will be analyzed by the system we are developing. Bucketing is a good way to create a security buffer that can be exploited whenever the scenario changes. The ensemble can be made up of completely different models, models belonging to the same family but differently parametrized (for example, different kernel SVMs) or a mixture of composite algorithms (such as PCA + SVM, and PCA + decision trees/random forests). The most important element is the cross-validation. As explained in the first chapter, splitting the dataset into training and test sets can be an acceptable solution only when the number of points and their variability is high enough to justify the belief that it correctly represents the final data distribution. This often happens in deep learning, where the dimensions of the datasets are quite large, and the computational complexity doesn't allow retraining of the model too many times.

Instead, in classical machine learning contexts, cross-validation is the only way to check the behavior of a model when trained with a large random subset and tested on the remaining subsample. Ideally, we'd like to observe the same performances, but it can also happen that the accuracy is higher in some folds and quite a bit lower in others. When this phenomenon is observed and the dataset is the final one, it probably means that the model is not able to manage one or more regions of the sample space and a boosting approach could dramatically improve the final accuracy.

Summary

In this chapter, we extended the concept of ensemble learning to a generic forward stage-wise additive model, where the task of each new estimator is to minimize a generic cost function. Considering the complexity of a full optimization, a gradient descent technique was presented that, combined with an estimator weight line search, can yield excellent performances, both in classification and in regression problems.

The remainder of the chapter covered how to build ensembles using a few strong learners, averaging their prediction or considering a majority vote. We discussed the main drawback of thresholded classifiers, and we showed how it's possible to build a soft-voting model that is able to trust the estimator that shows less uncertainty. Other useful topics are the stacking method, which consists of using an extra classifier to process the prediction of each member of the ensemble and how it's possible to create candidate ensembles that are evaluated using a cross-validation technique to find out the best estimator for each specific problem.

In the next chapter, we are going to begin discussing the most important deep learning techniques, introducing the fundamental concepts regarding neural networks and the algorithms involved in their training processes.

Further reading

- Alpaydin E., *Introduction to Machine Learning*, The MIT Press, 2010

- Breiman L., *Random Forests, Machine Learning*, 45, 2001

- Friedman J., Hastie T., Tibshirani R., *Additive Logistic Regression: A Statistical View of Boosting, Annals of Statistics*, 28/1998

- Zhu J., Rosset S., Zou H., Hastie T., *Multi-Class AdaBoost, Statistics, and Its Inference*, 02/2009

- Drucker H., *Improving Regressors Using Boosting Techniques*, ICML 1997

- *Starttech Educational Services LLP, Decision Trees, Random Forests, AdaBoost and XGBoost in Python*, Packt Publishing, 2019

- Lundberg S. M., Lee S., *A Unified Approach to Interpreting Model Predictions, Advances in Neural Information Processing Systems 30*, NIPS, 2017

- Bonaccorso G., *Machine Learning Algorithms Second Edition*, Packt Publishing, 2018

17
Modeling Neural Networks

This chapter is an introduction to the world of deep learning, whose methods make it possible to achieve *state-of-the-art* performance in many classification and regression fields often considered extremely difficult to manage (such as image segmentation, automatic translation, voice synthesis, and so on). The goal is to provide the reader with the basic instruments to understand the structure of a fully connected neural network using Keras (employing modern techniques to speed up the training process and prevent overfitting).

In particular, the topics covered in the chapter are as follows:

- The structure of a basic artificial neuron

- Perceptrons, linear classifiers, and their limitations

- Multilayer perceptrons with the most important activation functions (such as ReLU)

- Back-propagation algorithms based on the **stochastic gradient descent (SGD)** optimization method

Let's start this exploration with a formal definition of the computational unit that characterizes every neural network, the artificial neuron.

The basic artificial neuron

The building block of a neural network is an abstraction of a biological neuron, a quite simplistic but powerful computational unit that was proposed for the first time by F. Rosenblatt in 1957 to make up the simplest neural architecture, called a perceptron, which we are going to analyze in the next section. Contrary to Hebbian learning, which is more biologically plausible but has some strong limitations, the artificial neuron was designed with a pragmatic viewpoint and only its structure is based on a few of the elements that characterize a biological neuron.

However, recent deep learning research activities have unveiled the enormous power of this kind of architecture. Even though there are more complex and specialized computational cells, the basic artificial neuron can be summarized as the conjunction of two blocks, which are clearly shown in the following diagram:

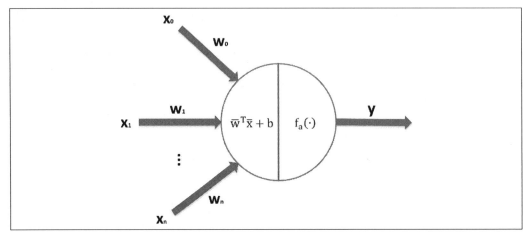

Structure of a generic artificial neuron

The input of a neuron is a real-valued vector $\bar{x} \in \mathbb{R}^n$, while the output is a scalar $y \in \mathbb{R}$. The first operation is linear:

$$z = \bar{w}^T \cdot \bar{x} + b$$

The vector $\bar{w} \in \mathbb{R}^n$ is called a weight vector (or synaptic weight vector, because, analogously to a biological neuron, it reweights the input values), while the scalar term $b \in \mathbb{R}$ is a constant called bias. In many cases, it's easier to consider only the weight vector. It's possible to get rid of the bias by adding an extra input feature equal to 1 and a corresponding weight:

$$\bar{x}^* = (x_1, x_2, \dots, x_n, 1)$$

In this way, the only element that must be learned is the weight vector. The following block is called an activation function, and it's responsible for remapping the input into a different subset. If the function is $f_a(z) = z$, the neuron is called linear and the transformation can be omitted. The first experiments were based on linear neurons that are much less powerful than non-linear ones, and this was a reason that led many researchers to consider the perceptron as a failure; but, at the same time, this limitation opened the door for a new architecture instead, that had the chance to show its excellent abilities. Let's now start our analysis with the first neural network ever proposed.

The perceptron

The perceptron was the name that Frank Rosenblatt gave to the first neural model in 1957. A perceptron is a neural network with a single layer of input linear neurons, followed by an output unit based on the *sign(x)* function (alternatively, it's possible to consider a bipolar unit whose output is -1 and 1). The architecture of a perceptron is shown in the following diagram:

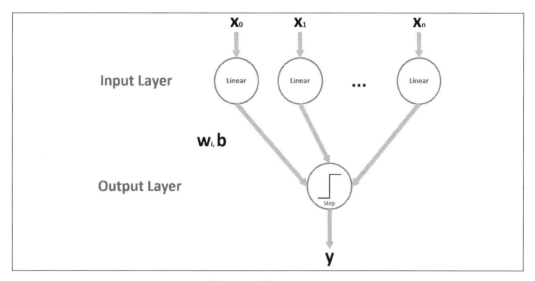

Structure of a perceptron

Even though the diagram might appear quite complex, a perceptron can be summarized by the following equation:

$$y_i = sign(\bar{w}^T \cdot \bar{x}_i + b) \ \ where \ \ \bar{w}, \bar{x}_i \in \mathbb{R}^n \ \ and \ y_i \in \{0,1\}$$

All the vectors are conventionally column-vectors; therefore, the dot product $\bar{w}^T \cdot \bar{x}_i$ transforms the input into a scalar, then the bias is added, and the binary output is obtained using the step function, which outputs 1 when $z > 0$ and 0 otherwise. At this point, a reader could object that the step function is non-linear; however, a non-linearity applied to the output layer is only a filtering operation that has no effect on the actual computation.

Indeed, the output is already decided by the linear block, while the step function is employed only to impose a binary threshold (transforming the continuous output into a discrete one). Moreover, in this analysis, we're considering only single-value outputs (even if there are multi-class variants) because our goal is to show the dynamics and also the limitations, before moving on to more generic architectures that can be used to solve extremely complex problems.

A perceptron can be trained with an online algorithm (even if the dataset is finite) but it's also possible to employ an offline approach that repeats for a fixed number of iterations or until the total error becomes smaller than a predefined threshold. The procedure is based on the squared error loss function (remember that, conventionally, the term loss is applied to single samples, while the term cost refers to the sum/average of every single loss):

$$L(\bar{x}_i, y_i; \overline{w}, b) = \frac{1}{2}(\overline{w}^T \cdot \bar{x}_i + b - y_i)^2 = \frac{1}{2}(w_1 x_i^{(1)} + w_2 x_i^{(2)} + \cdots + w_n x_i^{(n)} + b - y_i)$$

When a sample is presented, the output is computed, and if it is wrong, a weight correction is applied (otherwise the step is skipped). For simplicity, we don't consider the bias, as it doesn't affect the procedure. Our goal is to correct the weights so as to minimize the loss. This can be achieved by computing the partial derivatives with respect to w_j:

$$\frac{\partial L}{\partial w_j} = \left(w_j x_i^{(j)} - y_i\right) x_i^{(j)}$$

Let's suppose that $w^{(0)} = (0, 0)$ (ignoring the bias) and the data point, $\bar{x} = (1, 1)$, has the label $y = 1$. The perceptron misclassifies the sample because $sign(\overline{w}^T \cdot \bar{x}) = 0$ (or -1 if the representation $sign(x) \in \{-1, 1\}$ is employed). The partial derivatives are both equal to -1; therefore, if we subtract them from the current weights, we obtain $w^{(1)} = (1, 1)$ and now the sample is correctly classified because $sign(\overline{w}^T \cdot \bar{x}) = 0$. Therefore, including a learning rate η, the weight update rule becomes as follows:

$$w_i^{(t+1)} = \begin{cases} w_i^{(t)} - \eta\left(w_j x_i^{(j)} - y_i\right) x_i^{(j)} & if \ sign(\overline{w}^T \cdot \bar{x}_i) \neq y_i \\ w_i^{(t)} & otherwise \end{cases}$$

When a sample is misclassified, the weights are corrected proportionally to the difference between the actual linear output and the true label. This is a variant of a learning rule called the delta rule, which represents the first step toward the most famous training algorithm, employed in almost any supervised deep learning scenario (we're going to discuss it in the next sections). The algorithm has been proven to converge to a stable solution in a finite number of states as the dataset is linearly separable. The formal proof is quite tedious and very technical, but those readers who are interested can find it in Minsky M. L., Papert S. A., *Perceptrons*, The MIT Press, 1969.

In this chapter, the role of the learning rate becomes more and more important, in particular when the update is performed after the evaluation of a single sample (as in a perceptron) or a small batch. In this case, a high learning rate (that is, one greater than 1.0) can cause instability in the convergence process because of the magnitude of single corrections.

When working with neural networks, it's usually better to use a small learning rate and repeat the training session for a fixed number of epochs. In this way, single corrections are limited, and they can only become stable if they're confirmed by the majority of samples/batches, which drives the network to converge to an optimal solution. If instead, the correction is the consequence of an outlier, a small learning rate can limit its action, avoiding destabilization of the whole network for just a few noisy samples. We'll discuss this problem further across the next few sections.

Now, we can describe the full perceptron algorithm and close this section with some important considerations:

1. Select a value for the learning rate η (such as $\eta = 0.1$). As usual, smaller values allow more precise modifications but increase the computational cost, while larger values speed up the training phase but reduce the learning accuracy.

2. Append a constant column (set equal to 1.0) to the sample vector X. Therefore, the resulting vector will be $X_b \in \mathbb{R}^{M \times (n+1)}$.

3. Initialize the weight vector $\bar{w} \in \mathbb{R}^{n+1}$ with random values sampled from a normal distribution with a small variance (such as $\sigma^2 = 0.05$).

4. Set an error threshold *Thr* (such as *Thr* = 0.0001).

5. Set a maximum number of iterations N_{max}.

6. Set $i = 0$.

7. Set $e = 1$.

8. While $i < N_{max}$ and $e > Thr$:

    a. Set $e = 0$.

    b. For $k = 1$ to M:

        i. Compute the linear output $l_k = \bar{w}^T \cdot \bar{x}_k$ and the thresholded one $t_k = sign(l_k)$.

        ii. If $t_k \neq y_k$:

            1. Compute $\Delta w_j = \eta(l_k - y_k)x_k^{(j)}$.

            2. Update the weight vector.

     i.   Set $e = e + (l_k - y_k)^2$ (alternatively, it's possible to use the absolute value $e = e + |l_k - y_k|$).

  c. Set $e = {}^e/_M$.

The algorithm is very simple, and you should have noticed an analogy with logistic regression. Indeed, this method is based on a structure that can be considered as a perceptron with a sigmoid output activation function (that outputs a real value that can be considered as a probability). The main difference is the training strategy — in logistic regression, the correction is performed after the evaluation of a cost function based on the negative log likelihood:

$$L(X, Y; \bar{w}, b) = -\log \prod_{i=1}^{M} p(y_i | \bar{x}_i; \bar{w}, b)$$

$$= -\sum_{i=1}^{M} \log p(y_i | \bar{x}_i; \bar{w}, b) =$$

$$-\sum_{i=1}^{M} \left[y_i \log \sigma(\bar{w}^T \cdot \bar{x}_i + b) + (1 - y_i) \log\left(1 - \sigma(\bar{w}^T \cdot \bar{x}_i + b)\right) \right]$$

This cost function is the well-known cross-entropy, and in *Chapter 2, Loss functions and Regularization*, we showed that minimizing it is equivalent to reducing the Kullback-Leibler divergence between the true and predicted distribution. In almost all deep learning classification tasks, we're going to employ cross-entropy, thanks to its robustness and convexity (convexity is a convergence guarantee in logistic regression, but unfortunately, the property is normally lost in more complex architectures where the cost function is non-convex).

Example of a Perceptron with scikit-learn

Even if the algorithm is very simple to implement from scratch, I prefer to employ the scikit-learn implementation Perceptron, to focus our attention on the limitations that led to non-linear neural networks. The historical problem that showed the main weakness of the perceptron was based on the XOR dataset. It's easier to build this first, and visualize the structure, before we explain it:

```
import numpy as np

from sklearn.preprocessing import StandardScaler
from sklearn.utils import shuffle

np.random.seed(1000)

nb_samples = 1000
nsb = int(nb_samples / 4)

X = np.zeros((nb_samples, 2))
Y = np.zeros((nb_samples, ))

X[0:nsb, :] = np.random.multivariate_normal(
        [1.0, -1.0], np.diag([0.1, 0.1]), size=nsb)
Y[0:nsb] = 0.0

X[nsb:(2 * nsb), :] = np.random.multivariate_normal(
        [1.0, 1.0], np.diag([0.1, 0.1]), size=nsb)
Y[nsb:(2 * nsb)] = 1.0

X[(2 * nsb):(3 * nsb), :] = \
        np.random.multivariate_normal(
        [-1.0, 1.0], np.diag([0.1, 0.1]), size=nsb)
Y[(2 * nsb):(3 * nsb)] = 0.0

X[(3 * nsb):, :] = np.random.multivariate_normal(
        [-1.0, -1.0], np.diag([0.1, 0.1]), size=nsb)
Y[(3 * nsb):] = 1.0

ss = StandardScaler()
X = ss.fit_transform(X)

X, Y = shuffle(X, Y, random_state=1000)
```

The plot showing the true labels is shown here:

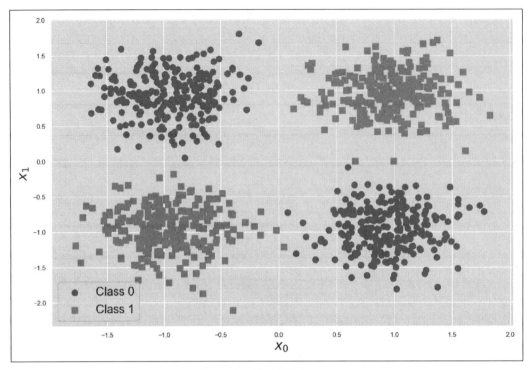

Example of the XOR dataset

As it's possible to see, the dataset is split into four blocks that are organized as the output of a logical XOR operator. Considering that the separation hypersurface of a two-dimensional perceptron (as well as the separation hypersurface of logistic regression) is a line; it's easy to understand that any possible final configuration can achieve an accuracy that is about 50% (a random guess). To get confirmation, let's try to solve this problem:

```
from sklearn.linear_model import Perceptron
from sklearn.model_selection import cross_val_score

pc = Perceptron(penalty='l2', alpha=0.1,
                n_jobs=-1, random_state=1000)
print("Perceptron Avg. CV score: {:.3f}".
      format(np.mean(cross_val_score(pc, X, Y, cv=10))))
```

The output of the previous snippet is:

```
Perceptron Avg. CV score: 0.504
```

This value confirms that, in this case, a perceptron is approximately equal to a random guess, therefore, it doesn't offer any advantages and there's no way to overcome this limitation. Conversely, for linearly separable scenarios, a scikit-learn implementation offers the possibility to add a regularization term (see *Chapter 2, Loss functions and Regularization*) through the parameter penalty (it can be `'l1'`, `'l2'`, or `'elasticnet'`) to avoid overfitting, induce sparsity, and improve the convergence speed (the strength can be specified using the parameter `alpha`). This is not always necessary, but as the algorithm is offered in a production-ready package, the designers decided to add this feature. Nevertheless, the average cross-validation accuracy is slightly higher than 0.5 (you're invited to test any other possible hyperparameter configuration). The corresponding plot (which can change with different random states or subsequent experiments) is shown here:

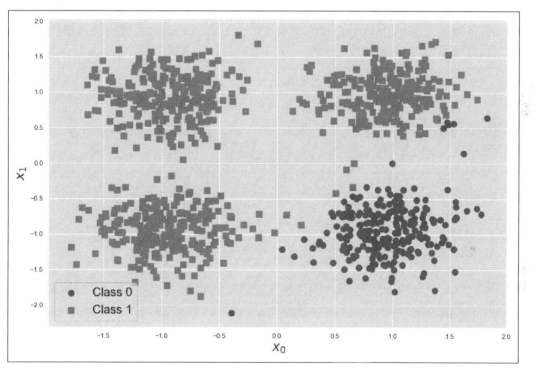

XOR dataset labeled using a Perceptron

It's obvious that a perceptron is another linear model without specific peculiarities, and its employment is discouraged in favor of other algorithms, such as logistic regression or SVM. After 1957, for a few years, many researchers didn't hide their disillusionment and considered the neural network as a promise never fulfilled. It was necessary to wait until a simple modification to the architecture, together with a powerful learning algorithm, officially opened the door to a new fascinating machine learning branch (later called deep learning).

In scikit-learn > 0.19, the class `Perceptron` allows adding `max_iter` or `tol` (tolerance) parameters. If not specified, a warning will be issued to inform you about future behavior. This piece of information doesn't affect the actual results.

Multilayer Perceptrons (MLPs)

The main limitation of a perceptron is its linearity. How is it possible to exploit this kind of architecture by removing such a constraint? The solution is easier than you might speculate. Adding at least one non-linear layer between the input and output leads to a highly non-linear combination, parametrized with a larger number of variables. The resulting architecture, called a **Multilayer Perceptron (MLP)** and containing a single (just for simplicity) hidden layer, is shown in the following diagram:

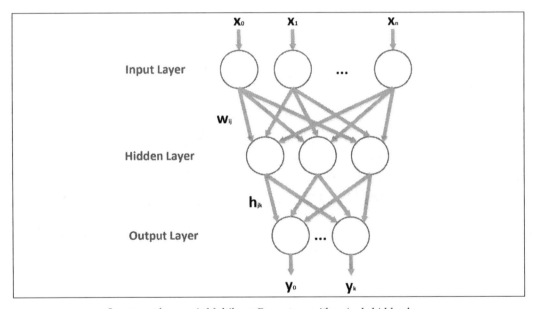

Structure of a generic Multilayer Perceptron with a single hidden layer

This is a so-called feed-forward network, meaning that the flow of information begins in the first layer, always proceeds in the same direction, and ends at the output layer. Architectures that allow partial feedback (for example, in order to implement local memory) are called recurrent networks and will be analyzed in the next chapter.

In this case, there are two weight matrices, W and H, and two corresponding bias vectors, b and c. If there are m hidden neurons, $\bar{x}_i \in \mathbb{R}^{n \times 1}$ (column vector), and $\bar{y}_i \in \mathbb{R}^{k \times 1}$, the dynamics are defined by the following transformations:

$$\begin{cases} \bar{z} = f_h(W^T \bar{x} + \bar{b}) \;\; where \;\; W \in \mathbb{R}^{n \times m} \;\; and \;\; \bar{b} \in \mathbb{R}^{m \times 1} \\ \bar{y} = f_a(H^T \bar{z} + \bar{c}) \;\; where \;\; H \in \mathbb{R}^{m \times k} \;\; and \;\; \bar{c} \in \mathbb{R}^{k \times 1} \end{cases}$$

A fundamental condition for any MLP is that at least one hidden-layer activation function $f_h(\bar{x})$ is non-linear. It's straightforward to prove that m linear hidden layers are equivalent to a single linear network and, hence, an MLP falls back into the case of a standard perceptron. In general, all hidden layers have non-linear activations, while the last one can also have a linear output to represent, for example, unbounded quantities (for example, in regression tasks). Conventionally, the activation function is fixed for a given layer, but there are no limitations on their combinations. In particular, the output activation is normally chosen to meet a precise requirement (such as multi-label classification, regression, image reconstruction, and so on). That's why the first step of this analysis concerns the most common activation functions and their features.

We can now have a deeper insight into the most common activation functions, discussing their features and their limitations.

Activation functions

In general, any continuous (also step-wise) and differentiable function could be employed as an activation function. The continuity property allows us to take all values in the domain D (generally $D = \mathbb{R}$, so $f(x)$ is defined for any x), while the differentiability is a fundamental condition to optimize neural networks. Even so, some functions have particular properties that allow us to achieve good accuracy while improving the learning process speed. They're commonly used in state-of-the-art models, and it's important to understand their properties in order to make the most reasonable choice.

Sigmoid and Hyperbolic Tangent

These two activations are very similar, with a very simple but important difference. Let's start defining them:

$$f_{sigmoid}(x) = \sigma(x) = \frac{1}{1 + e^{-x}} \;\; and \;\; f_{tanh}(x) = \tanh x = \frac{e^x - e^{-x}}{e^x + e^{-x}}$$

The corresponding plots are shown here:

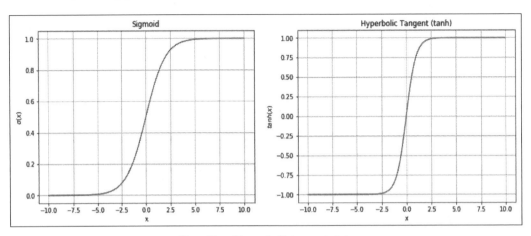

Sigmoid and hyperbolic tangent plots

A sigmoid $\sigma(x)$ is bounded between 0 and 1, with two asymptotes ($\sigma(x) \rightarrow 0$ when $x \rightarrow -\infty$ and $\sigma(x) \rightarrow 1$ when $x \rightarrow +\infty$). Similarly, the hyperbolic tangent (tanh) is bounded between -1 and 1 with two asymptotes corresponding to the extreme values. Analyzing the two plots, we can discover that both functions are almost linear in a short range (about (-2, 2)), and they become almost flat immediately after. This means that the gradient is high and about constant when x has small values around 0 and it falls down to about 0 for larger absolute values. A sigmoid perfectly represents a probability or a set of weights that must be bounded between 0 and 1, and therefore, it can be a good choice for some output layers.

However, the hyperbolic tangent is completely symmetric, and it's preferable for optimization purposes because its performance is normally superior. This activation function is often employed in intermediate layers, whenever the input is normally small. The reason will be clear when the back-propagation algorithm is analyzed; however, it's obvious that large absolute inputs lead to almost constant outputs, and since the gradient is about 0, the weight correction can become extremely slow (this problem is formally known as vanishing gradient). For this reason, in many real-world applications, the next family of activation functions is often employed.

Rectifier activation functions

These functions are all linear (or quasi-linear for Swish) when $x > 0$, while they differ when $x < 0$. Even if some of them are not differentiable when $x = 0$, the derivative is always set equal to 0 in this case. The most common functions are as follows:

$$\begin{cases} f_{ReLU}(x) = \max(0, x) \\ f_{LeakyReLU}(x) = \max(0, \alpha x) \; with \; \alpha \leq 1 \\ f_{ELU}(x) = \begin{cases} x \; if \; x > 0 \\ \alpha(e^x - 1) \; otherwise \end{cases} \\ f_{Swish}(x) = \dfrac{x}{1 + e^{-\alpha x}} = x\sigma(\alpha x) \end{cases}$$

The corresponding plots are shown here:

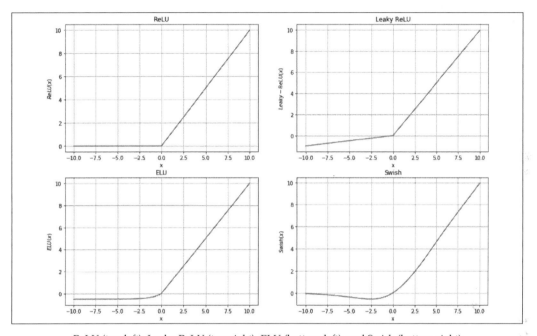

ReLU (top-left), Leaky ReLU (top-right), ELU (bottom-left), and Swish (bottom-right)

The most basic function (and also the most commonly employed) is the ReLU, which has a constant gradient when $x > 0$, while it is null for $x < 0$. This function is very often employed in visual processing when the input is normally greater than 0 and has the extraordinary advantage of mitigating the vanishing gradient problem, as a correction based on the gradient is always possible. On the other hand, ReLU is null (together with its first derivative) when $x < 0$, therefore every negative input doesn't allow any modification. In general, this is not an issue, but there are some deep networks that perform much better when a small negative gradient is allowed. This consideration drove the creation of the other variants, which are characterized by the presence of the hyperparameter α, which controls the strength of the negative tail. Common values between 0.01 and 0.1 allow behavior that is almost identical to ReLU, but with the possibility of a small weight update when $x < 0$.

The last function, called Swish and proposed in Ramachandran P., Zoph P., Le V. L., *Searching for Activation Functions*, arXiv:1710.05941 [cs.NE], is based on the sigmoid and offers the extra advantage of converging to 0 when $x \to 0$, so the non-null effect is limited to a short region bounded between $(-b, 0)$ with $b > 0$. This function can improve the performance of some particular visual processing deep networks, as discussed in the aforementioned paper. However, I always suggest starting the analysis with ReLU (which is very robust and computationally inexpensive) and switching to an alternative only if no other techniques can improve the performance of a model.

Softmax

This function characterizes the output layer of almost all classification networks, as it can immediately represent a discrete probability distribution. If there are k outputs, y_i, the softmax, is computed as follows:

$$f^{(i)}_{softmax}(x) = \frac{e^{y_i}}{\sum_{j=1}^{k} e^{y_j}}$$

In this way, the output of a layer containing k neurons is normalized so that the sum is always 1. It goes without saying that, in this case, the best cost function is cross-entropy. In fact, if all true labels are represented with one-hot encoding, they implicitly become probability vectors with 1 corresponding to the true class. The goal of the classifier is hence to reduce the discrepancy between the training distribution of its output by minimizing the function (see *Chapter 2*, *Loss functions and Regularization*):

$$L(Y ; \hat{Y}; \bar{\theta}) = -\sum_{i=1}^{k} y_i \log \hat{y}_i \quad where \; \hat{y}_i \; is \; a \; prediction$$

We can now discuss the training approach employed in an MLP (and almost all other neural networks).

The back-propagation algorithm

This algorithm is more of a methodology than an actual algorithm. In fact, it was designed to be flexible enough to adapt to any kind of neural architecture without any substantial changes. Therefore, in this section we'll define the main concepts without focusing on a particular case. Those who are interested in implementing it will be able to apply the same techniques to different kinds of networks with minimal effort (assuming that all requirements are met).

The goal of a training process using a deep learning model is normally achieved by minimizing a cost function. Let's suppose we have a network parameterized with a global vector $\bar{\theta}$. In that case, the cost function (using the same notation for loss and cost but with different parameters to disambiguate) is defined as follows:

$$L(\bar{\theta}) = \frac{1}{M} \sum_{i=1}^{M} L(\bar{x}_i, \bar{y}_i;\ \bar{\theta})$$

We've already explained that the minimization of the previous expression (which is the empirical risk) is a way to minimize the real expected risk and, therefore, maximize the accuracy. Our goal is to find an optimal parameter set so that the following applies:

$$\bar{\theta}_{opt} = \underset{\bar{\theta}}{\operatorname{argmin}}\, L(\bar{\theta})$$

If we consider a single loss function (associated with a data point $\bar{x}_i$ and a true vectorial label $\bar{y}_i$), we know that such a function can be expressed with an explicit dependence on the predicted value:

$$L(\bar{x}_i, \bar{y}_i;\ \bar{\theta}) = L(\bar{y}_i, \hat{y}_i)$$

In the previous expression, the parameters have been embedded in the prediction. From calculus (without the excessive mathematical rigor that can be found in many books about optimization techniques), we know that the gradient of $L(\bar{y}_i, \hat{y}_i)$, a scalar function, computed at any point (we are assuming the L is differentiable) as a vector with components:

$$\nabla_{\bar{\theta}} L = \left(\frac{\partial L}{\partial \theta_1}, \frac{\partial L}{\partial \theta_2}, \dots, \frac{\partial L}{\partial \theta_T} \right)^T$$

As $\nabla_{\bar{\theta}} L$ always points in the direction of the closest maximum, so the negative gradient points in the direction of the closest minimum. Hence, if we compute the gradient of L, we have a ready-to-use piece of information that can be used to minimize the cost function. Before proceeding, it's useful to expose an important mathematical property called the chain rule of derivatives:

$$\frac{\partial f_1(f_2(\dots f_n(x) \dots))}{\partial x} = \frac{\partial f_1}{\partial f_2} \frac{\partial f_2}{\partial f_3} \dots \frac{\partial f_n}{\partial x}$$

Now, let's consider a single step in an MLP (starting from the bottom) and let's exploit the chain rule:

$$\bar{y} = f_a(H^T \bar{z} + \bar{c})$$

Each component of the vector y is independent of the others, so we can simplify the example by considering only an output value:

$$\hat{y}_i = f_a\left(\sum_{j=1}^{k} h_{ji}\bar{z}_j + c_i\right)$$

In the previous expression (discarding the bias), there are two important elements — the weights, h_j (which are the columns of H), and the expression, $\bar{z}_j$, which is a function of the previous weights. As L is, in turn, a function of all predictions $\hat{y}_i$, applying the chain rule (using the variable t as the generic argument of the activation functions), we get the following:

$$\frac{\partial L}{\partial h_{ij}} = \frac{\partial L}{\partial \hat{y}_i}\frac{\partial \hat{y}_i}{\partial t}\frac{\partial t}{\partial h_{ij}} = \frac{\partial L}{\partial \hat{y}_i}\frac{\partial \hat{y}_i}{\partial t}\bar{z}_j = \delta_i \bar{z}_j$$

As we normally cope with vectorial functions, it's easier to express this concept using the gradient operator. Simplifying the transformations performed by a generic layer, we can express the relations (with respect to a row of H, so to a weight vector $\bar{h}_i$ corresponding to a hidden unit, $\bar{z}_i$) as follows:

$$\begin{cases} L = p(\bar{y}) \ where \ \bar{y} \in \mathbb{R}^{k \times 1} \\ \bar{y} = \bar{q}(\bar{h}_i) \ where \ \bar{h}_i \in \mathbb{R}^{m \times 1} \end{cases}$$

Employing the gradient and considering the vectorial output $\bar{y}$ can be written as $\bar{y} = (y_1, y_2, \dots, y_m)$, we can derive the following expression:

$$\nabla_{\bar{h}_i}L = J_{\bar{h}_i}(\bar{y})^T \nabla_{\bar{y}}L = \begin{pmatrix} \frac{\partial \bar{y}_1}{\partial h_1} & \cdots & \frac{\partial \bar{y}_k}{\partial h_1} \\ \vdots & \ddots & \vdots \\ \frac{\partial \bar{y}_1}{\partial h_m} & \cdots & \frac{\partial \bar{y}_k}{\partial h_m} \end{pmatrix}\begin{pmatrix} \frac{\partial L}{\partial \bar{y}_1} \\ \vdots \\ \frac{\partial L}{\partial \bar{y}_k} \end{pmatrix} = \begin{pmatrix} \frac{\partial L}{\partial h_1} \\ \vdots \\ \frac{\partial L}{\partial h_m} \end{pmatrix}$$

In this way, we get all the components of the gradient of L computed with respect to the weight vectors, $\bar{h}_i$. If we move back, we can derive the expression of $\bar{z}_j$:

$$\bar{z}_j = f_h \left(\sum_{p=1}^{m} w_{pj} \bar{x}_p + b_j \right)$$

Reapplying the chain rule, we can compute the partial derivative of L with respect to w_{pj} (to avoid confusion, the argument of the prediction $\hat{y}_i$ is called t_1, while the argument of $\bar{z}_j$ is called t_2):

$$\frac{\partial L}{\partial w_{pj}} = \frac{\partial L}{\partial \hat{y}_i} \frac{\partial \hat{y}_i}{\partial t_1} \frac{\partial t_1}{\partial \bar{z}_j} \frac{\partial \bar{z}_j}{\partial t_2} \frac{\partial t_2}{\partial w_{pj}} = \delta_i h_{ji} \frac{\partial \bar{z}_j}{\partial t_2} \bar{x}_p$$

Observing this expression (which can easily be rewritten using the gradient) and comparing it with the previous one, it's possible to understand the philosophy of the back-propagation algorithm, presented for the first time in Rumelhart D. E., Hinton G. E., Williams R. J., *Learning representations by back-propagating errors*, Nature 323, 1986. The data points are fed into the network and the cost function is computed. At this point, the process starts from the bottom, computing the gradients with respect to the closest weights and reusing a part of the calculation δ_i (proportional to the error) to move back until the first layer is reached. The correction is indeed propagated from the source (the cost function) to the origin (the input layer), and the effect is proportional to the responsibility of each different weight (and bias). Considering all the possible different architectures, writing all the equations for a single example would be useless.

A very important phenomenon that is worth considering was already outlined in the previous section and now it should be clearer: the chain rule is based on multiplications, and therefore, when the gradients start to become smaller than 1, the multiplication effect forces the last values to be close to 0. This problem is known as vanishing gradient and can really stop the training process of very deep models that use saturating activation functions (such as sigmoid or tanh). Rectifier units provide a good solution for many specific issues, but sometimes when functions such as hyperbolic tangent are necessary, other methods such as normalization must be employed to mitigate the phenomenon. We are going to discuss some specific techniques in this chapter and in the next one, but a generic best practice is to always work with normalized datasets and, if necessary, to also test the effect of whitening.

Stochastic gradient descent (SGD)

Once the gradients have been computed, the cost function can be moved in the direction of its minimum. However, in practice, it is better to perform an update after the evaluation of a fixed number of training samples (a batch).

Indeed, the algorithms that are normally employed don't compute the global cost for the whole dataset, because this operation could be very computationally expensive. An approximation is obtained with partial steps, limited to the experience accumulated with the evaluation of a small subset. According to some literature, the expression stochastic gradient descent (SGD) should be used only when the update is performed after every single sample. When this operation is carried out on every k points, the algorithm is also known as mini-batch gradient descent; however, conventionally, SGD is referred to as all batches containing $k \geq 1$ data points, and we are going to use this expression from now on.

The process can be expressed considering a partial cost function computed using a batch containing k data points:

$$L(\bar{\theta}) = \frac{1}{k} \sum_{i=1}^{k} L(\bar{x}_i, \bar{y}_i; \bar{\theta})$$

The algorithm performs gradient descent by updating the weights according to the following rule:

$$\bar{\theta}^{(t+1)} = \bar{\theta}^{(t)} - \eta \nabla_{\bar{\theta}} L$$

If we start from an initial configuration $\bar{\theta}_{start}$ and a target $\bar{\theta}_{opt}$, the stochastic gradient descent process can be imagined like the path shown in the following diagram:

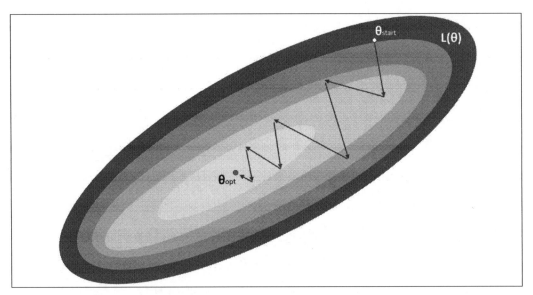

Graphical representation of the optimization process based on SGD

The weights are moved toward the minimum $\bar{\theta}_{opt}$, with many subsequent corrections that could also be wrong considering the whole dataset. For this reason, the process must be repeated several times (epochs), until the validation accuracy reaches its maximum. In a perfect scenario, with a convex cost function L, this simple procedure converges to the optimal configuration.

Unfortunately, a deep network is a very complex and non-convex function where plateaus and saddle points are quite common (see *Chapter 1, Machine Learning Model Fundamentals*). In such a scenario, a vanilla SGD wouldn't be able to find the global optimum and, in many cases, would not even find a close point. For example, in flat regions, the gradients can become so small (also considering the numerical imprecisions) as to slow down the training process until no change is possible (so $\bar{\theta}^{(t+1)} \approx \bar{\theta}^{(t)}$). In the next section, we are going to present some common and powerful algorithms that have been developed to mitigate this problem and dramatically accelerate the convergence of deep models.

Before moving on, it's important to mark two important elements. The first one concerns the learning rate, η. This hyperparameter plays a fundamental role in the learning process. As is also shown in the figure, the algorithm proceeds, jumping from one point to another one (which is not necessarily closer to the optimum). Together with the optimization algorithms, it's absolutely important to correctly tune up the learning rate. A high value (such as 1.0) can move the weights too rapidly, increasing the instability. In particular, if a batch contains a few outliers (or simply non-dominant samples), a large η will consider them as representative elements, correcting the weights so as to minimize the error. However, subsequent batches might better represent the data-generating process, and therefore, the algorithm must partially revert its modifications in order to compensate for the incorrect update. For this reason, the learning rate is usually quite small with common values bounded between 0.0001 and 0.01 (in some particular cases, $\eta = 0.1$ can also be a valid choice).

On the other hand, a very small learning rate leads to minimal corrections, slowing down the training process. A good trade-off, which is often the best practice, is to let the learning rate decay as a function of the epoch. In the beginning, η can be higher, because the probability of being close to the optimum is almost null; so, larger jumps can be easily adjusted. While the training process goes on, the weights are progressively moved toward their final configuration and, hence, the corrections become smaller and smaller. In this case, large jumps should be avoided, preferring fine-tuning. That's why the learning rate is decayed. Common techniques include exponential decay or linear decay. In both cases, the initial and final values must be chosen according to the specific problem (testing different configurations) and the optimization algorithm. In many cases, the ratio between the start and end value is about 10, and sometimes even larger.

Another important hyperparameter is the batch size. There are no silver bullets that allow us to automatically make the right choice, but some considerations can be made. As SGD is an approximate algorithm, larger batches can result in corrections that are probably more similar to the ones obtained considering the whole dataset. However, when the number of samples is extremely high, we don't expect the deep model to map them with a one-to-one association, but instead, our efforts are directed to improving the generalization ability. This feature can be re-expressed by saying that the network must learn a smaller number of abstractions and reuse them in order to classify new samples.

A batch, if sampled correctly, contains a part of these abstract elements and part of the corrections automatically improve the evaluation of a subsequent batch. You can imagine a waterfall process, where a new training step never starts from scratch. However, the algorithm is also called mini-batch gradient descent, because the usual batch size normally ranges from 16 to 512 (larger sizes are uncommon, but always possible), which are values smaller than the number of total samples (in particular, in deep learning contexts). A reasonable default value could be 32 data points, but I always suggest testing larger values, comparing performance in terms of training speed and final accuracy.

When working with deep neural networks, all the values (the number of neurons in a layer, batch size, and so on) are normally powers of two. This is not a constraint, but only an optimization tip (above all, when using GPUs), as the memory can be more efficiently filled when the blocks are based on 2^N elements. However, this is only a suggestion, whose benefits could also be negligible; so, don't be afraid to test architectures with different values. For example, in many papers, the batch size is 100 and some layers have 1,000 neurons.

Weight initialization

A very important element is the initial configuration of a neural network. How should the weights be initialized? Let's imagine we that have set them all to zero. As all neurons in a layer receive the same input, if the weights are 0 (or any other common, constant number), the output will be equal. When applying the gradient correction, all neurons will be treated in the same way; so, the network is equivalent to a sequence of single-neuron layers. It's clear that the initial weights must be different to achieve a goal called *symmetry breaking*, but which is the best choice?

If we knew (also approximately) the final configuration, we could set them to easily reach the optimal point in a few iterations, but unfortunately, we have no idea where the minimum is located.

Therefore, some empirical strategies have been developed and tested, with the goal of minimizing the training time (obtaining *state-of-the-art* accuracy). A general rule of thumb is that the weights should be small (compared to the input sample variance). Large values lead to large outputs that negatively impact on saturating functions (such as tanh and sigmoid), while small values can be more easily optimized because the corresponding gradients are relatively larger, and the corrections have a stronger effect. The same is also true for rectifier units because maximum efficiency is achieved by working in a segment crossing the origin (where the non-linearity is actually located). For example, when coping with images, if the values are positive and large, a ReLU neuron becomes almost a linear unit, losing a lot of its advantages (that's why images are normalized, so as to bound each pixel value between 0 and 1 or -1 and 1).

At the same time, ideally, the activation variances should remain almost constant throughout the network, as well as the weight variances after every back-propagation step. These two conditions are fundamental in order to improve the convergence process and to avoid the vanishing and exploding gradient problems (the latter, which is the opposite of vanishing gradient, will be discussed in *Chapter 19, Deep Convolutional Networks*).

A very common strategy considers the number of neurons in a layer and initializes the weights as follows:

$$w_{ij} \sim N\left(0, \frac{1}{n}\right)$$

This method is called variance scaling and can be applied using the number of input units (Fan-In), the number of output units (Fan-Out), or their average. The idea is very intuitive: if the number of incoming or outgoing connections is large, the weights must be smaller, so as to avoid large outputs. In the degenerate case of a single neuron, the variance is set to 1.0, which is the maximum value allowed (in general, all methods keep the initial values for biases equal to 0.0 because it's not necessary to initialize them with a random value).

Other variations have been proposed, even if they all share the same basic ideas. LeCun proposed initializing the weights as follows:

$$w_{ij} \sim U\left(-\sqrt{\frac{3}{n_{fan-in}}}, \sqrt{\frac{3}{n_{fan-in}}}\right)$$

Another method, called Xavier initialization (presented in Glorot X., Bengio Y., *Understanding the difficulty of training deep feedforward neural networks*, Proceedings of the 13th International Conference on Artificial Intelligence and Statistics, 2010), is similar to LeCun initialization, but it's based on the average of the number of units of two consecutive layers (to mark the sequentiality, we have substituted the terms Fan-In and Fan-Out with explicit indices):

$$w_{ij} \sim U\left(-\sqrt{\frac{6}{n_k + n_{k+1}}}, \sqrt{\frac{6}{n_k + n_{k+1}}}\right)$$

This is a more robust variant, as it considers both the incoming connections and also the outgoing ones (which are in turn incoming connections). The goal (widely discussed by the authors in the aforementioned papers) is to try to meet the two previously presented requirements. The first one is to avoid oscillations in the variance of the activations of each layer (ideally, this condition can avoid saturation). The second one is strictly related to the back-propagation algorithm, and it's based on the observation that, when employing variance scaling (or an equivalent uniform distribution), the variance of a weight matrix is proportional to the reciprocal of $3n_k$. Therefore, the averages of Fan-In and Fan-Out are multiplied by three, trying to avoid large variations in the weights after the updates. Xavier initialization has been proven to be very effective in many deep architectures, and it's often the default choice.

Other methods are based on a different way to measure the variance during both the feed-forward and back-propagation phases and trying to correct the values to minimize residual oscillations in specific contexts. For example, He, Zhang, Ren, and Sun (in He K., Zhang X., Ren S., Sun J., *Delving Deep into Rectifiers: Surpassing Human-Level Performance on ImageNet Classification*, arXiv:1502.01852 [cs.CV]) analyzed the initialization problem in the context of convolutional networks (we are going to discuss them in the next chapter) based on ReLU or variable Leaky-ReLU activations (also known as PReLU – parametric ReLU), deriving an optimal criterion (often called the He initializer), which is slightly different from the Xavier initializer:

$$w_{ij} \sim U\left(-\sqrt{\frac{6}{n_{fan-in}}}, \sqrt{\frac{6}{n_{fan-in}}}\right)$$

All these methods share some common principles, and in many cases, they are interchangeable. As already mentioned, Xavier is one of the most robust and, in the majority of real-life problems, there's no need to look for other methods; however, you should always be aware that the complexity of deep models must often be faced using empirical methods based on sometimes simplistic mathematical assumptions. Only validation with a real dataset can confirm whether a hypothesis is correct or it's better to continue the investigation in another direction.

Example of MLP with TensorFlow and Keras

Keras (`https://keras.io`) is a powerful Python toolkit that allows modeling and training complex deep learning architectures with minimal effort. Thanks to its flexibility, it has been incorporated into TensorFlow, which has become its predefined backend. Therefore, from now on, we are going to refer to TensorFlow 2.0 (for further details, I suggest the book Holdroyd T., *TensorFlow 2.0 Quick Start Guide*, Packt Publishing, 2019). When it's not necessary to use advanced features, we employ the Keras API through TensorFlow. If you want to use another backend, you'll have to install Keras separately and follow the instructions in the documentation to configure it properly.

 Tensorflow can be installed using the command `pip -U install tensorflow` (or `tensorflow-gpu` for GPU support). All of the required documentation can be found on the official page at `https://www.tensorflow.org/`.

In this example, we want to build a small MLP with a single hidden layer to solve the XOR problem (the dataset is the same as was created in the previous example). The simplest and most common way is to instantiate the class `Sequential`, which defines an empty container for an indefinite model. In this initial part, the fundamental method is `add()`, which allows adding a layer to the model. For our example, we want to employ four hidden layers with hyperbolic tangent activation and two `softmax` output layers.

The following snippet defines the MLP:

```
import tensorflow as tf

model = tf.keras.models.Sequential([
        tf.keras.layers.Dense(4, input_dim=2,
                              activation='tanh'),
        tf.keras.layers.Dense(2, activation='softmax')
])
```

The Dense class defines a fully connected layer (a classical MLP layer), and the first parameter is used to declare the number of desired units. The first layer must declare the input_shape or input_dim, which specify the dimensions (or the shape) of a single sample (the batch size is omitted as it's dynamically set by the framework). All the subsequent layers compute the dimensions automatically. One of the strengths of Keras is the possibility to avoid setting many parameters (such as weight initializers), as they will be automatically configured using the most appropriate default values (for example, the default weight initializer is Xavier).

In the next examples, we're going to explicitly set some of them, but I suggest you check the official documentation to get acquainted with all the possibilities and features. The other layer involved in this experiment is **activation**, which specifies the desired activation function (it's also possible to declare it using the parameter activation implemented by almost all layers, but I prefer to decouple the operations to emphasize the single roles, and also because some techniques — such as batch normalization — are normally applied to the linear output before the activation).

At this point, we must ask Keras to compile the model (using the preferred backend):

```
model.compile(optimizer='adam',
              loss='categorical_crossentropy',
              metrics=['accuracy'])
```

The parameter optimizer defines the stochastic gradient descent algorithm that we want to employ. Using optimizer='sgd', it's possible to implement a standard version (as described in the previous paragraph). In this case, we're employing Adam (with the default parameters), which is a much more performant variant that will be discussed in the next chapter. The parameter loss is used to define the cost function (in this case, cross-entropy) and metrics is a list of all the evaluation scores we want to be computed ('accuracy' is enough for many classification tasks). Once the model is compiled, it's possible to train it:

```
from sklearn.model_selection import train_test_split

X_train, X_test, Y_train, Y_test = \
        train_test_split(X, Y, test_size=0.3,
                              random_state=1000)

model.fit(X_train,
              tf.keras.utils.to_categorical(
          Y_train, num_classes=2),
              epochs=100,
              batch_size=32,
              validation_data=
              (X_test,
              tf.keras.utils.to_categorical(
                 Y_test, num_classes=2)))
```

The output of the previous snippet is:

```
Train on 700 samples, validate on 300 samples
Epoch 1/100
700/700 [==============================] - 1s 2ms/sample - loss:
0.7453 - accuracy: 0.5114 - val_loss: 0.7618 - val_accuracy: 0.4767
Epoch 2/100
700/700 [==============================] - 1s 1ms/sample - loss:
0.7304 - accuracy: 0.5129 - val_loss: 0.7465 - val_accuracy: 0.4833
Epoch 3/100
700/700 [==============================] - 1s 2ms/sample - loss:
0.7177 - accuracy: 0.5143 - val_loss: 0.7342 - val_accuracy: 0.4900
...
Epoch 99/100
700/700 [==============================] - 1s 1ms/sample - loss:
0.0995 - accuracy: 0.9914 - val_loss: 0.0897 - val_accuracy: 0.9967
Epoch 100/100
700/700 [==============================] - 1s 2ms/sample - loss:
0.0977 - accuracy: 0.9914 - val_loss: 0.0878 - val_accuracy: 0.9967
```

The operations are quite simple. We've split the dataset into training and test/validation sets (in deep learning, cross-validation is seldom employed), and then, we have trained the model setting `batch_size=32` and `epochs=100`. The dataset is automatically shuffled at the beginning of each epoch, unless setting `shuffle=False`. In order to convert the discrete labels into one-hot encoding, we have used the utility function `to_categorical`. In this case, the label 0 becomes (1, 0) and the label 1 (0, 1). The model converges before reaching 100 epochs; therefore, I invite you to optimize the parameters as an exercise. However, at the end of the process, both accuracies are extremely close to 1.

The final classification plot is shown here:

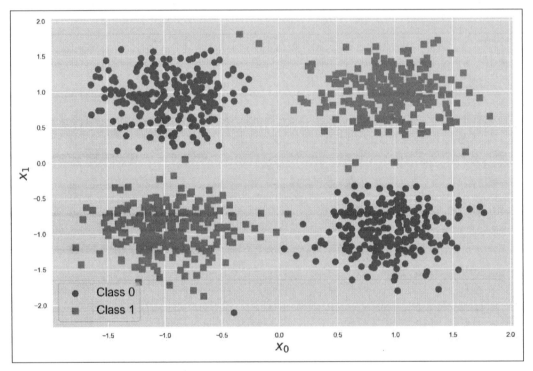

MLP classification of the XOR dataset

Only a few points (which can also be considered as outliers) have been misclassified, but it's clear that the MLP successfully separated the XOR dataset. To get confirmation of the generalization ability, we've plotted the decision surfaces for a hyperbolic tangent hidden layer and a ReLU one:

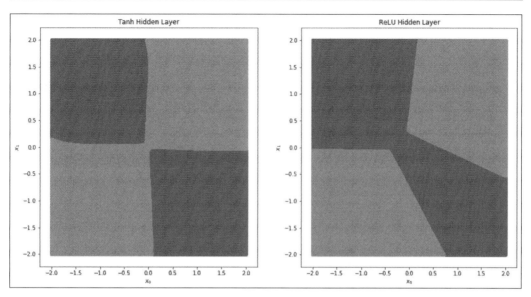

MLP decision surfaces with Tanh (left) and ReLU (right) hidden layer

In both cases, the MLPs delimited the areas in a reasonable way. However, while a hyperbolic tangent hidden layer seems to be overfitted (this is not true in our case, as the dataset represents exactly the data-generating process), the ReLU layer generates less smooth boundaries with an apparent lower variance (in particular, for considering the outliers of a class). We know that the final validation accuracies confirm an almost perfect fit, and the decision plots (which are easy to create with two dimensions) show acceptable boundaries in both cases, but this simple exercise is useful to understand the complexity and the sensitivity of a deep model and to gain a better comprehension about the best way to structure it. For these reasons, it's absolutely necessary to select a valid training set (representing the ground truth) and employ all possible techniques to avoid overfitting (as we're going to discuss later). The easiest way to detect such a situation is to check the validation loss. A good model should reduce both training and validation loss after each epoch, reaching a plateau for the latter. If, after n epochs, the validation loss (and, consequently, the accuracy) begins to increase, while the training loss keeps decreasing, it means that the model is overfitting the training set.

Another generally valid empirical indicator that the training process is evolving correctly is that, at least at the beginning, the validation accuracy should be higher than the training accuracy. This might seem strange, but we need to consider that the validation set is slightly smaller and less complex than the training set; therefore, if the capacity of the model is not saturated with training samples, the probability of misclassification is higher for the training set than for the validation set.

When this trend is inverted, the model is very likely to overfit after a few epochs. The advice is generally correct, however it's important to remember that the complexity of these models sometimes leads to unpredictable behaviors. Hence, before aborting a training process, it's always helpful to wait for at least one third of the total epochs. To verify these concepts, I invite you to repeat the exercise using a large number of hidden neurons (so as to dramatically increase the capacity), but they will be clearer when working with much more complex and unstructured datasets.

Summary

In this chapter, we started our exploration of the deep learning world by introducing the basic concepts that led the first researchers to improve algorithms until they achieved the top results we can achieve nowadays. The first part explained the structure of a basic artificial neuron, which combines a linear operation followed by an optional non-linear scalar function. A single layer of linear neurons was initially proposed as the first neural network, with the name of the perceptron.

Even though it was quite powerful for many problems, this model soon showed its limitations when working with non-linear separable datasets. A perceptron is not very different from logistic regression, and there's no concrete reason to employ it. Nevertheless, this model opened the doors to a family of extremely powerful models obtained by combining multiple non-linear layers. The multilayer perceptron, which has been proven to be a universal approximator, is able to manage almost any kind of dataset, achieving high-level performance when other methods fail.

In the next section, we analyzed the building blocks of an MLP. We started with the activation functions, describing their structures and features, and focused on the reasons they are the main choice for specific problems. Then, we discussed the training process, considering the basic idea behind the back-propagation algorithm and how it can be implemented using the stochastic gradient descent method. Even though this approach is quite effective, it can be slow when the complexity of the network is very high. For this reason, many optimization algorithms were proposed. In this chapter, we analyzed the role of momentum and how it's possible to manage adaptive corrections using RMSProp. Then, we combined momentum and RMSProp to derive a very powerful algorithm called Adam. In order to provide a complete picture, we also presented two slightly different adaptive algorithms, called AdaGrad and AdaDelta.

In the next chapter, we are going to discuss the most important neural network optimization strategies (including RMSProp and Adam) and how to use regularization and other techniques that improve the overall performances of the models both in terms of speed and accuracy.

Further reading

- Minsky M. L., Papert S. A., *Perceptrons*, The MIT Press, 1969

- Ramachandran P., Zoph P., Le V. L., *Searching for Activation Functions*, arXiv:1710.05941 [cs.NE]

- Rumelhart D. E., Hinton G. E., Williams R. J., *Learning representations by back-propagating errors*, Nature 323, 1986

- Glorot X., Bengio Y., *Understanding the difficulty of training deep feedforward neural networks*, Proceedings of the 13th International Conference on Artificial Intelligence and Statistics, 2010

- He K., Zhang X., Ren S., Sun J., *Delving Deep into Rectifiers: Surpassing Human-Level Performance on ImageNet Classification*, arXiv:1502.01852 [cs.CV]

- Holdroyd T., *TensorFlow 2.0 Quick Start Guide*, Packt Publishing, 2019

- *Kingma D. P., Ba J., Adam: A Method for Stochastic Optimization, arXiv:1412.6980 [cs.LG]*

- Duchi J., Hazan E., Singer Y., *Adaptive Subgradient Methods for Online Learning and Stochastic Optimization*, Journal of Machine Learning Research 12, 2011

- Zeiler M. D., *ADADELTA: An Adaptive Learning Rate Method*, arXiv:1212.5701 [cs.LG]

- Hornik K., *Approximation Capabilities of Multilayer Feedforward Networks*, Neural Networks, 4/2, 1991

- Cybenko G., *Approximations by Superpositions of Sigmoidal Functions*, Mathematics of Control, Signals, and Systems, 2 /4, 1989

18
Optimizing Neural Networks

In this chapter, we're going to discuss the most important optimization algorithms that have been derived from the basic **Stochastic Gradient Descent** (**SGD**) approach. This method can be quite ineffective when working with very high-dimensional functions, forcing the models to remain stuck in sub-optimal solutions. The optimizers discussed in this chapter have the goals of speeding up convergence and avoiding any sub-optimality. Moreover, we'll also discuss how to apply L_1 and L_2 regularization to a layer of a deep neural network, and how to avoid overfitting using these advanced approaches.

In particular, the topics covered in the chapter are as follows:

- Optimized SGD algorithms (Momentum, RMSProp, Adam, AdaGrad, and AdaDelta)
- Regularization techniques and dropout
- Batch normalization

After having discussed the basic concepts of neural modeling in the previous chapter, we can now start discussing how to improve the convergence speed and how to implement the most common regularization techniques.

Optimization algorithms

When we discussed the back-propagation algorithm in the previous chapter, we showed how the SGD strategy can be easily employed to train deep networks with large datasets. This method is quite robust and effective; however, the function to optimize is generally non-convex and the number of parameters is extremely large.

These conditions dramatically increase the probability of finding saddle points (instead of local minima) and can slow down the training process when the surface is almost flat (as shown in the following figure, where the point (0, 0) is a saddle point).

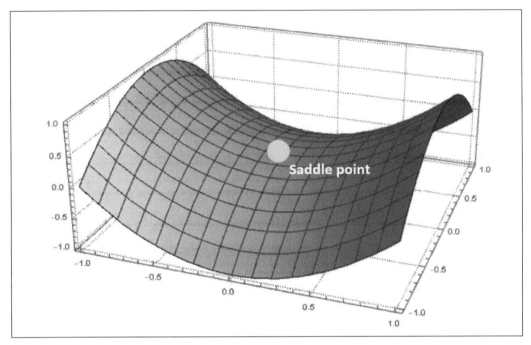

Example of saddle point in a hyperbolic paraboloid

Considering the previous example, as the function is $f(x,y) = x^2 - y^2$, the partial derivatives and the Hessian are:

$$\frac{\partial f}{\partial x} = 2x \ \text{ and } \ \frac{\partial f}{\partial y} = -2y \text{ and } \mathcal{H} = \begin{pmatrix} 2 & 0 \\ 0 & -2 \end{pmatrix}$$

Hence, the point the first partial derivatives vanishes at (0, 0), so the point is a candidate to be an extreme. However, the Hessian has the eigenvalues that are solutions of the equation $(2 - \lambda)(-2 - \lambda) = 0$, which leads to $\lambda_1 = 2$ and $\lambda_2 = -2$, therefore the matrix is neither positive nor negative (semi-)definite and the point (0, 0) is a saddle point. It goes without saying that these kind of points are quite dangerous during the optimization process, because they can be located at the center of valleys where the gradient tends to vanish. In those cases, even many corrections can result in minimal movement. A common result of applying a *vanilla* SGD algorithm to these systems is shown in the following diagram:

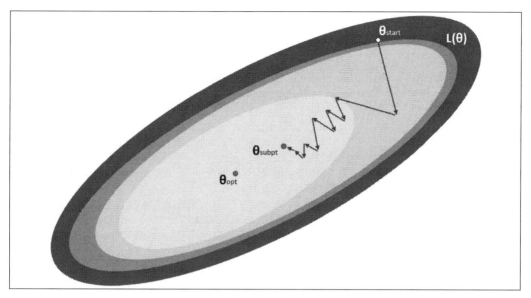

Graphical representation of a real optimization process

Instead of reaching the optimal configuration, $\bar{\theta}_{opt}$, the algorithm reaches a sub-optimal parameter configuration, $\bar{\theta}_{subopt}$, and loses the ability to perform further corrections because the gradients tend to vanish and, consequently, their contribution becomes negligible. To mitigate all these problems and their consequences, many SGD optimization algorithms have been proposed, with the purpose of speeding up convergence (also when the gradients become extremely small) and avoiding the instabilities of ill-conditioned systems.

Gradient perturbation

A common problem arises when the hypersurface is flat (plateaus) – the gradients become close to zero. A very simple way to mitigate this problem is based on adding a small homoscedastic noise component to the gradients:

$$\nabla_{\bar{\theta}} L^n = \nabla_{\bar{\theta}} L + \bar{n}(t) \;\; where \; \bar{n}(t) \sim N(0, \Sigma(t))$$

The covariance matrix is normally diagonal with all elements set to $\sigma^2(t)$, and this value is decayed during the training process to avoid perturbations when the corrections are very small. This method is conceptually reasonable, but its implicit randomness can yield undesired effects when the noise component is dominant. As it's very difficult to tune up the variances in deep models, other (more deterministic) strategies have been proposed.

Momentum and Nesterov momentum

A more robust way to improve the performance of SGD when plateaus are encountered is based on the idea of momentum (analogous to physical momentum). More formally, momentum is obtained by employing the weighted moving average of subsequent gradient estimations instead of the punctual value:

$$\bar{v}^{(t+1)} = \mu\bar{v}^{(t)} - \eta\nabla_{\bar{\theta}}L$$

The new vector $\bar{v}^{(t+1)}$ contains a component that is based on the past history (and weighted using the parameter μ, which is a forgetting factor) and a term referred to the current gradient estimation (multiplied by the learning rate). With this approach, abrupt changes become more difficult. When the exploration leaves a sloped region to enter a plateau, the momentum doesn't become immediately null, but for a time (proportional to μ) a portion of the previous gradients will be kept, making it possible to traverse flat regions. The value assigned to the hyperparameter μ is normally bounded between 0 and 1. Intuitively, small values imply a short memory as the first term decays very quickly, while values close to 1.0 (for example, 0.9) allow a longer memory, less influenced by local oscillations. Like many other hyperparameters, μ needs to be tuned according to the specific problem, considering that a high momentum is not always the best choice. High values could slow down the convergence when very small adjustments are needed, but at the same time, values close to 0.0 are normally ineffective because the memory contribution decays too early. Using momentum, the update rule becomes as follows:

$$\bar{\theta}^{(t+1)} = \bar{\theta}^{(t)} + \bar{v}^{(t+1)}$$

A variant is provided by Nesterov momentum, which is based on the results obtained in the field of mathematical optimization by Y. Nesterov, which has been proven to speed up the convergence of many algorithms. The idea is to determine a temporary parameter update based on the current momentum and then apply the gradient to this vector to determine the next momentum (it can be interpreted as a look-ahead gradient evaluation aimed to mitigate the risk of an incorrect correction considering the moving history of each parameter):

$$\begin{cases} \bar{\theta}_N^{(t+1)} = \bar{\theta}^{(t)} + \mu\bar{v}^{(t)} \\ \bar{v}^{(t+1)} = \mu\bar{v}^{(t)} - \eta\nabla_{\bar{\theta}}L\left(\bar{\theta}_N^{(t+1)}\right) \end{cases}$$

This algorithm showed a performance improvement in several deep models; however, its usage is still limited because, as you'll see later in this chapter, newer algorithms very soon outperformed the standard SGD with momentum, and they became the first choice in almost any real-life task.

SGD with Momentum in TensorFlow and Keras

When using TensorFlow/Keras, it's possible to customize the SGD optimizer by directly instantiating the SGD class and using it while compiling the model:

```
import tensorflow as tf

sgd = tf.keras.optimizers.SGD(lr=0.0001,
                              momentum=0.8,
                              nesterov=True)

model.compile(optimizer=sgd,
              loss='categorical_crossentropy',
              metrics=['accuracy'])
```

The class SGD accepts the parameter lr (the learning rate η with a default set equal to 0.01), momentum (the parameter μ), nesterov (a Boolean indicating whether Nesterov momentum is employed), and an optional decay parameter to indicate whether the learning rate must be decayed over the updates with the following formula:

$$\eta^{(t+1)} = \frac{\eta^{(t)}}{1 + decay}$$

Obviously, when *decay = 0*, the learning rate remains constant throughout the training process. With positive values, it starts decaying with a speed inversely proportional to *decay*.

In the following figure, three decayed learning rates are shown:

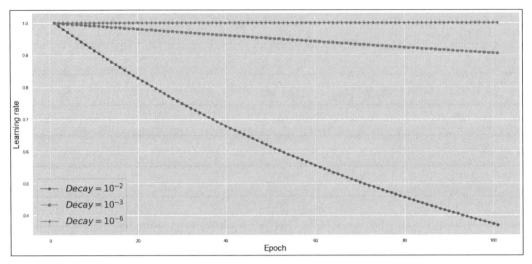

Plot of a learning rate decayed over 100 epochs with 3 different decay values

As it's possible to see, with the default value of *decay* = 10^{-2}, a hypothetical initial learning rate η = 1.0 reaches 0.5 after about 50 epochs and it's slightly lower than 0.4 at the end of the training process. As expected, exponentially smaller decays have a dramatic impact on the learning rate. For example, *decay* = 10^{-3} reaches 0.9 at the end of the process, while *decay* = 10^{-6} has almost no impact. We are going to use this very value in most of our examples; in particular, when the number of epochs is not extremely large (for example, $n < 200$) and, with an almost constant learning rate, we keep observing a constant training/validation loss decrease throughout the process. Instead, in cases where the performance becomes worse after a number of epochs, it probably means that the algorithm has reached the basin of a minimum but keeps on jumping on the sides without reaching it. In these cases, smaller learning rates can help to improve the accuracy with a proportionally longer training process.

RMSProp

RMSProp was proposed by G. Hinton as an adaptive algorithm, partially based on the concept of momentum. Instead of considering the whole gradient vector, it tries to optimize each parameter separately to increase the corrections of slowly changing weights (which probably need more drastic modifications) and decreases the update magnitudes of quickly changing ones (which are normally the more unstable). The algorithm computes the exponentially weighted moving average of the changing speed of every parameter considering the square of the gradient (which is insensitive to the sign):

$$\bar{v}^{(t+1)}(\bar{\theta}_i) = \mu \bar{v}^{(t)} + (1 - \mu)\left(\nabla_{\bar{\theta}} L(\bar{\theta}_i)\right)^2$$

The weight update is then performed, as follows:

$$\bar{\theta}_i^{(t+1)} = \bar{\theta}_i^{(t)} - \frac{\eta}{\sqrt{\bar{v}^{(t+1)}(\bar{\theta}_i) + \delta}} \nabla_{\bar{\theta}} L(\bar{\theta}_i)$$

The parameter δ is a small constant (such as 10^{-6}) that is added to avoid numerical instabilities when the changing speed becomes null. The previous expression could be rewritten in a more compact way:

$$\bar{\theta}_i^{(t+1)} = \bar{\theta}_i^{(t)} + \mu(\bar{\theta}_i)\nabla_{\bar{\theta}} L(\bar{\theta}_i)$$

Using this notation, it is clear that the role of RMSProp is adapting the learning rate for every parameter so that it can increase it when necessary (almost *frozen* weights) and decrease it when the risk of oscillations is higher. In a practical implementation, the learning rate is always decayed over the epochs using an exponential or linear function.

RMSProp in TensorFlow and Keras

The following snippet shows the usage of RMSProp with TensorFlow/Keras:

```
import tensorflow as tf

rmp = tf.keras.optimizers.RMSprop(lr=0.0001,
                                  rho=0.8,
                                  epsilon=1e-6,
                                  decay=1e-2)

model.compile(optimizer=rmp,
              loss='categorical_crossentropy',
              metrics=['accuracy'])
```

The learning rate and decay are the same as SGD. The parameter `rho` corresponds to the exponential moving average weight μ, and epsilon ϵ is the constant added to the changing speed to improve the stability. As with any other algorithm, if the user wants to use the default values, it's possible to declare the optimizer without instantiating the class (for example, `optimizer='rmsprop'`).

Adam

Adam (a contraction of **Adaptive Moment Estimation**) is an algorithm proposed by Kingma and Ba (in Kingma D. P., Ba J., *Adam: A Method for Stochastic Optimization*, arXiv:1412.6980 [cs.LG]) to further improve the performance of RMSProp. The algorithm determines an adaptive learning rate by computing the exponentially weighted averages of both the gradient and its square for every parameter:

$$\begin{cases} \bar{g}^{(t+1)}(\bar{\theta}_i) = \mu_1 \bar{g}^{(t)}(\bar{\theta}_i) + (1-\mu_1)\nabla_{\bar{\theta}}L(\bar{\theta}_i) \\ \bar{v}^{(t+1)}(\bar{\theta}_i) = \mu_2 \bar{v}^{(t)}(\bar{\theta}_i) + (1-\mu_2)\left(\nabla_{\bar{\theta}}L(\bar{\theta}_i)\right)^2 \end{cases}$$

In the aforementioned paper, the authors suggest unbiasing the two estimations (which concern the first and second moment) by dividing them by $1-\mu_i$, so the new moving averages become as follows:

$$\begin{cases} \hat{g}^{(t+1)}(\bar{\theta}_i) = \dfrac{\bar{g}^{(t+1)}(\bar{\theta}_i)}{1-\mu_1} \\ \hat{v}^{(t+1)}(\bar{\theta}_i) = \dfrac{\bar{v}^{(t+1)}(\bar{\theta}_i)}{1-\mu_2} \end{cases}$$

The weight update rule for Adam is as follows:

$$\bar{\theta}_i^{(t+1)} = \bar{\theta}_i^{(t)} - \frac{\eta \hat{g}^{(t+1)}(\bar{\theta}_i)}{\sqrt{\hat{v}^{(t+1)}(\bar{\theta}_i) + \delta}}$$

Analyzing the previous expression, it is possible to understand why this algorithm is often called RMSProp with momentum. In fact, the term $\hat{g}^{(t+1)}(\bar{\theta}_i)$ acts just like the standard momentum, computing the moving average of the gradient for each parameter (with all the advantages of this procedure), while the denominator acts as an adaptive term with the same exact semantics of RMSProp. For this reason, Adam is very often one of the most widely employed algorithms, even if, in many complex tasks, its performance is comparable to a standard RMSProp. The choice must be made considering the extra complexity due to the presence of two forgetting factors. In general, the default values (0.9) are acceptable, but sometimes it's better to perform an analysis of several scenarios before deciding on a specific configuration.

Another important element to remember is that all momentum-based methods can lead to instabilities (oscillations) when training some deep architectures. That's why RMSProp is very diffused in almost any research paper; however, don't consider this statement as a limitation, because Adam has shown outstanding performance on many tasks. It's helpful to remember that, whenever the training process seems unstable, also with low learning rates, it's preferable to employ methods that are not based on momentum (the inertial term, in fact, can slow down the fast modifications necessary to avoid oscillations).

Adam in TensorFlow and Keras

The following snippet shows the usage of Adam with TensorFlow/Keras:

```
import tensorflow as tf

adam = tf.keras.optimizers.Adam(lr=0.0001,
                                beta_1=0.9,
                                beta_2=0.9,
                                epsilon=1e-6,
                                decay=1e-2)

model.compile(optimizer=adam,
              loss='categorical_crossentropy',
              metrics=['accuracy'])
```

The forgetting factors, μ_1 and μ_2, are represented by the parameters `beta_1` and `beta_2`. All the other elements are the same as the other algorithms. The choice of parameters has been evaluated by the authors considering a large parameter space and it's generally not necessary to change them (except for the learning rate). In particular cases when there are no other solutions, it's advisable to slightly reduce the forgetting factors and the decay (for instance, in our next examples, we are often going to employ a much smaller decay equal to 10^{-6}, which avoids the rapid decay of the learning rate). This process can be repeated to check whether a more conservative configuration yields better performance. If the desired result is not achieved, it's preferable to change architecture, because drastic changes to the parameters might produce instabilities that worsen the training phase.

AdaGrad

This algorithm has been proposed by Duchi, Hazan, and Singer (in Duchi J., Hazan E., Singer Y., *Adaptive Subgradient Methods for Online Learning and Stochastic Optimization*, Journal of Machine Learning Research 12, 2011). The idea is very similar to RMSProp, but in this case, the whole history of the squared gradients is taken into account:

$$\bar{v}^{(t+1)}(\bar{\theta}_i) = \bar{v}^{(t)}(\bar{\theta}_i) + \left(\nabla_{\bar{\theta}} L(\bar{\theta}_i)\right)^2$$

The weights are updated exactly as in RMSProp:

$$\bar{\theta}_i^{(t+1)} = \bar{\theta}_i^{(t)} - \frac{\eta}{\sqrt{\hat{v}^{(t+1)}(\bar{\theta}_i) + \delta}} \nabla_{\bar{\theta}} L(\bar{\theta}_i)$$

However, as the squared gradients are non-negative, the implicit sum $\bar{v}^{(t)}(\bar{\theta}_i) \to \infty$ when $t \to \infty$. As the growth continues until the gradients are non-null, there's no way to keep the contribution stable while the training process proceeds. The effect is normally quite strong at the beginning, but vanishes after a limited number of epochs, yielding a null learning rate. AdaGrad keeps on being a powerful algorithm when the number of epochs is very limited, but it cannot be a first-choice solution for the majority of deep models (the next algorithm was proposed to solve this problem).

AdaGrad with TensorFlow and Keras

The following snippet shows the use of AdaGrad with TensorFlow/Keras:

```
import tensorflow as tf

adg = tf.keras.optimizers.Adagrad(lr=0.0001,
                                  epsilon=1e-6,
                                  decay=1e-2)

model.compile(optimizer=adg,
              loss='categorical_crossentropy',
              metrics=['accuracy'])
```

The AdaGrad implementation has no other parameters except for the ones discussed in the theoretical part. As for other optimizers, there's normally no need to change either epsilon or decay, while it's always possible to tune up the learning rate.

AdaDelta

AdaDelta is an algorithm (proposed in Zeiler M. D., *ADADELTA: An Adaptive Learning Rate Method*, arXiv:1212.5701 [cs.LG]) in order to address the main issue of AdaGrad, which arises to manage the whole squared gradient history. First of all, instead of the accumulator, AdaDelta employs an exponentially weighted moving average, like RMSProp:

$$\bar{v}^{(t+1)}(\bar{\theta}_i) = \mu \bar{v}^{(t)}(\bar{\theta}_i) + (1 - \mu)\left(\nabla_{\bar{\theta}} L(\bar{\theta}_i)\right)^2$$

However, the main difference with RMSProp is based on the analysis of the update rule. When we consider the operation $\bar{x} + \Delta\bar{x}$, we assume that both terms have the same unit; however, the author noticed that the adaptive learning rate $\eta(\bar{\theta}_i)$ obtained with RMSProp (as well as AdaGrad) is unitless (instead of having the unit of $\bar{\theta}_i$). In fact, as the gradient is split into partial derivatives that can be approximated as $\Delta L/\Delta\bar{\theta}_i$ and the cost function L is assumed to be unitless, we obtain the following relations:

$$unit_{\nabla_{\bar{\theta}} L(\bar{\theta}_i)} = \frac{1}{unit_{\bar{\theta}_i}} \quad and \quad unit_{\Delta\bar{\theta}_i} \propto \frac{unit_{\nabla_{\bar{\theta}} L(\bar{\theta}_i)}}{\sqrt{unit_{\bar{v}^{(t+1)}(\bar{\theta}_i)}}} \propto \frac{\frac{1}{unit_{\bar{\theta}_i}}}{\sqrt{\frac{1}{\left(unit_{\Delta\bar{\theta}_i}\right)^2}}} \propto 1$$

Therefore, Zeiler proposed applying a correction term proportional to the unit of each weight $\bar{\theta}_i$. This factor is obtained by considering the exponentially weighted moving average of every squared difference:

$$\bar{u}^{(t+1)}(\bar{\theta}_i) = \mu \bar{u}^{(t)}(\bar{\theta}_i) + (1 - \mu)(\Delta\bar{\theta}_i)^2$$

The resulting updated rule hence becomes as follows:

$$\bar{\theta}_i^{(t+1)} = \bar{\theta}_i^{(t)} - \frac{\eta\sqrt{\bar{u}^{(t)}(\bar{\theta}_i)}}{\sqrt{\bar{v}^{(t+1)}(\bar{\theta}_i) + \delta}} \nabla_{\bar{\theta}} L(\bar{\theta}_i)$$

This approach is indeed more similar to RMSProp than AdaGrad, but the boundaries between the two algorithms are very thin, in particular when the history is limited to a finite sliding window. AdaDelta is a powerful algorithm, but it can outperform Adam or RMSProp only on very particular tasks (such as where the problem is ill-conditioned).

My suggestion is to employ a method and, before moving to another one, try to optimize the hyperparameters until the accuracy reaches its maximum. If the performance keeps on being bad and the model cannot be improved in any other way, it's a good idea to test other optimization algorithms.

AdaDelta in TensorFlow and Keras

The following snippet shows the usage of AdaDelta with TensorFlow/Keras:

```
import tensorflow as tf

add = tf.keras.optimizers.Adadelta(lr=0.0001,
                                   rho=0.9,
                                   epsilon=1e-6,
                                   decay=1e-2)
model.compile(optimizer=add,
              loss='categorical_crossentropy',
              metrics=['accuracy'])
```

The forgetting factor, μ, is represented by the parameter rho (ρ). As for the other methods, it's necessary to pay attention to different parameter configurations because they can yield instabilities. Unfortunately, contrary to simpler machine learning algorithms, the effect of small changes is often unpredictable because of the complexity of the function subject to optimization. The default choices are generally obtained after performing a grid search with a set of general-purpose tasks and selecting the best parameter set.

Regularization and Dropout

Overfitting is a common issue in deep models. Their extremely high capacity can often become problematic even with very large datasets because the ability to learn the structure of the training set is not always related to the ability to generalize. A deep neural network can easily become an associative memory, but the final internal configuration might not be the most suitable to manage samples belonging to the same distribution because that distribution was never presented during the training process. It goes without saying that this behavior is proportional to the complexity of the separation hypersurface.

A linear classifier has a minimal chance of overfitting, and a polynomial classifier is incredibly more prone to do so. A combination of hundreds, thousands, or more non-linear functions yields a separation hypersurface that is beyond any possible analysis.

In 1991, Hornik (in Hornik K., *Approximation Capabilities of Multilayer Feedforward Networks*, Neural Networks, 4/2, 1991) generalized a very important result obtained 2 years before by the mathematician Cybenko (and published in Cybenko G., *Approximations by Superpositions of Sigmoidal Functions, Mathematics of Control, Signals, and Systems*, 2 /4, 1989). Without any mathematical detail (which is, however, not very complex), the theorem states that an MLP (not the most complex architecture!) can approximate any function that is continuous in a compact subset of $\mathbb{R}^n$. It's clear that such a result formalized what almost any researcher already intuitively knew, but its power goes beyond the first impact because the MLP is a finite system (not a mathematical series) and the theorem assumes a finite number of layers and neurons.

Obviously, the precision is proportional to the complexity; however, there are no unacceptable limitations for almost any problem. However, our goal is not learning an existing continuous function, but managing samples drawn from an unknown data-generating process with the purpose of maximizing the accuracy when a new sample is presented. There are no guarantees that the function is continuous or that the domain is a compact subset.

Regularization

In *Chapter 2*, *Loss functions and Regularization*, we presented the main regularization techniques based on a slightly modified cost function:

$$L_r(X, Y; \bar{\theta}) = \frac{1}{M} \sum_{i=1}^{M} L(\bar{x}_i, \bar{y}_i; \bar{\theta}) + g(\bar{\theta})$$

The additional term $g(\bar{\theta})$ is a non-negative function of the weights (such as L_2 norm) that forces the optimization process to keep the parameters as small as possible. When working with saturating functions (such as tanh), regularization methods based on the L_2 norm try to limit the operating range of the function to the linear part, reducing its capacity. Of course, the final configuration won't be the optimal one (that could be the result of an overfitted model) but the suboptimal trade-off between training and validation accuracy (alternatively, we can say between bias and variance).

A system with a bias close to 0 (and a training accuracy close to 1.0) could be extremely rigid in the classification, succeeding only when the samples are very similar to ones evaluated during the training process. That's why this price is often paid considering the advantages obtained when working with new samples. L_2 regularization can be employed with any kind of activation function, but the effect could be different.

For example, ReLU units have an increased probability of becoming linear (or constantly null) when the weights are very large. Trying to keep them close to 0.0 means forcing the function to exploit its non-linearity without the risk of extremely large outputs (which can negatively affect very deep architectures). This result can sometimes be more useful, because it allows training bigger models in a smoother way, obtaining better final performance.

In general, it's almost impossible to decide whether regularization can improve the result without several tests, but there are some scenarios where it's very common to introduce a dropout (we discuss this approach in the next section) and tune up its hyperparameter. This is more an empirical choice than a precise architectural decision, because many real-life examples (including state-of-the-art models) have obtained outstanding results employing this regularization technique. I suggest you prefer rational skepticism to blind trust and double-check models before picking a specific solution. Sometimes, an extremely high-performing network turns out to be ineffective when a different (but analogous) dataset is chosen. That's why testing different alternatives can provide the best experience in order to solve specific problem classes.

Regularization in TensorFlow and Keras

Before moving on, I want to show how it's possible to implement L_1 (helpful to enforce sparsity), L_2, or ElasticNet (the combination of L_1 and L_2) regularization using TensorFlow and Keras. The framework provides a fine-grained approach that allows imposing a different constraint on each layer. For example, the following snippet shows how to add an `l2` constraint with the strength parameter set to `0.05` on a generic fully connected layer:

```
import tensorflow as tf

l2 = tf.keras.regularizers.l2(0.05)
...
tf.keras.layers.Dense(10, activity_regularizer=l2)

...
```

The `keras.regularizers` package contains the functions `l1()`, `l2()`, and `l1_l2()`, which can be applied to dense and convolutional layers (we're going to discuss them in the next chapter). These layers allow us to impose regularization on the weights (`kernel_regularizer`), on the bias (`bias_regularizer`), and on the activation output (`activation_regularizer`), even if the first one is normally the most widely employed.

Alternatively, it's possible to impose specific constraints on the weights and biases in a more selective way. The following snippet shows how to set a maximum norm (equal to 1.5) on the weights of a layer:

```
import tensorflow as tf

kc = tf.keras.constraints.max_norm(1.5)
...
tf.keras.layers.Dense(10, kernel_constraint=kc)

...
```

Keras, in the `keras.constraints` package, provides some functions that can be used to impose a maximum norm on the weights or biases `max_norm()`, a unit norm along an axis `unit_norm()`, non-negativity `non_neg()`, and upper and lower bounds for the norm `min_max_norm()`. The difference between this approach and regularization is that it is applied only if necessary. Considering the previous example, imposing L_2 regularization always has an effect, while a constraint on the maximum norm is inactive until the value is lower than the predefined threshold.

Dropout

This method has been proposed by Hinton and co. (in Hinton G. E., Srivastava N., Krizhevsky A., Sutskever I., Salakhutdinov R. R., *Improving neural networks by preventing co-adaptation of feature detectors*, arXiv:1207.0580 [cs.NE]) as an alternative to prevent overfitting and allow bigger networks to explore more regions of the sample space. The idea is rather simple—during every training step, given a predefined percentage n_d, a dropout layer randomly selects $n_d N$ incoming units and sets them to 0.0 (the operation is only active during the training phase, while it's completely removed when the model is employed for new predictions).

This operation can be interpreted in many ways. When more dropout layers are employed, the result of their selection is a sub-network with a reduced capacity that can, with more difficultly, overfit the training set. The overlap of many trained sub-networks makes up an implicit ensemble whose prediction is an average over all models. If the dropout is applied on input layers, it works like a weak data augmentation, by adding random noise to the samples (setting a few units to zero can lead to potentially corrupted patterns). At the same time, employing several dropout layers allows exploring several potential configurations that are continuously combined and refined.

This strategy is clearly probabilistic, and the result can be affected by many factors that are impossible to anticipate; however, several tests have confirmed that the employment of dropout is a good choice when networks are very deep because the resulting sub-networks have a residual capacity that allows them to model a wide portion of the samples, without driving the whole network to freeze its configuration, overfitting the training set. On the other hand, this method is not very effective when networks are shallow or contain a small number of neurons (in these cases, L_2 regularization is probably a better choice).

According to the authors, dropout layers should be used in conjunction with high learning rates and maximum norm constraints on the weights. In this way, in fact, the model can easily learn more potential configurations that would be avoided when the learning rate is kept very small. However, this is not an absolute rule because many state-of-the-art models use a dropout together with optimization algorithms, such as RMSProp or Adam, and not excessively high learning rates.

The main drawback of a dropout is that it slows down the training process and can lead to unacceptable sub-optimality. The latter problem can be mitigated by adjusting the percentages of dropped units, but in general, it's very difficult to solve it completely. For this reason, some new image-recognition models (such as residual networks) avoid dropout and employ more sophisticated techniques to train very deep convolutional networks that overfit both training and validation sets.

Dropout with TensorFlow and Keras

We can now test the effectiveness of the dropout technique with a more challenging classification problem. The dataset is the classical MNIST handwritten digits, but Keras allows downloading and working with the original version, which is made up of 70,000 (60,000 training and 10,000 test) 28 × 28 grayscale images. Even if this is not the best strategy, because a convolutional network should be the first choice to manage images, we want to try to classify the digits considering them as flattened 784-dimensional arrays.

The first step is loading and normalizing the dataset so that each value becomes a float bounded between 0 and 1:

```
import tensorflow as tf
import numpy as np

(X_train, Y_train), (X_test, Y_test) = \
        tf.keras.datasets.mnist.load_data()

width = height = X_train.shape[1]
```

```
X_train = X_train.reshape(
        (X_train.shape[0], width * height)).\
                astype(np.float32) / 255.0
X_test = X_test.reshape(
        (X_test.shape[0], width * height)).\
                astype(np.float32) / 255.0

Y_train = tf.keras.utils.to_categorical(
        Y_train, num_classes=10)
Y_test = tf.keras.utils.to_categorical(
        Y_test, num_classes=10)
```

At this point, we can start testing a model without dropout. The structure, which is common to all experiments, is based on three fully connected ReLU layers (2048-1024-1024) followed by a softmax layer with 10 units. Considering the problem, we can try to train the model using an Adam optimizer with $\eta = 0.0001$ and a decay set equal to 10^{-6}:

```
model = tf.keras.models.Sequential([
        tf.keras.layers.Dense(2048,
                        input_shape=(width*height,),
                        activation='relu'),
        tf.keras.layers.Dense(1024, activation='relu'),
        tf.keras.layers.Dense(1024, activation='relu'),
        tf.keras.layers.Dense(10, activation='softmax')
])

model.compile(optimizer=
                tf.keras.optimizers.Adam(
                        lr=0.0001, decay=1e-6),
                loss='categorical_crossentropy',
                metrics=['accuracy'])
```

The model is trained for 200 epochs with a batch size of 256 data points:

```
history_nd = model.fit(X_train, Y_train,
                        epochs=200,
                        batch_size=256,
                        validation_data=(X_test, Y_test))
```

The output of the previous snippet is:

```
Train on 60000 samples, validate on 10000 samples
Epoch 1/200
60000/60000 [==============================] - 3s 50us/sample - loss:
0.3997 - accuracy: 0.8979 - val_loss: 0.1672 - val_accuracy: 0.9503
```

```
Epoch 2/200
60000/60000 [==============================] - 2s 37us/sample - loss:
0.1371 - accuracy: 0.9605 - val_loss: 0.1138 - val_accuracy: 0.9640
Epoch 3/200
60000/60000 [==============================] - 2s 36us/sample - loss:
0.0887 - accuracy: 0.9740 - val_loss: 0.0893 - val_accuracy: 0.9716

...

Epoch 199/200
60000/60000 [==============================] - 3s 43us/sample - loss:
2.9862e-09 - accuracy: 1.0000 - val_loss: 0.1380 - val_accuracy: 0.9845
Epoch 200/200
60000/60000 [==============================] - 3s 42us/sample - loss:
2.9624e-09 - accuracy: 1.0000 - val_loss: 0.1380 - val_accuracy: 0.9845
```

Even without further analysis, we can immediately notice that the model is overfitted. After 200 epochs, the training accuracy is 1.0 with a loss close to 0.0, while the validation accuracy is reasonably high, but with a validation loss slightly lower than the one obtained at the end of the second epoch.

To better understand what happened, it's useful to plot both accuracy and loss during the training process:

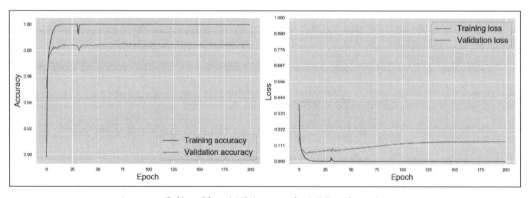

Accuracy (left) and loss (right) curves for MLP without dropout

As it's possible to see, the validation loss reached a minimum during the first 10 epochs and then immediately started to grow (this is sometimes called a *U-curve* because of its shape). At the same moment, the training accuracy reached 1.0. From that epoch on, the model started overfitting, learning the perfect structure of the training set, but losing the generalization ability. In fact, even if the final validation accuracy is rather high, the loss function indicates a lack of robustness when new samples are presented.

As the loss is categorical cross-entropy, the result can be interpreted as saying that the model has learned a distribution that partially mismatches the validation set distribution.

As our goal is to use the model to predict new samples, this configuration is not acceptable. Therefore, we try again, using some dropout layers. As suggested by the authors, we also increment the learning rate to 0.1 (switching to a momentum SGD optimizer in order to avoid explosions due to the adaptivity of RMSProp or Adam), initialize the weight with a uniform distribution (-0.05, 0.05), and impose a maximum norm constraint set to 2.0. This choice allows the exploration of more sub-configurations without the risk of excessively high weights. The dropout is applied to 25% of input units and to all ReLU fully connected layers with the percentage set to 50%:

```
import tensorflow as tf

model = tf.keras.models.Sequential([
        tf.keras.layers.Dropout(0.25,
                        input_shape=(width*height,),
                        seed=1000),
        tf.keras.layers.Dense(2048,
                kernel_initializer='uniform',
                kernel_constraint=
                tf.keras.constraints.max_norm(2.0),
                activation='relu'),
        tf.keras.layers.Dropout(0.5, seed=1000),
        tf.keras.layers.Dense(1024,
                kernel_initializer='uniform',
                kernel_constraint=
                tf.keras.constraints.max_norm(2.0),
                activation='relu'),
        tf.keras.layers.Dropout(0.5, seed=1000),
        tf.keras.layers.Dense(1024,
                kernel_initializer='uniform',
                kernel_constraint=
                tf.keras.constraints.max_norm(2.0),
                activation='relu'),
        tf.keras.layers.Dropout(0.5, seed=1000),
        tf.keras.layers.Dense(10, activation='softmax')
])

model.compile(optimizer=
        tf.keras.optimizers.SGD(lr=0.1, momentum=0.9),
        loss='categorical_crossentropy',
```

```
                    metrics=['accuracy'])
```

The training process is performed with the same parameters:

```
history = model.fit(X_train, Y_train,
                    epochs=200,
                    batch_size=256,
                    validation_data=(X_test, Y_test))
```

The output of the previous block is:

```
Train on 60000 samples, validate on 10000 samples

Epoch 1/200

60000/60000 [==============================] - 3s 53us/sample - loss:
0.4993 - accuracy: 0.8393 - val_loss: 0.1497 - val_accuracy: 0.9559

Epoch 2/200

60000/60000 [==============================] - 3s 45us/sample - loss:
0.2299 - accuracy: 0.9295 - val_loss: 0.1118 - val_accuracy: 0.9654

...

Epoch 199/200

60000/60000 [==============================] - 3s 52us/sample - loss:
0.0195 - accuracy: 0.9938 - val_loss: 0.0516 - val_accuracy: 0.9878

Epoch 200/200

60000/60000 [==============================] - 5s 77us/sample - loss:
0.0185 - accuracy: 0.9944 - val_loss: 0.0510 - val_accuracy: 0.9875
```

The final condition is dramatically changed. The model is no longer overfitted (even if it's possible to improve it in order to increase the validation accuracy) and the validation loss is lower than the initial one. To get confirmation, let's analyze the accuracy/loss plots:

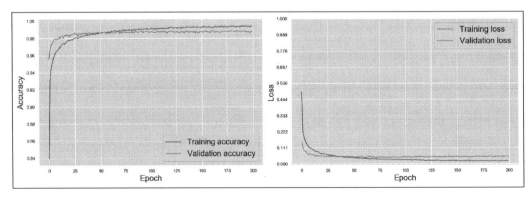

Accuracy (left) and loss (right) curves for MLP with dropout

The result shows some imperfections because the validation loss is almost flat for many epochs; however, the same model, with a higher learning rate and a weaker algorithm, achieved a better final performance (0.988 validation accuracy) and a superior generalization ability. *State-of-the-art* models can also reach a validation accuracy equal to 0.995, but our goal was to show the effect of dropout layers in preventing overfitting and, moreover, yielding a final configuration that is much more robust to new samples or noisy ones. I invite you to repeat the experiment with different parameters, bigger or smaller networks, and other optimization algorithms, trying to further reduce the final validation loss.

TesorFlow/Keras also implements two additional dropout layers. `GaussianDropout` (https://keras.io/layers/core/) multiplies the input samples by Gaussian noise:

$$\hat{x}_i = \bar{x}_i \cdot \bar{n} \ where \ \bar{n} \sim N\left(1.0, \frac{\rho}{1-\rho}\right)$$

The value for the constant ρ can be set through the parameter rate (bounded between 0 and 1) when $\rho \to 1$, $\sigma^2 \to \infty$, while small values yield a null effect as $\bar{n} \approx 1$. This layer can be very useful as an input layer, in order to simulate a random data augmentation process.

The other class is `AlphaDropout`, which works like the previous one, but renormalizes the output to keep the original mean and variance (this effect is very similar to the one obtained by employing the technique described in the next paragraph together with noisy layers).

When working with probabilistic layers (such as dropout), I always suggest setting the random seed (`np.random.seed(...)` and `tf.random.set_seed(...)` when a TensorFlow backend is used). In this way, it's possible to repeat the experiments, comparing the results without any bias. If the random seed is not explicitly set, every new training process will be different and it won't be easy to compare the performance, for example, after a fixed number of epochs.

Batch normalization

Let's consider a mini-batch containing k data points:

$$\bar{n} \approx 1$$

Before traversing the network, we can measure the sample mean and variance:

$$\bar{X}_b = \frac{1}{k}\sum_{i=1}^{k}\bar{x}_i \ \ and \ \ Var(X_b) = \frac{1}{k-1}\sum_{i=1}^{k}(\bar{x}_i - \bar{X}_b)^2$$

After the first layer (for simplicity, let's suppose that the activation function, $f_a(x)$, is always the same), the batch is transformed into the following:

$$X_b^{(1)} = \{f_a(\bar{w}_1^T\bar{x}_1 + \bar{b}_1), f_a(\bar{w}_2^T\bar{x}_2 + \bar{b}_2), ..., f_a(\bar{w}_k^T\bar{x}_k + \bar{b}_k)\}$$

In general, there's no guarantee that the new mean and variance are the same. On the contrary, it's easy to observe a modification that increases throughout the network. This phenomenon is called covariate shift, and it's responsible for a progressive training speed decay due to the different adaptations needed in each layer. Ioffe and Szegedy (in Ioffe S., Szegedy C., *Batch Normalization: Accelerating Deep Network Training by Reducing Internal Covariate Shift*, arXiv:1502.03167 [cs.LG]) proposed a method to mitigate this problem, which is called batch normalization (BN).

The idea is to renormalize the linear output of a layer (before or after applying the activation function) so that the batch has null mean and unit variance. Therefore, the first task of a BN layer is to compute:

$$\bar{X}_b^{(j)} = \frac{1}{k}\sum_{i=1}^{k}\bar{x}_i^{(j)} \ \ and \ \ Var\left(X_b^{(j)}\right) = \frac{1}{k-1}\sum_{i=1}^{k}\left(\bar{x}_i^{(j)} - \bar{X}_b^{(j)}\right)^2$$

Then, each sample is transformed into a normalized version (the parameter δ is included to improve the numerical stability):

$$\hat{x}_i^{(j)} = \frac{\bar{x}_i^{(j)} - \bar{X}_b^{(j)}}{\sqrt{Var\left(X_b^{(j)}\right) + \delta}}$$

However, as the BN has no computational purpose other than speeding up the training process, the transformation must always be an identity (in order to avoid distorting and biasing the data); therefore, the actual output will be obtained by applying the linear operation:

$$\bar{y}_i^{(j)} = \alpha^{(j)}\hat{x}_i^{(j)} + \beta^{(j)}$$

The two parameters $\alpha^{(j)}$ and $\beta^{(j)}$ are variables optimized by the SGD algorithm; therefore, each transformation is guaranteed not to alter the scale and the position of data. These layers are active only during the training phase (like dropout), but contrary to other algorithms, they cannot be simply discarded when the model is used to make predictions on new samples because the output would be constantly biased. To avoid this problem, the authors suggest approximating both the mean and variance of X_b by averaging over the batches (assuming that there are N_b batches with k data points):

$$\mu = \frac{1}{N_b} \sum_{i=1}^{N_b} \bar{X}^{(i)} \quad and \quad \sigma^2 = \frac{k}{N_b(k-1)} \sum_{i=1}^{N_b} Var\left(X_b^{(i)}\right)$$

Using these values, the BN layers can be transformed into the following linear operations:

$$y_i^{(j)} = \frac{\alpha^{(j)}}{\sqrt{\sigma^2 + \delta}} \bar{x}_i + \left(\beta^{(j)} - \frac{\alpha^{(j)}\mu}{\sqrt{\sigma^2 + \delta}} \right)$$

It's not difficult to prove that this approximation becomes more and more accurate when the number of batches increases and that the error is normally negligible. However, when the batch size is very small, the statistics can be quite inaccurate; therefore, this method should be used considering the representativeness of a batch. If the data-generating process is simple, even a small batch can be enough to describe the actual distribution.

When instead P_{data} is more complex, BN requires larger batches to avoid incorrect adjustments (a feasible strategy is to compare global mean and variance with the ones computed sampling some batches and trying to set the batch size that minimizes the discrepancy). However, this simple process can dramatically reduce the covariate shift and improve the convergence speed of very deep networks (including the famous residual networks).

Moreover, BN allows us to employ higher learning rates, since the layers are implicitly saturated and can never explode. Additionally, it has been proven that BN also has a secondary regularization effect even if it doesn't work on the weights. The reason is not very different from the one proposed for L_2, but in this case, there's a residual effect due to the transformation itself (partially caused by the variability of the parameters $\alpha^{(j)}$ and $\beta^{(j)}$), which can encourage the exploration of different regions of the sample space. However, this is not the primary effect, and it's not a good practice to employ this method as a regularizer.

Example of batch normalization with TensorFlow and Keras

In order to show the features of this technique, let's repeat the previous example using an MLP without dropout but applying BN after each fully connected layer before the ReLU activation. This example is very similar to the first one, but in this case, we'll increase the Adam learning rate to `0.001`, keeping the same decay:

```python
import tensorflow as tf

model = tf.keras.models.Sequential([
        tf.keras.layers.Dense(2048,
                        input_shape=(width*height,),
                        activation='relu'),
        tf.keras.layers.Dense(1024),
        tf.keras.layers.BatchNormalization(),
        tf.keras.layers.Activation('relu'),
        tf.keras.layers.Dense(1024),
        tf.keras.layers.BatchNormalization(),
        tf.keras.layers.Activation('relu'),
        tf.keras.layers.Dense(10),
        tf.keras.layers.BatchNormalization(),
        tf.keras.layers.Activation('softmax'),
])

model.compile(optimizer=
                tf.keras.optimizers.Adam(lr=0.001,
                                    decay=1e-6),
                loss='categorical_crossentropy',
                metrics=['accuracy'])
```

We can now train using the same parameters again:

```python
history_bn = model.fit(X_train, Y_train,
                    epochs=200,
                    batch_size=256,
                    validation_data=(X_test, Y_test))
```

The output of the previous snippet is:

```
Train on 60000 samples, validate on 10000 samples
Epoch 1/200
60000/60000 [==============================] - 13s 224us/sample - loss:
0.3881 - accuracy: 0.9556 - val_loss: 0.3788 - val_accuracy: 0.9769
Epoch 2/200
```

```
60000/60000 [==============================] - 13s 222us/sample - loss:
0.1966 - accuracy: 0.9842 - val_loss: 0.1916 - val_accuracy: 0.9805

...

Epoch 199/200

60000/60000 [==============================] - 12s 208us/sample - loss:
7.6897e-07 - accuracy: 1.0000 - val_loss: 0.0710 - val_accuracy: 0.9889
Epoch 200/200

60000/60000 [==============================] - 12s 207us/sample - loss:
6.6039e-07 - accuracy: 1.0000 - val_loss: 0.0719 - val_accuracy: 0.9890
```

The model is again overfitted, but now the final validation accuracy is only slightly higher than the one achieved using the dropout layers. Let's plot the accuracy and loss to better analyze the training process:

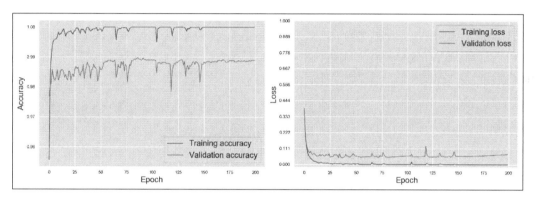

Accuracy (left) and loss (right) curves for MLP with batch normalization

The effect of the BN improved the performance and slowed down the overfitting. At the same time, the elimination of the covariate shift avoided the U-curve keeping a quite low validation loss (even though it's possible to observe a slight performance decrease at the end of the training process). Moreover, the model reached a validation accuracy of about 0.99 during epochs 135-140 with a residual positive trend, which is, however, not substantial.

Analogous to the previous example, this solution is imperfect, but it's a good starting point for further optimization. It would be a good idea to continue the training process for a larger number of epochs, monitoring both the validation loss and accuracy. Moreover, it's possible to mix dropout and BN or experiment with the Keras AlphaDropout layer. However, if, in the first example (without dropout), peak training accuracy was associated with a starting positive trend for the validation loss.

In this case, the learned distribution doesn't seem to be very different from the validation set one. In other words, BN is not preventing overfitting the training set, but it's avoiding a decay in the generalization ability (observed when there was no BN). I suggest repeating the test with other hyperparameter and architectural configurations in order to decide whether this model can be used for prediction purposes or whether it's better to look for other solutions.

Summary

In this chapter, we analyzed the role of momentum and how it's possible to manage adaptive corrections using RMSProp. Then, we combined momentum and RMSProp to derive a very powerful algorithm called Adam. In order to provide a complete picture, we also presented two slightly different adaptive algorithms, called AdaGrad and AdaDelta.

In the next sections, we discussed regularization methods and how they can be plugged into a Keras model. An important section was dedicated to a very diffused technique called dropout, which consists of setting to zero (dropping) a fixed percentage of samples through random selection. This method, although very simple, prevents the overfitting of very deep networks and encourages the exploration of different regions of the sample space, obtaining a result not very dissimilar to the ones analyzed in *Chapter 15, Fundamentals of Ensemble Learning*. The last topic was the batch normalization technique, which is a method for reducing the mean and variance shift (called covariate shift) caused by subsequent neural transformations. This phenomenon can slow down the training process as each layer requires different adaptations and it's more difficult to move all the weights in the best direction. Applying BN means very deep networks can be trained in a shorter time, thanks also to the possibility of employing higher learning rates.

In the next chapter, we are going to continue this exploration, analyzing very important advanced layers such as convolutions (which achieve extraordinary performance on image-oriented tasks) and recurrent units (for the processing of time series), and discussing some practical applications that can be experimented with and readapted using Keras and TensorFlow.

Further reading

- Glorot X., Bengio Y., *Understanding the difficulty of training deep feedforward neural networks*, Proceedings of the 13th International Conference on Artificial Intelligence and Statistics, 2010

- He K., Zhang X., Ren S., Sun J., *Delving Deep into Rectifiers: Surpassing Human-Level Performance on ImageNet Classification*, arXiv:1502.01852 [cs.CV]

- Holdroyd T., *TensorFlow 2.0 Quick Start Guide*, Packt Publishing, 2019

- *Kingma D. P., Ba J., Adam: A Method for Stochastic Optimization, arXiv:1412.6980 [cs.LG]*

- Duchi J., Hazan E., Singer Y., *Adaptive Subgradient Methods for Online Learning and Stochastic Optimization*, Journal of Machine Learning Research 12, 2011

- Zeiler M. D., *ADADELTA: An Adaptive Learning Rate Method*, arXiv:1212.5701 [cs.LG]

- Hornik K., *Approximation Capabilities of Multilayer Feedforward Networks*, Neural Networks, 4/2, 1991

- Cybenko G., *Approximations by Superpositions of Sigmoidal Functions*, Mathematics of Control, Signals, and Systems, 2 /4, 1989

- Hinton G. E., Srivastava N., Krizhevsky A., Sutskever I., Salakhutdinov R. R., *Improving neural networks by preventing co-adaptation of feature detectors*, arXiv:1207.0580 [cs.NE])

- Ioffe S., Szegedy C., *Batch Normalization: Accelerating Deep Network Training by Reducing Internal Covariate Shift*, arXiv:1502.03167 [cs.LG]

Deep Convolutional Networks

19

In this chapter, we continue our pragmatic exploration of the world of deep learning, analyzing deep convolutional networks. Deep convolutional networks represent the most accurate and best performing visual processing technique for almost any purpose. Results like the ones obtained in fields such as real-time image recognition, self-driving cars, and deep reinforcement learning have been possible thanks to the expressivity of this kind of network. Employing this technique together with all the elements discussed in the previous chapters makes it possible to achieve extraordinary results in the fields of video processing, decoding, segmentation, and generation.

In particular, in this chapter, we are going to discuss the following topics:

- Deep convolutional networks
- Convolutions, atrous convolutions
- Separable convolutions, and transpose convolutions
- Pooling and other support layers

At this point, we can start discussing the basic concepts of deep convolutional networks, trying to understand why such kind of operator is so helpful in solving visual detection tasks.

Deep convolutional networks

In the previous chapter, we saw how a multi-layer perceptron can achieve very high accuracy when working with an image dataset that is not very complex, such as the MNIST handwritten digits dataset. However, as the fully-connected layers are horizontal, the images, which in general are three-dimensional structures (*width* x *height* x *channels*), must be flattened and transformed into one-dimensional arrays where the geometric properties are definitively lost.

With more complex datasets, where the distinction between classes depends on details and on their relationships, this approach can yield moderate accuracy, but it can never reach the precision required by production-ready applications.

The conjunction of neuroscientific studies and image processing techniques suggested experimenting with neural networks where the first layers work with bidimensional structures (without the channels), trying to extract a hierarchy of features that are strictly dependent on the geometric properties of the image. In fact, as confirmed by neuroscientific research about the visual cortex, a human being doesn't decode an image directly. The process is sequential and starts by detecting low-level elements such as lines and orientations; progressively, it proceeds by focusing on sub-properties that define more and more complex shapes, different colors, structural features, and so on, until the amount of information is enough to resolve any possible ambiguity (for further scientific details, I recommend the book Stone J. V., *Vision and Brain*: *How We Perceive the World*, The MIT Press, 2012).

For example, we can imagine the decoding process of an eye as a sequence made up of these filters (of course, this is only a didactic example): directions (dominant horizontal dimension), a central circle inside an ellipsoidal shape, a darker center (pupil) and a clear background (bulb), a smaller darker circle in the middle of the pupil, the presence of eyebrows, and so on. Even if the process is not biologically correct, it can be considered as a reasonable hierarchical process where a higher-level sub-feature is obtained after lower-level filtering.

This approach has been synthesized using the bidimensional convolutional operator, which was already known as a powerful image processing tool. However, in this case, there's a very important difference: the structure of the filters is not pre-imposed but learned by the network using the same back-propagation algorithm employed for MLPs. In this way, the model can adapt the weights with a final goal in mind (which is the classification output), without taking into account any pre-processing steps. In fact, a deep convolutional network, more than an MLP, is based on the concept of end-to-end learning, which is a different way to express what we have described before.

The input is the source; in the middle, there's a flexible structure; and, at the end, we define a global cost function, measuring the accuracy of the classification. The learning process has to back-propagate the errors and correct the weights to reach a specific goal, but we don't know exactly how this process works. What we can easily do is analyze the structure of the filters at the end of the learning phase, discovering that the network has specialized the first layers on low-level details (such as orientations) and the last ones on high-level, sometimes recognizable, ones (such as the components of a face).

It's not surprising that such models achieved state-of-the-art performance in tasks such as image recognition, segmentation (detecting the boundaries of different parts composing an image), and tracking (detecting the position of moving objects). Nevertheless, deep convolutional networks have become the first block of many different architectures (such as deep reinforcement learning or neural style transfer) and, even with a few known limitations, continue to be the first choice for solving several complex real-life problems. The main drawback of such models (which is also a common objection) is that they require very large datasets to reach high accuracies. All the most important models are trained with millions of images and their generalization ability (that is, the main goal) is proportional to the number of different data points.

There were researchers who noticed that a human being learns to generalize without this huge amount of experience, and, in the coming decades, we are likely to observe improvements with this viewpoint. However, deep convolutional networks have revolutionized many artificial intelligence fields, allowing results that were considered almost impossible just a few years ago.

In this section, we are going to discuss different kinds of convolutions and how they can be implemented using TensorFlow and Keras; therefore, for specific technical details, I continue suggesting you check out the official documentation and the book Holdroyd T., *TensorFlow 2.0 Quick Start Guide*, Packt Publishing, 2019.

Convolutional operators

Even if we work only with finite and discrete convolutions, it's useful to start providing the standard definition based on integrable functions. For simplicity, let's suppose that $f(t)$ and $k(t)$ are two real functions of a single variable with support in $\mathbb{R}$. The convolution of $f(t)$ and $k(t)$ (conventionally denoted as $f(t) * k(t)$), which we are going to call a kernel, is defined as follows:

$$f(t) * k(t) = \int_{-\infty}^{\infty} f(\tau)k(t - \tau)d\tau$$

The expression may not be very easy to understand without a mathematical background, but it can become exceptionally simple with a few considerations. First of all, the integral sums all values of τ; therefore, the convolution is a function of the remaining variable, t. The second fundamental element is a sort of dynamic property: the kernel is reversed ($-\tau$) and transformed into a function of a new variable, $z = t - \tau$. Without deep mathematical knowledge, it's possible to understand that this operation shifts the function along the τ (independent variable) axis.

In the following graphs, there's an example based on a parabola:

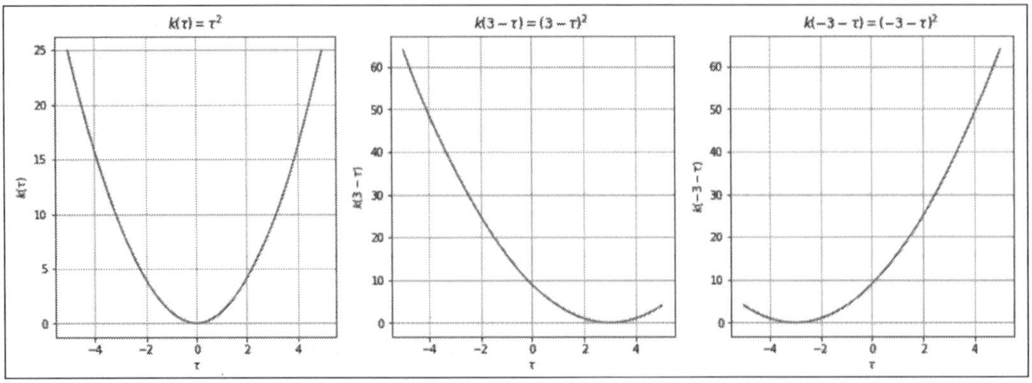

Examples of shifted convolutional quadratic kernels

The first diagram is the original kernel (which is also symmetric). The other two plots show, respectively, a forward and a backward shift. It should be clearer now that a convolution multiplies the function $f(\tau)$ times the shifted kernel and computes the area under the resulting curve. As the variable t is not integrated, the area is a function of t and defines a new function, which is the convolution itself. In other words, the value of the convolution of $f(t)$ and $k(t)$ computed for $t = 5$ is the area under the curve obtained by the multiplication $f(\tau)k(5 - \tau)$ (of course, the variable to be integrated out is τ). By definition, a convolution is:

- Commutative $(f * k = k * f)$
- Distributive $(f * (k + g) = (f * k) + (f * g))$
- Moreover, it's also possible to prove that it's also associative $(f * (k * g) = (f * k) * g))$

However, in deep learning, we never work with continuous convolutions; therefore, I've omitted all the properties and mathematical details, focusing the attention on the discrete case. The reader who is interested in the theory can find further details in *Circuits, Signals, and Systems*, Siebert W. M., MIT Press. A common practice is, instead, to stack multiple convolutions with different kernels (often called filters) to transform an input containing n channels into an output with m channels, where m corresponds to the number of kernels.

This approach allows the unleashing of the full power of convolutions, thanks to the synergic actions of different outputs. Conventionally, the output of a convolution layer with n filters is called a feature map ($w(t)$ x $h(t)$ x n) because its structure is no longer related to a specific image but resembles the overlap of different feature detectors. In this chapter, we often talk about images (considering a hypothetical first layer), but all the considerations are implicitly extended to any feature map.

Bidimensional discrete convolutions

The most common type of convolution employed in deep learning is based on bidimensional arrays with any number of channels (such as grayscale or RGB images). For simplicity, let's analyze a single-layer (channel) convolution because the extension to n layers is straightforward. If $X \in \mathbb{R}^{w \times h}$ and $k \in \mathbb{R}^{n \times m}$, the convolution $X * k$ is defined as (the indexes start from 0):

$$(X * k)(x, y) = \sum_{\substack{i \in (0, n-1) \\ j \in (0, m-1)}} k(i, j) X(x + i)(y + j)$$

It's clear that the previous expression is a natural derivation of the continuous definition. In the following graph, there's an example with a 3×3 kernel:

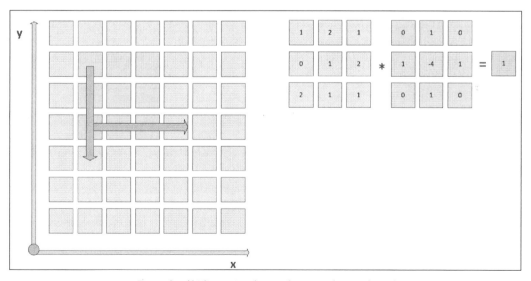

Example of bidimensional convolution with a 3x3 kernel

The kernel is shifted horizontally and vertically, yielding the sum of the element-wise multiplication of corresponding elements. Therefore, every operation leads to the output of a single pixel. The kernel employed in the example is called the discrete Laplacian operator (because it's obtained by discretizing the real Laplacian); let's observe the effect of this kernel on a complete grayscale diagram:

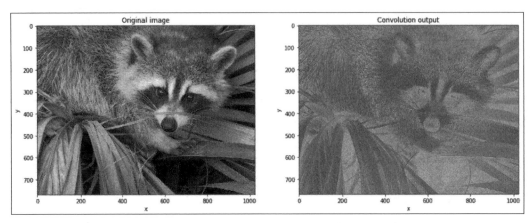

Example of convolution with a discrete Laplacian kernel

As we can see, the effect of the convolution is to emphasize the borders of the various shapes. The reader can now see how variable kernels can be tuned up in order to fulfil precise requirements. However, instead of trying to do it manually, a deep convolutional network leaves these tasks to the learning process, which is subject to a precise goal expressed as the minimization of a cost function. A parallel application of different filters yields complex overlaps that can simplify the extraction of those features that are really important for a classification. The main difference between a fully-connected layer and a convolutional one is the ability of the latter to work with an existing geometry, which encodes all the elements needed to distinguish an object from another one.

These elements cannot be immediately generalizable (think about the branches of a decision tree, where a split defines a precise path towards a final class), but require subsequent processing steps to perform a necessary disambiguation. Considering the previous photo, for example; the eyes and nose are rather similar. How is it possible to segment the picture correctly? The answer is provided by a double analysis: there are subtle differences that can be discovered by fine-grained filters and, above all, the global geometry of real objects is based on internal relationships that are almost invariant.

For example (only for didactic purposes), eyes and nose should make up an isosceles triangle, because the symmetry of a face implies the same distance between each eye and the nose.

This consideration can be made apriori, like in many visual processing techniques, or, thanks to the power of deep learning, it can be left to the training process. As the cost function and the output classes implicitly control the differences, a deep convolutional network can learn what is important to reach a specific goal, discarding at the same time all those details that are useless.

In the previous section, we have said that the feature extraction process is mainly hierarchical. Now, it should be clear that different kernel sizes and subsequent convolutions achieve precisely this objective. Let's suppose that we have a 100 x 100 image and a 3 x 3 kernel. The resulting image will be 98 x 98 pixels (we will explain this concept later). However, each pixel encodes the information of a 3 x 3 block and, as these blocks are overlapping, two consecutive pixels will share some knowledge but, at the same time, they emphasize the difference between the corresponding blocks.

In the following diagram, the same Laplacian kernel is applied to a simple white square on a black background:

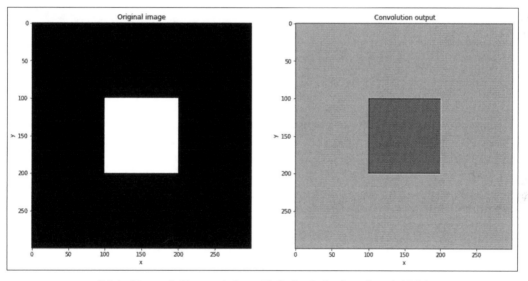

Original image (left); convolution with the Laplacian kernel result (right)

Even if the image is very simple, we can see that the result of a convolution enriched the output image with some very important pieces of information: the borders of the square are now clearly visible (they are black and white) and they can be immediately detected by thresholding the image. The reason is straightforward: the effect of the kernel on the compact surfaces is compact too but, when the kernel is shifted upon the border, the effect of the difference becomes visible. Three adjacent pixels in the original image can be represented as (0, 1, 1), indicating the horizontal transition between black and white.

After the convolution, the result is approximately (0.75, 0.0, 0.25). All the original black pixels have been transformed into a light gray, the white square became darker, and the border (which is not marked in the original picture) is now black (or white, depending on the shift direction). Reapplying the same filter to the output of the previous convolution, we obtain the following:

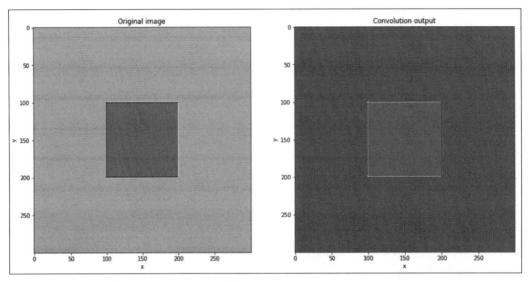

Second application of the Laplacian kernel

A sharp eye can immediately notice three results: the compact surfaces (black and white) are becoming more and more similar, the borders are still visible, and, above all, the top and lower left corners are now more clearly marked with white pixels. Therefore, the result of the second convolution added a finer-grained piece of information, which was much more difficult to detect in the original image. Indeed, the effect of the Laplacian operator is very straightforward, and it's useful only for didactic purposes. In real deep convolutional networks, the filters are trained to perform more complex processing operations that can reveal details (together with their internal and external relationships) that are not immediately exploited to classify the image. Their isolation (obtained thanks to the effect of many parallel filters) allows the network to mark similar elements (such as the corners of the square) in a different way and make more accurate decisions.

The purpose of this example is to show how a sequence of convolutions allows the generation of a hierarchical process that will extract coarse-grained features at the beginning and very high-level ones at the end, without losing the information that's already been collected. Metaphorically, we could say that a deep convolutional network starts placing labels indicating lines, orientations, and borders and proceeds by enriching the existing ontology with further details (such as corners and particular shapes). Thanks to this ability, such models can easily outperform any MLP and reach almost to the Bayes level if the number of training samples is large enough. The main drawback of these models is their inability to easily recognize objects after the application of affine transformations (such as rotations or translations). In other words, if a network is trained with a dataset containing only faces in their natural position, it will achieve poor performance when a rotated (or upside-down) sample is presented. In the next sections, we are going to discuss a couple of methods that are helpful for mitigating this problem (in the case of translations); however, a new experimental architecture called a capsule network (which is beyond the scope of this book) has been proposed in order to solve this problem with a slightly different and much more robust approach (the reader can find further details in Sabour S., Frosst N., Hinton G. E., *Dynamic Routing Between Capsules*, arXiv:1710.09829 [cs.CV]).

Strides and Padding

Two important parameters common to all convolutions are padding and strides. Let's consider the bidimensional case, but keep in mind that the concepts are always the same. When a kernel (n x m with $n, m > 1$) is shifted upon an image and it arrives at the end of a dimension, there are two possibilities. The first one, called valid padding, consists of not continuing even if the resulting image is smaller than the original. In particular, if X is a w x h matrix, the resulting convolution output will have dimensions equal to $(w - n + 1)$ x $(h - m + 1)$. However, there are many cases when it's useful to keep the original dimensions, for example, to be able to sum different outputs. This approach is called same padding and it's based on the simple idea of adding $n - 1$ blank columns and $m - 1$ blank rows to allow the kernel to shift over the original image, yielding a number of pixels equal to the initial dimensions. In many implementations, the default value is set to valid padding.

The other parameter, called strides, defines the number of pixels to skip during each shift. For example, a value set to (1,1) corresponds to a standard convolution, while the following diagram shows strides set to (2,1):

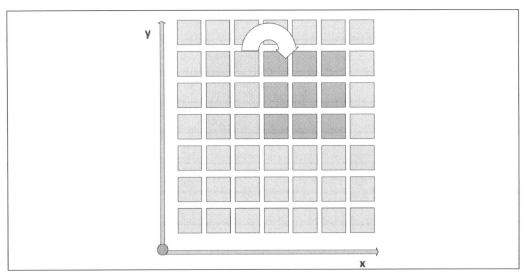

Example of bidimensional convolution with strides=2 on the x-axis

In this case, every horizontal shift skips a pixel. Larger strides force a dimensionality reduction when a high granularity is not necessary (for example, in the first layers), while strides set to (1, 1) are normally employed in the last layers to capture smaller details. There are no standard rules to find out the optimal value and testing different configurations is always the best approach. Like any other hyperparameter, the right choice of strides and padding require an overall evaluation of the entire configuration and cannot be easily limited to a few single considerations. However, some general pieces of information about the dataset (and therefore about the underlying data generating process) can help in making a reasonable initial decision. For example, if we are working with pictures of buildings whose dimension is vertical, it's possible to start picking a value of (1, 2) because we can assume that there's more informative redundancy in the y axis than in the x axis. This choice can dramatically speed up the training process, as the output has one dimension, which is half (with the same padding) of the original one. In this way, larger strides produce partial denoising and can improve the training speed. At the same time, the information loss could have a negative impact on the accuracy. If that happens, it probably means that the scale isn't high enough to allow skipping some elements without compromising the semantics. For example, an image with very small faces could be irreversibly damaged with large strides, yielding an inability to detect the right feature and a consequent worsening of the classification accuracy.

Atrous convolution

In some cases, a stride larger than one could be a good solution because it reduces the dimensionality and speeds up the training process, but it can lead to distorted images where the main features are not detectable anymore. An alternative approach is provided by atrous convolution (also known as dilated convolution). In this case, the kernel is applied to a larger image patch, but skips some pixels inside the area itself (that's why someone called it convolution with holes). In the following graph, there's an example with (3 x 3) and the dilation rate set to 2:

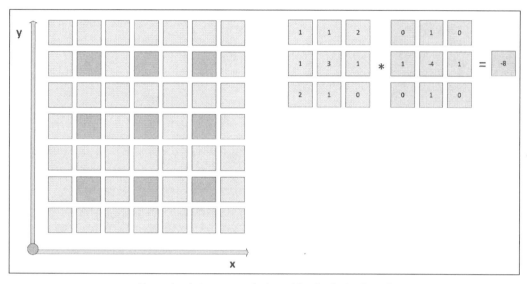

Example of atrous convolution with a Laplacian kernel

Every patch is now 9 x 9, but the kernel remains a 3 x 3 Laplacian operator. The effect of this approach is more robust than increasing the strides because the kernel perimeter will always contain a group of pixels with the same geometrical relationships. Of course, fine-grained features could be distorted, but as the strides are normally set to (1, 1), the final result is normally more coherent. The main difference with a standard convolution is that in this case, we are assuming that farther elements can be taken into account to determine the nature of an output pixel. For example, if the main features don't contain very small details, an atrous convolution can consider larger areas, focusing directly on elements that a standard convolution can detect only after several operations. The choice of this technique must be made considering the final accuracy, but just like for the strides, it can be considered from the beginning whenever the geometric properties can be detected more efficiently, considering larger patches with a few representative elements.

Even if this method can be very effective in particular contexts, it isn't normally the first choice for very deep models. In the most important image classification models, standard convolutions (with or without larger strides) are employed because they have been proven to yield the best performance with very generic datasets (such as ImageNet or Microsoft Coco). However, I suggest the reader experiments with this method and compares the results. In particular, it would be a good idea to analyze which classes are better classified and try to find a rational explanation for the observed behavior.

 In some frameworks, such as Keras, there are no explicit layers to define an atrous convolution. Instead, a standard convolutional layer normally has a parameter to define the dilation rate (in TensorFlow/Keras, it's called `dilation_rate`). Of course, the default value is 1, meaning that the kernel will be applied to patches matching its size.

Separable convolution

If we consider an image $X \in \mathbb{R}^{w \times h}$ (single channel) and a kernel $k \in \mathbb{R}^{n \times m}$, the number of operations is $n \cdot m \cdot w \cdot h$. When the kernel is not very small and the image is large, the cost of this computation can be quite high, even with GPU support. An improvement can be achieved by taking into account the associated property of convolutions. In particular, if the original kernel can be split into the dot product of two vectorial kernels, $k^{(1)}$ with dimensions $(n \times 1)$ and $k^{(2)}$ with dimensions $(1 \times m)$, the convolution is said to be separable. This means that we can perform an $(n \times m)$ convolution with two subsequent operations:

$$X * k \sim \left(X * \begin{pmatrix} k_1^{(1)} \\ \vdots \\ k_n^{(1)} \end{pmatrix} \right) * \begin{pmatrix} k_1^{(2)} & \cdots & k_m^{(2)} \end{pmatrix}$$

The advantage is clear because now the number of operations is $(n + m) \cdot w \cdot h$. In particular, when $nm >> n + m$, it's possible to avoid a large number of multiplications and speed up both the training and the prediction process.

A slightly different approach has been proposed in Chollet F., Xception: *Deep Learning with Depthwise Separable Convolutions*, arXiv:1610.02357 [cs.CV]. In this case, which is properly called depthwise separable convolution, the process is split into two steps.

The first one operates along the channel axis, transforming it into a single-dimensional map with a variable number of channels (for example, if the original diagram is 768 x 1024 x 3, the output of the first stage will be n x 768 x 1024 x 1). Then, a standard convolution is applied to the single layer (which can actually have more than one channel). In most implementations, the default number of output channels for the depthwise convolution is 1 (this is conventionally expressed by saying that the depth multiplier is 1). This approach allows a dramatic parameter reduction with respect to a standard convolution. In fact, if the input generic feature map is $X \in \mathbb{R}^{w \times h \times p}$ and we want to perform a standard convolution with q kernels $k^{(i)} \in \mathbb{R}^{n \times m}$, we need to learn $n \cdot m \cdot w \cdot h$ parameters (each kernel $k^{(i)}$ is applied to all input channels). Employing depthwise separable convolution, the first step (working with only the channels) requires nmp parameters. As the output has still p feature maps and we need to output q channels, the process employs a trick: processing each feature map with q 1 x 1 kernels (in this way, the output will have q layers and the same dimensions). The number of parameters required for the second step is $p \cdot q$, so the total number of parameters becomes $(n \cdot m \cdot p) + (p \cdot q)$. Comparing this value with the one required for a standard convolution, we obtain an interesting result:

$$nmp + pq < nmpq \;\Rightarrow\; nm + q < nmq \;\Rightarrow\; nm < q(nm - 1) \;\Rightarrow\; q > \frac{nm}{nm - 1}$$

As this condition is easily true, this approach is extremely effective in optimizing the training and prediction processes, as well as the memory consumption in any scenario. It's not surprising that the Xception model has been immediately implemented in mobile devices, allowing real-time image classification with very limited resources. Of course, depthwise separable convolutions don't always have the same accuracy as standard ones because they are based on the assumption that the geometrical features observable inside a channel of a composite feature map are independent of each other. This is not always true because we know that the effect of multiple layers is based also on their combinations (which increases the expressivity of a network). However, in many cases the final result has an accuracy that's comparable to some *state-of-the-art* models; therefore, this technique can very often be considered as a valid alternative to a standard convolution.

Since version 2.1.5, Keras has introduced a layer called DepthwiseConv2D that implements depthwise separable convolution. This layer extends the existing SeparableConv2D.

Transpose convolution

A transpose convolution (sometimes also called deconvolution, even if the mathematical definition is different) is not very different from a standard convolution, but its goal is to rebuild a structure with the same features as the input sample. Let's suppose that the output of a convolutional network is the feature map $X \in \mathbb{R}^{w' \times h' \times p'}$ and we need to build an output element $Y \in \mathbb{R}^{w \times h \times 3}$ (assuming the w and h are the original dimensions). We can achieve this result by applying a transpose convolution with appropriate strides and padding to X. For example, let's suppose that $X \in \mathbb{R}^{128 \times 128 \times 256}$ and our output must be 512 x 512 x 3. The last transpose convolution must learn three filters with strides set to four and the same padding. We are going to see some practical examples of this method in the next chapter. However, there are no very important differences between transpose and standard convolution in terms of internal dynamics. The main difference is the cost function, because when a transpose convolution is used as the last layer, the comparison must be done between a target image and a reconstructed one. In the next chapter, we are also going to analyze some techniques to improve the quality of the output even when the cost function doesn't focus on specific areas of the image.

Pooling layers

In a deep convolutional network, pooling layers are extremely useful elements. There are two main kinds of these structures: max pooling and average pooling. They both work on patches $p \in \mathbb{R}^{n \times m}$, shifting horizontally and vertically according to the predefined stride value and transforming the patches into single pixels according to the following rules:

$$\begin{cases} f_{MaxPooling}(X) = \max_{i,j} X(i,j) \\ f_{AveragePooling}(X) = \frac{1}{n+m} \sum_{i=1}^{n} \sum_{j=1}^{m} X(i,j) \end{cases}$$

There are two main reasons that justify the use of these layers. The first one is dimensionality reduction with limited information loss (for example, if we set the strides to (2, 2), it's possible to halve the dimensions of an image/feature map). Clearly, pooling techniques can be more or less lossy (max pooling in particular), and the specific result depends on the single image.

In general, pooling layers try to summarize the information contained in a small chunk into a single pixel. This idea is supported by a perceptual-oriented approach; in fact, when the pools are not very large, it's rather unlikely to find high variances in subsequent shifts (natural images have very few isolated pixels). Therefore, all the pooling operations allow us to set up strides greater than one with a mitigated risk of compromising the information content. However, considering several experiments and architectures, I suggest that you set up larger strides in the convolutional layers (in particular, in the first layer of a convolutional sequence) instead of in pooling ones. In this way, it's possible to apply the transformation with minimal loss and to fully exploit the next fundamental property.

The second (and probably the most important) reason is that they slightly increase the robustness to translations and limited distortions with an effect that is proportional to the pool size. Let's consider the following diagram, representing an original image of a cross and the version after a 10-pixel diagonal translation

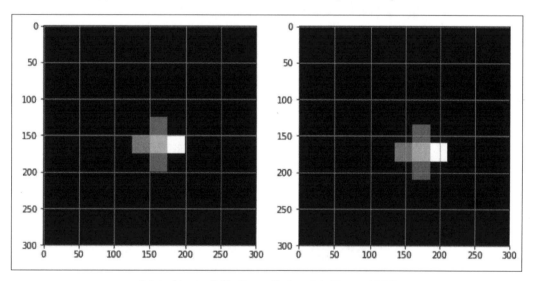

Original image (left); diagonally translated image (right)

This is a very simple example, and the translated image is not very different to the original one. However, in a more complex scenario, a classifier could fail to correctly classify an object in similar conditions.

Applying max pooling (with a (2 x 2) pool size and 2-pixel strides) on the translated image (while the left image is always the original one, which represents our *benchmark*), we get the following:

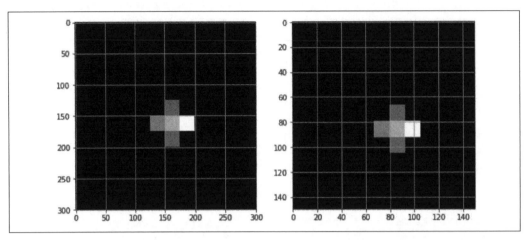

Original image (left); result of a max pooling on the translated image (right)

The reader must pay attention that pooling reduces the size of the images (for example, in our case, a (2 x 2) pool halves both dimensions), but we preferred to adopt the same scale to have a better visual comparison. The result is a larger cross, whose arms are slightly more aligned to the axis. When compared with the original image, it's easier for a classifier with a good generalization ability to filter out the spurious elements and recognize the original shape (which can be considered a cross surrounded by a noisy frame). Repeating the same experiment with average pooling (same parameters), we obtain the following:

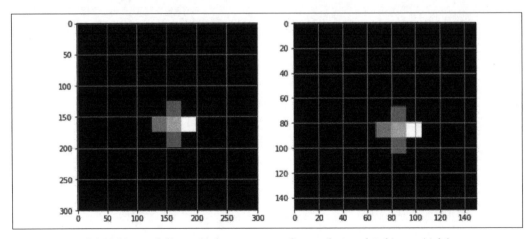

Original image (left); result of an average pooling on the translated image (right)

In this case, the picture is partially smoothed, but it's still possible to see a better alignment (thanks mainly to the fading effect). Also, if these methods are simple and somewhat effective, the robustness to invariant transformations is never dramatically improved and higher levels of invariance are possible only by increasing the pool size. This choice leads to coarser-grained feature maps whose amount of information is drastically reduced; therefore, whenever it's necessary to extend the classification to samples that can be distorted or rotated, it can be a good idea (which allows working with a dataset that better represents the real data generating process) to use a data augmentation technique to produce artificial images and to also train the classifier on them.

However, as pointed out in Goodfellow I., Bengio Y., Courville A., *Deep Learning*, The MIT Press, 2015, pooling layers can also provide robust invariance to rotations when they are used together with the output of a multiple convolution layer or a rotated image stack. In fact, in these cases, a single pattern response is elicited, and the effect of the pooling layer becomes similar to a collector that standardizes the output. In other words, it will produce the same result without an explicit selection of the best matching pattern. For this reason, if the dataset contains enough samples, pooling layers in intermediate positions of the network can provide moderate robustness to small rotations, increasing the generalization ability of the whole deep architecture.

As it's easy to see in the previous example, the main difference between the two variants is the final result. Average pooling performs a sort of very simple interpolation, smoothing the borders and avoiding abrupt changes. On the other hand, max pooling is less noisy and can yield better results when the features need to be detected without any kind of smoothing (which could alter their geometry). I always suggest testing both techniques because it's almost impossible to pick the best method with the right pool size according only to heuristic considerations (above all, when the datasets are not made up of very simple images).

Clearly, it's always preferable to use these layers after a group of convolutions, avoiding very large pool sizes that can irreversibly destroy the information content. In many important deep architectures, the pooling layers are always based on (2, 2) or (3, 3) pools, independently of their position, and the strides are always set to 1 or 2. In both cases, the information loss is proportional to the pool size/strides; therefore, large pools are normally avoided when small features must be detected together with larger ones (for example, foreground and background faces).

Other helpful layers

Even if convolution and pooling layers are the backbone of almost all deep convolutional networks, other layers can be helpful to manage specific situations.

They are the following ones:

- Padding layers: These can be employed to increase the size of a feature map (for example, to align it with another one) by surrounding it with a blank frame (*n* black pixels are added before and after each side). See `https://keras.io/layers/convolutional/` for information about Keras/ TensorFlow implementations.

- Upsampling layers: These increase the size of a feature map by creating larger blocks out of a single pixel. To a certain extent, they can be considered as a transformation that's opposite to a pooling layer, even if, in this case, the upsampling is not based on any kind of interpolation. These kinds of layers can be used to prepare the feature maps for transformations similar to the ones obtained with a transpose convolution, even if many experiments confirmed that using larger strides can yield very accurate results without the need for an extra computational step.

- Cropping layers: These are helpful for selecting specific rectangular areas of an image/feature map. They are particularly useful in modular architectures, where the first part determines the cropping boundaries (for example, of a face), while the second part, after having removed the background, can perform high-level operations such as detail segmentation (marking the areas of eyes, nose, mouth, and so on). The possibility of inserting these layers directly into a deep neural model avoids multiple data transfers. Unfortunately, many frameworks (such as TensorFlow/Keras) don't allow us to use variable boundaries, in effect limiting the number of possible use cases.

- Flattening layers: These are the conjunction link between feature maps and fully-connected layers. Normally, a single flattening layer is used before processing the output of the convolutional blocks, with a few dense layers terminating in a final Softmax layer (for classification). The operation is computationally very cheap as it works only with the metadata and doesn't perform any calculations.

Example of a deep convolutional network with TensorFlow and Keras

In the first example, we want to consider the complete MNIST handwritten digit dataset again, but instead of using an MLP, we are going to employ a small deep convolutional network. The first step consists of loading and normalizing the dataset:

```
import tensorflow as tf
import numpy as np
```

```
(X_train, Y_train), (X_test, Y_test) = \
        tf.keras.datasets.mnist.load_data()

width = height = X_train.shape[1]

X_train = X_train.reshape(
        (X_train.shape[0], width, height, 1)).\
                astype(np.float32) / 255.0
X_test = X_test.reshape(
        (X_test.shape[0], width, height, 1)).\
                astype(np.float32) / 255.0

Y_train = tf.keras.utils.to_categorical(
        Y_train, num_classes=10)
Y_test = tf.keras.utils.to_categorical(
        Y_test, num_classes=10)
```

We can now define the model architecture. The data points are quite small (28 × 28), so it might be helpful to use small kernels. This is not a general rule and it's useful to also evaluate larger kernels (in particular in the first layers); however, many state-of-the-art architectures confirmed that large kernel sizes with small images can lead to a performance loss. In our personal experiments, we have always obtained the best results when the largest kernels were 8 to 10 times smaller than the image dimensions (for example if the image is 100 x 100, the largest kernels should be smaller than 10 x 10, even if in many cases, the starting size is even smaller, like 5 x 5).

Our model is made up of the following layers:

1. Input dropout 25% to prevent overfitting.
2. Convolution with 16 filters, (3 × 3) kernel, strides equal to 1, ReLU activation, and the same padding (the default weight initializer is Xavier). TensorFlow/Keras implements the Conv2D class, whose main parameters are immediately understandable.
3. Dropout 50%.
4. Convolution with 32 filters, (3 × 3) kernel, strides equal to 1, ReLU activation, and the same padding.
5. Dropout 50%.
6. Average pooling with (2 × 2) pool size and strides equal to 1 (using the TensorFlow/Keras class AveragePooling2D).
7. Convolution with 64 filters, (3 × 3) kernel, strides equal to 1, ReLU activation, and the same padding.

8. Average pooling with (2 × 2) pool size and strides equal to 1.

9. Convolution with 64 filters, (3 × 3) kernel, strides equal to 1, ReLU activation, and the same padding.

10. Dropout 50%.

11. Average pooling with (2 × 2) pool size and strides equal to 1.

12. Flattening layer.

13. Fully-connected layer with 1,024 ReLU units.

14. Dropout 50%.

15. Fully-connected layer with 10 Softmax units.

The goal is to capture the low-level features (horizontal and vertical lines, intersections, and so on) in the first layers and use the pooling layers and all the subsequent convolutions to increase the accuracy when distorted samples are presented. Considering the capacity of the model, it's helpful to introduce dropout layers (or alternatively, L_2 regularization) to prevent overfitting. The effect of dropout in this and similar cases is dual. In fact, as pointed out by Goodfellow et al. (in Goodfellow I., Bengio Y., Courville A., *Deep Learning*, The MIT Press, 2015) and explained in the previous chapter, dropout has also the ability to transform a single model into a constrained bagging ensemble (for further details, please read *Chapter 9, Generalized Linear Models and Regression*).

By switching off the activation of random units during batch processing, the global model is split into a large number of dependent sub-models that specialize in classifying particular samples. Therefore, dropout avoids overfitting by exploiting all of the capacity of the model to cover the entire sample space without overlearning the detailed structure of the training set. Every single sub-model is fed with randomly sampled mini-batches and is forced to modify the weights to minimize the global cost function. However, the corrections become null for the units whose activation has been zeroed, hence, a part of the model remains unchanged, while a subset of units undergoes an update. This process avoids the overspecialization of the global model and, at the same time, improves the performances of the classifier by employing a strategy that is similar to bagging (except for the fact that the sub-models are dependent on each other).

At this point, we can create and compile the model (using the Adam optimizer with $\eta = 0.001$ and a decay rate equal to 10^{-5}):

```
model = tf.keras.models.Sequential([
        tf.keras.layers.Dropout(0.25,
                        input_shape=(width, height, 1),
                        seed=1000),
```

```
    tf.keras.layers.Conv2D(16,
                            kernel_size=(3, 3),
                            padding='same',
                            activation='relu'),
    tf.keras.layers.Dropout(0.5, seed=1000),

    tf.keras.layers.Conv2D(32,
                            kernel_size=(3, 3),
                            padding='same',
                            activation='relu'),
    tf.keras.layers.Dropout(0.5, seed=1000),
    tf.keras.layers.AveragePooling2D(
                            pool_size=(2, 2),
                                padding='same'),

    tf.keras.layers.Conv2D(64,
                            kernel_size=(3, 3),
                            padding='same',
                            activation='relu'),
    tf.keras.layers.AveragePooling2D(
                                pool_size=(2, 2),
                                padding='same'),

    tf.keras.layers.Conv2D(64,
                            kernel_size=(3, 3),
                            padding='same',
                            activation='relu'),
    tf.keras.layers.Dropout(0.5, seed=1000),
    tf.keras.layers.AveragePooling2D(
                                pool_size=(2, 2),
                                padding='same'),

    tf.keras.layers.Flatten(),

    tf.keras.layers.Dense(1024,
                            activation='relu'),
    tf.keras.layers.Dropout(0.5, seed=1000),

    tf.keras.layers.Dense(10,
                            activation='softmax')
])
```

The choice of the optimal batch size is almost never based on standardized criteria, but rather on practical considerations. The reason is that it's quite difficult to predict the behavior of a deep model with different batch sizes. However, some general considerations are possible. Stochastic Gradient Descent is an approximated algorithm that has been derived from Gradient Descent. In the latter case, the whole training set is processed before any change. Therefore, larger batches generally (but not always) improve the accuracy of the gradient estimation because they provide more information than smaller batches and, consequently, avoid further corrections. On the other side, smaller batches better fit into memory (particularly when working with GPUs) and, together with a reasonably small learning rate, offer a perfect trade-off between convergence speed and hardware requirements. Unfortunately, there are no golden rules for the choice of the batch size (except maybe for the proportionality to the power of 2, because of the better fit into the VRAM of GPUs), so I invite the reader to start with the largest possible value (proportional to about $\frac{1}{10}$ of the training set, for example) and decrease it to a size somewhere between $\frac{1}{100}$ to $\frac{1}{50}$ of the training set until the performance is satisfactory. It's worth mentioning that recent research (Masters D., Luschi C., *Revisiting Small Batch Training for Deep Neural Networks*, arXiv:1804.07612 [cs.LG]) showed that, on average, small batch sizes are preferable. In particular, the authors proved that a progressive increase of the batch size, together with a normal decay of the learning rate guarantees better convergence speed and performances. Unfortunately, these advices are often precious but they seldom a have general application. Some datasets (and neural architecture) can benefit, while others might show worse performances. Therefore, the optimal way to solve this problem is necessarily trying and evaluating, possibly following the most common guidelines in order to avoid known errors. It goes without saying that the batch size is only one of the hyperparameters that must be tuned up during a deep learning task; therefore, the optimal choice isn't independent of other values. As many researchers suggest, a thorough grid search is impossible, so they recommend sampling randomly from the parameter space (given a precise architecture) and to proceed by zooming into the regions where the performances are better. The process can be continued until the result meets the expected requirements. However, if the improvement is negligible, it's preferable to sample another random region rather than continually zooming into the same subspace.

We can now proceed to train the model with 200 epochs and a batch size of 256 data points, which is a value that offers a good trade-off between performance and computational cost:

```
model.compile(optimizer=
    tf.keras.optimizers.Adam(lr=0.001, decay=1e-5),
            loss='categorical_crossentropy',
            metrics=['accuracy'])
```

```
history = model.fit(X_train, Y_train,
                    epochs=200,
                    batch_size=256,
                    validation_data=(X_test, Y_test))
```

The output of the previous snippet is:

```
Train on 60000 samples, validate on 10000 samples

Epoch 1/200

60000/60000 [==============================] - 15s 257us/sample - loss:
0.4680 - accuracy: 0.8459 - val_loss: 0.1048 - val_accuracy: 0.9688

Epoch 2/200

60000/60000 [==============================] - 8s 127us/sample - loss:
0.1470 - accuracy: 0.9531 - val_loss: 0.0760 - val_accuracy: 0.9802

...

Epoch 199/200

60000/60000 [==============================] - 22s 370us/sample - loss:
0.0086 - accuracy: 0.9972 - val_loss: 0.0240 - val_accuracy: 0.9918

Epoch 200/200

60000/60000 [==============================] - 18s 297us/sample - loss:
0.0082 - accuracy: 0.9972 - val_loss: 0.0172 - val_accuracy: 0.9941
```

The final validation accuracy is now 0.9940, which means that only about 50 samples (out of 10,000) have been misclassified. To better understand the behavior, we can plot the accuracy and loss diagrams:

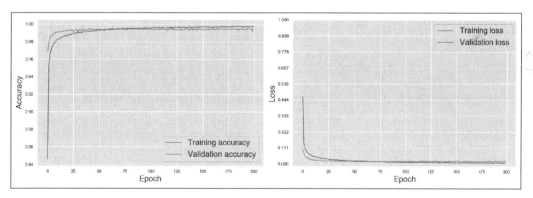

Accuracy plot (left); loss function plot (right)

As we can see, both validation accuracy and loss easily reach the optimal values. In particular, the initial validation accuracy is about 0.97, and the remaining epochs are required to improve the performance with all the samples whose shapes can lead to confusion (for example, malformed 8s that resemble 0s, or 7s that are very similar to 1s).

It's evident that the geometric approach employed by convolutions guarantees much greater robustness than a standard fully connected network, thanks also to the contribution of pooling layers, which reduce the variance due to noisy samples.

Example of a deep convolutional network with TensorFlow/Keras and data augmentation

In this example, we are going to use the Fashion MNIST dataset, which was freely provided by Zalando as a more difficult replacement for the standard MNIST dataset. In this case, instead of handwritten digits, there are miniature grayscale photographs of different articles of clothing. An example of a few images is shown in the following screenshot:

Example of images sampled from the Fashion MNIST dataset

However, in this case, we want to employ a utility class provided by TensorFlow/Keras (`ImageDataGenerator`) in order to create a data-augmented sample set to improve the generalization ability of the deep convolutional network. This class allows us to add random transformations (such as standardization, rotation, shifting, flipping, zooming, and shearing) and output the samples using a Python generator (with an infinite loop). Let's start loading the dataset (we don't need to standardize it, as this transformation is performed by the generator):

```
import tensorflow as tf

nb_classes = 10
train_batch_size = 256
test_batch_size = 100
nb_epochs = 100
steps_per_epoch = 1500

(X_train, Y_train), (X_test, Y_test) = \
        tf.keras.datasets.fashion_mnist.load_data()
```

At this point, we can create the generators, selecting the transformation that best suits our case. As the dataset is rather standard (all the samples are represented only in a few positions), we've decided to augment the dataset by applying a sample-wise standardization (which doesn't rely on the entire dataset), horizontal flip, zooming, small rotations, and small shears.

This choice has been made according to an objective analysis, but I suggest the reader repeats the experiment with different parameters (for example, adding whitening, vertical flip, horizontal/vertical shifting, and extended rotations). Of course, increasing the augmentation variability needs larger processed sets. In our case, we are going to use 384,000 training samples (the original size is 60,000), but larger values can be employed to train deeper networks:

```
import numpy as np

train_idg = tf.keras.preprocessing.image.\
        ImageDataGenerator(
        rescale=1.0 / 255.0,
        samplewise_center=True,
        samplewise_std_normalization=True,
        horizontal_flip=True,
        rotation_range=10.0,
        shear_range=np.pi / 12.0,
        zoom_range=0.25)

train_dg = train_idg.flow(
        x=np.expand_dims(X_train, axis=3),
        y=tf.keras.utils.to_categorical(
            Y_train, num_classes=nb_classes),
        batch_size=train_batch_size,
        shuffle=True,
        seed=1000)

test_idg = tf.keras.preprocessing.image.\
        ImageDataGenerator(
        rescale=1.0 / 255.0,
        samplewise_center=True,
        samplewise_std_normalization=True)

test_dg = train_idg.flow(
        x=np.expand_dims(X_test, axis=3),
        y=tf.keras.utils.to_categorical(
            Y_test, num_classes=nb_classes),
        shuffle=False,
        batch_size=test_batch_size,
        seed=1000)
```

Once an image data generator has been initialized, it must be fitted, specifying the input dataset and the desired batch size (the output of this operation is the actual Python generator). The test image generator is voluntarily kept without transformations except for normalization and standardization, in order to avoid validation on a dataset drawn from a different distribution. At this point, we can create and compile our network using 2D convolutions based on Leaky ReLU activations (to improve the ability to perform corrections also when the value is slightly below zero, where the ReLU gradient is null), batch normalization, and max pooling:

```
model = tf.keras.models.Sequential([
        tf.keras.layers.Conv2D(32,
                               kernel_size=(3, 3),
                               padding='same',
                      input_shape=(X_train.shape[1],
                                   X_train.shape[2], 1)),
        tf.keras.layers.BatchNormalization(),
        tf.keras.layers.LeakyReLU(alpha=0.1),

        tf.keras.layers.Conv2D(64,
                               kernel_size=(3, 3),
                               padding='same'),
        tf.keras.layers.BatchNormalization(),
        tf.keras.layers.LeakyReLU(alpha=0.1),

        tf.keras.layers.Conv2D(128,
                               kernel_size=(3, 3),
                               padding='same'),
        tf.keras.layers.BatchNormalization(),
        tf.keras.layers.LeakyReLU(alpha=0.1),

        tf.keras.layers.Conv2D(128,
                               kernel_size=(3, 3),
                               padding='same'),
        tf.keras.layers.BatchNormalization(),
        tf.keras.layers.LeakyReLU(alpha=0.1),

        tf.keras.layers.MaxPooling2D(pool_size=(2, 2)),

        tf.keras.layers.Flatten(),

        tf.keras.layers.Dense(1024),
        tf.keras.layers.BatchNormalization(),
        tf.keras.layers.LeakyReLU(alpha=0.1),
```

```
    tf.keras.layers.Dense(1024),
    tf.keras.layers.BatchNormalization(),
    tf.keras.layers.LeakyReLU(alpha=0.1),

    tf.keras.layers.Dense(nb_classes,
                          activation='softmax')
])

model.compile(loss='categorical_crossentropy',
              optimizer=tf.keras.optimizers.Adam(
                  lr=0.0001, decay=1e-5),
              metrics=['accuracy'])
```

All the batch normalizations are always applied to the linear transformation before the activation function. Considering the additional complexity, we are also going to use a callback, which is a class that TensorFlow/Keras uses in order to perform in-training operations. In our case, we want to reduce the learning rate when the validation loss stops improving. The specific callback is called ReduceLROnPlateau, and it's tuned in order to reduce η by multiplying it by 0.1 (after a number of epochs equal to the value of the patience parameter) with a cooldown period (the number of epochs to wait before restoring the original learning rate) of 1 epoch and a minimum $\eta = 10^{-6}$.

The training method is now fit_generator(), which accepts Python generators instead of finite datasets and the number of iterations per epoch (all the other parameters are the same as implemented by fit()). Before starting, it's important to remember that this model is rather more complex than the previous one and the training procedure might last several hours on slower GPUs:

```
history = model.fit_generator(
        generator=train_dg,
        epochs=nb_epochs,
        steps_per_epoch=steps_per_epoch,
        validation_data=test_dg,
        validation_steps=int(X_test.shape[0] /
                             test_batch_size),
        callbacks=[
            tf.keras.callbacks.ReduceLROnPlateau(
                factor=0.1, patience=1,
                cooldown=1, min_lr=1e-6)
        ])
```

The output of the previous snippet is:

```
Epoch 1/100
1500/1500 [==============================] - 471s 314ms/step - loss:
0.3457 - acc: 0.8722 - val_loss: 0.2863 - val_acc: 0.8952
Epoch 2/100
1500/1500 [==============================] - 464s 309ms/step - loss:
0.2325 - acc: 0.9138 - val_loss: 0.2721 - val_acc: 0.8990
Epoch 3/100
1500/1500 [==============================] - 460s 307ms/step - loss:
0.1929 - acc: 0.9285 - val_loss: 0.2522 - val_acc: 0.9112
...
Epoch 99/100
1500/1500 [==============================] - 449s 299ms/step - loss:
0.0438 - acc: 0.9859 - val_loss: 0.2142 - val_acc: 0.9323
Epoch 100/100
1500/1500 [==============================] - 449s 299ms/step - loss:
0.0443 - acc: 0.9857 - val_loss: 0.2136 - val_acc: 0.9339
```

In this case, the complexity is larger and the result is not as accurate as the one obtained with the standard MNIST dataset. The validation and loss plots are shown in the following graph:

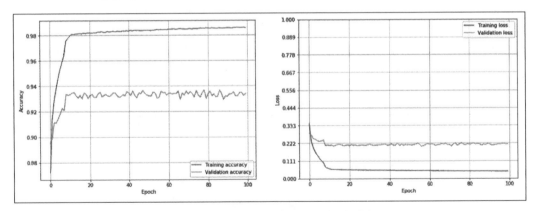

Accuracy plot (left); loss function plot (right)

The loss plot doesn't show a *U-curve*, but it seems that there are no real improvements starting from the 20th epoch. This is also confirmed by the validation plot, which oscillates between 0.935 and about 0.94. On the other hand, the training loss hasn't reached its minimum (nor has the training accuracy), mainly because of the batch normalizations (as explained in the previous chapter, in order to achieve a full unbiasedness, it's necessary to have very large batch sizes.

When this condition cannot be fully met, the result is generally slightly biased, but with a quite faster convergence speed). However, considering several benchmarks, the result is not bad (even if *state-of-the-art* models can reach a validation accuracy of about 0.96). I suggest that the reader tries different configurations (with and without dropout and other activations) based on deeper architectures with larger training sets. This example offers many chances to practice with this kind of model, as the complexity is not as great as to require dedicated hardware, but at the same time, there are many ambiguities (for example, between shirts and t-shirts) that can reduce the generalization ability.

Summary

In this chapter, we have presented the concept of a deep convolutional network, which is a generic architecture that can be employed in any visual processing task. The idea is based on hierarchical information management, aimed at extracting features starting from low-level elements and moving forward to the high-level details that can be helpful to achieve specific goals.

We discussed the concept of convolution and how it's applied in discrete and finite samples. We followed on by defining the properties of standard convolution, before analyzing some important variants such as atrous (or dilated) convolution, separable (and depth wise separable) convolution, and, eventually, transpose convolution. All these methods can work with 1D, 2D, and 3D samples, even if the most diffused applications are based on bidimensional (not considering the channels) matrices representing static images. In the same section, we also discussed how pooling layers can be employed to reduce the dimensionality and improve the robustness to small translations.

In the next chapter, we are going to discuss recurrent neural networks, which allow us to model temporal sequences with an accuracy that is often much larger than the one obtainable using standard time-series analysis algorithms.

Further reading

- Stone J. V., *Vision and Brain: How We Perceive the World*, The MIT Press, 2012
- Holdroyd T., *TensorFlow 2.0 Quick Start Guide*, Packt Publishing, 2019
- Sabour S., Frosst N., *Hinton G. E., Dynamic Routing Between Capsules*, arXiv:1710.09829 [cs.CV]

- Chollet F., *Xception: Deep Learning with Depthwise Separable Convolutions*, arXiv:1610.02357 [cs.CV]
- Goodfellow I., Bengio Y., Courville A., *Deep Learning*, The MIT Press, 2015
- Zipser D., *Advances in Neural Information Processing Systems*, II, 1990
- Masters D., Luschi C., *Revisiting Small Batch Training for Deep Neural Networks*, arXiv:1804.07612 [cs.LG]

20
Recurrent Neural Networks

In this chapter, we analyze **recurrent neural networks** (**RNNs**). In order for a neural network to fully manage the temporal dimension, it is necessary to introduce advanced recurrent layers, whose performance must be greater than any other regression method (in several contexts, like forecasting and deep reinforcement learning).

In particular, in this chapter, we are going to discuss the following topics:

- Recurrent neural networks
- LSTM and GRU cells
- Transfer learning

The first topic we need to discuss is the concept of the RNN focusing on its structure, abilities and limitations. Starting with this knowledge, we can continue the exploration of more complex algorithms that can outperform standard time-series methods.

Recurrent networks

All the neural network models that we analyzed in the previous chapter have a common feature. Once the training process is completed, the weights are frozen, and the output depends only on the input sample. Clearly, this is the expected behavior of a classifier, but there are many scenarios where a prediction must take into account the history of the input values. A time series is a classic example (review *Chapter 10*, *Introduction to Time-Series Analysis*, for further details). Let's suppose that we need to predict the temperature for the next week. If we try to use only the last known $x(t)$ value and an MLP trained to predict $x(t + 1)$, it's impossible to take into account temporal conditions, such as the season, the history of the season over the years, the position in the season, and so on.

The regressor will be able to associate the output that yields the minimum average error but, in real-life situations, this isn't enough. The only reasonable way to solve this problem is to define a new architecture for the artificial neuron in order to provide it with a memory. This concept is shown in the following diagram:

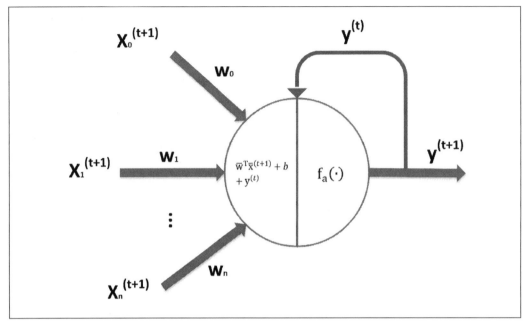

Example of the schematic of a recurrent neuron

Now, the neuron is no longer a pure feed-forward computational unit because the feedback connection forces it to remember its past and use it in order to predict new values. The new dynamic rule is now as follows:

$$\begin{cases} y^{(t+1)} = f_a(\bar{w}^T \cdot \bar{x}^{(t+1)} + b + y^{(t)}) \ if \ t > 0 \\ y^{(0)} = 0 \end{cases}$$

The previous prediction is fed back and summed to create a new linear output. The resulting value is transformed by the activation function in order to produce the actual new output (conventionally, the first output is null, but this is not a constraint). An immediate consideration concerns the activation function — this is a dynamic system that could easily become unstable. The only way to prevent this phenomenon is to employ saturating functions (such as the sigmoid or hyperbolic tangent). In fact, whatever the input is, the output can never explode by moving toward $+\infty$ or $-\infty$.

Suppose that, instead, we were to use a ReLU activation—under some conditions, the output will grow indefinitely, leading to an overflow. Clearly, the situation is even worse with a linear activation and could be very similar even when using a Leaky ReLU or ELU. Hence, it's obvious that we need to select saturating functions, but is this enough to ensure stability? Even if a hyperbolic tangent (and a sigmoid) has two stable points (-1 and +1), this isn't enough to ensure stability. Let's imagine that the output is affected by noise and oscillates around 0.0. The unit cannot converge toward a value and remains trapped in a limit cycle.

Luckily, the ability to learn the weights allows us to increase the robustness to noise, preventing limited changes in the input from inverting the dynamic of the neuron. This is a very important (and easy to prove) result that guarantees stability under very simple conditions, but again, what is the price that we need to pay? Is it simple and straightforward? Unfortunately, the answer is no; the price for stability is extremely high. However, before discussing this problem, let's show how a simple recurrent network can be trained.

Backpropagation through time

The simplest way to train an RNN is based on a representational trick. As the input sequences are limited and their lengths can be fixed, it's possible to restructure the simple neuron with a feedback connection as an unrolled feed-forward network. In the following diagram, there's an example with k timesteps:

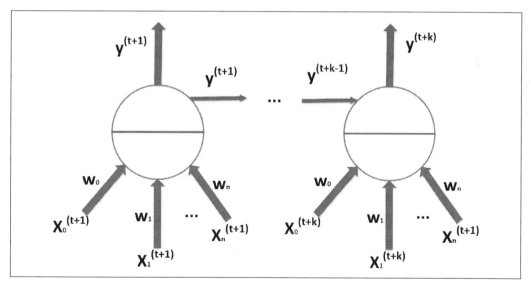

Example of an unrolled recurrent network

This network (which can be easily extended to a more complex architecture with several layers) is exactly like an MLP, but in this case, the weights of each clone are the same. The algorithm called **Back-Propagation Through Time (BPTT)** is the natural extension of the standard learning technique to unrolled recurrent networks. The procedure is straightforward. Once all the outputs have been computed, it's possible to determine the value of the cost function for every single network. At this point, starting from the last step, the corrections (the gradients) are computed and stored, and the process is repeated until the initial step. Then, all of the gradients are summed and applied to the network. As every single contribution is based on a precise temporal experience (made up of a local sample and a previous memory element), the standard backpropagation will learn how to manage a dynamic condition as if it were a point-wise prediction. However, we know that the actual network is not unrolled, and the past dependencies are theoretically propagated and remembered. I voluntarily used the word theoretically, because all practical experiments show completely different behavior than we are going to discuss. This technique is very easy to implement, but it can be very expensive for deep networks that must be unrolled for a large number of timesteps. For this reason, a variant called **Truncated Backpropagation Through Time (TBPTT)** has been proposed (in *Subgrouping reduces complexity and speeds up learning in recurrent networks*, Zipser D., Advances in Neural Information Processing Systems, II, 1990).

The idea is to use two sequence lengths t_1 and t_2 (with $t_1 \gg t_2$) — the longer one $(t_1 t_1)$ is employed for the feed-forward phase, while the shorter length one (t_2) is used to train the network. At first sight, this version seems like a normal BPTT with a short sequence; however, the key idea is to force the network to update the hidden states with more pieces of information and then compute the corrections according to the result of the longer sequence (even if the updates are propagated to a limited number of previous timesteps). Clearly, this is an approximation that can speed up the training process, but the final result is normally comparable with the one obtained by processing long sequences, in particular when the dependencies can be split into shorter temporal chunks (and therefore the assumption is that there are no very long dependencies).

Even if the BPTT algorithm is mathematically correct and it's not difficult to learn short-term dependencies (corresponding to short unrolled networks), several experiments confirmed that it's extremely difficult (or almost impossible) to learn long-term dependencies. In other words, it's easy to exploit past experiences whose contribution is limited to a short window (and therefore whose importance is limited because they cannot manage the most complex trends), but the network cannot easily learn all behaviors that, for example, have a seasonal component involving hundreds of timesteps. The reason for this limitation can be intuitively understood considering the standard behavior of the back-propagation algorithm.

Limitations of BPTT

In this approach, the gradients are propagated back, starting from the cost function and ending at the first layer. In a recurrent network, however, the timesteps are equivalent to a sort of *prolonged* model where the gradients have to traverse many more layers. During each derivation, the magnitude (as we are going to see soon) tends very often to reduce. As the correction is proportional to the gradient, this effect leads to models that are mathematically unable to correct the weights and, consequently, to learn. When working with long-term dependencies, this phenomenon is much more evident because the signal can be split into at least two different components:

$$x(t) = s(t) + l(t)$$

The term $s(t)$ contains high-frequency information regarding the short-term variations, while $l(t)$ is responsible for long-term dependencies (more complex decompositions are also possible, but this one is enough for our purposes). While the former element is quite fast, the latter is generally very slow and its contribution to the gradient tends to be reduced by the short-term component. Therefore, after a few timesteps, the gradient loses its information content relating to the long-term dependencies and leads the model to focus only on short-term variations, forgetting the structure of the long-term component.

In 1994, Bengio, Simard, and Frasconi provided a theoretical explanation of the problem (in Bengio Y., Simard P., Frasconi P., *Learning Long-Term Dependencies with Gradient Descent is Difficult*, IEEE Transactions on Neural Networks, 5/1994). The mathematical details are rather complex because they involve dynamic system theory. However, the final result is that a network whose neurons are forced to become robust to noise (the normal expected behavior) is affected by the vanishing gradients problem when $t \to \infty$. More generally, we can represent a vectorial recurrent neuron dynamic as follows:

$$\bar{y}^{(t+1)} = f_a\left(W^T \cdot \bar{x}^{(t+1)} + \bar{b} + \bar{y}^{(t)}\right)$$

The multiplicative effect of BPTT forces the gradients to be proportional to W^t. In general, it's possible to decompose W as $W = P\Lambda P^T$ with Λ diagonal containing the eigenvalues. Hence, $W^t = P\Lambda^t P^T$ and, if the largest absolute eigenvalue (also known as spectral radius) of W is smaller than 1, then the following applies:

$$\lim_{t \to \infty} W^t = \lim_{t \to \infty} P\Lambda^t P^T = P\left(\lim_{t \to \infty}\Lambda^t\right)P^T = P\begin{pmatrix} \lambda_1^t & 0 & 0 \\ 0 & \ddots & 0 \\ 0 & 0 & \lambda_n^t \end{pmatrix}P^T = 0$$

Conversely, the effect of an eigenvalue larger than 1 produces an exploding effect that forces the saturation of bounded units (such as sigmoid or hyperbolic tangent) or the overflow of unbounded ones (such as ReLU):

$$\lim_{t \to \infty} W^t = \infty$$

More simply, we can re-express the result by saying that the magnitude of the gradients is proportional to the length of the sequences and even if the condition is asymptotically valid, many experiments confirmed that the limited precision of numeric computations and the exponential decay due to subsequent multiplications can force the gradients to vanish or to explode even when the sequences are not extremely long (the former condition is much more likely than the latter). This seems to be the end of any RNN architecture, but luckily, more recent approaches have been designed and proposed to resolve this problem, allowing RNNs to learn both short-and long-term dependencies without particular complications. A new era of RNNs started, and the results were immediately outstanding.

Long Short-Term Memory (LSTM)

This model (which represents the state-of-the-art recurrent cell in many fields) was proposed in 1997 by Hochreiter and Schmidhuber (in Hochreiter S., Schmidhuber J., *Long Short-Term Memory*, Neural Computation, Vol. 9, 11/1997) with the emblematic name **Long Short-Term Memory** (**LSTM**). As the name suggests, the idea is to create a more complex artificial recurrent neuron that can be plugged into larger networks and trained without the risk of vanishing and, of course, exploding gradients. One of the key elements of classic recurrent networks is that they are focused on learning, but not on selectively forgetting. This ability is indeed necessary for optimizing the memory in order to remember what is really important and removing all those pieces of information that are not necessary to predict new values.

To achieve this goal, LSTM exploits two important features (it's helpful to discuss them before moving on to the model). The first one is an explicit state, which is a separate set of variables that store the elements required to build long-and short-term dependencies, including the current state. These variables are the building blocks of a mechanism called **Constant Error Carousel** (**CEC**), so named because it's responsible for the cyclical and internal management of the error provided by the backpropagation algorithm. This approach allows the correction of the weights without suffering the multiplicative effect anymore. The internal LSTM dynamics allow a better understanding of how the error is safely fed back; however, the exact explanation of the training procedure (which is always based on the gradient descent) is beyond the scope of this book, and can be found in the aforementioned paper.

The second feature is the presence of gates. We can simply define a gate as an element that can modulate the amount of information flowing through it. For example, if $y = ax$ and a is a variable bounded between 0 and 1, it can be considered a gate because when it's equal to 0, it blocks the input $\bar{x}$; when it's equal to 1, it allows the input to flow in without restriction; and when it has an intermediate value, it reduces the amount of information proportionally. In LSTMs, gates are managed by sigmoid functions, while the activations are based on hyperbolic tangents (whose symmetry guarantees better performance). At this point, we can show the structural diagram of an LSTM cell and discuss its internal dynamics:

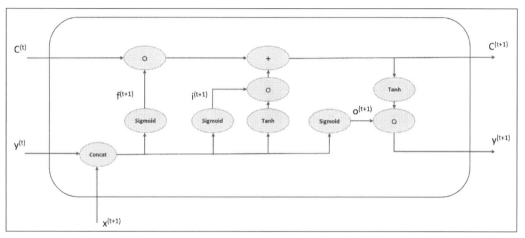

Structure of an LSTM cell. The functions $f(\cdot), i(\cdot), and\ o(\cdot)$ denote the cores of the forget, input, and output gates, respectively

The first (and most important) element is the memory state, which is responsible for the dependencies and for the actual output. In the diagram, it is represented by the upper line and its dynamics are represented by the following general equation:

$$C^{(t+1)} = g_1\left(C^{(t)}\right) + g_2\left(\bar{x}^{(t+1)}, \bar{y}^{(t)}\right)$$

So, the state depends on the previous value, on the current input, and on the previous output. Let's start with the first term, the forget gate. As the name suggests, it's responsible for the persistence of the existing memory elements or for their deletion. In the diagram, it's represented by the first vertical block, and its value is obtained by concatenating the previous output and the current input:

$$\bar{f}^{(t+1)} = \sigma\left(W_f \cdot \begin{pmatrix} \bar{y}^{(t)} \\ \bar{x}^{(t+1)} \end{pmatrix} + \bar{b}_f\right)$$

The operation is a classical neuron activation with a vectorial output. An alternative version can use two weight matrices and keep the input elements separated:

$$\bar{f}^{(t+1)} = \sigma\left(W_f \cdot \bar{x}^{(t+1)} + V_f \cdot \bar{y}^{(t)} + \bar{b}_f\right)$$

However, I prefer the previous version, because it can better express the homogeneity of input and output, and also their consequentiality. Using the forget gate, it's possible to determine the value of $g_1(C^{(t)})$ using the Hadamard (or elementwise) product:

$$g_1(C^{(t)}) = \bar{f}^{(t+1)} \circ C^{(t)}$$

The effect of this computation is filtering the content of $C^{(t)}$ that must be preserved and the validity degree (which is proportional to the value of $\bar{f}^{(t+1)}$). If the forget gate outputs a value close to 1, the corresponding element is still considered valid, while lower values determine a sort of obsolescence that can even lead the cell to completely remove an element when the forget gate value is 0, or close to it. The next step is to consider the amount of the input sample that must be considered to update the state. This task is achieved by the input gate (the second vertical block). The equation is analogous to the previous one:

$$\bar{i}^{(t+1)} = \sigma\left(W_i \cdot \begin{pmatrix} \bar{y}^{(t)} \\ \bar{x}^{(t+1)} \end{pmatrix} + \bar{b}_i\right)$$

However, in this case, we also need to compute the term that must be added to the current state. As already mentioned, LSTM cells employ hyperbolic tangents for the activations; therefore, the new contribution to the state is obtained as follows:

$$\hat{C}^{(t+1)} = \tanh\left(W_c \cdot \begin{pmatrix} \bar{y}^{(t)} \\ \bar{x}^{(t+1)} \end{pmatrix} + \bar{b}_c\right)$$

Using the input gate and the state contribution, it's possible to determine the function $g_2(\bar{x}^{(t+1)}, \bar{y}^{(t)})$:

$$g_2(\bar{x}^{(t+1)}, \bar{y}^{(t)}) = \bar{i}^{(t+1)} \circ \hat{C}^{(t+1)}$$

Hence, the complete state equation becomes as follows:

$$C^{(t+1)} = \left(\bar{f}^{(t+1)} \circ C^{(t)}\right) + \left(\bar{i}^{(t+1)} \circ \hat{C}^{(t+1)}\right)$$

Now, the inner logic of an LSTM cell is more evident. The state is based on the following:

- A dynamic balance between previous experience and its re-evaluation according to new experience (modulated by the forget gate)

- The semantic effect of the current input (modulated by the input gate) and the potential additive activation

There are many realistic scenarios. It's possible that a new input forces the LSTM to reset the state and store the new incoming value. On the other hand, the input gate can also remain closed, giving a very low priority to the new input (together with the previous output). In this case, the LSTM, considering the long-term dependencies, can decide to discard a sample that is considered noisy and not necessarily able to contribute to an accurate prediction. In other situations, both the forget and input gates can be partially open, letting only some values influence the state. All these possibilities are managed by the learning process through the correction of the weight matrices and the biases. The difference with BPTT is that the long-term dependencies are no longer impeded by the vanishing gradients problem.

The last step is determining the output. The third vertical block is called the output gate and controls the information that must transit from the state to the output unit. Its equation is as follows:

$$\bar{o}^{(t+1)} = \sigma \left(W_o \cdot \begin{pmatrix} \bar{y}^{(t)} \\ \bar{x}^{(t+1)} \end{pmatrix} + \bar{b}_o \right)$$

The actual output is hence determined as follows:

$$\bar{y}^{(t+1)} = \bar{o}^{(t+1)} \circ \tanh C^{(t+1)}$$

An important consideration concerns the gates. They are all fed with the same vector, which contains the previous output and the current input. As they are homogenous values, the concatenation yields a coherent entity that encodes a sort of inverse cause-effect relationship (this is an improper definition, as we are working with previous effect and current cause). The gates work like logistic regressions without thresholding; therefore, they can be considered as *pseudo*-probability vectors (not distributions, as each element is independent). The forget gate expresses the probability that the last sequence (effect, cause) is more important than the current state; however, only the input gate is responsible for granting it the right to influence the new state. Moreover, the output gate expresses the probability that the current sequence is able to let the current state flow out.

The dynamic is indeed very complex and has some drawbacks. For example, when the output gate remains closed, the output is close to zero, and this influences both the forget and input gates. As they control the new state and the CEC, they could limit the amount of incoming information and consequent corrections, leading to poor performance. A simple solution that can mitigate this problem is provided by a variant called peephole LSTM. The idea is to feed the previous state to every gate so that they can take decisions more independently. The generic gate equation becomes as follows:

$$\bar{g}^{(t+1)} = \sigma \left(W_g \cdot \begin{pmatrix} \bar{y}^{(t)} \\ \bar{x}^{(t+1)} \end{pmatrix} + U_g \cdot C^{(t)} + \bar{b}_g \right)$$

The new set of weights U_g (for all three gates) must be learned in the same way as the standard W_g and $\bar{b}_g$. The main difference between this and a classic LSTM is that the sequential dynamic forget gate → input gate → new state → output gate → actual output is now partially bypassed. The presence of the state in every gate activation allows them to exploit multiple recurrent connections, yielding better accuracy in many complex situations. Another important consideration is the learning process: in this case, the peepholes are closed and the only feedback channel is the output gate. Unfortunately, not every LSTM implementation supports peepholes; however, several studies confirmed that in most cases, all the models yield similar performances.

Xingjian et al. (in Xingjian S., Zhourong C., Hao W., Dit-Yan Y., Wai-kin W., Wang-Chun W., *Convolutional LSTM Network: A Machine Learning Approach for Precipitation Nowcasting*, arXiv:1506.04214 [cs.CV]) proposed a variant called convolutional LSTM, which clearly mixes convolutions and LSTM cells. The main internal difference concerns the gate computations, which now become (without peepholes, which can always be added, though):

$$\bar{g}^{(t+1)} = \sigma \left(W_g * \begin{pmatrix} \bar{y}^{(t)} \\ \bar{x}^{(t+1)} \end{pmatrix} + \bar{b}_g \right)$$

W_g is now a kernel that is convoluted with the input-output vector (which is usually the concatenation of two images). Of course, it's possible to train any number of kernels to increase the decoding power of the cell and the output will have a shape equal to batch size x width x height x kernels. This kind of cell is particularly useful for joining spatial processing with a robust temporal approach. Given a sequence of images (for example, satellite images and game screenshots), a convolutional LSTM network can learn long-term relationships that are manifested through geometric feature evolutions (for example, cloud movements or specific sprite strategies that it's possible to anticipate considering a long history of events).

This approach (even with a few modifications) is widely employed in deep reinforcement learning in order to solve complex problems where the only input is provided by a sequence of images. Of course, the computational complexity is very high, in particular, when many subsequent layers are used; however, the results outperformed any existing method and this approach became one of the first choices to manage this kind of problem.

Another important variant, which is common to many RNNs, is provided by a bidirectional interface. This isn't an actual layer, but a strategy that is employed in order to join the forward analysis of a sequence with the backward one. Two cellblocks are fed with a sequence and its inverse and the output, for example, are concatenated and used for further processing steps. In fields such as NLP, this method allows us to dramatically improve the accuracy of classifications and real-time translations. The reason is strictly related to the rules underlying the structure of a sequence. In natural language, a sentence $w_1 w_2 \ldots w_n$ has forward relationships (for example, a singular noun can be followed by *is*), but the knowledge of backward relationships (for example, the sentence *this place is pretty awful*) permits the common mistakes that, in the past, had to be corrected using post-processing steps (the initial translation of *pretty* could be similar to the translation of *nice*, but a subsequent analysis can reveal that *pretty* is not an adjective in this case; the adjective *nice* mismatches, and a special rule can be applied). Deep learning, on the other side, is not based on *special rules*, but on the ability to learn an internal representation that should be autonomous in making final decisions (without further external aids) and bidirectional LSTM networks help in reaching this goal in many important contexts.

Keras/TensorFlow has implemented LSTM classes since its origins. It also provides a bidirectional class wrapper that can be used with every RNN layer in order to obtain a double output (computed with the forward and backward sequences). Moreover, in Keras 2 there are optimized versions of LSTM based on NVIDIA CUDA (CuDNNLSTM), which provide very high performance when a compatible GPU is available. In the same package, it's possible to also find the ConvLSTM2D class, which implements a convolutional LSTM layer. In this case, the reader can immediately identify many of the parameters as they are the same as a standard convolutional layer.

Gated Recurrent Unit (GRU)

This model, named **Gated Recurrent Unit (GRU)**, proposed by Cho et al. (in Cho K., Van Merrienboer B., Gulcehre C., Bahdanau D., Bougares F., Schwenk H., Bengio Y., *Learning Phrase Representations Using RNN Encoder-Decoder for Statistical Machine Translation,* arXiv:1406.1078 [cs.CL]), can be considered to be a simplified LSTM with a few variations.

The structure of a generic full-gated unit is represented in the following diagram:

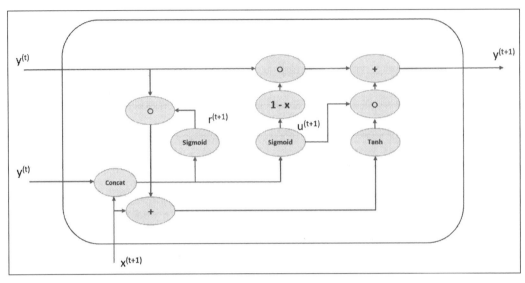

Structure of a GRU cell. The functions $r(\cdot)$ and $u(\cdot)$ represent
the cores of the reset and update gates, respectively

The main differences between this and LSTMs are the presence of only two gates and the absence of an explicit state. These simplifications can speed up both the training and the prediction phases while avoiding the vanishing gradient problem.

The first gate is called the reset gate (conventionally denoted with the letter r) and its function is analogous to the forget gate:

$$\bar{r}^{(t+1)} = \sigma\left(W_r \cdot \begin{pmatrix} \bar{y}^{(t)} \\ \bar{x}^{(t+1)} \end{pmatrix} + \bar{b}_r\right)$$

Similar to the forget gate, its role is to decide what content of the previous output must be preserved and to what degree. In fact, the additive contribution to new output is obtained as follows:

$$\hat{y}^{(t+1)} = \tanh\left(W_y \cdot \bar{x}^{(t+1)} + \bar{r}^{(t+1)} \circ \left(V_y \cdot \bar{y}^{(t)}\right) + \bar{b}_y\right)$$

In the previous expression, I've preferred to separate the weight matrices to better explain the behavior. The argument of tanh x is the sum of a linear function of the new input and a weighted term that is a function of the previous state. Now, it's clear how the reset gate works: it modulates the amount of history (accumulated in the previous output value) that must be preserved and what instead can be discarded.

However, the reset gate is not enough to determine the correct output with enough accuracy, considering both short-and long-term dependencies. In order to increase the expressivity of the unit, an update gate (with a role that's similar to the LSTM input gate) has been added:

$$\bar{u}^{(t+1)} = \sigma\left(W_u \cdot \begin{pmatrix} \bar{y}^{(t)} \\ \bar{x}^{(t+1)} \end{pmatrix} + \bar{b}_u\right)$$

The update gate controls the amount of information that must contribute to the new output (and hence to the state). As it's a value bounded between 0 and 1, GRUs are trained to mix old output and new additive contributions with an operation similar to a weighted average:

$$\bar{y}^{(t+1)} = \bar{u}^{(t+1)} \circ \hat{y}^{(t+1)} + \left(I - \bar{u}^{(t+1)}\right) \circ \bar{y}^{(t)}$$

Therefore, the update gate becomes a modulator that can select which components of each flow must be outputted and stored for the next operation. This unit is structurally simpler than an LSTM, but several studies have confirmed that its performance is, on average, equivalent to LSTM (for example, *Chung J., Gulcehre C., Cho K., Bengio Y., Empirical Evaluation of Gated Recurrent Neural Networks on Sequence Modeling,* arXiv:1412.3555v1 [cs.NE]). On the other side, there are some particular cases (for example, natural language modeling) when LSTM has even outperformed GRU (Mangal S., Joshi P., Modak R., *LSTM vs. GRU vs. Bidirectional RNN for script generation,* arXiv:1908.04332 [cs.CL]). My suggestion is that you test both models, starting with LSTM. The computational cost has been dramatically reduced by modern hardware and in many contexts the advantage of GRUs is often negligible. In both cases, the philosophy is the same: the error is kept inside the cell and the weights of the gates are corrected in order to maximize accuracy.

This behavior prevents the multiplicative cascade of small gradients and increases the ability to learn very complex temporal behaviors. However, a single cell/layer would not be able to successfully achieve the desired accuracy. In all these cases, it's possible to stack multiple layers made up of a variable number of cells. Every layer can normally output the last value or the entire sequence. The former is used when connecting the LSTM/GRU layer to a fully connected one, while the whole sequence is necessary to feed another recurrent layer. We are going to see how to implement these techniques with Keras in the following example.

Just like for LSTMs, Keras/TensorFlow implements the GRU class and its NVIDIA CUDA optimized version, CuDNNGRU.

Example of an LSTM with TensorFlow and Keras

In this example, we want to test the ability of an LSTM network to learn long-term dependencies. For this reason, we employ a dataset called Zuerich Monthly Sunspots containing the number of sunspots observed in all the months starting from 1749 to 2015 (collected by *SILSO data/image*, Royal Observatory of Belgium, Brussels).

 The CVS dataset can be downloaded from the page of SILSO data/ image, Royal Observatory of Belgium, Brussels at `http://sidc. be/silso/infossntotmonthly`.

As we are not interested in the dates, we need to parse the file in order to extract only the values needed for the time series (limited to 3,175 steps to simplify the partitioning into 15-step chunks):

```
import numpy as np
import pandas as pd


n_samples = 3175
sequence_length = 15


dataset_filename = 'ISSN_M_tot.csv'


df = pd.read_csv(dataset_filename, header=None).dropna()
data =  df[3].values[:n_samples - sequence_length].\
        astype(np.float32)
```

The values are unnormalized and, since LSTMs work with hyperbolic tangents, it's helpful to normalize them in the interval (-1, 1). We can easily perform this step using the scikit-learn class, `MinMaxScaler`:

```
from sklearn.preprocessing import MinMaxScaler

mmscaler = MinMaxScaler((-1.0, 1.0))
data = mmscaler.fit_transform(data.reshape(-1, 1))
```

The complete dataset is shown in the following diagram:

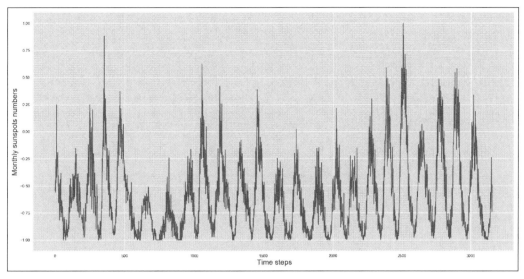

Zuerich Monthly Sunspots time-series

In order to train the model, we have decided to use 2,600 data points for training and the remaining 575 for validation (corresponding to about 48 years). The input of the model is a batch of sequences of 15 data points (shifted along the time axis) and the output is the subsequent month; therefore, before training, we need to prepare the dataset:

```
X_ts = np.zeros(shape=(n_samples - sequence_length,
                       sequence_length, 1),
                dtype=np.float32)
Y_ts = np.zeros(shape=(n_samples - sequence_length, 1),
                dtype=np.float32)

for i in range(0, data.shape[0] - sequence_length):
X_ts[i] = data[i:i + sequence_length]
Y_ts[i] = data[i + sequence_length]

X_ts_train = X_ts[0:2600, :]
Y_ts_train = Y_ts[0:2600]

X_ts_test = X_ts[2600:n_samples, :]
Y_ts_test = Y_ts[2600:n_samples]
```

Now, we can create and compile a simple model with a single stateful LSTM layer containing four cells, followed by a hyperbolic tangent output neuron (I always suggest that the reader experiments with more complex architectures and different parameters):

```
import tensorflow as tf

model = tf.keras.models.Sequential([
        tf.keras.layers.LSTM(4,
                             stateful=True,
                             batch_input_shape=
                             (20, sequence_length, 1)),
        tf.keras.layers.Dense(1,
                             activation='tanh')
    ])

model.compile(optimizer=
              tf.keras.optimizers.Adam(
                  lr=0.001, decay=0.0001),
              loss='mse',
              metrics=['mse'])
```

Setting the `stateful=True` parameter in the LSTM class forces TensorFlow/Keras not to reset the state after each batch (the default value is `False`). In fact, our goal is both learning long-term dependencies and considering the single batches as parts of the same sequence. Therefore, the internal LSTM state must reflect the overall trend and capture the seasonalities over a long series of batches. When an LSTM network is stateful, it's also necessary to specify the batch size in the input shape (through the `batch_input_shape` parameter). In our case, we have selected a batch size of 20 data points, which are concatenated to generate the whole sequence (assuming that the data points are sampled at regular intervals). The reader must remember that a stateless LSTM is always helpful for learning time-series, but the focus is restricted to shorter sequences. On the other side, when we are interested in predicting the future behavior given the entire past experience, the cells must keep the state and re-use it when a new batch is submitted.

The optimizer is Adam with a higher decay (to avoid instabilities) and a loss based on the Mean Square Error (which is the most common choice in this kind of scenario). At this point, we can train the model for 100 epochs, enough to reach a region where both training and validation loss functions stop decreasing:

```
model.fit(X_ts_train, Y_ts_train,
          batch_size=20,
          epochs=100,
          shuffle=False,
          validation_data=(X_ts_test, Y_ts_test))
```

The output of the previous snippet is:

```
Train on 2600 samples, validate on 560 samples
Epoch 1/100
2600/2600 [==============================] - 3s 1ms/sample - loss: 0.2676
- mse: 0.2676 - val_loss: 0.1020 - val_mse: 0.1020
Epoch 2/100
2600/2600 [==============================] - 0s 174us/sample - loss:
0.0670 - mse: 0.0670 - val_loss: 0.0893 - val_mse: 0.0893
...
Epoch 99/100
2600/2600 [==============================] - 1s 204us/sample - loss:
0.0160 - mse: 0.0160 - val_loss: 0.0182 - val_mse: 0.0182
Epoch 100/100
2600/2600 [==============================] - 0s 171us/sample - loss:
0.0159 - mse: 0.0159 - val_loss: 0.0181 - val_mse: 0.0181
```

This is an example whose purpose is only didactic; therefore, the final validation mean squared error is not extremely low (even if it's less than 2%). However, as it's possible to see in the following diagram (representing the predictions on the validation set), the model has successfully learned the global trend and several short-term dependencies:

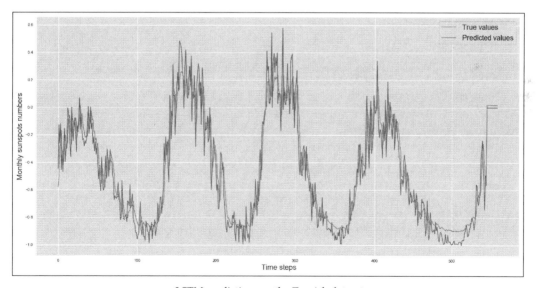

LSTM predictions on the Zuerich dataset

The model is still unable to achieve a very high accuracy to correspond with all the very rapid spikes, but it's able to correctly model the amplitude of the oscillations and the length of the tails. For the sake of intellectual honesty, we must consider that this validation is performed on true data; however, when working with time series, it's normal to predict a new value using the ground truth. In this case, it's like a moving prediction where each value is obtained using the training history and a set of real observations. It's clear that the model is able to predict the long-term oscillations and also some local ones (for example, the sequence starting from step 300), but it can be improved in order to have better performance across the whole validation set. To achieve this goal, it is necessary to increase the network's complexity and tune up the learning rate (this is a very interesting exercise on a real dataset).

Observing the previous diagram, it's possible to see that the model is relatively more accurate at some high frequencies (rapid changes), while it's more imprecise on others. This is not strange behavior because very oscillating functions need more non-linearity (think about the Taylor expansion and the relative error when it's truncated to a specific degree) to achieve high accuracies (this means employing more layers). My suggestion is that you repeat the experiment using more LSTM layers, considering that we need to pass the whole output sequence to the following recurrent layer (this can be achieved by setting the `return_sequences=True` parameter). The last layer, instead, must return only the final value (which is the default behavior). I also suggest testing the GRU layers, comparing the performance with the LSTM version, and picking the simplest (benchmarking the training time) and most accurate solution.

Transfer learning

We have discussed how deep learning is fundamentally based on black-box models that learn how to associate input patterns to specific classification/regression outcomes. The entire processing pipeline that is often employed to prepare the data for specific detections is absorbed by the complexity of the neural architecture. However, the price to pay for high accuracies is a proportionally large number of training samples. *State-of-the-art* visual networks are trained with millions of images and, obviously, each of them must be properly labeled. Even if there are many free datasets that can be employed to train several models, many specific scenarios need hard preparatory work that sometimes is very difficult to achieve.

Luckily, deep neural architectures are hierarchical models that learn in a structured way. As we have seen in the examples of deep convolutional networks, the first layers become more and more sensitive to detect low-level features, while the higher ones concentrate their work on extracting more detailed high-level features.

In several tasks, it's reasonable to think that a network trained, for example, with a large visual dataset (such as ImageNet or Microsoft Coco) could be reused to achieve a specialization in a slightly different task. This concept is known as transfer learning and it's one of the most useful techniques when it's necessary to create *state-of-the-art* models with brand new datasets and specific objectives.

For example, a customer can ask for a system to monitor a few cameras with the goal of segmenting the images and highlighting the boundaries of specific targets. The input is made up of video frames with the same geometric properties, since thousands of images employed in training make very powerful models (for example, Inception, ResNet, or VGG); therefore, we can take a pretrained model, remove the highest layers (normally dense ones ending in a softmax classification layer), and connect the flattening layer to an MLP that outputs the coordinates of the bounding boxes. The first part of the network can be frozen (the weights are not modified anymore), while the SGD is applied to tune up the weights of the newly specialized sub-network, as shown in the following diagram:

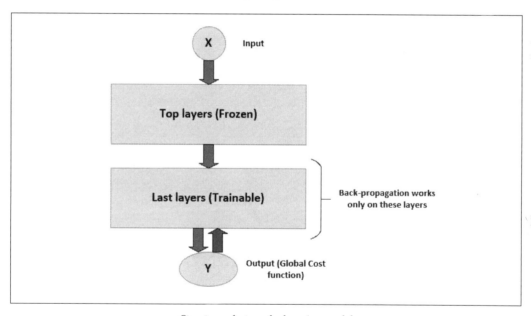

Structure of a transfer learning model

Clearly, such an approach can dramatically speed up the training process because the most complex part of the model is already trained and can also guarantee extremely high accuracy (with respect to a naive solution) thanks to the optimization already performed on the original model. Obviously, the most natural question is how does this method work? Is there any formal proof? Unfortunately, there are no complete mathematical proofs for all results, but there's enough evidence to assure us of this approach.

For example, *in* Parisotto E., Ba J., Salakhutdinov R., *Actor-Mimic Deep Multitask and Transfer Reinforcement Learning,* arXiv:1511.06342v4 [cs.LG], and in Taylor M., Stone P., *Transfer learning for reinforcement learning domains: A survey,* The Journal of Machine Learning Research, 10, 2009, it's possible to see how transfer learning can improve the effectiveness of deep models applied to reinforcement learning contexts. In this kind of situation, transferring (and adapting) the existing knowledge can save time and improve the reusability of existing models.

Generally speaking, the goal of a neural training process is to specialize each layer in order to provide a more particular (detailed, filtered, and so on) representation to the following one. Convolutional networks are a clear example of this behavior, but the same is observable in MLPs as well. The analysis of very deep convolutional networks showed how the content is still visual until reaching the flattening layer, where it's sent to a series of dense layers that are responsible for feeding the final softmax layer. In other words, the output of the convolutional block is a higher-level, segmented representation of the input, which is seldom affected by the specific classification problem.

For this reason, transfer learning is generally sound and doesn't normally require retraining of the lower layers. However, it's difficult to understand which model can yield the best performance, and it's very useful to know which dataset has been used to train the original network. General-purpose datasets (for example, ImageNet) are very useful in many contexts, while specific ones (such as Cifar-10 or Fashion; MNIST can be too restrictive). Luckily, TensorFlow/Keras offers (in the TensorFlow package tf.keras.applications) many models (even quite complex ones) that are always trained with ImageNet datasets and that can be immediately employed in a production-ready application. Even if using them is extremely simple, it requires a deeper knowledge of this framework, which is beyond the scope of this book. I invite the reader interested in this topic to take a look at Holdroyd T., *TensorFlow 2.0 Quick Start Guide,* Packt Publishing, 2019.

In the last few years, transfer learning has become more and more important because even if hardware prices are going down, training large models several times can produce an unacceptable delay in project schedules. In order to allow machine learning to become a standard approach, it's also necessary to find engineered solutions to problems that are normally reserved for research. Transfer learning is surely one such approach, and the data scientist should always consider it when coping with complex and large datasets that require deep networks.

On the other hand, not all problems are suitable to be solved using this approach. In some cases, the existing models are too generic and it's possible to freeze only a few initial layers to achieve reasonable accuracy.

In other scenarios, the structure of the training sets employed in pretrained models required neural architectures that are incompatible with a specific task. For example, a model trained to recognize different shapes of cars or trucks might struggle to work with biological cells whose features are bounded to very small (and often overalapping) areas. In such cases, a pretrained model has learned a much wider data generating process, with many regions corresponding to imperceptible differences. On the contrary, cell recognition often requires working on smaller regions with a finer discriminative ability. Transfer learning demands this role for the last layers (often fully connected), but sometimes, also the previous layers can be exploited to improve the final performances.

Like many other techniques described in the book, transfer learning is like a Swiss army knife that adapts to completely different tasks if they are virtually compatible with each other. Considering the effort required to train a brand new model, it's always a good idea to consider transfer learning as an alternative. However, it's also important to have a clear idea of the goals and make decisions that should always be both pragmatic and effective.

For example, it's necessary to select the right pretrained model. Some networks have been designed to work with particular kinds of samples (such as small or low-resolution images), while others have been trained with data sampled from a very generic data generating process. A model designed to work in a specific context is generally a good choice only if the usage is similar. For instance, a deep network designed to be implemented in a self-driving car has probably never been trained to identify objects that are different from the ones that we can encounter in a street.

Such models can be extremely effective if the destination domain overlaps the initial one, but they would probably be inaccurate when the geometric properties of the objects require the ability to discriminate at very different scales. Hence, the choice of the initial model should start with generic ones, leaving the last layers to be more and more selective with respect to particular details. On the other hand, a clear idea about the data generating process is seldom possible. Therefore, the data scientist must include some exploration time in the project schedule, possibly keeping all different versions of trained models in order to perform a final, comprehensive comparison.

Summary

In this chapter, we introduced the concept of RNNs, emphasizing the issues that normally arise when classic models are trained using the BPTT algorithm. In particular, we explained why these networks cannot easily learn long-term dependencies.

For this reason, new models have been proposed, whose performance was immediately outstanding. We discussed the most famous recurrent cell, called Long Short-Term Memory (LSTM), which can be used in layers that can easily learn all the most important dependencies of a sequence, allowing us to minimize the prediction error even in contexts with very high variance (such as stock market quotations). The last topic was a simplified version of the idea implemented in LSTMs, which led to a model called a **Gated Recurrent Unit (GRU)**. This cell is simpler and more computationally efficient, and many benchmarks confirmed that its performance is approximately the same as LSTM.

In the next chapter, we are going to discuss some models called autoencoders, whose main property is to create internal representations of an arbitrarily complex input distribution.

Further reading

- Holdroyd T., *TensorFlow 2.0 Quick Start Guide*, Packt Publishing, 2019
- Goodfellow I., Bengio Y., Courville A., *Deep Learning*, The MIT Press, 2015
- Zipser D., *Advances in Neural Information Processing Systems*, II, 1990
- Bengio Y., Simard P., Frasconi P., *Learning Long-Term Dependencies with Gradient Descent is Difficult*, IEEE Transactions on Neural Networks, 5/1994
- Hochreiter S., Schmidhuber J., *Long Short-Term Memory*, *Neural Computation*, Vol. 9, 11/1997
- Xingjian S., Zhourong C., Hao W., Dit-Yan Y., Wai-kin W., Wang-Chun W., *Convolutional LSTM Network: A Machine Learning Approach for Precipitation Nowcasting*, arXiv:1506.04214 [cs.CV]
- Cho K., Van Merrienboer B., Gulcehre C., Bahdanau D., Bougares F., Schwenk H., Bengio Y., *Learning Phrase Representations using RNN Encoder-Decoder for Statistical Machine Translation*, arXiv:1406.1078 [cs.CL]
- Mangal S., Joshi P., Modak R., *LSTM vs. GRU vs. Bidirectional RNN for script generation*, arXiv:1908.04332 [cs.CL]
- Chung J., Gulcehre C., Cho K., Bengio Y., *Empirical Evaluation of Gated Recurrent Neural Networks on Sequence Modeling*, arXiv:1412.3555v1 [cs.NE]
- Parisotto E., Ba J., Salakhutdinov R., *Actor-Mimic Deep Multitask and Transfer Reinforcement Learning*, arXiv:1511.06342v4 [cs.LG]
- Taylor M., Stone P., *Transfer learning for reinforcement learning domains: A survey*, The Journal of Machine Learning Research, 10, 2009

21
Autoencoders

In this chapter, we're going to look at an unsupervised model family whose performance has been boosted by modern deep learning techniques. Autoencoders offer a different approach to classic problems such as dimensionality reduction or dictionary learning; however, unlike many other algorithms, they don't suffer the capacity limitations that affect many famous models. Moreover, they can exploit specific neural layers (such as convolutions) to extract pieces of information based on specialized criteria. In this way, the internal representations can be more robust to different kinds of distortion, and much more efficient in terms of the amount of information they can process.

In particular, we will discuss the following:

- Standard autoencoders
- Denoising autoencoders
- Sparse autoencoders
- Variational autoencoders

We can now start discussing the main concepts of autoencoders, focusing on the structural components and their features. In the next sections, we're going to further expand these concepts in order to solve more complex problems.

Autoencoders

In the previous chapters (in particular, *Chapter 3*, *Introduction to Semi-Supervised Learning* and *Chapter 4*, *Advanced Semi-Supervised Classification* on semi-supervised learning), we discussed how real datasets are very often high-dimensional representations of samples that lie on low-dimensional manifolds (this is one of the semi-supervised pattern's assumptions, but it's generally true).

As the complexity of a model is proportional to the dimensionality of the input data, many techniques have been analyzed and optimized in order to reduce the actual number of valid components. For example, PCA selects features according to their relative explained variance, while ICA and generic dictionary learning techniques look for basic atoms that can be combined to rebuild the original samples. In this chapter, we're going to analyze a family of models based on a slightly different approach, but whose capabilities are dramatically increased by the employment of deep learning methods. A generic autoencoder is a model that is split into two separate (but not completely autonomous) components called an encoder and a decoder. The task of the encoder is to transform an input sample into an encoded feature vector, while the task of the decoder is the opposite: rebuilding the original sample using the feature vector as input. The following diagram shows a schematic representation of a generic model:

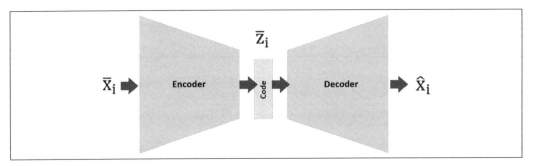

Schema of a generic autoencoder

More formally, we can describe the encoder as a parametrized function:

$$\bar{z}_i = e(\bar{x}_i; \bar{\theta}_e) \ where \ \bar{x}_i \in X$$

The output $\bar{z}_i$ is a vectorial code whose dimensionality is normally quite a bit lower than the input's dimensionality. Analogously, the decoder is described as follows:

$$\hat{x}_i = d(\bar{z}_i; \bar{\theta}_d)$$

The goal of a standard algorithm is to minimize a cost function that is proportional to the reconstruction error. A classic method is based on the **mean squared error (MSE)** (working on a dataset with a sample size equal to M):

$$C(X; \bar{\theta}_e, \bar{\theta}_d) = \frac{1}{M} \sum_{i=1}^{M} \|\bar{x}_i - \hat{x}_i\|^2 = \frac{1}{M} \sum_{i=1}^{M} \|\bar{x}_i - d(e(\bar{x}_i; \bar{\theta}_e); \bar{\theta}_d)\|^2$$

This function depends only on the input samples (which are constant) and the parameter vectors; therefore, this is a de facto unsupervised method where we can control the internal structure and the constraints imposed on the $\bar{z}_i$ code. From a probabilistic viewpoint, if the input samples $\bar{x}_i$ are drawn from a $p(X)$ data-generating process, our goal is to find a $q(X)$ parametric distribution that minimizes the Kullback–Leibler divergence with $p(X)$. Considering the previous definitions, we can define a conditional distribution $q(\hat{X}|X)$ as follows:

$$q(\hat{x}_i|\bar{x}_i) = q(d(e(\bar{x}_i; \bar{\theta}_e); \bar{\theta}_d)|\bar{x}_i)$$

Therefore, the Kullback–Leibler divergence becomes the following:

$$D_{KL}(p||q) = \sum_i p(\bar{x}_i)\log\frac{p(\bar{x}_i)}{q(d(e(\bar{x}_i; \bar{\theta}_e); \bar{\theta}_d)|\bar{x}_i)} = -H(p) + H(p,q)$$

The first term represents the negative entropy of the original distribution, which is constant and isn't involved in the optimization process. The second term is the cross entropy between p and q. If we assume Gaussian distributions for p and q, the MSE is proportional to the cross entropy (for optimization purposes, it's equivalent to it), and therefore this cost function is still valid under a probabilistic approach. Alternatively, it's possible to consider Bernoulli distributions for p and q, and the cross entropy becomes the following:

$$H(p,q) = -\sum_i \bar{x}_i \log \hat{x}_i + (1 - \bar{x}_i)\log(1 - \hat{x}_i)$$

The main difference between the two approaches is that while an MSE can be applied to $\bar{x}_i \in \mathbb{R}^q$ (or multidimensional matrices), Bernoulli distributions need $\bar{x}_i \in (0,1)^q$ (formally, this condition should be $\bar{x}_i \in \{0,1\}^q$; however, the optimization can also be performed successfully when the values are not binary). The same constraint is necessary for the reconstructions; therefore, when using neural networks, the most common choice is to employ sigmoid layers. To be precise, if the data-generating process is assumed to be Gaussian, the cross entropy becomes the MSE. I invite you to check this, but the calculation is extremely easy because we have:

$$\log p(\bar{x}) = \log \alpha e^{-\frac{\|\bar{x}-\bar{\mu}\|^2}{2\beta^2}} = \log \alpha - \frac{\|\bar{x} - \bar{\mu}\|^2}{2\beta^2}$$

Excluding the terms not subject to optimization, it's straightforward to understand that the actual cross entropy between the original distribution and the autoencoder distribution is indeed equivalent to an MSE cost function.

Example of a deep convolutional autoencoder with TensorFlow

This example (like all the others in this and the following chapters) is based on TensorFlow 2.0 (for information about the installation of TensorFlow, please refer to the information provided on the official page: https://www.tensorflow.org/). As explained in the previous chapters, TensorFlow has evolved to incorporate Keras and offers extraordinary flexibility in creating and training deep models. We'll approach this example pragmatically, which means we won't explore all the features; they're beyond the scope of this book. However, interested readers can refer to the book Holdroyd T., *TensorFlow 2.0 Quick Start Guide*, Packt Publishing, 2019.

In this example, we are going to create a deep convolutional autoencoder and train it using the Fashion MNIST dataset. The first step is loading the data (using the Keras helper function), normalizing the data, and, in order to speed up the computation, limiting the training set to 1,000 data points:

```
import tensorflow as tf
import numpy as np

nb_samples = 1000
nb_epochs = 400
batch_size = 200
code_length = 256

(X_train, _), (_, _) = \
        tf.keras.datasets.fashion_mnist.load_data()
X_train = X_train.astype(np.float32)[0:nb_samples] \
            / 255.0

width = X_train.shape[1]
height = X_train.shape[2]

X_train_g = tf.data.Dataset.\
    from_tensor_slices(np.expand_dims(X_train, axis=3)).\
    shuffle(1000).batch(batch_size)
```

The generator `X_train_g` is based on the utility class `Dataset` provided by TensorFlow 2.0. It allows you to select the block of data needed for training and testing purposes (in our case, there's no test generator), automatically shuffle it (to remove potential collinearities), and return batches at every call.

At this point, we can create a class inheriting from `tf.keras.Model`, setting up the whole architecture, which is made up of the following:

The encoder (all layers have padding "same" and ReLU activation):

- Convolution with 32 filters, kernel size equal to (3 × 3), and strides (2 × 2)
- Convolution with 64 filters, kernel size equal to (3 × 3), and strides (1× 1)
- Convolution with 128 filters, kernel size equal to (3 × 3), and strides (1 × 1)

The decoder:

- Transpose convolution with 128 filters, kernel size equal to (3 × 3), and strides (2 × 2)
- Transpose convolution with 64 filters, kernel size equal to (3 × 3), and strides (1× 1)
- Transpose convolution with 32 filters, kernel size equal to (3 × 3), and strides (1 × 1)
- Transpose convolution with 1 filter, kernel size equal to (3 × 3), strides (1 × 1), and a sigmoid activation

As the images are (28 x 28), it makes things easier for us if we resize each batch to have dimensions of (32 x 32), to easily manage all of the subsequent operations that are based on sizes that are a power of 2.

The encoder performs a series of convolutions, starting with larger strides (2 x 2) to capture high-level features and proceeds with 64 and 128 convolutions with (1 x 1) strides to learn more and more detailed features. As explained in *Chapter 19, Deep Convolutional Networks*, convolutions work in a sequential fashion, therefore, a standard architecture generally follows a hierarchical sequence, with a few top-level convolutions and more low-level ones. In this case, the size of the images is very small, and therefore it's a good idea to keep (3 x 3) kernels through the encoder network. In the case of larger images, instead, the first convolutions should also involve larger kernels, while the last ones must focus on smaller details and the size should be smaller (the *normal* minimum value is (2 x 2)).

The decoder has a symmetric architecture because it's based on transpose convolutions (that is, deconvolutions). Therefore, once the code is reshaped, the first filters have to work with detailed features, while the last ones must generally focus on high-level elements (for example, borders). The last transpose convolution is responsible for building the output, which must match the input size. Since we're working with grayscale images in our example, we're employing a single filter, while RGB images require three filters. A practical discussion can be had about the strides. When the networks have a very large capacity, it's possible to use the strides to adjust the output of a transpose convolution layer (multiplying each dimension by the corresponding stride value) in order to match the final desired dimensions. This can be a clever trick to add further convolutions (or to remove them) without altering the output. Instead, if the reconstructions' quality doesn't meet the expected requirements, it's sometimes preferable to resize the images using a specialized high-order function (like we do in the input phase). Your choice must be made by evaluating the MSE and, if possible, also through a visual inspection of the results.

TensorFlow 2.0, when working with classes derived from `tf.keras.Model`, requires the definition of the variables in the constructor, while the methods are free to manipulate them to obtain specific results. In our case, we have:

- The constructor, with all layers required for both the encoder and the decoder
- The encoder method
- The decoder method
- The resizing method as a utility function
- The overload of the `call()` method to invoke the main operation directly using the model instance:

```
class DAC(tf.keras.Model):
    def __init__(self):
        super(DAC, self).__init__()

        # Encoder layers
        self.c1 = tf.keras.layers.Conv2D(
            filters=32,
            kernel_size=(3, 3),
            strides=(2, 2),
            activation=tf.keras.activations.relu,
            padding='same')

        self.c2 = tf.keras.layers.Conv2D(
            filters=64,
            kernel_size=(3, 3),
```

```
            activation=tf.keras.activations.relu,
            padding='same')

        self.c3 = tf.keras.layers.Conv2D(
            filters=128,
            kernel_size=(3, 3),
            activation=tf.keras.activations.relu,
            padding='same')

        self.flatten = tf.keras.layers.Flatten()

        self.dense = tf.keras.layers.Dense(
            units=code_length,
            activation=tf.keras.activations.sigmoid)

        # Decoder layers
        self.dc0 = tf.keras.layers.Conv2DTranspose(
            filters=128,
            kernel_size=(3, 3),
            strides=(2, 2),
            activation=tf.keras.activations.relu,
            padding='same')

        self.dc1 = tf.keras.layers.Conv2DTranspose(
            filters=64,
            kernel_size=(3, 3),
            activation=tf.keras.activations.relu,
            padding='same')

        self.dc2 = tf.keras.layers.Conv2DTranspose(
            filters=32,
            kernel_size=(3, 3),
            activation=tf.keras.activations.relu,
            padding='same')

        self.dc3 = tf.keras.layers.Conv2DTranspose(
            filters=1,
            kernel_size=(3, 3),
            activation=tf.keras.activations.sigmoid,
            padding='same')

    def r_images(self, x):
        return tf.image.resize(x, (32, 32))
```

```
        def encoder(self, x):
            c1 = self.c1(self.r_images(x))
            c2 = self.c2(c1)
            c3 = self.c3(c2)
            code_input = self.flatten(c3)
            z = self.dense(code_input)
            return z

        def decoder(self, z):
            decoder_input = tf.reshape(z, (-1, 16, 16, 1))
            dc0 = self.dc0(decoder_input)
            dc1 = self.dc1(dc0)
            dc2 = self.dc2(dc1)
            dc3 = self.dc3(dc2)
            return dc3

        def call(self, x):
            code = self.encoder(x)
            xhat = self.decoder(code)
            return xhat

    model = DAC()
```

Once we have also defined an instance of our class (called *model* for simplicity), we can define the optimizer, which is Adam with $\eta = 0.001$:

```
optimizer = tf.keras.optimizers.Adam(0.001)
```

The next step consists of defining a helper function to collect information about the training loss. In our case, it's enough to compute the mean of the loss function over each batch:

```
train_loss = tf.keras.metrics.Mean(name='train_loss')
```

Now we need to create the training function, which is one of the innovations introduced in TensorFlow 2.0. Let's define it first:

```
@tf.function
def train(images):
    with tf.GradientTape() as tape:
        reconstructions = model(images)
        loss = tf.keras.losses.MSE(
            model.r_images(images), reconstructions)
    gradients = tape.gradient(
        loss, model.trainable_variables)
    optimizer.apply_gradients(
```

```
        zip(gradients, model.trainable_variables))
    train_loss(loss)
```

This function is marked with a decorator that informs TensorFlow that it's going to work with the variables defined in the model. To apply the backpropagation algorithm, we need to perform the following steps:

- Activate a `GradientTape` context that will take care of computing the gradients of all trainable variables.
- Run the model (the feed-forward phase).
- Evaluate the loss function (in our case, it's a standard mean square error).
- Compute the gradients.
- Ask the optimizer to apply the gradients to all trainable variables (of course, each algorithm performs all the necessary additional operations).
- Accumulate the training loss.

The corresponding Python commands are straightforward and only a little different from the previous TensorFlow versions. Once this function has been declared, it's possible to start the training process:

```
for e in range(nb_epochs):
    for xi in X_train_g:
        train(xi)
    print("Epoch {}: Loss: {:.3f}".
        format(e+1, train_loss.result()))

    train_loss.reset_states()
```

The output of the previous snippet is:

```
Epoch 1: Loss: 0.136
Epoch 2: Loss: 0.090

...

Epoch 399: Loss: 0.001
Epoch 400: Loss: 0.001
```

Hence, at the end of the training process, the average mean square error is 0.001. Considering that the images are resized to 32 x 32 and the values are in the range (0,1), the **mean absolute error (MAE)** ranges between 0 and 1,024. Therefore, an error equal to 0.001 guarantees a high reconstruction quality (it's equivalent to an MAE that is equal to about 0.03 or 3% of the maximum error) of about 97%. Whenever the MSE is considered a reliable reconstruction metric, this approach can also be generalized to data points different from images.

It's also interesting to analyze the length of the code (for instance, the encoder output). As it's standardized in the range (0,1), a total average close to 0.5 indicates that about 50% of the values are active, while the remaining ones are close to 0 (without taking into account the standard deviation). A value slightly larger than 0.5 indicates that the code is very dense, while a value slightly lower than 0.5 is a sign of sparsity because more than 50% of the units have a very low activation:

```
codes = model.encoder(np.expand_dims(X_train, axis=3))
print("Code mean: {:.3f}".format(np.mean(codes)))
print("Code STD: {:.3f}".format(np.std(codes)))
```

The output of the previous block is:

Code mean: 0.554

Code STD: 0.241

As expected (considering that we haven't imposed any constraints), our code is moderately dense. This also means that it's not generally possible to drastically reduce the code length (in the example, it was set equal to 256) without a significant loss of information. The reason for this is directly connected to the entropy of the code. For example, in the case of two images, we know that the optimal encoding requires a single binary unit; however, with complex images, we should consider the full joint probability distribution to estimate the optimal length, and this is

generally intractable. Therefore, a good strategy is to start with a length of about $1/5$ of the dimensionality and to proceed by reducing it until the mean square error remains below a fixed threshold. It goes without saying that a part of the information managed by an autoencoder is stored in the weights of the model; hence, a deeper architecture is normally able to manage shorter code, while a very shallow network requires more information in the code.

We can now visualize some original images and their reconstructions:

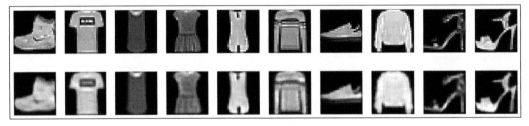

Original images (first row) and their reconstructions (second row)

We can see how the loss of information is limited to secondary details and the autoencoder has successfully learned how to reduce the dimensionality of the input samples.

As an exercise, I invite the reader to split the code into two separate sections (encoder and decoder) and to optimize the architecture in order to achieve better accuracy on the whole Fashion MNIST dataset.

Denoising autoencoders

Autoencoders can be used to determine under-complete representations of a dataset. However, Bengio et al. (in Vincent P., Larochelle H., Lajoie I., Bengio Y., Manzagol P., *Stacked Denoising Autoencoders: Learning Useful Representations in a Deep Network with a Local Denoising Criterion*, from the Journal of Machine Learning Research, 11/2010) proposed using autoencoders to denoise the input samples rather than learning the exact representation of a sample in order to rebuild it from low-dimensional code.

This is not a brand-new idea, because, for example, Hopfield networks (proposed a few decades ago) had the same purpose, but their limitations in terms of capacity led researchers to look for different methods. Nowadays, deep autoencoders can easily manage high-dimensional data (such as images) with a consequent space requirement. That's why many people are now reconsidering the idea of teaching a network how to rebuild a sample image starting from a corrupted one. Formally, there are not many differences between denoising autoencoders and standard autoencoders. However, in this case, the encoder must work with noisy samples:

$$\bar{z}_i = e(\bar{x}_i + \bar{n}_i; \bar{\theta}_e) \ where \ \bar{x}_i \in X$$

The decoder's cost function remains the same. If the noise is sampled for each batch, repeating the process for a sufficiently large number of iterations allows the autoencoder to learn how to rebuild the original image when some fragments are missing or corrupted. To achieve this goal, the authors suggested different possible kinds of noise. The most common choice is to sample Gaussian noise, which has some helpful features and is coherent with many real-world noisy processes:

$$\bar{z}_i = e(\bar{x}_i + \bar{n}_i(t); \bar{\theta}_e) \ where \ \bar{x}_i \in X \ and \ \bar{n}_i(t) \sim N(0, \Sigma)$$

Another possibility is to employ an input dropout layer, zeroing some random elements:

$$\bar{z}_i = e(\bar{x}_i \circ \bar{n}_i; \bar{\theta}_e) \ where \ \bar{x}_i \in X \ and \ \bar{n}_i(x, y) \sim B(0, 1)$$

This choice is clearly more drastic, and the rate must be properly tuned. A very large number of dropped pixels can irreversibly delete many pieces of information and the reconstruction can become more difficult and rigid (our purpose is to extend the autoencoder's ability to other samples drawn from the same distribution). Alternatively, it's possible to mix up the Gaussian noise and the dropout's, switching between them with a fixed probability. Clearly, the models must be more complex than standard autoencoders because now they have to cope with missing information.

The same concept applies to the code length: very under-complete code wouldn't be able to provide all the elements needed to reconstruct the original image in the most accurate way. I suggest testing all the possibilities, in particular when the noise is constrained by external conditions (for example, old photos or messages transmitted through channels affected by precise noise processes). If the model must also be employed for never-before-seen samples, it's extremely important to select samples that represent the true distribution, using data augmentation techniques (limited to operations compatible with the specific problem) whenever the number of elements is not enough to reach the desired level of accuracy.

Example of a denoising autoencoder with TensorFlow

This example doesn't require any dramatic modification of the model previously defined. In fact, the denoising ability is an intrinsic property that every autoencoder has. In order to test it, we only need to consider that the training function now needs both the noisy images and the original ones:

```
model = DAC()

@tf.function
def train(noisy_images, images):
    with tf.GradientTape() as tape:
        reconstructions = model(noisy_images)
        loss = tf.keras.losses.MSE(
            model.r_images(images), reconstructions)
    gradients = tape.gradient(
        loss, model.trainable_variables)
    optimizer.apply_gradients(
        zip(gradients, model.trainable_variables))
    train_loss(loss)
```

As it's possible to see, the mean square error is now computed between the reconstructions and the original images (which are not the input of the model anymore), while the model is fed with the noisy images. If the noise is randomly sampled at each training step, the autoencoder learns the structure of the manifold where the data lies and, at the same time, it becomes robust to small variations of the input. This result is a consequence of the smoothness assumption (see *Chapter 3, Introduction to Semi-Supervised Learning*) and of the fact that the mean of a set of corrupted data points defines an attractor basin. Hence, the noisy input yields slightly different code that is decoded as the closest mean. Of course, if the variation is too large, considering the high non-linearity of the model, the probability of recovering the original image becomes smaller and smaller. For our purposes, we are going to consider clipped Gaussian noise:

$$\bar{x}_{noisy} = clip_{(0,1)}(\bar{x} + \bar{n}(t)) \ where \ \bar{n}(t) \sim N(0, I)$$

In this way, the noisy images are always implicitly normalized, assuming values in the range (0,1):

```
for e in range(nb_epochs):
        for xi in X_train_g:
            xn = np.clip(xi +
                np.random.normal(
                    0.0, 0.2,
                    size=(batch_size, width, height, 1)),
                0.0, 1.0)
            train(xn, xi)
        print("Epoch {}: Loss: {:.3f}".
            format(e + 1, train_loss.result()))
        train_loss.reset_states()
```

The output of the previous snippet is:

```
Epoch 1: Loss: 0.146
Epoch 2: Loss: 0.100

...

Epoch 399: Loss: 0.002
Epoch 400: Loss: 0.002
```

Considering the capacity of these models, it's not surprising to see that the final loss is almost the same as a standard autoencoder. Therefore, we can be sure that any noisy image (based on clipped Gaussian noise with the unit variance/identity covariance matrix) will be correctly recovered.

We can see some examples in the following figure:

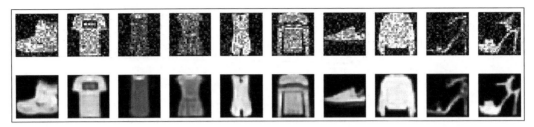

Noisy images (first row) and their reconstructions (second row)

The denoising autoencoder has successfully learned to rebuild the original images (with an MAE equal to about 0.04 and, therefore, an accuracy of about 96%) in the presence of Gaussian noise. I invite you to test other methods (such as using an initial dropout) and increase the noise level to understand what the maximum corruption is that this model can effectively remove.

Sparse autoencoders

In general, standard autoencoders produce dense internal representations. This means that most of the values are different from zero. In some cases, however, it's more useful to have sparse code that can better represent the atoms belonging to a dictionary. In this case, if $\bar{z}_i = (0,0, ..., \bar{z}_i^{(n)}, 0 ..., 00, \bar{z}_i^{(n)}, ..., 0,0)$, we can consider each sample as the overlap of specific atoms weighted accordingly. To achieve this objective, we can simply apply an L_1 penalty to the code layer, as explained in *Chapter 2, Loss functions and Regularization*. The loss function for a single sample, therefore, becomes the following:

$$\hat{L}(\bar{x}_i; \bar{\theta}_e, \bar{\theta}_d) = L(\bar{x}_i; \bar{\theta}_e, \bar{\theta}_d) + \alpha \|\bar{z}_i\|_1$$

In this case, we need to consider the extra hyperparameter α, which must be tuned to increase the sparsity without a negative impact on the accuracy. As a general rule of thumb, I suggest starting with a value equal to 0.01 and then reducing it until the desired result has been achieved. In most cases, higher values yield very poor performance, and therefore they are generally avoided. A different approach has been proposed by Andrew Ng (in 2011 Stanford Machine Learning lecture notes Ng. A, *Sparse Autoencoder*, CS294A, Stanford University). If we consider the code layer as a set of independent Bernoulli random variables, we can enforce sparsity by considering a generic reference Bernoulli variable with a very low mean (for example, $p_r = 0.01$) and adding the Kullback–Leibler divergence between the generic element $\bar{z}_i^{(j)}$ and p_r to the cost function. For a single sample, the extra term is as follows (where p is the code length):

$$L_{D_i} = \sum_{j=1}^{p} D_{KL}(\bar{z}_i^{(j)} || p_r) = \sum_{j=1}^{p} p_r \log \frac{p_r}{\bar{z}_i^{(j)}} + (1 - p_r) \log \frac{1 - p_r}{1 - \bar{z}_i^{(j)}}$$

The resulting loss function becomes the following:

$$\hat{L}(\bar{x}_i; \bar{\theta}_e, \bar{\theta}_d) = L(\bar{x}_i; \bar{\theta}_e, \bar{\theta}_d) + \alpha L_{D_i}$$

The effect of this penalty is similar to L_1 (with the same considerations about the α hyperparameter), but many experiments have confirmed that the resulting cost function is easier to optimize, and it's possible to achieve the same level of sparsity that reaches higher reconstruction accuracies. When working with sparse autoencoders, the code length is often longer because of the assumption that a single element is made up of a small number of atoms (compared to the dictionary size). As a result, I suggest that you evaluate the level of sparsity with different code lengths and select the combination that maximizes the former and minimizes the latter.

Adding sparseness to the Fashion MNIST deep convolutional autoencoder

In this example, we are going to add an L_1 regularization term to the cost function that was defined in the first exercise. As we are employing only 1,000 images, we prefer to use larger potential code equal to 24 x 24 = 576 values. Assuming a partial overlap due to the categories, we expect a final sparsity that's much more extensive than in the first example, but not lower than 10% of the maximum length (which corresponds to a perfect clustering). Smaller values are very unlikely and require much longer, over-complete dictionaries. In fact, considering the nature of the features, many different images share the same details (for example, shirts and t-shirts or coats) and this leads to a minimum density that can be reduced by only leveraging the extreme capacity of some deep models that, in the end, obtain an almost 1-to-1 association between data points (for example, a complete overfitting of the training set without almost any generalization ability). Of course, this is neither our goal nor the objective of any real deep learning task.

Let's start by defining the parameters:

```
nb_samples = 1000
nb_epochs = 400
batch_size = 200
code_length = 576
alpha = 0.1
```

At this point, we can redefine the class, where the code dense layer has an additional L_1 regularization constraint with a coefficient of $\alpha = 0.1$. This value can be increased to induce more sparsity, but the result will suffer a quality loss due to the sub-optimality of the solution. However, as this constraint is imposed only on a limited number of activations, there's room for the other weights to partially compensate the error and yield a very small final loss:

```python
class SparseDAC(tf.keras.Model):
    def __init__(self):
        super(DAC, self).__init__()

        self.c1 = tf.keras.layers.Conv2D(
            filters=32,
            kernel_size=(3, 3),
            strides=(2, 2),
            activation=tf.keras.activations.relu,
            padding='same')

        self.c2 = tf.keras.layers.Conv2D(
            filters=64,
            kernel_size=(3, 3),
            activation=tf.keras.activations.relu,
            padding='same')

        self.c3 = tf.keras.layers.Conv2D(
            filters=128,
            kernel_size=(3, 3),
            activation=tf.keras.activations.relu,
            padding='same')

        self.flatten = tf.keras.layers.Flatten()

        self.dense = tf.keras.layers.Dense(
            units=code_length,
            activation=tf.keras.activations.sigmoid,
            activity_regularizer=
            tf.keras.regularizers.l1(alpha))

        self.dc0 = tf.keras.layers.Conv2DTranspose(
            filters=128,
            kernel_size=(3, 3),
            activation=tf.keras.activations.relu,
            padding='same')
```

```python
        self.dc1 = tf.keras.layers.Conv2DTranspose(
            filters=64,
            kernel_size=(3, 3),
            activation=tf.keras.activations.relu,
            padding='same')

        self.dc2 = tf.keras.layers.Conv2DTranspose(
            filters=32,
            kernel_size=(3, 3),
            activation=tf.keras.activations.relu,
            padding='same')

        self.dc3 = tf.keras.layers.Conv2DTranspose(
            filters=1,
            kernel_size=(3, 3),
            activation=tf.keras.activations.relu,
            padding='same')

    def r_images(self, x):
        return tf.image.resize(x, (24, 24))

    def encoder(self, x):
        c1 = self.c1(self.r_images(x))
        c2 = self.c2(c1)
        c3 = self.c3(c2)
        code_input = self.flatten(c3)
        z = self.dense(code_input)
        return z

    def decoder(self, z):
        decoder_input = tf.reshape(z, (-1, 24, 24, 1))
        dc0 = self.dc0(decoder_input)
        dc1 = self.dc1(dc0)
        dc2 = self.dc2(dc1)
        dc3 = self.dc3(dc2)
        return dc3

    def call(self, x):
        code = self.encoder(x)
        xhat = self.decoder(code)
        return code, xhat


model = SparseDAC()
```

The training function is slightly different because the model outputs both the code and the reconstructions:

```
@tf.function
def train(images):
    with tf.GradientTape() as tape:
        _, reconstructions = model(images)
        loss = tf.keras.losses.MSE(
            model.r_images(images), reconstructions)
    gradients = tape.gradient(
        loss, model.trainable_variables)
    optimizer.apply_gradients(
        zip(gradients, model.trainable_variables))
    train_loss(loss)
```

After the training procedure (which is identical to the first example), we can recompute both the mean and standard deviation of the code:

```
codes = model.encoder(np.expand_dims(X_train, axis=3))
print("Code mean: {:.3f}".format(np.mean(codes)))
print("Code STD: {:.3f}".format(np.std(codes)))
```

The output of the previous snippet is:

```
Code mean: 0.284
Code STD: 0.249
```

As you can see, the mean is now lower (with almost the same standard deviation and minimal random variations), indicating that more code values are closer to 0. I invite you to implement the other strategy, considering that it's easier to create a constant vector filled with small values (for example, 0.01) and exploit the vectorization properties offered by TensorFlow. I also suggest simplifying the Kullback–Leibler divergence by splitting it into an entropy term $H(p_r)$ (which is constant) and a cross-entropy $H(\bar{z}, p_r)$ term.

Variational autoencoders

A **variational autoencoder (VAE)** is a generative model proposed by Kingma and Wellin (in their work Kingma D. P., Wellin M., *Auto-Encoding Variational Bayes*, arXiv:1312.6114 [stat.ML]) that partially resembles a standard autoencoder, but it has some fundamental internal differences. The goal, in fact, is not finding an encoded representation of a dataset, but determining the parameters of a generative process that is able to yield all possible outputs given an input data-generating process.

Let's take the example of a model based on a learnable parameter vector $\bar{\theta}$ and a set of latent variables $\bar{z}$ that have a probability density function $p(\bar{z}; \bar{\theta})$. Our goal can, therefore, be defined as the research of the $\bar{\theta}$ parameters that maximize the likelihood of the marginalized distribution $p(\bar{x}; \bar{\theta})$ (obtained through the integration of the joint probability $p(\bar{x}, \bar{z}; \bar{\theta})$):

$$p(\bar{x}; \bar{\theta}) = \int p(\bar{x}, \bar{z}; \bar{\theta}) d\bar{z} = \int p(\bar{x}|\bar{z}; \bar{\theta}) p(\bar{z}; \bar{\theta}) d\bar{z}$$

If this problem could be easily solved in closed form, a large set of samples drawn from the $p(\bar{x})$ data-generating process would be enough to find a good approximation for $p(\bar{x}; \bar{\theta})$. Unfortunately, the previous expression is intractable in the majority of cases because the true prior $p(\bar{z})$ is unknown (this is a secondary issue, as we can easily make some helpful assumptions) and the posterior distribution $p(\bar{x}|\bar{z}; \bar{\theta})$ is almost always close to zero. The first problem can be solved by selecting a simple prior (the most common choice is $\bar{z} \sim N(0, I)$), but the second one is still very hard because only a few $\bar{z}$ values can lead to the generation of acceptable samples. This is particularly true when the dataset is very high-dimensional and complex (for example, images). Even if there are millions of combinations, only a small number of them can yield realistic samples (if the images are photos of cars, we expect four wheels in the lower part, but it's still possible to generate samples where the wheels are at the top).

For this reason, we need to exploit a method to reduce the sample space. Variational Bayesian methods are based on the idea of employing proxy distributions, which are easy to sample, and, in this case, whose densities are very high (that is, the probability of generating a reasonable output is much higher than the true posterior). In this case, we define an approximate posterior, considering the architecture of a standard autoencoder. In particular, we can introduce a distribution $q(\bar{z}|\bar{x}; \bar{\theta}_q)$ that acts as an encoder (that doesn't behave deterministically anymore), which can be easily modelled with a neural network. Our goal, of course, is to find the best $\bar{\theta}_q$ parameter set to maximize the similarity between q and the true posterior distribution $p(\bar{z}|\bar{x}; \bar{\theta})$. This result can be achieved by minimizing the Kullback–Leibler divergence:

$$D_{KL}\left(q(\bar{z}|\bar{x}; \bar{\theta}_q) \| p(\bar{z}|\bar{x}; \bar{\theta})\right) = \sum_{\bar{z}} q(\bar{z}|\bar{x}; \bar{\theta}_q) \log \frac{q(\bar{z}|\bar{x}; \bar{\theta}_q)}{p(\bar{z}|\bar{x}; \bar{\theta})} = E_{\bar{z}}\left[\log q(\bar{z}|\bar{x}; \bar{\theta}_q)\right] - E_{\bar{z}}\left[\log p(\bar{z}|\bar{x}; \bar{\theta})\right]$$
$$= E_{\bar{z}}\left[\log q(\bar{z}|\bar{x}; \bar{\theta}_q)\right] - E_{\bar{z}}\left[\log p(\bar{x}|\bar{z}; \bar{\theta}) - \log p(\bar{z}; \bar{\theta}) + \log p(\bar{x}; \bar{\theta})\right]$$

In the last formula, the term $\log p(\bar{x}; \bar{\theta})$ doesn't depend on $\bar{z}$, and therefore it can be extracted from the expected value operator and the expression can be manipulated to simplify it:

$$\log p(\bar{x}; \bar{\theta}) - D_{KL}\left(q(\bar{z}|\bar{x}; \bar{\theta}_q)||p(\bar{z}|\bar{x}; \bar{\theta})\right) = E_{\bar{z}}[\log q(\bar{z}|\bar{x}; \bar{\theta}_q) - \log p(\bar{x}|\bar{z}; \bar{\theta}) - \log p(\bar{z}; \bar{\theta})] = E_{\bar{z}}[\log p(\bar{x}|\bar{z}; \bar{\theta})] - D_{KL}(q(\bar{z}|\bar{x}; \bar{\theta}_q)||p(\bar{z}; \bar{\theta}))$$

The equation can be also rewritten as follows:

$$\log p(\bar{x}; \bar{\theta}) = E_{\bar{z}}[\log p(\bar{x}|\bar{z}; \bar{\theta})] - D_{KL}(q(\bar{z}|\bar{x}; \bar{\theta}_q)||p(\bar{z}; \bar{\theta})) + D_{KL}(q(\bar{z}|\bar{x}; \bar{\theta}_q)||p(\bar{z}|\bar{x}; \bar{\theta})) = ELBO_{\bar{\theta}} + D_{KL}(q(\bar{z}|\bar{x}; \bar{\theta}_q)||p(\bar{z}|\bar{x}; \bar{\theta}))$$

On the right-hand side, we now have the term **ELBO** (short for **evidence lower bound**) and the Kullback–Leibler divergence between the probabilistic encoder $q(\bar{z}|\bar{x}; \bar{\theta}_q)$ and the true posterior distribution $p(\bar{z}|\bar{x}; \bar{\theta})$. The ELBO is the only quantity needed in a variational approach (for further details about this technique, which is beyond the scope of this book, please see Bishop C. M., *Pattern Recognition and Machine Learning, Springer*, 2011). As we want to maximize the log probability of a sample under the $\bar{\theta}$ parametrization and considering that the KL divergence is always non-negative, we can only work with the ELBO (which is a lot easier to manage than the other term). Indeed, the loss function that we are going to optimize is the negative ELBO. To achieve this goal, we need two more important steps.

The first one is choosing an appropriate structure for $q(\bar{z}|\bar{x}; \bar{\theta}_q)$. As $p(\bar{z}; \bar{\theta})$ is assumed to be normal, we can supposedly model $q(\bar{z}|\bar{x}; \bar{\theta}_q)$ as a multivariate Gaussian distribution, splitting the probabilistic encoder into two blocks fed with the same lower layers:

- A mean generator $\mu(\bar{z}|\bar{x}; \bar{\theta}_q)$ that outputs a vector $\bar{\mu}_i \in \mathbb{R}^p$
- A covariance generator (assuming a diagonal matrix) $\Sigma(\bar{z}|\bar{x}; \bar{\theta}_q)$ that outputs a vector $\bar{\sigma}_i \in \mathbb{R}^p$ so that $\Sigma_i = diag(\bar{\sigma}_i)$

In this way, $q(\bar{z}|\bar{x}; \bar{\theta}_q) = N\left(\mu(\bar{z}|\bar{x}; \bar{\theta}_q), \Sigma(\bar{z}|\bar{x}; \bar{\theta}_q)\right)$, and therefore the second term on the right-hand side is the Kullback-Leibler divergence between two Gaussian distributions, which can be easily expressed as follows (p is the dimension of both the mean and covariance vector):

$$D_{KL}(N(\mu(\bar{z}|\bar{x}; \bar{\theta}_q), \Sigma(\bar{z}|\bar{x}; \bar{\theta}_q)||N(0, I)) = \frac{1}{2}\left[tr\left(\Sigma(\bar{z}|\bar{x}; \bar{\theta}_q) + \mu(\bar{z}|\bar{x}; \bar{\theta}_q)^T\mu(\bar{z}|\bar{x}; \bar{\theta}_q) - \log|\Sigma(\bar{z}|\bar{x}; \bar{\theta}_q)| - p\right)\right]$$

This operation is simpler than expected because, as Σ is diagonal, the trace corresponds to the sum of the elements $\Sigma_1 + \Sigma_2 + \cdots + \Sigma_p$ and $\log|\Sigma| = \log\Sigma_1\Sigma_2 \ldots \Sigma_p = \log\Sigma_1 + \log\Sigma_2 + \cdots + \log\Sigma_p$.

At this point, maximizing the right-hand side of the previous expression is equivalent to maximizing the expected value of the log probability to generate acceptable samples and minimizing the discrepancy between the normal prior and the Gaussian distribution synthesized by the encoder. Everything seems much simpler now, but there is still a problem to solve. We want to use neural networks and the stochastic gradient descent algorithm, and therefore we need differentiable functions.

As the Kullback-Leibler divergence can be computed only using mini-batches with n elements (the approximation becomes closer to the true value after a sufficient number of iterations), it's necessary to sample n values from the distribution $N\left(\mu(\bar{z}|\bar{x}; \bar{\theta}_q), \Sigma(\bar{z}|\bar{x}; \bar{\theta}_q)\right)$ and, unfortunately, this operation is not differentiable. To solve this problem, the authors suggest a reparameterization trick: instead of sampling from $q(\bar{z}|\bar{x}; \bar{\theta}_q)$, we can sample from a normal distribution, $\epsilon \sim N(0, I)$, and build the actual samples as $\mu(\bar{z}|\bar{x}; \bar{\theta}_q) + \epsilon \Sigma(\bar{z}|\bar{x}; \bar{\theta}_q)^2$. Considering that ϵ is a constant vector during a batch (both the forward and backward phases), it's easy to compute the gradient with respect to the previous expression and optimize both the decoder and the encoder. The last element to consider is the first term on the right-hand side of the expression that we want to maximize:

$$E_{\bar{z}}[\log p(\bar{x}|\bar{z}; \bar{\theta})] = \sum_{\bar{z}} p(\bar{z}|\bar{x}; \bar{\theta}) \log p(\bar{x}|\bar{z}; \bar{\theta}) = -H(p(\bar{z}|\bar{x}; \bar{\theta}), p(\bar{x}|\bar{z}; \bar{\theta}))$$

This term represents the negative cross entropy between the actual distribution and the reconstructed one. As discussed in the first section, there are two feasible choices: Gaussian or Bernoulli distributions. In general, VAEs employ a Bernoulli distribution with input samples and reconstruction values constrained between 0 and 1. However, many experiments have confirmed that the MSE can speed up the training process, and therefore I suggest that you test both methods and pick the one that guarantees the best performance (both in terms of accuracy and training speed).

Example of a VAE with TensorFlow

Let's continue working with the Fashion MNIST dataset to build a VAE. The first step requires loading and normalizing it:

```
import tensorflow as tf

(X_train, _), (_, _) = \
    tf.keras.datasets.fashion_mnist.load_data()
X_train = X_train.astype(np.float32)[0:nb_samples] \
/ 255.0
```

```
width = X_train.shape[1]
height = X_train.shape[2]
```

As explained, the output of the encoder is now split into two components: the mean and covariance vectors (both with dimensions equal to (width x height)) and the decoder input is obtained by sampling from a normal distribution and projecting the code components. The complete model class is as follows (all the parameters are the same as the first example, which is a reference for all the other ones):

```
class DAC(tf.keras.Model):
    def __init__(self, width, height):
        super(DAC, self).__init__()

        self.width = width
        self.height = height

        self.c1 = tf.keras.layers.Conv2D(
            filters=32,
            kernel_size=(3, 3),
            strides=(2, 2),
            activation=tf.keras.activations.relu,
            padding='same')

        self.c2 = tf.keras.layers.Conv2D(
            filters=64,
            kernel_size=(3, 3),
            activation=tf.keras.activations.relu,
            padding='same')

        self.c3 = tf.keras.layers.Conv2D(
            filters=128,
            kernel_size=(3, 3),
            activation=tf.keras.activations.relu,
            padding='same')

        self.flatten = tf.keras.layers.Flatten()

        self.code_mean = tf.keras.layers.Dense(
            units=width * height)

        self.code_log_variance = tf.keras.layers.Dense(
            units=width * height)

        self.dc0 = tf.keras.layers.Conv2DTranspose(
```

```
                filters=63,
                kernel_size=(3, 3),
                strides=(2, 2),
                activation=tf.keras.activations.relu,
                padding='same')

            self.dc1 = tf.keras.layers.Conv2DTranspose(
                filters=32,
                kernel_size=(3, 3),
                strides=(2, 2),
                activation=tf.keras.activations.relu,
                padding='same')

            self.dc2 = tf.keras.layers.Conv2DTranspose(
                filters=1,
                kernel_size=(3, 3),
                padding='same')

        def r_images(self, x):
            return tf.image.resize(x, (32, 32))

        def encoder(self, x):
            c1 = self.c1(self.r_images(x))
            c2 = self.c2(c1)
            c3 = self.c3(c2)
            code_input = self.flatten(c3)
            mu = self.code_mean(code_input)
            sigma = self.code_log_variance(code_input)
            code_std = tf.sqrt(tf.exp(sigma))
            normal_samples = tf.random.normal(
                mean=0.0, stddev=1.0,
                shape=(batch_size, width * height))
            z = (normal_samples * code_std) + mu
            return z, mu, code_std

        def decoder(self, z):
            decoder_input = tf.reshape(z, (-1, 7, 7, 16))
            dc0 = self.dc0(decoder_input)
            dc1 = self.dc1(dc0)
            dc2 = self.dc2(dc1)
            return dc2, tf.keras.activations.sigmoid(dc2)

        def call(self, x):
            code, cm, cs = self.encoder(x)
```

```
        logits, xhat = self.decoder(code)
        return logits, cm, cs, xhat
```

The structure is very similar to a standard deep autoencoder, but, in this case, the encoder performs two additional steps:

1. Samples from a normal distribution $\epsilon \sim N(0, I)$

2. Performs the transformation $\mu + \epsilon \Sigma^2$ (in the code, instead of the variance, the standard deviation is employed; therefore, there's no need to square the second term)

The decoder outputs both the reconstructions (filtered by a `sigmoid`) and the `logits` (that is, the values before the application of the `sigmoid`). This helps in defining the loss function:

```
optimizer = tf.keras.optimizers.Adam(0.001)
train_loss = tf.keras.metrics.Mean(name='train_loss')


@tf.function
def train(images):
    with tf.GradientTape() as tape:
        logits, cm, cs, _ = model(images)
        loss_r = \
            tf.nn.sigmoid_cross_entropy_with_logits(
            logits=logits, labels=images)
        kl_divergence = 0.5 * tf.reduce_sum(
            tf.math.square(cm) + tf.math.square(cs) -
            tf.math.log(1e-8 + tf.math.square(cs)) - 1,
            axis=1)
        loss = tf.reduce_sum(loss_r) + kl_divergence
    gradients = tape.gradient(
        loss, model.trainable_variables)
    optimizer.apply_gradients(
        zip(gradients, model.trainable_variables))
    train_loss(loss)
```

As you can see, the only differences in the training functions are:

*   The use of sigmoid cross entropy as a reconstruction loss (which is numerically more stable than a direct computation)

*   The presence of the Kullback-Leibler divergence as a regularization term

The training process is very similar to the first example in this chapter, as the sampling operations are performed directly by TensorFlow. For simplicity, the whole training block is reported in the following snippet:

```
model = DAC(width, height)

X_train_g = tf.data.Dataset.\
        from_tensor_slices(
        np.expand_dims(X_train, axis=3)).\
        shuffle(1000).batch(batch_size)

for e in range(nb_epochs):
for xi in X_train_g:
            train(xi)
        print("Epoch {}: Loss: {:.3f}".
            format(e + 1, train_loss.result()))
        train_loss.reset_states()
```

The output of the previous snippet is:

Epoch 1: Loss: 102563.508

Epoch 2: Loss: 82810.648

...

Epoch 399: Loss: 38469.824

Epoch 400: Loss: 38474.977

The result after 400 epochs is shown in the following figure:

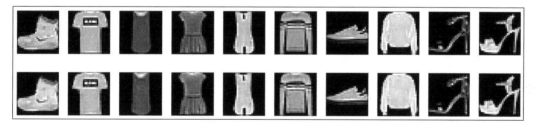

Original images (first row) and their reconstructions (second row)

The quality of the reconstructions is visually better than the standard deep autoencoder and, contrary to the latter, many secondary details have also been successfully reconstructed.

In this and also in the previous examples, the results may be slightly different because of TensorFlow random seed (whose default is 1000). Even when there is no explicit sampling, the initialization of neural networks requires many sampling steps that lead to moderately different initial configurations.

As an exercise, I invite the reader to use the RGB datasets (such as Cifar-10, which is found at `https://www.cs.toronto.edu/~kriz/cifar.html`) to test the generation ability of the VAE by comparing the output samples with the one drawn from the original distribution.

Summary

In this chapter, we presented autoencoders as unsupervised models that can learn to represent high-dimensional datasets with lower-dimensional code. They are structured into two separate blocks (which, however, are trained together): an encoder, responsible for mapping the input sample to an internal representation, and a decoder, which must perform the inverse operation, rebuilding the original image starting from the code.

We have also discussed how autoencoders can be used to denoise samples and how it's possible to impose a sparsity constraint on the code layer to resemble the concept of standard dictionary learning. The last topic was about a slightly different pattern called a VAE. The idea is to build a generative model that is able to reproduce all the possible samples belonging to a training distribution.

In the next chapter, we are going to briefly introduce a very important model family called **generative adversarial networks (GANs)**, which are not very different from the purposes of a VAE, but which have a much more flexible approach.

Further reading

- Vincent P., Larochelle H., Lajoie I., Bengio Y., Manzagol P., *Stacked Denoising Autoencoders: Learning Useful Representations in a Deep Network with a Local Denoising Criterion*, Journal of Machine Learning Research, 11/2010

- Ng. A, Sparse Autoencoder, CS294A, *Machine Learning lecture notes, Stanford University*, 2011

- Kingma D. P., Wellin M., *Auto-Encoding Variational Bayes*, arXiv:1312.6114 [stat.ML]

- Holdroyd T., *TensorFlow 2.0 Quick Start Guide*, Packt Publishing, 2019

- Bishop C. M., *Pattern Recognition and Machine Learning*, Springer, 2011

- Goodfellow I., Bengio Y., *Courville A., Deep Learning*, The MIT Press, 2016

- Bonaccorso G., *Machine Learning Algorithms Second Edition*, Packt Publishing, 2018

22

Introduction to Generative Adversarial Networks

In this chapter, we're going to provide a brief introduction to a family of generative models based on some game theory concepts. Their main peculiarity is an adversarial training procedure that is aimed at learning to distinguish between true and fake samples, driving, at the same time, another component that generates samples more and more similar to the training examples.

In particular, we will be discussing:

- **Adversarial training and standard Generative Adversarial Networks (GANs)**
- **Deep Convolutional GANs (DCGANs)**
- **Wasserstein GANs (WGANs)**

We can now introduce the concept of adversarial training of neural models, its connection to game theory and its applications to GANs.

Adversarial training

The brilliant idea of adversarial training, proposed by Goodfellow et al. (in Goodfellow I. J., Pouget-Abadie J., Mirza M., Xu B., Warde-Farley D., Ozair S., Courville A., Bengio Y., *Generative Adversarial Networks*, arXiv:1406.2661 [stat.ML] – although this idea has been, at least in theory, discussed earlier by other authors), ushered in a new generation of generative models that immediately outperformed the majority of existing algorithms. All of the derived models are based on the same fundamental concept of adversarial training, which is an approach partially inspired by game theory.

Let's suppose that we have a data-generating process, $p_{data}(\bar{x})$, that represents an actual data distribution and a finite number of data points that we suppose are drawn from p_{data}:

$$X = \{\bar{x}_1, \bar{x}_2, \dots, \bar{x}_M\} \ where \ \bar{x}_i \in \mathbb{R}^n$$

Our goal is to train a model called a generator, whose distribution must be as close as possible to p_{data}. This is the trickiest part of the algorithm because instead of standard methods (for example, variational autoencoders), adversarial training is based on a minimax game between two players (we can simply say that, given an objective, the goal of both players is to minimize the maximum possible loss, but in this case, each of them works on different parameters). One player is the generator, which we can define as a parameterized function of a noise sample:

$$\hat{x}_i = G\left(\bar{z}_i; \bar{\theta}_g\right) \ where \ \bar{z}_i \sim U(-1,1)$$

The generator is fed with a noise vector (in this case, we have employed a uniform distribution, but there are no particular restrictions; therefore, we are simply going to say that $\bar{z}_i$ is drawn from a random noise distribution p_{noise}), and outputs a value that has the same dimensionality as the samples drawn from p_{data}. Without any further control, the generator distribution will be completely different to the data-generating process, but this is the moment for the other player to enter the scene. The second model is called the discriminator (or critic), and it is responsible for evaluating the samples drawn from p_{data} and the ones produced by the generator:

$$p_i = D(\bar{x}_i; \bar{\theta}_d) \ where \ p_i \in (0,1)$$

The role of this model is to output a probability that must reflect the fact that the sample is drawn from p_{data}, instead of being generated by $G\left(\bar{z}_i; \bar{\theta}_g\right)$. What happens is very simple: the first player (the generator) outputs a sample, $\bar{x}_i$. If x actually belongs to p_{data}, the discriminator will output a value close to 1, while if it's very different from the other true samples, $D(\bar{x}_i; \bar{\theta}_d)$ will output a very low probability. The real structure of the game is based on the idea of training the generator to deceive the discriminator by producing samples that could potentially be drawn from p_{data}. This result can be achieved by trying to maximize the log-probability, $\log D(\bar{x}_i; \bar{\theta}_d)$, when x is a true sample (drawn from p_{data}), while minimizing the log-probability, $\log\left(1 - D\left(G\left(\bar{z}_i; \bar{\theta}_g\right); \bar{\theta}_d\right)\right)$, with $\bar{z}_i$ sampled from a noise distribution.

The first operation forces the discriminator to become more and more aware of the true samples (this condition is necessary to avoid being deceived too easily).

The second objective is a little bit more complex because the discriminator has to evaluate a sample that can be acceptable or not. Let's suppose that the generator is not smart enough, and outputs a sample that cannot belong to p_{data}. As the discriminator is learning how p_{data} is structured, it will very soon distinguish the wrong sample, outputting a low probability. Hence, by minimizing $\log\left(1 - D\left(G\left(\bar{z}_i; \bar{\theta}_g\right); \bar{\theta}_d\right)\right)$, we are forcing the discriminator to become more and more critical when the samples are quite different from the ones drawn from p_{data}, and the generator becomes more and more able to produce acceptable samples. On the other hand, if the generator outputs a sample that belongs to the data-generating process, the discriminator will output a high probability, and the minimization falls back into the previous case.

The authors expressed this minimax game using a shared value function, $V(G, D)$, that must be minimized by the generator and maximized by the discriminator:

$$V(G, D) = E_{\bar{x} \sim p_{data}}[\log D(\bar{x}_i; \bar{\theta}_d)] + E_{\bar{z} \sim p_{noise}}\left[\log\left(1 - D\left(G\left(\bar{z}_i; \bar{\theta}_g\right); \bar{\theta}_d\right)\right)\right] = V_{data}(D) + V_{noise}(G, D)$$

This formula represents the dynamics of a non-cooperative game between two players (for further information, refer to Tadelis S., *Game Theory*, Princeton University Press, 2013) that theoretically admits a special configuration, called a Nash equilibrium, that can be described by saying that if the two players know each other's strategy, they have no reason to change their own strategy if the other player doesn't.

In this case, both the discriminator and generator will pursue their strategies until no change is needed, reaching a final, stable configuration, which is potentially a Nash equilibrium (even if there are many factors that can prevent reaching this goal). A common problem is the premature convergence of the discriminator, which forces the gradients to vanish because the loss function becomes flat in a region close to 0. As this is a game, a fundamental condition is the possibility of providing information to allow the player to make corrections. If the discriminator learns how to separate true samples from fake ones too quickly, the generator convergence slows down, and the player can remain trapped in a sub-optimal configuration.

In general, when the distributions are rather complex, the discriminator is slower than the generator; but in some cases, it is necessary to update the generator more times after each single discriminator update. Unfortunately, there is no rule of thumb; but, for example, when working with images, it's possible to observe the samples generated after a sufficiently large number of iterations. If the discriminator loss has become very small and the samples appear corrupted or incoherent, it means that the generator did not have enough time to learn the distribution, and it's necessary to slow down the discriminator.

The authors (in the aforementioned paper) showed that given a generator characterized by a distribution $p_g(\bar{x})$, the optimal discriminator is:

$$D_{opt}^G(\bar{x}) = \frac{p_{data}(\bar{x})}{p_{data}(\bar{x}) + p_g(\bar{x})}$$

At this point, considering the previous value function $V(G, D)$ and using the optimal discriminator, we can rewrite it in a single objective (as a function of G) that must be minimized by the generator:

$$V'(G) = E_{\bar{x} \sim p_{data}} \left[\log D_{opt}^G(\bar{x}; \bar{\theta}_d) \right] + E_{\bar{x} \sim p_g} \left[\log(1 - D_{opt}^G(\bar{x}; \bar{\theta}_d)) \right]$$

To better understand how a GAN works, we need to expand the previous expression:

$$V'(G) = E_{\bar{x} \sim p_{data}} \left[\log \frac{p_{data}(\bar{x})}{p_{data}(\bar{x}) + p_g(\bar{x})} \right] + E_{\bar{x} \sim p_g} \left[\log \frac{p_g(\bar{x})}{p_{data}(\bar{x}) + p_g(\bar{x})} \right]$$

Applying some simple manipulations, we get the following:

$$\frac{1}{2} V'(G) + 2 \log 2$$

$$= \frac{1}{2} E_{\bar{x} \sim p_{data}} \left[\log \frac{p_{data}(\bar{x})}{p_{data}(\bar{x}) + p_g(\bar{x})} \right] + \frac{1}{2} E_{\bar{x} \sim p_g} \left[\log \frac{p_g(\bar{x})}{p_{data}(\bar{x}) + p_g(\bar{x})} \right]$$

$$+ \frac{1}{2} 2 \log 2 = \frac{D_{KL}\left(p_{data} \| \frac{p_{data} + p_g}{2}\right) + D_{KL}\left(p_g \| \frac{p_{data} + p_g}{2}\right)}{2} = D_{JS}(p_{data} \| p_g)$$

The last term represents the Jensen-Shannon divergence between p_{data} and p_g. This measure is similar to the Kullback-Leibler divergence, but it's symmetrical and bounded between 0 and log 2. When the two distributions are identical, $D_{JS} = 0$, but if their supports (the value sets where $p(\bar{x}) > 0$) are disjoint, $D_{JS} = \log 2$ (while $D_{KL} \to \infty$). Therefore, the value function can be expressed as:

$$V'(G) = 2D_{JS}(p_{data} \| p_g) - 2 \log 2$$

Now, it should be clearer that a GAN tries to minimize the Jensen-Shannon divergence between the data-generating process and the generator distribution. In general, this procedure is quite effective; however, when the supports are disjoint, a GAN has no information about the true distance.

This consideration (analyzed with more mathematical rigor in Salimans T., Goodfellow I., Zaremba W., Cheung V., Radford A., and Chen X., *Improved Techniques for Training GANs*, arXiv:1606.03498 [cs.LG]) explains why training a GAN can become quite difficult and, consequently, why the Nash equilibrium cannot be found in many cases. For these reasons, we are going to analyze an alternative approach in the next section.

The complete GAN algorithm (as proposed by the authors) is:

1. Set the number of epochs, N_{epochs}.
2. Set the number of discriminator iterations, N_{iter} (in most cases, $N_{iter} = 1$).
3. Set the batch size, k.
4. Define a noise-generating process, N (for example, $N = U(-1,1)$).
5. For $e = 1$ to N_{epochs}:

    a. Sample k values from X.

    b. Sample k values from N.

    c. For $i = 1$ to N_{iter}:

        i. Compute the gradients, $\nabla_d V(G, D)$ (only with respect to the discriminator variables). The expected value is approximated with a sample mean.

        ii. Update the discriminator parameters by stochastic gradient ascent (as we are working with logarithms, it's possible to minimize the negative loss).

    d. Sample k values from N.

    e. Compute the gradients, $\nabla_g V_{noise}(G, D)$ (only with respect to the generator variables).

    f. Update the generator parameters by stochastic gradient descent.

As these models need to sample noisy vectors in order to guarantee reproducibility, I suggest setting the random seed in both NumPy (`np.random.seed(...)`) and TensorFlow (`tf..random.set_seed(...)`). The default value chosen for all of these experiments is 1,000.

Deep Convolutional GANs

After discussing the basic concepts of adversarial training, we can apply them to a practical example of DCGANs. In fact, even if it's possible to use only dense layers (MLPs), as we want to work with images, it's preferable to employ convolutions and transpose convolutions to obtain the best results.

Example of DCGAN with TensorFlow

In this example, we want to build a DCGAN (proposed in Radford A., Metz L., Chintala S., *Unsupervised Representation Learning with Deep Convolutional Generative Adversarial Networks*, arXiv:1511.06434 [cs.LG]) with the Fashion-MNIST dataset (obtained through the TensorFlow/Keras helper function). As the training speed is not very high, we limit the number of samples to 5,000, but I suggest repeating the experiment with larger values. The first step is loading and normalizing (between -1 and 1) the dataset:

```
import tensorflow as tf
import numpy as np

nb_samples = 5000

(X_train, _), (_, _) = \
        tf.keras.datasets.fashion_mnist.load_data()
X_train = X_train.astype(np.float32)[0:nb_samples]/255.0
X_train = (2.0 * X_train) - 1.0

width = X_train.shape[1]
height = X_train.shape[2]

code_length = 100
```

According to the original paper, the generator is based on four transpose convolutions with kernel sizes equal to (4, 4) and strides equal to (2, 2). The input is a single multi-channel pixel (1 × 1 × code_length) that is expanded by subsequent convolutions. The number of filters is 1024, 512, 256, 128, and 1 (we are working with grayscale images). The authors suggest employing a symmetric-valued dataset (that's why we have normalized between -1 and 1), batch normalization after each layer, and leaky ReLU activation (with a default negative slope set equal to 0.3):

```
generator = tf.keras.models.Sequential([
    tf.keras.layers.Conv2DTranspose(
        input_shape=(1, 1, code_length),
        filters=1024,
```

```
        kernel_size=(4, 4),
        padding='valid'),
    tf.keras.layers.BatchNormalization(),
    tf.keras.layers.LeakyReLU(),


    tf.keras.layers.Conv2DTranspose(
        filters=512,
        kernel_size=(4, 4),
        strides=(2, 2),
        padding='same'),
    tf.keras.layers.BatchNormalization(),
    tf.keras.layers.LeakyReLU(),


    tf.keras.layers.Conv2DTranspose(
        filters=256,
        kernel_size=(4, 4),
        strides=(2, 2),
        padding='same'),
    tf.keras.layers.BatchNormalization(),
    tf.keras.layers.LeakyReLU(),


    tf.keras.layers.Conv2DTranspose(
        filters=128,
        kernel_size=(4, 4),
        strides=(2, 2),
        padding='same'),
    tf.keras.layers.BatchNormalization(),
    tf.keras.layers.LeakyReLU(),


    tf.keras.layers.Conv2DTranspose(
        filters=1,
        kernel_size=(4, 4),
        strides=(2, 2),
        padding='same',
        activation='tanh')
])
```

The strides are set to work with 64 × 64 images and, as the Fashion-MNIST dataset has 28 × 28 samples, which cannot be generated with power-of-two modules, we are going to resize the samples while training. Contrary to older TensorFlow versions, in this case we don't need to declare any variable scope because the training scope will be managed using the GradientTape contexts.

Moreover, all Keras-derived models inherit the parameter "training" to enable/disable dropout and batch normalization. The output of the generator is already normalized in the range (-1,1), thanks to hyperbolic tangent activation.

The discriminator is almost the same as a generator (the only main differences are the inverse convolution sequence and the absence of batch normalization after the first layer):

```
discriminator = tf.keras.models.Sequential([
    tf.keras.layers.Conv2D(
        input_shape=(64, 64, 1),
        filters=128,
        kernel_size=(4, 4),
        strides=(2, 2),
        padding='same'),
    tf.keras.layers.LeakyReLU(),


    tf.keras.layers.Conv2D(
        filters=256,
        kernel_size=(4, 4),
        strides=(2, 2),
        padding='same'),
    tf.keras.layers.BatchNormalization(),
    tf.keras.layers.LeakyReLU(),


    tf.keras.layers.Conv2D(
        filters=512,
        kernel_size=(4, 4),
        strides=(2, 2),
        padding='same'),
    tf.keras.layers.BatchNormalization(),
    tf.keras.layers.LeakyReLU(),


    tf.keras.layers.Conv2D(
        filters=1024,
        kernel_size=(4, 4),
        strides=(2, 2),
        padding='same'),
    tf.keras.layers.BatchNormalization(),
    tf.keras.layers.LeakyReLU(),


    tf.keras.layers.Conv2D(
```

```
        filters=1,
        kernel_size=(4, 4),
        padding='valid')
])
```

The discriminator is still a fully convolutional network, even if the output (with a single filter) is a vector of values representing the logits of the samples. As explained in the chapter about regression models, the logit can be immediately transformed into an actual probability by using the sigmoid function, but in this case, we prefer to output the original value, letting TensorFlow perform the transformation in a more robust way when computing the loss function. Of course, if it's necessary to obtain the probability, all we need to do is use the appropriate function:

```
p = tf.math.sigmoid(discriminator(x, training=False))
```

We can also create a couple of helper functions to run both generator and discriminator by taking care of converting the output every time:

```
def run_generator(z, training=False):
    zg = tf.reshape(z, (-1, 1, 1, code_length))
    return generator(zg, training=training)


def run_discriminator(x, training=False):
    xd = tf.image.resize(x, (64, 64))
    return discriminator(xd, training=training)
```

At this point, we need to define the optimizers and the loss meters:

```
optimizer_generator = \
    tf.keras.optimizers.Adam(0.0002, beta_1=0.5)
optimizer_discriminator = \
    tf.keras.optimizers.Adam(0.0002, beta_1=0.5)


train_loss_generator = \
    tf.keras.metrics.Mean(name='train_loss')
train_loss_discriminator = \
    tf.keras.metrics.Mean(name='train_loss')
```

Both networks will be trained using the Adam optimizer with $\eta = 0.0002$ and $\beta_1 = 0.5$. This choice has been suggested by the authors after testing different configurations, and results in fast convergence and average-to-good generative quality.

At this point, we can define the training function using two different `GradientTape` contexts (for the generator and the discriminator):

```python
@tf.function
def train(xi):
    zn = tf.random.uniform(
        (batch_size, code_length), -1.0, 1.0)

    with tf.GradientTape() as tape_generator, \
            tf.GradientTape() as tape_discriminator:
        xg = run_generator(zn, training=True)
        zd1 = run_discriminator(xi, training=True)
        zd2 = run_discriminator(xg, training=True)

        loss_d1 = tf.keras.losses.\
            BinaryCrossentropy(from_logits=True)\
            (tf.ones_like(zd1), zd1)
        loss_d2 = tf.keras.losses.\
            BinaryCrossentropy(from_logits=True)\
            (tf.zeros_like(zd2), zd2)
        loss_discriminator = loss_d1 + loss_d2

        loss_generator = tf.keras.losses.\
            BinaryCrossentropy(from_logits=True)\
            (tf.ones_like(zd2), zd2)

    gradients_generator = \
        tape_generator.gradient(
        loss_generator,
        generator.trainable_variables)
    gradients_discriminator = \
        tape_discriminator.gradient(
        loss_discriminator,
        discriminator.trainable_variables)

    optimizer_discriminator.apply_gradients(
        zip(gradients_discriminator,
            discriminator.trainable_variables))
    optimizer_generator.apply_gradients(
        zip(gradients_generator,
            generator.trainable_variables))
```

```
train_loss_discriminator(loss_discriminator)
train_loss_generator(loss_generator)
```

After generating the noise ($z_n \sim U(-1,1)$), the generator is invoked, followed by a double call to the discriminator to obtain the evaluation for a true image batch and an equal number of generated samples. The next step is defining the loss functions. As we are working with logarithms, there can be stability problems when the values become close to 0. For this reason, it's preferable to employ the built-in TensorFlow class `tf.keras.losses.BinaryCrossentropy`, which guarantees numerical stability in every case. This class must be initialized by selecting whether the input is either a probability (bounded between 0 and 1) or a logit (unbounded). As we are working with the linear output of the final 2D convolution, we are also imposing `from_logits=True` in order to ask the algorithm to apply the sigmoid transformation internally. In general, the output (given the logits) is:

$$L = -x_{label} \log \sigma(x_{logit}) - (1 - x_{label}) \log \left(1 - \sigma(x_{logit})\right)$$

Therefore, setting the label equal to 1 forces the second term to be null, and vice versa. The training step is split into two parts, which act on the discriminator and generator variables separately. Contrary to older versions of TensorFlow, we don't need to worry about the reuse of discriminator variables because every time we call the model, the same instance will be used. However, as the training procedure is split, we can simply compute the gradients of both generator and discriminator and apply the corrections only to the respective models (even if the discriminator is also fed with the output of the generator, which becomes part of the same computational graph). Therefore, when the discriminator is trained, the generator variables remain unchanged if this model generated a batch that contributed to the final loss function.

We can now implement the training cycle with a code length equal to 100 epochs and a batch size of 128 (the reader is free to change these values and observe the effects as an exercise):

```
nb_epochs = 100
batch_size = 128


x_train_g = tf.data.Dataset.from_tensor_slices(
        np.expand_dims(X_train, axis=3)).\
        shuffle(1000).batch(batch_size)


for e in range(nb_epochs):
```

```
for xi in x_train_g:
            train(xi)


        print("Epoch {}: "
            "Discriminator Loss: {:.3f}, "
            "Generator Loss: {:.3f}".
            format(e + 1,
                train_loss_discriminator.result(),
                train_loss_generator.result()))


    train_loss_discriminator.reset_states()
    train_loss_generator.reset_states()
```

Once the training process has finished, we can generate some images (50) by executing the generator with a matrix of noise samples:

```
Z = np.random.uniform(-1.0, 1.0,
                    size=(50, code_length)).\
        astype(np.float32)
Ys = run_generator(Z, training=False)
Ys = np.squeeze((Ys + 1.0) * 0.5 * 255.0).\
        astype(np.uint8)
```

The result (which depends on the random seed) is shown in the following screenshot:

Samples generated by a DCGAN trained with the Fashion-MNIST dataset

As an exercise, I invite the reader to employ more complex convolutional architectures and an RGB dataset such as CIFAR-10 (`https://www.cs.toronto.edu/~kriz/cifar.html`).

Mode collapse

We have seen that a GAN is a generative model that learns to reproduce a data-generating process p_{data}. In the best cases, the artificial distribution $q(\bar{x} ; \bar{\theta})$ is close enough to p_{data} according to a predefined metric (for example, Kullback-Leibler divergence). Unfortunately, however, this case is often impossible to achieve, and the distribution learned by the GAN is only partially overlapped onto the data-generating process. From a generic viewpoint, the discrepancy might have two different aspects:

- The two distributions differ in many regions; therefore, the GAN isn't able to output any correct examples.

- The two distributions have a strong overlap limited to a single region.

In the first case, the model is clearly underfitted and it's necessary to increase its capacity and tune up the learning algorithm in order to achieve better performance. In the second case, the GAN instead remained stuck in a high-probability region and discarded all the remaining ones. This particular phenomenon is called mode collapse, and it's a common problem that affects these models. Given a distribution $p(\bar{x})$, the mode is $\bar{x}_M$ corresponding to $\max p(\bar{x})$. For example, a normal distribution is monomodal and the mode is clearly $x = 0$. Conversely, a mixture of Gaussians is a multi-modal distribution where all local maxima are associated with different modes, as shown in the following figure:

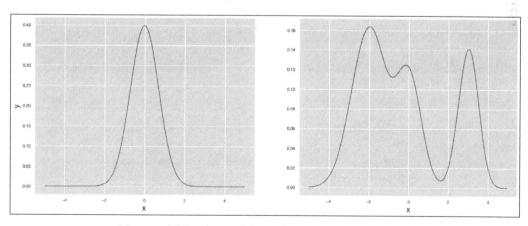

Mono-modal distribution (left). Multi-modal distribution (right)

From a statistical viewpoint, a mode is very likely to be a data point, therefore it's not surprising that a GAN learns to output it (and all its neighbors) with high probability. However, real-world data distributions are multi-modal, and it's also extremely difficult (or impossible) to know where the modes are located. Therefore, a GAN that learns to reproduce only a region of p_{data} collapses in small subspace and lose the ability to output other samples. Even if mode collapse has been discovered and studied, unfortunately, there are no explicit solutions. Models with a more flexible distance function (such as the one that we are going to study in the next section) can mitigate the problem and reduce its probability. However, the usage of GANs should always include a massive test phase to check whether any regions of the data-generating process are completely missing.

The test is not simple, but in some cases (for example, with images), it's possible to sample many values from the GAN, measure their frequencies, and compare them with the expected ones. For example, if we know that the Fashion-MNIST dataset has 10 different classes. After training the GAN and sampling 1,000 images, we should expect about 100 images for each class. If, for instance, all images are shoes or shoes are completely missing, it means that the GAN has collapsed. In the first case, the effect is dramatic and it's probably due to a bad shuffling, class imbalance, or very low capacity. Hence, the simplest solution is to check the dataset and, if it's perfectly balanced, to increase the capacity of the model. In the second case, the problem is tougher because a specific class is completely missing. If all other images are correctly reproduced, the problem may depend on the overspecialization of the units.

For example, a convolutional generator can become more and more specialized and output only shirts and other similar shapes. This is a sort of overfitting (even if the accuracy with respect to the training set is not saturated), and one potential mitigating strategy is based on the usage of dropout layers or other regularization techniques. In particular, dropout is able to limit the overspecialization even when the capacity is very large and should be employed as a first choice. Layer regularization is also a reasonable approach, but it increases the computational complexity and might yield only a sub-optimal result.

On the other hand, when the generator collapses around a mode, the information provided to the discriminator will become very limited and it will consequently lose the chance to be able to discriminate between noise and other valid classes. The usage of dropout (also in the discriminator) may help to leave some free capacity that can be used to limit the overfitting. In this way, the gradients are forced to vanish more slowly and the double feedback generator $\rightarrow$ discriminator (and vice-versa) can be active for a longer time. This is clearly not a general-purpose solution (the problem is extremely complex), but it's a strategy that should be kept in mind when working with GANs because, contrary to other models, they could fail in a way that is not easy to immediately verify.

Wasserstein GAN

As explained in the previous section, one of the most difficult problems with standard GANs is caused by the loss function based on the Jensen-Shannon divergence, whose value becomes constant when two distributions have disjointed supports. This situation is quite common with high-dimensional, semantically structured datasets. For example, images are constrained to having particular features in order to represent a specific subject (this is a consequence of the manifold assumption discussed in *Chapter 3, Introduction to Semi-Supervised Learning*). The initial generator distribution is very unlikely to overlap a true dataset, and in many cases, they are also very far from each other. This condition increases the risk of learning the wrong representation (a problem known as mode collapse), even when the discriminator is able to distinguish between true and generated samples (such a condition arises when the discriminator learns too quickly with respect to the generator). Moreover, the Nash equilibrium becomes harder to achieve, and the GAN can easily remain blocked in a sub-optimal configuration.

In order to mitigate this problem, Arjovsky, Chintala, and Bottou (in Arjovsky M., Chintala S., Bottou L., *Wasserstein GAN*, arXiv:1701.07875 [stat.ML]) proposed employing a different divergence, called the Wasserstein distance (or Earth Mover's distance), which is formally defined as follows:

$$D_W(p_{data}||p_g) = \inf_{\mu \in \Pi(p_{data}, p_g)} E_{(x,y) \sim \mu}[\|x - y\|]$$

The term $\Pi(p_{data}, p_g)$ represents the set of all possible joint probability distributions between p_{data} and p_g. Hence, the Wasserstein distance is the infimum (considering all joint distributions) of the set of expected values of $\|x - y\|$, where x and y are sampled from the joint distribution μ.

The Wasserstein distance can be directly employed also when the couple $\bar{x}, \bar{y} \in \mathbb{R}^p$ represent, for example, word embeddings obtained from algorithms like Word2Vec/ Doc2Vec (for further details, see Mikolov T., Sutskever I., Chen K., Corrado G. S., Dean J., *Distributed representations of words and phrases and their compositionality. Advances in Neural Information Processing Systems*, arXiv:1310.4546) or fastText (Bojanowski P., Grave E., Joulin A., Mikolov T., *Enriching Word Vectors with Subword Information*, arXiv:1607.04606 [cs.CL]). Using these algorithms, the words (or also *n-grams*) of a text are transformed into high-dimensional vectors, whose distance is proportional to the actual semantic distance of the words/sentences. Therefore, a GAN can be trained to generate sequences of words sampled from a semantically-acceptable distribution (for example, "An apple is a fruit" and "A car is a fruit" should be considered as drawn from different distributions even if their composition is very similar).

This topic is very interesting and quite complex at the same time. If, in fact, a slightly corrupted image can go undetected by the human eye (or simply be considered a normal image), a sentence with a semantic mistake is almost always immediately identified as flawed. Therefore, these models must be trained with very large corpora (even when using pretrained vectors, like fastText based on Wikipedia) in order to guarantee reliable results.

The main property of the Wasserstein distance is that even when two distributions have disjointed support, its value is proportional to the actual distributional distance. The formal proof is not very complex, but it's easier to understand the concept intuitively. In fact, given two distributions with disjointed support, the infimum operator forces taking the shortest distance between each possible couple of samples. Clearly, this measure is more robust than the Jensen-Shannon divergence, but there's a practical drawback: it's extremely difficult to compute. As we cannot work with all possible joint distributions (nor with an approximation), a further step is necessary to employ this loss function. In the aforementioned paper, the authors proved that it's possible to apply a transformation, thanks to the Kantorovich-Rubinstein theorem (the topic is quite complex, but the reader can find further information *in* Edwards D. A., *On the Kantorovich–Rubinstein Theorem*, Expositiones Mathematicae, 2011):

$$D_W(p_{data} \| p_g) = \frac{1}{L} \sup_{\|f\| \le L} E_{\bar{x} \sim p_{data}}[f(\bar{x})] - E_{\bar{x} \sim p_g}[f(\bar{x})]$$

The first element to consider is the nature of $f(\bar{x})$. The theorem requires considering only L-Lipschitz functions, which means that $f(\bar{x})$ (assuming a real-valued function of a single variable defined over a set D) must obey:

$$|f(x_1) - f(x_2)| \le L|x_1 - x_2| \ \forall \ x_1, x_2 \in D$$

At this point, the Wasserstein distance is proportional to the supremum (with respect to all L-Lipschitz functions) of the difference between two expected values, which are extremely easy to compute. In a WGAN, the $f(\bar{x})$ function is represented by a neural network; therefore, we have no warranties about the Lipschitz condition. To solve this problem, the author suggested a very simple procedure: clipping the discriminator (which is normally called the critic), and whose responsibility is to represent the parameterized function $f(\bar{x})$) variables after applying the corrections. If the input is bounded, all of the transformations will yield a bounded output; however, the clipping factor must be small enough (0.01, or even smaller) to avoid the additive effect of multiple operations leading to an inversion of the Lipschitz condition.

This is not an efficient solution (because it slows down the training process when it's not necessary), but it permits the exploitation of the Kantorovich-Rubinstein theorem even when there are no formal constraints imposed on the function family.

Using a parameterized function (such as a Deep Convolutional Network), the Wasserstein distance becomes as follows (omitting the term L, which is constant):

$$D_W(p_{data}||p_g) = \max_{\bar{\theta}_c \in \Theta_c} E_{\bar{x} \sim p_{data}}[f(\bar{x}; \bar{\theta}_c)] - E_{\bar{z} \sim p_{noise}}[f(g(\bar{z}; \bar{\theta}_g); \bar{\theta}_c)] = \max_{\bar{\theta}_c \in \Theta_c}(W_{data} - W_{noise})$$

In the previous expression, we explicitly extracted the generator output, and in the last step, separated the term that will be optimized separately. The reader has probably noticed that the computation is simpler than a standard GAN because in this case, we have to average over only the $f(\bar{x})$ values of a batch (there's no more need for a logarithm). However, as the Critic variables are clipped, the number of required iterations is normally larger, and in order to compensate the difference between the training speeds of the Critic and generator, it's often necessary to set $N_{critic} > 1$ (the authors suggest a value equal to 5, but this is a hyperparameter that must be tuned in every specific context).

The complete WGAN algorithm is:

1. Set the number of epochs, N_{epochs}.
2. Set the number of Critic iterations, N_{critic} (in most cases, $N_{critic} = 5$).
3. Set the batch size, k.
4. Set a clipping constant c (for example, $c = 0.01$).
5. Define a noise-generating process N (for example, $N = U(-1,1)$).
6. For $e = 1$ to N_{epochs}:

    a. Sample k values from X.

    b. Sample k values from N.

    c. For $i = 1$ to N_{critic}:

       i. Compute the gradients, $\nabla_c D_W(p_{data}||p_g)$ (only with respect to the Critic variables). The expected values are approximated by sample means.

       ii. Update the Critic parameters by stochastic gradient ascent.

       iii. Clip the Critic parameters in the range $(-c, c)$.

    d. Sample k values from N.

e. Compute the gradients, $\nabla_g W_{noise}$ (only with respect to the generator variables).

f. Update the generator parameters by stochastic gradient descent.

We can now implement a WGAN using TensorFlow. As we are going to see, the loss function is now much simpler, but it's important to clip the variables in order to guarantee the L-Lipschitz condition.

Example of WGAN with TensorFlow

This example can be considered a variant of the previous one because it uses the same dataset, generator, and discriminator structures. The only main difference is that in this case, the discriminator has been renamed `critic()` and the helper function is `run_critic()`. Moreover, to simplify the training process, we have also introduced another helper function that runs the whole model and computes the simplified loss functions, which are:

$$\begin{cases} L_{critic} = \dfrac{1}{batch\ size} \sum critic(\bar{x}_{generator}) - critic(\bar{x}_{noise}) \\ L_{generator} = -\dfrac{1}{batch\ size} \sum critic(\bar{x}_{generator}) \end{cases}$$

The snippet to run the model is:

```
def run_model(xi, zn, training=True):
    xg = run_generator(zn, training=training)
    zc1 = run_critic(xi, training=training)
    zc2 = run_critic(xg, training=training)


    loss_critic = tf.reduce_mean(zc2 - zc1)
    loss_generator = tf.reduce_mean(-zc2)


    return loss_critic, loss_generator
```

The two loss functions are simpler than a standard GAN as they work directly with the Critic outputs, computing the sample mean over a batch. In the original paper, the authors suggest using RMSProp as the standard optimizer in order to avoid the instabilities that a momentum-based algorithm can produce. However, Adam, with lower forgetting factors ($\beta_1 = 0.5$ and $\beta_2 = 0.9$) and a learning rate $\eta = 0.00005$, is faster than RMSProp, and doesn't lead to instabilities. I suggest testing both options, trying to maximize the training speed while preventing the mode collapse:

```
import tensorflow as tf

optimizer_generator = \
    tf.keras.optimizers.Adam(
        0.00005, beta_1=0.5, beta_2=0.9)
optimizer_critic = \
    tf.keras.optimizers.Adam(
        0.00005, beta_1=0.5, beta_2=0.9)


train_loss_generator = \
    tf.keras.metrics.Mean(name='train_loss')
train_loss_critic = \
    tf.keras.metrics.Mean(name='train_loss')
```

We can now define the training functions which, for simplicity, are now separated. The main reason is that we need to perform more critic iterations for each generator step. Moreover, the critic variables must be clipped in the range (-0.01, 0.01) (as suggested by the authors) to meet the requirements of the Kantorovich-Rubinstein theorem and, consequently, use the simplified loss function:

```
@tf.function
def train_critic(xi):
    zn = tf.random.uniform(
        (batch_size, code_length), -1.0, 1.0)

    with tf.GradientTape() as tape:
        loss_critic, _ = run_model(xi, zn,
                                   training=True)


    gradients_critic = tape.gradient(
        loss_critic,
        critic.trainable_variables)
    optimizer_critic.apply_gradients(
        zip(gradients_critic,
            critic.trainable_variables))


    for v in critic.trainable_variables:
        v.assign(tf.clip_by_value(v, -0.01, 0.01))


    train_loss_critic(loss_critic)
```

```
@tf.function
def train_generator():
    zn = tf.random.uniform(
        (batch_size, code_length), -1.0, 1.0)
    xg = tf.zeros((batch_size, width, height, 1))


    with tf.GradientTape() as tape:
        _, loss_generator = run_model(xg, zn,
                                      training=True)


    gradients_generator = tape.gradient(
        loss_generator,
        generator.trainable_variables)
    optimizer_generator.apply_gradients(
        zip(gradients_generator,
            generator.trainable_variables))


    train_loss_generator(loss_generator)
```

The structures of each function are straightforward and don't need detailed explanations. However, it's very important to notice that the critic variables are clipped after the gradients are applied. Carrying out this operation before the gradients are applied leads to an inconsistency because the gradients can push the values outside the predefined range and the critic can lose the property to be Lipschitz-continuous. Therefore, when running the generator training step, the loss function might not be accurate anymore.

The complete training procedure is shown in the following snippet:

```
nb_samples = 10240
nb_epochs = 100
nb_critic = 5
batch_size = 64
code_length = 256


x_train = tf.data.Dataset.from_tensor_slices(
        np.expand_dims(X_train, axis=3)).\
        shuffle(1000).batch(nb_critic * batch_size)


for e in range(nb_epochs):
    for xi in x_train:
            for i in range(nb_critic):
```

```
        train_critic(xi[i * batch_size:
                            (i + 1) * batch_size])


    train_generator()


print("Epoch {}: "
      "Critic Loss: {:.3f}, "
      "Generator Loss: {:.3f}".
      format(e + 1,
             train_loss_critic.result(),
             train_loss_generator.result()))


    train_loss_critic.reset_states()
    train_loss_generator.reset_states()
```

In this example, we have decided to employ a larger training set (10,240 images), batch size equal to 64, and 5 critic steps per iteration. I invite the reader to employ a larger training set (of course, the computational cost will grow proportionally) and to also test a different number of critic steps. The optimal choice in this case is based on the original paper. However, a simple way to find a suitable value is to monitor both losses during the training. If the generator converges much faster than the critic (that is, it stabilizes very quickly to a steady value), n_{critic} must be increased.

Ideally, both components should have the same training speed in order to guarantee a constant flow of information (depending on the magnitude of the gradients) from the critic to the generator and vice-versa. If the latter stops modifying the variables very early, the generator stops receiving information to improve the quality of reproduction of p_{data} and the GAN will likely reach a mode collapse. On the other hand, a very large n_{critic} value can force the model to hyperspecialize the critic before the generator has reached a satisfactory accuracy, leading to an underfitted GAN with very poor performance.

The result of the generation of 50 random samples is shown in the following screenshot:

Samples generated by a WGAN trained with the Fashion-MNIST dataset

As we can see, the quality is slightly higher than the DCGAN, and the samples are smoother and better defined. I invite the reader to also test this model with an RGB dataset because the final quality is normally excellent (with a proportionally longer training time).

 When working with these models, the training time can be very long. To avoid waiting to see the initial results (and to perform the required tuning), I suggest using Jupyter. In this way, it's possible to stop the learning process, check the generator ability, and restart it without any problem. Of course, the graph must remain the same, and the variable initialization (which, in TensorFlow 2, happens when defining the models) must be performed only at the beginning.

Summary

In this chapter, we discussed the main principles of adversarial training and explained the roles of two players: the generator and discriminator. We described how to model and train them using a minimax approach whose double goal is to force the generator to learn the true data distribution p_{data} and get the discriminator to distinguish perfectly between true samples (belonging to p_{data}) and unacceptable ones. In the same section, we analyzed the inner dynamics of a GAN and some common problems that can slow down the training process and lead to a sub-optimal final configuration.

One of the most difficult problems experienced with standard GANs arises when the data-generating process and the generator distribution have disjointed support. In this case, the Jensen-Shannon divergence becomes constant and doesn't provide precise information about the distance. An excellent alternative is provided by the Wasserstein measure, which is employed in a more efficient model, called WGAN. This method can efficiently manage disjointed distributions, but it's necessary to enforce the L-Lipschitz condition on the Critic. The standard approach is based on clipping the parameters after each gradient ascent update. This simple technique guarantees the L-Lipschitz condition, but it's necessary to use very small clipping factors, and this can lead to a slower conversion. For this reason, it's normally necessary to repeat the training of the Critic a fixed number of times (such as five) before each single generator training step.

In the next chapter, we are going to introduce another probabilistic generative neural model, based on a particular kind of neural network, called the Restricted Boltzmann Machine.

Further reading

- Goodfellow I. J., Pouget-Abadie J., Mirza M., Xu B., Warde-Farley D., Ozair S., Courville A., Bengio Y., *Generative Adversarial Networks*, arXiv:1406.2661 [stat.ML]

- Tadelis S., *Game Theory*, Princeton University Press, 2013

- Radford A., Metz L., Chintala S., *Unsupervised Representation Learning with Deep Convolutional Generative Adversarial Networks*, arXiv:1511.06434 [cs.LG]

- Salimans T., Goodfellow I., Zaremba W., Cheung V., Radford A., and Chen X., *Improved Techniques for Training GANs*, arXiv:1606.03498 [cs.LG]

- Arjovsky M., Chintala S., Bottou L., *Wasserstein GAN*, arXiv:1701.07875 [stat.ML]

- Edwards D. A., *On the Kantorovich-Rubinstein Theorem, Expositiones Mathematicae*, 2011

- Holdroyd T., *TensorFlow 2.0 Quick Start Guide*, Packt Publishing, 2019

- Goodfellow I., Bengio Y., Courville A., *Deep Learning*, The MIT Press, 2016

- Mikolov T., Sutskever I., Chen K., Corrado G. S., Dean J., *Distributed representations of words and phrases and their compositionality. Advances in Neural Information Processing Systems*, arXiv:1310.4546

- Bojanowski P., Grave E., Joulin A., Mikolov T., *Enriching Word Vectors with Subword Information*, arXiv:1607.04606 [cs.CL]

- Bonaccorso G., *Hands-On Unsupervised Learning with Python*, Packt Publishing, 2019

23
Deep Belief Networks

In this chapter, we're going to present two probabilistic generative models that employ a set of latent variables to represent a specific data generation process. **Restricted Boltzmann Machines** (**RBMs**), proposed in 1986, are the building blocks of a more complex model, called a **Deep Belief Network** (**DBN**), which is capable of capturing complex relationships among features at different levels (in a way not dissimilar to a deep convolutional network). Both models can be used in unsupervised and supervised scenarios as preprocessors or, as is usual with DBN, fine-tuning the parameters using a standard backpropagation algorithm.

In particular, we will discuss:

- **Markov random fields** (**MRF**)
- RBM, including the **Contrastive Divergence** (**CD-k**) algorithm
- DBN with supervised and unsupervised examples

We can now discuss the fundamental theoretical concept behind this model family: the Markov random fields, showing their properties and how they can be applied to solve many specific problems.

Introduction to Markov random fields

Let's consider a set of random variables, $X = \{\bar{x}_i\}$ (normally drawn from the same distribution family despite there being no restrictions about the distributions that demand this must be so), organized in an undirected graph, $G = \{V, E\}$, as shown in the following diagram:

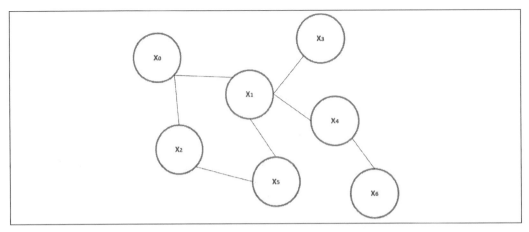

Example of a probabilistic undirected graph

Before analyzing the properties of the graph, we need to remember that two random variables, a and b, are conditionally independent given the random variable, c, if:

$$p(a, b|c) = p(a|c)p(b|c)$$

If all generic couples of subsets of variables $S_i, S_j \subseteq X$ are conditionally independent given a separating subset S_k (so that all connections between variables belonging to S_i to variables belonging to S_j pass through S_k), the graph is called a **Markov random field (MRF)**.

Given $G = \{V, E\}$, a subset containing vertices such that every couple is adjacent is called a clique (the set of all cliques is often denoted as $cl(G)$). For example, consider the graph shown earlier. The set $\{x_0, x_1\}$ is a clique. Moreover, if x_0 and x_5 are connected, $\{x_0, x_1, x_5\}$ would be a clique too, as in the following figure:

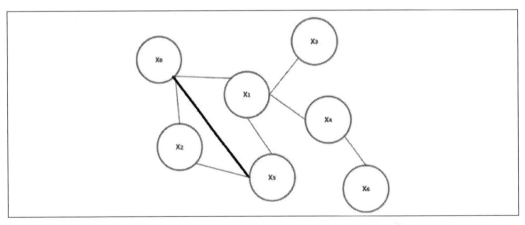

Example of a probabilistic undirected graph with connection between x_0 and x_5

A maximal clique is a clique that cannot be expanded by adding new vertices. A particular family of MRF is made up of all those graphs whose joint probability distribution can be factorized as:

$$p(\bar{x}) = \alpha \prod_{i \in cl(G)} \rho_i(\bar{x})$$

In this case, α is the normalizing constant and the product is extended to the set of all maximal cliques. According to the Hammersley-Clifford theorem, if the joint probability density function is strictly positive, the MRF can be factorized and all the $\rho_i(\bar{x})$ functions are strictly positive too. Hence $p(\bar{x})$, after some straightforward manipulations based on the properties of logarithms, can be rewritten as a Gibbs (or Boltzmann) distribution:

$$p(\bar{x}) = \alpha e^{\log \prod_{i \in cl(G)} \rho_i(\bar{x})} = \alpha e^{\sum_{i \in cl(G)} \log \rho_i(\bar{x})} = \frac{1}{Z} e^{-E(\bar{x})}$$

The term $E(\bar{x})$ is called energy, as it derives from the first application of such a distribution in statistical physics. The term $1/Z$ is now the normalizing constant employing the standard notation. In our scenarios, we always consider graphs containing observed $\{\bar{x}_i\}$ and latent variables $\{\bar{h}_j\}$. Therefore, it's useful to express the joint probability as:

$$p(\bar{x}, \bar{h}) = \frac{1}{Z} e^{-E(\bar{x}, \bar{h})}$$

Whenever it's necessary to marginalize to obtain $p(\bar{x})$, we can simply sum over the set $\{\bar{h}_j\}$:

$$p(\bar{x}) = \sum_j \frac{1}{Z} e^{-E(\bar{x}, \bar{h}_j)}$$

Unfortunately, $p(\bar{x}, \bar{h})$ is generally intractable and the marginalization can also be extremely complex (if not impossible). However, as we are going to see, it's generally possible to work the conditional distributions $p(\bar{x} | \bar{h})$ and $p(\bar{h} | \bar{x})$, which are easier to manage and allow us to model networks where the hidden units represent latent states that are never considered alone or in a joint probability distribution, but rather in conditional forms. The most common application of this approach is the Restricted Boltzmann Machine, which we are going to discuss in the next section.

Restricted Boltzmann Machines

A **Restricted Boltzmann Machine (RBM)**, originally called a Harmonium, is a neural model proposed by Smolensky (in Smolensky P., *Information processing in dynamical systems: Foundations of harmony theory*, Parallel Distributed Processing, Vol 1, The MIT Press, 1986) that is made up of a layer of input (observable) neurons and a layer of hidden (latent) neurons. A generic structure is shown in the following diagram:

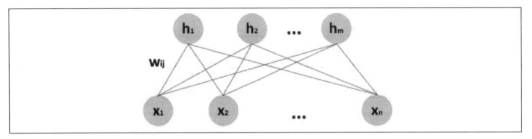

Structure of an RBM

As the undirected graph is bipartite (there are no connections between neurons belonging to the same layer), the underlying probabilistic structure is an MRF. In the original model (even if this is not a restriction), all the neurons are assumed to be Bernoulli-distributed ($x_i, h_j = \{0,1\}$), with a bias b_i (for the observed units) and c_j (for the latent neurons). The resulting energy function is:

$$E(\bar{x}, \bar{h}) = -\sum_i \sum_j w_{ij} \bar{x}_i \bar{h}_j - \sum_i \bar{b}_i \bar{x}_i - \sum_j \bar{c}_j \bar{h}_j$$

An RBM is a probabilistic generative model that can learn a data-generating process, p_{data}, which is represented by the observed units but exploits the presence of the latent variables in order to model all the internal relationships.

If we summarized all the parameters in a single vector, $\bar{\theta} = \{w_{ij}, \bar{b}_i, \bar{c}_j\}$, the Gibbs distribution becomes:

$$p(\bar{x}, \bar{h}; \bar{\theta}) = \frac{1}{Z} e^{-E(\bar{x}, \bar{h}; \bar{\theta})} = \frac{e^{-E(\bar{x}, \bar{h}; \bar{\theta})}}{\sum_i \sum_j e^{-E(\bar{x}_i, \bar{h}_j; \bar{\theta})}}$$

The training goal of an RBM is to maximize the log-likelihood with respect to an input distribution. Hence, the first step is determining $L(\bar{\theta}; \bar{x})$ after the marginalization of the previous expression:

$$L(\bar{\theta}; \bar{x}) = \log p(\bar{x}; \bar{\theta}) = \log \sum_{\bar{h}} \frac{1}{Z} e^{-E(\bar{x},\bar{h};\bar{\theta})} = \log \sum_{\bar{h}} e^{-E(\bar{x},\bar{h};\bar{\theta})} - \log \sum_{\bar{x}} \sum_{\bar{h}} \frac{1}{Z} e^{-E(\bar{x},\bar{h};\bar{\theta})}$$

As we need to maximize the log-likelihood, it's useful to compute the gradient with respect to $\bar{\theta}$:

$$\nabla_{\bar{\theta}} L(\bar{\theta}; \bar{x}) = \nabla_{\bar{\theta}} \log \sum_{\bar{h}} e^{-E(\bar{x},\bar{h};\bar{\theta})} - \nabla_{\bar{\theta}} \log \sum_{\bar{x}} \sum_{\bar{h}} \frac{1}{Z} e^{-E(\bar{x},\bar{h};\bar{\theta})}$$

Applying the chain rule of derivatives, we get:

$$\nabla_{\bar{\theta}} L(\bar{\theta}; \bar{x}) = -\sum_{\bar{h}} \frac{e^{-E(\bar{x},\bar{h};\bar{\theta})}}{\sum_{\bar{h}} e^{-E(\bar{x},\bar{h};\bar{\theta})}} \nabla_{\bar{\theta}} E(\bar{x}, \bar{h}; \bar{\theta}) + \sum_{\bar{x}} \sum_{\bar{h}} \frac{e^{-E(\bar{x},\bar{h};\bar{\theta})}}{\sum_{\bar{x}} \sum_{\bar{h}} e^{-E(\bar{x},\bar{h};\bar{\theta})}} \nabla_{\bar{\theta}} E(\bar{x}, \bar{h}; \bar{\theta})$$

Using the conditional and joint probability equalities, the previous expression becomes:

$$\nabla_{\bar{\theta}} L(\bar{\theta}; \bar{x}) = -\sum_{\bar{h}} p(\bar{h}|\bar{x}; \bar{\theta}) \nabla_{\bar{\theta}} E(\bar{x}, \bar{h}; \bar{\theta}) + \sum_{\bar{x}} \sum_{\bar{h}} p(\bar{x}, \bar{h}; \bar{\theta}) \nabla_{\bar{\theta}} E(\bar{x}, \bar{h}; \bar{\theta})$$

Considering the full joint probability, after some tedious manipulations (omitted for simplicity), it's possible to derive the following conditional expressions, where $\sigma(x)$ is the sigmoid function:

$$\begin{cases} p(\bar{h}_j = 1|\bar{x}) = \sigma\left(\sum_i w_{ij}\bar{x}_i + c_j\right) \\ p(\bar{x}_i = 1|\bar{h}) = \sigma\left(\sum_j w_{ij}\bar{h}_i + b_i\right) \end{cases}$$

At this point, we can compute the gradient of the log-likelihood with respect to each single parameter, w_{ij}, b_i, and c_j. Starting with w_{ij}, and considering that $\nabla_{w_{ij}} E(\bar{x}, \bar{h}; \bar{\theta}) = -\bar{x}_i\bar{h}_j$, we get:

$$\nabla_{w_{ij}} L(\bar{\theta}; \bar{x}) = \sum_{\bar{h}} p(\bar{h}|\bar{x}; \bar{\theta})\bar{x}_i\bar{h}_j - \sum_{\bar{x}} \sum_{\bar{h}} p(\bar{x}; \bar{h}; \bar{\theta})\bar{x}_i\bar{h}_j$$

If we transform the last full joint probability into a conditional one, the previous expression can be rewritten as:

$$\nabla_{w_{ij}} L(\bar{\theta}; \bar{x}) = \sum_{\bar{h}} p(\bar{h}|\bar{x}; \bar{\theta}) \bar{x}_i \bar{h}_j - \sum_{\bar{x}} p(\bar{x}; \bar{\theta}) \sum_{\bar{h}} p(\bar{h}|\bar{x}; \bar{\theta}) \bar{x}_i \bar{h}_j$$

Now, considering that all the units are Bernoulli-distributed, and isolating only the jth hidden unit, it's possible to apply the simplification:

$$\sum_{\bar{h}} p(\bar{h}|\bar{x}; \bar{\theta}) \bar{x}_i \bar{h}_j =$$

$$= \sum_{\bar{h}} \prod_i p(\bar{h}_i|\bar{x}; \bar{\theta}) \bar{x}_i \bar{h}_j == \sum_{\bar{h}_j} p(\bar{h}_j|\bar{x}; \bar{\theta}) \bar{x}_i \bar{h}_j \sum_{\bar{h}_{i \neq j}} p(\bar{h}_i|\bar{x}; \bar{\theta}) = \sum_{\bar{h}_j} p(\bar{h}_j|\bar{x}; \bar{\theta}) \bar{x}_i \bar{h}_j =$$

$$= p(\bar{h}_j = 1|\bar{x}) \bar{x}_i$$

Therefore, the gradient becomes:

$$\nabla_{w_{ij}} L(\bar{\theta}; \bar{x}) = p(\bar{h}_j = 1|\bar{x}) \bar{x}_i - \sum_{\bar{x}} p(\bar{x}; \bar{\theta}) p(\bar{h}_j = 1|\bar{x}) \bar{x}_i$$

Analogously, we can derive the gradient of $L(\bar{\theta}; \bar{x})$ with respect to b_i and c_j:

$$\begin{cases} \nabla_{b_i} L(\bar{\theta}; \bar{x}) = \bar{x}_i - \sum_{\bar{x}} p(\bar{x}; \bar{\theta}) \bar{x}_i \\ \nabla_{c_j} L(\bar{\theta}; \bar{x}) = p(\bar{h}_j = 1|\bar{x}) - \sum_{\bar{x}} p(\bar{x}; \bar{\theta}) p(\bar{h}_j = 1|\bar{x}) \end{cases}$$

Hence, the first term of every gradient is very easy to compute, while the second one requires summing over all observed values. As this operation is impracticable, the only feasible alternative is an approximation based on sampling, using a method such as Gibbs sampling (for further information, see *Chapter 11, Bayesian Networks and Hidden Markov Models*).

However, as this algorithm samples from the conditionals $p(\bar{x}|\bar{h})$ and $p(\bar{h}|\bar{x})$, rather than from the full joint distribution $p(\bar{x}, \bar{h})$, it requires the associated Markov chain to reach its stationary distribution, π, in order to provide valid samples. Since we don't know how many sampling steps are required to reach π, Gibbs sampling may also be an unfeasible solution due to its potentially high computational cost.

Contrastive Divergence

In order to solve this problem, Hinton proposed (in Hinton G., *A Practical Guide to Training Restricted Boltzmann Machines*, Dept. Computer Science, University of Toronto, 2010) an alternative algorithm called CD-k. The idea is very simple but extremely effective: instead of waiting for the Markov chain to reach the stationary distribution, we sample a fixed number of times starting from a training sample at $t = 0$, $\bar{x}^{(0)}$ and computing $\bar{h}^{(1)}$ by sampling from $p(\bar{h}^{(1)}|\bar{x}^{(0)})$. Then, the hidden vector is employed to sample the reconstruction, $\bar{x}^{(2)}$, from $p(\bar{x}^{(2)}|\bar{h}^{(1)})$. This procedure can be repeated any number of times, but in practice, a single sampling step is normally enough to ensure quite good accuracy. At this point, the gradient of the log-likelihood is approximated as (considering t steps):

$$\nabla_{\bar{\theta}} L(\bar{\theta}; \bar{x}) \approx -\sum_p p(\bar{h}^{(p)}|\bar{x}^{(0)}; \bar{\theta})\nabla_{\bar{\theta}} E(\bar{x}^{(0)}, \bar{h}^{(p)}; \bar{\theta}) + \sum_p p(\bar{h}^{(p)}|\bar{x}^{(t)}; \bar{\theta})\nabla_{\bar{\theta}} E(\bar{x}^{(t)}, \bar{h}^{(p)}; \bar{\theta})$$

The single gradients with respect to w_{ij}, b_i, and c_j can be easily obtained considering the preceding procedure. The term contrastive derives from the approximation of the gradient of $L(\bar{\theta}; \bar{x})$ computed at $\bar{x}^{(0)}$ with a weighted difference between a term called the positive gradient and another defined as the negative gradient. This approach is analogous to the approximation of a derivative with this incremental ratio:

$$\frac{\partial L}{\partial x} \approx \frac{1}{2h}L(x + h) - \frac{1}{2h}L(x - h) \; if \; h \to 0$$

The complete RBM training algorithm, based on a single-step CD-k is (assuming that there are M training data points):

1. Set the number N_h of hidden units.
2. Set the number of training epochs N_{epochs}.
3. Set a learning rate η (for example, $\eta = 0.01$).
4. For $e = 1$ to N_{epochs}:

    a. Set $\Delta w = 0$, $\Delta b = 0, \Delta c = 0$.

    b. For $i = 1$ to M:

        i. Sample $\bar{h}^{(i)}$ from $p(\bar{h}|\bar{x}^{(i)})$.

        ii. Sample a reconstruction $\bar{x}^{(i+1)}$ from $p(\bar{x}^{(i+1)}|\bar{h}^{(i)})$.

        iii. Accumulate the updates for weights and biases:

1. $\Delta w = \Delta w + p(\bar{h} = 1 | \bar{x}^{(i)}) \bar{x}^{(i)} - p(\bar{h} = 1 | \bar{x}^{(i+1)}) \bar{x}^{(i+1)}$ (as the outer product)

2. $\Delta b = \Delta b + \bar{x}^{(i)} - \bar{x}^{(i+1)}$

3. $\Delta c = \Delta c + \left[p(\bar{h} = 1 | \bar{x}^{(i)}) - p(\bar{h} = 1 | \bar{x}^{(i+1)}) \right]$

   c. Update weights and biases:

      i. $w = w + \eta \Delta w$

      ii. $b = b + \eta \Delta b$

      iii. $c = c + \eta \Delta c$

The outer product between two vectors is defined as:

$$\bar{a} \otimes \bar{b} = \bar{a} \cdot \bar{b}^T = \begin{pmatrix} a_1 \\ \vdots \\ a_n \end{pmatrix} \cdot (b_1 \quad \cdots \quad b_m) = \begin{pmatrix} a_1 b_1 & \cdots & a_1 b_m \\ \vdots & \ddots & \vdots \\ a_n b_1 & \cdots & a_n b_m \end{pmatrix}$$

If vector $\bar{a}$ has $(n, 1)$ shape and $\bar{b}$ has $(m, 1)$ shape, the result is a matrix with a (n, m) shape.

Deep Belief Networks

A belief or Bayesian network is a concept already explored in *Chapter 11, Bayesian Networks and Hidden Markov Models*. In this particular case, we are going to consider Belief networks where there are visible and latent variables, organized into homogeneous layers. The first layer always contains the input (visible) units, while all the remaining ones are latent. Hence, a DBN can be structured as a stack of RBMs, where each hidden layer is also the visible one of the subsequent RBM, as shown in the following diagram (the number of units can be different for each layer):

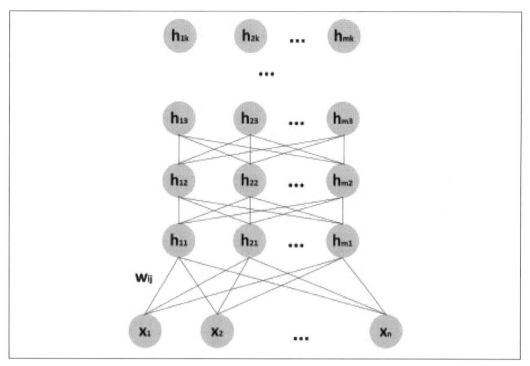

Structure of a generic DBN

The learning procedure is usually greedy and stepwise (as proposed in Hinton G. E., Osindero S., Teh Y. W., *A fast learning algorithm for deep belief nets*, Neural Computation, 18/7, 2006). The first RBM is trained with the dataset and optimized to reconstruct the original distribution using the CD-k algorithm. At this point, the internal (hidden) representations are employed as input for the next RBM, and so on until all the blocks are fully trained. In this way, the DBN is forced to create subsequent internal representations of the dataset that can be used for different purposes. Of course, when the model is trained, it's possible to infer from the recognition (inverse) model sampling from the hidden layers and compute the activation probability as ($\bar{x}$ represents a generic cause):

$$p(\bar{x}_i = 1|\bar{h}) = \sigma\left(\sum_j w_{ij}\bar{h}_j + b_i\right)$$

As a DBN is always a generative process, in an unsupervised scenario it can perform a component analysis/dimensionality reduction, with an approach that is based on the idea of creating a chain of sub-processes that are able to rebuild an internal representation. While a single RBM focuses on a single hidden layer and hence cannot learn sub-features, a DBN greedily learns how to represent each sub-feature vector using a refined hidden distribution.

The concept behind this process isn't all that different from a cascade of convolutional layers, with the main difference being that in this case, the learning procedure is greedy. Another distinction with methods such as PCA is that we don't know exactly how the internal representation is built. As the latent variables are optimized by maximizing the log-likelihood, there are possibly many optimal points, but we cannot easily impose constraints on them.

However, DBNs show very powerful properties in different scenarios, even if their computational cost is normally considerably higher than other methods. One of the main problems (common to the majority of deep learning methods) concerns the right choice of hidden units in every layer. As they represent latent variables, their number is a crucial factor for the success of a training procedure. The right choice is not immediate because it's necessary to know the complexity of the data-generating process. However, as a rule of thumb, I suggest starting with a couple of layers containing 32/64 units and proceeding to increase the number of hidden neurons and the layers until the desired accuracy is reached (in the same way, I suggest starting with a small learning rate, such as $\eta = 0.01$, increasing it if necessary).

As the first RBM is responsible for reconstructing the original dataset, it's very useful to monitor the log-likelihood (or the error) after each epoch in order to understand whether the process is learning correctly (decreasing error) or it's saturating the capacity. It's clear that an initial bad reconstruction leads to subsequently worse representations. As the learning process is greedy, in an unsupervised task there's no way to improve the performance of lower layers when the previous training steps are finished. Therefore, I always suggest tuning up the parameters so that the first reconstruction is very accurate. Of course, all the considerations about overfitting are still valid, so, it's also important to monitor the generalization ability with validation samples. However, in a component analysis, we assume we're working with a distribution that is representative of the underlying data-generating process, so the risk of finding previously seen features should be minimal.

In a supervised scenario, there are generally two options whose first step is always a greedy training of the DBN. However, the first approach performs a subsequent refinement using a standard algorithm, such as backpropagation (considering the whole architecture as a single deep network), while the second one uses the last internal representation as the input of a separate classifier.

It goes without saying that the first method has many more degrees of freedom because it works with a pre-trained network whose weights can be adjusted until the validation accuracy reaches its maximum value. In this case, the first greedy step works with the same assumption that has been empirically confirmed by observing the internal behavior of deep models (similar to convolutional networks). The first layers learn how to detect low-level features, while all the subsequent ones increase the details. Therefore, the backpropagation step presumably starts from a point that is already quite close to the optimum and can converge more quickly.

Conversely, the second approach is analogous to applying the kernel trick to a standard **Support Vector Machine** (**SVM**). In fact, the external classifier is generally a very simple one (such as a logistic regression or an SVM) and the increased accuracy is normally due to an improved linear separability obtained by projecting the original samples onto a sub-space (often higher-dimensional) where they can be easily classified. In general, this method yields worse performance than the first one because there's no way to tune up the parameters once the DBN is trained. Therefore, when the final projections are not suitable for a linear classification, it's necessary to employ more complex models and the resulting computational cost can be very high without a proportional performance gain. As deep learning is generally based on the concept of end-to-end learning, training the whole network can be useful to implicitly include the pre-processing steps in the complete structure, which becomes a black box that associates input samples with specific outcomes. On the other hand, whenever an explicit pipeline is requested, greedy training the DBN and employing a separate classifier could be a more suitable solution.

Example of an unsupervised DBN in Python

In this example, we are going to use a Python library freely available on GitHub (`https://github.com/albertbup/deep-belief-network`) that allows working with supervised and unsupervised DBN using NumPy (CPU-only) or TensorFlow (CPU or GPU support for versions before 2.0) with the standard scikit-learn interface. The package can be installed using the `pip install git+git://github.com/albertbup/deep-belief-network.git` command. However, as we are focusing our attention on TensorFlow 2.0, we are going to employ the NumPy interface.

Our goal is to create a lower-dimensional representation of a subset of the MNIST dataset (as the training process can be quite slow, we'll limit it to 400 samples), which is made up of data points $\bar{x}_i \in \mathbb{R}^{784}$. The first step is loading (using the TensorFlow/Keras helper function), shuffling, and normalizing the dataset:

```
import numpy as np
import tensorflow as tf

from sklearn.utils import shuffle
```

```
(X_train, Y_train), (_, _) = \
        tf.keras.datasets.mnist.load_data()
X_train, Y_train = shuffle(X_train, Y_train,
                                  random_state=1000)

width = X_train.shape[1]
height = X_train.shape[2]

nb_samples = 400

X = X_train[0:nb_samples].reshape(
        (nb_samples, width * height)).\
            astype(np.float32) / 255.0
Y = Y_train[0:nb_samples]
```

At this point, we can create an instance of the UnsupervisedDBN class, setting three hidden layers with 512, 256, and 64 sigmoid units respectively (as we want to bind the values between 0 and 1), while we don't need to specify the input dimensionality as it is automatically detected from the dataset. It's easy to understand that the final goal of the model is to perform a sequential dimensionality reduction. The first RBM reduces the dimension from 784 to 512 (about 65%), and the second halves it as there 256 latent variables in the layer. Once this second representation has been optimized, the third RBM divides the dimension by 4, obtaining an output $\bar{y}_i \in \mathbb{R}^{64}$. It's important to notice that, contrary to PCA, in this case, the interdependencies between single variables (which, in this case, are pixels) are fully captured by the model.

The learning rate η (learning_rate_rbm), is set equal to 0.05, the batch size (batch_size) to 64, and the number of epochs for each RBM (n_epochs_rbm) to 100. The default value for the number of CD-k steps is 1, but it's possible to change it using the contrastive_divergence_iter parameter. All these values can be freely changed to improve the performance (for example, to get a smaller loss) or to speed up the training process. Our choice is based on a trade-off between accuracy and speed:

```
from dbn import UnsupervisedDBN

unsupervised_dbn = UnsupervisedDBN(
        hidden_layers_structure=[512, 256, 64],
        learning_rate_rbm=0.05,
        n_epochs_rbm=100,
        batch_size=64,
        activation_function='sigmoid')

X_dbn = unsupervised_dbn.fit_transform(X)
```

The output of this snippet is:

```
[START] Pre-training step:
>> Epoch 1 finished        RBM Reconstruction error 48.407841
>> Epoch 2 finished        RBM Reconstruction error 46.730827

...

>> Epoch 99 finished       RBM Reconstruction error 6.486495
>> Epoch 100 finished      RBM Reconstruction error 6.439276
[END] Pre-training step
```

As explained, the training process is sequential and split into pre-training and fine-tuning phases. Of course, the complexity is proportional to the number of layers and hidden units. Once this step is complete, the X_dbn array contains the values sampled from the last hidden layer. Unfortunately, this library doesn't implement an inverse transformation method, but we can use the t-SNE algorithm to project the distribution onto a bidimensional space:

```
from sklearn.manifold import TSNE

tsne = TSNE(n_components=2,
            perplexity=10,
            random_state=1000)
X_tsne = tsne.fit_transform(X_dbn)
```

The corresponding plot is shown in the following figure:

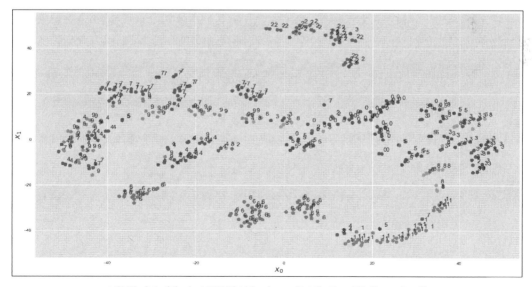

t-SNE plot of the last DBN hidden layer distribution (64-dimensional)

As you can see, even if there are still a few anomalies, the hidden low-dimensional representation is globally coherent with the original dataset. Each group containing the same digits is organized in compact clusters that preserve many geometrical properties of the original manifold where the dataset lies. For example, the group containing the digits representing a 9 is very close to the one containing the images of 7s. The groups of 3s and 8s are also very close to one another.

This result confirms that a DBN can be successfully employed as a pre-processing layer for classification purposes, but in this case, rather than reducing the dimensionality, it's often preferable to increase it in order to exploit the redundancy so we can use a simpler linear classifier (to better understand this concept, think about augmenting a dataset with polynomial features). I invite the reader to test this ability by pre-processing the whole MNIST dataset and then classifying it using logistic regression, comparing the results with a direct approach.

Example of a supervised DBN in Python

In this example, we are going to employ the Wine dataset (provided by scikit-learn), which contains data points $\bar{x}_i \in \mathbb{R}^{13}$ representing the chemical properties of three different wine classes. This dataset is not extremely complex, and it can be successfully classified with simpler methods; however, the example has only a didactic purpose and can be useful for understanding how to work with this kind of data.

The first step is to load the dataset and standardize the values by removing the mean and dividing by the standard deviation (this is very important when using, for example, ReLU units, which are equivalent to linear ones when the input is positive):

```
from sklearn.datasets import load_wine
from sklearn.preprocessing import StandardScaler

wine = load_wine()

ss = StandardScaler()
X = ss.fit_transform(wine['data'])
Y = wine['target']
```

At this point, we can create train and test sets:

```
from sklearn.model_selection import train_test_split

X_train, X_test, Y_train, Y_test = \
        train_test_split(X, Y,
                              test_size=0.25,
                              random_state=1000)
```

The model is based on an instance of the SupervisedDBNClassification class, which implements the backpropagation method. The parameters are very similar to the unsupervised case, but now we can also specify the stochastic gradient descent (SGD) learning rate (`learning_rate`), the number of backpropagation epochs (`n_iter_backprop`), and an optional dropout (`dropout_p`). The algorithm performs an initial greedy training (whose computational cost is normally higher than the SGD phase), followed by fine-tuning. Considering the structure of the training set, we have chosen to have two hidden ReLU layers containing 16 and 8 units and to apply a dropout of 0.1 to prevent overfitting.

Considering the general behavior of these models, the two RBMs will try to find an internal representation of p_{data} in order to obtain the most accurate classification. In our case, the first RBM expands the dimensionality to 16 units, therefore, the hidden layer should encode some interdependency features more explicitly. The second RBM, instead, reduces the dimensionality to 8 units and it's mainly responsible to discover the manifold where the dataset lies. The choice of the structure of the network is similar to any other procedure employed in deep learning and should follow the Occam's Razor principle. Therefore, I suggest starting with very simple models and proceed by adding new layers or expanding the existing ones. Of course, the usage of dropout is highly recommended whenever the risk of overfitting is large (for example, when the dataset is very small and it's impossible to retrieve new data points):

```
from dbn import SupervisedDBNClassification

classifier = SupervisedDBNClassification(
        hidden_layers_structure=[16, 8],
        learning_rate_rbm=0.001,
        learning_rate=0.01,
        n_epochs_rbm=20,
        n_iter_backprop=100,
        batch_size=16,
        activation_function='relu',
        dropout_p=0.1)

classifier.fit(X_train, Y_train)
```

The output of the previous snippet shows the pre-training and fine-tuning losses for each epoch:

```
[START] Pre-training step:
>> Epoch 1 finished        RBM Reconstruction error 12.488863
>> Epoch 2 finished        RBM Reconstruction error 12.480352
...
>> Epoch 99 finished       ANN training loss 1.440317
```

```
>> Epoch 100 finished        ANN training loss 1.328146
[END] Fine tuning step
```

At this point, we can evaluate our model using a scikit-learn classification report:

```
from sklearn.metrics.classification import \
    classification_report

Y_pred = classifier.predict(X_test)
print(classification_report(Y_test, Y_pred))
```

The output is:

	precision	recall	f1-score	support
0	0.92	1.00	0.96	11
1	1.00	0.90	0.95	21
2	0.93	1.00	0.96	13
accuracy			0.96	45
macro avg	0.95	0.97	0.96	45
weighted avg	0.96	0.96	0.96	45

The validation accuracy (in terms of both precision and recall) is very large (close to 0.96), but this is really a simple dataset that needs only a few minutes of training. I invite the reader to test the performance of a DBN in the classification of the MNIST/ Fashion MNIST dataset, comparing the results with the one obtained using a deep convolutional network. In this case, it's important to monitor the reconstruction error of each RBM, trying to minimize it before running the backpropagation phase. At the end of this exercise, you should be able to answer this question: which is preferable, an end-to-end or a pre-processing-based approach?

Summary

In this chapter, we presented the MRF as the underlying structure of an RBM. An MRF is represented as an undirected graph whose vertices are random variables. In particular, for our purposes, we considered MRFs whose joint probability can be expressed as a product of the positive functions of each random variable. The most common distribution, based on an exponential, is called the Gibbs (or Boltzmann) distribution and it is particularly suitable for our problems because the logarithm cancels the exponential, yielding simpler expressions.

An RBM is a simple bipartite, undirected graph made up of visible and latent variables, with connections only between different groups.

The goal of this model is to learn a probability distribution, thanks to the presence of hidden units that can model the unknown relationships. Unfortunately, the log-likelihood, although very simple, cannot be easily optimized because the normalization term requires summing over all the input values. For this reason, Hinton proposed an alternative algorithm, called CD-k, which outputs an approximation of the gradient of the log-likelihood based on a fixed number (normally 1) of Gibbs sampling steps.

Stacking multiple RBMs allows us to model DBNs, where the hidden layer of each block is also the visible layer of the following one. DBNs can be trained using a greedy approach, maximizing the log-likelihood of each RBM in sequence. In an unsupervised scenario, a DBN is able to extract the features of a data-generating process in a hierarchical way, and therefore the application includes component analysis and dimensionality reduction. In a supervised scenario, a DBN can be greedily pre-trained and fine-tuned using the backpropagation algorithm (considering the whole network) or sometimes using a pre-processing step in a pipeline where the classifier is generally a very simple model (such as logistic regression).

In the next chapter, which is available online, we're going to introduce the concept of reinforcement learning, discussing the most important elements of systems that can autonomously learn to play a game or allow a robot to walk, jump, and perform tasks that are extremely difficult to model and control using classic methods.

Further reading

- Smolensky P., *Information processing in dynamical systems: Foundations of harmony theory*, Parallel Distributed Processing, Vol 1, The MIT Press, 1986

- Hinton G., *A Practical Guide to Training Restricted Boltzmann Machines*, Dept. Computer Science, University of Toronto, 2010

- Hinton G. E., Osindero S., Teh Y. W., *A fast learning algorithm for deep belief nets*, Neural Computation, 18/7, 2006

- Goodfellow I., Bengio Y., Courville A., *Deep Learning*, The MIT Press, 2016

- Bonaccorso G., *Hands-On Unsupervised Learning with Python*, Packt Publishing, 2019

24
Introduction to Reinforcement Learning

In this chapter, we're going to introduce the fundamental concepts of **Reinforcement Learning (RL)**, which is a set of approaches that allows an agent to learn how to behave in an unknown environment thanks to rewards that are provided after each possible action. RL has been studied for decades, but it has matured into a powerful approach in the last few years, with advances making it possible to employ deep learning models together with standard (and often simple) algorithms in order to solve extremely complex problems (such as learning how to play an Atari game perfectly).

In particular, we will discuss:

- The concept of the **Markov Decision Process (MDP)**
- The concepts of environment, agent, policy, and reward
- The policy iteration algorithm
- The value iteration algorithm
- The TD(0) algorithm

We can now introduce the main concepts that characterize a reinforcement learning scenario, focusing on the features of each element and how they interact to reach a global objective.

Fundamental concepts of RL

Imagine that you want to learn to ride a bike, and ask a friend for advice. They explain how the gears work, how to release the brake and a few other technical details. In the end, you ask the secret to keeping your balance.

What kind of answer do you expect? In an imaginary supervised world, you should be able to perfectly quantify your actions and correct errors by comparing the outcomes with precise reference values. In the real world, you have no idea about the quantities underlying your actions and, above all, you will never know what the right value is.

Increasing the level of abstraction, the scenario we're considering can be described as: a generic agent performs actions inside an environment and receives feedback that is somehow proportional to the competence of its actions. According to this **Feedback**, the **Agent** can correct its actions in order to reach a specific goal. This basic schema is represented in the following diagram:

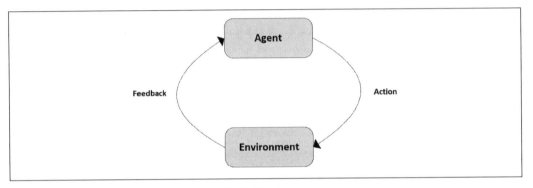

Basic RL schema

Returning to our initial example, when you ride a bike for the first time and try to keep your balance, you will notice that the wrong movement causes an increase in the slope, which in turn increases the horizontal component of the gravitational force, pushing the bike laterally. As the vertical component is compensated, the result is a rotation that ends when the bike falls to the ground completely. However, as you can use your legs to control your balance, when the bike starts falling, thanks to Newton's third law, the force on your leg increases and your brain understands that it's necessary to make a movement in the opposite direction.

Even though this problem can be easily expressed in terms of physical laws, nobody learns to ride a bike by computing forces and momentums. This is one of the main concepts of RL: an agent must always make its choices considering a piece of information, usually defined as a reward that represents the response provided by the environment. If the action is correct, the reward will be positive, otherwise, it will be negative. After receiving a reward, an agent can fine-tune the strategy, called the policy, in order to maximize the expected future reward.

For example, after a few rides, you will be able to slightly move your body so as to keep your balance while turning, but in the beginning, you'll probably need to extend your leg to avoid falling down.

Hence, your initial policy suggested an incorrect action, which received repeated negative rewards; so your brain corrected it by increasing the probability of choosing another action. The implicit hypothesis that underlies this approach is that an agent is always rational, meaning that its goal is to maximize the expected return of its actions (nobody decide to fall off their bike just to find out how it feels).

Before discussing the single components of an RL system, it's necessary to add a couple of fundamental assumptions. The first one is that an agent can repeat experiences an infinite number of times. In other words, we assume that it's possible to learn a valid policy (possibly the optimal one) only if we have enough time. Clearly, this is unacceptable in the animal world, and we all know that many experiences are extremely dangerous; however, this assumption is necessary to prove the convergence of some algorithms. Indeed, sub-optimal policies can sometimes be learned very quickly, but it's necessary to iterate many times to reach the optimal one.

In real artificial systems, we always stop the learning process after a finite number of iterations, but it's almost impossible to find valid solutions if some experiences prevent the agent from continuing to interact with the environment. As many tasks have final states (either positive or negative), we assume that the agent can play any number of episodes (somewhat analogous to the epochs of supervised learning), exploiting the experience previously learned.

The second assumption is a little bit more technical and it's usually known as the Markov property.

The Markov Decision Process

When the agent interacts with the environment, it observes a sequence of states. Even though it might seem like an oxymoron, we assume that each state is stateful. We can explain this concept with a simple example; suppose that you're filling a tank and every 5 seconds you measure the level. Imagine that at $t = 0$, the level $L = 10$ and the water is flowing in. What do you expect at $t = 1$? Obviously, $L > 10$. In other words, without external unknown causes, we assume that a state contains the previous history, so that the sequence, even if discretized, represents a continuous evolution where no jumps are allowed.

When an RL task satisfies this property, it's called a **Markov Decision Process (MDP)** and it's very easy to employ simple algorithms to evaluate the actions. Luckily, the majority of natural events can be modeled as MDPs (when you're walking toward a door, every step in the right direction must decrease the distance), but there are some games that are implicitly stateless.

For example, if you want to employ an RL algorithm to learn how to guess the outcome of a probabilistic sequence of independent events (such as tossing a coin), the result could be dramatically wrong. The reason is clear: any state is independent of the previous ones and every attempt to build up a history is a failure. Therefore, if you observe a sequence of 0, 0, 0, 0... you are not justified in increasing the value of betting on 0 unless, after considering the likelihood of the events, you suppose that the coin is loaded.

However, if there's no reason to do so, the process isn't an MDP and every episode (event) is completely independent. All the assumptions that we, either implicitly or explicitly, make are based on this fundamental concept, so pay attention when evaluating new, unusual scenarios because you may discover that the employment of a specific algorithm isn't theoretically justified.

Environment

The environment is the entity within which the agent has to reach its goals. For our purposes, a generic environment is a system that receives an input action, a_t (we use the index t because this is a natural time process), and outputs a tuple composed of a state, s_{t+1}, and a reward, r_{t+1}. These two elements are the only pieces of information provided to the agent to make its next decision. If we are working with an MDP and the sets of possible actions, A, and states, S, are discrete and finite, the problem is a defined finite MDP (in many continuous cases, it's possible to treat the problem as a finite MDP by discretizing the spaces). If there are final states, the task is called episodic and, in general, the goal is to reach a positive final state in the shortest amount of time or maximize a score. The schema of the cyclic interaction between an agent and an environment is shown in the following diagram:

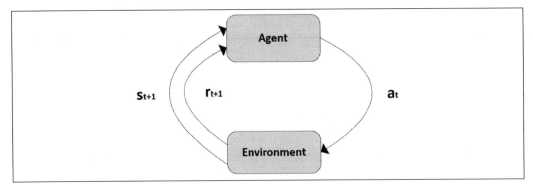

Agent-environment interaction schema

A very important feature of an environment is its internal nature. It can be either deterministic or stochastic. A deterministic environment is characterized by a function that associates each possible action in a specific state s_t to a well-defined successor s_{t+1}, with a precise reward r_{t+1}:

$$(s_{t+1}, r_{t+1}) = f(s_t, a_t) \; where \; a_t \in A \; and \; s_t, s_{t+1} \in S$$

Conversely, a stochastic environment is characterized by a transition probability between the current state s_t and a set of possible successors s_{t+1}^i given an action a_t:

$$T(s_t, s_{t+1}^i, a_t) = (p(s_t, s_{t+1}^1, a_t), \dots, p(s_t, s_{t+1}^i, a_t), \dots)$$

If a state s_i has a transitional probability $T(s_t, s_{t+1}^i, a_t) = 1 \; \forall \; a_t \in A$, the state is defined as absorbing. In general, all ending states in episodic tasks are modeled as absorbing ones, to avoid any further transition. When an episode is not limited to a fixed number of steps, the only criterion to determine its end is to check whether the agent has reached an absorbing state. As we don't know which state will be the successor, it's necessary to consider the expected value of all possible rewards considering the initial state s_t and the action a_t:

$$E[r_{t+1}^i; s_t, a_t]$$

In general, it's easier to manage stochastic environments because they can be immediately converted into deterministic ones by setting all probabilities to zero except the one corresponding to the actual successor (for example, $T(s_t, s_{t+1}^i, a_t) = (0,0,\dots,0,1,0,\dots,0))$. In the same way, the expected return can be set equal to r_{t+1}. Knowledge of $T(s_t, s_{t+1}^i, a_t)$, as well as $E[r_{t+1}^i]$, is necessary to employ some specific algorithms, but it can become problematic when finding a suitable model for the environment requires extremely complex analysis. In all those cases, model-free methods can be employed and, therefore, the environment is considered as a black box, whose output at time t (subsequent to an action performed by the agent a_{t-1}), is the only available piece of information for the evaluation of a policy.

Rewards

We have seen that rewards (sometimes negative rewards are called penalties, but it's preferable to use a standardized notation) are the only feedback provided by the environment after each action. However, there are two different approaches to the use of rewards. The first one is the strategy of a very short-sighted agent and consists of taking into account only the reward just received.

The main problem with this approach is clearly the inability to consider longer sequences that can lead to a very high reward. For example, an agent has to traverse a few states with a negative reward (for example, -0.1), but after them, they arrive at a state with a very positive reward (for example, +5.0). A *short-sighted* agent couldn't find out the best policy because it would simply try to avoid the immediate negative rewards. On the other hand, it's better to suppose that a single reward contains a part of the future rewards that will be obtained following the same policy. This concept can be expressed by introducing a discounted reward, which is defined as:

$$R_t = \sum_{i=0}^{\infty} \gamma^i r_{i+t+1} = r_{t+1} + \gamma r_{t+1} + \cdots + \gamma^k r_{k+t+1} + \cdots$$

In the previous expression, we are assuming an infinite horizon with a discount factor γ, which is a real number bounded between 0 and 1 (not included). When $\gamma = 0$, the agent is extremely short-sighted, because of $R_t = r_{t+1}$, but when $\gamma \to 1$, the current reward takes into account the future contributions discounted in a way that is inversely proportional to the time-step. In this way, very close rewards will have a higher weight than very distant ones. If the absolute value of all rewards is limited by a maximum immediate absolute reward $|r_i| \le |r_{max}|$, the previous expression will always be bounded. In fact, considering the properties of a geometric series, we get:

$$|R_t| = \left| \sum_{i=0}^{\infty} \gamma^i r_{i+t+1} \right| \le \sum_{i=0}^{\infty} \gamma^i |r_{i+t+1}| \le |r_{max}| \sum_{i=0}^{\infty} \gamma^i = \frac{|r_{max}|}{1 - \gamma}$$

Clearly, the right choice of γ is a crucial factor in many problems and cannot be easily generalized. As in many other similar cases, I suggest testing different values, picking the one that minimizes the convergence speed while yielding a quasi-optimal policy. Of course, if the tasks are episodic with length $T(e_i)$, the discounted reward becomes:

$$R_t = \sum_{i=0}^{T(e_i)-t-1} \gamma^i r_{i+t+1} = r_{t+1} + \gamma r_{t+1} + \cdots + \gamma^{T(e_i)} r_{T(e_i)+t+1}$$

A checkerboard environment in Python

We are going to consider an example based on a checkerboard environment representing a tunnel. The goal of the agent is to reach the ending state (the lower-right corner), avoiding 10 wells that are negative absorbing states. The rewards are:

- **Ending state**: +5.0
- **Wells**: -5.0
- **All other states**: -0.1

Selecting a small negative reward for all non-terminal states is helpful to force the agent to move forward until the maximum (final) reward has been achieved. Let's start modeling an environment that has a 5 × 15 matrix:

```python
import numpy as np

width = 15
height = 5

y_final = width - 1
x_final = height - 1

y_wells = [0, 1, 3, 5, 5, 7, 9, 11, 12, 14]
x_wells = [3, 1, 2, 0, 4, 1, 3, 2, 4, 1]

standard_reward = -0.1
tunnel_rewards = np.ones(shape=(height, width)) * \
                    standard_reward

for x_well, y_well in zip(x_wells, y_wells):
    tunnel_rewards[x_well, y_well] = -5.0

tunnel_rewards[x_final, y_final] = 5.0
```

The graphical representation of the environment (in terms of rewards) is shown in the following chart:

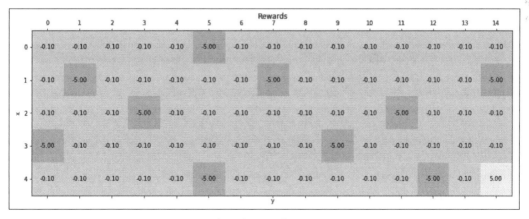

Rewards in the tunnel environment

The agent can move in four directions: up, down, left, and right. Clearly, in this case, the environment is deterministic because every action moves the agent to a predefined cell. We assume that whenever an action is forbidden (such as trying to move to the left when the agent is in the first column), the successor state is the same one (with the corresponding reward).

Policy

Formally, a policy is a deterministic or stochastic law that the agent follows in order to maximize its return. Conventionally, all policies are denoted by the letter π. A deterministic policy is usually a function of the current state that outputs a precise action:

$$a_{t+1} = \pi(s_t)$$

A stochastic policy, analogously to environments, outputs the probability of each action (in this case, we are assuming we work with a finite MPD):

$$\pi(s_t) = \left(p\left(a_{t+1} = a^{(1)}\right), \dots, p\left(a_{t+1} = a^{(n)}\right), \dots\right)$$

However, contrary to the environment, an agent must always pick a specific action, transforming any stochastic policy into a deterministic sequence of choices. In general, a policy where $\pi(s_t, a) > 0 \; \forall \, a \in A$ is called soft and it's often very useful during the training process because it allows more flexible modeling without the premature selection of a suboptimal action. Instead, when $\pi(s_t, a_i) = 0 \; \forall \, i \neq j$ and $\pi\left(s_t, a_j\right) = 1$, the policy is also defined as hard. This transformation can be performed in many ways, but the most common one is to define a policy that is greedy with respect to a value (we're going to discuss this concept in the next section). This means that, at every step, the policy will select the action that maximizes the value of the successor state. Obviously, this is a very rational approach, which could be too pragmatic. In fact, when the values of some states don't change, a greedy policy will always force the agent to perform the same actions.

Such a problem is known as the exploration-exploitation dilemma and arises when it would be better to allow the agent to evaluate alternative strategies that could initially appear to be suboptimal. In other words, we want the agent to explore the environment before starting to exploit the policy, to know whether the policy is really the best one or whether there are hidden alternatives. To solve this problem, it's possible to employ an ϵ-greedy policy, where the value ϵ is called the exploration factor and represents a probability.

In this case, the policy will pick a random action with probability ϵ and a greedy one with probability $1 - \epsilon$. In general, at the beginning of the training process, ϵ is kept very close to 1.0 to incentivize the exploration and it's progressively decreased when the policy becomes more stable. In many **Deep RL (DRL)** applications, this approach is fundamental, in particular when there are no models of the environment. The reason is that greedy policies can be initially wrong and it's necessary to allow the agent to explore many possible state and action sequences before forcing a deterministic decision.

Policy iteration

In this section, we are going to analyze a strategy to find an optimal policy based on complete knowledge of the environment (in terms of transition probability and expected returns). The first step is to define a method that can be employed to build a greedy policy. Let's suppose we're working with a finite MDP and a generic policy π; we can define the intrinsic value of a state s_t as the expected discounted return obtained by the agent starting from s_t and following the stochastic policy π:

$$V(s_t; \pi) = E_\pi[R_t; s_t] = E_\pi\left[\sum_{i=0}^{\infty} \gamma^i r_{i+t+1}; s_t\right]$$

In this case, we are assuming that, as the agent will follow π, the state s_a is more useful than s_b if the expected return starting from s_a is greater than the one obtained starting from s_b. Unfortunately, trying to directly find the value of each state using the previous definition is almost impossible when $\gamma > 0$. However, this is a problem that can be solved using dynamic programming (for further information, please refer to R. A. Howard, *Dynamic Programming and Markov Process*, The MIT Press, 1960), which allows us to solve the problem iteratively.

In particular, we need to turn the previous formula into a Bellman equation:

$$V(s_t; \pi) = E_\pi\left[\sum_{i=0}^{\infty} \gamma^i r_{i+t+1}; s_t\right] = E_\pi\left[r_{t+1} + \gamma \sum_{i=0}^{\infty} \gamma^i r_{i+t+2}; s_t\right] = E_\pi[r_{t+1}; s_t] + \gamma E_\pi\left[\sum_{i=0}^{\infty} \gamma^i r_{i+t+2}; s_t\right]$$

The first term on the right-hand side can be expressed as:

$$E_\pi[r_{t+1}; s_t] = \sum_{a_k} \pi(s_t) \sum_{s_k} T(s_t, s_k; a_k) E[r_{t+1}; s_k, a_k]$$

In other words, it is the weighted average of all expected returns considering that the agent is in the state s_t and evaluates all possible actions and the consequent state transitions. For the second term, we need a small trick. Let's suppose we start from s_{t+1}, so that the expected value corresponds to $V(s_{t+1}; \pi)$; however, as the sum starts from s_t, we need to consider all possible transitions starting from s_t. In this case, we can rewrite the term as:

$$E_\pi \left[\sum_{i=0}^{\infty} \gamma^i r_{i+t+2}; s_t \right] = \sum_{a_k} \pi(s_t) \sum_{s_k} T(s_t, s_k; a_k) V(s_k; \pi)$$

Again, the first terms take into account all possible transitions starting from s_t (and ending in s_{t+1}), while the second one is the value of each ending state. Therefore, the complete expression becomes:

$$V(s_t; \pi) = \sum_{a_k} \pi(s_t) \sum_{s_k} T(s_t, s_k; a_k) [E[r_{t+1}; s_k, a_k] + \gamma V(s_k; \pi)]$$

For a deterministic policy, instead, the formula is:

$$V(s_t; \pi) = \sum_{s_k} T(s_t, s_k; \pi(s_t)) [E[r_{t+1}; s_k, \pi(s_t)] + \gamma V(s_k; \pi)]$$

The previous equations are particular cases of a generic discrete Bellman equation for a finite MDP that can be expressed as a vectorial operator L_π applied to the value vector:

$$L_\pi V = R + \gamma T V$$

It's easy to prove that there is a unique fixed point that corresponds to $V(s; \pi)$, so $L_\pi V(s; \pi) = V(s; \pi)$. However, in order to solve the system, we need to consider all equations at the same time because, both on the left-hand and on the right-hand side of the Bellman equation, there is the $V(s; \pi)$ term. Is it possible to transform the problem into an iterative procedure, so that a previous computation can be exploited for the following one? The answer is yes and it's the consequence of an important property of L_π. Let's consider the infinity norm of the difference between two value vectors computed at time t and $t+1$:

$$\left\| L_\pi V^{(t+1)} - L_\pi V^{(t)} \right\|_\infty = \left\| R + \gamma T V^{(t+1)} - R - \gamma T V^{(t)} \right\|_\infty = \gamma \left\| T V^{(t+1)} - T V^{(t)} \right\|_\infty \leq \gamma \left\| V^{(t+1)} - V^{(t)} \right\|_\infty$$

As the discount factor $\gamma \in (0,1)$, the Bellman operator L_π is a γ-contraction that reduces the distance between the arguments by a factor of γ (they get more and more similar). The Banach Fixed-Point Theorem states that a contraction $L: D \to D$ on a metric space D admits a unique fixed point $d^* \in D$, which can be found by repeatedly applying the contraction to any $d^{(0)} \in D$.

Hence, we know about the existence of a unique fixed point $V(s; \pi)$, which is the goal of our research. If we now consider a generic starting point $V(')$, and we compute the norm of the difference with $V(s; \pi)$, we obtain:

$$\left\|V^{(t)} - V(s; \pi)\right\|_\infty = \left\|L_\pi V^{(t-1)} - L_\pi V(s; \pi)\right\|_\infty \leq \gamma \left\|V^{(t-1)} - V(s; \pi)\right\|_\infty$$

Repeating this procedure iteratively until $t = 0$, we get:

$$\gamma \left\|V^{(t-1)} - V(s; \pi)\right\|_\infty \leq \gamma^2 \left\|V^{(t-2)} - V(s; \pi)\right\|_\infty \leq .. \leq \gamma^{t+1}\left\|V^{(0)} - V(s; \pi)\right\|_\infty$$

The term $\gamma^{t+1} \to 0$, while continuing the iterations over the distance between $V(')$ and $V(s; \pi)$ gets smaller and smaller, authorizing us to employ the iterative approach instead of the one-shot closed method. Hence, the Bellman equation becomes:

$$V^{(i+1)}(s_t) = \sum_{a_k} \pi(s_t) \sum_{s_k} T(s_t, s_k; a_k)\left[E[r_{t+1}; s_k, a_k] + \gamma V^{(i)}(s_k)\right]$$

This formula allows us to find the value for each state (the step is formally called policy evaluation), but of course, it requires a policy. In the first step, we can randomly select the actions because we don't have any other piece of information, but after a complete evaluation cycle, we can start defining a greedy policy with respect to the values. In order to achieve this goal, we need to introduce a very important concept in RL, the Q function (which must not be confused with the Q function defined in the EM algorithm), which is defined as the expected discounted return obtained by an agent starting from state s_t and selecting a specific action at:

$$Q(s_t, a_t; \pi) = E_\pi[R_t; s_t, a_t] = E_\pi\left[\sum_{i=0}^{\infty} \gamma^i r_{i+t+1}; s_t, a_t\right]$$

The definition is very similar to $V(s, \pi)$, but in this case, we include the action, a_t, as a variable. Clearly, it's possible to define a Bellman equation for $Q(s_t, a_t; \pi)$ by simply removing the policy/action summation:

$$Q(s_t, a_t; \pi) = \sum_{s_k} T(s_t, s_k; a_t)[E[r_{t+1}; s_k, a_t] + \gamma V(s_k; \pi)]$$

Sutton and Barto (in Sutton R. S., Barto A. G., *Reinforcement Learning*, The MIT Press, 1998) proved a simple but very important theorem (called the Policy Improvement Theorem), which states that given the deterministic policies π_1 and π_2, if $Q(s, \pi_2(s); \pi_2) \geq V(s; \pi_1) \, \forall s \in S$, then π_2 is better than or equal to π_1. The proof is very compact and can be found in their book, however, the result can be understood intuitively. If we consider a sequence of states, $s_1 \to s_2 \to \ldots \to s_n$ and $\pi_2(s_i) = \pi_1(s_i) \, \forall i < m < n$, while $\pi_2(s_i) \geq \pi_1(s_i) \, \forall i \geq m$, the policy π_2 is at least equal to π_1 and it becomes better if at least inequality is strict. Conversely, if $Q(s, \pi_2(s); \pi_2) \geq V(s; \pi_1)$, this means that $\pi_2(s) \geq \pi_1(s)$ and, again, $Q(s, \pi_2(s); \pi_2) > V(s; \pi_1)$ if there's at least a state s_i, where $\pi_2(s_i) > \pi_1(s_i)$.

Hence, after a complete policy evaluation cycle, we are authorized to define a new greedy policy as:

$$\pi^{(k+1)}(s_t) = \underset{a_t}{\operatorname{argmax}} \, Q\left(s_t, a_t; \pi^{(k)}\right)$$

This step is called policy improvement and its goal is to set the action associated with each state as the one that leads to the transition to the successor state with the maximum value. It's not difficult to understand that an optimal policy will remain stable when $V^{(t)} \to V(s; \pi)$. In fact, when $t \to \infty$, the Q function will converge to a stable fixed point determined by $V(s; \pi)$ and the term $\underset{a_t}{\operatorname{argmax}} \, Q\left(s_t, a_t; \pi^{(k)}\right)$ will always select the same actions. However, if we start with a random policy, in general, a single policy evaluation cycle isn't enough to assure the convergence. Therefore, after a policy improvement step, it's often necessary to repeat the evaluation and continue alternating the two phases until the policy becomes stable (that's why the algorithm is called policy iteration). In general, the convergence is quite fast, but the actual speed depends on the nature of the problem, the number of states and actions, and the consistency of the rewards.

The complete policy iteration algorithm (as proposed by Sutton and Barto) is:

1. Set an initial deterministic random policy $\pi(s)$.
2. Set the initial value array $V(s) = 0 \, \forall s \in S$.
3. Set a tolerance threshold *Thr* (for example, *Thr* = 0.0001).
4. Set a maximum number of iterations N_{iter}.
5. Set a counter $e = 0$.

6. While $e < N_{iter}$:

   a. $e = e + 1$.

   b. While $Avg(|V(s) - V_{old}(s)|) > Thr$:

      i. Set $V_{old}(s) = V(s) \forall s \in S$.

      ii. Perform a policy evaluation step reading the current value from $V_{old}(s)$ and updating $V(s)$.

   c. Set $\pi_{old}(s) = \pi(s) \forall s \in S$.

   d. Perform a policy improvement step.

   e. If $\pi_{old}(s) = \pi(s)$:

      i. Break (Main while loop)

7. Output the final deterministic policy $\pi(s)$.

 In this case, as we have full knowledge of the environment; there's no need for an exploration phase. The policy is always exploited as it's built to be greedy to the real value (obtained when $t \rightarrow \infty$).

Policy iteration in the checkerboard environment

We want to apply the policy iteration algorithm in order to find an optimal policy for the tunnel environment. Let's start by defining a random initial policy and a value matrix with all values (except the terminal states) equal to 0:

```
import numpy as np

nb_actions = 4

policy = np.random.randint(0, nb_actions,
                           size=(height, width)).\
    astype(np.uint8)
tunnel_values = np.zeros(shape=(height, width))
```

The initial random policy ($t = 0$) is shown in the following chart:

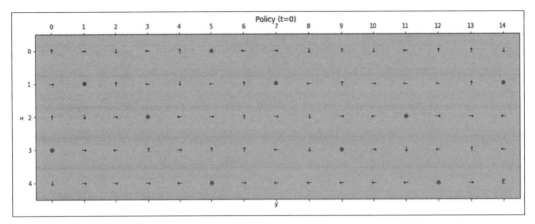

Initial ($t = 0$) random policy

The states denoted by $\otimes$ represent the wells, while the final positive one is represented by the capital letter E.

Hence, the initial value matrix ($t = 0$) is:

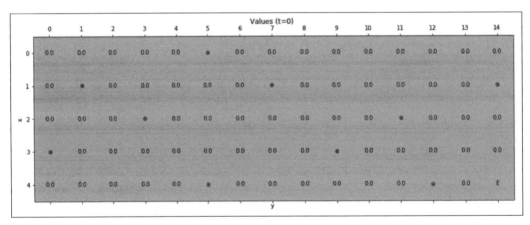

Initial ($t = 0$) value matrix

At this point, we need to define the functions to perform the policy evaluation and improvement steps. As the environment is deterministic, the processes are slightly simpler because of the generic transition probability:

$$T(s_i, s_j; a_k) = \begin{cases} 1 \text{ for the only possible successor} \\ 0 \text{ otherwise} \end{cases}$$

In the same way, the policy is deterministic and only a single action is taken into account. The policy evaluation step is performed, freezing the current values and updating the whole matrix $V^{(t+1)}$ with $V^{(t)}$; however, it's also possible to use the new values immediately. I invite the reader to test both strategies in order to find the fastest way. In this example, we are employing a discount factor, $\gamma = 0.9$ (it goes without saying that an interesting exercise consists of testing different values and comparing the result of the evaluation process and the final behavior):

```
import numpy as np

def is_final(x, y):
    if (x, y) in zip(x_wells, y_wells) \
            or (x, y) == (x_final, y_final):
        return True
    return False
```

The code for policy evaluation is shown in the following snippet:

```
def policy_evaluation():
    old_tunnel_values = tunnel_values.copy()

    for i in range(height):
        for j in range(width):
            action = policy[i, j]

            if action == 0:
                if i == 0:
                    x = 0
                else:
                    x = i - 1
                y = j

            elif action == 1:
                if j == width - 1:
                    y = width - 1
                else:
                    y = j + 1
                x = i

            elif action == 2:
                if i == height - 1:
                    x = height - 1
                else:
                    x = i + 1
                y = j
```

```
        else:
            if j == 0:
                y = 0
            else:
                y = j - 1
            x = i

        reward = tunnel_rewards[x, y]
        tunnel_values[i, j] = \
            reward + \
            (gamma * old_tunnel_values[x, y])
```

In an analogous way, we can define the code necessary to perform the policy improvement step:

```
def policy_improvement():
    for i in range(height):
        for j in range(width):
            if is_final(i, j):
                continue

            values = np.zeros(shape=(nb_actions,))

            values[0] = (tunnel_rewards[i - 1, j] +
                        (gamma *
                          tunnel_values[i - 1, j])) \
                if i > 0 else -np.inf
            values[1] = (tunnel_rewards[i, j + 1] +
                        (gamma *
                          tunnel_values[i, j + 1])) \
                if j < width - 1 else -np.inf
            values[2] = (tunnel_rewards[i + 1, j] +
                        (gamma *
                          tunnel_values[i + 1, j])) \
                if i < height - 1 else -np.inf
            values[3] = (tunnel_rewards[i, j - 1] +
                        (gamma *
                          tunnel_values[i, j - 1])) \
                if j > 0 else -np.inf

            policy[i, j] = np.argmax(values).\
                astype(np.uint8)
```

Once the functions have been defined, we start the policy iteration cycle (with a maximum number of epochs, N_{iter} = 100,000, and a tolerance threshold equal to 10^{-5}):

```
nb_max_epochs = 100000
tolerance = 1e-5

e = 0

gamma = 0.85
old_policy = np.random.randint(0,
                                nb_actions,
                                size=(height, width)).astype(np.uint8)

while e < nb_max_epochs:
e += 1
        old_tunnel_values = tunnel_values.copy()
        policy_evaluation()

        if np.mean(np.abs(tunnel_values -
                        old_tunnel_values)) < \
                tolerance:
            old_policy = policy.copy()
        policy_improvement()

        if np.sum(policy - old_policy) == 0:
            break
```

At the end of the process (in this case, the algorithm converged after 182 iterations, but this value can change with different initial policies), the value matrix is:

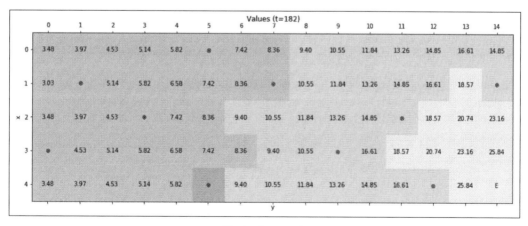

Final value matrix

Analyzing the values, it's possible to see how the algorithm discovered that they are an implicit function of the distance between a cell and the ending state. Moreover, the policy always avoids the wells because the maximum value is always found in an adjacent state. It's easy to verify this behavior by plotting the final policy:

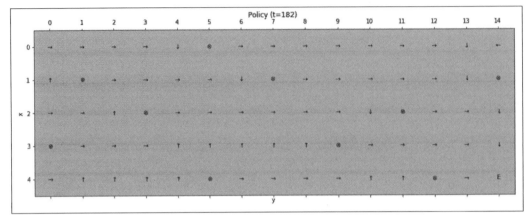

Final policy

Picking a random initial state, the agent will always reach the ending one, avoiding the wells and confirming the optimality of the policy iteration algorithm.

Value iteration

An alternative approach to policy iteration is provided by the value iteration algorithm. The main assumption is based on the empirical observation that the policy evaluation step converges rather quickly and it's reasonable to stop the process after a fixed number of steps (normally 1). In fact, policy iteration can be thought of as a game where the first player tries to find the correct values considering a stable policy, while the other player creates a new policy that is greedy with respect to the new values.

Clearly, the second step compromises the validity of the previous evaluation, forcing the first player to repeat the process. However, as the Bellman equation uses a single fixed point, the algorithm converges to a solution characterized by the fact that the policy doesn't change anymore and, consequently, the evaluation becomes stable. This process can be simplified by removing the policy improvement step and continuing the evaluation in a greedy fashion. Formally, each step is based on the following update rule:

$$V^{(i+1)}(s_t) = \max_{a_t} \sum_{s_k} T(s_t, s_k; a_k)\big[E[r_{t+1}; s_k, a_k] + \gamma V^{(i)}(s_k)\big]$$

Now the iteration doesn't consider the policy anymore (assuming implicitly that it will be greedy with respect to the values) and selects $V^{(i+1)}$ as the maximum possible value among all $V^{(i)}(a_t)$. In other words, value iteration anticipates the choice that is made by the policy improvement step by selecting the value that corresponds to the action that is likely ($p \to 1$) to be selected. It's not difficult to extend the convergence proof presented in the previous section to this case, therefore, $V^{(\infty)} \to V^{(opt)}$, just as in policy iteration. However, the average number of iterations is normally smaller because we are starting with a random policy that can contrast the value iteration process. When the values become stable, the optimal greedy policy is simply obtained as:

$$\pi^{(opt)}(s_t) = \operatorname*{argmax}_{a_t} Q^{(opt)}(s_t, a_t)$$

This step is formally equivalent to a policy improvement iteration, which, however, is done only once, at the end of the process.

The complete value iteration algorithm (as proposed by Sutton and Barto) is:

1. Set the initial value array $V(s) = 0 \ \forall s \in S$.
2. Set a tolerance threshold Thr (for example, $Thr = 0.0001$).
3. Set a maximum number of iterations N_{iter}.
4. Set a counter $e = 0$.
5. While $e < N_{iter}$:

    a. $e = e + 1$.
    b. While $Avg(|V(s) - V_{old}(s)|) > Thr$:

        i.   Set $V_{old}(s) = V(s) \ \forall s \in S$.
        ii. Perform a value evaluation step reading the current value from $V_{old}(s)$ and updating $V(s)$.

6. Output the final deterministic policy $\pi(s) = \operatorname*{argmax}_{a} Q(s, a)$.

Value iteration in the checkerboard environment

To test this algorithm, we need to set an initial value matrix with all values equal to 0 (they can also be randomly chosen but, as we don't have any prior information on the final configuration, every initial choice is probabilistically equivalent):

```
import numpy as np


tunnel_values = np.zeros(shape=(height, width))
```

At this point, we can define the two functions to perform the value evaluation and the final policy selection (the function is_final() is the one defined in the previous example):

```
import numpy as np


def is_final(x, y):
    if (x, y) in \
            zip(x_wells, y_wells) or \
            (x, y) == (x_final, y_final):
        return True
    return False
```

We can now define the value evaluation function:

```
def value_evaluation():
    old_tunnel_values = tunnel_values.copy()

    for i in range(height):
        for j in range(width):
            rewards = np.zeros(shape=(nb_actions,))
            old_values = np.zeros(shape=(nb_actions,))

            for k in range(nb_actions):
                if k == 0:
                    if i == 0:
                        x = 0
                    else:
                        x = i - 1
                    y = j

                elif k == 1:
                    if j == width - 1:
                        y = width - 1
```

```
                    else:
                        y = j + 1
                    x = i

                elif k == 2:
                    if i == height - 1:
                        x = height - 1
                    else:
                        x = i + 1
                    y = j

                else:
                    if j == 0:
                        y = 0
                    else:
                        y = j - 1
                    x = i

                rewards[k] = tunnel_rewards[x, y]
                old_values[k] = old_tunnel_values[x, y]

            new_values = np.zeros(shape=(nb_actions,))

            for k in range(nb_actions):
                new_values[k] = rewards[k] + \
                                (gamma * old_values[k])

            tunnel_values[i, j] = np.max(new_values)
```

The next function we need is the policy selection one, shown in the following
snippet:

```
def policy_selection():
    policy = np.zeros(shape=(height, width)).\
        astype(np.uint8)

    for i in range(height):
        for j in range(width):
            if is_final(i, j):
                continue

            values = np.zeros(shape=(nb_actions,))

            values[0] = (tunnel_rewards[i - 1, j] +
                        (gamma *
```

```
                                   tunnel_values[i - 1, j])) \
                if i > 0 else -np.inf
            values[1] = (tunnel_rewards[i, j + 1] +
                    (gamma *
                    tunnel_values[i, j + 1])) \
                if j < width - 1 else -np.inf
            values[2] = (tunnel_rewards[i + 1, j] +
                    (gamma *
                    tunnel_values[i + 1, j])) \
                if i < height - 1 else -np.inf
            values[3] = (tunnel_rewards[i, j - 1] +
                    (gamma *
                    tunnel_values[i, j - 1])) \
                if j > 0 else -np.inf

            policy[i, j] = np.argmax(values).\
                astype(np.uint8)

    return policy
```

The main differences are in the `value_evaluation()` function, which now has to consider all possible successor states and select the value corresponding to the action that leads to the state with the highest value. Instead, the `policy_selection()` function is equivalent to `policy_improvement()`, but as it is invoked only once, it outputs directly to the final optimal policy. At this point, we can run a training cycle (assuming the same constants as before):

```
e = 0

policy = None

while e < nb_max_epochs:
e += 1
        old_tunnel_values = tunnel_values.copy()
        value_evaluation()

        if np.mean(np.abs(tunnel_values -
                        old_tunnel_values)) < \
                tolerance:
            policy = policy_selection()
                break
```

The final value configuration (after 127 iterations) is shown in the following chart:

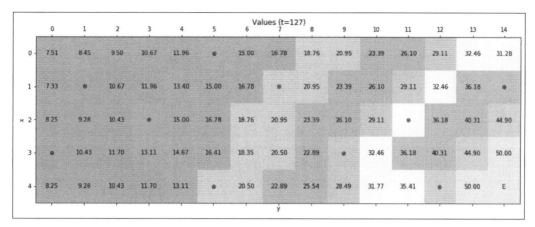

Final value matrix

As in the previous example, the final value configuration is a function of the distance between each state and the ending one, but in this case, the choice of $\gamma = 0.9$ isn't optimal. In fact, the wells close to the final state aren't considered very dangerous anymore. Plotting the final policy can help us understand the behavior:

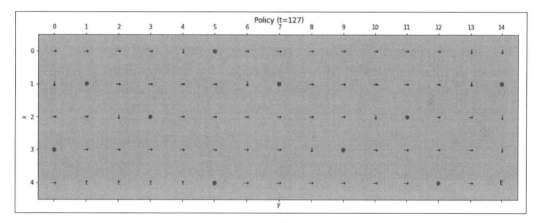

Final policy

As expected, the wells that are far from the target are avoided, but the two that are close to the final state are accepted as reasonable penalties. This happens because the value iteration algorithm is very greedy with respect to the value and the discount factor $\gamma < 1.0$; the effect of negative states can be compensated for by the final reward. In many scenarios, these states are absorbing, therefore their implicit reward is $+\infty$ or $-\infty$, meaning that no other actions can change the final value.

I invite the reader to repeat the example with different discount factors (remember that an agent with $\gamma \rightarrow 1$ is very short-sighted and will avoid any obstacle, even reducing the efficiency of the policy) and change the values of the final states. Moreover, you should be able to answer the question: What is the agent's behavior when the standard reward (whose default value is -0.1) is increased or decreased?

The TD(0) algorithm

One of the problems with dynamic programming algorithms is the need for full knowledge of the environment in terms of states and transition probabilities. Unfortunately, there are many cases where these pieces of information are unknown before the direct experience. In particular, states can be discovered by letting the agent explore the environment, but transition probabilities require us to count the number of transitions to a certain state and this is often impossible. Moreover, an environment with absorbing states can prevent visiting many states if the agent has learned a good initial policy. For example, in a game, which can be described as an episodic MDP, the agent discovers the environment while learning how to move forward without ending in a negative absorbing state.

A general solution to these problems is provided by a different evaluation strategy, called **Temporal Difference (TD)** RL. In this case, we start with an empty value matrix and we let the agent follow a greedy policy with respect to the value (except for the initial one, which is generally random). Once the agent observes a transition $s_i \rightarrow s_j$, due to an action, a_i, it updates the estimation of $V(s_i)$ with a reward. The process is structured in episodes (which is the most natural way) and ends when a maximum number of steps have been done or a terminal state is met. In particular, the TD(0) algorithm updates the value according to the rule:

$$V^{(t+1)}(s_i) = V^{(t)}(s_i) + \alpha\left(r_{ij} + \gamma V^{(t)}(s_j) - V^{(t)}(s_i)\right)$$

The constant α is bounded between 0 and 1 and acts as a learning rate. Each update considers a variation with respect to the current value $V(t)(s_i)$, which is proportional to the difference between the actual return and the previous estimation. The term $r_{ij} + \gamma V^{(t)}(s_j)$ is analogous to the one employed in the previous methods and represents the expected value given the current return and the discounted value starting from the successor state. However, as $V(t)(s_j)$ is an estimation, the process is based on a bootstrap from the previous values. In other words, we start from an estimation to determine the next one, which should be closer to the stable fixed point. Indeed, TD(0) is the simplest example of a family of TD algorithms that are based on a sequence (usually called a backup) that can be generalized as (considering k steps):

$$R_t^k = r_{t+1} + \gamma^2 r_{t+2} + \cdots + \gamma^{k-1} r_{k-1} + \gamma^k V^{(t)}(s_{t+k})$$

As we're using a single reward to approximate the expected discounted return, TD(0) is usually called a one-step TD method (or one-step backup). A more complex algorithm can be built considering more subsequent rewards or alternative strategies. We're going to analyze a generic variant called TD(λ) in the next chapter and explain why this algorithm corresponds to a choice of $\lambda = 0$. TD(0) has been proven to converge, even if the proof (which can be found for a model-based approach in Van Hasselt H., Wiering M. A., *Convergence of Model-Based Temporal Difference Learning for Control*, Proceedings of the 2007 IEEE Symposium on Approximate Dynamic Programming and Reinforcement Learning (ADPRL 2007)) is more complex because it's necessary to consider the evolution of the Markov process. In fact, in this case, we are approximating the expected discounted return with both a truncated estimation and a bootstrap value $V(s_j)$, which is initially (and for a large number of iterations) unstable. However, assuming the convergence for $t \rightarrow \infty$, we get:

$$V^{(\infty)}(s_i) = V^{(\infty)}(s_i) + \alpha\big(r_{ij} + \gamma V^{(\infty)}(s_j) - V^{(\infty)}(s_i)\big) = r_{ij} + \gamma V^{(\infty)}(s_j)$$

The last formula expresses the value of the state s_i, assuming that the greedy optimal policy forces the agent to perform the action that causes the transition to s_j. Of course, at this point, it's natural to ask under which conditions the algorithm converges. In fact, we are considering episodic tasks and the estimation $V^{(\infty)}(s_i)$ can be correct only if the agent performs a transition to s_i an infinite number of times, selecting all possible actions an infinite number of times. Such a condition is often expressed by saying that the policy must be **Greedy in the Limit with Infinite Explorations** (GLIE). In other words, the real greediness is achieved only as an asymptotic state when the agent is able to explore the environment without limitations for an unlimited number of episodes.

This is probably the most important limitation of TD Reinforcement Learning, because, in real-life scenarios, some states can be very unlikely and, hence, the estimation can never accumulate the experience needed to converge to the actual value. We are going to analyze some methods to solve this problem in the next chapter, but in our example, we employ a random start. In other words, as the policy is greedy and could always avoid some states, we force the agent to start each episode in a random nonterminal cell. In this way, we allow deep exploration even with a greedy policy. Whenever this approach is not feasible (because, for example, the environment dynamics are not controllable), the exploration-exploitation dilemma can be solved only by employing an ε-greedy policy, which selects a fraction of suboptimal (or even wrong) actions. In this way, it's possible to observe a higher number of transitions paying the price of slower convergence.

However, as pointed out by Sutton and Barto, TD(0) converges to the maximum-likelihood estimation of the value function determined by the MDP, finding the implicit transition probabilities of the model. Therefore, if the number of observations is high enough, TD(0) can quickly find an optimal policy, but at the same time, it's also more sensitive to biased estimations if some couples' state-action is never experienced (or experienced very seldom). In our example, we don't know which the initial state is, hence selecting a fixed starting point yields a policy that is extremely rigid and almost completely unable to manage noisy situations.

For example, if the starting point is changed to an adjacent (but never explored) cell, the algorithm could fail to find the optimal path to the positive terminal state. On the other hand, if we know that the dynamics are well defined, TD(0) will force the agent to select the actions that are most likely to produce the optimal result given the current knowledge of the environment. If the dynamics are partially stochastic, the advantage of an ε-greedy policy can be understood considering a sequence of episodes where the agent experiences the same transitions and the corresponding values are increased proportionally. If, for example, the environment changes one transition after many experiences, the agent has to face a brand-new experience when the policy is already almost stable.

The correction requires many episodes and, as this random change has a very low probability, it's possible that the agent will never learn the correct behavior. Instead, by selecting a few random actions, the probability of encountering a similar state (or even the same one) increases (think about a game where the state is represented by a screenshot) and the algorithm can become more robust with respect to very unlikely transitions.

The complete TD(0) algorithm is:

1. Set an initial deterministic random policy $\pi(s)$.
2. Set the initial value array $V(s) = 0 \ \forall \ s \in S$.
3. Set the number of episodes $N_{episodes}$.
4. Set a maximum number of steps per episode N_{max}.
5. Set a constant α (for example, $\alpha = 0.1$).
6. Set a constant γ (for example, $\gamma = 0.9$).
7. Set a counter $e = 0$.
8. For $i = 1$ to $N_{episodes}$:
    a. Observe the initial state s_i.
    b. While s_j is non-terminal and $e < N_{max}$:

i. $e = e + 1$.

ii. Select the action $a_t = \pi(s_i)$.

iii. Observe the transition $(a_t, s_i) \rightarrow (s_j, r_{ij})$.

iv. Update the value function for the state s_i.

v.   Set $s_i = s_j$.

9. Update the policy to be greedy with respect to the value function
    $$\pi(s) = \underset{a}{\operatorname{argmax}} Q(s, a).$$

At this point, we can test the TD(0) algorithm in the checkerboard environment.

TD(0) in the checkerboard environment

The first step in testing TD(0) in the checkerboard environment is to define an initial random policy, and a value matrix with all elements equal to 0:

```
import numpy as np

policy = np.random.randint(0,
                           nb_actions,
                           size=(height, width)).\
         astype(np.uint8)
tunnel_values = np.zeros(shape=(height, width))
```

As we want to select a random starting point at the beginning of each episode, we need to define a helper function that must exclude the terminal states (all the constants are the same as previously defined):

```
import numpy as np

xy_grid = np.meshgrid(np.arange(0, height),
                      np.arange(0, width),
                      sparse=False)
xy_grid = np.array(xy_grid).T.reshape(-1, 2)

xy_final = list(zip(x_wells, y_wells))
xy_final.append([x_final, y_final])

xy_start = []

for x, y in xy_grid:
    if (x, y) not in xy_final:
        xy_start.append([x, y])
```

```
    xy_start = np.array(xy_start)


def starting_point():
    xy = np.squeeze(xy_start[
                np.random.randint(0,
                                    xy_start.shape[0],
                                    size=1)])
        return xy[0], xy[1]
```

Now we can implement the function to evaluate a single episode (setting the maximum number of steps equal to 500 and the constant to $\alpha = 0.25$):

```
max_steps = 1000
alpha = 0.25

def episode():
    (i, j) = starting_point()
    x = y = 0

    e = 0

    while e < max_steps:
        e += 1

        action = policy[i, j]

        if action == 0:
            if i == 0:
                x = 0
            else:
                x = i - 1
            y = j

        elif action == 1:
            if j == width - 1:
                y = width - 1
            else:
                y = j + 1
            x = i

        elif action == 2:
            if i == height - 1:
                x = height - 1
            else:
```

```
                    x = i + 1
              y = j

         else:
             if j == 0:
                 y = 0
             else:
                 y = j - 1
             x = i

         reward = tunnel_rewards[x, y]
         tunnel_values[i, j] += \
             alpha * (reward +
                     (gamma * tunnel_values[x, y]) -
                     tunnel_values[i, j])

         if is_final(x, y):
             break
         else:
             i = x
             j = y
```

The function to determine the greedy policy with respect to the values is the same as was already implemented in the previous examples; however, we report it to guarantee the consistency of the example:

```
def policy_selection():
    for i in range(height):
        for j in range(width):
            if is_final(i, j):
                continue

            values = np.zeros(shape=(nb_actions,))

            values[0] = (tunnel_rewards[i - 1, j] +
                        (gamma *
                        tunnel_values[i - 1, j])) \
                   if i > 0 \
                   else -np.inf
            values[1] = (tunnel_rewards[i, j + 1] +
                        (gamma *
                        tunnel_values[i, j + 1])) \
                   if j < width - 1 \
                   else -np.inf
            values[2] = (tunnel_rewards[i + 1, j] +
```

```
                        (gamma *
                         tunnel_values[i + 1, j])) \
            if i < height - 1 \
            else -np.inf
        values[3] = (tunnel_rewards[i, j - 1] +
                        (gamma *
                         tunnel_values[i, j - 1])) \
            if j > 0 \
            else -np.inf

        policy[i, j] = np.argmax(values).\
            astype(np.uint8)
```

At this point, we can start a training cycle with 5,000 episodes:

```
n_episodes = 5000

for _ in range(n_episodes):
    episode()
    policy_selection()
```

The final value matrix is shown in the following chart:

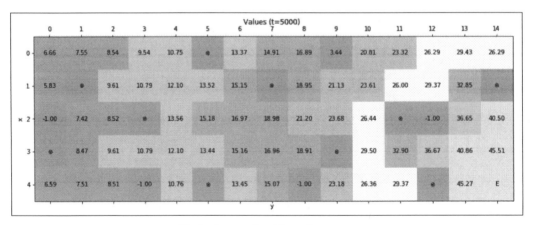

Final value matrix with random starts

As in the previous examples, the final values are inversely proportional to the distance from the final positive state. Let's analyze the resulting policy to understand whether the algorithm converged to a consistent solution:

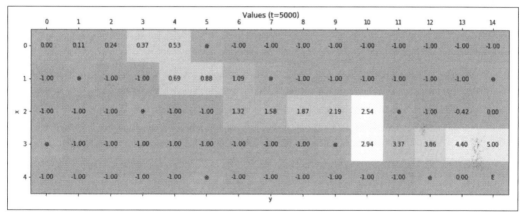

Final policy with random starts

As can be seen, the random choice of the starting state is allowed to find the best path independently from the initial condition. To better understand the advantage of this strategy, let's plot the final value matrix when the initial state is fixed to the cell (0, 0), corresponding to the upper-left corner:

Final value matrix with a fixed initial state (0, 0)

Without any further analysis, it's possible to see that many states have never been visited or have been visited only a few times, and the resulting policy is therefore extremely greedy with respect to the specific initial state. The blocks containing values equal to -1.0 indicate states where the agent often has to pick a random action because there's no difference in the values, hence it can be extremely difficult to solve the environment with a different initial state.

The resulting policy confirms this analysis:

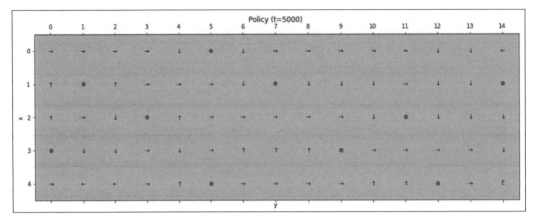

Final policy with a fixed initial state (0, 0)

As it's possible to see, the agent is able to reach the final state only when the initial point allows us to cross the trajectory starting from (0, 0). In all these cases, it's possible to recover the optimal policy, even if the paths are longer than the ones obtained in the previous example. Instead, states such as (0, 4) are clearly situations where there's a loss of policy. In other words, the agent acts without any knowledge or awareness and the probability of success converges to 0. As an exercise, I invite the reader to test this algorithm with different starting points (for example, a set of fixed ones) and higher α values. The goal is also to answer these questions: Is it possible to speed up the learning process? Is it necessary to start from all possible states in order to obtain a globally optimal policy?

Summary

In this chapter, we introduced the most important RL concepts, focusing on the mathematical structure of an environment as an MDP, and on the different kinds of policy and how they can be derived from the expected reward obtained by an agent. In particular, we defined the value of a state as the expected future reward considering a sequence discounted by a factor, γ. In the same way, we introduced the concept of the Q function, which is the value of an action when the agent is in a specific state.

These concepts directly employed the policy iteration algorithm, which is based on a Dynamic Programming approach assuming complete knowledge of the environment. The task is split into two stages; during the first one, the agent evaluates all the states given the current policy, while in the second one, the policy is updated in order to be greedy with respect to the new value function.

In this way, the agent is forced to always pick the action that leads to a transition that maximizes the obtained value.

We also analyzed a variant, called value iteration, that performs a single evaluation and selects the policy in a greedy manner. The main difference from the previous approach is that now the agent immediately selects the highest value, assuming that the result of this process is equivalent to a policy iteration. Indeed, it's easy to prove that, after infinite transitions, both algorithms converge on the optimal value function.

The last algorithm is called TD(0) and it's based on a model-free approach. In fact, in many cases, it's difficult to know all the transition probabilities and, sometimes, even all possible states are unknown. This method is based on the TD evaluation, which is performed directly while interacting with the environment. If the agent can visit all the states an infinite number of times (clearly, this is only a theoretical condition), the algorithm has been proven to converge to the optimal value function more quickly than other methods.

In the next chapter, we'll continue the discussion of RL algorithms, introducing some more advanced methods that can be immediately implemented using deep convolutional networks.

Further reading

- R. A. Howard, *Dynamic Programming and Markov Process*, The MIT Press, 1960
- Sutton R. S., Barto A. G., *Reinforcement Learning*, The MIT Press, 1998
- Van Hasselt H., Wiering M. A., *Convergence of Model-Based Temporal Difference Learning for Control*, Proceedings of the 2007 IEEE Symposium on Approximate Dynamic Programming and Reinforcement Learning (ADPRL 2007)

25
Advanced Policy Estimation Algorithms

In this chapter, we'll complete our exploration of the world of **Reinforcement Learning (RL)**, focusing our attention on complex algorithms that can be employed to solve difficult problems. The topic of RL is extremely large, and we couldn't cover it in its entirety even if we dedicated an entire book to it; this chapter is instead based on many practical examples that you can use as a basis to work on more complex scenarios.

The topics that will be discussed in this chapter are:

- The TD(λ) algorithm
- Actor-Critic TD(0)
- SARSA
- Q-learning, including a simple visual input and a neural network
- Direct policy search through policy gradient

We can now start analyzing the natural extension of TD(0) algorithm, which helps take into account a longer sequence of transitions, obtaining a more accurate estimation of the value function.

TD(λ) algorithm

In the previous chapter, we introduced the temporal difference strategy, and we discussed a simple example called TD(0). In the case of TD(0), the discounted reward is approximated by using a one-step backup.

Hence, if the agent performs an action at in the state s_t, and the transition to the state s_{t+1} is observed, the approximation becomes the following:

$$R_t^1 = r_{t+1} + \gamma V(s_{t+1})$$

If the task is episodic (as in many real-life scenarios) and has $T(e_i)$ steps, the complete backup for the episode e_i is as follows:

$$R_t^{T(e_i)} = R_t = r_{t+1} + \gamma^2 r_{t+2} + \cdots + \gamma^{T(e_i)-1} r_{T(e_i)-1} + \gamma^{T(e_i)} V^{(t)}(s_{t+T(e_i)})$$

The previous expression ends when the MDP process reaches an absorbing state; therefore, R_t is the actual value of the discounted reward. The difference between TD(0) and this choice is clear: in the first case, we can update the value function after each transition, whereas with a complete backup, we need to wait for the end of the episode. We can say that this method (which is called Monte Carlo, because it's based on the idea of averaging the overall reward of an entire sequence) is exactly the opposite of TD(0); therefore, it's reasonable to think about an intermediate solution, based on k-step backups.

In particular, our goal is to find an online algorithm that can exploit the backups once they are available. Let's imagine a sequence of four steps. The agent is in the first state and observes a transition; at this point, only a one-step backup is possible, and it's a good idea to update the value function in order to improve the convergence speed. After the second transition, the agent can use a two-step backup; however, it can also consider the first one-step backup in addition to the newer, longer one. So, we have two approximations:

$$\begin{cases} R_t^1 = r_{t+1} + \gamma V(s_{t+1}) \\ R_t^2 = r_{t+1} + \gamma r_{t+2} + \gamma^2 V(s_{t+2}) \end{cases}$$

Which of the preceding is the most reliable? Obviously, the second one depends on the first one (particularly when the value function is almost stabilized), and so on until the end of the episode. Hence, the most common strategy is to employ a weighted average that assigns a different level of importance to each backup (assuming the longest backup has k steps):

$$\tilde{R}_t = \lambda_1 R_t^1 + \lambda_2 R_t^2 + \cdots + \lambda_k R_t^k \quad and \quad \sum_i \lambda_i = 1$$

Watkins (in Watkins C.I.C.H., *Learning from Delayed Rewards*, Ph.D. Thesis, University of Cambridge, 1989) proved that this approach (with or without averaging) has the fundamental property of reducing the absolute error of the expected R_t^k with respect to the optimal value function $V(s; \pi)$. In fact, he proved that the following inequality holds:

$$\max_{s^*} \left| E_\pi \left[R_t^k; s^* \right] - V(s^*; \pi) \right| \leq \gamma^k \max_s |V(s) - V(s; \pi)|$$

As γ is bounded between 0 and 1, the right-hand side is always smaller than the maximum absolute error $V(s) - V(s; \pi)$, where $V(s)$ is the value of a state during an episode. Therefore, the expected discounted return of a k-step backup (or of a combination of different backups) yields a more accurate estimation of the optimal value function if the policy is chosen to be greedy with respect to it. This is not surprising, as a longer backup incorporates more actual returns, but the importance of this theorem resides in its validity when an average of different k-step backups are employed.

In other words, it provides us with the mathematical proof that an intuitive approach actually converges, and it can also effectively improve both the convergence speed and the final accuracy. However, managing k coefficients is generally problematic, and in many cases, useless. The main idea behind TD(λ) is to employ a single factor, λ, that can be tuned in order to meet specific requirements. The theoretical analysis (or *forward view*, as referred to by Sutton and Barto) is based, in a general case, on an exponentially decaying average. If we consider a geometric series with λ bounded between 0 and 1 (exclusive), we get:

$$\sum_{i=0}^{\infty} \lambda^i = \frac{1}{1 - \lambda} \implies (1 - \lambda) \sum_{i=0}^{\infty} \lambda^i = 1 \implies \sum_{i=0}^{\infty} (1 - \lambda)\lambda^i = 1$$

Hence, we can consider the averaged discounted return $R_t^{(\lambda)}$ with infinite backups as:

$$R_t^{(\lambda)} = \sum_{i=1}^{\infty} (1 - \lambda)\lambda^{i-1} R_t^i = (1 - \lambda) \sum_{i=1}^{\infty} \lambda^{i-1} R_t^i$$

Before defining the finite case, it's helpful to understand how $R_t^{(\lambda)}$ was built. As λ is bounded between 0 and 1, the factors decay proportionally to λ, so the first backup has the highest impact, and all of the subsequent ones have smaller and smaller influences on the estimation. This means that, in general, we are assuming that the estimation of R_t has more importance to the immediate backups (which become more and more precise), and we exploit the longer ones only to improve the estimated value.

Now, it should be clear that $\lambda = 0$ is equivalent to TD(0) (discussed in the previous chapter), because only the one-step backup remains in the sum (remember that $0^0 = 1$), while larger values involve all of the remaining backups. Let's now consider an episode e_i whose length is $T(e_i)$. Conventionally, if the agent reached an absorbing state at $t = T(e_i)$, all of the remaining $t + i$ returns are equal to R_t (this is straightforward, as all of the possible rewards have already been collected); therefore, we can truncate $R_t^{(\lambda)}$:

$$R_t^{(\lambda)} = \sum_{i=1}^{T(e_i)-t-1} (1-\lambda)\lambda^{i-1}R_t^i + \lambda^{T(e_i)-t-1}R_t$$

The first term of the previous expression involves all of the non-terminal states, while the second is equal to R_t discounted proportionally to the distance between the first time step and the final state. Again, if $\lambda = 0$, we obtain TD(0), but we are now also authorized to consider $\lambda = 1$ (because the sum is always extended to a finite number of elements). When $\lambda = 1$, we obtain $R_t^{(\lambda)} = R_t$, which means that we need to wait until the end of the episode to get the actual discounted reward.

As explained previously, this method is normally not a first-choice solution, because when the episodes are very long, the agent selects the actions with a value function that is not up to date in the majority of cases. Therefore, TD(λ) is normally employed with λ values less than 1 in order to obtain the advantage of an online update, together with a correction based on the new states. To achieve this goal without looking at the future (we want to update $V(s)$ as soon as new pieces of information are available), we need to introduce the concept of eligibility trace $e(s)$ (sometimes, in the context of computational neuroscience, $e(s)$ is also called stimulus trace).

An eligibility trace for a state s is a function of time that returns the weight (greater than 0) of the specific state. Let's imagine a sequence, $s_1, s_2, ..., s_n$, and consider a state, s_i. After a backup $V(s_i)$ is updated, the agent continues its exploration. When is a new update of s_i (given longer backups) important? If s_i is not visited anymore, the effect of longer backups must be smaller and smaller, and s_i is said to not be eligible for changes in $V(s)$. This is a consequence of the previous assumption that shorter backups must generally have higher importance. So, if s_i is an initial state (or is immediately after the initial state) and the agent moves to other states, the effect of s_i must decay. Conversely, if s_i is revisited, it means that the previous estimation of $V(s_i)$ is probably wrong, and hence s_i is eligible for a change.

To better understand this concept, imagine a sequence $s_1, s_2, s_1, \dots$. It's clear that when the agent is in s_1, as well as in s_2, it cannot select the right action; therefore, it's necessary to reevaluate $V(s)$ until the agent is able to move forward.

The most common strategy (which is also discussed in Sutton R. S., Barto A. G., *Reinforcement Learning*, The MIT Press, 1998) is to define the eligibility traces in a recursive fashion. After each time step, $e_t(s)$ decays by a factor equal to $\gamma\lambda$ (to meet the requirement imposed by the forward view); but when the state s is revisited, $e_t(s)$ is also increased by 1 ($e_t(s) = \gamma\lambda e_{t-1}(s) + 1$). In this way, we impose a jump in the trend of $e(s)$ whenever we desire to emphasize its impact. However, as $e(s)$ decays independently of the jumps, the states that are visited and revisited later have a lower impact than the ones that are revisited very soon.

The reason for this choice is very intuitive: the importance of a state revisited after a long sequence is clearly lower than the importance of a state that is revisited after a few steps. In fact, the estimation of R_t is obviously wrong if the agent moves back and forth between two states at the beginning of the episode, but the error becomes less significant when the agent revisits a state after having explored other areas. For example, a policy can allow an initial phase in order to reach a partial goal, and then it can force the agent to move back to reach a terminal state.

By exploiting the eligibility traces, TD(λ) can achieve very fast convergence in more complex environments, with a trade-off between a one-step TD method and a Monte Carlo one (which is normally avoided). At this point, the reader might wonder if we are sure about the convergence, and luckily, the answer is positive. Dayan proved (in Dayan P., *The convergence of TD (λ) for General λ*, Machine Learning 8, 3–4/1992) that TD(λ) converges for a generic λ with only a few specific assumptions and the fundamental condition that the policy is **Greedy in the Limit with Infinite Exploration (GLIE)**. The proof is very technical, and it's beyond the scope of this book; however, the most important assumptions (which are generally met) are:

- The **Markov Decision Process (MDP)** has absorbing states (in other words, all of the episodes end in a finite number of steps).
- All of the transition probabilities are not null (all states can be visited an infinite number of times).

The first condition is obvious. The absence of absorbing states yields infinite explorations, which are not compatible with a TD method (sometimes it's possible to prematurely end an episode, but this can either be unacceptable (in some contexts) or a sub-optimal choice (in many others)). Moreover, Sutton and Barto (in the aforementioned book) proved that TD(λ) is equivalent to employing the weighted average of discounted return approximations, but without the constraint of looking ahead in the future (which is clearly impossible).

The complete TD(λ) algorithm (with an optional forced termination of the episode) is:

1. Set an initial deterministic random policy $\pi(s)$.
2. Set the initial value array $V(s) = 0 \ \forall \ s \in S$.
3. Set the initial eligibility trace array $e(s) = 0 \ \forall \ s \in S$.
4. Set the number of episodes $N_{episodes}$.
5. Set a maximum number of steps per episode N_{max}.
6. Set a constant α (for example, $\alpha = 0.1$).
7. Set a constant γ (for example, $\gamma = 0.9$).
8. Set a constant λ (for example, $\lambda = 0.5$).
9. Set a counter $e = 0$.
10. For $i = 1$ to $N_{episodes}$:

    a. Create an empty state list L.
    b. Observe the initial state s_i and append s_i to L.
    c. While s_i is non-terminal and $e < N_{max}$:

        i. $e = e + 1$.
        ii. Select the action $a_t = \pi(s_i)$.
        iii. Observe the transition $(a_t, s_i) \to (s_j, r_{ij})$.
        iv. Compute the TD error as $TD_{error} = r_{ij} + \gamma V(s_j) - V(s_i)$.
        v. Increment the eligibility trace $e(s_i) = e(s_i) + 1$.
        vi. For $s \in L$:

            1. Update the value $V(s) = V(s) + \alpha TD_{error} e(s)$.
            2. Update the eligibility trace $e(s) = \gamma \lambda e(s)$.

        vii. Set $s_i = s_j$ and append s_j to L.

    d. Update the policy to be greedy with respect to the value function $\pi(s) = \underset{a}{\mathrm{argmax}} \, Q(s, a)$.

The reader can better understand the logic of this algorithm by considering the TD error and its backpropagation. Even if this is only a comparison, it's possible to imagine the behavior of TD(λ) as similar to the **stochastic gradient descent (SGD)** algorithms employed to train a neural network.

In fact, the error is propagated to the previous states (analogous to the lower layers of an MLP) and affects them proportionally to their importance, which is defined by their eligibility traces. Hence, a state with a higher eligibility trace can be considered more responsible for the error; therefore, the corresponding value must be corrected proportionally. This isn't a formal explanation, but it can simplify comprehension of the dynamics without an excessive loss of rigor.

TD(λ) in a more complex checkerboard environment

At this point, we want to test the TD(λ) algorithm with a slightly more complex checkerboard environment – a tunnel environment, where the initial state is on one side, and the final state on the other.

To add a little complexity, along with the absorbing states we'll also consider some intermediate positive states, which can be imagined as checkpoints. An agent should learn the optimal path from any cell to the final state, trying to pass through the highest number of checkpoints possible. Let's start by defining the new structure:

```python
import numpy as np

width = 15
height = 5

y_final = width - 1
x_final = height - 1

y_wells = [0, 1, 3, 5, 5, 6, 7, 9, 10, 11, 12, 14]
x_wells = [3, 1, 2, 0, 4, 3, 1, 3, 1, 2, 4, 1]

y_prizes = [0, 3, 4, 6, 7, 8, 9, 12]
x_prizes = [2, 4, 3, 2, 1, 4, 0, 2]

standard_reward = -0.1
tunnel_rewards = np.ones(shape=(height, width)) * \
                 standard_reward

def init_tunnel_rewards():
    for x_well, y_well in zip(x_wells, y_wells):
        tunnel_rewards[x_well, y_well] = -5.0

    for x_prize, y_prize in zip(x_prizes, y_prizes):
        tunnel_rewards[x_prize, y_prize] = 1.0
```

```
        tunnel_rewards[x_final, y_final] = 5.0

    init_tunnel_rewards()
```

The reward structure is shown in the following diagram:

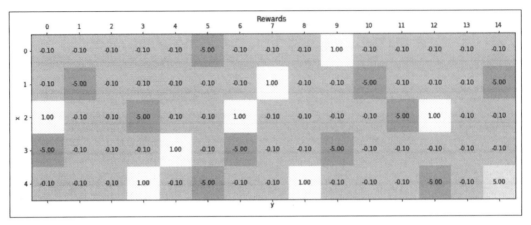

Reward schema in the new tunnel environment

At this point, we can proceed to initialize all of the constants (in particular, we have chosen $\lambda = 0.6$, which is an intermediate solution that guarantees an accuracy close to a Monte Carlo method, without compromising the learning speed):

```
nb_actions = 4
max_steps = 1000
alpha = 0.25
lambd = 0.6
gamma = 0.95

tunnel_values = np.zeros(shape=(height, width))
eligibility_traces = np.zeros(shape=(height, width))
policy = np.random.randint(0, nb_actions,
                           size=(height, width)).\
        astype(np.uint8)
```

In Python, the keyword lambda is reserved; we used the truncated expression `lambd` to declare the constant. As we want to start from a random cell, we need to repeat the same procedure presented in the previous chapter; but in this case, we are also including the checkpoint states:

```
xy_grid = np.meshgrid(np.arange(0, height),
                      np.arange(0, width),
                      sparse=False)
```

```
xy_grid = np.array(xy_grid).T.reshape(-1, 2)

xy_final = list(zip(x_wells, y_wells)) + \
           list(zip(x_prizes, y_prizes))
xy_final.append([x_final, y_final])

xy_start = []

for x, y in xy_grid:
    if (x, y) not in xy_final:
        xy_start.append([x, y])

xy_start = np.array(xy_start)

def starting_point():
    xy = np.squeeze(xy_start[
                    np.random.randint(
                        0, xy_start.shape[0],
                        size=1)])
    return xy[0], xy[1]
```

We can now define the `episode()` function, which implements a complete TD(λ) cycle. As we don't want the agent to roam around trying to pass through the checkpoints an infinite number of times, we have decided to reduce the reward during the exploration, to incentivize the agent to pass through only the necessary checkpoints—trying, at the same time, to reach the final state as soon as possible:

```
def is_final(x, y):
    if (x, y) in zip(x_wells, y_wells) or \
            (x, y) == (x_final, y_final):
        return True
    return False

def episode():
    (i, j) = starting_point()
    x = y = 0

    e = 0

    state_history = [(i, j)]

    init_tunnel_rewards()
    total_reward = 0.0

    while e < max_steps:
```

```
e += 1

action = policy[i, j]

if action == 0:
    if i == 0:
        x = 0
    else:
        x = i - 1
    y = j

elif action == 1:
    if j == width - 1:
        y = width - 1
    else:
        y = j + 1
    x = i

elif action == 2:
    if i == height - 1:
        x = height - 1
    else:
        x = i + 1
    y = j

else:
    if j == 0:
        y = 0
    else:
        y = j - 1
    x = i

reward = tunnel_rewards[x, y]
total_reward += reward

td_error = reward + \
            (gamma * tunnel_values[x, y]) - \
            tunnel_values[i, j]
eligibility_traces[i, j] += 1.0

for sx, sy in state_history:
    tunnel_values[sx, sy] += \
        (alpha * td_error *
         eligibility_traces[sx, sy])
```

```
            eligibility_traces[sx, sy] *= \
                (gamma * lambd)

        if is_final(x, y):
            break
        else:
            i = x
            j = y

        state_history.append([x, y])

        tunnel_rewards[x_prizes, y_prizes] *= 0.85

    return total_reward
```

It's also necessary to create a function to perform the policy selection:

```
def policy_selection():
    for i in range(height):
        for j in range(width):
            if is_final(i, j):
                continue

            values = np.zeros(shape=(nb_actions,))

            values[0] = (tunnel_rewards[i - 1, j] +
                        (gamma *
                        tunnel_values[i - 1, j])) \
                if i > 0 else -np.inf
            values[1] = (tunnel_rewards[i, j + 1] +
                        (gamma *
                        tunnel_values[i, j + 1])) \
                if j < width - 1 else -np.inf
            values[2] = (tunnel_rewards[i + 1, j] +
                        (gamma *
                        tunnel_values[i + 1, j])) \
                if i < height - 1 else -np.inf
            values[3] = (tunnel_rewards[i, j - 1] +
                        (gamma *
                        tunnel_values[i, j - 1])) \
                if j > 0 else -np.inf

            policy[i, j] = np.argmax(values).\
                astype(np.uint8)
```

The `is_final()` and `policy_selection()` functions are the same ones defined in the previous chapter, and need no explanation. Even if it's not really necessary, we have decided to implement a forced termination after a number of steps, equal to `max_steps`. This is helpful at the beginning because as the policy is not ε-greedy, the agent can remain stuck in a looping exploration that never ends. We can now train the model for a fixed number of episodes (alternatively, it's possible to stop the process when the value array doesn't change anymore):

```
n_episodes = 5000

total_rewards = []

for _ in range(n_episodes):
    e_reward = episode()
    total_rewards.append(e_reward)
    policy_selection()
```

The `episode()` function returns the total rewards; therefore, it's useful to check how the agent learning process evolved:

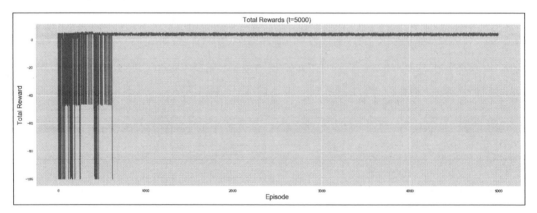

Total rewards achieved by the agent

At the beginning (for about 500 episodes), the agent employs an unacceptable policy that yields very negative total rewards. However, in under 1,000 iterations, the algorithm reaches an optimal policy that is only slightly improved by the following episodes. The oscillations are due to the different starting points; however, the total rewards are never negative, and as the checkpoint weights decay, this is a positive signal, indicating that the agent reaches the final positive state. To confirm this hypothesis, we can plot the learned value function:

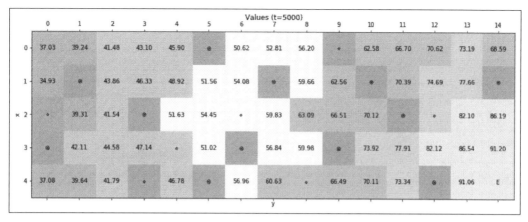

Final value matrix

The values are coherent with our initial analysis; in fact, they tend to be higher when the cell is close to a checkpoint, but at the same time, the global configuration (considering a policy that's greedy with respect to $V(s)$) forces the agent to reach the ending state whose surrounding values are the highest. The last step is checking the actual policy, with a particular focus on the checkpoints:

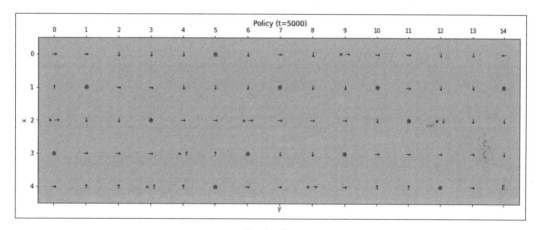

Final policy

As it's possible to observe, the agent tries to pass through the checkpoints, but when it's close to the final state, it (correctly) prefers to end the episode as soon as possible. I invite the reader to repeat the experiment using different values for the constant λ, and changing the environment dynamics for the checkpoints.

What happens if their values remain the same? Is it possible to improve the policy with a larger λ?

It's important to remember that, as we are extensively using random values, successive experiments can yield different results due to different initial conditions. However, the algorithm should always converge to an optimal policy when the number of episodes is high enough.

Actor-Critic TD(0) in the checkerboard environment

In this example, we want to employ an alternative algorithm called Actor-Critic, together with TD(0). In this method, the agent is split into two components, a critic, which is responsible for evaluating the quality of the value estimation, and an actor, which selects and performs an action. As pointed out by Dayan (in Dayan P., Abbott L. F., *Theoretical Neuroscience*, The MIT Press, 2005), the dynamics of the Actor-Critic approach are similar to the interleaving policy evaluation and policy improvement steps. In fact, the knowledge of the critic is obtained through an iterative process, and its initial evaluations are normally sub-optimal. The structural schema is shown in the following diagram:

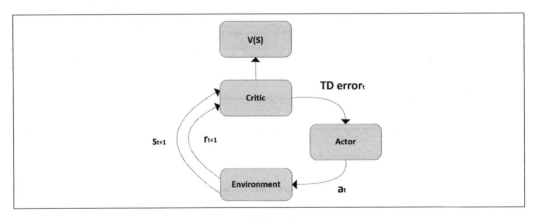

Actor-Critic schema

In this particular case, it's preferable to employ a ϵ-greedy soft policy based on the softmax function. The model stores a matrix (or an approximating function) called policy importance, where each entry $p_i(s, a)$ is a value representing the preference for a specific action in a certain state. The actual stochastic policy is obtained by applying the softmax with a simple trick to increase the numerical stability when the exponentials become very large:

$$\pi(s,a) = \frac{e^{p_i(s,a)}}{\sum_{a_k} e^{p_i(s,a_k)}} = \frac{e^{-\max_a p_i(s,a)} e^{p_i(s,a)}}{e^{-\max_a p_i(s,a)} \sum_{a_k} e^{p_i(s,a_k)}} = \frac{e^{p_i(s,a) - \max_a p_i(s,a)}}{\sum_{a_k} e^{p_i(s,a_k) - \max_a p_i(s,a)}}$$

After performing the action a in the state s_i and observing the transition to the state s_j with a reward r_{ij}, the critic evaluates the TD error:

$$TD_{error} = r_{ij} + \gamma V(s_j) - V(s_i)$$

If $V(s_i) < r_{ij} + \gamma V(s_j)$, the transition is considered positive, because the value is increasing. Conversely, when $V(s_i) > r_{ij} + \gamma V(s_j)$, the critic evaluates the action as negative because the previous value was higher than the new estimation. A more general approach is based on the concept of advantage, which is defined as:

$$A(s,a;\pi) = Q(s,a;\pi) - V(s;\pi)$$

Normally, one of the terms from the previous expression can be approximated because we often don't have enough knowledge to compute, for example, the effect of each action in each state. In our case, we cannot compute the Q function directly; hence, we approximate it with the term $r_{ij} + \gamma V(s_j)$. It's clear that the role of the advantage is analogous to the one of the TD errors (which is an approximation) and must represent the confirmation that an action in a certain state is a good or bad choice. An analysis of **All Advantage Actor-Critic (A³C)** algorithms (in other words, improvements of the standard policy gradient algorithm) is beyond the scope of this book. However, the reader can find some helpful pieces of information in Schulman J., Moritz P., Levine S., Jordan M. I., Abbeel P., *High-Dimensional Continuous Control Using Generalized Advantage Estimation*, ICLR 2016.

Of course, an Actor-Critic correction is not enough. To improve the policy, it's necessary to employ a standard algorithm (such as TD(0), TD(λ), or least square regression, which can be implemented using a neural network) in order to learn the correct value function, $V(s)$. As for many other algorithms, this process can converge only after a sufficiently high number of iterations, which must be exploited to visit the states many times, experimenting with all possible actions. Hence, with a TD(0) approach, the first step after evaluating the TD error is updating $V(s)$ using the rule defined in the previous chapter:

$$V(s_i) = V(s_i) + \alpha \left(r_{ij} + \gamma V(s_j) - V(s_i) \right) = V(s_i) + \alpha TD_{error}$$

The second step is more pragmatic; in fact, the main role of the critic is actually to criticize every action, deciding when it's better to increase or decrease the probability of selecting it again in a certain state. This goal can be achieved by simply updating the policy importance:

$$p_i(s_i, a) = p_i(s_i, a) + \rho T D_{error}$$

The role of the learning rate ρ is extremely important; in fact, incorrect values (in other words, values that are too high) can yield initial wrong corrections that may compromise the convergence. It's essential to not forget that the value function is almost completely unknown at the beginning, and therefore the critic has no chance to increase the right probability with awareness.

For this reason, I always suggest starting with a very small value (such as $\rho = 0.0001$) and increase it only if the convergence speed of the algorithm is effectively improved. As the policy is based on the softmax function, after a critic update, the values will always be renormalized, resulting in an actual probability distribution. After an adequately large number of iterations, with the right choice of both ρ and γ, the model is able to learn both a stochastic policy and a value function. Therefore, it's possible to employ the trained agent by always selecting the action with the highest probability (which corresponds to an implicitly greedy behavior):

$$\pi(s) = \underset{a}{\operatorname{argmax}} \, \pi(s, a)$$

Let's now apply this algorithm to the tunnel environment. The first step is defining the constants (as we are looking for a long-sighted agent, we are setting the discount factor $\gamma = 0.99$):

```
import numpy as np

tunnel_values = np.zeros(shape=(height, width))

gamma = 0.99
alpha = 0.25
rho = 0.001
```

At this point, we need to define the policy importance array, and a function to generate the softmax policy:

```
nb_actions = 4

policy_importances = np.zeros(
    shape=(height, width, nb_actions))
```

```
def get_softmax_policy():
    softmax_policy = policy_importances - \
                     np.amax(policy_importances,
                             axis=2, keepdims=True)
    return np.exp(softmax_policy) / \
           np.sum(np.exp(softmax_policy),
                  axis=2, keepdims=True)
```

The functions needed to implement a single training step are very straightforward, and the reader should already be familiar with their structure:

```
def select_action(epsilon, i, j):
    if np.random.uniform(0.0, 1.0) < epsilon:
        return np.random.randint(0, nb_actions)

    policy = get_softmax_policy()
    return np.argmax(policy[i, j])


def action_critic_episode(epsilon):
    (i, j) = starting_point()
    x = y = 0

    e = 0

    while e < max_steps:
        e += 1

        action = select_action(epsilon, i, j)

        if action == 0:
            if i == 0:
                x = 0
            else:
                x = i - 1
            y = j

        elif action == 1:
            if j == width - 1:
                y = width - 1
            else:
                y = j + 1
            x = i

        elif action == 2:
```

```
        if i == height - 1:
            x = height - 1
        else:
            x = i + 1
        y = j

    else:
        if j == 0:
            y = 0
        else:
            y = j - 1
        x = i

    reward = tunnel_rewards[x, y]
    td_error = reward + \
                (gamma * tunnel_values[x, y]) - \
                tunnel_values[i, j]

    tunnel_values[i, j] += (alpha * td_error)
    policy_importances[i, j, action] += \
        (rho * td_error)

    if is_final(x, y):
        break
    else:
        i = x
        j = y
```

At this point, we can train the model with 50,000 iterations, and 30,000 explorative ones (with a linear decay of the exploration factor):

```
n_episodes = 50000
n_exploration = 30000

for t in range(n_episodes):
    epsilon = 0.0

    if t <= n_exploration:
        epsilon = 1.0 - (float(t) /
                        float(n_exploration))

    action_critic_episode(epsilon)
```

The resulting greedy policy is shown in the following figure:

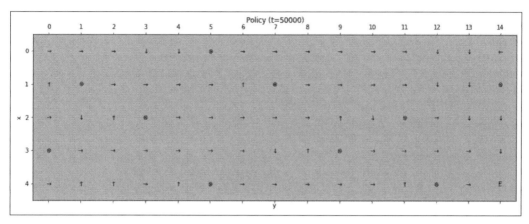

Final greedy policy

The final greedy policy is consistent with the objective, and the agent always reaches the final positive state by avoiding the wells. This kind of algorithm can appear more complex than necessary; however, in complex situations, it turns out to be extremely effective. In fact, the learning process can be dramatically improved thanks to the fast corrections performed by the critic. Moreover, the author has noticed that the Actor-Critic is more robust to wrong (or noisy) evaluations with respect to algorithms like SARSA or Q-Learning, which can suffer from instabilities that are, instead, reduced by the estimation of the advantage term.

As the policy is learned separately, the effect of small variations in $V(s)$ cannot easily change the probabilities $\pi(s, a)$ (in particular, when an action is generally much stronger than the others). On the other hand, as discussed previously, it's necessary to avoid premature convergence in order to let the algorithm modify the importance/probabilities, without an excessive number of iterations. The right trade-off can be found only after a complete analysis of each specific scenario, and unfortunately, there are no general rules that work in every case. My suggestion is to test various configurations, starting with small values (and, for example, a discount factor of $\gamma \in (0.7, 0.9)$), evaluating the total reward achieved after the same exploration period.

Complex deep learning models (such as asynchronous A3C; see Mnih V., Puigdomènech Badia A., Mirza M., Graves A., Lillicrap T. P., Harley T., Silver D., Kavukcuoglu K., *Asynchronous Methods for Deep Reinforcement Learning*, arXiv:1602.01783 [cs.LG] for further information) are based on a single network that outputs both the softmax policy (whose actions are generally proportional to their probability) and the value.

Instead of employing an explicitly ϵ-greedy soft policy, it's possible to add a maximum-entropy constraint to the global cost function:

$$\max H(\pi) = -\max \sum_i \pi(s, a_i) \log \pi(s, a_i) = \min \sum_i \pi(s, a_i) \log \pi(s, a_i)$$

As the entropy is at its maximum when all of the actions have the same probability, this constraint (with an appropriate weight) forces the algorithm to increase the exploration probability until an action becomes dominant and there's no more need to avoid a greedy selection. This is a sound and easy way to employ an adaptive ϵ-greedy policy, because as the model works with each state separately, the states where the uncertainty is very low can become greedy; it's possible to automatically keep a high entropy whenever it's necessary to continue the exploration in order to maximize the reward.

The effect of double correction, together with a maximum-entropy constraint, improves the convergence speed of the model, encourages the exploration during the initial iterations, and yields very high final accuracy. I invite the reader to implement this variant with other scenarios and algorithms. In particular, at the end of this chapter, we are going to experiment with an algorithm based on a neural network. As the example is pretty simple, I suggest using TensorFlow to create a small network based on the Actor-Critic approach (a good starting point is the article at `https://blog.tensorflow.org/2018/07/deep-reinforcement-learning-keras-eager-execution.html`). The reader can employ a **Mean Squared Error (MSE)** loss for the value and softmax cross-entropy for the policy. Once the models work successfully with our toy examples, it will be possible to start working with more complex scenarios (like the ones proposed in OpenAI Gym at `https://gym.openai.com`).

SARSA algorithm

SARSA (the name is derived from the sequence state-action-reward-state-action) is a natural extension of TD(0) to the estimation of the Q function. Its standard formulation (which is sometimes called one-step SARSA, or SARSA(0), for the same reasons explained in the previous chapter) is based on a single next reward r_{t+1}, which is obtained by executing the action a_t in the state s_t. The temporal difference computation is based on the following update rule:

$$Q(s_t, a_t; \pi) = Q(s_t, a_t; \pi) + \alpha\big(r_{t+1} + \gamma Q(s_{t+1}, a_{t+1}; \pi) - Q(s_t, a_t; \pi)\big)$$

The equation is equivalent to TD(0), and if the policy is chosen to be GLIE, it has been proven (in Singh S., Jaakkola T., Littman M. L., Szepesvári C., *Convergence Results for Single-Step On-Policy Reinforcement-Learning Algorithms*, Machine Learning, 39/2000) that SARSA converges to an optimal policy $\pi^{opt}(s)$ with a probability of 1 when all couples (state, action) are experienced an infinite number of times. This means that if the policy is updated to be greedy with respect to the current value function induced by Q, it holds that:

$$p\left(\lim_{k\to\infty} \pi^{(k)}(s) = \pi^{opt}(s)\right) = 1 \; \forall\, s \in S$$

The same result is valid for the Q function. In particular, the most important conditions required by the proof are:

- The learning rate $\alpha \in (0,1)$ with the constraints $\sum \alpha = \infty$ and $\sum \alpha^2 < \infty$.
- The variance of the rewards must be finite.

The first condition is particularly important when α is a function of the state and the time step; however, in many cases, it is a constant bounded between 0 and 1, and hence, $\sum \alpha^2 = \infty$. A common way to solve this problem (above all when a large number of iterations are required) is to let the learning rate decay (in other words, exponentially) during the training process. Instead, to mitigate the effect of very large rewards, it's possible to clip them in a suitable range (for example, (-1,1)).

In many cases, it's not necessary to employ these strategies, but in more complex scenarios, they can become crucial in order to ensure the convergence of the algorithm. Moreover, as pointed out in the previous chapter, these kinds of algorithms need a long exploration phase before starting to stabilize the policy. The most common strategy is to employ a ϵ-greedy policy, with a temporal decay of the exploration factor. During the first iterations, the agent must explore without caring about the returns of the actions. In this way, it's possible to assess the actual values before the beginning of a final refining phase characterized by a purely greedy exploration, based on a more precise approximation of $V(s)$.

The complete SARSA(0) algorithm (with an optional forced termination of the episode) is:

1. Set an initial deterministic random policy $\pi(s)$.
2. Set the initial value array $Q(s, a) = 0 \; \forall\, s \in S$ and $a \in A$.
3. Set the number of episodes $N_{episodes}$.

    4. Set a maximum number of steps per episode N_{max}.

    5. Set a constant α (for example, $\alpha = 0.1$).

    6. Set a constant γ (for example, $\gamma = 0.9$).

    7. Set an initial exploration factor $\epsilon^{(0)}$ (for example, $\epsilon^{(0)} = 1$).

    8. Define a policy to let the exploration factor ϵ decay (linear or exponential).

    9. Set a counter $e = 0$.

    10. For $i = 1$ to $N_{episodes}$:

        1. Observe the initial state s_i.

        2. While s_i is non-terminal and $e < N_{max}$:

            1. $e = e + 1$.

            2. Select the action $a_t = \pi(s_i)$ with an exploration factor $\epsilon^{(e)}$.

            3. Observe the transition $(a_t, s_i) \rightarrow (s_j, r_{ij})$.

            4. Select the action $a_{t+1} = \pi(s_j)$ with an exploration factor $\epsilon^{(e)}$.

            5. Update the $Q(s_t, a_t)$ function (if s_j is terminal, set $Q(s_{t+1}, a_{t+1}) = 0$).

            6. Set $s_i = s_j$.

The concept of eligibility trace can also be extended to SARSA (and other TD methods); however, that is beyond the scope of this book. A reader who is interested can find all of the algorithms (together with their mathematical formulations) in Sutton R. S., Barto A. G., *Reinforcement Learning*, The MIT Press, 1998.

SARSA in the checkerboard environment

We can now test the SARSA algorithm in the original tunnel environment (all of the elements that are not redefined are the same as the previous chapter). The first step is defining the $Q(s, a)$ array and the constants employed in the training process:

```
import numpy as np

nb_actions = 4

Q = np.zeros(shape=(height, width, nb_actions))

x_start = 0
y_start = 0
```

```
max_steps = 2000
alpha = 0.25
```

As we want to employ a ϵ-greedy policy, we can set the starting point to $(0, 0)$, forcing the agent to reach the positive final state. We can now define the functions needed to perform a training step:

```
def is_final(x, y):
    if (x, y) in zip(x_wells, y_wells) or \
            (x, y) == (x_final, y_final):
        return True
    return False


def select_action(epsilon, i, j):
    if np.random.uniform(0.0, 1.0) < epsilon:
        return np.random.randint(0, nb_actions)
    return np.argmax(Q[i, j])

def sarsa_step(epsilon):
    e = 0

    i = x_start
    j = y_start

    while e < max_steps:
        e += 1

        action = select_action(epsilon, i, j)

        if action == 0:
            if i == 0:
                x = 0
            else:
                x = i - 1
            y = j

        elif action == 1:
            if j == width - 1:
                y = width - 1
            else:
                y = j + 1
            x = i
```

```
        elif action == 2:
            if i == height - 1:
                x = height - 1
            else:
                x = i + 1
            y = j

    else:
        if j == 0:
            y = 0
        else:
            y = j - 1
        x = i

    action_n = select_action(epsilon, x, y)
    reward = tunnel_rewards[x, y]

    if is_final(x, y):
        Q[i, j, action] += alpha * \
                        (reward -
                         Q[i, j, action])
        break

    else:
        Q[i, j, action] += alpha * \
                        (reward +
                         (gamma *
                          Q[x, y, action_n]) -
                         Q[i, j, action])

        i = x
        j = y
```

The select_action() function has been designed to select a random action with the probability ε, and a greedy one with respect to $Q(s, a)$, with the probability $1 - \epsilon$. The sarsa_step() function is straightforward and executes a complete episode updating $Q(s, a)$ (that's why this is an online algorithm). At this point, it's possible to train the model for 20,000 episodes (I invite the reader to test also smaller values to learn to evaluate the convergence speed) and employ a linear decay for ϵ during the first 15,000 episodes (when t > 15,000, ϵ is set equal to 0 in order to employ a purely greedy policy):

```
n_episodes = 20000
n_exploration = 15000

for t in range(n_episodes):
    epsilon = 0.0

    if t <= n_exploration:
        epsilon = 1.0 - (float(t) /
                        float(n_exploration))

    sarsa_step(epsilon)
```

As usual, let's check the learned values (considering that the policy is greedy, we're going to plot $V(s) = \max_a Q(s, a)$):

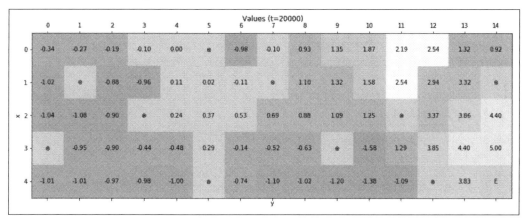

Final value matrix (as $V(s) = \max_a Q(s, a)$)

As expected, the Q function has been learned in a consistent way, and we can get confirmation by plotting the resulting policy:

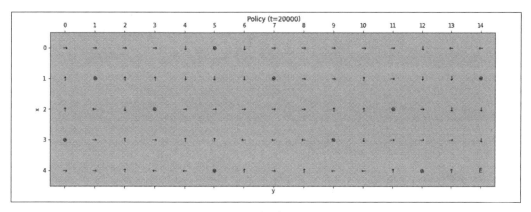

Final policy

The policy is coherent with the initial objective, and the agent avoids all negative absorbing states, always trying to move toward the final positive state. However, some paths seem longer than expected. As an exercise, I invite the reader to retrain the model for a larger number of iterations, adjusting the exploration period. Moreover, is it possible to improve the model by increasing (or decreasing) the discount factor γ? Remember that $\gamma \to 0$ leads to a short-sighted agent, which is able to select actions only considering the immediate reward, while $\gamma \to 1$ forces the agent to take into account a larger number of future rewards.

This particular example is based on a long environment because the agent always starts from $(0, 0)$ and must reach the farthest point; therefore, all intermediate states have less importance, and it's helpful to look at the future to pick the optimal actions. Using random starts can surely improve the policy for all initial states, but it's interesting to investigate how different γ values can affect the decisions; hence, I suggest repeating the experiment in order to evaluate the various configurations and increase awareness about the different factors that are involved in a TD algorithm.

Q-learning

This algorithm was proposed by Watkins (in Watkins C.I.C.H., *Learning from delayed rewards*, Ph.D. Thesis, University of Cambridge, 1989 and furtherly analyzed in Watkins C.I.C.H., Dayan P., *Technical Note Q-Learning*, Machine Learning 8, 1992) as a more efficient alternative to SARSA. The main feature of Q-learning is that the TD update rule is immediately greedy with respect to the $Q(s_{t+1}, a)$ function (assuming that the agent received the reward r_t after performing the action a_t while in the state s_t):

$$Q(s_t, a_t; \pi) = Q(s_t, a_t; \pi) + \alpha(r_t + \gamma \max_a Q(s_{t+1}, a; \pi) - Q(s_t, a_t; \pi))$$

The key idea is to compare the current $Q(s_t, a_t)$ value with the maximum Q value achievable when the agent is in the successor state. Assuming $\alpha = 1$, the previous equation can be transformed into a TD_{error} structure:

$$TD_{error} = r_t + \gamma \max_a Q(s_{t+1}, a; \pi) - Q(s_t, a_t; \pi)$$

The first term is the current reward, the second is the discounted maximum reward that the agent can theoretically achieve using its current knowledge and the last one is the estimation of the Q function. As the policy must be GLIE, the convergence speed can be increased by avoiding wrong estimations due to the selection of a Q value that won't be associated with the final action.

Instead, by choosing the maximum Q value (with the current knowledge), the algorithm will move toward the optimal solution faster than SARSA, and moreover, the convergence proof is less restrictive.

In fact, Watkins and Dayan (in the aforementioned papers) proved that if $|r_i| < R \; \forall \, i$, the learning rate $\alpha \in (0,1)$ (in the case of Q-learning, α must be always smaller than 1) with the same constraints imposed for SARSA ($\sum \alpha = \infty$ and $\sum \alpha^2 < \infty$), then the estimated Q function converges with probability 1 to the optimal one:

$$p \left(\lim_{k \to \infty} Q^{(k)}(s, a) = Q^{opt}(s, a) \right) = 1 \; \forall \, s \in S \; and \; a \in A$$

As discussed for SARSA, the conditions on the rewards and the learning rate can be managed by employing a clipping function and a temporal decay, respectively. In almost all deep Q-learning applications, these are extremely important factors to guarantee the convergence; therefore, I invite the reader to consider them whenever the training process isn't able to converge to an acceptable solution.

The complete Q-learning algorithm (with an optional forced termination of the episode) is:

1. Set an initial deterministic random policy $\pi(s)$.
2. Set the initial value array $Q(s, a) = 0 \; \forall \, s \in S \; and \; a \in A$.
3. Set the number of episodes $N_{episodes}$.
4. Set a maximum number of steps per episode N_{max}.
5. Set a constant α (for example, $\alpha = 0.1$).
6. Set a constant γ (for example, $\gamma = 0.9$).
7. Set an initial exploration factor $\epsilon^{(0)}$ (for example, $\epsilon^{(0)} = 1$).
8. Define a policy to let the exploration factor ϵ decay (linear or exponential).
9. Set a counter $e = 0$.
10. For $i = 1$ to $N_{episodes}$:

    a. Observe the initial state s_i.
    b. While s_i is non-terminal and $e < N_{max}$:

        i. $e = e + 1$.
        ii. Select the action $a_t = \pi(s_i)$ with an exploration factor $\epsilon^{(e)}$.
        iii. Observe the transition $(a_t, s_i) \to (s_j, r_{ij})$.

    iv. Select the action $a_{t+1} = \pi(s_j)$ with an exploration factor $\epsilon^{(e)}$.

    v. Update the $Q(s_t, a_t)$ function (if s_j is terminal, set $Q(s_{t+1}, a_{t+1})$) using $\max\limits_{a} Q(s_{t+1}, a)$.

    vi. Set $s_i = s_j$.

Q-learning in the checkerboard environment

Let's repeat the previous experiment with the Q-learning algorithm. As all of the constants are the same (as well as the choice of a ϵ-greedy policy and the starting point set to $(0, 0)$), we can directly define the function that implements the training for a single episode:

```python
import numpy as np

def q_step(epsilon):
    e = 0

    i = x_start
    j = y_start

    while e < max_steps:
        e += 1

        action = select_action(epsilon, i, j)

        if action == 0:
            if i == 0:
                x = 0
            else:
                x = i - 1
            y = j

        elif action == 1:
            if j == width - 1:
                y = width - 1
            else:
                y = j + 1
            x = i

        elif action == 2:
            if i == height - 1:
                x = height - 1
            else:
```

```
            x = i + 1
        y = j

    else:
        if j == 0:
            y = 0
        else:
            y = j - 1
        x = i

    reward = tunnel_rewards[x, y]

    if is_final(x, y):
        Q[i, j, action] += alpha * \
                        (reward -
                         Q[i, j, action])
        break

    else:
        Q[i, j, action] += alpha * \
                        (reward +
                         (gamma *
                          np.max(Q[x, y])) -
                         Q[i, j, action])

        i = x
        j = y
```

We can now train the model for 5,000 iterations, with 3,500 explorative ones:

```
n_episodes = 5000
n_exploration = 3500

for t in range(n_episodes):
    epsilon = 0.0

    if t <= n_exploration:
        epsilon = 1.0 - (float(t) /
                        float(n_exploration))

    q_step(epsilon)
```

The resulting value matrix (defined as in the SARSA experiment) is:

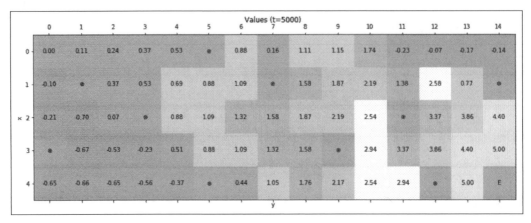

Final value matrix

Again, the learned Q function (and, obviously, also the greedy $V(s)$) is coherent with the initial objective (in particular, considering the starting point set to $(0, 0)$), and the resulting policy can immediately confirm this result:

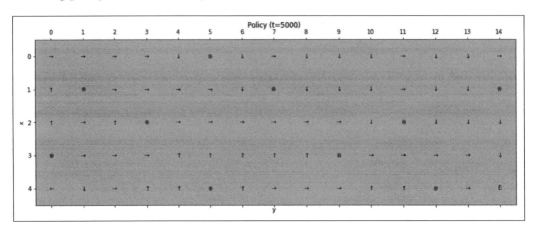

Final policy

The behavior of Q-learning is not very different from SARSA (even if the convergence is faster), and some initial states are not perfectly managed. This is a consequence of our choice; therefore, I invite the reader to repeat the exercise using random starts and comparing the training speed of Q-learning and SARSA.

Q-learning modeling the policy with a neural network

Now, we want to test the Q-learning algorithm using a smaller checkerboard environment and a neural network (with TensorFlow/Keras). The main difference from the previous examples is that now, the state is represented by a screenshot of the current configuration; hence, the model must learn how to associate a value with each input image and action. This isn't actual deep Q-learning (which is based on deep convolutional networks and requires more complex environments than we have space to discuss in this book), but it shows how such a model can learn an optimal policy with the same input provided to a human being. In order to reduce the training time, we are considering a square checkerboard environment, with four negative absorbing states and a positive final one:

```python
import numpy as np

width = 5
height = 5
nb_actions = 4

y_final = width - 1
x_final = height - 1

y_wells = [0, 1, 3, 4]
x_wells = [3, 1, 2, 0]

standard_reward = -0.1
tunnel_rewards = np.ones(shape=(height, width)) * \
                 standard_reward

for x_well, y_well in zip(x_wells, y_wells):
    tunnel_rewards[x_well, y_well] = -5.0

tunnel_rewards[x_final, y_final] = 5.0
```

A graphical representation of the rewards is shown in the following figure:

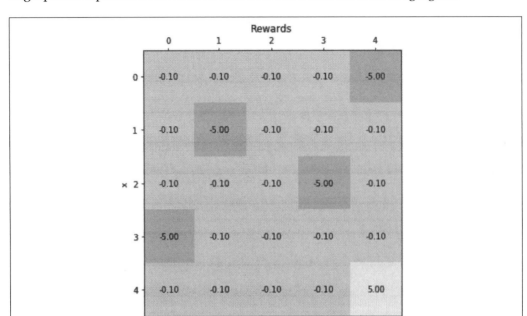

Rewards in the smaller checkerboard environment

As we want to provide the network with a graphical input, we need to define a function to create a matrix representing the tunnel:

```
def reset_tunnel():
    tunnel = np.zeros(shape=(height, width),
                      dtype=np.float32)

    for x_well, y_well in \
            zip(x_wells, y_wells):
        tunnel[x_well, y_well] = -1.0

    tunnel[x_final, y_final] = 0.5
    return tunnel
```

The reset_tunnel() function sets all values equal to 0, except for (which is marked with -1) and the final state (defined by 0.5). The position of the agent (defined with the value 1) is directly managed by the training function. At this point, we can create and compile our neural network. As the problem is not very complex, we are employing an MLP with the following structure:

- Input layer
- Hidden layer with six neurons with hyperbolic tangent activation
- Hidden layer with four neurons with hyperbolic tangent activation
- Output layer with nb_actions neurons with linear activation (as they represent the Q function values):

```
import tensorflow as tf

model = tf.keras.models.Sequential([
        tf.keras.layers.Dense(6,
                              input_dim=width * height,
                              activation='tanh'),
        tf.keras.layers.Dense(4,
                              activation='tanh'),
        tf.keras.layers.Dense(nb_actions,
                              activation='linear')
])

optimizer = tf.keras.optimizers.Adam(0.01)

model.compile(optimizer, loss='mse')
```

The input is a flattened array, while the output is the Q function (all of the values corresponding to each action). The network is trained using RMSprop and an MSE loss function (our goal is to reduce the MSE between the actual value and the prediction). In order to train and query the network, it's helpful to create two dedicated functions:

```
def train(state, q_value):
    model.train_on_batch(
        np.expand_dims(state.flatten(), axis=0),
        np.expand_dims(q_value, axis=0))


def get_Q_value(state):
    return model.predict(
        np.expand_dims(state.flatten(), axis=0))[0]

def select_action_neural_network(epsilon, state):
    Q_value = get_Q_value(state)

    if np.random.uniform(0.0, 1.0) < epsilon:
        return Q_value, \
                np.random.randint(0, nb_actions)

    return Q_value, np.argmax(Q_value)
```

The behavior of these functions is straightforward. The only element that may be new to the reader is the use of the `train_on_batch()` method. Contrary to `fit()`, this function allows us to perform a single training step, given a batch of input-output couples (in our case, we always have a single couple). As our goal is finding an optimal path to the final state, starting from every possible cell, we are going to employ random starts:

```
xy_grid = np.meshgrid(np.arange(0, height),
                      np.arange(0, width), sparse=False)
xy_grid = np.array(xy_grid).T.reshape(-1, 2)

xy_final = list(zip(x_wells, y_wells))
xy_final.append([x_final, y_final])

xy_start = []

for x, y in xy_grid:
    if (x, y) not in xy_final:
        xy_start.append([x, y])

xy_start = np.array(xy_start)

def starting_point():
    xy = np.squeeze(xy_start[
            np.random.randint(0,
                              xy_start.shape[0],
                              size=1)])
    return xy[0], xy[1]
```

Now, we can define the functions needed to perform a single training step:

```
def is_final(x, y):
    if (x, y) in zip(x_wells, y_wells) or \
            (x, y) == (x_final, y_final):
        return True
    return False

def q_step_neural_network(epsilon, initial_state):
    e = 0
    total_reward = 0.0

    (i, j) = starting_point()

    prev_value = 0.0
    tunnel = initial_state.copy()
    tunnel[i, j] = 1.0
```

```
while e < max_steps:
    e += 1

    q_value, action = \
        select_action_neural_network(epsilon, tunnel)

    if action == 0:
        if i == 0:
            x = 0
        else:
            x = i - 1
        y = j

    elif action == 1:
        if j == width - 1:
            y = width - 1
        else:
            y = j + 1
        x = i

    elif action == 2:
        if i == height - 1:
            x = height - 1
        else:
            x = i + 1
        y = j

    else:
        if j == 0:
            y = 0
        else:
            y = j - 1
        x = i

    reward = tunnel_rewards[x, y]
    total_reward += reward

    tunnel_n = tunnel.copy()
    tunnel_n[i, j] = prev_value
    tunnel_n[x, y] = 1.0

    prev_value = tunnel[x, y]

    if is_final(x, y):
        q_value[action] = reward
        train(tunnel, q_value)
```

```
            break

        else:
            q_value[action] = reward + \
                            (gamma *
                            np.max(
                        get_Q_value(tunnel_n)))
            train(tunnel, q_value)

            i = x
            j = y

            tunnel = tunnel_n.copy()

    return total_reward
```

The `q_step_neural_network()` function is very similar to the one defined in the previous example. The only difference is the management of the visual state. Every time there's a transition, the value 1.0 (denoting the agent) is moved from the old position to the new one, and the value of the previous cell is reset to its default (saved in the `prev_value` variable).

Another secondary difference is the absence of α because there's already a learning rate set in the SGD algorithm, and it doesn't make sense to add another parameter to the model. We can now train the model for 2,000 iterations, with 1,200 explorative ones:

```
n_episodes = 2000
n_exploration = 1200

total_rewards = []

for t in range(n_episodes):
    tunnel = reset_tunnel()

    epsilon = 0.0

    if t <= n_exploration:
        epsilon = 1.0 - (float(t) /
                    float(n_exploration))

    t_reward= q_step_neural_network(epsilon, tunnel)
    total_rewards.append(t_reward)
```

When the training process has finished, we can analyze the total rewards, in order to understand whether the network has successfully learned the Q function (the bold line is a smoothed version using a Savitzky-Golay filter):

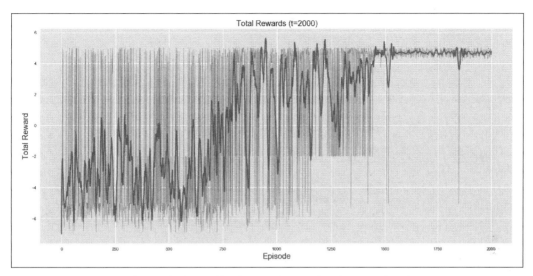

Total rewards obtained by the neural network Q-learning algorithm

It's clear that the model is working well, because after the exploration period, the total reward becomes stationary after 1,000 episodes, with only small oscillations due to the different path lengths (however, the final plot can be different because of the internal random state employed by TensorFlow/Keras). To see a confirmation, let's generate the trajectories for all of the possible initial states, using the greedy policy (equivalent to $\epsilon = 0$):

```
trajectories = []
tunnels_c = []

for I, j in xy_start:
    tunnel = reset_tunnel()

    prev_value = 0.0

    trajectory = [[I, j, -1]]

    tunnel_c = tunnel.copy()
    tunnel[i, j] = 1.0
    tunnel_c[i, j] = 1.0

    final = False
```

```
e = 0

while not final and e < max_steps:
    e += 1

    q_value = get_Q_value(tunnel)
    action = np.argmax(q_value)

    if action == 0:
        if I == 0:
            x = 0
        else:
            x = I - 1
        y = j

    elif action == 1:
        if j == width - 1:
            y = width - 1
        else:
            y = j + 1
        x = i

    elif action == 2:
        if I == height - 1:
            x = height - 1
        else:
            x = I + 1
        y = j

    else:
        if j == 0:
            y = 0
        else:
            y = j - 1
        x = i

    trajectory[e - 1][2] = action
    trajectory.append([x, y, -1])

    tunnel[I, j] = prev_value

    prev_value = tunnel[x, y]

    tunnel[x, y] = 1.0
```

```
        tunnel_c[x, y] = 1.0

        i = x
        j = y

        final = is_final(x, y)

    trajectories.append(np.array(trajectory))
    tunnels_c.append(tunnel_c)

  trajectories = np.array(trajectories)
```

Twelve random trajectories are shown in the following figure:

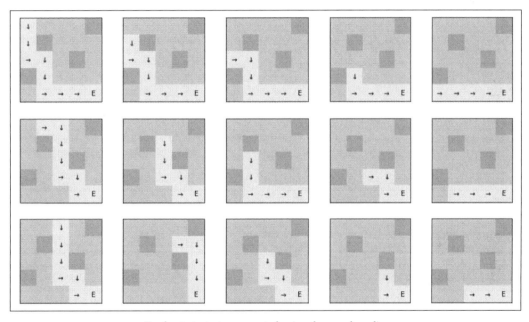

Twelve trajectories generated using the greedy policy

The agent always follows the optimal policy, independent from the initial state, and never ends up in a well. Even if this example is quite simple, it's helpful to introduce the reader to the concept of deep Q-learning (for further details, the reader can check the introductory paper, Li Y., *Deep Reinforcement Learning: An Overview*, arXiv:1701.07274 [cs.LG]). In a general case, the environment can be a more complex game (like Atari or Sega), and the number of possible actions is very limited. Moreover, there's no possibility to employ random starts, but it's generally a good practice to skip a number of initial frames, in order to avoid a bias to the estimator.

Clearly, the network must be more complex (involving convolutions to better learn the geometric dependencies), and the number of iterations must be extremely large.

Many other tricks and specific algorithms can be employed in order to speed up the convergence, but they are beyond the scope of this book. However, the general process and its logic are almost the same, and it's not difficult to understand why some strategies are preferable and how the accuracy can be improved. As an exercise, I invite the reader to create more complex environments, with or without checkpoints and stochastic rewards. It's not surprising to see how the model will be able to easily learn the dynamics with a sufficiently large number of episodes. Moreover, as suggested in the Actor-Critic section, it's a good idea to use TensorFlow to implement such a model, comparing the performances with Q-learning.

Direct policy search through policy gradient

The last method we're going to discuss doesn't employ a proxy to find the optimal policy, but rather looks for it directly. In this context, we always assume we're working with a stochastic environment where the transitions are not fully deterministic. For example, a robot can assign a high probability to a transition but, in order to increase the robustness, it has also to include a noise term that can lead the transition to a different state. Therefore, we need to include a transition probability $p(s_i \rightarrow s_j | a_k) \; \forall \; s_i, s_j \in S$ and a_k in A.

Given this element, we can evaluate the overall probability of an entire sequence (that normally ends in a final state): $S_k = (s_1, s_2, ..., s_k)$. To do so, we need to define a parameterized policy $\pi(s, \bar{\theta})$; therefore, the probability of S_k can be expressed as a conditional one: $p(S_k | \pi)$. The full expression requires us to explicitly separate the state transition component from the policy and to introduce the actions (which were implicit in the previous expressions):

$$p(S_k | \pi) = p(s_1) \prod_i p(s_i \rightarrow s_{i+1} | a_i) \pi(a_i | s_i; \bar{\theta})$$

This term represents the actual probability that an agent with a knowledge encoded in the parameter set $\bar{\theta}$ can experience such a sequence. At this point, we can easily define a cost function by considering the expected discounted reward with respect to the generic distribution $p(S_t | \pi)$:

$$L(\bar{\theta}) = \int p(S_t|\pi)R(S_t)dS_t$$

As the agent must maximize the expected future reward, $L(\bar{\theta})$ must be maximized. Of course, we cannot work with the integral, hence, we need to approximate it with a sample mean:

$$L(\bar{\theta}) \approx \frac{1}{N}\sum p(S_t|\pi)R(S_t)$$

In the previous formula, N is the total number of evaluated sequences, but in practice, it's easy to consider it as the batch size. In fact, our goal is to optimize $L(\bar{\theta})$ using a stochastic gradient ascent approach (such as RMSProp or Adam). Unfortunately, $p(S_t|\pi)$ is not immediately helpful because we don't know $p(s_i \rightarrow s_{i+1}|a_i)$. However, we can perform some straightforward manipulations to compute the gradient $\nabla L(\bar{\theta})$:

$$\nabla L(\bar{\theta}) \approx \frac{1}{N}\sum \nabla p(S_t|\pi)R(S_t)$$

To simplify the previous expression, we need to remember that:

$$\frac{d}{dx}f(x) = f(x)\frac{1}{f(x)}\frac{d}{dx}f(x) = f(x)\frac{d}{dx}\log f(x)$$

Therefore, by applying this trick, we obtain:

$$\nabla L(\bar{\theta}) \approx \frac{1}{N}\sum p(S_t|\pi)\nabla\log p(S_t|\pi)\,R(S_t) = \frac{1}{N}\sum p(S_t|\pi)\sum_i \nabla\log\pi(a_i|s_i;\,\bar{\theta})\,R(S_t)$$

$$= Avg_{p(S_t|\pi)}\left[\sum_i \nabla\log\pi(a_i|s_i;\,\bar{\theta})\,R(S_t)\right]$$

In other words, we are approximating the true gradient with a sample mean where the only complexity is the computation of the gradient of $\log\pi(a_i|s_i;\,\bar{\theta})$. Once we have computed the gradient, we can update the parameter vector:

$$\bar{\theta} = \bar{\theta} + \alpha\nabla L(\bar{\theta})$$

This problem can be solved either using directly the previous formula or, preferably, employing a more complex optimization algorithm like Adam. Of course, in practical implementations, it's important to remember that the goal is now a maximization; therefore, the sign of the logarithm must be inverted. In general, the expression $\sum_i \log \pi(a_i|s_i; \bar{\theta})\, R(S_t)$ is obtained using a *dummy* cross-entropy where $p = 1$:

$$H(p,\pi) = -\sum_i p \log \pi(a_i|s_i; \bar{\theta})R(S_t) = -\sum_i \log \pi(a_i|s_i; \bar{\theta})R(S_t)$$

Therefore, using a standard deep learning framework, it's enough to minimize $H(p,\pi)$.

Example of policy gradient with OpenAI Gym Cartpole

In this example, we want to test the policy gradient algorithm using a simple problem provided by OpenAI Gym (see `https://gym.openai.com/envs/CartPole-v0/`, where all installation instructions are also provided).

The goal is to find an optimal policy to balance a pole that is hinged upon a cart (as initially proposed by Barto et al. in Barto A., Sutton R., Anderson C., *Neuronlike Adaptive Elements That Can Solve Difficult Learning Control Problem*, IEEE Transactions on Systems, Man, and Cybernetics, 1983). The cart can be moved in both directions, but the problem is considered solved when it remains very close to the center (± 2.4 metric units) and the pole remains in a position of $\pm 15°$ from the vertical line.

It's interesting to notice that this problem has been studied for a long time because its physical formulation is quite complex, and directly modeling a control system is consequently extremely difficult. Conversely, RL can solve this kind of problem using only a limited number of experiments, using a policy that can be easily parameterized such as an MLP.

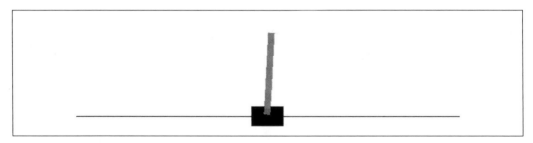

Screenshot of the CartPole-v0 problem

The first step is initializing the environment:

```
import gym

env = gym.make('CartPole-v0')
env.seed(1000)
```

The state is a four-dimensional vector $\bar{s} \in \mathbb{R}^4$ containing the following pieces of information:

- Position of the cart x
- Angle of the pole τ
- Linear speed of the cart (first derivative $\frac{dx}{dt}$)
- Angular speed of the pole (first derivative $\frac{d\tau}{dt}$)

There are only two possible actions (either {-1,1} or {0,1}) indicating the movement at constant speed in one of the two directions. The policy is parameterized using a neural network employing ReLU units, which are very easy to optimize:

```
import tensorflow as tf

policy = tf.keras.models.Sequential([
    tf.keras.layers.Dense(32,
                          activation='relu',
                          input_dim=4),
    tf.keras.layers.Dense(32,
                          activation='relu'),
    tf.keras.layers.Dense(2,
                          activation='relu')
])

optimizer = tf.keras.optimizers.Adam()
```

As we want to employ the more robust functions provided by TensorFlow to compute the cross-entropy, the output is not directly a Softmax, but rather two ReLU neurons, which can represent two logits perfectly. The optimizer is Adam with the default learning rate $\eta = 0.001$. As we need to compute the gradients while selecting an action, we have created a single function:

```
def policy_step(s, grads=False):
    with tf.GradientTape() as tape:
        actions = policy(s, training=True)
        action = tf.random.categorical(
            actions, 1)
```

```
        action = tf.keras.utils.to_categorical(action, 2)
        loss = tf.squeeze(
            tf.nn.softmax_cross_entropy_with_logits(
                action, actions))

    if grads:
        gradients = tape.gradient(
            loss, policy.trainable_variables)
        return np.argmax(action), gradients

    return np.argmax(action)
```

If the parameter `grads` is set to `True`, the function computes and returns the gradients; otherwise, it only returns the actions that have been selected. The structure of the function is very easy:

- The policy is evaluated using the current state.

- An action is selected using a random choice based on the probability vector (p_0, p_1) (using the logits). If the policy has high entropy, $p_0 \approx p_1$, the action is completely random. This behavior encourages exploration. However, when the policy becomes more and more stable, one probability $p_i \rightarrow 1$ and, consequently $\pi(s_i) \rightarrow 1$. In this case, the agent starts exploiting the policy, with a very limited chance to perform further explorations.

- The loss function is computed, as explained in the theoretical part, using a numerically stable cross-entropy.

- The gradients are computed.

In order to perform the gradient ascent, it's also necessary to create an empty vector based on all trainable variables and a utility function to compute the discounted reward according to the formula:

$$R_{S_k} = \sum_i \gamma^{i-1} r_i$$

The code for both functions is shown in the following snippet:

```
def create_gradients():
    gradients = policy.trainable_variables
    for i, g in enumerate(gradients):
        gradients[i] = 0
    return gradients

def discounted_rewards(r):
```

```
dr = []
da = 0.0
for t in range(len(r)-1, -1, -1):
    da *= gamma
    da += r[t]
    dr.append(da)
return dr[::-1]
```

Since we need to evaluate all possible sub-sequences, the discounted reward is computed considering all starting points from $i = 1$ to $i = T$, where T is the length of the sequence. It's also important to remember that the order is always inverted because the elements are appended to the tail of the list; therefore, the most recent transition is the last one.

At this point, we can start the training loop using $\gamma = 0.99$ to give more importance to the whole sequence. The environment provides a reward equal to 1.0 when the action is positive, and 0.0 when it's negative. Therefore, it's hard to understand whether a sequence should be considered a success. A simple trick is to penalize the last action if the episode is ended before the natural length (which is equal to 200 steps). In our case, every negative terminal state has a reward equal to -5.0, but this value can be tuned up further in order to maximize the convergence speed.

The batch size is equal to 5, and we're going to perform 2,000 episodes (of course, I invite the reader to test different values and observe the results):

```
nb_episodes = 2000
max_length = 200
batch_size = 5
gamma = 0.99

gradients = create_gradients()
global_rewards = []

for e in range(nb_episodes):
state = env.reset()

    e_gradients = []
    e_rewards = []
    done = False
    total_reward = 0.0
    t = 0

    while not done and t < max_length:
        env.render()
```

```
        state = np.reshape(state, (1, 4)).\
            astype(np.float32)
        action, grads = policy_step(state,
                                    grads=True)
        state, reward, done, _ = env.step(action)

        total_reward += reward
        e_rewards.append(
            reward if not done else -5)

        grads = np.array(grads)
        e_gradients.append(grads)
        t += 1

    global_rewards.append(total_reward)

    d_rewards = discounted_rewards(e_rewards)
    for i, g in enumerate(e_gradients):
        gradients += g * d_rewards[i]

    if e > 1 and e % batch_size == 0:
        optimizer.apply_gradients(
            zip(gradients / batch_size,
                policy.trainable_variables))
        gradients = create_gradients()

    print("Finished episode: {}. "
          "Total reward: {:.2f}".
          format(e + 1, total_reward))

env.close()
```

For each episode, the previous snippet performs a loop where it samples a state from the environment, performs an action (computing the gradients), observes the new state, and stores the immediate reward. Every five episodes, the sequences corrected using the discounted rewards are aggregated into the term $\frac{1}{N} \sum_{i} \nabla \log \pi(a_i | s_i; \bar{\theta}) R(S_t)$ and the gradients are applied using the Adam optimizer.

The plot with the rewards is shown in the following figure. The highlighted line is a smoothed version:

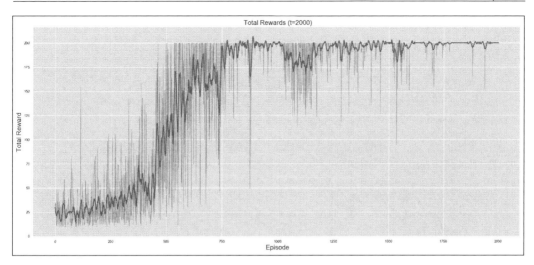

Rewards of policy gradient applied to the CartPole-v0 problem

As we can see, the algorithm reaches the maximum score (equal to 200) very quickly, but it keeps oscillating (with substantial flattening after 1,500 episodes). This is a drawback of this method. In fact, while the estimation is unbiased, its variance is generally quite large. There are different approaches to mitigate this problem, but they might worsen the overall performance. For example, increasing the batch size reduces the number of corrections and yields a more stable policy. Another method, which is likely to be the best one, is called baseline subtraction and consists of using a slightly different cost function:

$$Avg_{p(S_t|\pi)} \left[\sum_i \nabla \log \pi(a_i|s_i; \bar{\theta}) (R(S_t) - \beta) \right]$$

The term β doesn't alter the unbiasedness, but it can be chosen in order to minimize the variance of the gradient. However, when using small batch sizes, this term must be recomputed before each update and it has only a limited effect due to the small sample size. Therefore, it's often preferable to employ an optimization algorithm with a decaying learning rate to limit the corrections when the policy has reached good stability and to employ a slightly larger number of explorative episodes where the oscillation is large. As an exercise, I invite the reader to test these different approaches to learn more about the advantages and the drawbacks of this method.

Summary

In this chapter, we presented the natural evolution of TD(0) based on an average of backups with different lengths. The algorithm, called TD(λ), is extremely powerful, and it ensures faster convergence than TD(0), with only a few (non-restrictive) conditions. We also showed how to implement the Actor-Critic method with TD(0) in order to learn about both a stochastic policy and a value function.

In later sections, we discussed two methods based on the estimation of the Q function: SARSA and Q-learning. They are very similar, but the latter has a greedy approach, and its performance (in particular the training speed) results in it being superior to SARSA. The Q-learning algorithm is one of the most important models for the latest developments. In fact, it was the first RL approach employed with a deep convolutional network to solve complex environments (like Atari games). For this reason, we also presented a simple example based on an MLP that processes visual input and outputs the Q values for each action. Moreover, we introduced the concept of direct policy search with an example based on OpenAI Gym, a free set of environments in which it's possible to experiment with RL algorithms.

The world of RL is extremely fascinating, and hundreds of researchers work every day to improve algorithms and solve more and more complex problems. I invite the reader to check the references in order to find useful resources that can be exploited to obtain a deeper understanding of the models and their developments. Moreover, I suggest reading the blog posts written by the Google DeepMind team, which is a pioneer in the field of deep RL. I also suggest searching for papers freely available on arXiv (for example, Mnih V., Kavakcuoglu K., Silver D., Graves A., Antonoglou I, Wierstra D., Riedmiller M., *Playing Atari with Deep Reinforcement Learning*, arXiv:1312.5602v1 [cs.LG] or Mnih, V., Kavukcuoglu, K., Silver, D. et al. Human-level control through deep reinforcement learning. Nature 518, 529–533 (2015)).

I'm happy to end this book on this topic, because I believe that RL can provide new and powerful tools that will dramatically change our lives.

Further reading

- Sutton R. S., Barto A. G., *Reinforcement Learning*, The MIT Press, 1998
- Watkins C.I.C.H., *Learning from Delayed Rewards*, Ph.D. Thesis, University of Cambridge, 1989
- Dayan P., *The convergence of TD (λ) for General λ*, Machine Learning 8, 3–4/1992

- Dayan P., Abbott L. F., *Theoretical Neuroscience*, The MIT Press, 2005

- Schulman J., Moritz P., Levine S., Jordan M. I., Abbeel P., *High-Dimensional Continuous Control Using Generalized Advantage Estimation*, ICLR 2016

- Singh S., Jaakkola T., Littman M. L., Szepesvári C., *Convergence Results for Single-Step On-Policy Reinforcement-Learning Algorithms*, Machine Learning, 39/2000

- Watkins C.I.C.H., *Learning from delayed rewards*, Ph.D. Thesis, University of Cambridge, 1989

- Watkins C.I.C.H., Dayan P., *Technical Note Q-Learning*, Machine Learning 8, 1992

- Liu R., Zou J., *The Effects of Memory Replay in Reinforcement Learning*, Workshop on Principled Approaches to Deep Learning, ICML 2017

- Li Y., *Deep Reinforcement Learning: An Overview*, arXiv:1701.07274 [cs.LG]

- Mnih V., Kavakcuoglu K., Silver D., Graves A., Antonoglou I, Wierstra D., Riedmiller M., *Playing Atari with Deep Reinforcement Learning*, arXiv:1312.5602v1 [cs.LG]

- Mnih V., Kavukcuoglu K., Silver D., Graves A., Antonoglou I., Wierstra D., Riedmiller M., *Playing atari with deep reinforcement learning*. arXiv preprint arXiv:1312.5602, 2013

- Mnih V., Puigdomènech Badia A., Mirza M., Graves A., Lillicrap T. P., Harley T., Silver D., Kavukcuoglu K., *Asynchronous Methods for Deep Reinforcement Learning*, arXiv:1602.01783 [cs.LG]

- Barto A., Sutton R., Anderson C., *Neuronlike Adaptive Elements That Can Solve Difficult Learning Control Problem*, IEEE Transactions on Systems, Man, and Cybernetics, 1983

- Mnih, V., Kavukcuoglu, K., Silver, D. et al. *Human-level control through deep reinforcement learning*. Nature 518, 529–533 (2015)

This book took a lot of hard work, and I hope to have provided the reader with some really helpful insights about important machine learning algorithms and applications. I understand perfectly that the complexity of some topics can make them difficult to explain in easy to understand way, and I apologize to the reader if some points have not been made clear enough. However, I hope to have given a very small contribution to the dispersion of these wonderful concepts; through the bibliography, the reader eager to learn more can find very helpful resources and original papers. In each of them, she will find other references, because this process is destined to continue for a long time. Learning is changing! Learning also requires the ability to move on, taking what we need with us and leaving behind what we don't need anymore. Finally, I wish to all my readers a fantastic career in data science, and hope you maintain a constant desire to learn new ideas and to improve existing knowledge. The road is always ahead; travel on it with wonder, driven by AI!

Other Books You May Enjoy

If you enjoyed this book, you may be interested in these other books by Packt:

Python Machine Learning - Third Edition

Sebastian Raschka, Vahid Mirjalili

ISBN: 978-1-78995-575-0

- Master the frameworks, models, and techniques that enable machines to 'learn' from data
- Use scikit-learn for machine learning and TensorFlow for deep learning
- Apply machine learning to image classification, sentiment analysis, intelligent web applications, and more
- Build and train neural networks, GANs, and other models
- Discover best practices for evaluating and tuning models
- Predict continuous target outcomes using regression analysis
- Dig deeper into textual and social media data using sentiment analysis

Deep Learning with TensorFlow 2 and Keras - Second Edition

Antonio Gulli, Amita Kapoor, Sujit Pal

ISBN: 978-1-83882-341-2

- Build machine learning and deep learning systems with TensorFlow 2 and the Keras API

- Use Regression analysis, the most popular approach to machine learning

- Understand ConvNets (convolutional neural networks) and how they are essential for deep learning systems such as image classifiers

- Use GANs (generative adversarial networks) to create new data that fits with existing patterns

- Discover RNNs (recurrent neural networks) that can process sequences of input intelligently, using one part of a sequence to correctly interpret another

- Apply deep learning to natural human language and interpret natural language texts to produce an appropriate response

- Train your models on the cloud and put TF to work in real environments

- Explore how Google tools can automate simple ML workflows without the need for complex modeling

Machine Learning with R - Third Edition

Brett Lantz

ISBN: 978-1-78829-586-4

- Discover the origins of machine learning and how exactly a computer learns by example
- Prepare your data for machine learning work with the R programming language
- Classify important outcomes using nearest neighbor and Bayesian methods
- Predict future events using decision trees, rules, and support vector machines
- Forecast numeric data and estimate financial values using regression methods
- Model complex processes with artificial neural networks — the basis of deep learning
- Avoid bias in machine learning models
- Evaluate your models and improve their performance
- Connect R to SQL databases and emerging big data technologies such as Spark, H2O, and TensorFlow

Leave a review - let other readers know what you think

Please share your thoughts on this book with others by leaving a review on the site that you bought it from. If you purchased the book from Amazon, please leave us an honest review on this book's Amazon page. This is vital so that other potential readers can see and use your unbiased opinion to make purchasing decisions, we can understand what our customers think about our products, and our authors can see your feedback on the title that they have worked with Packt to create. It will only take a few minutes of your time, but is valuable to other potential customers, our authors, and Packt. Thank you!

Index

Made in the USA
Middletown, DE
02 September 2020